Praise for *Dean Acheson*
Douglas Brinkley

"Brinkley has written a fascinating portrait of Dean Acheson, with all his strengths and weaknesses, and given us an illuminating perspective on American foreign policy in the Cold War, with all its strengths and weaknesses. Highly recommended."—Stephen E. Ambrose

"Brinkley here tells an informative and gripping story of Acheson's life after he had ended his tenure as Truman's last secretary of state. The book places Acheson's contributions to American foreign policy during this period in enlightened perspective. Its mixture of politics and personalities mirror the complexities of a dangerous, unsettled time."—Forrest C. Pogue

"Brinkley, having done with Tim Hoopes the definitive book illuminating the days of James Forrestal, now gives us definitive insights to a later period that covers the Presidency of General Dwight D. Eisenhower who, aided by John Foster Dulles, attempted to run U.S. foreign policy and much of the free world's foreign policy through bluff rather than through building situations of strength. It is a tale of Acheson's wit and character overcoming the frustrations of being the advisor to lesser men."—Paul H. Nitze

"A splendid study of that bold and bristling figure as he observed foreign affairs in his outspoken years of so-called retirement."—Arthur Schlesinger, Jr.

"Cool, lucid account of the later years of a towering cold-war figure. . . . Even Acheson, for all his crustiness, would have respected the clear, concise writing and objectivity of this fine political biography."—*Kirkus Reviews*

"[Acheson] will always be remembered as one of the five or six Americans whose achievements as secretary of state gave them claim to greatness. . . . Brinkley has done well to present him with such dispassionate scholarship."
—*The Economist*

"A balanced, well-rendered account of a previously neglected period in the life of one of the most important figures in the history of postwar United States foreign policy."—Walter L. Hixson, *Journal of American History*

"Pithy and elegantly phrased, the book shows a command of the complexities of international politics from the end of the Truman administration to Acheson's death at the age of 78 in 1971. . . . With great skill Brinkley give us Dean Acheson's continuing preoccupation with the world at whose creation he believed he had presided."—D. K. Adams, *International Affairs*

Dean Acheson

THE

COLD WAR YEARS

1953–71

Douglas Brinkley

Yale University Press   *New Haven and London*

Frontispiece: Former President Harry S Truman with Dean Acheson at Yale University in 1958. Courtesy of Manuscripts and Archives, Yale University Library.

Published with assistance from the Kingsley Trust Association Publication Fund established by the Scroll and Key Society of Yale College.

Copyright © 1992 by Yale University.
All rights reserved.
This book may not be reproduced, in whole or in part, including illustrations, in any form (beyond that copying permitted by Sections 107 and 108 of the U.S. Copyright Law and except by reviewers for the public press), without written permission from the publishers.

Designed by James J. Johnson.
Set in ITC Berkeley type by
Tseng Information Systems, Inc., Durham, North Carolina.
Printed in the United States of America by Vail-Ballou Press, Binghamton, New York.

Library of Congress Cataloging-in-Publication Data

Brinkley, Douglas.
    Dean Acheson : the Cold War years, 1953–1971 / Douglas Brinkley.
    p. cm.
    Includes bibliographical references (p.) and index.
    ISBN 0-300-04773-8 (cloth)
           0-300-06075-0 (pbk.)

1. Acheson, Dean, 1893–1971. 2. Statesmen—United States—Biography. 3. United States—Foreign relations—1945–1989.
I. Title.
E748.A15B75   1992
973.921′092—dc20
[B]   91-48188
                                     CIP

A catalogue record for this book is available from the British Library.

The paper in this book meets the guidelines for permanence and durability of the Committee on Production Guidelines for Book Longevity of the Council on Library Resources.

10 9 8 7 6 5 4 3

For

    Jules Davids
    Townsend Hoopes
    J. Robert Schaetzel
    William J. vanden Heuvel

CONTENTS

Illustrations follow page 174
Acknowledgments ix
Introduction: Intimidating Seniority 1

Chapter One	Into the Fray against John Foster Dulles	6
Chapter Two	A Democrat Looks at His Party and at Eisenhower's Foreign Policy	38
Chapter Three	The Changing Political Climate in Europe, 1957–60	75
Chapter Four	JFK, NATO Review, and the Berlin Crisis of 1961	108
Chapter Five	The Cuban Missile Crisis	154
Chapter Six	Strains in the Atlantic Alliance, 1962–63	175
Chapter Seven	Repairing Cracks in NATO, 1964–67	203
Chapter Eight	The Vietnam War, 1961–68	237
Chapter Nine	Reconciled with Nixon	263
Chapter Ten	Southern Africa Policy, 1961–71	303
	Epilogue: Death at Harewood	329
	Notes	331
	Bibliography	393
	Index	417

ACKNOWLEDGMENTS

My interest in Dean Acheson dates from my graduate student years at Georgetown University. My fellowship assignment was with Jules Davids, the university's distinguished professor of diplomatic history. During the three years I worked for Professor Davids, I benefited from his vast knowledge of American foreign policy. Davids often spoke of Acheson in glowing terms, and after reading *Present at the Creation* for one of his seminars, I too became intrigued by this most literate and influential statesman.

It is difficult to be a student in Washington and not get caught up in the international scene. After only a few months in Washington, I had become close friends with students from Mexico, Nigeria, Italy, Argentina, the People's Republic of China, Israel, Iran, West Germany, Great Britain, France, and Spain. Conversations naturally turned to what was happening "back home." These out-of-class conversations particularized and personalized what I was learning from books. It is one thing to read that there are 20,000 *desaparecidos* in Argentina; it is quite another to hear a friend tell how her mother was abducted one hot March evening in Buenos Aires never to be seen again.

To help overcome the high cost of living in Washington, I moonlighted for two Washington institutions, Second Story Books and Idle Times Books. The owners, staff, and clientele of these stores were also influential teachers. They showed me the beauty and value of maintaining wide-ranging interests and passions.

In 1985 I also served as a museum assistant at the Phillips Collection of Modern Art. A connection made at the Phillips proved a turning point in my academic life. A frequent patron of the museum who knew I was studying U.S. diplomatic history asked whether I would like to meet the woman for whom she worked—Alice Acheson, the wife of the former secretary of state. Naturally, I said yes. To my surprise the next morning at 9:00 A.M. sharp, the phone rang. It was Mrs. Acheson, wanting to know whether I would join her for lunch to discuss her husband's career. Two gin and tonics and a sandwich later, I found myself sitting in Dean Acheson's P Street study in Old Georgetown, conversing with an elegant, strong-willed woman who had argued about art with Winston Churchill and discussed the Civil War with Harry Truman. She spoke of Portugal and Cambodia, and also of Sherwood Anderson and Archibald MacLeish, with insight and vitality. At conversation's end, she extended an open invitation to return whenever I was in the neighborhood. Over the next few months, I stopped back several times.

I began thinking about writing my doctoral dissertation on Dean Acheson's career after he stepped down as secretary of state in 1953. At that time the only books written exclusively about Acheson were Gaddis Smith's *Dean Acheson* and David S. McLellan's *Dean Acheson: The State Department Years*. Neither book dealt with the last eighteen years of Acheson's life, a time when he had served as an adviser to presidents Kennedy, Johnson, and Nixon. Smith's epilogue, indeed, had called for such a study. The void was partially filled when Walter Isaacson and Evan Thomas published *The Wise Men: Six Friends and the World They Made*—a masterful group biography of Acheson, Charles Bohlen, Averell Harriman, George Kennan, Robert Lovett, and John McCloy. The daunting task of combining the eventful lives of six eminent American foreign-policy makers in one volume allowed Isaacson and Thomas only to sketch Acheson's last eighteen years. Still, I found their portrait of Acheson during these years not only accurate and compelling, but indispensable.

I approached Alice Acheson about the dissertation possibility. She thought a political biography of her husband's postsecretarial years a splendid idea and told me to get in touch with her son, David, a well-known Washington attorney, coeditor of *Among Friends: Personal Letters of Dean Acheson*, and executor of his father's estate. No one has been more cooperative from start to finish of my writing than David Acheson. At an early stage in the project he made his Rolodex available, helping me gain access to Acheson associates like Paul H. Nitze and Charles Tyroler II. When research seemed to be at a dead end, I could always call David to supply a missing piece of the puzzle or to share a vignette that would illuminate his father. We also worked closely to sponsor a successful conference on Dean Acheson held at Johns Hopkins University's Paul H. Nitze School of Advanced International Studies in 1989. As I neared completion of *Dean Acheson: The Cold War Years, 1953–71* and my evaluation of certain aspects of Acheson's political views as elder statesman grew critical, we disagreed but never parted company. Despite sharp differences between us over his father's views on southern Africa, David nevertheless commented on the final draft of the book and loaned me family photographs. An objective biographer can ask for nothing more from the subject's family. I thank David Acheson and Alice Acheson for the many kind courtesies extended to me over this six-year period. Their generosity and friendship remain my most valued legacy of writing this book.

This project has gone through two distinct phases. In its first form it was a doctoral dissertation entitled "'Intimidating Seniority': Dean Acheson as Elder Statesman, 1953–1971." During the dissertation phase the following diplomats and scholars took time out from busy schedules to offer constructive criticism, moral support, and professional advice: Stephen Ambrose, George W. Ball, Lucius Battle, McGeorge Bundy, William P. Bundy, Honoré Catudal, Eleanor Dulles, John Gaddis, Richard Immerman, Larry Kaplan, Frederick Marks III, Charles Burton Marshall, Paul H. Nitze, Forrest Pogue, Ronald Steel, G. E. Thomas, and Charles Tyroler II. At Georgetown University I had the good fortune of receiving help and guidance from professors Jules Davids, Thomas Dodd, Walter Laqueur, Maurice Matloff, David Newsom, David Painter, and Nancy Bernkopf Tucker. Professor Tucker, whose *Patterns in the Dust: Chinese-American Relations and the Recognition Controversy, 1949–1950* is the best study of Acheson's China policy, gave unstintingly of her time and energy in criticizing every portion of the study. Her flexibility, encouragement, and advice helped me overcome many obstacles during the final push to complete the dissertation.

The leap from graduate student to assistant professor is perhaps the most daunting in the academic hierarchy and the transformation of a dissertation to a book the most humbling—just when you think you are finished, you must start all over again. For the past three years, I have continued researching Dean Acheson's postsecretarial years, incorporating new source material and refining many of the dissertation's conclusions. Throughout the phase of refining the dissertation into a book I incurred a number of new debts. Werner Abelhauser, Larry Berman, Robert Bowie, William P. Bundy, John Gillingham, George Herring, Melvyn Leffler,

Thomas Noer, Ronald Pruessen, Gary Reichard, Arthur Schlesinger, Jr., Thomas Schwartz, and Pascaline Winand read select chapters, and I am forever grateful for their help. From the beginning, Gaddis Smith, Larned Professor of History at Yale University, was my most astute and helpful reader.

The Dean Acheson Papers, housed at the Sterling Library, Yale University, proved to be the archival backbone of this book. Acheson considered these papers to be his private papers, as opposed to the papers he created as a lawyer and publicly as a civil servant. First opened to scholars in 1982, this wonderful collection of correspondence, memorandums, manuscripts of books and articles, speech and lecture files, and assorted memorabilia proved an untapped treasure trove, especially rich for the period after Acheson left public office in 1953 until his death in 1971. When I first began researching, only Walter Isaacson and Evan Thomas had made systematic use of the collection. Dean Acheson was a prolific and lively correspondent, and a few hours at the Sterling Library led me to conclude that where possible I would let Acheson speak for himself, a principle to which I have adhered. It is commonplace for scholars to thank archivists for their assistance, but in my case a mere thank you to the staff at the Sterling Library is inadequate. Judith Schiff, Diane Kaplan, Susan Brady, Essie Lucky-Barros, William R. Massa, Jr., and Katharine Morton made researching a joy. They made me feel an important part of the library team and were fun to work with.

The Harry S Truman Library staff, under the supervision of director Benjamin Zobrist, confirmed their heralded reputation as one of the most courteous, knowledgeable, and efficient groups of archivists in the country. Dennis Bilger, Donna Clark, George Curtis, Ray Geselbracht, Anita Heaver, Niel Johnson, Philip Lagerquist, and Elizabeth Safly never let me down, and I look forward to working with the "Missouri Gang" on other projects in the near future.

I also want to thank the staffs of the John F. Kennedy Library, the Lyndon B. Johnson Library, and the many other depositories cited in the notes. They graciously provided me with the documents and photographs that made the book possible. The Harry S Truman Library Institute (on the Acheson-Truman relationship), John F. Kennedy Library Foundation (on the Democratic Advisory Council, 1957–60), Hofstra University's Center for American-Netherlands Studies (on Acheson and NATO) and the Jean Monnet Council (on the Acheson-Monnet relationship) provided research grants that helped support this book. The European University

Institute in Florence, Italy, invited me to spend a semester as a research fellow to participate in seminars on the European community and to work on the book. Richard Griffiths, director of the Historical Research Project, deserves a special thanks for the many thoughtful courtesies he extended me while in Italy. I spent the last three summers at the Roosevelt Study Center in Middelburg, the Netherlands, running a student exchange program. Kees van Minnen, director of the center, made available to me their collection of microfilm including the Kennedy White House files and allowed me to make the center my European base of operations.

My friends and colleagues at New College, Hofstra University, provided me with constant encouragement and moral support to finish this book. Special thanks are in order to Dean David Christman, Tammy Cimalore, John Allen Gable, Linda Longmire, and Robert Sobel.

I am grateful to Helaine Randerson, who line-edited many drafts of the manuscript. Her knowledge of cold war history and her editorial sense improved this book immeasurably. Sue Wolfarth did a first-class job of word-processing and helping me prepare the manuscript for publication. The staff of Hofstra University's secretarial services deserve mention for tolerating my many rush-order word-processing requests with a smile.

It has been an honor to work with Yale University Press. Yale was the natural publisher, given Acheson's longstanding ties to the university. A graduate of the class of 1915 and member of the Yale Corporation for twenty years, he chose Yale as the depository for his papers.

My editor, Chuck Grench, has done a superb job of keeping me on schedule and recommending many stylistic changes which have enhanced the book. Cynthia Wells, my production editor, did a prodigious job of line editing. Not only did she tighten the rambling prose, but in the process acquired the nickname "Queen of the Query." She was terrific.

This study could not have been completed without the untiring and selfless encouragement and love of Dianne Hilsky. Dianne helped me in so many ways that it would be impossible to recount or acknowledge properly. Likewise, my gratitude to my parents, Edward and Anne Brinkley of Laguna Niguel, California, is boundless. Throughout the years they have steadfastly supported me in every possible way. Their love and reassurance have been generous and inspirational, for they paradoxically served to keep us geographically apart, which has been difficult for all of us.

For the past six years four individuals have taught me the value of combining my life as a historian with serving the larger community. Jules

Davids taught me that teaching must never be considered a secondary concern for a professor. The distinguished author and former under secretary of the air force Townsend Hoopes taught me that writing contemporary history takes courage and that the historian must never evade the larger moral obligation to communicate the truth. "If you don't have any enemies, you don't stand for anything," he once told me. Ambassador J. Robert Schaetzel taught me how important it is to bring new talent onto the national scene to tackle the seemingly insurmountable problems our nation faces. Ambassador William J. vanden Heuvel taught me that commitment, persistence, and energy can overcome almost any obstacle and that a worthy goal for one's public life is to fight for a world where Franklin D. Roosevelt's Four Freedoms flourish. This book is dedicated to them.

Dean Acheson: The Cold War Years, 1953–71

Introduction: Intimidating Seniority

Dean Gooderham Acheson, secretary of state under President Harry S Truman (1949–1953), was a major architect of United States foreign policy in the decade following the Second World War, and his achievements during this period establish him as one of the most imaginative, productive, and distinguished statesmen in America's history. In the immediate aftermath of the war, America was confronted with what seemed a fateful choice: to return to its traditional political and military isolationism as a means of walling off the turmoil of the outside world, or to play a dominant role in shaping the postwar world. In fact, the choice was dictated by America's supreme power and influence at the time. Dean Acheson was a leading advocate of the view that America must accept responsibilities conferred by compelling circumstance.

Acheson's career was a classic example of the rise of a patrician in the comfortable embrace of the American Establishment. The son of an Episcopal bishop of Connecticut, he attended Groton School, was graduated from Yale in 1915, and, after serving in the Navy during World War I, received a law degree from Harvard in 1918 and became private secretary to Supreme Court justice Louis Brandeis. In 1921 he began the practice of law in Washington with the new firm of Covington, Burling & Rublee, with which he would be affiliated for the rest of his life. In 1933 President Franklin D. Roosevelt appointed Acheson under secretary of the treasury, but he soon resigned in protest over Roosevelt's decision to take the dollar off the gold standard. For the next eight years he polished his reputation as one of the country's most incisive lawyers. In early 1940 he helped to craft an arrangement whereby the president could legally transfer fifty over-age destroyers to the British Navy in exchange for leases on British naval and air bases off the Atlantic coast of Canada and in the Caribbean—without requesting congressional approval. After his reelection to an unprecedented third term, Roosevelt rewarded Acheson by appointing him assistant secretary of state. For the next eleven years, he served the State Department with distinction, but he departed government under a cloud of controversy and public disapproval related to the stalemated Korean War, the Communist victory in the Chinese civil war, and the witchhunt known as McCarthyism. In 1953 observers of the American scene assumed that Dean Acheson's career had gone into eclipse. In fact, in the following two decades he engineered his own resurrection as a major influence on American foreign policy.

Near the end of his life, he could cheerfully caricature "the elder statesman" who was so addicted to Washington-style power that he continued to haunt the capital, write dull tomes, and give interminable speeches long after his government service had ended.[1] "One would love to get one's hands on the levers of control; and yet one would hesitate, if asked to do so," Acheson wrote professor Hans J. Morgenthau of the University of Chicago. "Responsibility is so hellishly more difficult than 'comment'—that foul word."[2] Not only did the elder statesman miss his glory days, but he also was incapable of believing that the new generation could manage government affairs properly. In 1969, Acheson wrote sardonically to his friend Anthony Eden, the former British prime minister: "If you and I could run the world, we could do a much better job than those who fail to run it now. Or so we think."[3] If Acheson could banter in the late 1960s about the foibles and absurdities of elder statesmanship, he was in the previous fifteen years no less deadly serious about retaining a position of influence in U.S. foreign policy.

The story of Acheson's struggle against the political death of relinquishing office is one of distinguished service to his country, but this service was marred by growing egotism, accentuated by a gay and reckless brilliance. Acheson's illustrious governmental career had given him unparalleled foreign-policy credentials, and his wide experience, coupled with his personal qualities of pragmatism, stoicism, and articulate self-assurance, led President Kennedy to say that Dean Acheson possessed an "intimidating seniority."[4]

From 1960 to 1971 Acheson served his country in various capacities: as head of several influential NATO task forces, and as special envoy, diplomatic troubleshooter, ambassador plenipotentiary, political consultant, and foreign-policy adviser and comforter. During the Eisenhower presidency, he took the intellectual lead in criticizing Republican foreign policy, providing the Democratic Party with well-articulated positions for the 1956 and 1960 presidential elections. Later, Richard Nixon recognized the importance of gaining the public backing of an increasingly conservative Acheson for basic elements of his own foreign policy.

Acheson was able to retain a voice in U.S. foreign policy on nearly all issues of international significance until his death in 1971. He did so by writing powerful polemics that candidly expressed his views, by appearing on television and radio news shows, by lecturing to college and university audiences, by testifying before congressional committees, and by giving dozens of addresses at private meetings and international conferences. By staying in touch with a network of distinguished European statesmen, such as Jean Monnet, Robert Schuman, Konrad Adenauer, Anthony Eden, and Dirk Stikker, Acheson could present himself in Washington as America's unofficial authority on European affairs.

Acheson wrote six books after he left office. Three of them—*A Democrat Looks at His Party* (1955), *A Citizen Looks at Congress* (1957), and *Power and Diplomacy* (1958)—fall into a category he often derided as tracts intended "to make a new and better world." The other three—*Sketches from Life of Men I Have Known* (1961), *Morning and Noon* (1965), and the Pulitzer Prize–winning *Present at the Creation* (1969)—are graceful reminiscences that, taken together, trace Acheson's life from his Connecticut Valley childhood in the 1890s to 1953, when he stepped down as secretary of state. The three memoirs, especially, offer the historian and student of diplomacy invaluable insights into the circumstances and values that led to a remarkably constructive and effective public career. Toward the end of his life Acheson began making preparations to publish an anthology of his scattered writings and speeches. Three volumes were eventually published posthumously with the assistance of Acheson's longtime personal secretary, Barbara Evans, and his only son, David: *Fragments of My Fleece* (1971), *Grapes from Thorns* (1972), and *This Vast External Realm* (1973). These further support his reputation as a gifted literary craftsman. In fact, anyone who reads one of the memoirs, or some of the more than one hundred articles and speeches Acheson wrote after leaving office, or a few of the hundreds of letters by Acheson housed at the Harry S Truman Presidential Library in Independence, Missouri, and the Sterling Library at Yale University must concur with the assessment of the historians Robert H. Ferrell and David S. McLellan: the only other secretaries of state who approached Acheson's literary flair were "Jefferson, whose writings appeared largely in the form of discursive letters, together with an occasional state paper or philosophical utterance; and John Hay, whose poetry, so popular in his own time, is now happily forgotten."[5]

As secretary of state and later as elder statesman, Acheson's political philosophy was anchored in the classic realpolitik concepts of balance of power and strong alliances. One of NATO's founding fathers, Acheson passionately believed that the political, military, and economic link between North America and Western Europe must be the cornerstone of the American foreign-policy structure. His key belief, forged in the crucible of the Second World War, was that the United States could no longer cling to an illusionary isolationism but must accept the burdens and responsibilities that circumstance had imposed. For better or for worse, America must henceforth be wedded to the fate of Europe and committed to containing communist expansion. To Acheson, the cold war was the fundamental foreign-policy reality, and security for the West depended on dealing with Soviet and Chinese communism from "positions of strength."

Along with his distinguished qualities, Acheson possessed several unattractive characteristics, which advancing age and the loss of political power seemed to exacerbate. An innate impatience led to intemperate, painful-to-behold verbal assaults on those with whom he disagreed; he became increasingly inflexible, insensitive, and ad hominem. His sharp tongue was known as one of Washington's more lethal weapons. Chester Bowles noted in 1963 that Acheson "likes not only to disagree with people but to destroy them if he can."[6] In 1957 Acheson visited his old friend David K. E. Bruce, then serving as U.S. ambassador to Germany. Bruce recorded in his diary that he found Acheson "devastating, clever, bitter and not constructive. . . . Dean is overfull of bile and it is sad."[7] Paul Nitze, whose admiration for Acheson is unqualified, admits that Acheson's wit could do more than charm; it could cut: "[Dean] had a hard time resisting the temptation to score points, even on those he was fond of. I was confident that he was fond of me, but at one point, after I had decided, contrary to his advice, to devote most of my time to arms control negotiation, he told a number of mutual friends that 'Paul has gone soft on communism.'"[8] Averell Harriman complained in 1970 that Acheson and other unreconstructed cold warriors "bring out their old, broken swords and charge into battle with the same vehemence that they used to.

The world has changed considerably since those years after the war. . . . Some people close their minds, often by the age of 40 or 45; others are able to keep them open. Some people's minds freeze. Acheson's hasn't changed since 1952."[9] Robert Bowie, an important foreign-policy adviser from Truman's administration to Carter's, has commented that there were two Dean Achesons, "the one who was in government and the less attractive elder statesman."[10] Clark Clifford believes that Acheson became increasingly acerbic during his postsecretarial years because he had been deeply wounded by the Republican assaults on him during the Truman presidency "and never fully recovered."[11]

But if Dean Acheson the elder statesman was viewed by some as a cold war relic, a high-browed anachronism rigid in outlook and haughty in demeanor, he remains appealing nevertheless for his unflinching candor, personal integrity, and diplomatic acumen. The most esteemed of a vanishing breed of gentlemen diplomats, he maintained his unique patrician identity in an increasingly bureaucratized Washington that seemed to place a higher premium on "image" than on substance. His influence when he was out of office could not begin to match the central role he held in foreign policy when he had President Truman's undivided attention. Nevertheless, from 1953 to 1971 there were few American figures who loomed larger in international affairs.

CHAPTER ONE

Into the Fray against John Foster Dulles

On January 20, 1953, three-quarters of a million people gathered at the Capitol in Washington, D.C., for the inauguration of General Dwight D. Eisenhower as the thirty-fourth president of the United States. Eisenhower, supreme commander of the Allied forces during World War II, was succeeding Harry S Truman, who had occupied the office since April 1945. Truman had decided not to run for another term in 1952, concluding that he was too unpopular to be reelected. Having announced in March of that year that he would not run again, Truman in effect became a lame-duck president for his last ten months in office, leading to what his secretary of state Dean Acheson called a "virtual interregnum of more than a year."[1]

Following Eisenhower's inaugural address, Acheson and his wife, Alice, hurried back to their home in old Georgetown near the corner of Twenty-eighth and P streets, where they would be hosting a farewell luncheon for Mr. and Mrs. Truman, the cabinet and other top-ranking administration officials, and friends of the former president. Once at the house, Acheson was stunned to find the entire block packed with throngs of people cheering and chanting "We want Harry" in pep-rally fashion. When Citizen Truman arrived, the crowd erupted into a thunderous ovation. While Truman and former vice-president Alben Barkley addressed the gathering, Acheson stood behind them, beaming with pleasure. Then the crowd called for him to speak. The six-foot-tall, immaculately dressed Acheson stepped forward and the crowd quieted as he began, "My dear friends and neighbors, thank you from the bottom of my heart for coming here and greeting a lot of old has-beens."[2]

The "old has-beens" and their wives, thirty-eight guests in all, went inside to dine on stuffed chicken washed down with a good many cocktails. The burdens of public service lifted from their shoulders, Truman, Acheson, and the others let loose, trading stories and reminiscing about the days when they were in power. Truman later wrote Acheson that he had never been "at a luncheon of this sort where everybody seemed to be having the best time they ever had."[3] As the luncheon began winding down, Acheson went outside to tell reporters about the affair: "We ended as we began, with love and devotion to our chief, his wife and their daughter which I believe has never been equaled in the history of the United States."[4] The effusive utterance was heartfelt. Acheson and Truman had worked well as a team in government; once they left public office their relationship, always characterized by deep mutual respect and loyalty, grew into intimate friendship that lasted until Acheson's death in 1971. They wrote, visited, and consoled each other often during these years.[5]

Later that evening, as dusk fell over the capital, Acheson and the rest of the cabinet went to Union Station to bid the Trumans bon voyage on their journey back to Independence, Missouri. "This is the first time you sent me home in a blaze of glory," Truman told the five thousand well-wishers, who responded by spontaneously singing "Auld Lang Syne." Then, with a toot of the whistle, Harry S Truman's train pulled out of the station, leaving Washington and the tumultuous years of the Truman administration behind it.[6]

Dean Acheson had been a key figure in the Truman administration. Sworn in as President Truman's secretary of state on January 21, 1949, Acheson succeeded in office the man he admired more than any other living person, General George C. Marshall. Acheson had served as under secretary of state for Marshall and his predecessor James F. Byrnes from August 1945 to July 1947, when he temporarily retired from the State Department. During those years Acheson was responsible for implementing the Bretton Woods agreement, which led to the establishment of the World Bank; contributed to the assistance program to Greece and Turkey under the Truman Doctrine; helped lay the groundwork for the Marshall Plan, developed to rebuild war-torn Europe; and worked to organize an effective American atomic policy.[7]

Thus when Acheson became secretary of state in 1949 he already was regarded throughout Washington as a chief architect of postwar foreign policy. During his tenure as secretary Acheson was instrumental in the creation of NATO (the North Atlantic Treaty Organization), the rebuilding of West Germany, and the formulation of a peace treaty with Japan, while orchestrating an era of bipartisanship in foreign policy. Although Acheson's European policy was largely successful, energized by a vigorous NATO and by the creation of the European Coal and Steel Community (ECSC), rapidly moving developments surrounding the fall in China of the pro-Western leader Chiang Kai-shek and, later, the Korean War occupied much of his energy. For all of the good cheer Acheson had displayed on inauguration day, he was deeply troubled by the war still raging in Korea, a war he had helped steer the United States into by taking advantage of the Soviet boycott of the United Nations Security Council to secure UN support for American intervention.[8]

The Election of 1952

The presidential election of 1952 was dominated by discussion of the war in Korea and by the hysterical anticommunist fervor of McCarthyism. Many Americans, including most Republicans, believed Senator Joseph McCarthy's accusations that Dean Acheson—"this pompous diplomat in striped pants with a phony British accent"—had "lost" China, had pursued a "no-win" policy in the Korean War, and was now "coddling" communists in the State Department. In a political atmosphere suffused with longing for victory and virtue, the Republican war hero, Dwight D. ("Ike") Eisenhower, handily defeated his Democratic opponent, Adlai E. Stevenson, taking 39 states and receiving 442 electoral votes, with a remarkable show of strength even in the traditionally Democratic South.[9]

Few presidential campaigns have been as personally vituperative as the 1952 Stevenson-Eisenhower face-off; the cutthroat duel between Truman and Ike was no small part of the friction. President Truman had appointed Eisenhower army chief of staff in 1945 and had assigned him to command the forces being organized under NATO in 1951. He had flirted with the idea of working to nominate Ike as the Democratic candidate for president in 1948. But the two had never liked each other. Relations between them had been only correct prior to the 1952 election; events during the presidential campaign that year turned what little goodwill there might have been between them into a permanent feud. In response to Eisenhower's continuous attacks on his administration's record, Truman himself went on the offensive and took a few public potshots at Ike before election day. A typical line was "The General doesn't know any more about politics than a pig knows about Sunday."[10] Their postelection animosity reached such a pitch that on inauguration day Eisenhower committed two breaches of protocol designed to humiliate Truman: Ike refused to enter the White House or even to leave his car to greet the president, as it was customary for the president-elect to do before the two departed together for the inauguration ceremony; earlier he had declined the outgoing president's invitation to lunch.[11]

Acheson believed that Eisenhower had run a dishonest campaign based on demagoguery and political hucksterism. Acheson and Truman were enraged by Eisenhower's pledge that if elected he personally would go to Korea. They were convinced Ike shamefully was using the bitter conflict as a vehicle for self-promotion, in contemptuous disregard for the American soldiers dying in the war. Further, Eisenhower's acquiescence in the Republican witchhunts to eliminate supposed communist subversives from government; his exaggerated promise to "liberate" the peoples of Eastern Europe from Soviet domination; his repudiation of the Yalta agreements; his support for reelection of the right-wing extremist senators Joseph McCarthy of Wisconsin and William E. Jenner of Indiana; his refusal to defend his own mentor, George C. Marshall, from outrageous disloyalty charges; the casual disrespect he showed toward President Truman; and his sheer hypocrisy in criticizing a foreign policy he himself had been instrumental in formalizing and executing convinced Acheson that Eisenhower had turned duplicity into an art form unmatched in recent American political history.[12]

Acheson had spent election day evening, November 4, 1952, at a friend's house, anxiously listening to the returns on the radio. When it appeared certain that Eisenhower had won a landslide victory over Stevenson, Acheson rose to address the small gathering, mostly young associates from the government. Defeat was not necessarily a bad thing, Acheson said. The Democrats had been in power for twenty years, and perhaps the change in party leadership would do the country some good: "Whatever we may have thought of some of the men who will come into the new administration when they have been so critical of us, there's no sense in continuing to voice these past opinions of the new man. We must give them a chance.... Above all, we shouldn't organize ourselves into factions that are anti-this or anti-that. We shouldn't form anti-Dulles clubs, if he is the next Secretary of State, or anti-anybody clubs." After the new administration had been in office a year, he continued, the Democrats would be in a position to assess its policies and to propose alternative policies and fresh insights into how to solve the pressing issues of the day. "There is no sense in having our ideas simply ideas of how badly the Republicans are doing things," Acheson concluded.[13]

Throughout the campaign Acheson kept a low public profile, making only a handful of speeches, none of them on Stevenson's behalf. Among Republican attacks on his loyalty and competence was the charge, which Eisenhower endorsed, that Acheson had helped precipitate the war in Korea by mysteriously excluding mention of that country as part of the "defense perimeter" of the United States in an important speech at the National Press Club in Washington on January 12, 1950.[14] If the Democrats were to win, party strategists had reasoned, it was best to keep some distance between Dean Acheson and the Stevenson entourage. The Republicans, sensing a political opportunity to exploit, ran harder against the Truman-Acheson record than they did against Stevenson. Acheson also understood that even if by some stroke of luck Stevenson were to be elected, there would be no place for the controversial Dean Acheson in his administration. Although Acheson accepted the reality that he was a political liability, he was nonetheless annoyed when Stevenson attempted to distance himself and the party from specific foreign-policy positions Acheson had formulated during the Truman years. But, not wanting to break ranks with his party's nominee, he kept quiet.

During the election campaign and in the twelve-week interval that followed Ike's landslide victory, Acheson attended to his multifarious duties at State, focusing primarily on pursuing the prisoner-of-war negotiations in Korea (the main obstacle to achieving an armistice), finding a suitable settlement to the Anglo-Iranian oil dispute, worrying about the future of the European Defense Community (EDC) and of continued French control in Indochina, and reviewing the pile of loyalty cases that cluttered his desk. Having played no role in Stevenson's campaign and containing his displeasure with Ike's political tactics within the confines of administration circles, Acheson remained the epitome of the public servant to the end, briefing President-elect Eisenhower on the pressing foreign-policy issues he would soon have to confront.[15]

The Changing of the Guard

When Eisenhower announced the appointment of John Foster Dulles as his secretary of state, Acheson was among the first to congratulate Dulles and to put himself at his disposal. "All of us in the Department stand ready to help you in any way we can to assure the smoothest possible transition," Acheson wrote Dulles. "When you have decided on your top people, we will be glad to have any or all of them come and sit with us in any way that you think would be useful."[16] Although Acheson and Dulles met only once during the interregnum, Dulles was given an office at State and was kept abreast of the pressing problems facing the department. Despite the animosity of the campaign, the transition at Foggy Bottom appeared orderly and amicable, with Dulles seeking and Acheson offering recommendations on a number of posts and policies. But on the day before the actual changing of command was to take place Acheson made his contempt for Dulles known by resigning early as secretary of state to avoid being the official who signed Dulles's commission.[17]

This last-minute gesture did not come as a shock to many in the State Department. Although he did not make it a public issue, it is safe to say that there were few men in Washington whom Dean Acheson loathed more thoroughly than his successor as secretary of state. This had not always been the case. "My relations with JFD were entirely cordial while I was in the State Department," Acheson later noted. "Thereafter, I saw JFD only once. I was never invited to the State Department or the White House, nor ever consulted on any subject."[18]

Dulles, an old Washington hand, was in many ways perfectly cast for the position of secretary of state. During the Second World War, as an international lawyer of great distinction, he undertook several diplomatic assignments for the Roosevelt administration. In 1945 President Truman appointed him to serve as a senior Republican member of the bipartisan U.S. delegation to the San Francisco Conference where the UN Charter was drawn up. Truman also named him to the delegation that accompanied Secretary of State Marshall to the Moscow Conference in 1947, where major cold war issues were addressed. But Dulles's single greatest achievement during the Truman years, perhaps the most formidable of his entire governmental career, was his successful negotiation in 1951 of the peace treaty with Japan which restored Japan's sovereignty while retaining the presence of U.S. bases.[19]

Truman reluctantly had appointed Dulles as a special representative of the president with the rank of ambassador to negotiate the treaty with Japan. Acheson was not enthusiastic at the prospect of having Dulles as a consultant, but he understood the benefits that would accrue from having a leading Republican foreign-policy spokesman work for him. Acheson knew Dulles was a competent international lawyer but thought him limited, a member of that one-dimensional species of humanity Acheson called "the single-minded concentrators," those who can focus on only one objective at a time. He believed that, unlike himself, Dulles had no wide-angle vision, no ability to see the big picture. Acheson was prepared to entrust Dulles with the specific task of concluding a peace treaty with the Japanese. However, he never would have dreamt of allowing Dulles to serve on, say, his State Department Policy Planning Staff, which in 1950 was headed by the then-Republican Paul H. Nitze, for he considered Dulles incapable of contributing new ideas or of even comprehending in broad geopolitical terms the intricate web of nation-states, each with its own political agenda and unique history. Dulles was like a bull in a china shop, Acheson believed; without careful monitoring he could trample a delicate alliance or create turmoil within the State Department itself.[20]

Although Acheson did not like Dulles, he found the GOP's most prominent foreign-policy spokesman tolerable, especially because Dulles had given enthusiastic and much-needed support to the Truman Doctrine, the Marshall Plan, and NATO, and perhaps even more important, to Truman and Acheson's handling of the war in Korea. It was Dulles's abrupt reversal of his position on the Truman administration's management of foreign policy that confirmed for Acheson what he had suspected all along: Dulles was a dishonest coward, an unprincipled opportunist whose primary concern was advancing his own position in government.[21]

Acheson's shock over Dulles's policy reversal is not surprising. Dulles had been on a special government mission to South Korea early in 1950. On June 24, 1950, when communist North Korean troops crossed the 38th parallel and invaded anticommunist South Korea, he was in Asia working on the peace treaty with Japan. When he heard of the invasion, he immediately cabled the White House through army channels to urge U.S. intervention: "To sit by while Korea is overrun by unprovoked armed attack would start a disastrous chain of events leading most probably to world war."[22] Dulles returned to Washington shortly thereafter, where he praised Truman's decisiveness: "The President of the United States, with bipartisan backing, has given our nation and indeed the entire free world fine leadership." Even as late as the spring of 1952 Dulles characterized President Truman's decision to defend South Korea as "courageous, righteous and in the national interest."[23]

Acheson, among others, therefore was astonished when Dulles wrote, in the GOP platform for the election of 1952, that the Truman administration had "plunged us into war in Korea without the consent of our citizens through their authorized representatives in Congress."[24] To appease the Republican McCarthyites, Dulles had repudiated Truman and Acheson's use of the United Nations as a vehicle for legitimating U.S. intervention in Korea. He thereby lost his integrity and credibility in Acheson's eyes.

And as if his volte-face on Korea were not enough, Dulles, who, Acheson knew, had been around the State Department long enough to know better, pronounced Yalta a willful "betrayal" of Eastern Europe by the Democrats. He wrote in the Republican platform that "the government of the United States, under Republican leadership, will repudiate all commitments contained in secret understandings such as those of Yalta which aid Communist enslavement."[25] Here was the one-dimensional Dulles at his lowest and most deceitful, Acheson believed—like Faust himself, willing to sell his soul to the McCarthyite devils in return for being appointed secretary of state in a Republican administration. For the end of attracting voters of Eastern European descent and showcasing his hardline anticommunist credentials for the Old Guard Republicans, he was irresponsible enough to jettison containment as the primary objective of American foreign policy and substitute liberation without giving a second thought to the broader implications. Acheson doubted whether a man who would do or say anything to enhance his political profile was morally qualified to be entrusted with a high post in government, particularly the responsible and sensitive position of secretary of state.

Acheson, apparently determined to maintain his statesmanlike pledge of election night 1952, chose not to pop off publicly at the new administration, despite what must have been an enormous temptation. He prepared to return to law practice at Covington & Burling in Washington, resigned to watch in self-imposed silence as the events of 1953, including Stalin's death on March 5 and the accompanying changes in the Soviet Union, unfolded. As much as he disliked Dulles, Acheson was not going to start any anti-Dulles clubs. Perhaps Dulles's distorted rhetoric and pliant principles would give way to clearheadedness once he assumed the responsibilities of his position, Acheson wistfully hoped. However, as Dulles's first days in office turned to months, and he appeared consistently to be placating rabidly isolationist Republican senators, Acheson found it increasingly difficult to bite his tongue: Dulles was proving to be a more ruinous secretary than even Acheson had anticipated.[26]

Private Citizen

A few days after Eisenhower's inauguration Acheson, accompanied by his wife of thirty-five years, Alice, left for a seven-week vacation on the island of Antigua in the British West Indies. As they had done in years past, in years to come the Achesons would escape Washington winters at Antigua's Mill Reef Club, often in the company of John Cowles, the publisher of the *Minneapolis Star and Tribune*, and Archibald MacLeish, the eminent playwright and poet, who had been a college friend at Yale.[27]

This winter's stay in Antigua was particularly therapeutic for Acheson, as it gave him the opportunity to put his years as secretary of state into perspective, to spend time with his three children, David, Mary, and Jane, and to prepare himself for his new life as lawyer and elder statesman. Acheson was able to read more widely and to contemplate what kind of figure he would cut on the pages of history. It also gave him time to reflect, admiringly, on President Harry S Truman. On February 10 Acheson wrote Truman the first letter in what would become an almost two-decade-long correspondence. "One of the glorious things which I have read—and which you probably know—is Paul Wilstach's edition of the correspondence between John Adams and Jefferson," Acheson wrote his old boss, clearly hoping the two of them could emulate their predecessors. "If you do not know it, by all means get it. They were two robust old codgers, I think one gets a wholly new affection for Adams."[28] Acheson had more in mind than mere exchange of news with Truman; he wanted to make a record. Acheson also had with him the Oliver Wendell Holmes, Jr.–Harold Laski correspondence, and to his surprise he found his own name mentioned in letters from the 1920s. "To suddenly read about yourself—particularly when you have forgotten the episode entirely—gives the strangest sense that you are dead and the consciousness reading the book is another's," he wrote his son, David.[29]

Acheson's letters from this vacation are filled with references to the Adams-Jefferson and Holmes-Laski letters. So impressed was he by these volumes that he decided to correspond with selected thinkers and political leaders around the world. From 1953 on, Acheson's letters began to change, growing longer and more discursive in the manner of Victorian statesman, displaying more candor and Holmesian wit than ever before, informing the recipient with precision of his views about the changing world. Acheson was writing with posterity in mind and was careful to retain a duplicate of all outgoing correspondence. Only an occasional note written while traveling would slip by his longtime personal secretary, Barbara Evans, without a file copy.[30]

The Achesons returned at the end of March, intending to spend April at their eighteenth-century country home, Harewood, in Sandy Spring, Maryland, some twenty miles north of Washington. Acheson had purchased Harewood in 1923, and from that time until his death in 1971, the rural retreat served as an island of tranquility, where, freed from the distractions of Washington, he was able to indulge his passions for gardening, writing and cabinetmaking. "I kept sane, when I was Secretary of State," Acheson told a reporter years after he had retired from government, "by making furniture in my workshop."[31]

As April drew to a close Acheson was reluctant to return to his Washington law practice. "I am a spry and very lazy lad of sixty summers," he wrote Truman from Harewood. "After nearly three months off, the very thought of work is repulsive to me. That is, work in an office. Out here on the farm Alice has me painting the porch furniture, plowing the garden, wheelbarrowing manure for her roses, building a new wood fence and taking the grandchildren down to the next farm to see horses, cattle, pigs, and puppies."[32] What really bothered Acheson, however, was not work, but toiling in the oppressive atmosphere of Eisenhower's and McCarthy's Washington. In the foreign-policy realm he worried that America's credibility as leader of the free world might be in jeopardy. On June 16, 1953, workers' demonstrations in East Germany were met with Soviet tanks and troops sent to restore order. Dulles, with his doctrine of liberation and his self-styled Policy of Boldness, seemed a captive of his own rhetoric, unwilling and unable to help the dissidents achieve democratic freedoms. The empty campaign promises of liberation were exposed for all to see, Acheson pointed out—privately.

Even more worrisome to Acheson was his fear that the Republicans would cut a quick deal with the Communists over Korea for the sake of political expediency. "I most earnestly hope that Foster [Dulles] and Ike do not appease these Chinese Communists to get a truce in Korea," Acheson wrote Truman on April 6, 1953. "As you know so well, we could always have had a truce on their terms."[33] Acheson's concerns were unnecessary. The final general shape of the Korean armistice agreement had been ironed out earlier between the United States and the People's Republic of China (PRC) at Panmunjom, South Korea, under the Truman administration. But then talks had stalled over the prisoner-of-war provisions. It was not until March 30, 1953, when the Chinese suggested letting the issue be decided by an international authority, that the Eisenhower administration resumed negotiations for an armistice. On July 27, 1953, the PRC accepted the truce proposals put forth by the UN. The Korean War ended, and Eisenhower had achieved an unmitigated foreign-policy success. Acheson complained privately that Ike and Dulles unfairly were taking all of the credit. Acheson maintained that, for its own political reasons, Communist China had by May 1953 decided to accept terms on the prisoner-of-war issue essentially identical to those offered by the Truman administration in December 1952 and rejected then by the PRC.[34]

When asked by Adlai Stevenson to explain the PRC's dramatic change of heart, Acheson replied, "First: they may well have reasoned that they could always get an armistice on the terms available in [19]52 and that in Ike's campaign promise to end the Korean War they might do better. Second: the Communist Party Congress in [19]52 foreshadowed the change in tactics which developed faster after Stalin's death."[35] It is clear that Acheson gave little weight to the Eisenhower administration's public threats of employing increased U.S. air power in Korea, enlarging the South Korean army, and placing nuclear weapons on Okinawa as significant in bringing about the negotiated settlement; it was the Truman administration's efforts, plus internal changes in Sino-Soviet policy, that produced the desired result.

Besides having to endure Eisenhower's crowing over Korea, there were other more fundamental reasons why Acheson was unhappy in what he called Ike's Washington miasma. In a brief farewell address to his State Department associates on January 16, Acheson had read them their rights, as he put it: the right not to be "vilified," not to have their loyalty and patriotism questioned, and not to have "slander and libel" broadcast against them.[36] Yet after only a few short weeks out of office, Acheson looked on in horror as Dulles purged the foreign service of those too closely associated with Achesonian policies. He wrote Truman that he believed this sacrifice of the careers and besmirching of the reputations of some of America's most distinguished diplomats and foreign-service experts in order to placate "primitive" right-wing Republican senators like Joseph McCarthy, William Jenner, William Knowland, and Styles Bridges was "not only criminal but frightening in what it may mean regarding the quality of advice which the Secretary of State, and ultimately, the President will receive."[37] The willful tarring of reputations Acheson viewed as egregious and distasteful, a repetition of the unforgiveable Palmer Raids and Red Scare witchhunts that occurred after World War I.

The treatment of Paul Nitze was particularly rankling to Acheson. Nitze had come to Washington from Wall Street in 1940, and he held various governmental positions during World War II, including vice-chairman of the U.S. Strategic Bombing Survey from 1944 to 1946. Nitze then moved to the State Department, where he eventually became director of the State Department Policy Planning Staff from 1950 to 1953. He had first come to Acheson's attention through his work on the congressional legislation that became the Marshall Plan. In 1950 Nitze, in his capacity as chief of policy planning, drafted a seminal and comprehensive review of national security policy known as NSC-68. The review document, written just weeks before the Korean War began, urged the United States to take responsibility for defending the West from communist aggression. It concluded that this could be accomplished only if the defense budget were greatly increased so as to meet Soviet expansionism and maintain a strategic superiority in both nuclear weapons and conventional forces. The U.S. economy, the review argued, could sustain an increase in military expenditures without demanding heavy taxation or producing runaway inflation.[38]

Acheson shared Nitze's view of the Soviet military threat and the need for massive U.S. rearmament in order to effect an unassailable military posture. On first meeting Nitze, Acheson had thought the young Republican another brash, over-ambitious Wall Street operator, but by 1950 he had come full circle and considered Nitze an invaluable adviser because of his clear, incisive mind.[39] Acheson regarded the strategic premises Nitze and his staff developed as the foreign policy bible for the new cold war era. NSC-68 laid out, he believed, "the conflicting aims and purposes of the two superpowers: the priority given by the Soviet rulers to the Kremlin design, world domination, contrasted with the American aim, an environment in which free societies could exist and flourish. Throughout 1950, the year my immolation in the Senate began, I went about the country preaching this premise of NSC-68."[40]

Because some voices on Capitol Hill demanded that anyone who had worked with Acheson must be assigned to a new department or fired, Dulles sacrificed, in Acheson's view, the most astute young mind in Washington—Paul Nitze. Acheson wrote Truman that Dulles's mistreatment of Nitze, the Republican who had formulated the policy "under which the rearmament took place and under which Ike himself operated in Europe," was a disgraceful display of "plain cowardice and utter folly" unparalleled in the annals of the State Department.[41] "Dulles' people seem to me like Cossacks quartered in a grand city hall, burning the paneling to cook with," Acheson complained to his former special assistant, Lucius Battle.[42] Nitze was briefly picked up by Secretary Charles E. Wilson at Defense, but by June Wilson informed Nitze that he would have to resign from government: his association with Acheson's foreign policy had made him an undesirable, at least in the eyes of certain influential Old Guard Republican senators and the right-wing *Washington Times-Herald.* When Nitze double-checked with Dulles to make sure he agreed with Wilson, the new secretary of state not only agreed but, to Nitze's shock, helped him write a resignation letter.[43]

Nitze was the first Truman administration official to "call on" Acheson after his return to Covington & Burling in May 1953. The gesture initiated a weekly luncheon date at the Metropolitan Club that would extend over the next two decades. "Dean was incredibly grateful," Nitze recalls. "It clearly turned our work relationship into a personal one." By the summer of 1953, Acheson and Nitze had become in the minds of many an inseparable Washington tandem.[44]

Acheson's return to Covington & Burling, the prestigious Washington law firm which he had first joined in 1921 and with which he would remain affiliated for the rest of his life, was unenthusiastic. The prize student of Louis Brandeis and Felix Frankfurter, Acheson was regarded as one of the outstanding legal minds of his generation, but by 1953 he was not engaged by the notion of practicing law. After the exhilarating years as secretary of state, the narrow focus of private practice appeared unfulfilling and uninviting to a man of Acheson's intellectual scope. Justice Frankfurter, Acheson's law professor and mentor at Harvard, his closest friend and daily walking companion, recalled that Acheson was afraid that in the transition from public to private life "he might go stale." "The difference in the two schemes of life," Frankfurter noted, "is about that between French cooking and hardtack."[45]

For the next seventeen years Acheson handled many important cases for Covington & Burling, affirming his reputation as a noted appellate lawyer, but his heart was not in the private practice of law. Acheson's years as secretary of state—trying to negotiate an end to the Korean War, providing American leadership to NATO, the delicate task of directing strategic U.S. planning, administering the State Department bureaucracy, and dining in the White House with the likes of Truman and Churchill—left him unhappy handling routine legal cases. He missed the prestige and accoutrements of high office and soon began using his law office, facing Lafayette Park directly across from the White House, as a convenient base for his true passions—foreign affairs and politics.[46]

By the autumn of 1953 Dean Acheson was anxious to get back into the action. Though he was struggling to overcome a bacterial infection he had contracted on a recent trip abroad, Acheson was slowly starting to feel reenergized. Since July he, along with some other associates from the Truman administration, had been participating in a series of tape-recorded debriefing seminars on their governmental experiences, held at the Institute for Advanced Study in Princeton, New Jersey, under the direction of J. Robert Oppenheimer. "The idea [was] not to write history," Acheson noted, "but to aid those who may some day do so."[47] In preparing for the sessions Acheson was struck anew by what he had known all along—the remarkable job Harry S Truman had done as president. That autumn Acheson delivered two public speeches, notable only for their outpouring of affection and admiration for his old boss.[48]

Earlier Acheson had endured McCarthyite accusations of appeasement, blindness, and softness on communism with unruffled dignity, but finally he broke his self-imposed silence to throw a few punches of his own. On October 1 at a Woodrow Wilson Foundation dinner held in his honor, Acheson gave his first major address since leaving office. He was openly contemptuous of Eisenhower for slashing military and foreign-aid budgets. He also chided his arch-nemesis, Senator Joseph R. McCarthy, for his "insults" to allies of the United States and for his "totalitarian" methods.[49] Dean Acheson had reentered the foreign-policy arena. His address was received positively in Democratic circles; Adlai Stevenson praised him, for instance, and party leader and former secretary of the air force Thomas K. Finletter encouraged him to speak out even more strongly.[50] When in early 1954 John Foster Dulles announced his new policy of massive retaliation, Acheson stepped forward to become one of its most vehement and outspoken critics, a role he played for the duration of both Eisenhower administrations.

Disagreement over Defense

On January 12, 1954, Secretary of State John Foster Dulles enunciated before the Council on Foreign Relations a new nuclear defense policy, a companion piece to Eisenhower's New Look doctrine, which called for heavy cuts in defense and foreign-aid spending. Dulles announced that American policy would no longer be based, as it had been under Truman, on expensive reflex responses to communist advances like those in Greece, Turkey, Korea, and Berlin. Instead, more reliance would be placed on "deterrent power, a less local defensive power." The United States would "depend primarily upon a great capacity to retaliate, instantly, by means and at places of our own choosing."[51] America's response would be massive not only in the sense of inflicting great damage, but also in that it might enlarge the scope of action beyond the limits of the initial aggression, in terms of both territory and method. The United States might use nuclear weapons, and the war might be brought to the aggressor's home field. Although Dulles's so-called massive retaliation speech did not preclude the need for limited forces, it certainly minimized their importance.[52]

Acheson reacted to the policy with fear and disbelief—fear that every border incident would be converted into an all-out war and disbelief in a policy he saw as a dangerous, politically motivated bluff. "Defense on the cheap," Acheson said of Dulles's reliance on nuclear weapons. It was an Orwellian attempt "to persuade the country that it got stronger by getting weaker."[53] The fears engendered by Dulles's rhetoric were widespread, and although it was his critics who originated the phrase "massive retaliation," in popular parlance the term came to stand for the essential features of the Eisenhower-Dulles defense policies.

Dulles realized his speech had many world leaders believing the administration was threatening to use nuclear warheads against unfriendly nations and tried to dispel that impression. However, neither Dulles's personal explanation to journalists nor his testimony on Capitol Hill nor an article for *Foreign Affairs* proved effective. Although the article, for example, was relatively cautious in tone, it retained the basic tenets of the first pronouncement. Nuclear weapons would be stressed over conventional in making up the American arsenal. And American leaders would reserve the right to enlarge the territorial scope of a conflict by attacking what they perceived as the source of aggression, for instance, Moscow, or Peking.[54]

The policy of massive retaliation was a response to both domestic and international pressures. In large part, Dulles was attempting to explain and justify the New Look program, for the president viewed national security and American prosperity as two sides of the same coin. The nation's wealth provided the capital necessary for defense, and conversely, the military's ultimate purpose was to protect the economic system that supported America's standard of living. Because the threat of communism was indeterminate and American economic capabilities were clearly finite, defense planning had to be geared to the long haul rather than for the immediate crisis, as had been the case under the Truman-Acheson regime. Dulles argued that were the United States to continue to maintain a state of constant mobilization, the steadily increasing defense budget—which Truman envisioned as costing $74 billion per year in his 1952 budget plan—would stifle the American economy and, in turn, damage national security. The New Look defense decrease was an effort to plan for the long term; a reduced annual military budget of $38 to $40 billion would be in balance with the American economy. Massive retaliation would provide the "maximum military strength within economic capabilities," or the "biggest bang for the buck."[55]

Fundamental to this policy was the announcement to friends and enemies alike that the United States reserved the option *not* to intervene militarily in local and limited communist aggressions outside of Europe—like Korea—which would require a large arsenal of conventional weapons along with a huge investment in manpower. Military planning would stress air and nuclear power. Ground troops would be retained as a symbol of America's commitment to Western Europe; large contingents of manpower beyond this were unnecessary. Massive retaliation also was conceived as a response to the domestic backlash against the Korean War. The doctrine ostensibly would not permit a long-lasting war, for the United States could use its most powerful weaponry to terminate the conflict immediately.[56]

The doctrine became the subject of a well-publicized series of critical assessments published in the *New York Times Magazine*. The first was by Chester Bowles, former Democratic governor of Connecticut and ambassador to India, who characterized the policy as immoral and concluded it reduced the chances for international nuclear disarmament to nil.[57] This set the stage for Acheson.

On March 28, 1954, Acheson's article appeared, causing a swirl of controversy.[58] From then on, Acheson led the Democrats in denouncing Eisenhower-Dulles foreign policy, which he saw as a return to Republican isolationist tendencies of the 1920s and 1930s, and in defending the Truman administration's strategies. Acheson believed that the new administration had restructured U.S. defenses to meet preconceived budget goals rather than providing the strength needed to guarantee America's national survival. Acheson's wrong-headed equation of massive retaliation with the entire New Look defense program, as authorized in NSC-162/2 (October 1953), failed to address the policy's sensible budgetary concerns. Acheson's state of mind is revealed in a letter he wrote Truman shortly after his article appeared. "I become too worked up over the fraud of the New Look to be quiet any longer."[59]

Dulles was frustrated with Acheson's article, feeling the former secretary had relied on misleading quotations and had charged the administration unfairly with wanting to dispense with conventional defensive forces.[60] Freed of the burden of governmental responsibility, Acheson had begun to relish lobbing criticisms at the "ins," especially at those, like Dulles, whose rhetorical gaffes made particularly tempting targets.[61] Acheson, a practitioner of realpolitik in foreign relations, had described massive retaliation as weakening America's position of strength, an abandonment of NSC-68. He pointed out that America's atomic monopoly had neither deterred the Soviets from blockading Berlin in 1948 nor prevented the Chinese from intervening in the Korean War. Furthermore, the Soviets now had their own nuclear capability. What had not been a deterrent to aggression in the past (that is, U.S. capability to wage war with atomic weapons in an aggressor's homeland) was even less likely to be a deterrent in the future.

Acheson argued that the policy represented a mutual suicide pact of the superpowers, founded in an escalating game of tit-for-tat. Should the United States call a nuclear attack, this could only lead to counter-retaliation by the Soviets. Massive retaliation, Acheson concluded, certainly could not be used often, nor could it be used effectively in the face of a similarly armed foe.

Most important to Acheson, the policy precluded a forceful American response to limited aggression. The former secretary accused Eisenhower and Dulles of misinterpreting the usefulness of conventional forces. Their purpose, Acheson maintained, was not necessarily to defeat an aggressor but to exact, with some certainty, a cost an aggressor would be unwilling to pay. Because of the uncertainty associated with the U.S. use of nuclear weapons, they were not a credible deterrent, whereas ground forces were.

Acheson defended the policy outlined in NSC-68, which, though expensive, would put the West on a permanent wartime footing, ready to do battle anywhere against communist encroachment.[62] "There is no bargain basement where peace is sold cheap," he wrote Adlai Stevenson.[63] The free world would disintegrate if it opted for inexpensive, mechanical solutions to dangers that could only be met by sustained effort. A flexible defense force was essential to thwarting communist expansionism and winning the cold war. Although Dulles had supported the concept of a flexible defense establishment, Acheson believed such statements were belied by the administration's simultaneous push to reduce military expenditures and deemphasize ground forces. Acheson distorted, or misread, massive retaliation as promising nuclear war as a response to any Soviet or Chinese violation of the status quo, which was certainly not the case.[64]

Western Europe, as Acheson had predicted, found Washington's newfound reliance on unilateral nuclear deterrence difficult to appreciate or comprehend. The initial European reaction had two components: fear that Europe might be dragged into an unwanted nuclear war and fear that the United States might not value Europe enough to risk massive retaliation for its defense. Acheson took these concerns seriously, for if a coalition is to be held together by consent rather than force, the members must believe their basic interests are recognized by the coalition leader—in this case, the United States. The unilateral nature of the doctrine of massive retaliation eroded the postwar trans-Atlantic bonds of trust.

That is not to say that Acheson supported the idea of Western European nations developing their own nuclear arsenal. He was opposed to this on two grounds: First, it was not wise to "hasten the dissemination of nuclear weapons."[65] Second, should NATO members devote their limited resources to creating independent nuclear forces, little would be left with which to finance adequate conventional forces. Acheson began to make what would become a perennial call for increasing NATO conventional forces and emphasizing continued U.S. participation and financial assistance for the defense of Europe.[66]

A Difference of Style

Throughout the fifties, in speeches, articles, and stinging off-the-cuff remarks, Acheson pounded away at massive retaliation's hollow deterrence capabilities and the failure of what he called the "Dullesian approach" to instill confidence in America's allies. Disagreement over defense strategy afforded Acheson a useful hook on which to hang his opposition to most of Dulles's proposals. Acheson painted the New Look as dangerously irresponsible, due to its disregard of consultation with the NATO allies, the reckless brandishing of atomic weapons, and the inclination to gamble with war and peace. As for Ike's perennial call for a balanced budget, Acheson could point out by 1959 that while masquerading as a fiscal conservative Eisenhower presided over the largest peacetime deficit in American history. These assaults on Eisenhower provided the Democratic Party with useful campaign rhetoric.[67]

Throughout the 1950s the differences between the two men were exaggerated by Dulles's overblown rhetoric and Acheson's equally overblown counterattacks. In reality, their analyses of deterrent policy were not as far apart as many historians have assumed. Both believed that the United States had to be strong militarily in order to prevent nuclear war; that it had to make its strength known to prevent miscalculation; and that, when challenged by communist aggression, it had to demonstrate a will to resist. By 1957 Dulles himself began to modify his earlier position, pointing out that due to Soviet nuclear gains the U.S. would have to expand its stockpile of flexible small-yield nuclear weapons, as their "destructiveness and radiation effects . . . [could be] confined substantially to predetermined targets."[68] The disagreement between the two statesmen was not over whether to deter and contain Sino-Soviet expansionism, but over the most effective means of doing so. Acheson himself confirmed this picture years later; in 1969, when asked if he saw significant differences in the foreign policies pursued by himself and by Dulles, he responded, "No. What we did when I was in office set the pattern which has been followed more or less up to the present time. Foster's problems stemmed not from foreign policy, but from the way he handled particular situations."[69] It was Dulles's style that infuriated Acheson, for he saw it as a pious and self-righteous foreign policy built unacceptably on a foundation of moralistic bombast and sleazy political ploys.

The Republicans had made Acheson's life nearly intolerable during his last years in government. Now that the shoe was on the other foot, the former secretary derived tremendous satisfaction from kicking Eisenhower and Dulles around as often and as hard as he could. The statesmanlike qualities Acheson had so brilliantly exhibited while in government had fallen by the wayside only a year after leaving office. The "attack of the primitives" clearly had scarred Acheson, leading him to coarsen his method of foreign-policy analysis and turning him into a caustic, and at times vengeful, man.

Acheson's letters to friends from 1953 until 1960 are filled with barbs aimed at denigrating Eisenhower and Dulles, and unfortunately not just on policy issues: their physical appearance, their manhood, the clothes they wore, the churches they attended, the hobbies they pursued, even the illnesses they contracted (including Eisenhower's heart attack and Dulles's bout with cancer) were all fair game for Acheson's acerbic tongue and virulent pen. Dulles's Presbyterianism in particular seems to have touched a raw nerve in Acheson, the son of an Episcopal bishop.[70]

It was Dulles's tendency to mix religious moralism with foreign affairs that inflamed Acheson. He thought it the height of hypocrisy for a man like Dulles, whom he saw as utterly lacking in personal integrity, to impose moral standards on others. Of course, the record shows that Acheson himself used moralistic discourse in foreign-policy pronouncements; for instance, he called preventive war "immoral and wrong from every point of view."[71] He described the decision of the People's Republic of China to enter the Korean War as demonstrating a "complete disregard of any kind of moral standard."[72] He went so far as to state that "just as the foundations of freedom in the United States are based on morality and moral purpose and moral responsibility, so relationships in the world are based on moral conviction and moral responsibility."[73] Speaking before a group of ministers of foreign affairs in 1951, Acheson sounded like John Foster Dulles himself as he declared: "Our cause is above all, the cause of freedom, of international morality."[74]

A year after he left the State Department Acheson was still applying the morality yardstick to conduct in foreign affairs, most notably in his criticism of Dulles's doctrine of massive retaliation. In his article "'Instant Retaliation': The Debate Continued," he formulated his opposition to the deterrence strategy in these terms: "It would violate the deepest moral convictions of the people who are the final arbitrators of policy.... We must by our very nature be defenders, not offenders.... That is the basis of our moral position in the world."[75]

With time Acheson became more vociferous in his objection to Dulles's moralistic maxims. In his book *Power and Diplomacy* (1958) Acheson referred to Dulles's "sanctimonious self-righteousness which, joined with a sly worldliness, beclouds the dangers and opportunities of our time with an unctuous film."[76] Nevertheless, the book itself to a large degree defends the substance of the Dullesian foreign policy. As Arthur Schlesinger, Jr., pointed out, "*Power and Diplomacy* is, so to speak, Dulles minus Norman Vincent Peale." Acheson later took Schlesinger to task for equating him with the contemptible Mr. Dulles.[77] Again, in a speech delivered at the University of Florida at Gainesville on February 28, 1958, and subsequently published in the *Yale Review* under the title "Morality, Moralism, and Diplomacy," Acheson took another swipe at Dulles, maintaining that "seldom [do] those who demand a moral policy appeal to the principles of truth, honor, and courage. Instead, they use morality as a prop to practice duplicity, conspiracy, and treachery."[78]

The historian is left to ponder why Acheson, who as secretary of state had discussed the relationships of nations in moralistic terms, only four years after leaving office denounced the intrusion of morality into foreign-policy issues with such vehemence. Part of the answer is that as secretary of state Acheson was forced to articulate foreign-policy stances in language that would elicit the response he was seeking from the audience he addressed; thus, for example, he denounced in moral terms the PRC's entry into the Korean War. It is also reasonable to surmise that Secretary Acheson employed moralistic phrases in an attempt to recapture the confidence of Americans who had been led to doubt his loyalty and patriotism. Interestingly enough, Acheson's moralistic speeches were all delivered at the height of the relentless attack on him by McCarthy, that is, from February 1950 onward.[79]

One might argue that Acheson as elder statesman, freed from the straitjacket of responsibility and the daily pressures of decision, could step back and examine the relevance of moralism in international affairs. Yet one cannot help but believe that it was not so much moralism in foreign-policy making that Acheson objected to as moralism as practiced by that "psalm-singing Presbyterian Wall Street lawyer" John Foster Dulles.[80]

One of the difficulties in evaluating the Acheson-Dulles disagreement over deterrence is determining where strategic concerns ended and partisan politics, tainted with personal animosity, began. By the summer of 1954, with congressional elections only months away, Acheson, Truman, Stevenson, Lyndon Johnson, and a handful of other national Democratic leaders had seized upon Dulles's foreign-policy rhetoric as a campaign issue, a counterissue to Eisenhower's successful ending of the Korean War. They saw massive retaliation as an ill-conceived containment strategy and a dangerous political hoax. The Eisenhower administration then provided what some Democrats regarded as conclusive proof of the Republican sham: it refused to send immediate assistance to the French besieged at Dienbienphu in Indochina, and it allowed the supranational European army, the European Defense Community, to fall by the wayside.

Controversy over Indochina and the European Defense Community

By spring 1954 Acheson was convinced the beleaguered French garrison at Dienbienphu in Indochina would fall to the communist Viet Minh, under the command of Ho Chi Minh, if the United States did not go in and bail out the ten thousand French soldiers stranded there. He knew well the difficulties involved in establishing a coordinated policy in Indochina; Acheson had become frustrated with the French, who, he said, seemed "paralyzed."[81] But, Acheson maintained, since France, a loyal NATO ally, was the only nation preventing communism from taking over Indochina, the United States was bound to support their colonialist efforts.

On November 18, 1952, President Truman, Acheson, and others briefed President-elect Eisenhower on the increasingly volatile situation. Acheson advised Eisenhower that the lack of an aggressive French military posture and "fence-sitting by the population" were the region's central problems, and the new administration must be prepared to intervene at a moment's notice to prevent the communists from gaining control of the French colony. One never knew when or if the Chinese would enter the conflict, but if they did, "the new administration must be prepared to act," Acheson warned, without international support if necessary.[82]

Eisenhower's public pronouncements initially echoed Acheson's assessment. In his inaugural address, Eisenhower asserted that his administration would be even tougher than Truman's in stopping the spread of communism in Asia. Fifteen months later arguing what came to be known as his "falling dominoes theory," Eisenhower flatly stated that the defeat of communism in Southeast Asia was essential to American security interests.[83] Acheson hoped Ike would be true to his word. He realized that the administration was anxious to find a way to keep Vietnam out of communist hands but thought Eisenhower "did not have enough nerve" to commit troops to the region.[84] Although he offered no solutions or policy alternatives publicly, except for his constant demand for stronger executive leadership, privately Acheson was saying that the first step should be to persuade the French and Indochinese to make a public request for U.S. military intervention, with a promise attached from both "not to run out on us after we have picked up the baby."[85]

The scope of the bail-out Acheson had in mind is revealing. When Ranald MacDonald, an old Yale classmate and friend, suggested to Acheson in April that perhaps the United States could send in some specialists and just let the "local boys do the fighting," Acheson dismissed the idea as "plain baloney. There has got to be more force from the outside, . . . that means us and some others." Acheson considered the French position to be so eroded that negotiations could be effectively ruled out, as all the West could do is "take what the other side wants."[86] Nevertheless, he was emphatically against the type of massive bombing campaign proposed by Chairman of the Joint Chiefs of Staff Arthur Radford, because of the possibility the Soviets would supply China with bombs, which could lead the United States into an all-out war with the Chinese.[87]

Eisenhower and Dulles were equally concerned about not starting a war with China over Vietnam. But Acheson believed that the blustery rhetoric of massive retaliation confused not only China, but also America's allies, about the administration's intentions in the region. Acheson's cure was some straight talk from Eisenhower, affirming that the United States had no desire to destroy the communist regime in China with military force. "'New Looks'—which are not new and look about as far as an ostrich with its head in the sand—'United Fronts,' without knowing with whom or about what we want to be united, intervention alone one day, and the next only on conditions as long as a life insurance contract and involving no American boy anywhere on his own feet—these shifts, twists and turns have people groggy," Acheson wrote Truman in June. "And the grog is that prohibition hooch which makes some people go crazy and blinds others."[88]

Dulles had made a fatal error, Acheson believed, by letting it be known that the United States would not send ground troops to Indochina and by announcing that the administration would not take any actions without congressional blessing. Acheson thought such statements played directly into Viet Minh hands. He believed that the only way to bolster sagging French morale and undermine the communist rebels was to send U.S. ground troops to Vietnam. Acheson reckoned that Eisenhower, whom he viewed as obsessed by his public-opinion-poll ratings and intent on maintaining good relations with Congress, would never commit American forces to fight in another unpopular Asian land war during an election year.[89] Acheson himself, however, was unsure just what the magnitude of a U.S. intervention should be. He confessed that spring to his journalist friend James ("Scotty") Reston that he was glad Dulles, and not he, bore the onerous burden of decision.[90]

A few months later, despite administration rhetoric, it became apparent that Ike would allow France to negotiate northern Vietnam into Ho Chi Minh's communist hands. On July 21, the president of France, Joseph Laniel, and the premier of Vietnam, Bao Dai, signed an agreement in Geneva that temporarily severed Vietnam along the 17th parallel, with the North under the control of communist forces, while a pro-Western government headed by the American-educated Ngo Dinh Diem assumed charge of the South. Under the Geneva accords Vietnam was to be reunified by free elections in 1956. The United States refused to sign these accords but did "take note" of the agreement. Acheson was appalled.[91]

Acheson thought Dulles and Under Secretary of State Walter Bedell Smith, who headed the American delegation at Geneva, utter incompetents. The same Republicans who had bludgeoned Acheson for losing China had just let half of Vietnam—a region Eisenhower and Dulles continually had characterized as essential to America's global policy and national security—fall into the communist camp. Acheson was concerned that these men, though they had initially thundered their determination to roll back and liberate, would not even try to contain communism in Asia. "I think the chances of hanging on to southern Vietnam are less than 50-50," Acheson prophetically forecast to Scotty Reston shortly after Geneva.[92] Not only was it likely that Vietnam would be lost, but the United States's decision against rescuing France at Dienbienphu would damage relations with the embittered French government.

Some Republicans continued to scapegoat Truman and Acheson for the Indochina crisis. Postmaster General Arthur E. Summerfield blamed the Vietnamese rebellion on the "tragic legacy of Communist intrigue growing in large part out of the Truman-Acheson foreign policy which let Nationalist China fall."[93] Vice-President Richard M. Nixon reiterated this theme in a June 26 speech.[94] Senator William E. Jenner went a step further by attributing the Indochina upheaval to what he called "the Acheson cease-fire in Korea," asserting there was still an "Acheson fifth column" at work under the administration of John Foster Dulles. "By some hidden route" they had been able to undermine Eisenhower's initially correct thinking on Asian policy.[95] The continued Republican immolation only served to exacerbate Acheson's already well-established abhorrence for the Republican administration.

To Acheson, the real lesson of Dienbienphu and Geneva was that nuclear capability, because it was not credible, did not deter communist use of force. "At the time the policy of 'massive retaliation' was proclaimed, its application to the war in Indochina between the French forces and Ho Chi Minh's Communist forces was also proclaimed," Acheson later reflected. "The collapse of the French was the domino which would tumble the other Southeast Asian dominoes. Despite a confused succession of American threats, the President backed off. The French fortress of Dienbienphu fell to the Communists and the American bluff was called for all the world to see."[96]

America's failure to rescue the French in Vietnam, Acheson believed, had damaging repercussions on plans for the European Defense Community (EDC), which aimed at rearming Germany in the context of a larger European defense program. Refusing to concede that for all practical purposes the EDC had been dead by the time Eisenhower took office, Acheson insisted that there was a direct correlation between America's abandonment of the French Fourth Republic in Vietnam and the French National Assembly's rejection of the European Defense Community Treaty on August 30, 1954. Paris, Acheson asserted, after a four-year struggle to negotiate and ratify it, ultimately decided the treaty was another American attempt to undermine French military power, prestige, sovereignty, and honor.[97]

After the Second World War, France consistently had opposed German rearmament. At a meeting of the Western Big Three on September 12, 1950, Secretary of State Acheson, motivated by the outbreak of the Korean War, pressured Britain and France to accept German rearmament as part of an American plan designed to enhance Western European security. Ten German divisions should be organized and put under the command of the NATO commander-in-chief, Acheson argued. The French foreign minister, Robert Schuman, considered any reformation of a German army unacceptable, and the meeting ended in deadlock. Later that year, at the urging of Jean Monnet—president of the ECSC's High Authority—Prime Minister René Pleven of France devised his own plan for gradually integrating German forces into a larger European army under a European ministry of defense and responsible to a European assembly. French public opinion was hostile to the notion of a supranational European defense organization, for it would permit Germans in military uniform to parade once more on French soil and to march side by side with the French in moral equivalence. Although France had signed the EDC treaty on May 27, 1952, this by no means signaled that ratification was certain; the battle was just beginning. The treaty still required ratification by six European parliaments—those of Belgium, France, Luxembourg, the Netherlands, West Germany, and Britain.[98]

Although it would have a separate organization, the EDC was to be considered an integral part of the unified NATO command. Acheson was delighted at the prospect of a European army, for it would reduce the balance-of-payments gap, strengthen NATO, and ease the burden on American finances at a time when the cold war required Washington to assume a global military posture. The majority of French citizens did not share Acheson's optimism about the reliability of a remilitarized German ally, so Acheson launched a behind-the-scenes public relations campaign to convince them.[99] Sensitive to French public opinion, Acheson telegraphed the American ambassador in Paris on September 6, 1952, to use "every means at our disposal . . . to dispel picture of US forcing a reluctant France to accept EDC. We are all agreed any attitude on our part indicating desire to buy this ratification could only make matters worse by seemingly confirming impression EDC is Amer[ican] project primarily benefiting us."[100]

Shortly after the EDC treaty was signed, Acheson, with U.S. Ambassador to France David K. E. Bruce as point man, reiterated American support for the EDC and for the general concept of European unity. On January 14, 1953, at his farewell news conference, Acheson focused on the need to move forward with the EDC, admitting that getting the French to ratify the treaty was an uphill struggle.[101] Acheson knew it would be up to President-elect Dwight D. Eisenhower to move forward on the plan and on steps toward creating other European unity programs.

French opposition to the EDC, which continued to grow, coincided with the rise of Gaullist sentiments of maintaining French sovereignty. Many French politicians, including Gaullists and Socialists, thought the death of Stalin and the end of the Korean War made German rearmament less important. The new secretary of state, John Foster Dulles, attempted to pressure France by promising an "agonizing reappraisal" of U.S. policy toward Western Europe should the EDC fail. But by 1954, following their recent reverses in Indochina, the French viewed the EDC as another inroad into their weakened military prestige. In August of that year the National Assembly, under the new government of Premier Pierre Mendès-France, rejected the treaty. Acheson thought the rejection "threw Europe into a serious crisis," for with it, plans for a proposed European political community had also collapsed. To a deeply disappointed Acheson, the ECSC appeared an isolated outpost of integration in a Europe moving swiftly to reassert nationalistic lines.[102]

Acheson blamed Eisenhower and Dulles's condescending attitude toward the French before, during, and after the fall of Dienbienphu for the rejection of the EDC by America's oldest ally. Instead of dealing tactfully with France, as Acheson had done as secretary of state, Dulles had issued his insulting agonizing reappraisal ultimatum. Acheson also faulted Eisenhower and Dulles's other escalating threats to Europe—ending arms deliveries to the Continent, withdrawing six military divisions from Germany, hinting that all foreign aid might be halted if a European army that included German troops did not materialize. In an essay praising former French foreign minister Robert Schuman, Acheson wrote: "EDC, and perhaps the beginning of the political community of

Europe, would not have been impossible if pressure had been maintained for another year, and it could have affected profoundly all that followed in the decade of the fifties."[103] Members of the French assembly had bitterly complained of "improper and intolerable" interference in domestic affairs. "Nor was there any 'agonizing reappraisal' afterward," Acheson scoffed. "The only effect the threat had was to leave France in a brooding, morose, and suspicious frame of mind toward anything which later came its way with a Washington postmark."[104]

The Geneva Conference of 1955

With the Korean War and the Indochina conflict apparently settled, McCarthy witchhunts in remission, and the Stalinist position of the Soviets relaxed, events in 1955 augured well for reduction of cold war tensions. Winston Churchill had returned as British prime minister in 1953, and he and other world leaders were pressing for a U.S.-USSR summit meeting. The Soviets had taken two steps that persuaded Eisenhower a superpower conference might prove fruitful. Moscow announced its readiness to reach an agreement with the West regarding Austria's status and also let it be known it was prepared to begin serious arms reduction talks.

After sidestepping the issue of Austria's future for nearly a decade, on May 15, 1955, the Soviet Union finally joined with Britain, France, and the United States in signing the Austrian State Treaty. This pact restored Austria's pre–1938 frontiers, forbade a future union between Germany and Austria, and called for the removal of all foreign troops from Austria by December 31, 1955. A neutral Austria, no longer under Soviet influence, most certainly would gravitate toward the West.[105]

Undoubtedly, Eisenhower and Dulles had achieved a U.S. foreign-policy success. Even Democrats praised the outcome, although many thought partial credit was owed the Truman administration, as Dulles agreed. "As I signed the Austrian Peace Treaty a few minutes ago I thought gratefully of your contribution notably at the Paris Peace Conference of 1949," he cabled Acheson from Vienna in a rare gesture of bipartisan spirit.[106] Dulles also cabled General George C. Marshall, who, like Acheson, had been secretary of state during some hard-fought treaty negotiations with the Soviets. The Austrian treaty was one accomplishment by Dulles of which Acheson wholeheartedly approved; after all, he himself had struggled in vain to achieve such an agreement.[107] But just when

Acheson was finally willing to concede that the Eisenhower administration had done something right, the president scheduled a Big Four (U.S., U.K., USSR, France) summit conference at Geneva's Palais des Nations for mid-July 1955.

The convening of the conference must be seen against the backdrop of contemporary international developments. After Stalin's death in 1953, the Soviet leadership moved steadily, if cautiously, to cast off Stalin's "two-camp" adversarial posture and increase intercourse with noncommunist countries. Nikita Khrushchev had managed by 1955 to become first among equals in a Soviet leadership struggle which included Nikolai Bulganin and Georgi Malenkov. There had been no summit meeting since Potsdam in 1945, and this conference was seen as an opportunity for Moscow to open a new dialogue with Washington.

In addition to resolving the Austrian issue, the Soviets had recently undertaken a political fence-mending trip to President Josip Broz Tito's Yugoslavia and established relations with Chancellor Konrad Adenauer's German Federal Republic. After Geneva, they put forth new disarmament proposals at the United Nations disarmament committee meeting in London and negotiated for a formal peace treaty with Japan. Khrushchev and Bulganin also went on a political visit to India, Burma, and Afghanistan. No one doubted that these activities signified a major diplomatic blitz, an attempt to establish a new direction for the Soviet Union in international affairs.

At the same time, the Soviets were facing pressures from China. In March and April of 1955, the Chinese Communists threatened Taiwan's offshore islands of Quemoy and Matsu, and it took coercion by Moscow to end their threats. Simultaneously the Chinese attempted to seize leadership of the neutral and nonaligned underdeveloped nations at the Asian-African Conference held in Bandung, Indonesia. These assertions of independence on the part of the Chinese Communists may have been one cause of the Soviet search for a true modus vivendi with the West.

The Geneva conference should also be seen in the context of changing strategic realities. By the mid-fifties, Soviet nuclear capacity had grown rapidly. A massive hydrogen-bomb testing program had been initiated in 1954, and in numbers of weapons and in delivery capability, the Soviet Union was beginning to close the gap between itself and the United States. The nuclear stalemate called for reevaluation by both sides of strategic assumptions and tactical operational procedures. Believe as they might in the moral superiority of the United States vis-à-vis the

Soviet Union, Eisenhower and Dulles could not ignore the changed strategic situation. On the whole, the year 1955 seemed to many perhaps the most promising year since 1945 for the relaxation of international tensions. Dean Acheson, however, did not view "B. and K." (Bulganin and Khrushchev) diplomacy that way.

Acheson's analysis went like this: what the West was witnessing was the Soviet's continued pursuit of its longtime goals, only now by more subtle means—negotiation. He noted to Reston, "The great forces that are operating in connection with present developments and that make for adjustments are not registered on a fever chart—they are not up one week and down another. They are much more even."[108] Bulganin and Khrushchev make a few self-serving overtures to the West, Acheson observed, and suddenly a "thaw" in the cold war is proclaimed by many so-called foreign-policy experts. It was obvious to him that the Soviets simply were maneuvering to improve their global image. The United States had a unique opportunity to make life harder for them. Moscow would use political gains at a summit to consolidate the regime internally and to promote the image of a Soviet Union bent on "peaceful coexistence" (Khrushchev's phrase, which Acheson considered "flabby and unrevealing"[109]). The Soviet Union also was coping with serious economic difficulties—especially in the perennial problem area of agriculture—and desperately desired to reduce international pressures in order to focus its energies on internal concerns. Eisenhower's obligation, Acheson asserted, was to maintain relentless pressure on the Soviets so that the inherent weaknesses of communism and virtues of capitalism would emerge and eventually bring about the collapse of the totalitarian state.[110]

Buttressing Acheson's views was the creation on May 14, 1955, of the Warsaw Pact defense alliance of European communist nations, which he construed rightly as a Soviet response to U.S. integration of West German troops into NATO. The pact, Acheson feared, confronted the West with a more solidified and dangerous communist military and political force, making the chance of any significant breakthrough at a summit next to impossible.[111] As the two sides would come to Geneva with different premises and objectives, it was difficult for the former secretary to see how either compromise on the German question or disarmament could be achieved. "They [the Kremlin] deny the goodness of truth," Acheson told the newspaperman C. L. Sulzberger. "They regard everything as an instrument. They want only to produce results. There are no basic values—like the individual human spirit—important to them. They see as fundamental their immediate objectives. And they twist the human spirit by the will of the state."[112] How could Eisenhower expect to gain any concessions at Geneva from such a reprehensible regime?

The conference took place in Geneva from July 18 to 23. President Eisenhower, and the new British prime minister, Anthony Eden; the French premier, Edgar Faure; and the Soviet premier, Nikolai Bulganin, discussed the reunification of Germany, European security, and disarmament. When talks stalled over the German issue, Eisenhower gained favorable publicity by offering his Open Skies plan, which would have permitted among the signatories reconnaissance photography of any territory as a means of assuring against a surprise enemy attack. Each nation would provide a complete blueprint of its military facilities for purposes of aerial reconnaissance; an inspection procedure would serve to verify this information. The UN General Assembly endorsed the plan, but the Soviet Union rejected it outright as an American espionage scheme that would infringe on Soviet territorial sovereignty.[113]

Acheson's predictions were borne out. The conference made no great strides in easing cold war tensions. Not only did Acheson distrust Soviet motives but he also questioned Eisenhower's motives; he thought the president was using the summit to enhance his personal political popularity. Acheson believed Eisenhower already had shown his absence of political scruples by turning his back on George C. Marshall in order to embrace Joseph R. McCarthy. But, to Acheson's lasting irritation, Eisenhower emerged from Geneva with the domestic image of a warm, serious, conscientious statesman who wanted conciliation of the rival powers, not that of an unprincipled politician.

While the president was turning the "Spirit of Geneva" (a media catchphrase born at the conference) into a "spirit of Eisenhower" public relations coup, the Soviets had managed to use the summit to gain the West's "grudging acquiescence" to Soviet domination of Eastern Europe, Acheson told friends.[114] What had happened to Eisenhower's 1952 campaign pledge to liberate the Soviet "satellites" (by 1955 transfigured by the alchemy of the Warsaw Pact into Soviet allies) from Kremlin domination? Acheson wondered aloud.

For their part Eisenhower and Dulles had learned to turn a deaf ear to Acheson and his accusations, although at times they considered him not just a partisan attacker but a downright obstructionist of U.S. policy. At a National Security Council meeting in January 1955 a perturbed Dulles complained to Eisenhower that Acheson, Nitze, and some other

Democrats were circulating a memorandum to select congressmen that criticized the Formosa Resolution, the mutual defense treaty Eisenhower recently had signed with the Taiwanese government. "This memorandum was plainly designed to obfuscate the issues and throw monkey wrenches into the Administration's plans," Dulles lamented. Dulles, who wanted to find a way to squelch the memorandum, went so far as to charge that its authors' activities "bordered on the traitorous—at a time when our national security policies were faced with such severe difficulties."[115] Although Acheson's analysis of the Formosa Resolution, the New Look, massive retaliation, the Geneva Conference, the failure of EDC, and the situation in Indochina annoyed both men, they never responded publicly, convinced Acheson was so entrenched in partisan warfare that no matter what defense policy they implemented or what terminology they employed, he would have rebuked them.

In an interview with the journalist Arthur Krock in 1960 Eisenhower spoke of the element of "hate" some saw as the cause of Acheson's strident rhetoric and feudist impulses. Ike recalled one of his teachers in Kansas, who admonished his pupils that hate was always destructive to one's aims. The teacher advised his students to exorcise hate "by writing on a card the name of the one for whom he felt hatred and putting the card in a drawer after which he forgot the location of the drawer and the name of the individual."[116] This was apparently Eisenhower's course of action with regard to Dean Acheson. Not once during his eight years as president did he invite Acheson to the White House for consultation—or even to attend a social function.

In 1969 in a televised interview Eric Sevareid asked Acheson why he thought President Eisenhower had slighted him. Was there some sort of personal animosity? Acheson responded, "The curious thing is he did the same thing to Mr. Truman. Mr. Truman was never invited to the White House. When Mr. Truman called on President Eisenhower when President Eisenhower was in Kansas City, Eisenhower wouldn't even see him. Now why? It seemed to me—the only explanation I could think of is that people dislike people whom they have unjustly injured. And I think Eisenhower had the feeling that he had unjustly said things about Mr. Truman, and unjustly said things about me, so that it made it embarrassing for him to have a pleasant social relation. I thought it was bad manners, but I never cared much whether he did or didn't."[117]

Acheson kept most of his character assaults private, within a small coterie of European and American friends; his public speeches and writing focus primarily on specific foreign-policy disagreements with the Republicans. Only occasionally, at dinner parties or informal gatherings and particularly if he had been drinking a bit, would Acheson's penchant for the witty and shocking phrase get the best of him, and out would fly some outrageous condemnation of Eisenhower or Dulles, to either the astonishment or delight of those present. These outbursts, along with the many letters aimed at belittling the president and the secretary of state, may lead one to ask whether or not Acheson's serious foreign-policy critiques from 1954 to 1960 were not in large part driven by personal malice. His recorded dislike of Eisenhower and Dulles unmasks his public persona as an objective observer and critic of the Eisenhower era. But, although personal criticism and vindictiveness may be considered unbefitting a former secretary of state, distinguished diplomat, and well-known proponent of bipartisanship, they are right in line with the hatchet-wielding, hard-boiled, rough-and-tumble world of American party politics—and it was in that world that Acheson would find his new niche.

CHAPTER TWO

A Democrat Looks at His Party and at Eisenhower's Foreign Policy

Dean Acheson's partisan assaults during Eisenhower's first two years in office did not indicate any wavering of support for the foreign-policy prerogatives of the president. In an essay written in September of 1954 about the recently defeated Bricker Amendment—which would have restricted the president's treaty-making power—he argued that any curb on the exercise of presidential power in the foreign-policy realm endangered national security. He asserted that the Constitution wisely gave authority over international affairs to the president. Restriction on the preeminent presidential role would result "in a negative and vacillating foreign policy, the impairment of our world position and danger to our national security."[1] To Acheson, the root of the current problem lay not in an excessive allowance for presidential power but in the person of the officeholder, in Dwight Eisenhower himself. The only solution was the eviction of the current tenant of the White House through the electoral process.

February of 1955 was not too soon to endorse a Democratic candidate and prime the campaign pump against the still-popular war hero. Acheson was well aware that Ike would be difficult to unseat in view of the exceptional vote-getting abilities he had demonstrated in 1952 and his continuing high approval ratings in opinion polls. He thought only two Democrats had even a glimmer of a chance of defeating him: Adlai E. Stevenson and W. Averell Harriman. From Independence, Missouri, where he was spending a few days with the Trumans, Acheson announced at a press conference attended by the former president that Adlai Stevenson was his "strong choice" as the nominee in 1956 and that Truman concurred.[2] "Acheson was perfectly prepared to support

Stevenson early on," Paul Nitze recalled. "He considered Stevenson more a wordsmith than a solid leader but he had the best chance of beating Eisenhower and that is what mattered more than anything to Dean."[3]

Taking leave of the Trumans, Acheson returned to Washington to continue his law practice as well as his involvement with Yale University. Throughout the 1950s he was senior fellow (trustee) of the Yale Corporation and took an active part in university concerns ranging from fundraising campaigns to a drive to outlaw new fraternities. Acheson's deep devotion to Yale and his commitment to furthering the university's mission of educational excellence always occupied a large amount of his time and energy.[4] At the same time, his thoughts were turning to ways to put a Democrat back in the White House. Acheson recalled a remark made by a former client—a Republican tycoon. After a long evening together drinking scotch and letting talk ramble, the client inquired whether he might ask a rather blunt question. Certainly, Acheson replied. "You are counsel for my company," the man began. "Let us say to minimize the personal side that this means you are intelligent and experienced. And yet you are a Democrat. How can this be?"[5]

Convinced that his client was not being facetious, Acheson decided to set down a reply, hoping in the process to shed some light on the Democratic Party itself. He began pondering how individuals arrive at their political convictions and their party allegiance. By June 1955 Acheson had completed his first book, the aptly titled *A Democrat Looks at His Party*. In September a prepublication excerpt appeared in *Harper's Magazine* while Acheson was in London casually discussing NATO affairs with Prime Minister Anthony Eden and Foreign Minister Harold Macmillan.[6] In the article he condemned Dulles's threats of atomic retaliation as "a classic illustration of the way a leader among free nations should not proceed."[7] Acheson's pen drew blood, and he returned to Washington the target of a counterattack.

Senator Wallace F. Bennett, a Republican from Utah, leaped on Acheson for making an "untimely attack" on the secretary of state on the eve of the Big Four foreign ministers' meeting in Geneva. He accused Acheson of "undermining" U.S. foreign policy and aiding the communist cause just as he had when he was secretary of state.[8] A new battle between Acheson and his Republican detractors had begun. The Republicans, hoping to keep Acheson a political liability for the Democrats, took the offensive. They painted a picture of the "Red Dean" at it again, ready to surrender America to the communists. On the right, the *National Review* went so far as to commission Joseph McCarthy to review Acheson's book.⁹ This tactic backfired, however. T. S. Eliot, for instance, whom some cited as the "patron saint of the new conservatism," told Russell Kirk, a protégé of William Buckley, that it was "ill-advised" to allow McCarthy to attack Acheson under the guise of a book review, and he cancelled his subscription.¹⁰

The Senate Republican Policy Committee continued the attack in a memorandum that insinuated that Dean Acheson and Alger Hiss, the former State Department official accused of treason and convicted of perjury in 1949, were working jointly for the nomination of a "left-winger" as the Democratic presidential candidate. "For a time the two friends were separated," the memorandum read. "Hiss was serving a prison sentence for perjury. Acheson, after the Republican victory of 1952, returned to his law practice. But now the appearance of the articles [the second was a piece Hiss had written for *Pocketbook* magazine defending Yalta] suggest that the two friends are together again."¹¹

In mid-November Acheson's already controversial book was published. Reviewers were generally positive. The Pulitzer Prize–winning biographer William S. White wrote that Acheson's "polished, gravely witty, sprightly and lucid" look at the Democratic Party was "a memorable work, far more than a perceptive analysis of a political party. Unobtrusively and perhaps unintentionally it is also the uncomplaining testament of a man who has borne in dignity and strength lashes of a kind that few have known in the history of the country."¹²

A Democrat Looks at His Party was, in fact, a mélange of party history, politics, and topical issues, written with the 1956 presidential election in mind. It was simultaneously a considered, temperate view of the historical achievements of the Democratic Party. Acheson tackled his subject the way a skillful lawyer prepares a brief—marshalling the evidence to present his client's case in the most favorable light.

He dissected with contempt the abuses of the loyalty programs and other security measures inaugurated under both Democratic and Republican administrations in the days of McCarthy. He went on to evaluate Roosevelt's New Deal, Truman's Fair Deal, and the origins of the modern welfare state. He explained that the Republicans were a single-interest (big business) party while the Democrats represented many and diverse constituencies (including property interests). He praised Democrats for believing in strong executive leadership and chastised Republicans for their reliance on Congress. Overall, he concluded, Democrats generally are pragmatists, who regard government as an instrument for getting things done, whereas the Republicans of the 1950s were so out of touch with the majority of hard-working Americans that they were incapable of determining what was best for the country.

Acheson lauded the foreign-policy decisions of the Truman administration, his own included. Again he deplored massive retaliation and the deterioration of morale and competence in the State Department under Dulles's tenure. The remedy was obvious: for American foreign policy to be coherent once more, the people must elect a Democrat in 1956.

The impact of Acheson's book on both parties was apparent. The Republican Party commissioned their own "egghead," Arthur Larson (then serving as under secretary of labor), to write a GOP reply, entitled *A Republican Looks at His Party*.[13] Senator John F. Kennedy of Massachusetts, noting Acheson's great success, wrote an essay entitled "A Democrat Looks at Foreign Policy" for *Foreign Affairs*. It contained the seeds of his later New Frontier program.[14]

Spurred by his book's success, Acheson himself lashed out again at the Eisenhower administration. In a speech before the Women's National Democratic Club he scored the dubious military advantages of the Baghdad Pact and the Southeast Asian (SEATO) defense alliances.[15] Under the Baghdad Pact, signed during the spring of 1955, Turkey, Iraq, Iran, Pakistan, and Britain pledged mutual security and an anti-Soviet defense. (Subsequent events would take Iraq out of the pact, which was reorganized in September 1959 as the Central Treaty Organization, CENTO.) Notwithstanding Dulles's initiatives in creating the "Northern Tier" regional defense organization and probably to the dismay of the signatories, the United States declined membership. It participated only as an observer and member of several committees; in time the United States signed bilateral agreements with each CENTO member.

In Acheson's view, the political consequences of the Baghdad Pact were to divide and embitter the Arab nations, increase Egypt's resentment of the West, multiply India's controversies with the United States (because of U.S. arms shipments to Pakistan), and arouse suspicion and fear in Moscow.[16] Rather than uniting the Middle Eastern nations and promoting the virtues of the free world, the Baghdad Pact, Acheson charged, had the countries in the region "at each other's throats," which gave the Soviet Union an "unparalleled opportunity" to increase its influence in the region.[17]

Acheson added that he saw no problem with neutrality, and he urged the Eisenhower administration to stop pressuring nations to choose between East and West. "It should be all right with us if they want to stand apart," he said, "so long as they do not fall under Sino-Soviet imperialism." Dulles's "pactomania" would only serve to alienate countries excluded and to force them into Moscow and Peking's open arms.[18] Acheson's criticism of pactomania ignores the fact that the Truman administration signed formal alliances with forty-one countries, including the Rio Treaty (1947), the North Atlantic Treaty (1949), the ANZUS Treaty (1951), and the Japanese and Philippine security treaties (1951).

Acheson's concerns soon were borne out as Egypt's president, Colonel Gamal Abdel Nasser, turned vehemently against the Baghdad Pact and the West. "Seen through the eyes of Colonel Nasser [the Baghdad Pact] was the supreme double-cross," Acheson explained to fellow Democrats. The Egyptian leader "turned all the vitriolic guns of his propaganda on the Baghdad Pact and on those whom he chose to regard as Arab Benedict Arnolds who would sell their fellows to the Western colonial imperialists and exploiters."[19] The Eisenhower administration had earmarked the colonel as its chosen instrument for solving the Middle East tangle. So strong was Eisenhower's faith in Nasser that in October 1954 the president had supported the British withdrawal of troops from the Suez Canal Zone. Nasser's seizure (and later nationalization) of the Suez Canal Company in 1956 was conclusive evidence for Acheson of the decline of American diplomacy under John Foster Dulles. As for Eisenhower, Acheson concurred with Winston Churchill, who, according to his wartime private secretary, thought the general "both weak and stupid."[20]

Disaster at Suez

The controversy over Suez is crucial to the study of Dean Acheson's postsecretarial years, for it marks his reemergence as a Democratic spokesman for world affairs. From Acheson's point of view the administration's bungling of the Suez situation allowed him to take the offensive, without care for assaults from the Republican right. He would continue his one-man onslaught from the sidelines until John F. Kennedy's victory over Richard M. Nixon in the 1960 presidential election.[21]

By autumn of 1956, several pounds lighter, his health restored, and his depression gone, Acheson led a vociferous chorus of criticism of the administration's handling of the Suez crisis.[22] Acheson did not saddle Eisenhower with sole responsibility for the debacle but did insist he bear the brunt. "A leader of a coalition is responsible for it as a captain is responsible for his ship," Acheson later observed.[23]

The seizure of Suez and its aftermath occurred in the midst of the 1956 presidential campaign. Throughout, Acheson tried to persuade the Democratic nominee, Adlai Stevenson, to make Suez a campaign issue. Stevenson was avoiding being seen or associated with the former secretary; Dean Acheson was still a political liability as far as he was concerned. He listened privately to what Acheson had to say, and then in most cases disregarded his advice.

In this instance Acheson's analysis overvalued the play of personalities and undervalued the importance of the shifting balance of power in the Middle East and rising Arab nationalism. He thought Nasser's July 19 seizure of the Suez Canal was precipitated by Dulles's abrupt refusal to finance the Aswan High Dam project on the Nile River, and that the manner in which Dulles had withdrawn the offer was almost a deliberate insult to Egypt's national pride. "Mr. Dulles now claims that his policy of the Aswan Dam had nothing to do with creating the Suez Crisis because Nasser has admitted that he had been thinking of seizing the canal company for two years," Acheson wrote in September 1956. "This is no defense; it is an indictment of Mr. Dulles. Without the shock and insult of the decision on the Aswan Dam, Nasser might have gone on thinking idly of seizing the canal company for another two years but doing nothing about it; and by that time many things would have happened to change the course of events in the Middle East."[24]

Acheson also charged that Dulles was so obsessed by politics that he was incapable of behaving in a statesmanlike manner. Rather than thinking of ways to get the canal back, Dulles was treating the seizure as a fait accompli. Acheson thought an immediate and forceful Western response was called for. "Paul Nitze and I lunch regularly and try to figure out what should be done—like the discussions at the lunches at the Soldiers Home," Acheson wrote Henry Byroade, the assistant secretary of state for Near Eastern, South Asian, and African affairs, shortly after the seizure.

> One turn we called rightly was in telling Scotty Reston when Foster pulled the rug on the Aswan Dam to hold his hat for Nasser was going to come back vigorously. . . . After the seizure we thought the soundest move was for the British to reoccupy the Canal zone at once—if they had the force to do it—on the ground that the Egyptians had with force, and contrary to the presuppositions of the withdrawal,

struck at a vital British interest. But the trouble is that there was no force—a part of the penalty for . . . falling for this massive retaliation deterrent."[25]

Although he was aware that British military intervention could be risky, particularly if met by resistance from the United Arab Republic (the union of Egypt and Syria), Acheson did not think resistance was likely. As for getting out of Egypt once the British were in, Acheson concluded that it would have required "the nerve to get out immediately on Nasser's fall with the threat of coming back if the Canal was touched again."[26]

Given these views, one would assume Acheson would have held London partially responsible for failing immediately to reclaim the canal. But instead he, like Anthony Eden, chose to pin most of the blame on Dulles.[27] Recognition of the shift in the balance of power in the Middle East was implicit in British withdrawal from the region beginning in 1954. The vacuum proved an irresistible temptation for the Soviets. Nasser was revered as a pan-Arab statesman throughout much of the Middle East while, Acheson believed, he simultaneously was becoming a puppet of Moscow.[28] Even before the canal crisis, Acheson had charged that the new Soviet leaders were "as ruthless and dangerous as the old ones";[29] by August he accused Dulles of playing into the hands of the Kremlin. That summer Acheson's letters to family and friends overflowed with mockery of Dulles's handling of the crisis.[30]

It soon became clear that Eisenhower was prepared to accept what the British and French found unacceptable—Egyptian control of the canal. As the London Conference of August 15–23 was dispatching a group of delegates to negotiate with Nasser for international supervision and mediation, Dulles made it known that the United States would not "shoot its way through the Canal."[31] While Britain and France talked eagerly of resorting to force, the American delegation suggested economic sanctions through a Suez Canal Users Association but let it be known that Washington would not help defray the association's cost. To Acheson, the London Conference, which Nasser boycotted, seemed to be "subsiding into acceptance [of the Egyptian seizure of the canal] and humiliation for Britain and France, their resentment against us and the very possible disappearance of Eden."[32]

In mid-October Eisenhower, Nixon, and Dulles were all saying a peaceful solution was just around the corner. Acheson thought this rhetoric masked the administration's sheepish inaction. "I think it a grave mistake to let the idea get abroad that little people can use force to interfere with the vital interests of big people without incurring any risk of riposte in force," Acheson wrote Assistant Secretary Byroade. "Of course, if the big people are not really big but are only living on past glories that is another matter. But then they should not talk big. And so far as the idea that people will not love those who stand up strongly for their rights, the answer to me, is that respect is what we want or can get."[33]

While negotiations with Egypt were under way, French, British, and Israeli representatives held secret military planning sessions. The three nations, believing they had to act to protect their interests, kept their plans secret from the United States as they prepared for a joint military action to reclaim the canal. First, Israeli troops launched a surprise raid in the Sinai desert that nearly destroyed Nasser's army on October 29; on October 31 British and French planes bombed several Egyptian military targets and Israel fortified its position in the Sinai.

Although the Israeli Sinai campaign was a resounding military success, the badly executed Anglo-French invasion was a disaster. By late December the humiliated and discredited Anglo-French troops withdrew from Egypt. The European nations had gambled on a show of force to reclaim the canal, as Acheson had urged, only to come up empty-handed. The defeat cost them dearly. Far from being overthrown, Nasser in fact was rescued from domestic foes by the failed intervention. The defeat inflated his reputation among Arab nationalists to mythic proportions. Also to be reckoned in the costs of the open political defeat was the rapid decline of British and French influence among revolutionary Arab states. The United States felt compelled to join the Soviet Union and the Arab-Asian bloc in the United Nations in condemning Israel, Britain, and France and ordering them to withdraw their forces. Nasser, a man "defeated, humiliated, and ripe for oblivion," Acheson charged, "was given a victory unprecedented and complete."[34]

Acheson adamantly opposed the UN resolution. He believed no stakes were high enough to justify censuring Britain and France and siding with the Soviets. He found it unthinkable that the country's oldest and dearest allies should have felt it necessary to maneuver behind America's back. "In the Suez Crisis Dulles couldn't have done worse," Acheson commented in an interview in 1969. "He ended up siding with the Russians and attacking our friends. A complete mess."[35] Although Acheson acknowledged that siding with Britain and France would have damaged U.S. relations with the unaligned nations, he insisted that, not anticolonialism, but maintaining strength and unity with the heart of the free world—Western Europe—was America's primary foreign-policy objective.[36]

In *Power and Diplomacy*, which was published in 1958, Acheson restated the four main principles to be derived from the Suez fiasco: maintaining loyalty to those engaged in a common enterprise; fostering candid discussion of interests affecting associated nations; sacrificing, if necessary, to obtain joint action among allies; and declining to line up with an enemy of the alliance. Although he continued to call Dulles's withdrawal of financial help for Egypt's Aswan Dam the main blunder of the drama, he admitted that in the last phase the British and French, in desperation, had acted "deceitfully" in not informing Washington of their intentions.[37]

Acheson the private citizen asserted that had he, rather than Dulles, been in charge there would have been no crisis. The claim requires examination. A year after Acheson left government, he admitted to "a feeling of dissatisfaction with everything we did in the Middle East" during the Truman years.[38] The Eurocentric Acheson never, whether in office or after, recognized the strength of the currents running against the old European imperial tradition. Although Dulles, as executor of Eisenhower's policy, did appreciate these trends, he lacked the competence and finesse to deal astutely with the leaders of the former colonies. There is one point on which no doubt can be entertained: Acheson would never have sided with the Soviets in the UN, not only as a matter of principle but also because he viewed the institution with utter contempt, seeing it solely as a drain on American power. Eisenhower and Dulles, on the other hand, motivated by determination to preserve the UN, felt they had no other choice but to side with the Soviets.[39]

Whether or not Dulles's diplomacy was effective—especially in the Suez crisis—is still hotly debated. Dulles partisans and Eisenhower revisionists insist that the secretary—with the hidden-handed maneuvering of the president—saved the United Nations and gave heart to countries emerging from colonialism.[40] Acheson and other critics counter that the vacillating Dulles behaved deceptively during Suez, gravely injuring the Western alliance and thereby buttressing the Soviet Union. Dulles's deceptiveness was all-pervasive, Acheson charged, as demonstrated by his refusal to aid Hungarian rebels in October and November of 1956, while Soviet tanks rolled through Budapest killing thousands. He made mockery of Republican promises to liberate Eastern Europe.[41] Fortunately, the economic and political repercussions of Suez and Hungary were neither as serious nor as long-lasting as Acheson predicted.

Dulles's failures brought into sharp relief Acheson's own glittering record as secretary of state. Not surprisingly, Harry Truman told reporters at a news conference in November, "If Ike had had sense enough to keep Dean Acheson as Secretary of State he would not be in all this trouble."[42] Dulles's woes and the favorable reception of *A Democrat Looks at His Party* had invigorated Acheson, restoring his puckish, self-assured style for the first time since he had stepped down as secretary of state.

The 1956 Presidential Election

The man who had triumphed with *A Democrat Looks at His Party* and who was chomping at the bit as he sensed an opportunity to draw Republican blood over foreign policy, was virtually ignored by his party and its leaders (Truman excepted, of course) in the 1956 presidential election. Acheson and Truman had supported their party's presidential candidate early on but were unenthusiastic about what they termed Stevenson's "soft" style and chronic indecisiveness. Both men also still were nettled by the way Stevenson had distanced himself from the Truman administration during the 1952 campaign. When Robert Bowie and McGeorge Bundy were at Harvard in 1952 Secretary of State Acheson came to campus. Acheson was asked his opinion of Adlai Stevenson as president. "Well," Acheson said, "Adlai has a third-rate mind that he can't make up."[43]

Stevenson and Acheson had become acquainted in the early 1930s when both of them worked in FDR's first administration. Their paths crossed once more during the Second World War and again in 1952 when Stevenson, then governor of Illinois, became the Democratic presidential candidate and titular head of the party. Acheson's wife, Alice, and Stevenson's sister, Buffy Ives, were childhood friends, a friendship that survived until 1958, when Dean Acheson "expressed less than total enthusiasm" for Stevenson as a presidential candidate. "This outraged Adlai's adoring sister," Acheson later wrote, "and led her quite foolishly to cut Alice out of her life." Acheson never disliked Stevenson, but he shared Harold Macmillan's assessment that "he would have made a good staff officer, but he did not have the stuff of command in him."[44]

Acheson nonetheless preferred Stevenson, warts and all, to Eisenhower, and in late June 1956 he was asked by the Democratic National Committee to head a group assigned to write position papers on foreign policy. The papers would serve as the basis for the party platform. Acheson accepted the assignment and with the help of two vice-chairmen, Paul Nitze and Senator Mike Mansfield of Montana, immediately went to work.[45] Most of what Acheson himself wrote, however, was excised or drastically rewritten by the resolutions committee at the convention. Under the direction of Chairman John McCormack of Massachusetts, the committee discarded Acheson's call for a new American foreign policy based on a set of overarching philosophical principles in favor of an ad hoc plank of specific policies focused on particular areas of the globe in a bid for the votes of various ethnic groups. Acheson later said that only "half a sentence" of his draft appeared in the final approved version.[46]

What Acheson had written was blue-penciled not over substance but because his language was too venomous to be incorporated into a party platform. Acheson's pronouncements also had failed to take domestic political considerations into account. For example, his reference to Dulles's "inept and gratuitous statement on Goa" (the secretary of state had condemned India's takeover of the Portuguese colony of Goa) was deleted. The resolutions committee did not disagree with Acheson, but it feared that his statement might offend voters of Portuguese background in Rhode Island and Massachusetts and, very possibly, Catholic voters in general.[47] Still, some of Acheson's notions—for instance, his recommendation that a new Democratic administration pursue a policy of "intelligent neglect" toward Communist China—were readily adopted.[48] Likewise, the Acheson-Nitze slogan "Peace can be lost without a shot being fired" was used in the 1956 campaign by many Democratic office-seekers.[49]

In the months before Chicago, Truman had lobbied Stevenson and others to let Acheson—"the greatest Secretary of State in history," Truman rhapsodized—address the convention. Truman's appeal was rejected on the ground that there were no votes to be gained from a speech by Acheson.[50] Pained by the snub, Acheson elected to remain in Washington and listen to Adlai Stevenson's nomination over the radio. What he heard reinforced his conviction that his fellow Democrats had made a strategic blunder by not staging a frontal assault on the Eisenhower-Dulles foreign-policy issues—massive retaliation, Indochina, the Baghdad Pact, and the deepening crisis over Suez.

After the convention the party continued to follow a policy of "intelligent neglect" toward Acheson. While the Democratic National Committee pressed Harry Truman, Eleanor Roosevelt, Averell Harriman, Chester Bowles, and other party veterans into service, Acheson remained on the sidelines; not once was he invited to make a national speech for Stevenson.[51]

Undaunted, on September 26 Acheson unleashed perhaps the most devastating denunciation of Eisenhower's foreign-policy record made in the entire campaign. The text of his speech was published in full by the *New York Times*. In it Acheson charged Eisenhower with "fail[ing] to serve the interest of the country." America's allies, he argued, were "scared to death" by the president's boasts and threats, and four years of Ike had given the Soviets numerous cold war gains. "This administration has been playing Russian roulette with an atomic pistol," Acheson said of Eisenhower's massive retaliation policy. The New Look program, Acheson lashed out, was likely to result in the very kind of war its budgetary "high policy" sought to avoid—nuclear disaster.[52]

The next day Eisenhower was asked if he would like to comment on Acheson's caustic remarks. "Well," he said, "if this campaign were going to be settled on the basis of misleading wisecracks, why, I would think the betting would be very considerably different than it would be if it is settled just on facts and on the record."[53]

Many Democrats wondered why Acheson never once mentioned Stevenson by name in what was billed as a campaign address. Yet the attention Acheson's speech received made other party members wonder whether Stevenson was not taking too polite an approach to the campaign. Believing their candidate would be unable to alter the prevailing perception of Eisenhower as an authority on foreign affairs and the person responsible for bringing an end to the unpopular Korean War, Stevenson's chief advisers had geared the campaign toward domestic issues.[54] Shortly after his speech, Acheson once more appealed to Stevenson to change strategy and forcefully challenge the Republican foreign-policy record before it was too late. "I just don't believe the professionals who know how to elect mayors and governors have any competence to judge what moves people when they are choosing the man in whose hands, more than any other, will be our destinies. There is such a thing as gallop-polling ourselves into a frustrating paralysis," he argued. "Go forward with confidence and power" and do not "struggle through ineptitude to some puny end," he implored.[55]

Stevenson did not heed Acheson's advice. When the Eisenhower-

Nixon ticket handily defeated the Stevenson-Kefauver ticket on November 5, 1956, Acheson was not surprised. The Democrats' retention of control of both houses of Congress was some consolation, he noted. A year later, in response to a letter asking why he thought the Democrats lost the presidential election, Acheson replied: "In foreign policy at least . . . there was not enough conviction among those directing campaign strategy that the American people are capable of adult thought and should have been told forcefully all that should have been done and of the policy of drift."[56]

The Eisenhower Doctrine

During Eisenhower's first term as president, Acheson had targeted his attacks on John Foster Dulles in particular. To Dulles, who had been hospitalized in November following a cancer operation, the landslide victory of 1956 was a bittersweet personal triumph. Shortly after the election he proudly showed Eisenhower the findings of a poll that gave him a two-thirds public approval rating, in sharp contrast to Acheson's two-thirds disapproval rating during his last year in office.[57] But Dulles was dying, and Acheson's public criticisms, which grew even more scathing, were aimed more often at the soldier-president himself. Acheson's first opportunity to skewer his adversary in his second term of office came with the unveiling of Eisenhower's new Middle Eastern policy, known as the Eisenhower Doctrine, in January 1957.

How and when Eisenhower and Dulles developed the new policy remains unclear. On New Year's Day of 1957, the pair briefed leaders of the new Congress on their plan to request a joint resolution giving the president broad powers to act in the event of a Middle Eastern crisis. Eisenhower told them, "The existing vacuum in the Middle East must be filled by the United States before it is filled by Russia. . . . Should there be a Soviet attack there I can see no alternative but that the United States move in immediately to stop it."[58]

On January 5, 1957, Eisenhower went before a joint session of Congress to set forth a landmark proposal for an extension of America's security frontiers to the Middle East—a region, according to the president, that had "abruptly reached a new and critical stage in its long important history."[59] General approval by the nonaligned nations of the unilateral policy of the United States during the Suez affair had induced the administration to take over the former Anglo-French role of powerbroker in Middle Eastern affairs.

Eisenhower did not define the Middle East formally, but the term was taken to encompass the region extending from Libya to Pakistan and from Turkey to the Sudan. The doctrine focused on the danger of communism: the president pledged support to any country that requested assistance to resist "overt armed aggression from any nation controlled by International Communism." Eisenhower asked for congressional authority to use military force against communist incursions in the region and proposed a two-year, $400 million program of economic aid. How the money was to be spent was not specified.[60]

The 85th Congress had returned the Democrats to majority status in both houses, a status reflected in the makeup of the three committees that would play pivotal roles in subsequent hearings. The Senate Committee on Foreign Relations and Armed Services Committee held joint hearings. On the House side the hearings were held by the Committee on Foreign Affairs. Activities on the Hill began on January 6, when Secretary Dulles testified before the House Committee on Foreign Affairs on behalf of the president's proposal. He invoked in its support the Truman Doctrine, which states that "totalitarian regimes imposed upon free peoples, by direct or indirect aggression, undermine the foundations of international peace and hence the security of the United States."[61]

The president's proposal encountered unexpected resistance from a variety of quarters. Speaking before a Democratic Party gathering shortly after Dulles's testimony, Acheson drew enthusiastic applause when he characterized the resolution as fighting "an enemy that's not going to attack, with forces that don't exist, to carry out a policy you haven't decided upon yet."[62] On January 10, in his first official excursion into foreign policy since his retirement from government, Acheson testified before the House Foreign Affairs Committee on the joint Middle East resolution.

His reservations centered on Eisenhower's request for legislative authority to use American military forces "against overt armed aggression by the Soviet Union or a nation controlled by the Soviet Union." Acheson thought this an attempt to "legislate" foreign policy, which was "not only unnecessary but undesirable," particularly in the unpredictable waters of U.S.–Middle Eastern affairs. The president already had the authority to employ armed forces to defend vital American interests abroad when an emergency arose without having to seek congressional approval. Acheson went on to argue that Eisenhower's proposal failed to grapple with the more probable form of Soviet aggression in the Middle East: "support for dissident elements within the nation to be undermined." He also pointed out that Soviet penetration in the region would likely target Egypt and Syria (the new United Arab Republic), who were not apt to seek aid from the West.⁶³

The real problems in the Middle East—dispute over ownership of the Suez Canal and continuing Arab-Israeli antagonism—were not addressed by the Eisenhower Doctrine, Acheson contended. While he supported economic aid for the Middle East, he noted that such aid was "already amply authorized by law." What the United States had to do was coordinate programs for economic development in the region and simultaneously remove Egypt's leverage over Western Europe by supplying Europe with cheap American oil. Were the United States to implement these two measures, the issue of management and control of the canal could be settled on terms fair to all sides, Acheson assured the committee.⁶⁴

As to Israel, although Acheson had been opposed to its creation as a nation in 1948, it was now an existing state for which the United States was largely responsible. By 1957 he saw Israel as America's only trustworthy ally in the region; therefore it deserved respect, not condemnation by the United States in the UN. A measure of Acheson's changed view toward Israel is revealed in a letter to Eugene Milligan, a foreign service officer at the American Embassy in Pakistan. Acheson deplores the Eisenhower administration's "pompous, bullying, and sanctimonious manner" toward Tel Aviv. "I hope," he writes, on the issue of Israel remaining in Gaza, "the Israelis have nerve enough to stand up to us because I do not believe the great golfer and the Presbyterian elder between them will do anything about it."⁶⁵

After a stormy nine-week debate, Congress passed a slightly watered-down resolution, which was signed into law on March 8, 1957. Events proved Acheson and other critics correct. The Eisenhower Doctrine failed as a policy because of its overreliance on military posturing and its fundamental misreading of pan-Arab political currents. Most analysts now conclude that hostility to the West was the primary ingredient in the pan-Arabic movement in the 1950s. This hostility grew from a host of causes: the legacy of colonialism, the Palestine question, the creation of the Baghdad Pact, the Moscow-Cairo arms agreement, the outcome of the Aswan project, and the war that followed the nationalization of the Suez Canal. In this environment, the Eisenhower Doctrine could do little but offend. It served to weaken the regimes it sought to help, for any country that associated itself with the West was viewed as an enemy of pan-Arabism and came under pressure from Egypt and Syria. The 1957–58 crises in

Lebanon, Jordan, Syria, and Iraq can, to a large degree, be attributed to the close ties of these countries with the West. Acheson blamed all of these crises entirely on Eisenhower and his Middle Eastern doctrine based on "phony law and fuzzy morals."[66] Still, Acheson agreed with Eisenhower and Dulles that the cornerstone of U.S. Middle East policy was to keep the Soviets out of the region.

On July 15, 1958, at the request of President Camille Chamoun of Lebanon, President Eisenhower dispatched 15,000 U.S. troops to the beaches near Beirut to thwart a threatened invasion by the United Arab Republic under Nasser. Eisenhower was anxious both to stabilize Lebanon and to demonstrate his commitment to the principles outlined in his Middle East doctrine. "We frowned on England and France in 1956 when they sent troops to the Suez, now we are doing the same thing in sending our troops to quell an internal affair, our reason being to protect Americans in Lebanon and to protect the independence of Lebanon," Acheson told a Rotary Club gathering only a few days after the soldiers were dispatched. "Now that our Marines are in the Middle East, we have to decide what is the best and wisest move to make. What are we trying to accomplish with our troops there? If what we have done is not the wise thing, how are we to recover without loss of prestige in the world." He noted that Napoleon once said, "You can do almost anything with bayonets except sit on them." Acheson was not surprised that the intervention triggered another violent outburst of anti-Americanism throughout the region.[67]

In April 1957 Acheson delivered the first Edward R. Stettinius, Jr., Lectures, established at the University of Virginia to honor FDR's last secretary of state. He examined legislative-executive relationships in the federal government in terms of the stresses and strains of the modern world on a democracy. Acheson used the format of Woodrow Wilson's well-known book *Congressional Government*, in which the young Wilson made a strong case for placing both the formulation and execution of foreign affairs in the hands of Congress.[68] But Acheson disagreed with Wilson's thesis, arguing that the author had himself repudiated it when he assumed the presidency and had to face the onerous task of guiding the United States through the First World War. He thought Congress should be limited to approving or disapproving presidential proposals, not allowed to take the initiative. Acheson believed most members of Congress were parochial politicians ignorant of international affairs and thus not well equipped to frame foreign policy.

The lectures were published later in a slender volume entitled *A Citi-*

zen Looks at Congress. Although Acheson's second book did not generate the national attention and controversy of *A Democrat Looks at His Party*, it did reach number two on the *Washington Post* nonfiction bestsellers list.[69]

The Creation of the Democratic Advisory Council

Only a few weeks after losing the presidential election the Democratic Party began reorganizing. The Democratic National Committee (DNC) was determined to develop a coordinated party policy with which to challenge the Republicans in the 1960 election. Out of this reorganization Dean Acheson came forth as the Democrats' leading official foreign-policy spokesman.

Prior to 1956 the DNC had no arm with the sole function of creating party policy. When a Democrat did not sit in the White House, the party's only official voices were those of the Democratic members of Congress, the defeated presidential candidate, and the DNC chairman. "The latter two have never been very effective spokesmen," Dean Acheson noted, "owing to the fact that, by hypothesis, they have just been through a losing campaign. The senior members of Congress are likely to come from the South . . . this has given the party voice a decidedly southern accent."[70]

After the 1956 defeat the DNC decided to develop a forward-looking agenda that could enable them to defeat the GOP presidential candidate—a new figure, as Eisenhower could not run for reelection in 1960.[71] By executive committee resolution the DNC authorized the formation of the Democratic Advisory Council (DAC) on November 27, 1956.[72] To balance Texans Lyndon Johnson as prospective Senate Majority Leader and Sam Rayburn as Speaker of the House, the non-Southern Democratic contingent was seeking a forum through which it could exert influence on the party. The DAC was intended to become the official "voice of the urban intellectual liberal, the creation of the friends and supporters of Adlai Stevenson."[73] Instead, once Dean Acheson became its chief foreign-policy spokesman, the tune the DAC sang changed from a liberal, Stevensonian air to the cold war refrain heard in the Truman administration, the very program the organization had wanted to leave behind.

Paul Butler of Indiana, the DNC chairman, modeled the DAC on the Finletter Group, a brain trust that provided Stevenson with position papers on civil rights, civil liberties, and foreign affairs from 1953 to 1956.

The group's organizer, Thomas K. Finletter, a secretary of the air force under Truman and a staunch Stevenson supporter, drafted specialists to help advance liberal objectives during the Democratic Party's "years in the wilderness." John Kenneth Galbraith, Arthur Schlesinger, Jr., Charles Murphy, James Warburg, Chester Bowles, W. Averell Harriman, and a host of other prominent Democrats became members. In 1956 the Finletter Group dissolved, and the DAC assumed its role.[74]

The DAC held its first organizational meeting in mid-December. Butler had attempted to recruit the party's congressional leaders, but of the twenty he invited, only Hubert Humphrey and Estes Kefauver finally accepted. Lyndon Johnson and Sam Rayburn refused to join, viewing the DAC as a preposterous attempt by Stevensonian Democrats to shape the party's future.[75] Butler did manage to recruit such party luminaries as Adlai Stevenson, Harry Truman, W. Averell Harriman, Herbert Lehman, and G. Mennen Williams, thereby giving the DAC both legitimacy and respectability. Butler persuaded Finletter and Phillip Perlman, the former solicitor general, to serve with him on the council's administrative committee. Eleanor Roosevelt signed on as a consultant, while Charles Murphy, former special counsel to President Truman, became the organization's special counsel. Adlai Stevenson's fundraising provided most of the DAC's financial support.[76] Dean Acheson had not been invited to join at this formative stage.

The administrative committee's first task was to find a director, someone acceptable to both the Stevenson and Truman wings of the party. At Finletter's suggestion, they hired Charles Tyroler II. Tyroler, who had run Estes Kefauver's Democratic presidential campaign in 1956, ultimately became the driving force behind the DAC. Throughout March and April of 1957 Tyroler visited often with Stevenson to discuss fundraising and organizational tactics. Tyroler believed the key ingredient for success was keeping Eleanor Roosevelt and Harry Truman content, for they gave the DAC intellectual and political legitimacy.[77]

The new organization developed two major advisory committees—for economic issues and for foreign policy—with the aim of garnering national attention through issuing policy memorandums, position papers, and statements. The strategy, according to Butler, was "big names talking about important matters." Other committees were added later.[78] John Kenneth Galbraith was named chairman of economic policy, which pleased the Stevenson group immensely.[79]

Finletter, Murphy, and Tyroler wanted Acheson as chairman of the foreign-policy committee both because he had more international experience than any other Democrat and because his appointment would keep "old boy Truman happy." Tyroler and Finletter had phoned the former president to seek his recommendation. Truman unhesitatingly responded, "There is only one man for the job—Dean Acheson." A few days later they went to see the former secretary at his Washington law office to offer him the chairmanship. Acheson, who by then had heard from Truman, opened the conversation by saying, "I know why you boys are here, and I'll take it."[80] On June 12, 1957, Acheson was named chairman of the DAC's committee on foreign policy, a political comeback of significant magnitude when one considers that as late as 1956 many Democrats still viewed association with him as political suicide.

Acheson had redeemed himself by the sheer magnitude of his intellect, by his unwavering self-confidence, and by retaining the trust and confidence of Harry S Truman. Had any Truman administration official been marked for permanent political retirement, it was Dean Acheson, and yet he had survived four years of McCarthyite attacks and general Republican slurs—as well as the cold shoulder from Stevenson and company—to reappear in 1957 as a principal player in the Democratic Party. During this period Acheson had remained Truman's most trusted adviser; many of the former president's foreign-affairs statements were cleared with Acheson before public release.[81] The two men were united in upholding the policies and principles they had established during Truman's presidency. Acheson's DAC appointment offered him an opportunity to shape party policy along the old Truman line.

Tyroler recalls that "Acheson was a somewhat lonely figure in the early fifties. The Republicans had done a real job on him. Many Democrats didn't want anything to do with him. Mr. Truman did, and others from his administration, but few from the Stevenson entourage. Acheson wasn't someone you wanted to have at the forefront of your campaign if you were running for president in 1952 or 1956."[82] In 1956, after Stevenson's second loss, the mood of the party hierarchy changed. Acheson was now seen as the perfect foreign-policy spokesman for building on what were now perceived as the Democratic Party's glory years—the 1940s.

Acheson told the DAC heads that he intended to make his committee the Democratic "think-tank" on all major foreign-policy issues and would therefore need some high-powered administrative assistance. He wanted his old colleague from the State Department, Paul Nitze, to serve as his vice-chairman. Finletter and Tyroler enthusiastically agreed.[83]

Acheson wanted the committee to develop policies with a national viewpoint, not to focus entirely on pending congressional issues.[84] He quickly went about enlisting party luminaries and foreign affairs experts to join his committee or to serve at least as occasional consultants.

His typical letter to prospective members opened with a clear statement of the committee's purpose and closed by insisting that, regardless of what Stevenson had believed in 1956, coherent discussion of foreign policy would attract votes: "I do not believe that there is 'no political mileage' in sensible discussion of foreign policy, and I don't believe either that a sound party position can be based on attempts to get the votes of national groups, protectionists, atomic pacifists, those who want to pay no taxes, and mothers of sons in their twenties. My idea of the Committee's function is to tell the Advisory Council what we think is the best foreign policy for the United States."[85]

By early September of 1957 Acheson had recruited twenty-seven members, including William Benton, Barry Bingham, Chester Bowles, Ben Cohen, Dorothy Fosdick, Philip Jessup, Estes Kefauver, Herbert Lehman, Hans Morgenthau, Edith Sampson, and G. Mennen Williams. Acheson dominated the first discussion, as he would all their meetings over the next three years. With Paul Nitze at his side, Acheson began intellectually muscling the Stevensonian liberals on the committee out of any meaningful role. Tyroler explained that this was possible in part because Acheson "would do his homework," while others came to the meetings "painfully unprepared." Acheson assumed authorship and control of nearly all DAC foreign-policy statements and press releases.[86]

The Democratic Party of 1957 had two schools of thought on foreign affairs, not defined clearly but nonetheless reflecting distinctly different emphases. The Stevenson-Bowles faction, although it did not deny the necessity of military strength, placed primary emphasis on economic aid to underdeveloped countries, expansion of world trade, and maintaining friendly relations with the neutrals in the United Nations. These "liberals" were optimists about agreements with the Soviets on arms control and lessening cold war tensions in general. They commanded the support of Senate Foreign Relations Committee members Hubert Humphrey and J. William Fulbright and considered Eleanor Roosevelt the spiritual leader of the Democratic Party.

The other faction, led by Acheson and Nitze, believed that the cold war was a reality, and because the Soviet Union was a Marxist, totalitarian state, negotiating with Moscow was a dangerous exercise in futility.

The key to understanding this faction is one word—power. They believed that the United States could maintain its hegemonic position in the world only by developing its military strength and maintaining a strong NATO alliance. Acheson was the intellectual leader of this faction, with Harry Truman its Grand Old Man. Lyndon Johnson and Sam Rayburn agreed with the emphasis on military strength and the Atlantic alliance and were vigorous supporters of the power faction.

Acheson's political rehabilitation also was nourished by his relationship with Lyndon Johnson, although domestic concerns, not foreign affairs, brought them together. In early 1957, when Johnson became Senate majority leader, he turned to Acheson for legal advice on the explosive issue of civil rights for black Americans. Within months Acheson became a trusted Johnson adviser. Johnson had power, understood it, and knew how to use it to achieve concrete results—a worldview congruent with Acheson's. The two corresponded frequently from 1957 through 1960 on the major international issues of the day: Quemoy and Matsu, Berlin, Khrushchev's visit to America, and the future of the Atlantic alliance. When Acheson was preparing an article on how to checkmate the Soviets during the 1958 Berlin crisis, he sought advice from Lyndon Johnson, whom he addressed as "the one man in the Democratic Party whose rare gifts of leadership and equally rare courage make possible the solution of this seemingly insoluble problem."[87] The connection served both men's interests, for Acheson could use his closeness to Johnson to bolster his own political power and prestige within the DAC, whereas with a respected member of the Eastern Establishment advising him on foreign and domestic policy issues, Johnson could escape being pigeonholed as a purely Southern politician. Johnson used flattery, a device to which Acheson was all-too-susceptible; he sent the former secretary warm personal notes on his birthday, on his mother's death, on Christmas and Easter, and included photos of himself with such adulatory inscriptions as "To Dean Acheson, a master logician and dedicated patriot."[88] For the time being Acheson and Johnson had achieved a mutually beneficial working relationship, but it eventually would see its share of ups and downs.

"America's Present Danger"

Acheson and Nitze wrote all DAC foreign-policy statements, although all of their press releases and, later, pamphlets required approval by the group's administrative council before release to the public. The statements began to turn the tables on the Republicans. Now it was Acheson accusing Eisenhower and Dulles of being soft on communism and of damaging America's prestige abroad. Acheson, doffing the bipartisan-foreign-policy cloak of the Truman years, was now saying, "The purpose of the opposition is to oppose." In a DAC-approved statement entitled "The Democratic Approach to Foreign Policy and United States Defense," he began by charging that the Eisenhower administration's miserly foreign aid would force America's allies to look to Moscow for capital and technical assistance. And, rather than cutting away at defense spending, he continued, the Democrats would increase it.[89]

The statement outlined four objectives the Democratic Party hoped to achieve by 1960: to rebuild confidence in the NATO alliance; to bolster American military strength and encourage allies to rebuild their military forces; to enable nations ready to industrialize to do so and thus add to the strength of the free world; and to regain the respect and confidence of "free men" and those longing for freedom throughout the world. The party could make these goals a reality by exerting pressure on Eisenhower and by taking advantage of a Democratic majority in both the House and Senate.

Coinciding with the release of "The Democratic Approach," the Gaither Committee—headed by H. Rowan Gaither, chairman of the board of the RAND Corporation, a West Coast think-tank—had prepared a top-secret report for President Eisenhower on the status of America's defense. In the wake of the first Soviet launching of an artificial satellite (Sputnik) on October 5, 1957, the Gaither Report of the Ford Foundation (entitled "Deterrence and Survival in the Nuclear Age") was written by a blue-ribbon commission from the private sector established by Eisenhower to advise the National Security Council. It called for a firmer stance with Moscow, more money for military research and development, and increased U.S. conventional forces. The authors asserted that the Soviet Union was spending 25 percent of its GNP for defense while the U.S. was spending only 10 percent.[90] They recommended that top priority be given to developing an invulnerable second-strike force, warning of a threat that could become critical by 1959 or early 1960 because of the "unexpected Soviet development of the ICBM [intercontinental ballistic missile]."[91] The report also urged that conventional forces be expanded to make limited wars to counter Soviet expanionism a viable option.

That both the Gaither Report and the DAC statement were strikingly similar to NSC-68 (which had recommended immense increases in U.S.

defense spending in order to provide a "limited war capability" and an expanded "nuclear weapon–missile deterrent capacity") was not a coincidence.[92] The principal author of NSC-68, Paul Nitze, was a consultant on strategic theory and resident arms expert for the Gaither Committee and played the largest role in drafting its final report while simultaneously collaborating with Acheson on the DAC foreign-policy advisory committee statement.[93]

Acheson's next statement for the DAC was a response to the president's State of the Union Address in January of 1958. It was entitled "America's Present Danger and What We Must Do About It." Acheson once again sounded the alarm about the deteriorating military power of the United States and demanded the administration increase nuclear capabilities in both manned aircraft and long-range missiles. He also argued again for an increase in conventional forces with special stress on airborne mobility.[94] Keynesian economic growth was the Acheson-DAC prescription for the Republicans' "one-sided disarmament" policy.[95] The New Deal economist Leon Keyserling, a member of the DAC economic committee, had convinced Acheson that deficit spending was necessary in order to maintain a viable national security system.[96]

"America's Present Danger" was a response as well to the recent successful launch of a second Sputnik satellite, this time with a dog aboard. The launchings had deeply concerned Acheson. He only hoped that the Soviet space feats would shake America out of its Eisenhower-induced complacency.

Acheson did not equate the success of Sputnik with Soviet parity in missile technology with the United States, but he did think that the Russians' triumph in space had damaged U.S. prestige abroad. He wrote to his friend John Cowles to explain his post-Sputnik concerns:

> My Airforce friends . . . tell me that they [the Soviets] are several years between a successful rocket and a successful intercontinental missile. Furthermore, they believe that intermediate missiles at our foreign bases, as well as bombers, are equal in strength to a Soviet intercontinental ballistic missile. But the real point [of Sputnik] . . . is not that there has been a break-through which enables the Russians to deliver an ultimatum which we cannot resist, but rather that the Russians have gained a great deal as an alternative center of power.[97]

Acheson did not believe the Soviets had a nuclear missile edge over the United States yet, but he feared that if defense-budget-cutting continued, America would eventually fall behind in missile technology. As a political strategist, he also realized that the Sputnik launchings could be a vehicle to unite Democrats of every stripe into a vocal chorus for increased military spending. Against the background of palpable Soviet successes in space, Acheson could blur the notion that a missile gap was a future danger into a warning of immediate threat. Thus he had a surefire hook with which to convince the American people that the defense program of the Eisenhower administration was woefully inadequate. It apparently never bothered Acheson that he was not telling the whole truth: there was no missile gap. The United States still maintained nuclear superiority; by 1961 the Soviets had only four ICBMs, compared to America's two hundred. For him, what counted was that there *would be* a missile gap in the near future, and the public had to be warned of the danger before it was too late, even if that meant exaggerating the present danger. Acheson insisted upon a missile gap in reverse, with the gap being on the Soviet side.[98]

From 1957 through 1960 the DAC received substantial support from the media. The *New York Times, New York Post, Washington Post,* and *Baltimore Sun* praised the committee for its public discussion of foreign-policy issues.[99] Nationally syndicated journalists such as Walter Lippmann, William Shannon, and Thomas Stokes analyzed DAC positions in their columns. In time the organization became known as the "Democratic shadow cabinet."[100] Although many journalists disagreed with the substance of Acheson's foreign-policy statements, they commended him for offering the public thoughtful alternatives to Eisenhower's policies. By 1958 the DAC had earned national acclaim, and Dean Acheson deserved a great deal of the credit.

The media attention spurred Acheson to develop a pamphlet series (with the title "Foreign and Military Policy for Peace and Security") modeled after Thomas Paine's *Common Sense*. His aim was to rally the nation against the Eisenhower-Dulles foreign policy.[101] Only half of the ten projected pamphlets ultimately were published. Unlike prior Acheson-DAC foreign-policy statements, these were targeted not so much at the press as at party activists across the nation, and thus they were longer and were typeset instead of typed. "The pamphlets," he wrote committee member Chester Bowles, "are directed primarily to those Democrats who are interested in doing some work for the Party in the next three years. They are intended to give them ammunition in talking to their neighbors, friends, and at various meetings they may attend. It is hoped that they will influence Members of Congress and perhaps help get better platforms which will make a little more sense than our platform made in 1956."[102] Acheson's constant jabs at the previous party platform set his fellow committee members to bickering among themselves over the substance of the pamphlets. An aging Acheson had no patience for coping with the disagreements within the DAC. Adhering to General Marshall's adage "Don't fight the problem, solve it," Acheson let the liberals do the squabbling while he kept writing.

Acheson's first pamphlet was published under the title "Where We Are: The World Today and How It Got That Way."[103] Although the pamphlet eventually received committee approval, some members, including Averell Harriman and John Kenneth Galbraith, felt that Acheson was issuing "declarations of war" when rapprochement was what was needed in a dangerous nuclear world.[104] Acheson, steadfastly refusing to recognize that anticolonial nationalism was responsible for much of the anti-American unrest in Africa, Asia, the Middle East, and Latin America, instead turned out DAC papers which charged the Eisenhower administration with permitting, and even encouraging, Sino-Soviet expansionism around the globe. Acheson's hard-line, Eisenhower-bashing, cold war stance was making him enemies among the more liberal and moderate committee members.

The first pamphlet also included a harsh personal attack on the president, who had been slowed down by the heart attack he had suffered in 1955:

> For months, stretching into years, we have heard that all was well. We have been bewitched into believing that an obviously aging and incapacitated man was fit to carry on the most mercilessly exacting office in the world. We were given dietary and physiological details; we watched doctors perform on super-quiz programs. All the time a misled and uninformed President has, quite honestly, misled us further.[105]

Acheson blamed the decline of American power and prestige under the Republicans not on any lack of patriotism but on a lack of will, vigor, and intelligence. He concluded the twenty-page pamphlet by urging the reader to vote for the Democrats in 1958.

Ranking number one at this time on Acheson's list of mindless, fickle administration policies was its handling of the crisis over the Chinese offshore islands of Quemoy and Matsu during the early fall of 1958. In

1954 and 1955 after Eisenhower had "unleashed" the Nationalist Chinese armed forces by withdrawing the U.S. Seventh Fleet from the Formosa Straits, a crisis had occurred that had brought the United States and the People's Republic of China (PRC) to the brink of war. Situated only a few miles off the Chinese mainland, the tiny Taiwanese islands of Quemoy and Matsu were used by Chiang Kai-shek, the Nationalist leader, as military bases for commando raids against the PRC. In autumn of 1954 the PRC began shelling the islands. President Eisenhower decided to defend Formosa's right to the outposts and let it be known he was contemplating the use of nuclear weapons. Acheson was aghast at this threat of massive retaliation over two insignificant rocks in the Pacific. In January 1955 Congress passed the Formosa Resolution, authorizing the president to send troops to defend Formosa and the surrounding islands. Acheson thought the resolution dangerously vague, for Chiang could interpret it as meaning the United States would risk war with Communist China to defend Quemoy and Matsu. Although the congressional resolution itself did not stop Peking's heavy bombardment of the islands, back-channel negotiations ensued between Chinese premier Chou En-lai and Dulles and by late May an informal cease-fire was attained.[106]

In August 1958 the PRC again began bombarding the offshore islands with heavy artillery. The Eisenhower administration responded with a conspicuous show of support for Chiang. Boisterous opposition to the administration's combative stance erupted throughout the Democratic Party. The partisan attack was not unexpected, but the administration was unprepared for the avalanche of discontent that rolled across America.

On September 6 Acheson, in his role as DAC spokesman, denounced Eisenhower's "horrendous" handling of the crisis: "We seem to be drifting, either dazed or indifferent, toward war with China, a war without friends or allies and over issues which the Administration has not presented to the people and which are not worth a single American life.... The decision seems now to have been made to defend Quemoy, even though it leads to World War." He charged that the administration had "most unwisely maneuvered itself, with the help of Chiang Kai-shek, into a situation of which it [had] lost control.... The attitude of the Administration is that nothing will be done to extricate ourselves from this position during periods of quiet, and that nothing can be done about it in times of crisis. This is an attitude which can not be tolerated."[107]

Acheson was convinced that making a symbolic stand over Quemoy was the height of recklessness. "You suggest that my views on Quemoy recall Mr. Chamberlain's policy toward Hitler," Acheson replied to a woman who had written to charge him with appeasement. "I can reply that my views much more resemble General Washington's when he withdrew from Long Island and thence to New Jersey where he took up a much more favorable position, as was proved at Trenton."[108] So strong were Acheson's objections to Eisenhower's nuclear blackmail that he found himself for the first time since leaving government opposed to former president Truman, who had endorsed Eisenhower's position. "The Administration should not be encouraged to make the stand here [Quemoy and Matsu]," Acheson admonished Truman. "It would be a disaster involving, as it well could, defense by atomic weapons. Please don't be hooked on one of these 'my country right or wrong' gambits. In this way Foster can always drive us like steers to the slaughter pen."[109]

Acheson began a two-pronged effort aimed at averting war with China while simultaneously leading the Democratic Party to an overwhelming victory in the upcoming November election. Events overtook his efforts, for after talks with Secretary of State Dulles in Formosa, Chiang Kai-shek announced his government would not use force to return to mainland China. His communiqué led Peking to stop bombing the islands. The second Quemoy-Matsu crisis ended with election day just over a week away.

Still, the Democrats did achieve, as Acheson had predicted, a landslide victory in 1958.[110] The Republicans—dogged by Sputnik, recession, and the Sherman Adams–Bernard Goldfine scandal, and lacking the popular Eisenhower at the head of the ticket—were handed one of the worst defeats in their history. The Democrats achieved control of both the House and Senate by nearly a two-to-one margin, having captured 62 percent of the vote. The White House in 1960 seemed within reach. "Now our party has just about two-thirds of the seats in each house and very little idea what to do with them," Acheson wrote Sir Patrick Devlin shortly after the election. "Senator Johnson of Texas, who will have the largest voice in any decision, comes out today for an activist policy. I am all for that. But to accomplish it is comparable to building the tower of Babel in the land of Shinar—the author or authors of Genesis lamentably did not know about the United States."[111]

The Achesonians vs. the Stevensonians

By early 1959, DAC statements were deemed even more newsworthy, for many read them as clues to the shape of the 1960 Democratic Party platform. For this reason within the DAC itself a number of members grew increasingly alarmed over Dean Acheson's uncompromising anti-Soviet posture. Later John Kenneth Galbraith explained,

> At each meeting Dean Acheson, aided by Paul Nitze, who was by now an unrelenting Cold Warrior . . . produced a paper attacking whatever John Foster Dulles had done in the preceding weeks. The attack was always for being too lenient toward Communism and the Soviet Union. Lehman, Stevenson, and Harriman would then take exception with a view to moderating the language. . . . I was not wholly passive. With the others I sought to mute the Acheson calls to battle. Acheson would then respond with a stand on some domestic issue that was well to the right of the irretrievably conservative [secretary of agriculture,] Ezra Taft Benson.[112]

Acheson, in turn, had little tolerance for Galbraith, whom he considered "an ineffectual gadfly."[113] Galbraith, as chairman of the DAC's economic committee, got tired of his adversary and friend Acheson constantly adding his unsolicited two-cents' worth on what should or should not constitute the Democratic Party's domestic agenda. To even up the score, Galbraith began venturing in on Acheson's foreign-policy meetings, offering liberal opinions and scolding Acheson for sounding like a right-wing reactionary.[114] Years later Averell Harriman, echoing similar comments made by Galbraith and Bowles, claimed, "We knocked Acheson out. The DAC kept the Democratic Party liberal. I took the lead in saying the rough things to Acheson that had to be said."[115]

In contrast, Tyroler insists that although Galbraith, Harriman, Stevenson, and others expressed disagreements, there was never any doubt that Acheson "was completely in control." Nitze's perception is similar: "Dean managed to carry the day even though the majority view wasn't consistent with his view. The pamphlets we produced reflect Dean Acheson, not those on the other side of the equation. Dean was in charge."[116]

In 1958 the chasm separating Stevenson and Acheson became unbridgeable, and tempers flared over every major foreign-policy issue discussed at DAC meetings. What infuriated Acheson was what he described as Stevenson's "indecisiveness": "He simply could not make up his mind about anything."[117] But by the late 1950s "decisiveness" to Acheson had come to mean agreeing with his position. Acheson's scorn for Stevenson is revealed in a story he enjoyed telling. In this account Stevenson, about to deliver a speech, asked an aide whether he had time to go to the bathroom. Assured that he did, Stevenson is reputed to have replied,

"Do I want to go to the bathroom?"[118] In letters and private conversation with family and friends, Acheson, with his genius for inventive barbs, referred to Stevenson by literally dozens of unflattering nicknames—"Fat Boy," a reference to Adlai's voracious eating habits and his potbelly, being the most common. When asked by reporters in January 1959 what Democrat was best suited for the presidency, Acheson ranked Stevenson sixth, below even Michigan governor "Soapy" Williams. "Adlai will never forgive me," Acheson predicted to Truman.[119]

Acheson's low opinion of Stevenson infected his relationship with two of Stevenson's supporters, William Benton and Chester Bowles, who had as young men founded a successful advertising agency. Writing to Eugene Rostow about the "Connecticut duo," Acheson scoffed that "time spent in the advertising business seems to create a permanent deformity like the Chinese habit of footbinding."[120] From the late 1940s through the 1950s Acheson had exchanged letters often with Benton, Bowles, and Stevenson; by 1960 his correspondence with them would come to a complete halt. Even Eleanor Roosevelt added her voice to the anti-Acheson chorus. At a press conference she suggested Acheson's proclivity for alarmist analysis was at least ten years behind the times: "I feel that he is dealing more with a situation that existed when he was laying down policy."[121] Earlier she had vehemently opposed Acheson's appointment as chairman of the foreign-policy committee of the DAC. For his part Acheson considered Eleanor Roosevelt too much of a "do-gooder" and wrote that at times he "found her very hard to take."[122]

Acheson was not unduly alarmed about his break with the liberal Stevensonian crowd; he continued writing his foreign-policy pamphlets and papers. By summer 1958, however, he had to contend with resistance from many DAC members, not just the Stevenson liberals. He complained to Harry Truman that "the statement on the Middle East which you and I like was strongly approved by Hubert Humphrey and Tom Finletter. However, Paul Butler, Charlie Murphy, Phil Perlman, and W. Averell Harriman opposed it, with the result being that Charles Tyroler did not issue it. They opposed it on what I thought was a silly ground—that it was not constructive. Why one has to be constructive in criticizing a fool step by someone else I do not know."[123]

The imprimatur of the first Acheson-written foreign-policy committee pamphlet read: "These pamphlets are recommendations for policy, prepared under the authority and supervision of the Advisory Council." The second pamphlet added: "They do not necessarily reflect the precise views of all members of the Advisory Council."[124] This second pamphlet, entitled "Why We Need Allies and They Need Us to Preserve the Free World" appeared in February 1959. In it Acheson denounced the Eisenhower administration for neoisolationism. He argued that the United States was part of a global community and must treat its NATO allies as equals, for lack of cooperation between the nations of the West would create a climate hospitable to communism.

The pamphlet closed with a call for the president "to awaken the nation, to tell it the truth, the whole harsh, distasteful truth, and point the way to action."[125] If Eisenhower was incapable of telling the American people the truth, it was the country's duty to elect a Democrat in 1960. Which Democrat, Acheson did not say, but already Hubert Humphrey, John F. Kennedy, and Stuart Symington were actively seeking the nomination.

Preparing for the 1960 Election

With a presidential election just around the corner, Acheson put together an itemized list of disasters wrought by the Eisenhower-Dulles foreign policy. "We have two pamphlets for the Advisory Committee in the press now," he wrote to Truman. "One takes Dulles apart in a way you will like. If he will only stay well for two weeks, we're in business."[126] John Foster Dulles did not stay well, and he died of cancer on May 24, 1959. Acheson silenced a dinner party at his country home, Harewood, by declaring, "Thank God Foster is underground."[127] He did recall the two pamphlets from the printers to delete the derogatory references to Dulles.[128] Three years after Dulles's death Acheson was still sparring with his ghost. "The dedicatory speeches by Messrs. Kennedy and Eisenhower at the so-called (and I hope only temporarily so) Dulles Airport had overwhelmed me with disgust," Acheson wrote Louis Halle in 1962. "They gave their apostolic blessing to the myth, and pushed forward the canonization of Caliban."[129]

The void left by Dulles was quickly filled by Richard Nixon. In a revised Acheson pamphlet titled "How to Lose Friends and Influence: The Decline of American Diplomacy, 1953–1959" Acheson attributes nearly all the diplomatic problems facing the United States to the failure of executive leadership. "A Canadian political party recently won a national election by waging an anti-U.S. campaign," he noted in evidence, and in Latin America Vice-President Nixon "was met by a hymn of hate, was stoned, and spat on."[130]

Acheson's charges of a failed Latin American policy were not of recent origin. In a June 1958 press conference, he had attacked Nixon's Latin American trip as a "Madison Avenue-conducted tour . . . causing more harm" to the United States's image there than any event in recent history. In general, he claimed earlier, Latin America had been "neglected" under the Eisenhower administration. The State Department countered with statistics showing that the amount of economic aid sent to the twenty Latin American republics in the previous five years had been more than double that sent in the five years of the Truman administration.[131]

Acheson also deplored the Eisenhower record elsewhere in the world. In Southeast Asia, for instance, half of French Indochina was "overrun by the Communists," he charged in his pamphlet. "Burma ordered a closing down of the U.S. Information Service libraries. Indonesia . . . went on an anti-U.S. rampage. India was alienated by our arming of Pakistan. And Japan squirmed restlessly under our China policy." As if this were not enough, the United States—in isolation, without allies—almost had become involved "in a foolish war with Communist China over the islands of Quemoy and Matsu."[132]

Next on the hit list was Middle East policy, which was in shambles under Eisenhower's haphazard direction. "The rising tide of anti-U.S. sentiment made an attack on anything American the easiest way to win local fame," Acheson asserted. Using this ploy, "Colonel Nasser of Egypt made common cause with the Soviet Union to destroy American and Western influence, and to imperil the lines of supply feeding oil into European industry." Syria and Yemen were also lost to "Nasserism." A revolution in Iraq was marked by assassination of all the pro-American Iraqi leaders, while Turkey, Iran, Pakistan, and Israel found themselves pinned between communism and Nasserism. "In a further sequel," Acheson wrote, "U.S. Marines were drawn into the morass of Lebanese civil strife; British paratroopers, into Jordan threatening to disintegrate into its desert sands. Saudi Arabia began to snuggle up to Egypt's Nasser."

All of this would not have occurred, Acheson contended, had Eisenhower not pursued a "go-it-alone diplomacy." He found the administration's performance "all the more fantastic," for Eisenhower had held "posts where he could be presumed to have gained exact knowledge about how our foreign policy had to be conducted," posts to which he had been appointed by Democratic presidents. Acheson closed this pamphlet as he had the others by urging the reader to vote the Democratic ticket in 1960.

The DAC released another pamphlet, entitled "The Military Forces We Need and How to Get Them," in June 1959.[133] It was written by Paul

Nitze and revised by Dean Acheson. They charged Eisenhower's New Look policy had destroyed America's defense capability. The administration's first priority should be "to assure nuclear adequacy—to retain a second strike capacity" by setting "goals high enough to permit a margin of insurance to cover faulty intelligence reports and possible rapid advances achieved by the Soviet Union without our knowledge." The authors also argued that the Air Force, Navy, and Army were in desperate need of modernization, which would require additional defense expenditures for the next four or five years of approximately $7.5 billion annually.

In a speech delivered at Colgate University shortly after the pamphlet's release, Acheson insisted that the U.S. economy could afford the additional defense expenditures and that indeed when the country's security was at stake the American people had no alternative. He called for the modernization of the army and an increase of 225,000 men at a cost of $3 billion annually. The Air Force, Acheson said, needed an additional $3 billion a year for jet tankers and missiles, and he estimated the Navy's needs for developing the Polaris submarine and missile at $1 billion. Expanded research at $500,000,000 annually brought the total necessary annual increase in military spending to $7.5 billion. Acheson did not specify how the additional revenue could be obtained.[134]

In November 1959 the DAC's political prestige was enhanced greatly by the addition to the group of two presidential candidates—Senators John Kennedy of Massachusetts and Stuart Symington of Missouri.[135] Both were tough critics of the Eisenhower administration's military, strategic, and foreign policies. Their membership in the foreign-policy committee provoked more intense scrutiny of committee pronouncements by the media and even brought the DAC a touch of the Kennedy glamour. In Washington the DAC was now commonly referred to as the "shadow government" or the "government in exile."[136]

Senator John F. Kennedy had nominated Adlai Stevenson at the 1956 Democratic National Convention. When Stevenson opened the vice-presidential nomination to the convention, Kennedy actively sought the vote and received widespread media attention, though he lost by a whisker to Senator Estes Kefauver of Tennessee. Kennedy immediately began preparing for a presidential bid in 1960. He demonstrated his voter appeal by winning reelection to the Senate in 1958 by a wide margin. Invited by Paul Butler to join the DAC in 1957, Kennedy first accepted, then declined. Unlike fellow senators and presidential hopefuls Hubert Humphrey and Estes Kefauver, Kennedy thought it unwise to be associated with the organization. He told Butler his decision was consonant with that of most House and Senate members, who had also declined.[137] As the battle for the Democratic nomination unfolded in late 1959, Kennedy, at the urging of Arthur Schlesinger, Jr., reversed himself and joined.[138] Acheson was not pleased with the "late arrival of the junior Senator from Massachusetts."[139] He associated the Kennedy clan with Joe McCarthy and called them all "uncouth Irishmen unfit for high public office."[140]

Acheson earlier had criticized the young Pulitzer Prize–winning senator's views on the Algerian conflict. The Senate speech that aroused Acheson's indignation—Kennedy's first major foreign-policy address—was made on July 2, 1957. Kennedy supported exerting U.S. influence on France to recognize the independence of Algeria. He thought France was repeating errors of the past, above all in its refusal to accept the reality of anticolonialism and Arab nationalism; he also bluntly criticized U.S. support of the French government in the struggle against the Algerian rebels.[141]

In Acheson's terms Kennedy had committed a mortal sin: criticizing a NATO ally. Speaking at the Fletcher School of Law and Diplomacy at Tufts University in October 1957, Acheson attacked Kennedy (though not by name). He later wrote that Kennedy's position showed a failure to understand the "humiliating agony of the loss of power" France was experiencing.[142] "This impatient snapping of our fingers," Acheson decried. "This seemed to me to be the wrong way to treat our oldest ally, a country which was still suffering under the defeats of World War II and a sense of inferiority for what had happened."[143] Furthermore, as Acheson saw it, if France pulled out of Algeria, chaos would reign.

If Acheson's acceptance of Kennedy's late entry into the DAC was grudging, he was delighted when Senator Stuart Symington joined. Symington, appointed the first secretary of the air force in 1947 by President Truman, was a leading advocate of increased defense spending. He insisted that the development of a large Air Force with nuclear capabilities should become the backbone of a modern U.S. defense system. Symington resigned in 1950 to protest defense budget cuts and was elected in 1952 from his adopted state of Missouri to the Senate, where he served until 1977.

As head of a subcommittee of the Senate Armed Forces Committee in 1956, Symington, already a presidential aspirant, endeared himself to Acheson with a majority report which claimed, "It is now clear that the U.S. . . . may have lost control of the air." The authors of the report charged the administration with placing the tight-fisted fiscal concerns of the New Look above national security and with a "tendency to either ignore or underestimate Soviet military progress." They called for increased defense spending.[144]

In 1959 Symington officially entered the contest for the Democratic presidential nomination. His platform attacked Eisenhower's weak defense program and blamed it for creating a missile gap. Acheson applauded Symington's zestful advocacy of increased defense spending and, together with Harry Truman, backed him for the presidency. Symington began attending DAC meetings. "Dean loved my attacks on Eisenhower's defense program," Symington recalled. "He felt that America had an obligation to handle the world. Not necessarily control it. But that we should establish a position well beyond the Monroe Doctrine. The U.S. had an obligation to the whole free world."[145]

While his personal choice for the presidency was Symington, Acheson had the political instincts to realize that the ticket most likely to defeat the Republicans in 1960 would be the Johnson-Kennedy combination. "Lyndon is the ablest man in national public life today," Acheson wrote Truman. "He has thousands of faults. But when we really take our hair down, he is a giant among pygmies. So I feel confident that if, with strong support and a united party, he took on the campaign, especially with Kennedy, we would have a chance for a fight in which I could join wholeheartedly, because there would not only be a real chance to win, but to win under circumstances where victory might really turn the tide for the great struggle of our time." Acheson confessed to Truman that his real worry was that Adlai Stevenson might get the nomination and "all we accomplish by electing him is to accept the formal responsibility for ultimate defeat."[146]

Shortly after the Kennedy and Symington memberships were confirmed, the DAC released a 10,000-word blueprint for the upcoming party platform titled "The Decision in 1960: The Need to Elect a Democratic President."[147] The foreign-policy section, written by Acheson and Nitze, was a synthesis of their prior anti-Eisenhower statements, with direct and personal attacks on Eisenhower replaced by a more statesmanlike tone. Because of its timely release just as the presidential race was intensifying, the council's blueprint received front-page news coverage and television exposure and editorial analysis throughout the country. Acheson and Nitze clearly were shaping the Democratic candidates' foreign-policy positions and angering many leading Republicans. When asked whether he thought their criticism of Republican foreign policy had been effective, Acheson replied with a grin, "Whenever you throw a brick up an alley and hear a squawk, you know you have hit a cat."[148]

Still, Acheson had become completely exasperated with the internal politics of the DAC. He thought many members were being adversely influenced by the "Butler liberals" who still listened to Adlai Stevenson and Eleanor Roosevelt, who wanted to create "peace agencies," and who preferred watered-down statements to his own hard-line attacks. Acheson confided to a friend his difficulties in being an effective DAC committee chairman: "The great weakness of being a head, but in not having the responsibility for action, is that every suggestion of any policy has some objectors and seems to mean some loss of support. The fundamental law of politics is that the greater the generalization the greater the area of agreement. Unanimity can be achieved on a statement which means nothing at all."[149]

Success for the DAC

Throughout 1959 and 1960 Acheson traveled the country denouncing Ike's record. The Democratic presidential candidates, he thought, were too deferential to the old war hero; if the Democrats were to defeat Nixon in the 1960 election, they would have to expose the administration's lies and corruption. "We shan't beat Nixon unless we get a candidate who believes in the democratic process, as a process of education, based on telling the truth, and will tell it militantly regardless of the supposed 'mileage' in it," he argued.[150] Acheson described Ike as exercising leadership, but in the wrong direction. He acknowledged that the president had taken on a "new vitality since he has escaped from the apron strings of Sherman Adams and Foster Dulles," but it was only a partial escape, "because [Secretary of the Treasury] George Humphrey remains his Svengali." "The President's leadership," Acheson wrote Louis Halle, "is the leadership of a nurse singing a lullaby to a baby, and I fear that the country to some extent is responding."[151] When Eisenhower announced his plan of taking a 20,000-mile goodwill trip around the world in November 1959, Acheson scoffed: "Locomotion," he told the press, "seems to have taken the place of policy and action."[152]

Acheson was buoyed by a nonpartisan Rockefeller Brothers Fund report which reached conclusions identical to those of the Gaither Report and the DAC foreign-policy group regarding the deficiencies of Eisenhower's defense program and the need to increase the military budget. Acheson, Truman, Symington, and Hubert Humphrey issued a joint statement—written by Acheson—praising the findings of "Mid-Century Challenge to U.S. Foreign Policy," which had been written under the direction of Professor Henry Kissinger of Harvard. "In our connection with the Democratic Advisory Council," they said, "we are not oblivious of the parallels between what this document says and what we have been saying. To the contrary, we are much encouraged to have our views implicitly confirmed from such an authoritative nonpartisan source."[153]

Throughout the spring and early summer of 1960 the DAC continued to release numerous foreign-policy statements. Many were written by Acheson, including "A Policy for the West Toward Underdeveloped Countries," "Nuclear Testing," "United States Space Program," and "The Summit Failure in Perspective."[154] Acheson appraised the DAC as "pretty effective" in influencing the presidential candidates and the Congress, pointing to "the excellence of our Foreign Policy pamphlets as the secret of the success."[155]

As the fight for the Democratic nomination intensified in the spring of 1960, Senators Humphrey, Kennedy, and Symington campaigned on many of the foreign-policy stances developed by the DAC. This gave the Democratic convention a sense of cohesiveness around issues such as the missile gap and the failure of executive leadership. Acheson's pointed attacks on Eisenhower had news value, as they typically were controversial, quotable, and dramatic. The DAC's activities brought mixed reviews. Arthur Krock, writing in the *New York Times*, complained that the DAC had achieved a "monopoly of the political publicity market . . . because the national prominence of these citizens effects widespread and generous use by the newspapers of excerpts, and often full texts of the long papers issued under their imprimatur." In contrast, Earl Mazo of the *New York Herald Tribune* called the DAC "the boldest, most imaginative and most controversial political innovation produced by a regular party organization in many years."[156]

For all practical purposes, the Democratic Advisory Council expired in July 1960 at the Democratic nominating convention. Acheson resigned as foreign-policy committee chairman shortly after Kennedy was nominated. The death certificate for the organization was signed at a harmony meeting between DAC chairmen and leaders of the Senatorial and Congressional Campaign Committee on March 10, 1961. The participants declared that the DAC had served a function when the Republicans were in control of the White House, but now that a Democrat was president, "policy should be made at the White House and by the leadership of Congress."[157]

The DAC provided a rich resource for the new president; Kennedy would eventually hire nearly a third of the group's 275 members for his administration.[158] Fellow committee members such as Bowles, Galbraith, Harriman, Nitze, and Williams were assigned top posts in either State or Defense. The DAC also supplied Kennedy with an intellectual framework, which he would dub the New Frontier. That the DAC foreign-policy committee was able to shape the discussion of the issues before the election and to influence the new president strongly afterward is a tribute to the determination and hard work of Dean Acheson and Paul Nitze. As always, Acheson had been ready to pay any price, bear any burden, meet any hardship, support any friend, oppose any foe, to put a Democrat in the White House.

CHAPTER THREE

The Changing Political Climate in Europe, 1957–60

In the spring of 1957 Dean Acheson shifted his attention from the Middle East to Europe, where views toward economic and political integration, German reunification, and the future of NATO were all in flux. Many Europeans had lost confidence in American leadership after Suez and Sputnik, and the "U.S. out of Europe" slogan arose throughout Britain, Germany, and the rest of Western Europe.

Although the tremors in the Atlantic alliance concerned Acheson, he was heartened by the formal creation of the European Economic Community (EEC), or Common Market, and the European Atomic Energy Commission (Euratom). These bodies were established on March 25, 1957, when the nations known as the Six (France, Belgium, the Netherlands, Germany, Luxembourg, and Italy) signed the Treaties of Rome. That the Rome agreements appeared to have been enacted without active American participation was evidence to Acheson of the declining importance of the United States in the Western coalition. Nonetheless, in the relaunching of the idea of a united Europe, he envisioned new political and economic opportunities to complement NATO in what he and other "Europeanists" called the Atlantic community.[1]

The immediate objectives of the EEC treaty were to establish a customs union with free movement of goods; to dismantle quotas and barriers to trade; and to encourage the free movement of people, services, and capital. Acheson most welcomed the treaty's provisions for common policies on matters such as agriculture and transportation, social issues, and external trade, and the allotment of capital to the community itself.

About Euratom, which was to provide for the joint development of nuclear energy for peaceful purposes while renouncing the acquisition of nuclear weapons, Acheson was elated, but he feared that the plan would meet opposition in France. He was right; before too long, under Charles de Gaulle, France turned away from Euratom, opting for a nuclear force of its own. Acheson nevertheless remained a staunch supporter of Euratom well into the 1960s, mainly at his French friend Jean Monnet's urging.[2] Monnet's steadfast support of Euratom is an interesting counterpoint to his initial refusal to support the Common Market. He had believed, mistakenly, that the French parliament would reject this challenge to their protectionist traditions, as it had the EDC.

"The success of the movement toward unity in the West of Europe is no longer in doubt," an optimistic Acheson wrote in an article for *Foreign Affairs*. "Only the rate of progress is undecided. The Coal and Steel Community, Euratom, and the Common Market have been accepted. A common community and political community are on the way." But, as the title of this article—"The Illusion of Disengagement"—indicates, Acheson did not favor withdrawing U.S. troops from the Continent, fearing this could lead to political upheaval in Europe.[3]

George F. Kennan and the Reith Lectures

George F. Kennan served under Secretary of State George C. Marshall as the director of the policy planning staff from 1947 through 1949. He gained international notice for an influential *Foreign Affairs* essay (1947) entitled "Sources of Soviet Conduct." In this article (better known as the "Mr. X" essay, as it was unsigned), Kennan called on the United States to adopt a firm policy of "containment" of Soviet expansionism. Kennan was appointed State Department counselor in 1949, a post he soon vacated as a consequence of policy differences with the new secretary of state, Dean Acheson. He was summoned back to Washington in late 1951 at the behest of Secretary Acheson and was appointed ambassador to the Soviet Union. While in Geneva in October 1952, Kennan was declared persona non grata by Stalin and denied reentry to Moscow because a few weeks earlier he had criticized Soviet treatment of Western diplomats.[4]

In 1948 Kennan had begun making the case for neutralizing Central Europe to Secretary of State Marshall and other senior State Department officials. When Acheson succeeded Marshall, he brushed aside Kennan's recommendations as dangerous and unenlightened. Almost a decade later, the issue would be joined once more, this time in a public forum. The occasion was an invitation to Kennan, who spent the 1957–58 academic year as a visiting professor at Oxford University, to deliver the BBC Radio's prestigious Reith Lectures on international affairs. The series of half-hour lectures was broadcast on six successive Sundays, beginning on November 10, 1957.[5]

Kennan, regarded by many as America's foremost Soviet specialist, hoped to use the forum to awaken Europeans to the realities of the superpower nuclear chess game in which they were passive pawns. He called for a joint Anglo-American and Soviet military withdrawal from Central Europe, offering specific disengagement proposals for Washington and Moscow, and supported a reunified, neutral Germany. Kennan believed both the United States and the Soviet Union had to adopt a "hands-off" policy in Europe for the sake of global stability in the nuclear age. Kennan's broadcasts did more than awaken the Europeans; they triggered a disengagement debate that produced reverberations on both sides of the Atlantic and set in motion a reexamination of the cold war status quo.

Kennan was motivated in part by the changing complexion of the nuclear world. In the decade since he had first advanced his disengagement proposals, the United States had lost its nuclear monopoly. There were rumblings that NATO was about to embark upon the deployment of tactical nuclear weapons in Western Europe, which Kennan felt would lead the Soviets to accelerate the dissemination of nuclear weapons in the Warsaw Pact countries.

Kennan's first talk was delivered only a month after the Soviet launching of Sputnik I, and the last aired on the eve of a pivotal NATO conference convened in Paris to discuss whether or not to deploy tactical nuclear weapons in Western Europe. The explosive material emerged in the third and fourth broadcasts, which dealt with the possibility of a unified, neutral Germany and the need for eventual U.S.-Soviet disengagement from Europe. Kennan argued that the excessive military buildup in Europe increased the likelihood of a war that would have dire consequences for civilization. To reduce this risk, Kennan urged the Europeans to pressure both Washington and Moscow to pull out of Europe—not to put in more troops and missiles. Washington should withdraw its troops from West Germany in exchange for withdrawal of Soviet troops from Eastern Europe. He contended that since Stalin's death, a liberalizing trend had emerged in the Soviet Union, making Moscow more inclined to diplomatic negotiations and domestic reforms than military adventurism.

All U.S. forces eventually should be withdrawn from the Continent and from Britain. Implicit in this argument was the belief that the United States had overcommitted itself in Europe; as the corollary to the end of its military presence, the NATO countries would have to mount paramilitary or militia forces for local defense.

Kennan stressed that in his plan the newly unified Germany would be placed under military restrictions, including a prohibition on nuclear weapons. In 1955 West Germany had become a member of NATO, to Kennan's dismay, and the United States had been pushing for West German rearmament. Kennan opposed this effort, and particularly wanted to keep nuclear weapons out of Germany. The man who had conceptualized the containment policy was now opposed to strengthening NATO and advocated instead the neutralization of Europe. Kennan's eloquent case against the whole NATO defense plan—the presence of German divisions, tactical atomic weapons, and missile bases in Europe—aroused a swirl of controversy.

In West Germany, where Kennan frequently lectured and where he had a wide following, his disengagement proposals received immediate attention from the press. The praise of Kennan in the New Year's message to the German people of President Theodor Heuss was interpreted by German journalists as an oblique endorsement of Kennan's disengagement proposals. Many journalists, including Fritz René Allemann of *Die Zeit* and Paul Sethe of *Die Welt*, regarded Kennan as an unofficial foreign-policy spokesman for the Democratic Party, or at least for Adlai Stevenson. (Stevenson had explicitly and bluntly repudiated this perception during the 1956 campaign: Mr. Kennan "is in no way connected with my staff and never has been," the *New York Times* quoted him as saying in June 1956.[6]) The Social Democratic Party (SPD) vigorously supported Kennan's plan, which to a great extent paralleled its own position.[7]

Because press and political support for Kennan's proposals in West Germany clearly conflicted with NATO policy and because that support was based, in part, on a misperception of Kennan's influence within the Democratic Party in the United States, the pro-NATO lobby felt impelled to clarify the situation. Dean Acheson—the chairman of the foreign-policy committee of the Democratic Advisory Council and a man respected throughout Europe as a tireless American proponent of a strong NATO—was called into action.

Reply to Kennan

The American Council on Germany, a New York City–based nonprofit organization, was the first with the counter-Kennan initiative. The group was headed by James B. Conant, formerly ambassador to Germany and president of Harvard University. Its mission was to clarify any misunderstandings that might appear in the American or West German press, particularly those considered detrimental to NATO or to continued harmonious American-German relations.[8]

Christopher Emmet, the executive vice-chairman of the council, wrote Dean Acheson on December 24, 1957, urging him to sign a joint statement criticizing the Kennan lectures. Emmet, a blue-blooded Atlanticist and conservative ideologue, argued that Acheson, as chairman of the foreign-policy committee of the DAC, should counter the European descriptions of Kennan as a "semi-official spokesman" and "super brain-truster" for the Democratic Party and deliver a rebuttal to his arguments. If Acheson preferred to write a separate statement, the council would arrange the widest possible press coverage, both in West Germany and in the United States.[9]

Emmet had long admired Acheson for his pivotal role in bringing West Germany into NATO and into the planning for the European Defense Community (EDC). He thought well of the defense of NATO made by Acheson in a recently published debate in *Western World* magazine. Acheson's opponent was Erich Ollenhauer, the leader of the SPD. Ollenhauer, a stubborn opponent of the Nazi regime who had been forced to emigrate first to France and later to England from 1938 to 1946, was also a staunch adversary of both Adenauer's Christian Democratic Party (CDU) and NATO.

The question posed to the discussants was "Is the North Atlantic Treaty Organization useful?" Acheson argued that NATO was not only useful but also necessary for the security of Western Europe: "The North Atlantic Treaty, its organization and its military forces, are [a] recognition of the truth that there can be no balance of power in Europe, or elsewhere, which will restrain Soviet power unless the weight of the United States is put into the scales."[10]

Ollenhauer countered that although NATO had been useful in 1949, it was now a roadblock to a unified Germany. He called for U.S. disengagement from Europe and the end of NATO.[11] "Ollenhauer's statement is a frightening one and I am afraid is only too typical of the paralysis of will and the growth of illusion current in Western Europe," Acheson wrote his friend W. Averell Harriman. "I have tried to get the Europeans to see the basic reality of the situation."[12]

In response to Emmet's request Acheson immediately wrote a powerful two-page statement entitled "Reply to Kennan." "It is, as you see," Acheson wrote Emmet, "written more for European than American readers. But it won't hurt some of our Democrats to learn that they don't agree with George."[13] Emmet—a vociferous and well-organized man—wanted to obtain the largest possible audience for Acheson's statement. He mailed copies to other council members, asking them to join in criticizing Kennan's proposals. Lack of publicity for their views in the United States was of little consequence, for "the most important thing is that an answer should be publicized in Germany, coming from the people whose names are known there, at least in intellectual and political circles, for their knowledge of the German problem." Emmet was confident that Acheson's statement would receive special attention in Great Britain, where he was greatly respected as an astute diplomat.[14] Both Emmet and Acheson were aware that the case for West German inclusion in NATO would need to be explained again and again to meet new criticisms and changing political conditions.

After covertly consulting a group of experienced newsmen, Emmet decided to release Acheson's statement in full for the Sunday, January 12, newspapers both at home and abroad. He gathered statements supporting Acheson's reply from former president Truman, Adlai Stevenson, W. Averell Harriman, and senators Lyndon Johnson, Estes Kefauver, Paul Douglas, and John F. Kennedy for release for the January 13 editions.[15] Emmet felt obliged to do whatever was necessary to publicize Acheson's statement because he was alarmed by what he saw as increasing evidence of a cumulative, growing emotionalism in Britain, as well as Germany, over Kennan's views. The next round of the Kennan-Acheson debate was about to begin.

In Acheson's rebuttal, published throughout Europe and the United States on January 12, 1958, he unequivocally disassociated himself and the Democratic Party from Kennan's proposals for the withdrawal of American and Soviet troops from continental Europe. Acheson attempted to disabuse Europeans of the notion that the views of this nominal Democrat and armchair intellectual represented those of the Democratic Party: "Most categorically they do not, as Mr. Kennan would, I am sure, agree."[16]

Acheson argued that Kennan's proposals were stale ideas, first expounded in 1949 when their author was part of the Truman administration, and did not meet new circumstances. This rehash of his "Plan A," which had had Kennan and Acheson at loggerheads in 1950, should be rejected now as it was then, Acheson argued. Its provisions were contrary to the expressed opinion of leading Democrats both in and out of Congress.

Acheson brusquely dismissed Kennan's "personal assurance" that the Soviet threat to Europe was one of subversion only, and that there was no danger of Soviet military attack:

> How can any man speak of "personal assurance" to any such effect? On what does the guarantee rest except divine revelation? . . . So long as we are giving personal assurances, I think I can give mine that Mr. Kennan's opinion is not shared by any responsible leader in the Democratic Party in the United States.[17]

Although Acheson paid tribute to Kennan's knowledge of Russian history and culture, he declared, in what became the most widely quoted paragraph of his reply:

> Mr. Kennan has never, in my judgment, grasped the realities of power relationships but takes a rather mystical attitude toward them. To Mr. Kennan there is no Soviet military threat in Europe.[18]

Acheson believed that without a U.S. military presence in Western Europe, independent national life could not be revived in Eastern Europe. Without a U.S. military deterrent to counter the Soviet military presence a united, pro-Western Germany would not be possible. Given the recent Soviet squelching of the Hungarian resistance by brute military force, Acheson argued, it was absurd to paint the Kremlin's leaders as sincere and accommodating partners bent on peace and freedom for Europe.

The full text was printed in nearly all of the major Western European newspapers. *Life International* added maps illustrating "Kennan's Europe" and "Acheson's Europe," effectively communicating Acheson's message to hundreds of thousands of readers abroad. The full text was published in Germany by the *Rheinischer Merkur* and in Switzerland by *Neue Zürcher Zeitung*, and it appeared as a paid advertisement by a German corporation in *Die Welt* and other leading papers.

In the United States, Acheson's statement received front-page coverage in both the *New York Times* and the *Herald Tribune*. Both *Time* and *Newsweek* covered the story in full, and *U.S. News and World Report* printed nearly all of Acheson's rebuttal. There was a lead editorial on Kennan and Acheson in the February 3 issue of *Life*. Later, the *Herald Tribune*, which had carried a number of "disengagement" articles by Aneurin Bevan, Cyrus Eaton, and other notables, in a lead editorial praised Adenauer's loyalty to NATO and endorsed Acheson's position.[19] James Reston observed of the Kennan-Acheson debate, "Next to the Lincoln Memorial in moonlight the sight of Mr. Dean G. Acheson blowing his top is without doubt the most impressive view in the capital."[20]

Kennan attributed Acheson's "indignant" response to misunderstandings and distortions of his proposals:

> I was charged with having advanced a "plan" for disengagement. I had advanced no such plan; on the contrary, I had said that only governmental planners were competent to draw one up. Time after time, my views were discussed as though I had proposed a unilateral American withdrawal from the Continent. I had never spoken in any terms other than those of mutual action. I was charged with advocating the dismantling of NATO. I had never suggested such a thing. I was charged with urging that we "trust" the Russians. For years, I had argued against the very use of the word "trust" in international relations, etc., etc.[21]

The coverage of Acheson's statement did not match the publicity Kennan had generated during the six-week period when he had the field to himself. His lectures were rebroadcast in full throughout Western Europe and North America. A survey taken in Britain showed an astonishing 72 percent of the population knew who George Kennan was and what his Reith Lectures proposed.[22] Advocacy of "disengagement" became the foreign-policy platform of the Labour Party under Hugh Gaitskell. "Acheson was saying the same old thing," Labourite Denis W. Healey later recalled. "Kennan had struck a responsive new chord with the British people."[23] Even such Conservative Party leaders as Harold Macmillan and Anthony Eden were receptive to Kennan's themes of neutralization and disengagement.[24]

Nevertheless, Acheson's hard-hitting text checked the uncritical praise being heaped on the Reith Lectures, and a real debate ensued. Acheson received letters of gratitude from around the world. The ascendant Henry Kissinger, then a professor of international relations at Harvard University, initiated a correspondence that would last until Acheson's death. He noted, "Your comment on Kennan was extremely well taken and very much needed."²⁵ Kissinger, like Acheson, believed the Soviet Union still posed a serious military threat to Western Europe. Kennan's "daring policy" toward disengagement of Western and communist troops in Central Europe made sense, Kissinger wrote, "only if we are ready to prevent the crushing of satellite revolutions."²⁶ Senator Paul H. Douglas of Illinois, speaking, he said, for thousands of Democrats across America, praised Acheson's reply to Kennan and had it printed in the *Congressional Record*.²⁷

Chancellor Adenauer, who had been hounded for weeks by the Social Democrats' endorsement of the "Kennan Plan for Germany," wrote Acheson, thanking him "heartily for the firmness of the way in which you dealt with the unrealistic thinking of Mr. Kennan. I believe that with this you did a very great service to everyone, and especially to us."²⁸ (He later agreed to write the introduction to the German edition of Acheson's third book, *Power and Diplomacy*.) The West German foreign minister, Heinrich von Brentano, reflected the general view of the ruling Christian Democratic Party in publicly mocking Kennan's "senseless proposals" and "werewolf policy" of suddenly turning on Adenauer, one of America's and NATO's most loyal and trustworthy friends.²⁹

By far the most unexpected congratulatory responses came from none other than John Foster Dulles and Richard Nixon. The two GOP leaders thanked Acheson for taking the wind out of Kennan's sails and endorsing current U.S. European policy. "I was glad to note your statement on the Kennan thesis," said Dulles in the only letter he wrote as secretary of state to Acheson. "His lectures were doing considerable harm abroad to United States policies which are common to both the preceding and present United States Administration."³⁰ Acheson replied that he was glad Dulles approved his statement and hoped his support would be of "some help in combating a very pernicious doctrine."³¹ Vice-President Nixon wrote Christopher Emmet a glowing letter thanking the American Council on Germany for enlisting Acheson. He added that the Eisenhower administration was "firmly opposed to the ideas propounded by Mr. Kennan" and was confident Acheson's reply would "prevent the people in European countries from adopting the mistaken idea that there is support for such a program by any responsible or influential American political leader."³² Considering the fierce Republican hostility toward Acheson during the Eisenhower Doctrine debate only months earlier, the Dulles and Nixon letters came as a shock. "I am getting too respectable to be safe," he wrote to the publisher Cass Canfield. "Alice is already suspicious of me. When I got a letter from Foster thanking me for my attack on George Kennan she was about ready to leave me."³³

But it was not all accolades. Some commentators criticized Acheson for claiming the role of spokesman for the Democratic Party and for displaying a narrow-minded, dismissive, and reductionist attitude. The columnist William Shannon pointed out in the *New York Post* that "if no prominent Democrat has endorsed Kennan, none has endorsed Acheson either."³⁴ (He overlooked the backing Truman had given to Acheson's views in an informal press conference. Truman had added insult to injury by saying that Kennan "was a good Ambassador when he had somebody to tell him what to do, but he's not a policy maker." That somebody, of course, had been Dean Acheson, Truman's secretary of state. "Acheson was his boss, just as he was Dulles's boss," Truman added.³⁵) In fact, no leading Democrat had spoken out publicly to offer Kennan support.

Acheson also was taken to task by friends for attacking Kennan so venomously. Sir Frederick Leith-Ross, a British confidant since the early Lend-Lease days of 1941, complained that Acheson "bludgeoned Kennan." According to Sir Fredrick, many in England agreed with Kennan's main thesis, "that we can't go on sitting on our respective backsides slinging insults at the Kremlin and that we should enter negotiations at whatever level may be acceptable to see what can be made of Bulganin's and Khrushchev's proposals, including the Polish proposal for a disengagement in Central Europe."³⁶

An irritated Acheson responded: "Your ideas inspired by Kennan depress me. Perhaps I bludgeoned him. The same thought seems to have occurred to others. Joe Alsop called it a brutal attack; the *Washington Post* savage. I felt savage about it, because, his lectures seemed to me, not only wooly-headed, which would have been unimportant, or mischievous, which one could have overlooked, but destructive in the extreme."³⁷ It made no difference to Acheson whether advocacy of withdrawing American and British troops from Europe came from "a nice man with a scholarly background" like Kennan or a Republican snake like Senator Jenner. It still added up to isolationism, and Acheson was against it.³⁸

The Soviet bloc recently had hinted that it was ready to negotiate a disengagement agreement, so long as NATO would promise not to transform West Germany into a nuclear power. On December 10, 1957, Foreign Minister Nikolai Bulganin publicly endorsed the Rapacki Plan, a proposal initiated by Foreign Minister Adam Rapacki of Poland that called for a "nuclear-free zone" in Central Europe. Bulganin promised that if U.S. and

British forces withdrew from the Continent, Soviet troops likewise would be recalled from East Germany and the other Warsaw Pact countries.

Bulganin issued a second statement displaying the new Soviet flexibility on January 9, 1958. This one called for the United States and USSR to suspend nuclear testing, outlaw nuclear weapons, and accept the Rapacki Plan. Eisenhower rejected the Soviet proposals but left open the possibility of a summit conference. He believed the Soviet plan had omitted too much that was essential to genuine demilitarization, specifically a means of inspecting nuclear stockpiles and verifying their elimination.[39]

Acheson, in rare agreement with Eisenhower, saw the plan as a ruse to eliminate the American presence in Europe while the Soviets remained free to interfere with a divided Germany. He was infuriated that Kennan appeared to favor the Rapacki Plan, for he saw this support as a propaganda advantage for the Soviet Union. The NATO nations were now bickering among themselves over the disengagement issue, instead of demonstrating unity, and Kennan's notions were introducing chaos into Acheson's vision of an economically integrated, American-dominated Western Europe.

The Illusion of Disengagement

In the midst of the Kennan-Acheson debate, Harvard University Press rushed into print Acheson's new book, *Power and Diplomacy*. Using his unique blend of pragmatism, nuanced expression, and stylish prose, Acheson focused on the global position of the United States and the direction in which its policies had been moving.[40]

In the first chapter, "Power Today: Its Location, Nature and Growth," Acheson made an explicit break with what the journalist Quincy Howe called the "school of moralistic diplomacy, founded by Woodrow Wilson and perpetuated by John Foster Dulles." Instead Acheson aligned himself "with the more worldly approach promoted today by a growing body of Americans who hold that while right may, perhaps, make might, self-righteousness makes only for disaster."[41] As Acheson saw it, World War II had destroyed the power structure of Western Europe (thereby unleashing nationalism in Asia and Africa), released the power of the atom, and produced the two new superpowers—the United States and Soviet Union. He reiterated his long-held positions that America's primary interests lay with Western Europe and that the United States should fortify its industrial might, increase its exports of goods and capital and extend the responsibilities of the federal government in order to maintain a favorable balance of power in the world. Most important, the United States had to maintain strong conventional and nuclear military establishments.[42]

Once again Acheson made clear he had no use for the Dulles doctrine of massive retaliation, particularly since he believed the United States lacked the will to retaliate. Thus, America needed to maintain sufficient conventional forces in Western Europe to check the spread of any localized conflict caused by Soviet aggression. Acheson also underscored his belief that there could be no such thing as a limited nuclear war and urged that nuclear weapons not be made available to any continental European nation. The United States and Britain would have to possess powerful long-range nuclear strike capabilities in order to convince the Soviets that in a nuclear showdown, the West would destroy them.

Although *Power and Diplomacy* was in part an indictment of Dulles's florid foreign-policy rhetoric, in retrospect one cannot escape the conclusion that Acheson stood much closer to Dulles and Eisenhower on the crucial issues threatening to divide the Western alliance than he did to George Kennan or most other diplomats concerned with Europe.

Acheson expressed doubts whether Washington and Moscow could find any common ground on which to build a relationship of mutual trust. He thought a "further process of evolution" would be necessary within the Soviet Union and its satellites before disarmament talks could go beyond generalities. Acheson called German neutrality an illusion and warned against Khrushchev's propaganda on behalf of a joint withdrawal of all foreign troops from Europe.[43]

On January 22, 1958, seventeen American experts on Germany from the fields of journalism, education, business, and government, led by James B. Conant, published a statement in which they expressed opposition to Kennan's proposal for a neutral Germany and withdrawal of American, British, and Soviet troops from Europe. They contended that Kennan's plan would reduce NATO "to a paper organization." Furthermore, "it would reverse the most helpful trend in German history and rebuff the people of West Germany, who have just voted in their 3rd successive national election to repudiate the tradition of German nationalism by integrating with the West."[44] Acheson was in full agreement. "The statement, headed by Ambassador Conant's name, is excellent," Acheson wrote Emmet. "You have done a most useful work in getting replies to Kennan before the Europeans and our own countrymen."[45]

Many in the group urged Acheson to inject their objections to Kennan's Reith Lectures with new vitality via a polished piece of candid Achesonian prose. An opportunity to do just that came when Hamilton Fish Armstrong, the editor of *Foreign Affairs*, invited him to submit an article. "It isn't my idea that you just rebut Kennan's arguments; you did that effectively in your public statement," Armstrong wrote Acheson. "Nor am I suggesting that you leave him out by name, if it seemed necessary or convenient to name him. However, the objective of an article by you, as I see it, would be, while continuing to argue why certain general ideas suggested by Kennan . . . are erroneous and dangerous, to go on from there to outline even more definitely than you do in your book how present policies should be intensified or what new policies should be initiated in order to kill the attraction which the wrong policies hold for so many persons in Europe, as well, of course, as in Asia and elsewhere."[46] Acheson was initially reluctant; having disposed of Kennan's naive lectures, he said, he himself did not want to become "another Pied Piper who can lead the dancing folk away from the realities of life to some other happy solution."[47] A few days later, however, he agreed, and he spent February and early March working on what would ultimately be titled "The Illusion of Disengagement," his most frequently reprinted essay.

In the meantime, stung by the Acheson attacks and exhausted from stresses of the autumn, Kennan was hospitalized shortly after delivering the lectures in Zurich with duodenal ulcers and an acute sinus infection. Recuperating in Switzerland gave him time to regroup. "If the Reith Lectures did nothing else, they served to illustrate the truth of the fact . . . that a great many influential people, both in Western Germany and in the other capitals, have no strong interest either in the unification of Germany or in the removal of Soviet forces from Eastern Europe," Kennan wrote to N. J. Bonn. "Some of them will not readily forgive me for having punctured the hypocrisy with which they have been accustomed to treat these particular questions. But I cannot feel . . . comfortable about the continuation of the present trend of NATO policy. We are now getting into very deep and dangerous waters, where the hazards involved far surpass anything involved in the question of German unification."[48]

When Acheson finished the *Foreign Affairs* article, he decided it was time to write Kennan in an attempt to reestablish friendly communication. The letter, accompanied by proofs of the article, began by praising Kennan's award-winning book *Soviet-American Relations, 1917–1920: The Decision to Intervene*: "How you make a scholarly work as fascinating as a detective story is a wonder and joy." Acheson then brought up the "battle" in which they were engaged and declared his hope that Kennan harbored no ill feelings toward him personally: "As to our difference over current policy, I shall save argument for public utterance. The enclosed proofs I send along not to harass you but so that, should you choose, you can see the whole thing rather than mere snatches, often misquoted. We have differed on this subject too long for it to affect my deep regard and affection for you."[49]

Kennan responded with a letter thanking his former boss for the proofs. He went on:

> There is no reason why you should not have stated your views publicly, as I had mine; and for that I bear no hard feelings. I could have wished that your statement had not been so promptly and eagerly exploited by people for whose integrity of motive I have not the same respect as I have for your own.
>
> As for the substance of the article, and of the previous statement, I too, shall have to leave this to be answered, if at all, in the same forum where it appeared. I can only say that it is a very good article; rarely, if ever, have I seen error so gracefully and respectably clothed. One hates to start plucking at such finery; but I suppose that in one way or another I will have to do so.[50]

Acheson still felt justified in using sharp, polemical tactics to gain media attention and stem the disengagement tide caused by what he considered ridiculous and radical proposals. "I can quite understand that the Kennan-Acheson brawl causes pain to our mutual friends," Acheson wrote his longtime associate Philip Jessup. "George always engenders more solicitude in others than he shows for others. But the self-deprecating garnishment of his lectures did not minimize their damaging, indeed reckless, content. I was not writing for our friends nor to put forward a gentle caveat. I was writing for the Germans to destroy as effectively as I could the corroding effect of what he has said and the belief that he was a seer in these matters."[51]

Acheson, with the lessons of Neville Chamberlain at Munich foremost in his mind, began his article by characterizing *disengagement* as a fashionable but dangerous word essentially synonymous with appeasement and isolationism: "'Disengagement,' it is called now; but it is the same futile—and lethal—attempt to crawl back into the cocoon of history. For us there is only one disengagement possible—the final one, the disengagement from life, which is death."[52]

Acheson accurately saw Kennan's concept of disengagement as reversing the national security strategy—centered around the elephantine growth of the U.S. military—that he had helped devise during the Truman years. "It is a conception, blended of monasticism and the diplomacy of earlier centuries, by which the United States would artfully maneuver its way between and around forces without attempting to direct or control them."[53]

Disengagement signified a craven, immoral appeasement of the Kremlin that would usher in a return to isolationism, as it led down the slippery slope of complete U.S. withdrawal from all its overseas bases. Europe would be left, he wrote to a friend, "with nothing more than George Kennan's militia force" and the noncredible possibility of American nuclear retaliation.[54] "As the withdrawal makes the military position weaker, our forces will be less desired wherever they may remain," Acheson wrote in his article. "If withdrawal is represented as advantageous for Germans, it would seem equally advantageous to Frenchmen, Icelanders, Moroccans, Saudi Arabians, and the rest would quickly follow. And once the idea caught hold, Americans would, of course, join in the general demand."[55] If Kennan got his way, Acheson's vision of Pax Americana would be reduced to an impotent and lonely Fortress America.

Acheson dismissed Kennan's belief that the United States should negotiate with the Soviet Union in order to lessen cold war tensions, even if only through the propaganda value of initiating such efforts. He insisted not only that Kennan underestimated the Soviets' negotiating skill, but also that Washington had to inspire in Western Europe more confidence in America's commitment to NATO:

> In the first place, it [Kennan's proposal] treats international negotiations as though all figures on the chessboard were made of wood or ivory; whereas, in fact, we are dealing with living people, subject to all the emotions of mankind. If I were a European and had to live through two or three years of American negotiations about withdrawing from the Continent, I think that very early in the game I would discount America's remaining and would prepare to face a new situation.[56]

Acheson wanted a return to the policies he had established when he was secretary of state—maximum-power policies designed to establish a secure, democratic world system through a global buildup of U.S. military and economic strength. The NATO alliance had to provide a defense capable of checking the smallest Soviet incursion in Western Europe and crushing any greater assault with heavy damage to the aggressor. This meant NATO had to develop modernized conventional (including American) forces capable of defending Europe from Soviet aggression. Kennan's disengagement proposals and Dulles's massive retaliation–brinkmanship approach to foreign policy were equally reprehensible to Acheson. However, even though Acheson had no use for Dulles's methods, he was defending the substance of the Eisenhower administration's European policy in his debate with Kennan.[57]

Kennan responded nine months later in an article in *Foreign Affairs* entitled "Disengagement Revisited." He contended that "the rosy prospects which Mr. Acheson and others" saw at the end of the cold war tunnel rested solely on the complete breakdown of the Soviet power system, a highly unlikely event. Referring indirectly to Acheson, Kennan asserted that among the fiercest opponents of the disengagement alternative were those fearful less of permanent Soviet control of Eastern Europe than of the reassertion of a powerful, united, and neutral Germany in European affairs.[58] Shortly after Kennan's article appeared, Senator John F. Kennedy—whom Acheson also had charged with naiveté in foreign affairs—wrote to Kennan, saying he thought the former diplomat had "disposed of the extreme rigidity of Mr. Acheson's position with great effectiveness and without the kind of *ad hominem* irrelevances in which Mr. Acheson unfortunately indulged last year."[59]

Kennan's Reith Lectures were published as *Russia, the Atom, and the West*. The release of this book intensified the already high profile of the debate, for newspapers and journals began comparing the works of the two opponents. Arthur Schlesinger, Jr., for instance, reviewed both books together under the headline, "The Great Debate: Kennan vs. Acheson." (Schlesinger tactfully ended his review with the comment, "The publication of these small volumes provides an opportunity to compare the advice which two experienced and thoughtful men are offering their party and their country."[60])

In June of 1958 Acheson accidentally bumped into George Kennan coming out of the American Embassy in London. Acheson thought Kennan "looked badly." The two managed to find an empty office in which to chat and had "a well-behaved, indeed affectionate reunion" for half an hour. "He was in one of his melancholy moods, when he appeared to regard all the troubles of the world as punishments for sin," Acheson wrote his Canadian friend James C. Bonbright. When Kennan mentioned he might forgo writing the third volume of his historical trilogy on U.S.-

Soviet relations and instead devote himself to speaking out on current affairs, Acheson cringed. He told Bonbright, "I devoutly hope that he will take the former course."[61]

In October Kennan wrote Acheson to praise a speech Acheson had given at the University of New Hampshire.[62] Acheson used this overture as an opportunity to end the public disengagement debate. "I promise not to write further on our disagreements growing out of the Reith Lectures," he wrote to Kennan. "Our agreements are more numerous and more agreeable to me."[63]

Yet for the rest of Acheson's life he continued to deride Kennan's "bizarre" views, constantly telling friends that "George is one of those fellows who can tell you everything except what to do about anything."[64] When Kennan was appointed ambassador to Yugoslavia by President John F. Kennedy in 1961, Acheson joked to Joseph Alsop that "Tito is going to have a field day playing with poor George's marshmallow mind."[65]

Kennan resigned as ambassador in 1963, not because of Tito, but in protest of unfair economic sanctions levied by Congress against Yugoslavia. Tired of being an ignored diplomat, Kennan returned to the scholar's life at the Institute for Advanced Study in Princeton, New Jersey. His relationship with Acheson remained correct but distant and tenuous. Although the public debate with Acheson was over, Kennan's ego had been bruised, and residual resentment persisted. He continued to try to convince people that private citizen Acheson had drawn the wrong conclusions from his Reith Lectures in the same way that Secretary of State Acheson had drawn the wrong conclusions from his containment strategy of the late 1940s. In an interview for the John F. Kennedy Library in March 1965, Kennan reiterated his complaints about the public criticism the Reith Lectures received. "These attacks were, indeed, to some extent personal, and I was deeply upset about them because Mr. Acheson, in particular, took occasion to reproach me publicly for recommendations I had made to him as his subordinate in government several years earlier—recommendations which he had not acceded to, which I had never taken to the public as an issue," Kennan explained. "This seemed to me to be improper because I felt that any man who serves in an advisory capacity in government has a right to give his honest advice to his superior. But the superior must not reproach him with it later, publicly, because it was his duty to give him his honest judgment."[66]

In 1967 Kennan published his elegantly written and critically acclaimed *Memoirs, 1925–50*. Acheson was not impressed; he told Stuart Symington he thought it the height of hypocrisy for a "footnote of the Truman presidency to masquerade as an important policymaker."[67] When a young lawyer friend, John P. Frank, expressed enthusiasm for the memoirs, Acheson replied with his most uninhibited written assessment of George F. Kennan:

> George's two volumes on Soviet-American relations in 1917–1920 are first class. It is a great pity that he did not stick at it and do the third. But this is George's weakness. He has messianic visions.
>
> You are right that he is a good historian where his knowledge comes from research or peripheral observation. But when he becomes too involved, and particularly involved in controversy, he is no good....
>
> My view about the Mr. X article, which one should read with his famous cables from Moscow, is that he said exactly what he meant— or as near it as an inherently literary and fuzzy mind could. Later when he found that Lippmann disagreed and thought him a coarse minded militarist like me, he could not stand it. He tried to interpret common sense out of it, thereby turning it to nonsense. George's writing has a sort of sad lyrical beauty about it which drugs the mind, like Lafcadio Hearn's. His memoranda impressed me until I had them retyped with verbs and adjectives omitted and the word "not" followed by "repeat not." Then one could judge them calmly. I was and am fond of George. He wrote as Holmes has Shakespeare say of himself, "Five thousand times of pure gold and a good deal of padding." Unfortunately it is mostly the padding which has survived. His reputation has outrun his professional performance. You overrate him.[68]

The Kennan-Acheson debate added the word *disengagement* to the vocabulary of statesmen and scholars alike. Beyond this, it was the opening salvo in what would become a perennial debate about the usefulness of NATO and the presence of U.S. military forces in Europe.[69] This in part explains the vigor of Acheson's attack on Kennan. Acheson sensed that another important battle over whether to maintain the status quo of NATO and Germany had begun. The cold war crises over Berlin between 1958 and 1961, along with post-Sputnik fears that the Soviet Union had neared parity in the area of intercontinental ballistic missiles, were largely responsible for bringing many West European policymakers in line with the Achesonian concept of a free world security system and for the recognition that Soviet expansionism and technological advances still posed dangers to the West.

The Berlin Deadline Crisis of 1958–59

Ever since the 1948–49 Soviet blockade and the subsequent Allied airlift in Berlin, Dean Acheson had viewed the divided city as the linchpin of the entire Western position in Europe and the most likely site of a cold war showdown with the Soviets. The loss of Berlin, he feared, would completely undermine the Atlantic alliance. Whatever the cost, America had to hold firm on Berlin.[70]

In November 1958 Soviet fear of West Germany's rearmament and possible acquisition of nuclear weapons led to a demand by Premier Khrushchev that the three Western powers—the United States, France, and Great Britain—begin negotiations on European security and a nuclear-free Germany, and within six months, end the four-power occupation of Berlin. If they did not, the Soviet Union would sign a separate peace treaty with East Germany, placing all access routes into West Berlin under East German control. The West then would have to negotiate directly with East Germany on the issue of access to Berlin. Presumably East Germany would insist that the three Western powers pull out. If the Allies refused to leave, it was conceivable the East Germans could starve them out by severing the approaches to the city. The Western powers would then have four options: pull out of Berlin completely, try bulldozing their way into the beleaguered city, attempt a 1948 style airlift, or recognize East Germany and force Adenauer's resignation. If the heavily armed East Germans resisted an Allied military assault, war would break out. Should the Soviets come to their aid, as Khrushchev promised they would, World War III appeared likely. A superpower showdown over Berlin seemed at hand.[71]

Eisenhower and Dulles rejected the Soviet demand that West Berlin be made a "free city" independent of either Eastern or Western control. They, like most other Western leaders, believed the only conceivable choice was to hold the line and hope Khrushchev's ultimatum was a bluff. Should concessions be made to the Soviets—concessions tantamount to abandoning the 2,250,000 "free" Germans of West Berlin—American prestige would be irreparably damaged, West Germany would no longer trust the United States, and NATO's future would be in jeopardy. Eisenhower opposed recognizing East Germany and announced that the United States would never relinquish its access rights to Berlin. Although the 1954 policy of massive retaliation had been modified somewhat over the years, Eisenhower and Dulles clung to it to sustain the Western presence in Berlin and to deter Khrushchev from following through on his ultimatum.

Khrushchev himself was led to believe the West would have to accept his proposal because of the apparent absence of a fallback position—for instance, ordering ground forces, both American and Allied, to West Berlin and declaring that any East German interference would be overcome by Western force. Encouraged by the Sputnik launchings of 1957, the Soviet premier was confident his country was on the road to achieving nuclear parity with the United States and that parity would force the West into accepting some form of his proposals. Dulles's nuclear brinkmanship was no longer credible to Khrushchev, if it ever had been. Khrushchev boasted of the Red Army's preponderant military influence in Europe. Only if the American resolve to stay in Berlin were backed by conventional military capacity, not nuclear weapons, would Khrushchev be foiled, for he was confident Washington would not risk nuclear war over Berlin.

Acheson saw Khrushchev's Berlin ultimatum as the gravest threat to the West since Korea, and distrusting Eisenhower's bland assurances, urged the United States to start making all-out preparations for war. Speaking at the Johns Hopkins School of Advanced International Studies in early December 1958, Acheson criticized Eisenhower's lack of conventional military preparedness for this Berlin deadline crisis. Eisenhower's overreliance on nuclear retaliation at the expense of developing conventional forces for the West's defense had given the Soviet Union the upper hand in Europe, he asserted. The prognosis was "dark," Acheson told the gathering, for the United States was afraid to exert leadership, Great Britain was divided in purpose, France was "in danger of fascist nationalism," Italy was "weak and divided," and Germany "an enigma when the Old Man [Adenauer] goes." He judged Khrushchev's six-month deadline the "cleverest part" of the Soviet ultimatum, for it left just enough time for the Eisenhower administration and the liberal Democratic appeasement crowd, as he saw it—George Kennan, J. William Fulbright, Mike Mansfield, Walter Lippmann, and various members of the Americans for Democratic Action (ADA)—to intellectualize their calls for inaction and fantasize about world peace in our time. Six days, Acheson argued, would have caused the Western nations to pull together for better or worse, but six months of talking necessitated a "theory" for staying in Berlin that would be mercilessly debated, the end result being compromise instead of assertiveness.⁷²

"The truth is," Acheson told the audience, "we have to stay because to get out will destroy us all." A straightforward decision to withdraw from Berlin was not an option; even a conventional war was preferable to that. At least such a tragic outcome would not lead Western Europe to lose confidence in America's commitment to NATO.⁷³

Christopher Emmet was alarmed by a recent speech on Berlin by Senator Mike Mansfield. Mansfield's speech, Emmet wrote to Acheson, presented problems for NATO, West European security, and Germany's future similar to those posed by the Reith Lectures, which Acheson had done so much to place in a proper perspective. Emmet urged Acheson, as chairman of the foreign-policy committee of the DAC, to write a forceful response to Mansfield's proposals. "I fully recognize that because of Senator Mansfield's position as Democratic Whip and member of the Foreign Relations Committee, it will be much harder to clear up a new misunderstanding than in the Kennan case, even though Senator Mansfield specifically stated that he spoke as an individual senator," Emmet wrote Acheson. "But this makes it all the more important to try to prevent the Senator's speech from being accepted as an expression of the Party point of view, in view of the certainty that it will be so interpreted abroad, especially in Britain and Germany."⁷⁴ Emmet was concerned that silence might be perceived in Europe as Democratic Party consent, as it would have been in the case of George Kennan had Acheson not forcefully spoken out.

The key points in Khrushchev's ultimatum were: East and West Germany had to negotiate unification; Berlin had to be evacuated of U.S., British, French, and Soviet troops and declared a free city, possibly under UN supervision; and the flow of East Germans to the West through Berlin had to be stopped. The main difference between Mansfield's proposal and Khrushchev's demands was that the senator wanted UN troops to replace Allied troops in Berlin. "But since we all know that a U.N. police force, such as that in the Gaza Strip, is not capable of fighting or designed to fight," Emmet wrote Acheson, "this would leave the people of Berlin with a token U.N. force surrounded by the Soviet armies of East Germany."⁷⁵

Acheson stood ready to denounce both Eisenhower's inactivity and Mansfield's naiveté. To his way of thinking West Berlin—the most militant anticommunist bastion in the world—could never be a neutral city. More than a mere showcase for Western capitalism and free enterprise, it was the political and spiritual center of democracy. Berlin symbolized the crusading spirit of freedom, holding out hope for the ultimate triumph of democracy over communism, of good over evil. A neutral Berlin with a UN police force, even if it remained a haven for refugees, would not be the same.[76] He agreed with Henry Kissinger that, as the United States had little bargaining power in Berlin and as the city was of supreme importance to NATO, the Allies should not offer to compromise but should make this the test case of all Soviet intentions.[77] Acheson believed the United States had to convince both the Soviets and the free world of its will to fight; this was the core of his get-tough policies of containment and deterrence. Because Berlin must be held and the United States was the only country powerful enough to hold it, Berlin was where the United States must take its stand.

Acheson's argument extended beyond the symbolic. There was reason to believe Khrushchev's aggressive and chancy Berlin ultimatum was motivated also by fear of unrest in East Germany and elsewhere behind the Iron Curtain, unrest that could erupt once more into a Hungarian-type revolution. Acheson thought the Soviets would not be able to repress such revolutions should they occur simultaneously in several satellites, and thus he considered Berlin a stimulus to revolutionary potential in all Eastern Europe, especially in East Germany; it was the crucial pressure point on the Soviets.[78]

Acheson had been crafting an article on the strategic importance of Berlin and the need for conventional military preparedness. "The effort is to wake the country up to the true gravity of the Berlin crisis, what is involved, and the soul searching decisions which may go by default, or be made in ignorance. If the words of the Constitution in Article II, Section 4 mean anything, Ike ought to be removed from office," Acheson wrote Truman.[79] On March 7, 1959, the finished product—"Wishing Won't Hold Berlin"—appeared in the *Saturday Evening Post*.[80]

Writing as the head of foreign policy for the DAC, Acheson characterized the Berlin crisis as an attempt by Khrushchev to test how the United States would respond now that the Soviets were approaching nuclear parity. The only viable alternative he saw was for the West to use conventional power to remove obstacles to traffic to and from Berlin, both on land and in the air. The crisis was a contest of wills, and it was Eisenhower's duty to convince the Soviets that the United States was "genuinely determined to keep traffic to Berlin open, at whatever risk, rather than abandon the people and permit the whole Western position to crumble." Given U.S.–Soviet comparative nuclear capacity, Acheson advocated the development of a conventional force strategy that included armed truck convoys, armed trains, and infantry and tank escorts to challenge Soviet recidivism in the Berlin corridors once and for all. Acheson urged "a real concerting of plans with our allies, a building-up of NATO power in Europe, an increase in American troop strength and a return of British and French divisions to the continent, possibly Turkish and Italian reinforcements, and a strengthening of NATO's tactical air force. At home the unwise demobilization of our army since Korea should be reversed and a crash ICBM program put into immediate effect."[81]

All this, Acheson importuned, must be initiated immediately, before the Soviet deadline of late May. Conventional war, even with a Western loss, Acheson saw as palatable: "Then, at least, the bitter experience of defeat would have driven home a lesson and might well have inspired the will to act upon that lesson. For there would then be only one course left open to the western alliance, which would have to be pursued with the utmost urgency, in the interests of simple survival"—the immediate unification of Western Europe under the leadership of France and Germany, with close political and military ties to the U.K. and North America, not an altogether undesirable outcome to Dean Acheson. The crucial step was for the West to prepare for conventional war. Acheson believed this action alone would be sufficient to cause Khrushchev to back down, for "the West would have disclosed the will to resist." Acheson was unconcerned that a direct Western military challenge might force Khrushchev into military response, lest he lose his prestige and power in the Soviet Union.[82]

Acheson admitted his call for a showdown could result in nuclear war. But he was convinced that when faced with a determined West, the Soviet Union would back down. As usual, Acheson viewed negotiations as dangerous. The West had to demonstrate bold, united resolve in Berlin at once; the longer the crisis remained "hot" the greater the risk of confrontation. Although Prime Minister Macmillan sided with Eisenhower, both Adenauer and de Gaulle shared Acheson's assessment: the short-term benefits of negotiating with Khrushchev as if his ultimatum were not a challenge to the West's position in Europe did not outweigh the long-term risks of failed negotiations followed by hostilities. "The Administration's and Macmillan's attitudes seem to me very depressing," Acheson wrote Walt W. Rostow in mid-March. "A lot of talk of firmness and nothing behind it. Big talk and no stick."[83]

Army Chief of Staff General Maxwell Taylor endorsed Acheson's call for nonnuclear military options. Taylor told the press that General Lauris Norstad, the Supreme Commander of Allied Forces, Europe (NATO), had requested additional forces to meet the Soviet ultimatum and that he personally supported the increase. Taylor, like Acheson, considered Eisenhower's New Look strategy, particularly the primacy of economic considerations in making defense policy, a serious threat to the survival of the free world. Accordingly, Taylor was only too glad to retire from his position in June.[84] Shortly after Taylor stepped down, Acheson wrote his ally a letter of appreciation for standing by his principles.[85]

In 1960 Taylor wrote a book entitled *The Uncertain Trumpet*, in which he blamed Eisenhower's policy of massive retaliation for inhibiting contingency planning for Berlin. Taylor recommended replacing massive retaliation with "the strategy of flexible response."[86] Acheson called Taylor's book "the only breath of fresh air" in the otherwise suffocating atmosphere of Eisenhower's last year in the White House.[87] He agreed with Taylor that if the United States wanted to minimize the probability of nuclear war, the country had to develop means to deter or to win small wars. Soon the Kennedy administration would adopt Taylor's term *flexible response* to describe its new military policy of increasing both nuclear and conventional forces.[88] As for Acheson, he was a committed believer in flexible response long before the phrase was in vogue.

On March 12, five days after Acheson's *Saturday Evening Post* article appeared, Eisenhower reiterated his position that the United States would defend Berlin without increased conventional forces: "We are certainly not going to fight a ground war in Europe. What good would it do to send a few more thousand or indeed even a few divisions of troops to Europe?"[89] The president clung to the threat of massive retaliation to deter the Soviets from acting on their ultimatum. Eisenhower was dealing with the deadline crisis by ignoring and postponing it; Acheson wanted the president to confront Khrushchev and reprimand him in the way his old boss had blasted V. M. Molotov when the Soviet foreign minister visited the White House in 1946. "Poor Eisenhower seems to have no idea that the problem is not *whether* we should be firm about Berlin, but *how* we can be," Acheson wrote his friend William Tyler, a senior Foreign Service officer serving with the American Embassy in Bonn. "After going through the regular incantations the other night, he [Eisenhower] then got on to a discussion of the military situation. If this represented his honest thought, it is a sheer miracle that we were able to defeat the Germans in the last war. Perhaps it was Generals Marshall and Bradley who pulled it off, with some help from Montgomery and Patton. However, I shall not go on. My arteries are not strong enough to think about Eisenhower."[90]

Stunned by Eisenhower's passivity, Acheson told Lyndon Johnson that any day America could expect "a shattering blow growing out of the Soviet thrust at Berlin, and through Berlin, at West Germany and Western Europe." Acheson urged upon Johnson two modes of vigorous action, which he hoped the Senate majority leader would advance in Congress. First, a "dramatic revival" of U.S. and NATO military power, nuclear and conventional, was needed; second, a substantial economic development program for underdeveloped countries must be pushed. The economic end could be met by increasing the Development Loan Fund, which would provide the undeveloped countries of Asia, Africa, and Latin America an alternative to Soviet solutions for their most pressing needs. As before, Acheson was urging an increase of approximately $7 billion annually to maintain the U.S. nuclear arsenal and increased conventional forces.[91]

Acheson thought the primary problem lay, not in getting congressional action for increasing military expenditures, but in gaining executive acceptance of a congressional mandate. Eisenhower appeared set on demonstrating the "willful refusal of an irritated authoritarian to open his mind to the facts." The hour was getting late; Acheson and the country needed Johnson's help. "May I urge that you and the Speaker [Sam Rayburn] consider a very private meeting with the President to ask him how he wishes to play it—cooperatively or hostilely," Acheson continued. "If the latter, the Senate's power of confirmation and the power of both houses to investigate whether the laws are faithfully executed could, in a very short time, bring about a healthy change of attitude throughout the Executive Branch. We often, and properly, hear from Congressional leaders of the duties which Congress owes the nation. Today these duties are plain, urgent, and mean." Acheson closed by letting Johnson know he would be available for briefing on the crisis.[92] A week later Johnson, at George Reedy's prompting, called Acheson into his office and told him of the impossibility of Congress strong-arming the president, although he promised to press for a stronger commitment to ground forces in Europe.[93]

On May 11, 1959, a Big Four foreign ministers' meeting convened in Geneva in an attempt to settle the German and Berlin problems. The three Western powers stood firm on their rights in Berlin granted under the Potsdam Accords of 1945. Christian Herter, the new secretary of state, who had replaced the dying John Foster Dulles, publicly acknowledged that U.S. conventional forces in Europe were insufficient to block a Soviet takeover in Berlin. Nevertheless, he remained ambiguous about the U.S. response should the Soviets refuse to negotiate. Militarily, the West would stand or fall on the existing arrangements.[94] Geneva conferences held in May and again in August resulted in a complete deadlock. Eisenhower decided it was time to meet the Soviet leader face to face to discuss Berlin and invited him to come to America in mid-September; Khrushchev accepted.

Acheson, of course, viewed these attempts to negotiate with Khrushchev as futile. "The plain fact of the matter is that the Russians want us out of Berlin, Germany, and Europe," he wrote a Princeton University professor. "I do not believe this is going to be negotiated one way or the other."[95] Eisenhower was turning U.S. foreign policy into a pageant of congeniality. Because of Ike's neglect of basic realities of power, Acheson wrote Truman, "he feels, as a beautiful woman might, that his charm must carry all."[96]

Speaking before a group of high-ranking reserve officers at a national strategy seminar in July, Acheson urged Western policymakers to tell Moscow they would stay in Berlin even if it meant war. Without that demonstration of resolve, Acheson told the officers, it would be "nonsensical" to believe the Soviets would agree to continue four-power occupation of Berlin. Offering a line to adopt with the Soviets, Acheson suggested: "We will adjust ourselves to whatever you do, but we're not going to get out of Berlin. If you think any little East Germans are going to stop us, you're quite wrong. You say this means war.... But the Soviets should be told that it means, 'You are going to start the war.'" Acheson wondered aloud how Eisenhower, having ruled out any ground or military action over Berlin, could still maintain that America was acting from a firm position. "Firm with what and about what?" Acheson asked rhetorically. The administration, he scoffed, had retained only one "secret weapon—Mr. Nixon," alluding sarcastically to a scheduled journey to the Soviet Union by the vice-president.[97]

On September 15, 1959, Khrushchev began his famous whirlwind tour of the United States, in which he visited Washington, D.C.; the United Nations; Iowa; California; and Pennsylvania. The final three days of his visit were spent at Eisenhower's Camp David retreat in the Maryland mountains, where meetings between the two leaders were cordial. Although no specific accomplishments were announced, Khrushchev did drop his deadline for negotiations regarding Berlin. For his part, Eisenhower agreed to a June 1960 summit meeting with the Soviet leader in Paris to decide the future status of Berlin. "The Spirit of Camp David," as the media dubbed the improved relations between Washington and Moscow, had temporarily postponed a superpower showdown over Germany and Berlin. Eisenhower had bought some time.[98]

The New Atlantic Community

In September 1959, with the disengagement debate with Kennan behind him and the latest crisis over Berlin on the back burner, Acheson carried to Europe his ideas for strengthening Western defenses: stepping up economic activity and industrial production in all Western countries and developing, beyond NATO, a wider form of economic and political integration between the United States and the Western countries.[99] Acheson hoped that Moscow's attempted intimidation tactics over Berlin would serve as a catalyst to cement Western unity. He had been warning of the futility of summit meetings since "the tragic experience of Geneva in 1955."[100] Recently he had written a historical study of summit meetings beginning with the Thirty Years' War (1618–48) and ending with the Geneva conference of 1955. In this span of three centuries he judged only two summit conferences successes, the Congress of Vienna and the Münster Conference.[101]

Acheson was a supporter of traditional diplomacy carried out by diplomats. Too much commotion commonly surrounded summit meetings, and the public expected too much of them, thus preventing any constructive result. He also thought the attempt to achieve results within a fixed period of time a dangerous way for nations to conduct business. Ultimately, he believed, negotiations by chiefs of state were unproductive. He called for a return to old-fashioned diplomacy. "Diplomatic problems used to be discussed by ambassadors," Acheson told the Italian press in Florence, the first stop on his itinerary. "Then, when the ambassadors ceased to seem up to the task, Foreign Ministers were called to deal with these problems. Soon they, too, were dismissed as 'not having sufficient authority,' and somebody thought of the summit meetings. We are nearing the moment when political meetings will only be held at a divine level."[102]

From Florence, Acheson and his wife traveled to Bonn, West Germany, where he first visited his friend Chancellor Adenauer and then spoke to a German-American conference attended by many distinguished citizens from the private sectors of both nations. There Acheson proposed that North America and Western Europe create a new Atlantic community organization, with ambitions far greater than those of NATO: to bring the Western countries closer in the face of mounting Soviet military and economic offensives.[103]

Acheson, who had been instrumental in bringing NATO into being, now admitted that attempts to turn it into a political organization had failed. He blamed Eisenhower's lack of innovative leadership. The elder statesman now advocated the creation of an expanded Atlantic community, a united political and economic assembly open to NATO members as well as to other European countries. Simultaneously NATO should be beefed up militarily. Acheson was championing the idea of a body empowered to take action in the name of the West, although his description of its prospective institutional authority and powers was vague. Four distinct benefits would accrue to the Atlantic community: real consultation over and coordination of foreign policies; reconciliation of trade wars between the European Common Market and European nations outside the pact; creation of stronger defense guarantees in a new treaty more specific than NATO; and coordination of a sound aid program to underdeveloped countries. The new supranational organization would offer more flexibility than NATO, Acheson believed, and could "increase everybody's production instead of merely redistributing trade." The first step toward realizing the community, Acheson told the gathering, would be a joint resolution of support for the concept in the U.S. Congress.[104]

Acheson was not the only person calling for "a new Atlantic community." By the late 1950s the hopeful phrase was being bandied about by Atlanticists of every shade with great variety, and less precision, in meaning and context. At the time the Treaties of Rome were signed in 1957 Acheson was a vocal advocate of what was being called the Clarence Strait–Theodore Achilles–Christian Herter "union of democracies" approach to an Atlantic community. These men believed in NATO as the primary institution to establish and expand North American–West European unity programs, and were hopeful that the organization could be extended into various political and economic realms. Acheson's September 1959 Bonn address signifies a shift away from this expanded NATO approach to advocacy of a new Atlantic community institution that could act in the name of the West. In essence Acheson was suggesting that Western governments work to transform the EEC into an Organization for Atlantic Cooperation that would include the United States, Canada,

Britain, and various neutral European nations. "Plainly, I am over my head and making no sense," Acheson wrote to a friend in England who was puzzled by his proposals. "But while the first is true, somehow I think the latter is not."[105]

Although it is highly dubious whether the Western allies—or any nation for that matter—would ever delegate authority to ministers free to make decisions without first consulting their home governments, or whether the neutral countries of Western Europe (Switzerland, Sweden, and Austria) would ever join such an all-pervasive trans-Atlantic organization, the "Acheson Plan," as a Socialist member of the Bundestag, Carlo Schmid, favorably dubbed it, nevertheless aroused public interest.[106] The *Washington Post* believed that Acheson's proposals for a broader-based alliance were either farfetched or ahead of their time. However, the paper defended Acheson by saying that "the more imaginative the concept, the greater will be the prospect that some more effective instrument will emerge."[107] Kurt Kiesinger, a leading member of Adenauer's Christian Democratic Party, said, "The Acheson Plan coming from a distinguished American is almost too good to be true." Speaking before the West German branch of the European Union, Foreign Minister Heinrich von Brentano committed his government to exploring new institutional avenues to tighten the bond between the United States and Europe.[108] Henry Kissinger, who attended the conference, wrote Acheson that he was reassured "to know that at a moment when one can almost despair about the level of political debate in America there exists someone like yourself who recalls us to our duties."[109] Accolades aside, by 1962 Acheson had resigned himself to the improbability of adding an economic and political dimension to NATO or of creating a new all-encompassing Atlantic community institution and instead adopted Jean Monnet's more loosely defined and realistic two-pillar (or dumbbell) approach to trans-Atlantic affairs known as the Atlantic Partnership.

Acheson continued his assessment of the Atlantic community in a month-long series of lectures in Kings College at Cambridge. His talks focused on the historical role of diplomacy in the ordering of Western nation-states. The West needed strength and cohesiveness to maintain a favorable balance of power over the brutal Soviet regime. "Some of the scholars raised their eyebrows over the insouciance of my history, but the audience was with me and we all had a good time," Acheson wrote to Felix Frankfurter.[110] However, after a month of eating halls, sherry parties, and evening discussions of the classics, Acheson was anxious to get back to the United States, where the next presidential election was less than a year away and his leadership of the foreign-policy committee of the DAC was needed to set the party straight—or so he thought.[111]

On his return Acheson found Washington bubbling with optimism over the scheduled superpower summit. How could so-called foreign-policy experts believe the United States could gain anything at the bargaining table when Khrushchev would be setting the agenda? Acheson wondered. All that would happen, he predicted, was that Eisenhower "will do what he does so well—dispense charm without content."[112]

In a speech before the fifth annual conference of parliament members of the NATO nations on November 18, Acheson urged the NATO countries to "hold tight" on all aspects of their position in Berlin. Talks with the Soviets would dilute the Western position. The "abnormality" of the Berlin crisis was the result of Soviet recidivism, not of American actions. Khrushchev was inviting America "to confer with an idea of coming to terms about our own existence. This is the kind of thing into which we are being led by the incredible view that any sort of a negotiation is good per se."[113]

He asked the NATO parliamentarians to decide "and decide for a decade" that a strong defense force was needed in Europe; then they should pledge to "make the effort and sacrifice to do it." Delays and Kennanesque debates had to cease at once if NATO were to survive and West Berlin remain free. "Do not dig this tree up each year and look at its roots," Acheson warned. If the West did go through with this superpower summit, Acheson added, negotiations should be held only on issues not defined by the Soviet Union, mainly arms limitations to bring nuclear power under international control.[114]

Acheson's speech was met with sharp criticism from the Eisenhower administration, the British Labour Party, and the Soviet government. Secretary of State Christian Herter charged Acheson with failing to understand that the Soviet position had changed drastically in the previous year. "What Acheson had done [in his speech] was to build up a number of straw men, and then knock them down," Herter told reporters. "The assumption he made was that the Russians would be insisting still on the same position that they held a year ago last November, when the crisis was first precipitated. Actually they have come a very long way from that." When pushed to explain how the situation had changed, the secretary drew a blank. After a long, embarrassing pause, he said that since

November 1958, the Soviets had "admitted our legal rights, admitted them several times and completely. They have furthermore moved away from the threat of taking unilateral action."[115]

Once again Acheson relished being at center stage and seeing the new secretary of state squirm. "I seemed to have caused quite a furor with my speech to the NATO Parliamentarians," Acheson crowed to his friend Bernadotte Schmidt. "Poor Chris Herter had a terrible time dealing with it in a press conference yesterday."[116]

Acheson's speech drew an even harsher response from George Brown, the defense spokesman for the Labour Party's shadow cabinet. Brown considered it "ridiculous" to contend, as Acheson had, that withdrawal of troops from Germany meant removal from all of Europe. "This is an old argument between me and the Labour Party," Acheson replied, and again he stressed that withdrawal of U.S. forces from anywhere in Europe would be playing into the Kremlin's hands.[117]

On November 22, *Pravda*, the Soviet Union's official newspaper, published the entire text of Acheson's address. This rare occasion of a reprinting of a Western speech was an attempt by Khrushchev to prove his repeated assertion that President Eisenhower was combating powerful, sinister voices in America in his efforts to help end the unbearable cold war anxieties.[118] Five days later, *Pravda* blasted Acheson and his speech in a three-column commentary under the headline "Man of Yesterday." The editorial's author, V. Kornilov, described Acheson as "the unregenerate champion of the 'cold war' of the Truman-Rockefeller School."[119]

Arthur Krock joined the chorus of critics in a *New York Times* editorial piece charging that the former secretary was an intransigent and callous reactionary, unfit for public service. Professor Hans J. Morgenthau, who had developed a close intellectual friendship with Acheson through the DAC, rushed to his defense. "Mr. Acheson did not say [as Krock charged] 'that the tensions of the cold war cannot even conceivably be relaxed by negotiation which does not end in Western surrender to the Soviet Union,'" Morgenthau underscored in a published rebuttal to Krock. "What Mr. Acheson said, and what he was correct in saying, was that to negotiate on the Western presence in Berlin on Khrushchev's terms is bound to lead to the surrender of the Western position." Morgenthau noted, "Acheson may be right today, as Churchill was in 1938, and what he has to say ought not be so contemptuously dismissed."[120]

An unanticipated event partially redeemed Acheson and the other summit skeptics. On May 1, 1960, the Soviets downed an American U-2 plane some thirteen hundred miles inside its territory. At first, Eisenhower publicly denied the U-2 was a spy plane. The much-touted Five Power summit meeting scheduled for May 15–18 collapsed when Moscow released details of the U-2's mission and displayed its pilot, who had been captured alive. The president of the United States was caught in a flat-out lie. Eisenhower ultimately assumed personal responsibility for the U-2 incident, the abortive summit, and—when he finally owned up to the truth—the additional furor created when, for the first time, a president publicly admitted that the United States had engaged in espionage.[121]

As could be expected, Acheson viewed the U-2 affair as an inexcusable blow to America's image around the globe. The worst part of the whole episode, he charged, was Eisenhower's lies. Truman never would have behaved in such a contemptible manner. Now, thanks to Eisenhower's bungling, the Soviets were having a propaganda field day at America's expense. "It looks as if we are in a very ridiculous position without friends," Acheson wrote Truman. "We have always been known for honesty and fair dealing as a nation and I really don't know how we are going to recover."[122]

The U-2 incident fueled Acheson's desire to get Ike out of the White House. Still, as 1959 drew to a close and the prospect of 1960 party conventions neared, Acheson was somber. He had spent the past eight years sparring with the Eisenhower administration and the Stevensonian liberals. He had of course maintained the support of the Trumanites, but his hawkish utterances, position papers, and press releases had alienated the progressive wing of his party and in the process managed to turn much of the press vehemently against him. Because Acheson's own party comrades, including the presidential aspirants, were afraid to go on the offensive against Ike, Acheson's one-man onslaught made them understandably uneasy and resentful.

Acheson was no newcomer to Democratic Party infighting. (After all, early in his career he had resigned as undersecretary of the treasury over a disagreement with FDR regarding the president's constitutional right to reduce the gold content of the dollar.) He remained determined to help guide his party to victory in 1960, using the DAC as his institutional vehicle, by attacking the GOP foreign-policy record and hailing the cold war accomplishments of the Truman administration right up until the last ballot was cast on election day. More than any other person Acheson deserves the credit, for better or for worse, for shifting the

Democratic Party's foreign-policy agenda away from Stevensonian liberalism and back to the conservative, unyielding cold war tradition of Harry Truman. John F. Kennedy would be the benefactor of the swing back to the tough-minded, action-oriented, European-dominated, anticommunist foreign-policy principles of the Truman-Acheson heyday.

CHAPTER FOUR

JFK, NATO Review, and the Berlin Crisis of 1961

Dean Acheson and John F. Kennedy were never close. The two men were separated by differences in age, in values, and in social attitudes, and also by Acheson's general distaste for the Kennedy clan. But saying they were not close is an incomplete conclusion, for the record reveals that Acheson significantly molded Kennedy's thinking—either directly or through his disciples still in government—on the affairs of the Atlantic community and on the major European crisis for the new president: Khrushchev's threat to sign a separate peace treaty with East Germany and the subsequent erection of the Berlin Wall. In the late 1950s the two occasionally discussed foreign-policy issues when Acheson visited Capitol Hill, and sometimes after a working dinner with various Democratic senators Kennedy drove his Georgetown neighbor home. "So we became acquaintances," Acheson later said of his relationship with Kennedy. "I would not say in any way that we were friends—we were acquaintances and he was extremely deferential to me, which made me feel even older than I otherwise would have felt."[1]

Acheson felt closer to Kennedy's wife, Jacqueline, for he had known her stepfather's family, the Auchinclosses, from his Groton and Yale days. Shortly after Acheson completed *Power and Diplomacy*, which criticized Senator Kennedy's statements supporting Algerian independence, Jacqueline Kennedy wrote Acheson, asking "how one capable of such an Olympian tone can become so personal when attacking someone for political differences." Acheson's reply was short and to the point: "The Olympians seem to me to have been a pretty personal lot."[2]

The distrust he felt of the Kennedy family was based on political issues and value clashes that dated back to the 1930s. Acheson's attitude toward the patriarch, Joseph Kennedy, bordered on repugnance. He had never forgiven "Bootlegging Joe" for his embrace of Neville Chamberlain at Munich, to Acheson the moral equivalent of embracing the Nazis. Acheson also thought Joe Kennedy's life represented the worst aspects of the American character: greed and isolationism, wealth created out of unproductive and unscrupulous Wall Street wheeling and dealing. To Acheson's mind the names Joe Kennedy and Joe McCarthy were synonymous, two corrupt and criminal Irishmen cut out of the same primitive political cloth.

Further, JFK's support of Algerian independence against France, a longtime NATO ally, violated one of Acheson's cardinal foreign-policy principles. Initially, Acheson dismissed John Kennedy's presidential run as a brazen attempt by his father, whose finger was to be found deep in every Kennedy pie, to buy the White House for his son. But after the West Virginia primary victory, Acheson began to resign himself to the notion of a Kennedy as the Democratic standard bearer.[3]

The 1960 Presidential Campaign

In an interview in 1964 Acheson admitted to a period of soul-searching, and arm twisting by Clark Clifford, before he decided to work to convince Truman, other Democratic notables, and perhaps most important, himself to rally behind JFK so that a unified party could go into the election "with some steam up."[4] This self-portrait of a party loyalist was hotly, and unfairly, disputed by Chester Bowles, who claimed that Acheson "tried to destroy Kennedy," because he was "vigorously, violently and vehemently opposed" to his candidacy and that he "tried so hard to get aboard the bandwagon" only after JFK received the nomination. He attributed this abrupt about-face to Acheson's lack of professional scruples.[5]

A month before the young Massachusetts senator received the nomination, Acheson channeled his energies into getting him elected. On July 17, 1960, only four days after the convention, Acheson wrote to compliment Kennedy on his commanding performance: "Your bearings and actions were as admirable as they were successful. Here in Maryland you will have no problem. The ticket will be enthusiastically supported by our great Democratic registered majority. You will find no lack of advisors on foreign policy. But you will need all your good judgment to disregard most of their advice. The only advice I offer is to get all the rest you can while you can."[6]

When Vice-President Richard Nixon became the Republican presidential nominee in late July, Acheson's resolve to put Kennedy in the White House was fortified. Nixon as president was intolerable to Acheson (although he thought even "Tricky Dick" would be an improvement on Eisenhower). Dirk Stikker, the former Dutch foreign minister, asked Acheson why he thought the youthful Kennedy was better equipped for the presidency than the seasoned Nixon. Acheson noted the good, talented people around Kennedy, a reply in keeping with his tendency to portray Kennedy favorably to his foreign correspondents. Acheson believed that both candidates shared similar personalities—"cold, calculating, intelligent, and uncommitted." Kennedy, however, would "have the freedom to innovate and to be what conservatives will call financially irresponsible which is necessary to do what has to be done."[7]

During the course of the campaign Acheson's respect for JFK's political savvy and cold war adamancy grew. Kennedy had overcome Truman's opposition, Johnson's bullying, and Stevenson's ego with the cunning and skill of a consummate politician. "This is by no means the same thing as saying that he arouses enthusiasm," Acheson wrote Truman in early August. "Neither candidate does that. If their joint appearances don't stir some interest, the campaign may turn out to be one of those pitcher's duels, where neither side gets a hit and the paying customers go to sleep."[8]

In stumping across the country trying to rebuild the fractured New Deal coalition, Kennedy had difficulty finding effective partisan foreign-policy issues. He had long since adopted the alleged missile gap with the Soviets, the government's failure to reduce the payment deficit, the decline of U.S. prestige abroad, and the Eisenhower administration's reluctance to act forcefully—all criticisms Acheson had been leveling at the Republicans since 1957—as his overriding foreign-policy themes. "I have premised my campaign," Kennedy wrote, sounding like a DAC pamphlet by Acheson, "on the single assumption that the American people are uneasy at the present drift in our national course, that they are disturbed by the relative decline in our vitality and prestige, and that they have the will and strength to start the United States moving again."[9] Couching his points in such generalities presented a problem for Kennedy because he had difficulty distinguishing his policies from Nixon's. In reality, both favored containing Soviet expansionism by maintaining a strong defense and an activist, alliance-oriented American foreign policy around the world.

Kennedy had tried to subdue qualms about his Catholicism by declaring, "I am not the Catholic candidate for President. I am the Democratic Party's candidate for President who happens to be a Catholic."[10] But Acheson remarked to Truman, "If Kennedy goes on talking about the religious business he will gain few Protestant votes and lose a lot of Catholic ones. His strongest point he can't make. He isn't a very good Catholic."[11] Acheson was apparently trying to reassure his old boss, who himself worried constantly about the prospect of a Catholic president. Shortly after the election Acheson took Truman to task on this point: "Do you really care about Jack's being a Catholic," Acheson asked. "I never have. It hasn't bothered me about de Gaulle or Adenauer or [Robert] Schuman or [Alcide] De Gasperi, so why Kennedy?"[12]

A turning point in the campaign occurred on September 26, when Kennedy's youthful charm and laserlike wit were displayed elegantly in the first of four televised debates with Nixon. Although who won the debate substantively was never clear, JFK's candid, relaxed style attracted many undecided voters. Impressed with Kennedy's "performance," Acheson remarked to friends that given the American preference for image over substance, the country deserved a flashy novice like JFK. (In a concession to the modern age, Acheson had rented a television to watch the much-touted debates. He became so annoyed by what he perceived as the candidates' side-stepping of the issues that he returned the set after the first debate.)[13]

In October, Kennedy campaign headquarters issued a provocative statement calling for the strengthening of the "non-Batista democratic anti-Castro forces in exile, and in Cuba itself, who offer eventual hope of overthrowing Castro." It criticized the Republican administration for not supporting these "fighters for freedom."[14] This was an attempt to counter Nixon's campaign charge that if elected JFK would turn Quemoy and Matsu over to communism. Press reaction was harsh. Kennedy himself apparently had misgivings, as he called Acheson to ask if he should pursue the issue in an upcoming debate. Acheson responded that he should stop talking about it immediately; trying to solve important foreign- or domestic-policy problems on the campaign stump was dangerous. The candidate would be "likely to get himself hooked into positions which would be difficult afterwards." Acheson thought "a political campaign ought to be conducted on broader bases than this, that or the other minutia of foreign policy." A candidate "ought to give the country his attitude of approach to large questions of government, not to small specific policies."[15] Heeding Acheson's and others' recommendation, Kennedy dropped Cuba from his campaign speeches.

In letters to acquaintances in Western Europe written during the autumn of 1960, Acheson portrayed Kennedy in a favorable light and predicted the Democrats would win the election. However, in letters to his American friends he feigned indifference. "The best campaign cheer I know is the current gag, anyway, they can't elect both of them," Acheson joked to Archibald MacLeish.[16]

By early November, as Kennedy's chances for election looked stronger, Acheson grew apprehensive, for he was unclear what path the senator would pursue if elected. He worried that Kennedy would insulate himself with the younger men prominently associated with the campaign who possessed little or no experience in government. In a letter to Dirk Stikker he proposed a surefire remedy for this problem: appointing Paul Nitze under secretary of state, a position where he could exercise a strong prophylactic influence on the department. (Acheson did offer up this proposal to the president-elect a few weeks later.) He went on to speculate that Kennedy would appoint either J. William Fulbright or Chester Bowles secretary of state and Adlai Stevenson ambassador to the UN or Great Britain. Senator Henry "Scoop" Jackson seemed the probable candidate for secretary of defense. "The rest of the cabinet is likely to be made up of Young Turks," Acheson wrote. "I do not mention myself, not because of modesty but because I will not be asked to participate, a situation which is not distasteful to me."[17]

On November 8, 1960, John F. Kennedy was elected the thirty-fifth president of the United States by a minuscule plurality—fewer than 119,000 votes out of a total of more than 68,000,000. He was the youngest man and the first Catholic to be elected president. "His election was a very considerable achievement and I think it attests to the inherent strength of the Democratic Party," he wrote Count Gustiniani of Italy shortly after Kennedy's victory. "I believe that he has qualities which will make him an able, vigorous, but tactful, leader, and that, after he has had the opportunity over a year or so to demonstrate these qualities, the country will respond and follow him because of them."[18]

Advice for the President-Elect

Soon after the election Kennedy invited himself to Acheson's Georgetown home to discuss possible cabinet appointments. Shortly before the president-elect appeared, photographers arrived to set up their paraphernalia; the meeting, Acheson realized, would not lack publicity. Kennedy, alone and on foot, settled himself in the living room. Acheson offered a martini, but Kennedy declined and asked for tea.[19] This did not sit well with Acheson; a friend noted that "he never trusted a man who wouldn't have a drink with him."[20] He was further annoyed by the photographers thrashing about his home trying to film their meeting. Washington and American politics certainly had changed for the worse since Acheson first came to the then-sleepy city in 1919 to serve as private secretary to Justice of the Supreme Court Louis Brandeis, a time when privacy was respected.

Kennedy solicited advice on three positions in his cabinet: secretary of state, secretary of defense, and secretary of the treasury. He assured Acheson that he was not planning to appoint either Stevenson or Bowles as secretary of state, but said he had no one else clearly in mind. He told Acheson "that one of his troubles was that he had spent too much time in the last few years on knowing people who could help him become President that he found he knew very few people who could help him be President," a remark Acheson found "both true and touching" and that he often repeated to friends.[21]

Kennedy had been considering offering State to Senator J. William Fulbright; he respected Fulbright as "the resident scholar" on the Hill and supported his call for a complete reassessment of U.S. foreign-policy objectives. Further, as Fulbright was chairman of the Senate Foreign Relations Committee, his appointment would be likely to enhance Kennedy's influence on Capitol Hill. Acheson thought Fulbright was a terrible choice. First, he was important to the new administration right where he was; the person next in line for the chairmanship might not be nearly as useful as Fulbright. Acheson was also convinced that Fulbright "was not as solid and serious a man as [JFK] needed" for such an important position. "I've always thought that he had some of the qualities of the dilettante," he told Kennedy. "He likes to criticize—he likes to call for brave, bold new ideas and he doesn't have a great many brave, bold new ideas." Acheson thought it "rather tiresome for people to say that other people ought to think of things. You either think of them or you don't, and if you don't you better shut up." Finally, Acheson felt Fulbright lacked the administrative experience necessary to run the Byzantine bureaucracy of the State Department.

Acheson suggested it might be "interesting" to ask David K. E. Bruce, under secretary of state in the last years of the Truman administration and an experienced diplomat, to fill the position for a while, in the meantime appointing Paul Nitze as under secretary to see how he developed. "Paul has great qualities—he's wholly unknown—it would be impossible to appoint him as Secretary of State now," Acheson told Kennedy, "but after a year or so he might develop into a very useful man." Unconvinced, Kennedy moved on to Acheson's longtime Republican friend, and president of the Chase Manhattan Bank, John J. McCloy. Both quickly concluded that McCloy's appointment would lead the public to think there was no Democrat qualified to be secretary of state. Acheson then brought up Dean Rusk. Kennedy knew the name but had never met Rusk and was uninformed about his professional background.[22]

Dean Rusk, former Rhodes scholar and professor of government, had joined the army during the Second World War and seen duty in the Far East. Afterwards he joined the State Department, serving as an indispensable adviser to Dean Acheson and Robert Lovett from 1946 to 1953 and working on the creation of Israel, the Berlin blockade, Korea, and the drafting of NSC-68. In 1950, just before the Korean War erupted, he forever endeared himself to Acheson by offering to be demoted from deputy under secretary to assistant secretary for Far Eastern Affairs to help deal with the vociferous criticism of the administration's Asian policies from the Republican right. Acheson praised Rusk for his magnanimity, telling him he deserved "a Purple Heart and a Congressional Medal of Honor, all in one."[23] Rusk's arduous assignment was to drum up bipartisan support for intervention in Korea and help explain why the Communists had won the civil war in China. He also helped formulate policy during the conflict. He supported taking military action but opposed the widening of the war into Communist China. When Eisenhower became president in 1952, Rusk left government to become president of the Rockefeller Foundation, where he helped expand the foundation's international activities.[24]

Later, in his memoirs of his State Department years, *Present at the Creation*, Acheson praised Rusk for serving "faithfully and successfully in this most difficult of posts."[25] In his account to Kennedy he added a caveat: a good lieutenant did not always make a good general. Acheson's judicious endorsement of Rusk fell on receptive ears, for Kennedy was determined to participate intimately in foreign-policy making himself. A staff officer as secretary of state would fit his objectives.

Kennedy was intending to send Clark Clifford to ask Robert Lovett to be secretary of the treasury. Acheson scoffed at the notion: Lovett would not do it—Treasury would have no appeal—and, in any case, if he wanted Lovett, Kennedy should call on him personally rather than send a messenger. Acheson warned, finally, that Lovett was a hypochondriac and that the "old rascal" would have affidavits from every doctor in New York asserting his imminent demise. (Apparently that is precisely what happened: "Bob came down wrapped up like a terrific invalid," Acheson recalled in 1964, "with all sorts of things around his neck—overshoes on and letters saying it would be unfair to the United States, unfair to the administration—to do this.") Acheson suggested Kennedy appoint Lovett secretary of defense for a brief period—just long enough to reorganize the Pentagon: "By the time he offended everybody in Washington, you would have to let him go home." But Kennedy put aside this notion; he had other ideas about Defense.[26]

What about appointing World Bank president Eugene Black secretary of the treasury? Kennedy asked. Acheson demurred, for he considered Black "a strong-minded, stubborn, conservative banker." Any Democratic president, Acheson asserted, would have to do many things a conservative banker would not wish to do. Furthermore, once Black was ensconced he would garner the support of the banking community and it would be impossible to get him out. Kennedy would be encumbered with a George Humphrey in his administration. JFK then asked Acheson for his recommendation. C. Douglas Dillon, was the reply. Dillon had been in the State Department and understood foreign policy. He was also well respected on Wall Street, where his father had made a fortune building the firm Dillon, Read & Co. into one of the country's most prestigious investment banks. Acheson argued that appointing a "sound money" Wall Street man like Dillon—and a Republican to boot—would reassure the financial community, which was nervous about the "easy money" propensities of the incoming Democrats.[27]

Kennedy raised the idea of appointing his brother Bobby deputy secretary of defense, to which Acheson responded that it would be a serious political blunder, for he would open himself up to charges of nepotism. However, if he was determined to put his brother somewhere, it should be as head of a department. "It would be wholly impossible for any cabinet officer to have the President's brother as his second in command—

with the known closeness of the two brothers to one another," Acheson told JFK. "If he were to be brought in at all, he ought to be given complete responsibility for a department of government, or be brought into the White House and be close to the President himself."[28]

Acheson sympathized with Kennedy's wish for a confidant with whom he could "just sort of put his feet up and talk things over," but when Kennedy said he was thinking of making Bobby attorney general, Acheson cringed. "I thought it was not a good idea because it was an exposed position," Acheson recalled. "I mentioned the civil rights business which was going to come up. Bobby and the President would be one person—they wouldn't be two people and whatever Bobby did the President would bear directly. They would just be regarded in the public mind as the same person—and that it was important in a difficult job like that to have a little buffer in between." Should a problem arise, the attorney general should be in a position to insulate the president from blame.[29]

Kennedy made one last request of Acheson: Would he serve as ambassador to NATO? Acheson thanked the president-elect for the offer but emphatically declined. "I said that I thought policies were more important than posts and that I could be of more help to him as an advisor and consultant than I could 3000 miles away talking about ideas which might or might not be the policies of the United States government." Acheson was more candid about his decision in a letter to Dirk Stikker. He explained that he had spent years cultivating personal and professional relationships with European statesmen and was not about to jeopardize them by abandoning his well-known principles in order to defend the overwrought rhetoric of the New Frontier. The only official position Dean Acheson might have taken was secretary of state, but this was not to be.[30]

Acheson felt Kennedy came away from their discussions reassured that the former secretary was on his side, while for his part he was impressed by Kennedy's "air of calmness, of authority, of seriousness, and of modesty."[31] Kennedy eventually offered Lovett all three top positions—State, Defense, and Treasury. Lovett declined them all but offered a suggestion of his own: appoint Dean Acheson secretary of state. Kennedy replied that this was impossible; Acheson had too many adversaries in the Democratic Party and was too much of a maverick. Lovett thought the next-best man was Dean Rusk. With both Acheson and Lovett endorsing Rusk, Kennedy went ahead and selected the little-known man from Cherokee County, Georgia, as his secretary of state.[32]

NATO Policy Review

Dean Rusk held Dean Acheson in high esteem. A few weeks before the presidential inauguration Rusk asked his former boss for help in adjusting to the secretaryship and Acheson agreed. Rusk met with Acheson often during January and February to get his advice on NATO and Berlin: "At times he had a sharp tongue, but you learned to get around that. He was always willing to pitch in and help out in a difficult situation. Kennedy had total respect for him. It was always worth listening to what Acheson had to say. This does not mean that we always followed his advice."[33]

In his early days in the office, Rusk pressed Acheson to accept the ambassadorship to NATO. Acheson again declined. Rusk then told the former secretary that the president wanted him to undertake a reevaluation of U.S. objectives vis-à-vis NATO. Would he become Kennedy's chief de facto consultant on Atlantic community affairs? Without hesitation, Acheson accepted. He wanted it made clear that he was not accepting a permanent post, as he desired to continue practicing law without incurring conflict-of-interest charges. Acheson wanted no position of confidence, no pay, no State Department office; he wanted only to provide the president with his ideas on NATO. Rusk agreed to the provisos, and soon after the inauguration Acheson went to work on his NATO policy review, a document intended to serve as a touchstone for high-level NATO discussions.

On February 8, President Kennedy made public Acheson's appointment as chairman of his Advisory Committee on NATO. One of Acheson's charges was to formulate possible responses to the issues raised by Khrushchev's threat to sign a peace treaty with East Germany making Berlin a "free city" theoretically independent of control by either East or West.

The appointment precipitated an outcry from some of the president's supporters who believed the Acheson review group would serve up hawkish, military-oriented solutions for essentially political and diplomatic problems, such as Berlin. A wary Walter Lippmann, for instance, feared that Kennedy "was handing American policy over to the hard-liners." They were, he wrote, "like old soldiers trying to relive the battles in which they won their fame and glory.... Their preoccupation with their own past history [prevents] them from dealing with the new phase of the Cold War."[34]

Other presidential supporters did not share Lippmann's concerns.

Kennedy's close friend and aide Theodore Sorensen maintained, "There was nothing unusual about Acheson heading a NATO review. Acheson was a gifted statesman, well-versed in European affairs, and Kennedy wanted his opinions on NATO and Germany. This does not mean that he agreed with Acheson or followed his advice."[35]

Arthur Schlesinger, Jr., appointed special assistant to the president, wrote that Kennedy selected Acheson because he considered him "one of the most intelligent and experienced men around and did not see why he should not avail himself of 'hard' views before making his own judgments."[36] Although JFK perceived the former secretary as "an old man from another era," he still maintained a "deep-rooted admiration for Acheson as a lawyer and diplomat." Personally, Kennedy "liked the cut of Acheson's jib," professionally he "admired his toughness."[37]

Other difficulties than political differences inhered in the assignment. How could Acheson be comfortable as a private adviser when he was not an intimate of the president? How would he deal with an intermediary—the secretary of state—who was a former subordinate and lacked Acheson's international experience and intellectual stature? "I know that JFK got a great sense of reinforcement from the fact that he had Acheson's first-hand advice," wrote McGeorge Bundy, Kennedy's special assistant for national security affairs, "but I think that the position was intrinsically a difficult one for Dean."[38] If Acheson was not exactly back on center stage, he was at least in the prompter's box, and he was alternately treated by Kennedy and the New Frontiersmen with detachment and deference, as an overbearing presence or foreign-policy sage. "As I come back, a rather pampered and tolerated ghost among the bright new spirits, I know that I seem a sort of ancient mariner whose warnings only take on meaning *ex post facto*," Acheson wrote in June 1961.[39]

Acheson had been asked by Kennedy "to reappraise our entire defense strategy, capacity, commitments and needs in the light of present and future dangers."[40] He was to be assisted by the new secretary of defense, Robert McNamara, and his civilian "whiz kids" in the Defense Department, including former RAND Corporation analysts Alain Enthoven, Charles Hitch, William Kaufmann, and Henry S. Rowen. Their first task, as Acheson saw it, was to summarize America's original expectations of NATO and the European integration movement. Next they would assess the results of the Soviet acquisition of nuclear power, the further development of thermonuclear weapons by the United States, and the birth of the European Common Market. Finally, Acheson would evaluate the current situation in light of European discontent over America's nuclear monopoly.

As secretary of defense from 1961 through 1967, McNamara, the hard-nosed former president of Ford Motors, worked tirelessly to modernize the armed forces and make the Pentagon more efficient by centralizing decision making in his own office. Acheson liked McNamara and supported his call for a buildup of U.S. military power, particularly in two areas: replacing liquid-fueled ICBMs with solid-fuel missiles that would give the U.S. a "second-strike capability" (that is, the ability to absorb a nuclear attack while retaining the capacity to launch a counterattack) and developing a large, mobile strike force to permit the U.S. to fight conventional or guerrilla wars without nuclear weapons. With a flexible military force in place, Washington would be able to counter Moscow-backed "wars of liberation" and provide Europe with a realistic defense posture. McNamara, like Acheson, believed that Eisenhower's New Look strategy had limited America's ability to respond vigorously in a crisis or nonnuclear war while simultaneously increasing the likelihood of a Soviet-American nuclear showdown.[41]

Acheson had other allies in the administration. Kennedy had named as, respectively, assistant secretary of defense for international security affairs and deputy assistant secretary, Paul Nitze and William P. Bundy—both devoted Achesonians. Acheson told his law partner Edward Burling that he agreed with Nitze "about 99 percent of the time."[42] Nitze and William P. Bundy, Acheson's son-in-law, did their best to make Acheson feel an integral part of the administration. It was with Nitze's help that Acheson made his first important contribution to the Kennedy program: "A Review of North Atlantic Problems for the Future," a seventy-four-page policy directive proposal written for National Security Council consideration. Divided into three sections—political, military, and economic—the report stressed the importance of consulting frankly with the NATO allies on all U.S. policies, even in their formative stages.[43] Acheson was assisted in preparing the report by Robert Bowie, Foy Kohler, Robert Komer, Walt W. Rostow, Henry Rowen, and Albert Wohlstetter. General Lauris Norstad, Supreme Commander, Allied Forces, Europe, had briefed Acheson on the many problems that plagued NATO.[44]

In this report were the seeds of Kennedy's ambitious new approach to European affairs, which would soon be dubbed the Grand Design: the notion of a European union within an Atlantic partnership. The Grand Design had concrete objectives: facilitating British entry into the European Common Market, in part by discrediting British perceptions of a "special relationship" between the United Kingdom and the United States; increasing U.S. exports by reducing trans-Atlantic tariff barriers; convincing Europe to bolster its conventional forces; and persuading European nations to forgo developing independent nuclear forces in favor of the multilateral force (MLF). The NATO policy review paper articulated how these objectives could be realized—with the exception of the MLF, which Acheson did not favor until late 1963.[45]

Acheson's report drew heavily on an earlier policy paper that carries the imprimatur of the Eisenhower administration: Robert Bowie's "The North Atlantic Nations: Tasks for the 1960's."[46] That Acheson would rely on Eisenhower policy, fierce opponent of the prior administration as he was, is not as surprising as it first appears, for Bowie (along with Christian Herter) was a member of a rare species—the Eisenhower appointees whom Acheson respected and with whom he often agreed. The Bowie Report, as it became known, had been commissioned by Assistant Secretary for Policy Planning Gerard Smith, who had assumed that post when Bowie left it to return to Harvard, where he served as director of the Center for International Affairs from 1957 to 1972. At the NATO Council meeting in December 1960 Secretary of State Herter outlined how a Polaris submarine force could be manned by crews drawn from at least three alliance nations, leaving the decision whether to move forward with this plan in the incoming president's hands. Echoing Bowie's projected ten-year plan for closer trans-Atlantic economic, political, and military cooperation, the Acheson Report argued that multilateral NATO conventional forces should be bolstered at once. Acheson parted company with Bowie and Herter, however, on NATO nuclear strategy. Although Acheson was concerned about European development of independent nuclear forces, he believed the United States had a global responsibility to maintain a strategic nuclear monopoly—not sharing even with Great Britain. Bowie and Herter, among others, proposed the creation of a multilateral nuclear force under NATO control to allay European fears of American nuclear hegemony and to end counterproductive competition by the Europeans to develop their own nuclear arsenals. Intrigued by the MLF idea, Acheson still insisted that Europeans first had to demonstrate their continued commitment to NATO by increasing their conventional forces.

The Acheson Report concluded that NATO's neglect of conventional preparedness was its most pressing concern. It attributed the problem to four interrelated factors: lack of innovative leadership in the alliance; the high cost of maintaining conventional forces, which made it politically unpopular to do so; the belief that the Warsaw Pact had such superior conventional forces that NATO troop increases were futile; and the fear that increasing NATO's nonnuclear capabilities would be seen as an admission that the U.S. strategic nuclear deterrent was a hollow threat. Acheson challenged all these assumptions.

Under the rubric "A Pragmatic Doctrine," the most comprehensive section of the Acheson Report urged the administration to give priority to NATO programs that prepared for the more likely contingencies, that is, threats short of nuclear or massive nonnuclear attack. U.S. forces, under NATO command, should be retained in Europe at their present strength for the foreseeable future and if necessary, one or more U.S. divisions should be converted into an overseas Strategic Army Corps unit to further demonstrate America's commitment to the Continent. Acheson, concerned about America's balance of payments deficit, realized that there was also a sound economic rationale for convincing Europe to buy U.S. conventional weapons.[47]

The report elaborated on why strong NATO conventional forces were essential: "The U.S. should propose that the objective of improving NATO's non-nuclear forces should be to create a capability for halting Soviet forces now in or rapidly deployable to Central Europe for a sufficient period to allow the Soviets to appreciate the wider risks of the course which they are embarked." Acheson's program included raising manning levels, modernizing equipment, and improving mobility of NATO's nonnuclear forces. Only then would the U.S. be in a position to press strongly for European execution of its portion as a matter of highest priority, particularly the development of a mobile task force to deal with threats to NATO's flanks. The United States had to push for greater NATO research and development on nonnuclear weaponry, and for coordinated, alliance-wide production of new military equipment. The president must articulate America's steadfast commitment to retaining nuclear weapons in Europe unless the allies consented to their withdrawal or replacement.

Acheson was attempting to incorporate counterforce options into U.S. strategic plans to meet the objection that the threat of nuclear retaliation to attacks on allies was not credible. The French and Germans in particular were skeptical that the United States would "risk Chicago for Hamburg."[48] If the U.S. developed strategic counterforce alternatives— namely large conventional forces in Europe—Acheson argued, the president would have new options that would not in any way jeopardize the national security of America itself. Acheson urged implementation of General Norstad's 1960 proposal that NATO maintain thirty active and thirty reserve divisions. Only such conventional muscle would deter Soviet aggression, for NATO could then resist a Warsaw Pact conventional attack without having to rely on nuclear weapons or passive resistance as its only responses. At the same time, if U.S. nuclear weapons were maintained in Europe, the Soviets would be less inclined to invade Western Europe, for fear of triggering a nuclear exchange.

Acheson also addressed the question of centralized coordination should the deterrents fail and nuclear war erupt. If support for independent nuclear forces like those of France and Britain prevailed, chaos would reign throughout the alliance. Acheson urged the administration argue against independent strategic deterrents. As for the MLF, Acheson was opposed, at least until the allies first fulfilled their conventional force requirements. Meanwhile, the United States must maintain its strategic nuclear advantage over the Soviet Union.

The political section of the report focused on recent difficulties in the alliance, pointing out that "a fertile source of disagreement between the U.S. and its NATO allies arises out of the relations between the latter and colonial and ex-colonial areas." These differences were often aired publicly in the United Nations; this had to stop. While postimperial world problems were not completely soluble, Acheson thought their disruptive consequences could be reduced if the United States would: cooperate with its allies in preparing their colonies for independence; aid the allies in helping emerging dependent areas to prepare for economic adjustments as their political relations changed; and resist voting on UN resolutions that did not advance solutions, while in private, making U.S. opinions and objectives clear.

Acheson urged Kennedy to make clear that he supported the EEC and believed British entry a necessity. At the same time, the United States had to convince the EEC not to set the price for British membership too high. The ultimate goal of the Atlantic community was to develop a genuine commonwealth "in which common institutions are increasingly developed to address common problems."[49]

The conventional buildup would be cemented with the assurance that any nation that used nuclear weapons against any member of the fifteen-nation alliance would be devastated immediately by U.S. nuclear power. A strong conventional deterrent and a U.S. nuclear advantage would permit the alliance to deter Soviet expansionism. With Western security thus guarded, a genuine Atlantic community could blossom, a free-market haven where trade barriers could be lifted and goods and capital could flow without undue restrictions.

Acheson's report was formally submitted in late March. The "concise, specific, and comprehensive treatment of these problems will make it an invaluable guide to policy," Rusk wrote to Acheson on April 5. The report's recommendations would be "rapidly translated into concrete action."[50]

On April 21 Kennedy adopted Acheson's review as his official "Policy Directive Regarding NATO and the Atlantic Nations," set forth in National Security Memorandum no. 40, and had it disseminated throughout the government for implementation. "These are excellent papers," President Kennedy wrote Acheson on April 24, 1961. "They will provide a basis for our policy toward the Atlantic nations. I am directing that specific actions be taken to ensure that their conclusions are urgently carried out." Kennedy saluted Acheson for adding "one more to the long list of distinguished services rendered your country."[51]

Paul Nitze and Roswell Gilpatric in the Defense Department began promoting Acheson's report publicly in an effort to convince the European allies to increase their conventional forces. Speaking before the Canadian Parliament, Kennedy himself said that the United States looked "to the possibility of eventually establishing a NATO sea-borne [nuclear] force, which would be truly multilateral in ownership and control," but he echoed Acheson's condition that conventional forces must first be increased.[52] Kennedy repeated this contingency before a meeting of NATO's military committee.[53]

Despite his adoption of the Acheson Report, President Kennedy was disturbed by the ongoing stationing of over 400,000 American troops in Europe with no fixed date of withdrawal in view. He had hoped Acheson's report would provide him with a list of specific U.S.-NATO action items. Acheson, both in private conversations and in his report, attempted to address these concerns by emphasizing to the president the importance to foreign policy of consistent, long-range plans and principles, not short-term policy initiatives that Washington could force or frighten the Europeans into swallowing. The Eisenhower attitude of "if you don't do exactly what we want, we'll go home," Acheson told the president, was the wrong way to treat allies. What was needed was determined American leadership to keep NATO strong and effective.[54]

"The American people will respond to vigorous and sensible leadership," Acheson wrote Dirk Stikker, then representative of the Netherlands to NATO. "But it must be based on a broad grasp of new realities based on Russian possession of nuclear weapons and a growing economic potential."[55] Kennedy had to adopt the Achesonian view of reality, illiberal or un-Kennanesque as it might be: as a consequence of a prolonged European civil war from 1914 to 1945, the world had become divided into two great power centers—the United States and the Soviet Union—and it would continue to be so divided well into the foreseeable future. One consequence was that the United States must be prepared to stay in Europe until the Soviet system collapsed.[56]

Part of Kennedy's problem, Acheson believed, was that he listened to irresolute "utopian do-gooders" like Stevenson, Bowles, and Galbraith while tuning out the irrefutable logic of pragmatic pros like himself and Nitze. Although Kennedy began increasing defense spending in accordance with the flexible response doctrine (which was formally adopted as NATO policy in 1967), Acheson was not satisfied. According to McGeorge Bundy, "Dean criticized the administration because he didn't get as much flexible response as he wanted. It's as simple as that."[57]

Substance aside, Acheson never was comfortable with the "best and the brightest" staffers with which Kennedy had insulated himself. "I seem to have noticed that each time an appointment other than that of a Cabinet officer is announced it is said that this job will be bigger, better, have more influence than it ever has been or had before," Acheson wrote John Cowles. "It seems to me that the doctrine of relativity may have some bearing here and that if everyone becomes bigger, except the cabinet officers, the result is that they become smaller."[58]

Bridging the Generation Gap

Acheson's doubts about breaking through the static of the "do-gooders" should have been allayed when he was drafted by the president for several new diplomatic assignments. In early April, Harold Macmillan came to Washington to discuss, among other topics, Berlin. The donnish British prime minister was concerned about establishing a rapport with the new American president. "How am I ever going to get along with that cocky young Irishman?" Macmillan asked a journalist friend.[59] Kennedy was a boyish-looking forty-three, Macmillan a tired sixty-six. As Arthur Schlesinger, Jr., has written pungently, this "languid Edwardian, who looked back to the sun-lit years before the First World War as a lost paradise, feared that the brisk young American, nearly a quarter of a century his junior, would consider him a museum piece."[60] Macmillan, a Tory statesman of vast experience in foreign affairs, was also convinced that the new administration knew little about conducting coalition diplomacy, that it was interested only in enhancing American power, and that it was insensitive to Great Britain's needs. Kennedy, sensing Macmillan's apprehension, thought it would be wise to have Dean Acheson preside over a meeting with the British leader on the need for Allied contingency plans. What better way to reassure Macmillan of his strong commitment to Europe than by calling on America's foremost Eurocentric statesman to enunciate his program. Kennedy's strategy backfired.

Acheson had drawn up a list of responses the Allies might have to take if Khrushchev forced the Berlin issue. He had not yet formally submitted his Berlin review to Kennedy, but on April 3 he had given the president what McGeorge Bundy called "a first-rate interim memorandum on Berlin."[61] "All courses of action are dangerous and unpromising but inaction is even worse," Acheson had written. If the Soviets provoked a crisis, and he predicted they soon would, then "a bold and dangerous course may be the safest." Since the entire Western position in Europe would be at stake, the U.S. would have to respond with "a willingness to fight for Berlin." Economic and political responses alone would not be sufficient, "nor would threatening to initiate general war be a solution. The threat would not carry conviction; it would invite a preemptive strike; and it would alienate allies and neutrals alike. The fight for Berlin must begin, at any rate, as a local conflict. The problem is how and where it will end. This uncertainty must be accepted."[62] Kennedy, apparently impressed with Acheson's stoutheartedness and insensitive to how these views might be perceived by the British, asked the former secretary to give Macmillan and Foreign Minister Alec Douglas-Home the benefits of his views. Dismissing any possibility of a negotiated settlement, Acheson delivered what, in his narrative of the meeting, Schlesinger has called a "bloodcurdling recital" of possible military countermeasures that left the British statesmen aghast.[63]

He closed his exposition by urging that an Allied division (about 15,000 men) be dispatched from the checkpoint at Helmstedt in West Germany and sent eastward toward Berlin to test access rights. If the Soviets elected to interfere with the armed convoy, which Acheson saw as highly unlikely, at least the West would know where the Soviets stood and could begin to rearm immediately, as it had done during the Korean War.

Macmillan and Home were shocked at Acheson's hard-line rhetoric. They responded that it would be suicidal to isolate a single division on the autobahn and tried shifting the discussion to diplomatic solutions. Lord Home characterized Acheson's bravado as misguided activism that offered no diplomatic alternatives to Khrushchev's proposal of a peace conference and a treaty. It seemed to both of the Britons that Acheson was accepting the possibility of nuclear war over Berlin. After all, Home argued, the Allies were only in Berlin by right of military conquest, and that right was wearing thin. To this, Acheson bitingly replied that perhaps "it was Western resolve that was wearing thin."[64]

Throughout the debate Kennedy remained noncommittal, asking questions only about the adequacy of existing military options. His central concern had been to develop a contingency plan that would convince Khrushchev that should the Soviets push for a showdown over Berlin, the West would meet it head-on with counterforce of some kind.

Macmillan returned to Britain a few days later flustered by Acheson's uncompromising stand on Berlin and Kennedy's seeming diffidence. Dean Acheson appeared to be in charge of policy making, to the detriment of what Macmillan believed was the important task for the West: to avoid confrontation with the Soviets, not to develop plans to instigate it.

Adlai Stevenson and Averell Harriman were also present at the meeting, and they too were alarmed by Acheson's hard-line stance on Berlin. "Maybe Dean is right," Stevenson later noted, "but his position [the need for a military showdown] should be the conclusion of a process of investigation, not the beginning. He starts at a point which we should not reach until we have explored and exhausted all the alternatives."[65] Schlesinger reminded the president that Acheson was only one of America's "elder statesmen in the field of foreign affairs." Harriman and Stevenson likewise had years of international experience, and they were opposed to Acheson's position. "All have served the republic brilliantly, and all are honorable and towering figures. As a rule of thumb," Schlesinger wrote Kennedy in early April, "I would vote with any two of them against the third."[66] These objections to Acheson's saber-rattling did not cause JFK to reconsider his advice; Acheson would soon be put in charge of America's Berlin policy.

Diplomatic Mission to Europe

In early April, President Kennedy and Secretary of State Rusk asked Acheson if he would take on a diplomatic mission to Europe. He was to pay courtesy calls on President de Gaulle, Chancellor Adenauer, and other leaders while in Europe to argue a private case in The Hague for his law firm. The goal was to inform Western Europe that the Kennedy administration was reevaluating NATO policy and wished to take into consideration the opinions of notable European statesmen. Acheson readily agreed. In the course of his month-long stay he would visit five capitals and discuss foreign policy with most heads of government and their cabinets.

A few days before Acheson left for Europe, Kennedy called him to the White House for consultation. The two strolled the White House grounds discussing NATO and enjoying the first warm day of spring. Suddenly, while leading Acheson to a bench in the Rose Garden, Kennedy abruptly shifted gears: "I want to talk to you about something else. Do you know anything about this Cuba proposal?" Acheson replied that he did not. Kennedy described the CIA plan for an invasion by Cuban exiles inherited from the Eisenhower administration. Alarmed, Acheson said he hoped the president was not serious about it. "I don't know if I'm serious or not," Kennedy replied, "but this is the proposal and I've been thinking about it and it is serious—in that sense, I've not made up my mind but I'm giving it very serious thought." An astounded Acheson told Kennedy that "it was not necessary to call in Price, Waterhouse [a large accounting firm] to discover that 1500 [invading] Cubans weren't as good as 250,000 Cubans."[67]

Ten days later, news of the Bay of Pigs fiasco reached the Continent. Kennedy's expectation that the Cuban people would rise up against Castro never materialized. Acheson thought it incredible that the United States had attempted such a preposterous and irresponsible maneuver; the Europeans he encountered reacted similarly. "They had tremendously high expectations of the new Administration," Acheson later recalled, "and when this thing happened they just fell miles down with a crash."[68]

In a speech before the Foreign Service Association in Washington Acheson spoke ruefully of the "promise in the air" when he first arrived in Europe and how Kennedy's ill-advised sponsorship of the Cuban invasion "brought this dream to an end with shattering impact . . . they began to have the sort of unbelieving attitude that somebody might have as he watched a gifted amateur practicing with a boomerang and suddenly knocking himself cold. They were amazed that so inexperienced a person should play with so lethal a weapon."[69] Kennedy's fair-haired-boy reputation had been badly tarnished.

To his former boss, Truman, Acheson wrote, "Why we ever engaged in this asinine Cuban adventure, I cannot imagine. Before I left it was mentioned to me and I told my informants how you and I turned down similar suggestions for Iran and Guatemala and why. I thought this Cuban idea had been put aside, as it should have been. It gave Europe as bad a turn as the U-2. The direction of this government seems surprisingly weak." The only possible explanation, Acheson thought, was that "mere inertia of the Eisenhower plan carried it to execution. All that the present administration did was to take out of it those elements of strength essential to its success."[70] Because of Kennedy's bungling, Acheson's talks with European leaders were now sidetracked by concerns about the Bay of Pigs. The main thrust of his mission, he realized, had changed from informing to reassuring.

Before the invasion, Acheson had visited his old friend Konrad Adenauer, a man who had been chancellor of Germany longer than anyone since Bismarck. Acheson's recently published book, the best-selling *Sketches from Life of Men I Have Known*, included a salute to Adenauer. "Like Sir Winston Churchill," Acheson wrote, "the Chancellor, while a shrewd politician, has a sense of acting on the stream of history. This gives perspective to his thought and continuity to his action. The qualities which arouse his admiration and confidence are decisiveness, resolution, and strength. He distrusts facility."[71] These were the very qualities that Acheson admired in Truman and Marshall.

As secretary of state, Acheson had worked closely with Adenauer, the former lord mayor of Cologne, in rebuilding Germany. The primary concern of both had been Germany's complete integration into Western Europe, and they were instrumental in the establishment of the German Federal Republic (FRG) as a partner in the Western alliance in 1949. Both envisioned the FRG as a citizen of Europe, cooperating in the development of common interests and burying forever the nationalistic rivalries of past centuries. Acheson considered his association with Adenauer from 1949 to 1953 and their mutual efforts in pursuing a security system for free nations and a genuine European community to be among his most rewarding experiences as secretary of state.

The tone of their relationship is reflected in a story Acheson told about his visit as Kennedy's emissary: When they arrived at Adenauer's estate, which was perched on a hillside overlooking the Rhine River near Bonn, they stopped before the hundred feet of treacherous-looking steps zigzagging to the entry. The eighty-four-year-old Adenauer said, "My friend, you are not as young as you were the first time we met, and I must urge you not to take these steps too fast." Acheson thanked the chancellor and replied, "If I find myself wearying, may I take your arm?" Adenauer smiled at Acheson and said, "Are you teasing me?" "I wouldn't dare," Acheson responded, "I wouldn't think of doing it."[72]

Adenauer, recalled Acheson, was "worried to death—just completely worried" about Washington's European policies now that Kennedy was president. Adenauer had enjoyed open and honest dealings with Truman-Acheson and Eisenhower-Dulles-Herter from 1949 to 1960, but he believed JFK had a deep-rooted, irrational hostility toward him, a belief fueled in part by a *Foreign Affairs* article Kennedy had written in 1957, in which he intimated that Adenauer had been in power for too long and perhaps it was time for a Social Democrat to become chancellor.[73] During the 1960 election Adenauer made it clear that he preferred Nixon to Kennedy. The chancellor feared that the young president would make a backroom deal with Khrushchev on Germany, Berlin disarmament, a nonnuclear zone, and so on, without consulting the Germans. However, perceiving that Acheson was working closely with the president, he felt reassured. "Going over with him the formulation of plans that was going forward in Washington and an explanation of our actions toward the Russians, he began to understand that this was not a conspiracy behind his back which would result in selling out German interests," Acheson recalled.[74]

Once confident that he had addressed Adenauer's unwarranted concerns, Acheson informed the chancellor that the Eisenhower plan to place a fleet of U.S. Polaris missile submarines under NATO control had been rejected by Kennedy for the time being; the United States and Britain would retain their nuclear monopoly. This news, of course, did not please Adenauer, and he said he would discuss it with the president during his upcoming visit to the White House.

Their five-hour conversation finished, the two statesmen went outside to play boccie, the Italian bowling game, at which the chancellor was adept. As the game started, a relieved Adenauer told Acheson, "You have lifted a stone from my heart." (The American embassy in Bonn used this phrase to open their cable to Kennedy on the successful Acheson-Adenauer conference.) The game grew intense, and when it appeared Acheson was gaining on Adenauer, the chancellor changed the rules and began taking carom shots off the sideboards as well as bowling straight balls. Acheson protested. Adenauer stopped bowling and replied, "You are now in Germany—in Germany I make the rules."[75]

Two days later Adenauer met with Kennedy for the first time. He reported to Acheson that his White House visit produced mixed results. Adenauer urged the United States to resume a leadership role in NATO lest the alliance disintegrate. Kennedy thought it unlikely that the alliance could soon collapse. The two also disagreed on how to enhance NATO's power to deter Soviet aggression. Kennedy clung to the conclusion of the Acheson Report on the primacy of increasing NATO conventional forces; Adenauer, concerned about the domestic costs of another policy reversal, argued that what was needed was an independent NATO nuclear force. As to Berlin, Adenauer repeated his view, wholeheartedly shared by Acheson and de Gaulle: Khrushchev was testing Western resolve and the NATO countries must hold firm on the beleaguered city, no matter the cost. He warned the president not to negotiate with the Soviets on Berlin; it would only serve to undermine NATO unity—a position Adenauer would repudiate before year's end.[76]

Adenauer left Washington apprehensive about the new American president. Although he was reassured that Kennedy was committed to NATO, he was unhappy with the administration's emphasis on "flexible options" at the expense of developing a multilateral nuclear arsenal. He also feared the young Kennedy was too eager to achieve a modus vivendi on Berlin with Khrushchev, that he was too idealistic to understand that the Kremlin had distorted Clausewitz's famous maxim to mean, Negotiation is war by other means. He hoped that Acheson would continue to impress upon Kennedy and his entourage of "cooks," "whiz kids," and "prima donnas" that the only negotiating technique the Soviets respected was firm talk and unflinching brute strength.[77] Since the Bay of Pigs had intervened between the Acheson-Adenauer visit and Adenauer's debriefing letter to Acheson at the end of April, the chancellor's worst fears were stoked by that misguided invasion attempt.[78]

Ten days after his meeting with Adenauer, Acheson flew to Paris to confer with President de Gaulle. This was Acheson's first meeting with the French president. He informed de Gaulle of President Kennedy's deep commitment to keeping the Atlantic alliance intact, then briefed the general on the conclusions of his NATO review and the administration's current thoughts on Berlin. Aware of de Gaulle's disenchantment with America's dominance in NATO, Acheson emphasized the importance of Western nations working together on fundamental foreign-policy conceptions, particularly regarding Central Europe.

Acheson found de Gaulle "courteous" but in disagreement over

NATO; he had his own nascent *force de frappe*, an independent nuclear force, to develop and favored his Tripartite Plan (Anglo-American-French) for Western decision making, not the existing NATO structure. De Gaulle accepted NATO as a military alliance; he no longer believed that as a political organization it served France's best interests. He asked Acheson directly whether he thought it practical and proper to transform a military alliance into some visionary Jean Monnet–inspired trans-Atlantic political institution. "Who knows," Acheson answered, "until we really try it?" "But it is illogical," de Gaulle persisted. "NATO was conceived as a military alliance, now you are trying to make it a political mechanism." "Quite right," Acheson said. "We Americans think less of logic in politics than you French do. With us the test is whether something works. If it does, logic conforms to a new verity."[79] When presented with this prospect, de Gaulle's response was to begin disengaging France, not from the Atlantic alliance, but from the military integration realized by NATO under American command. De Gaulle also expressed dismay at Kennedy's shift from massive retaliation to flexible response strategy. An American policy of increasing conventional forces while building up already superior nuclear forces did not address the concerns of France and left the United States in hegemonic control of the rest of Western Europe. France, which in February 1960 had become the fourth nation to trigger a nuclear explosion, was no longer as dependent on the United States as it had been when Acheson was secretary of state. Distrustful of the Anglo-Saxons' nuclear club, de Gaulle insisted on some control over nuclear weapons and the NATO forces in Europe. Acheson promised to relay these concerns to the president. "I thought that we at least put de Gaulle into a position where he could not say that nobody let him know anything until he was faced with it," was Acheson's gloomy assessment of their meeting.[80]

De Gaulle was nettled by the recent American military ventures in Cuba and Laos. Less than a month before, in response to communist advances in the area, Kennedy had ordered U.S. forces moved closer to Laos without consulting France or NATO. De Gaulle was angered and voiced his discontent to Acheson, as these military preparations jeopardized chances for a cease-fire in the Laotian civil war.[81] Nor did de Gaulle consider the region of traditional French hegemony of vital interest to the West.

André Fontaine, the renowned diplomatic correspondent of *Le Monde*, caught the heart of the issue: "The recent events in Cuba, like those in Laos, certainly will not help Mr. Acheson to convince the President of the republic. Everything leads to the conclusion that the latter is less inclined than ever to leave to the United States alone the essential responsibility for the defense of the Western world."[82]

Acheson encountered more harsh criticism of U.S. policy when he spoke to the prime ministers of Belgium and the Netherlands. "They had troubles," he said, "which largely were the result of their own stupidity or foolishness, or a lack of foresight but in order to blame somebody other than themselves, they blamed us."[83] In Brussels the Belgian Congo was the all-absorbing topic; in Holland the preoccupation was West New Guinea. Both NATO allies held the United States partially responsible for their colonial difficulties because of Washington's failure to back their policies in the United Nations. In February, to the chagrin of both countries, Secretary Rusk had testified before the Senate Foreign Relations Committee that the administration would support the UN peace-keeping missions and Secretary-General Dag Hammarskjöld's policies in the Congo and West New Guinea even though this meant voting against Belgium and the Netherlands. If, as Acheson was claiming, NATO unity was the top American priority, why, these Europeans asked, did the United States betray them at the United Nations? Acheson's reply, reflecting his bedrock contempt for the UN, was that what happened at Turtle Bay was unconnected to America's actual foreign policy. "Don't you know we are always stupid in the United Nations," he recalled telling representatives from both countries. "We have never been intelligent yet. This is an emotional attitude and we have a Department of Emotion which deals with the United Nations. This is not coordinated in any other way with the foreign policy of the United States." Characterizing the organization as a useless, feeble bastion of missionary idealism, Acheson promised Dutch and Belgian leaders he would do what he could to convince the administration to stop voting against NATO allies there.[84]

After meeting Prime Minister Amintore Fanfani in Rome Acheson attended what he described as a "so-called conference of intellectuals" in Bologna. On his way there he had purchased a copy of D. H. Lawrence's *Twilight in Italy* to read on the plane. He took to heart Lawrence's assertion that an understanding of Italian theater illuminated Italian oratory. "He [Lawrence] said oratory in Italy deals directly from words to the blood. There is no confusing interposition of thought in between." At the Bologna conference Acheson "discovered that if I took the ear phones off and did not listen to the rather prissy British women who translated and merely listened to the glorious flow of Italian syllables I was carried along and perfectly happy."[85]

How are we to interpret this story, which Acheson told about himself? Apparently he had been urged to attend to the content of Italian political discourse. Joe Cunningham, a Foreign Service officer in Florence, told Acheson that many Italians believed that if Washington so wished, it could put the Social Democrats in power throughout Europe. Then Europeans would not have to deal with "old characters like Fanfani and the Chancellor [Adenauer], de Gaulle, and the people of this sort who are passé." Leaving unmentioned the CIA's covert support of the Christian Democrats in the 1948 election, Acheson replied that this would constitute interference in the internal affairs of sovereign nations, a clear violation of American principles. "Well," Cunningham said, "they have the belief that this has been happening for quite a long time and since you put the Christian Democrats in, you could put them out."[86]

Acheson judged all the Europeans he met as self-absorbed, which reinforced his belief that the United States was the only country capable of leading the West by shouldering global responsibilities: "I began to have a reluctant feeling that we perhaps are the only nation in the world which is capable of having a broad outlook of the world, an outlook which perhaps can at times comprise some of the interests or many of the interests of the whole free world. Other countries looked at it from little segments. Segments of their own preconceptions and therefore we must not be too delicate about being vigorous in our leadership."[87] Acheson told McGeorge Bundy, "In the final analysis, the United States [is] the locomotive at the head of mankind, and the rest of the world the caboose."[88] The lesson he learned from this trip to Europe was that America had to act always "ahead of the discussion . . . doing things which we urge others to follow rather than making proposals and talking about them forever."[89]

Acheson's return to Washington was met with charges of conflict of interest, instigated by the Republican National Committee and taken up by several leading newspapers. The committee charged that "Dean Acheson is wearing two hats—one as a U.S. official, the other as a private attorney." How could Acheson discharge the duty of undivided loyalty when "one day he confers with Chancellor Konrad Adenauer of Germany as president Kennedy's representative; the very next he is at The Hague [Acheson had represented Cambodia against Thailand before the World Court] representing one U.S. ally against another as a private attorney."[90] The Republicans demanded to know how Kennedy would rectify this situation, but Kennedy sloughed off the charges and asked Acheson to write another report, this time solely on Berlin.

Acheson took up the assignment with zeal, for, alarmed by the Bay of Pigs fiasco, he had concluded that emotional and unsystematic responses were replacing "real policy." The so-called bright young men with whom Kennedy had surrounded himself were too indecisive, too impressed by theories and statistics. The president himself shared these faults. "Brains are no substitute for judgment," he wrote Truman. "Kennedy has abroad, at least, lost a very large part of the almost fanatical admiration which his youth and good looks inspired." He noted ruefully that morale in the State Department had "struck bottom."[91]

Acheson was upset by Kennedy and Rusk's unsophisticated attempts at diplomacy. Rusk, for instance, at a May 5, 1961, NATO Council meeting, in Oslo, had said that the United States considered all areas of the world vital and worth defending. Didn't Rusk understand that such a statement diminished Western Europe's position vis-à-vis the United States? Acheson sought nothing less than a resurrection of the attitudes and policies of the Truman years, and to bring this off he would have to go from monitoring the foreign-policy situation to becoming its militant impresario. He could no longer afford to treat his NATO policy review and his contingency plans for Berlin as mere position papers; his recommendations had to be implemented. Acheson's forebodings were reinforced when Khrushchev shocked Kennedy with a renewed Berlin ultimatum at a summit conference in Vienna in early June. Dean Acheson was more certain than ever that a showdown with the Soviets over Berlin was just around the bend.

Khrushchev's Berlin Ultimatum

The Vienna conference, which took place on June 3 and 4, 1961, was a hastily arranged meeting. The Soviets had postponed their plans to sign a separate peace treaty with East Germany until after the American elections. The new American president, cognizant of the dangers the United States faced if forced to choose between surrendering to Soviet demands on Berlin or risking nuclear war, wanted to avoid being maneuvered into having to make such a decision. Kennedy hoped he could persuade Khrushchev to maintain the status quo in Berlin, but instead the premier upped the ante, precipitating a crisis.

Khrushchev renewed his request for a negotiated settlement, which

Kennedy refused. The Soviet leader then announced a new six-month deadline: if the West did not agree to new terms regarding Berlin, he would unilaterally sign a peace treaty with the German Democratic Republic (GDR) and turn access controls over to the GDR, which the West did not recognize. If the West interfered, the result could be war. Kennedy reasserted the primacy of U.S. wartime rights in Berlin. Khrushchev replied, "I want peace, but if you want war that is your problem." Kennedy answered, "It is you, and not I, who wants to force a change." As Kennedy told the American public on his return from the summit, it was "a very sobering two days."[92]

During the summit Acheson was busy finishing his report for the president on alternative responses available to the West in Berlin, a report which in tone and substance closely resembled his 1959 article "Wishing Won't Hold Berlin." Khrushchev's renewal of the deadline threat made the study vital to national security, for it was the only "new" top-level Berlin contingency planning already in the works. The president returned from the summit convinced detailed military planning would have to be stepped up. The Western powers would have to clarify their priorities and decide what they would do in a series of contingencies. On June 15 Khrushchev turned up the heat by issuing a statement threatening grave consequences for the West if it did not sign a peace treaty by December 31. Kennedy next announced he was forming a special task force headed by Dean Acheson to monitor the Berlin crisis. Apparently, the scope of its mission was not clearly defined, for all the senior statesman knew about his new assignment was that Kennedy expected him to serve as the administration's chief crisis watcher on Berlin, ready to give warning and advice on all new developments.

Acheson's assignment to the Berlin problem was well received throughout Europe, particularly in West Germany, where it was known that Acheson wholeheartedly agreed with Chancellor Adenauer in opposing Khrushchev's efforts to force changes in Berlin's status—although the German chancellor wanted to rely on the threat of nuclear weapons to deter Soviet aggression against Berlin. The June 17, 1961, issue of the *New York Herald Tribune* quoted Acheson as saying, "The present status of the Western Allies in Berlin is highly satisfactory. Why fuss around with other ideas? Premier Khrushchev is the only one who wants it changed."[93]

Acheson's statement was particularly welcomed by the West Germans, for the two weeks following the summit gave evidence of declining American resolve. Senate Majority Leader Mike Mansfield proposed accepting the "free city" idea for West Berlin, along the lines of the Vatican in Italy if it was extended to East Berlin as well. This seemed to Mansfield to be a logical step toward German unification.[94] Bonn was alarmed by this proposal from one of the Democratic Party's leading senators. If the proposal were implemented, all Western occupation troops would in due course leave Berlin; Adenauer believed that the physical presence of Americans in Berlin and the threat of U.S. nuclear attack were the best deterrents to Soviet action against the divided city. The Mansfield proposal, which European newspapers interpreted as an administration trial balloon, also had powerful support from J. William Fulbright. These statements, reinforced by a report from Britain that the United States was contemplating a radical new approach to Berlin, led Europeans to believe that Kennedy might capitulate to Khrushchev's demands. The appointment of Acheson was a shrewd way to calm the fears aroused by Mansfield's proposal.

Joining Acheson on the task force were specialists from within the administration, such as Walt W. Rostow, deputy White House assistant on national security affairs; Foy Kohler, assistant secretary of state for European affairs; and Paul Nitze, among others. Acheson, saying he found a "shortage of talent" in State and Defense to help deal with the crisis, invited W. Averell Harriman on board. "It seems like old times," the former Truman administration official said to Acheson, as the two sat down to work.[95]

By the end of the month Acheson's initial concerns about the lack of coordination among and leadership in State, Defense, and the White House were allayed. He believed the administration finally had comprehended the urgency of the situation. "I am working hard on plans to meet a Berlin crisis toward the end of the year," he wrote to Truman. "It is a grim business, but I think that the Joint Chiefs and the State Department have now got the idea and that we shall make some progress." Acheson thought these chiefs not "nearly as good" as those who served during Truman's administration. "In fact, I am shocked—and I think the Secretary of Defense is, also, at the shoddy work which comes out of the military," he complained to Truman. "For what we spend on them we deserve something better than we get." Acheson also was worried by the lackluster performance of the president and secretary of state. "Both Kennedy and Dean Rusk seem to me to be better when they make speeches than when they act," he continued in his letter to Truman. "We have heard a lot about the necessity to make sacrifices but we haven't been asked to make any.

There are plenty to make if the Administration would just get started. Time is running out."⁹⁶

This letter does not mention the controversy that Acheson himself had stirred up in official Washington. In mid-June, at a Foreign Service Association (FSA) luncheon at the Shoreham Hotel, Acheson had delivered his first public broadside against the administration. He condemned its naiveté in conducting foreign affairs and lamented the declining role of the State Department. "The Department of State," he told the gathering, "not only must be the President's chief adviser and confidant in foreign affairs but it must be the chief managerial department and agency secretariat in the running of the whole government. And it has not been this and it is not this today."⁹⁷

Part of the problem, Acheson maintained, was that Kennedy and Rusk had given key positions to popular politicians and to eggheads, rather than to qualified diplomats. For the department to function properly once again, the president would have to be "quite ruthless" about cleaning out incompetents. Kennedy had shown a "treasonable" tendency "to be kind to people as many of them fail to show the promise of their youth." (Clearly Acheson's barb was aimed at Chester Bowles, John Kenneth Galbraith, Adlai Stevenson, and G. Mennen Williams.) Acheson acknowledged that a vigorous housecleaning would be difficult because the department was now "organized on the basis of the feudal system."

> Very often, in fact, I have said to the present Secretary and to the President that the department tends to become a Valois feudal monarchy. We have the Secretary presiding at the central court, rather more glamorously perhaps than before, certainly more plate glass around and blue carpet, but he is surrounded by his feudal lords.
> There is the grand monsieur of New York [Adlai Stevenson at the UN] who doesn't seem to take orders very much from anybody. There are the various dukes in Washington, the Duke of Michigan [G. Mennen Williams]. Each one of these is conducting vigorously his own armies and he marches up hills and down hills again and quite often all of them stage an entertaining battle for the rest of the world to look at within the United Nations. There you could get almost any view that you would want to listen to. Now, this is entertaining but it is not really good. Therefore, we must pull out of this sort of thing and the department has got to be pulled together, I trust it will be pulled together, and all of us, I know I, shall be in favor of as much blood-

shed as possible . . . Gentlemen, I hope that I have inspired you with all sorts of lethal thoughts. You will go back to your work assured there will be one less enemy alive tonight. This is what I am told is the function of the elder statesman. Always stay in the back and have other people killed.[98]

Word of Acheson's caustic remarks spread quickly through official Washington. When Kennedy caught wind of them, he ordered McGeorge Bundy to obtain a transcript of the talk. Bundy asked Lucius Battle, who had been present at the luncheon, to arrange for a transcript to be sent to the White House. He urged Battle, one of the few men to whom Acheson listened, to persuade the former secretary to show more discretion in the future. When Acheson learned from Battle that Kennedy was "very irritated" by the elder statesman's insolence, his defense was that he thought the speech was off the record. "You've got to be kidding," Battle told his former boss, "I know you know better than that."[99]

That Acheson's words had not missed their mark was confirmed by a former State Department official, John Ausland, who heard President Kennedy speak at an FSA lunch not long after Acheson's talk. "JFK remarked that he had not heard of our club until he got a report on Acheson's speech. The President told us: 'I understand that there was a lot of blood flowing and that some of it was mine.' "[100]

Not until August did Acheson write to the president to apologize for his hectoring. "Clark Clifford mentioned to me that some of my remarks at the foreign service association luncheon had bothered you. I am most distressed to have added any concern to the many that must occupy your mind. I continually err in regarding my humor as less mordant and more amusing than the facts warrant."[101]

Some of the reasons are clear for Acheson's public flagellation of an administration already bleeding from self-inflicted wounds. Acheson was infuriated with the way foreign policy was being made—by White House advisers instead of by the State Department—even though this system put him back on the world stage. Asked in the late sixties what he would have done had he been secretary of state while McGeorge Bundy was national security adviser, Acheson responded, "I'd cease being Secretary of State . . . I couldn't function."[102]

Beyond the structural issues of how foreign policy was made, Acheson was deeply disturbed by the flawed execution of foreign policy. Much of his European trip had been spent trying to explain and defend the inexplicable, he felt, and the handling of the Vienna Conference added fuel to his anger. Still, at a time when the country was confronted by a grave crisis—a crisis in which Acheson conceived nuclear war could result—and he was actively involved in advising the president, such a public attack on his own administration by this seasoned diplomat borders on the inexplicable.

McGeorge Bundy, who as a young scholar had edited a collection of Acheson's speeches and writings, was familiar with Acheson's acerbic wit, some of it delivered at his own expense.[103] He saw Acheson's misguided use of his sense of humor as a partial explanation: "Dean loved popping off," Bundy said. "If you have a wicked gift for a funny phrase it's very tempting to use it."[104] Abram Chayes, a legal adviser to the State Department, stressed Acheson's circumstances at the time: "Dean was riding high. He had the feeling that he was in control."[105] Bundy added that Acheson failed to realize that "when you are out you are out. He wasn't Secretary of State and he wasn't in charge anymore."[106] Acheson was setting the agenda on Berlin contingency planning until mid-July, when some of his recommendations were rejected as too rigid, for there were no other top-level plans in the works. Bundy nonetheless described Acheson's role as more of a "critical observer than an adviser" to the Kennedy White House.[107]

Bundy's implication that at some level Acheson still thought that he was the *real* secretary of state is not a wholly satisfying explanation of the FSA speech, for one can scarcely conceive of Acheson attacking the administration of Harry Truman in a similar way—no matter how wrong he thought Truman might be—out of respect for the office of the presidency. Notwithstanding the close personal relationship between Truman and Acheson, the latter was always punctilious about observing the protocol he felt due the office. Chayes seems closer to the mark. Acheson's understanding of the formal duties and obligations inherent in the hierarchical roles of government seems to have been replaced for a time by what might be characterized more aptly in terms of family dynamics, where the paterfamilias is duty-bound to set his son on the right path. In any case, the flap apparently blew over, and by the end of June Acheson was ready with his recommendations to the president on Berlin.

Report on the Berlin Crisis

Acheson's report, "The Berlin Crisis," was a summary of the stern measures he recommended to demonstrate the West's determination not to be forced out of Berlin. The secrecy accorded the document was so stringent that the few granted access were required to read it in a special White House office, and as of the 1990s portions of the paper remain classified.[108] On the same day Acheson submitted the report, June 28, he wrote Adenauer a lengthy, morale-boosting letter urging him to remain strong on Berlin: "There is . . . the greatest need for allied unity in the face of Khrushchev's threats. Why he has gone as far as he has is hard to see. He appears to believe so strongly in the weakness of the West that he goes very far in limiting his own freedom of maneuver. This creates a most dangerous situation, but one which we should not recoil from."[109]

A sense of urgency engulfed Washington the next morning, as Kennedy called on congressional leaders to attend a National Security Council meeting in the White House at which Dean Acheson would present his recommendations for Berlin. Dean Rusk, perhaps still smarting from Acheson's criticism, later recalled that Acheson entered the room "with a scowl on his face, as if he smelled a dead dog."[110] The former secretary read his report aloud, elaborating as he went and displaying his well-honed oratorical skills. It was at this NSC meeting that formal high-level planning for the Berlin crisis began. The top-secret report was divided into five sections: (1) a summary of the situation; (2) recommendations for U.S. military, political, and economic preparations; (3) discussion of the role of negotiations; (4) contingency plans dealing with the use of force; and (5) probabilities and consequences of failure.[111]

Acheson began with an assessment of what he thought Khrushchev was trying to accomplish in Berlin. The Soviets were testing American resolve; Berlin was not a problem but a pretext. Any attempt to negotiate would therefore be interpreted by the Soviets as a sign of American weakness. What specific objectives was Khrushchev trying to achieve by precipitating a crisis in Berlin? First, the Kremlin wanted "to stabilize the regime in East Germany," paving the way for its eventual recognition. Second, they wanted "to legalize the Eastern frontiers of Germany." Third, the Soviets needed "to neutralize Berlin as a first step and prepare for its eventual takeover by the German Democratic Republic." Fourth, Moscow desired "to weaken if not break up the NATO Alliance." Finally, Khrushchev longed "to discredit the United States or at least seriously damage its prestige," thereby giving the Soviet Union an unprecedented opportunity to extend its influence throughout Europe and, for that matter, the world.[112]

Acheson then examined the nuclear and conventional capabilities at Khrushchev's disposal for implementing his five objectives. He proceeded to what he saw as America's long-range goals. The administration should work toward the de-Sovietization of Berlin and the GDR; the stabilization of the countries of Eastern Europe, "by having them regain a substantial national identity"; and arms limitations talks with the Soviets "so that the possibility of successful offensive action either way in Europe would be greatly reduced." Khrushchev had made his move, Acheson believed, because eight years of Eisenhower-Dulles bluffing had diminished U.S. deterrent credibility. Therefore, it was the Kennedy administration's duty to convince the Soviet leader that he was dead wrong about America's lack of resolve: the United States would fight rather than surrender the freedom of the two million citizens of West Berlin.

Acheson pursued this line of thinking in what he termed the "action part" of his paper. The key point for the United States was to maintain the status quo ante in Berlin: "We could not expect Khrushchev to accept less, we ourselves should not accept less." To achieve this end, old-style nuclear blackmail à la Dulles could be taken out of mothballs, as Adenauer recommended, but he thought it "not a real capability because it would not be believed . . . It would be perfectly obvious to the Russians that we didn't mean it." Acheson also rejected the option advocated by some in the military of "a limited use of nuclear means—that is, to drop one bomb somewhere" as "most unwise." He explained, "If you drop one bomb, that wasn't a threat to drop that bomb—that was a drop—and once it happened, it either indicated that you were going to drop more, or you invited the other side to drop one back. This seemed to me to be irresponsible and not . . . adapted to the problem of Berlin."[113]

Acheson instead urged Kennedy to declare a national emergency and order an immediate buildup in both U.S. nuclear and conventional forces, including substantially increasing force strength in West Germany. He recommended that U.S. troops in Germany be reinforced immediately by two or three divisions and that domestic military reserves be increased by three to six divisions with the "ability to transport more at short notice." "This had risks," Acheson later recalled, "but it seemed to me that it was the only way of showing that we meant business without doing something very foolish."

Acheson agreed with what was known as the Eisenhower State Department's "three essentials" in Berlin and told Kennedy that he must be "irretrievably committed" to them at all costs, even if it meant nuclear war: the maintenance of Allied garrisons in West Berlin; freedom of air and surface access to and from West Berlin; and the continued freedom and viability of West Berlin. Should the Soviets interfere with Western access, an immediate airlift, similar to that of 1948, should be implemented. If the airlift did not work, either because of the greater supply needs for Berliners in the 1960s or the advent of more sophisticated Soviet disruption equipment, two U.S. armored divisions should be sent up the autobahn from West Germany to force open the ground access routes, a contingent too large to be stopped by the East Germans alone. Acheson acknowledged his approach involved grave risks, but he believed that the risks from the failure to act forcefully were far graver. In any case, Acheson was convinced that the odds were good that military preparations alone would be sufficient to deter Khrushchev from pushing the Berlin issue any further.[114]

If Khrushchev backed down on his ultimatum, Acheson was willing to offer the Soviet leader a face-saving formula so he could gracefully retreat. "He even sketched the outlines of a settlement," Schlesinger later noted, "suggesting that Khrushchev's treaty be accompanied by an exchange of declarations assuring the western position in Berlin, along with certain western concessions—perhaps guarantees against espionage and subversion from West Berlin, perhaps even recognition of the Oder-Neisse line—thrown in to make the result more palatable to Moscow."[115]

For the time being, Acheson told the group, official negotiations with the Soviets had to be ruled out. Instead, he proposed conversations be held at lower levels; there were plenty of "elderly unemployed" like himself who could be sent to interminable meetings. He stressed that the United States could converse indefinitely without negotiating at all and volunteered himself to do this "for three months on end."[116]

A wrenching debate erupted at the conclusion of what Schlesinger called Acheson's "brilliant and imperious" presentation.[117] Kennedy mediated the discussion, remaining noncommittal throughout. Acheson's views were met by a chorus of criticism at the meeting from the "softliners," including Dean Rusk (who agreed with Acheson on most other foreign-policy questions), Chester Bowles, W. Averell Harriman, Arthur Schlesinger, Jr., and Abram Chayes. "Everybody these days is in favor of a 'positive' approach to Berlin except me," Acheson wrote to a friend. "If a highway man wants my watch, I am in favor of a negative reply."[118]

Besides Acheson, the hard-liners in the administration included Walt W. Rostow, Paul Nitze, Allen Dulles of the CIA, the joint chiefs of staff, Deputy Under Secretary of State U. Alexis Johnson, and Assistant Secretary Foy Kohler. Johnson felt that "Acheson and some in the military were the real super hawks while the rest of us agreed with him only to varying degrees."[119] Kohler, the resident Achesonian at State, was "thrilled" that Acheson was taking charge of Berlin planning. "He was a hero of mine," Kohler recalled. "His hard-line stance was just what the doctor ordered."[120] The common denominator of this group was a long-held assumption that if Washington displayed an unshakable commitment to hold Berlin, as evidenced by increasing conventional forces and declaring a national emergency, the Soviets would surely back down. Those who saw themselves as hard-liners thought that negotiating with Khrushchev, or any display of Western flexibility, was dangerous, for it would encourage him to press on with more unacceptable demands, in turn increasing the danger of war. This analysis largely was shared by both Adenauer and de Gaulle. "I am glad . . . that President Kennedy has charged you with a review of the plans for Berlin," Adenauer wrote Acheson on July 21. "For the sake of all of us he could not have found a better man."[121]

The soft-liners rejected Acheson's premises as "dangerous in the extreme" and "designed in the main to escalate the crisis, intensifying it to the brink of war."[122] Shortly after the meeting Averell Harriman complained to Arthur Schlesinger, Jr., about his old friend's hawkishness: "How long is our policy to be dominated by that frustrated and rigid man? He is leading us down the road to war."[123] Schlesinger, Sorensen, Deputy Director of the Central Intelligence Agency Robert Amory, and senators J. William Fulbright and Mike Mansfield all found the report too inflexible, as had Prime Minister Macmillan and Foreign Minister Douglas-Home.

This group thought Khrushchev was engaged in a defensive operation in Berlin with the primary aim of halting the flood of East Germans to the West, while also consolidating the Soviet grip on the Warsaw Pact countries. Although the soft-liners did not disagree with Acheson's "three essentials" nor with his belief that a buildup in conventional forces was needed, they completely parted company with the elder statesman on the issue of negotiations with the Soviets. They argued that negotiations were compulsory to reduce the heightened tensions between the two superpowers; they were the alternative to confrontation. Acheson believed that Moscow was bent on world domination; Berlin was the main testing ground of Western resolve in the East-West struggle. The soft-liners thought the Soviet provocation in Berlin was not an expansionist move but instead was based on "nationalist" and "defensive" motives.[124]

At the end of the NSC meeting, Kennedy took two steps aimed at gathering more information to guide his decisions: he directed Special Assistant for National Security Affairs McGeorge Bundy to analyze the situation further in consultation with an interdepartmental group and to present his findings at the next NSC meeting, and he asked Acheson to start a second phase of policy recommendations—this time on negotiations. Having just forcefully advocated ruling out negotiations, Acheson was puzzled about exactly what was expected of him, but he nevertheless accepted the new assignment.[125]

It had become clear to Acheson that Kennedy, who had not given Berlin the attention it deserved before Vienna, was now going to assume personal control of policy development: in effect the president was going to be his own Berlin desk officer.

The NSC Deliberates

The next NSC meeting was held on July 13. President Kennedy and Secretary Rusk led the discussion on policy options for Berlin. Rusk, surprising many by switching his viewpoint, declared that the United States "was not currently in a good position to negotiate" with the Soviets and should wait until the crisis intensified before pressing for talks.[126] After a brief discussion of economic countermeasures that might be taken against Moscow, Robert McNamara offered the Defense Department's recommendations for countering Khrushchev's threats: declare a national emergency, call up the reserves and the National Guard, extend terms of service of those on active duty, return dependents from Europe, and request an additional $4.3 billion for defense (which would create a deficit of from $8 to $10 billion).[127]

Acheson immediately seconded McNamara's program, which was nearly identical to his own "Berlin Crisis" report. He argued that the true merit of these steps was the psychological impact they would have on Khrushchev. Paul Nitze recalled that "Acheson had the Pentagon completely on his side. We all believed that the declaration of a national emergency would convince the Soviets that we meant business."[128] Secretary Rusk disagreed with the Acheson-McNamara call for brinkmanship. Rusk maintained that such a display would "have a dangerous sound of mobilization," wrongly conveying that the United States was preparing for war. He cleverly supported this position by quoting Acheson's own words urging that the military buildup take place without a great deal of fanfare: "We should try to avoid actions which are not needed for sound military purposes and which would be considered provocative. . . . The more drastic of our preparations will be more impressive to Moscow, and perhaps, have a less disturbing effect on our allies, if taken later on as the crisis deepens, when they will be more suited to the immediacy of the threat."[129]

Rusk offered the alternative of a congressional resolution, rather than a national call to arms, as the basis for a military buildup. Vice-President Lyndon Johnson broke in to advise against turning the matter over to Congress; he believed the president should take the lead.[130] Acheson agreed with Johnson and added that "we must do what is sound and necessary in itself and not act for the sake of appearances." He warned the president that if he "left the call-up of Reserves to the end," it "would not affect Khrushchev's judgment" of the situation any more than "we could do by dropping bombs after he had forced the issue to the limit." The United States had to begin training soldiers at once, Acheson argued. Secretary Rusk agreed with him on this point. Acheson, along with Johnson and McNamara, called on Kennedy to endorse his "full program of decisive action."[131] As the discussion evolved it became apparent, Deputy Special Assistant Walt W. Rostow later noted, that "Kennedy was prepared to risk war to defend West Berlin but not to maintain access between the Soviet and Western Sectors."[132]

Acheson was disappointed in Kennedy and Rusk; they appeared dazed and confused, he thought. "I find to my surprise a weakness in decision at the top—all but Bob McNamara who impresses me as first class," Acheson wrote Truman on July 14, the day after the NSC meeting. "The decisions are incredibly hard, but they don't, like Bourbon, improve with aging." Acheson also found the New Frontiersmen's obsession with image irksome. "This is a terrible weakness," he continued. "It makes one look at oneself instead of at the problem. How will I look fielding this hot line drive to shortstop? This is a good way to miss the ball altogether." But Kennedy's group were not the only ones obsessed by image and perception; the difference was that Acheson gave the notion a slightly different spin, couching it in terms of symbolic importance. As Acheson saw it, the point Kennedy had to drive home to the Soviets was that the United States was in "deadly earnest about Berlin, which is only a symbol for our world position. This is what Khrushchev has under attack."[133]

At the following NSC meeting, on July 20, discussion again centered on Berlin. Acheson pressed the president to declare a national emergency immediately and to begin calling up the reserves no later than September. McNamara responded that it would be better not to make such a definite commitment for the time being, but instead to agree that a declaration of emergency would be announced and larger ground reserves called up should the situation worsen. McNamara opposed a fixed target date on the grounds that it did not make sense to accept a rigid timetable in advance. He did not want to have a large reserve force on hand with no mission. Acheson initially interpreted McNamara's proposed course of action as inaction, but Kennedy kept the discussion going until it was agreed that McNamara's flexible timetable allowed for a sufficiently speedy deployment should the crisis deepen. The turning point came when McNamara convinced even Acheson that in a rapidly developing crisis up to six Army and two Marine divisions could be deployed to Europe, although the details of implementation were not spelled out. The consensus was that the plans presented by Secretary McNamara were satisfactory. The president decided that Acheson's call for a national emergency was unnecessary.[134]

The President Addresses the Nation

On July 25 President Kennedy went on live national television and radio to outline his policy on West Berlin. It was a stern warning to the Soviets. As the journalist Hugh Sidey later wrote, "It brought back memories of other voices from the early 1940's. The talk was war talk."[135] Kennedy told the American public that Berlin could not be viewed in isolation but should be seen in the context of a communist global offensive. In alluding to the "challenge" the West faced in deterring Soviet expansionism, Kennedy reiterated Acheson's contention that Khrushchev's main motivation in Berlin was to test American resolve. Nevertheless, Kennedy was careful not to incorporate the "loud and clear" message Acheson had urged, lest the Soviets interpret it as a provocation for war.[136]

To gird his rhetoric with substance, Kennedy announced an immediate conventional military buildup, the third in his first six months in the White House. He called on Congress to appropriate $3.247 billion for defense, ordered the expansion of the military services, tripled draft calls for the coming months, called 150,000 reservists to active duty, reactivated ships and planes previously headed for retirement—including of B-47 bombers—and ordered the procurement of nonnuclear weapons, ammunition, and equipment. If not a declaration of national emergency in form, it unquestionably was in substance.

Kennedy went so far as to request $207 million for an expanded civil defense program, evoking for many the prospect of nuclear war. "In the coming months, I hope to let every citizen know what steps he can take without delay to protect his family in the case of attack." The president had made it clear that nuclear or general war with the Soviets was a distinct possibility. By adopting Acheson's views, JFK had made the Berlin crisis a test of both his and America's courage and determination.[137]

Although Kennedy had adopted Acheson's recommendations in substance, the former secretary was dissatisfied because the president had not declared a national emergency, and he continued to grumble loudly, if semi-privately, that Kennedy's speech had not been forceful enough.[138] Khrushchev was shocked by the martial tone of Kennedy's speech. Was the United States really considering war over Berlin? "There should be a conference," Khrushchev publicly responded on August 7. "Let us not create a war psychosis, let us clear the atmosphere, let us rely on reason and not on the power of thermonuclear weapons."[139]

Acheson's views had been fortified by meetings on July 29 and 30 with the anticommunist West German defense minister from Bavaria, Franz Josef Strauss, at Paul Nitze's farm in southern Maryland. They discussed at length Bonn's views on how to manage the Berlin crisis. Strauss referred to the great psychological toll Khrushchev's ultimatum was taking on the West Germans and argued for the use of tactical nuclear weapons in the event of Warsaw Pact aggression. He also outlined what U.S. measures Bonn would regard as unacceptable political solutions.[140]

On August 1 Acheson submitted to the president his final crisis position paper, entitled "Berlin: A Political Program," which presented a systematic long-term strategy for maintaining the status quo in Berlin without sacrificing Allied rights or Western European security. Acheson contended that if the strategic vision of the United States was to lead the free world, first it must stabilize Berlin and then all of Europe, de-Sovietize East Germany and restore a substantial national identity to the countries of Eastern Europe, and, finally, limit armaments so that the possibility of successful offensive action by either superpower in Europe would be greatly reduced.[141]

Soon after completing this report, Acheson told Harry Truman that he had decided it was time to "phase out" for a while. He summarized his labors of the previous two months: heading a task force, submitting three detailed reports to the president, and fighting mightily to dissuade JFK from negotiating with the Soviets. What would be the outcome of all this? He did not know. Unlike Truman, President Kennedy was unable to make a firm decision, electing instead to straddle the whole Berlin issue while the time-bomb ticked on. "To work for this crowd is strangely depressing," Acheson continued. "Nothing seems to get decided." Acheson also said he was startled by the number of press leaks emanating from the White House and the State Department.[142] The job just finished was to get up a program of international political action—negotiation with its public opening, fall back, and very private positions on Berlin and Germany, together with a propaganda campaign.

Acheson criticized Secretary of State Rusk not only for his failure to coordinate opposing factions but also for the mortal sin of failing to have a clear objective. "The State Department has all sorts of suggestions but no definitive recommendations. Rusk wants to approach everything piecemeal," he complained to Truman. "But how you lead anyone unless you first know where you yourself want to go, I do not know." Acheson felt that Kennedy had no confidence in Rusk and for that reason kept turning to Acheson to discuss Berlin. "But the man he ought to talk with is his Secretary of (a curious ship) State; and he ought to demand a written program of action which he could approve, change or disapprove," Acheson wrote, apparently having forgotten his own early question of whether Rusk, the "good lieutenant," could grapple with strategic issues. "Instead of this everything is kept nebulous. This is a good way to drift into trouble wholly unprepared. What is the new word? Disenchanted. I am becoming disenchanted."[143]

Acheson also castigated Truman for his recent claim that Khrushchev was just bluffing. Acheson believed, to the contrary, that the Soviet leader "sensed weakness and division in the West and intends to exploit it to the hilt. It wouldn't take more than an error or two on each side to carry us over the edge into nuclear war." The only way for the West to avert a nuclear catastrophe, short of accepting Khrushchev's terms, was "to run grave danger of war by preparations for ground action . . . to convince K [Khrushchev] that by pressing too far he might force us into a nuclear response."[144] Acheson's stance is epitomized in an August 4 letter to Anthony Eden: "We must take great risks to avoid greater ones."[145]

The Berlin Wall

Berlin weighed heavily on the president that summer. His advisers could debate endlessly on how best to deter the Soviets, but the final decision—including whether or when to use nuclear weapons—rested on his shoulders. Following a meeting in July with only McGeorge Bundy and

Acheson present, Kennedy asked the former secretary when he thought the United States might be forced to use nuclear weapons. "Acheson's answer was more measured and quiet than usual," Bundy recalled. "He said that he believed the President should himself give that question the most careful and private consideration, well before the time when the choice might present itself, and that he should reach his own clear conclusion in advance as to what he would do, and that he should tell no one at all what that conclusion was." For all his bellicosity at NSC meetings, Acheson's response was delivered, Bundy noted, "with an order and clarity that showed that it was itself the product of careful advance consideration." In retrospect, Bundy believes Acheson's message went beyond merely advising Kennedy to think through his decision carefully in advance about using nuclear weapons and harked back to the central conclusion of "Wishing Won't Hold Berlin": "The final right choice might be to accept defeat, and the loss of West Berlin, if the only remaining alternatives were to start a nuclear war."[146]

Believing he had done all he could to help the president, Acheson decided to "leave Washington and its Potomac miasma" and spend the rest of August with his wife and daughters at Martha's Vineyard.[147] On the morning of August 13, Acheson joined the family of Eliot Janeway, the political economist whose influential newssheet "The Janeway Letter" was distributed worldwide, for breakfast at the Harbor View Inn. The Janeways' son Michael came racing in with the *New York Herald Tribune*, which carried a front-page headline story announcing that shortly after midnight the Soviets had begun erecting a barbed-wire barricade around the 104-mile perimeter of East Berlin. (The first concrete slabs would be laid three days later.)

To Janeway's surprise, "Acheson's fair complexion turned beet red . . . he was just boiling over with indignation at Kennedy." Janeway thought the reason for this reaction was that no one from the administration had had the courtesy to inform Acheson about this startling and significant development; the head of the president's task force on Berlin had to learn about the Berlin Wall from the newspaper. Minutes passed and his color remained high; Acheson finally had to excuse himself from the table.[148]

President Kennedy had in fact turned to Acheson's final position paper when news of the Wall reached him at Hyannis Port, and on August 14 he sent a handwritten note thanking Acheson for his report and inviting him to discuss new developments in Berlin once he finished his "well-earned holiday."[149] It is clear that Kennedy revealed no sense of urgency about having his adviser by his side as events unfolded—perhaps because in none of his three reports did Acheson suggest the possibility that Khrushchev might wall in West Berlin.

One of Khrushchev's main concerns in Berlin was the drain of East German manpower to West Germany. During July 1961 alone thirty thousand East Germans, most of them skilled workers under the age of twenty-five, left for a better life in the West. They used Berlin as their corridor. The Soviet solution to the knotty problem was to construct a barricade designed to halt the exodus. Except for Allied and West German personnel, East German border transit was now unlawful. East Berlin's isolation was made nearly complete the next day when all telephone, telegraph, and postal communications within the city were cut off.

The president's offensive options had been finessed; the Soviets now had the United States in a defensive position. Because President Kennedy had never demanded direct access to East Berlin, he announced on August 18 that he would not use force to break through the barricade, but, through Dean Rusk, he protested its construction and ordered reinforcement of the U.S. garrison in Berlin. As an added gesture to West Berliners, JFK also sent Vice-President Johnson and General Lucius Clay, a hero of the 1948–49 Berlin airlift, to the walled-in Western sector of the city to bolster morale.

Kennedy put into effect some measures Acheson had recommended in his June 29 report. The Defense Department sent another division to West Germany, bringing the total to five; some National Guard and reserve units were called into federal service, and a general posture of military preparedness for conventional action was displayed. "This, I think, had a really profound effect on the Russians, far more than blustery talk would have about using nuclear weapons which would not impress them," Acheson later recalled. "We were actually making life uncomfortable for a quarter of a million of American citizens, they were quite aware the Government wouldn't have done this quite for fun."[150]

General Clay had suggested a more vigorous response to the Wall. McGeorge Bundy, at Kennedy's request, asked Acheson if he agreed. Acheson was adamantly opposed, saying the time for action had passed: "If we had acted vigorously on August 13 we might have been able to accomplish something." Acheson believed it would be "even more unwise," after the United States had "more or less accepted the Wall, to begin to take steps which looked as though we were trying to undo what we'd already done."[151]

The Berlin Wall had become a reality, a stinging rebuke to those who held progressive notions about the advancement of civilization and a thaw in the cold war. To others in the West the concrete excrescence marked the stillbirth of communist plans for global ascendency. President Kennedy drew sharp criticism from some European leaders for not stopping construction of the Wall with military force. Generals Clay and Norstad grumbled that the barricade should have been bulldozed back to Moscow, and McGeorge Bundy believed that for the next ten years Acheson probably thought that "the Wall would have come down in a day if Harry Truman had been President."[152]

Acheson's public stance was one of silence. He elected to stay out of the debate over the Wall for the time being; he had done all he could to steer the president to what he considered the proper course of action. But privately he fretted over the future of the divided city, particularly as he wrote to friends in September, for the Soviet deadline was not lifted until October. "I believe that sometime this autumn we are in for a most humiliating defeat over Berlin," he grimly wrote to Truman on September 21. "The worst of it is not that eight years of Eisenhower inaction and one of Kennedy may have made the result inevitable, but that it will probably be dressed up as statesmanship of the new order, a refreshing departure from the bankrupt inheritance of the Truman-Acheson reliance on military power."[153] In a letter meant to shock the dovish Joseph Johnson, president of the Carnegie Endowment for International Peace, Acheson went so far as to warn that if Khrushchev and GDR president Walter Ulbricht decided to escalate the crisis further, Kennedy might have "to strike the USSR with nuclear weapons" to protect Allied interests. This position, if taken as a serious one, belies McGeorge Bundy's interpretation of Acheson's advice to Kennedy as saying that in the final analysis it might be preferable for the U.S. to accept defeat in Berlin rather than hazard nuclear holocaust.[154]

Acheson was unable to think of the building of the Wall as a Soviet attempt to preserve the status quo that he himself worked so assiduously to maintain. Instead, Acheson saw this event as a dangerous escalation, a technical violation of the Four Power agreement foreshadowing further Soviet efforts to take over all of Berlin. To Acheson, an undivided free Berlin was the first stage in reunifying Germany. The Berlin Wall thus was not a symbol of the inherent weakness of the Soviet political system, as Kennedy had portrayed it, but rather a symbol of the failure of the United States to provide bold leadership for the Atlantic alliance when the chips were down. When faced with a direct Soviet challenge on a central issue of American policy, the United States stood idly by, nervous and disoriented. The Germans were frightened about the future, unsure about America's commitment and ripe for a turn toward *Ostpolitik*.[155]

The danger Acheson saw looming was not a Soviet military invasion through East Germany across Europe; the danger was now political. He feared the Wall would have a corrosive effect on NATO. It was essential, Acheson maintained in a letter to General Clay, that the economic, political, and military interdependence between North America and Western Europe progress, with "the unity of the West and the reunification of Germany within it" as the alliance's ultimate goal.[156] Power in Europe seemed to be moving eastward: first out of France into Germany, then out of Germany into the Soviet Union. Because of the geopolitical disparities existing among the European powers, only the infusion of American power, purpose, and breadth of vision could prevent NATO from breaking up. Acheson noted that in the wake of the building of the Wall and Kennedy's subsequent passivity, even Adenauer, indisputably Europe's most pro-American leader, was questioning both the nuclear credibility and commitment to Germany of the United States.

On November 21, Adenauer called on Acheson for a private hour before a meeting with President Kennedy. "I found him much changed since last April—aged, shrunken, slower, and so I thought confused," Acheson wrote Marshall Shulman at the Russian Research Center at Harvard.[157] His notes from the meeting record an about-face by the German chancellor that left Acheson in despair. His old friend voiced the belief that, as the Soviets had conventional arms superiority over NATO and the West was agreed that nuclear weapons must never be used (although Khrushchev should not know this), the inescapable conclusion was that the West must negotiate with the Soviets to deescalate the cold war. It was up to the Americans, he continued, to initiate the negotiations; he promised that West Germany would not criticize the attempt even if things turned out badly. Acheson could not believe he was hearing the chancellor's "hackneyed and repetitive" speech. He replied that Khrushchev had already succeeded: he had damaged Western resolve severely, as evidenced by the fact that Adenauer himself, that formidable foe of negotiations, had broken down and was ready to give in.[158]

Acheson told the chancellor that he could not understand why the West was always on the defensive, responding to Soviet actions instead of taking the initiative. He liked to consider himself an "offensive gardener," shaping an Atlantic alliance by insisting that the West build up its conventional forces in Germany to prevent direct Soviet intervention in Central Europe. This would buy time for "other forces"—another East German revolt or Hungarian Revolution—to disrupt the Warsaw Pact nations and undermine the Soviet stranglehold on Eastern Europe. If the West had at least thirty-five divisions in West Germany, plus another thirty-five in reserve, Acheson argued, then when the inevitable future crisis over Berlin erupted and the East Germans revolted, the West would be in a position to tell Moscow, "This is a German problem—you stay out of it and we stay out of it." If the Soviets elected to intervene, Western nonnuclear conventional forces would be able to push them back. The "garden" Acheson hoped for was of course a reunified Germany within a united, pro-American, broadly based Western alliance.[159]

On December 5, 1961, Acheson, with former under secretary of state William L. Clayton at his side, brought his advocacy of closer U.S.-European military and economic integration before a joint congressional subcommittee on economic policy. Acheson warned that to preserve the "indispensable coalition" with Western Europe, the United States had to respect the painful economic reorientation Europe was experiencing, in part due to the loss of colonial possessions, and move forward toward a bold new Atlantic community. If Kennedy's State Department was to have an enlightened policy on Europe, the administration must learn to consult with the Europeans, not merely to inform them of U.S. decisions.[160]

CHAPTER FIVE

The Cuban Missile Crisis

In the nine months following his testimony before Congress in December 1961, Acheson was not much involved with official Washington. He traveled extensively throughout the Far East and Europe from January through March, meeting world leaders and doing business for his law firm.[1] He spent much of the summer visiting with and consoling his friend Felix Frankfurter, who was convalescing after a serious stroke, but occasionally he advised President Kennedy on NATO matters and the deepening U.S. balance-of-payments crisis. During this period State Department and White House staffers were grappling with the rapidly deteriorating U.S.-Cuban relations. "Castro's Cuba"—a two-word phrase pronounced by those around Kennedy as if it were one indivisible word—was obsessing every department of government from State to Commerce. But Cuba did not have high priority on Acheson's list of concerns, for although Acheson thought the issues involved were important, he did not find them personally absorbing. Acheson felt he had fulfilled his obligation to the administration by warning JFK in October 1960 not to make Cuba a campaign issue in order to give himself room to maneuver later and had alerted the president to the likelihood of a fiasco at the Bay of Pigs. On the other hand, he had cautioned the president that Soviet adventurism in Cuba would be an intolerable violation of the Monroe Doctrine, that most cherished of American foreign-policy principles.

Acheson had actually met Fidel Castro by happenstance at Princeton University in April 1959, while the Cuban leader was making a whirlwind tour of the United States. At that time Castro was esteemed in America for having ousted the corrupt dictator Fulgencio Batista. Castro had spent the afternoon at Princeton discussing foreign affairs and the plight of the Cuban economy; at a dinner sponsored by the Woodrow Wilson School of Public and International Affairs he chanced upon the former secretary. Acheson came away from their lengthy talk together deeply impressed.

Charles Burton Marshall, a former State Department official who spoke with Acheson shortly after his return from Princeton, recalled, "Acheson was surprised at how blunt Castro was regarding future difficulties between the U.S. and Cuba." Acheson's appraisal went beyond the substance of what Castro had to say, Marshall explained: "He noted how well tailored Castro's jungle fatigues were, how well trimmed his beard was, how there was not a trace of dirt under his manicured nails, and most importantly how carefully he chose his words."[2] Acheson had sized up the man who had come down from the Sierra Maestra to gain control of Cuba as shrewd and purposeful—not ill informed, hotheaded, or feckless. In their private conversation, with only one interpreter from his entourage present, Castro told Acheson that because of the difficult economic problems facing Cuba, he would soon be forced to blame the Yankee colossus to the north for most of his country's problems. Castro foresaw the U.S. role in the new Cuba would be not ally, but adversary. Cuba would take its place in history as an antagonist of the United States. Castro's professions that his new regime was antitotalitarian and humanistic were met with skepticism from Acheson, but Acheson did credit the Cuban revolutionary with candor in portraying his studied antipathy for the United States. "This fellow Castro really knows what he is doing," Acheson told Marshall. "He is going to cause us some problems down the road."[3]

In 1959 Castro was not viewed as a Soviet puppet by Acheson or, for that matter, by the Eisenhower administration. At a seminar for the National War College in July, Acheson called for the United States to be "understanding and sympathetic" to Havana but not offer foreign aid while Cuba was in the midst of a revolution. Acheson reassured the audience that there was no reason to fret over Cuba's recent radical agrarian reform decree because Castro was not "a communist or anything of that sort at all."[4]

Acheson changed his mind a year later when in response to the United States's cutting Cuba's sugar quota, Castro nationalized all U.S. property in Cuba. To the American public Castro immediately became a Great Satan: a communist revolutionary madman, a profaner of private property, a pawn of the Kremlin. Acheson feared that Cuban-style revolution might spread throughout Latin America, challenging United States hegemony.

By early autumn of 1962 the official Washington grapevine was filled with rumors that the Soviets were shipping offensive weapons into Cuba. On October 8 Acheson wrote Harry Truman that he was glad he did not have to deal with it: "Two presidents [Eisenhower and Kennedy] have pretty well loused it up."[5] Acheson's relief at being on the sidelines was short-lived. Eight days later, on the morning of October 16, President Kennedy received definitive evidence that the Soviets were shipping offensive strategic weapons into Cuba; later that day he invited Acheson to advise him on the gravest challenge of the nuclear age. Acheson was to join the secret crisis management contingent of the National Security Council, which came to be known as ExCom (Executive Committee).[6]

Acheson had learned from administration officials in July that Soviet missiles of some sort were being received in Cuba. "We did not know definitely what kind of missiles they were," he recalled later. "Our information was consistent with their being defensive SAM's [surface-to-air missiles]. Similarly, we knew sites were being constructed from which all Cubans were excluded but they could have been SAM sites."[7]

U.S. naval planes had, for some time, photographed routinely at mast level all ships bound for Cuba. A photograph of a Soviet vessel taken in early October revealed on its deck what were without a doubt crates of IL-28s, bombers capable of carrying nuclear weapons to targets within a 750-mile radius. With clear evidence of a buildup of offensive capability in Cuba, U-2 surveillance flights were ordered immediately. The surveillance was delayed by air turbulence and cloud cover from Hurricane Ella, but when the weather finally cleared, the entire island was surveyed and nearly all its surface photographed stereoscopically. Pictures taken on October 14 provided incontrovertible evidence that the Soviets had introduced into Cuba surface-to-surface medium-range ballistic missiles (MRBMs) and were rapidly constructing sites for intermediate-range ballistic missiles (IRBMs), both with nuclear delivery systems. The MRBMs, with a range of 1,020 nautical miles, could reach Washington, D.C.; the IRBMs, with a range of 2,200 nautical miles, were capable of destroying every major American city except Seattle. The U-2 photographs were quickly and quietly developed and sent on to President Kennedy on the morning of October 16. From that moment on, daily intensive U-2 reconnaissance of Cuba was maintained throughout the entire period of the crisis. The Soviet Union denied there were offensive nuclear weapons in what was now perceived as their new Caribbean beachhead.[8]

Acheson first was shown photographs of a Soviet ballistic missile installation under construction near San Cristóbal, Cuba, on October 16 at

Dean Rusk's office. The secretary of state asked Acheson what he thought the president should do about the installations. Acheson examined the photographs for some minutes and reflected, finally responding that the United States could not afford to wait and see if the missiles were made operative. Immediate action to eliminate the missile sites was required.[9] This initial assessment of the situation would never change. "I was very much afraid that if we delayed dealing with them [the missiles] we would get into a situation where we could never deal with them," Acheson said in an interview in 1964. "The danger of the situation would become very much accentuated if these weapons got into a firing stance." Acheson argued that if the president waited until nuclear weapons "were pointed at our hearts and ready to shoot," the task of eliminating them would be next to impossible.[10]

Acheson and Rusk, carrying a briefcase of photographs, joined the ExCom advisory group already in session and deeply divided. Three distinct views had emerged in the group: (1) as the weapons in Cuba did not alter the balance of power, no action was required; (2) the missiles were posing an acute danger and should be removed by military action before they became operational; and (3) a naval blockade against weapons should be established to enforce a demand that Khrushchev remove the missiles.[11] Acheson, the only member of the group who did not hold an official position in the administration, became the leading proponent of the second option, what the foreign-policy analyst Ronald Steel called the "bomb-first-talk-later" position. Its advocates in ExCom included, in addition to Paul Nitze and Maxwell Taylor, the Establishment Republicans C. Douglas Dillon and John McCone.[12]

Secretary of Defense Robert McNamara took the lead in arguing that "a missile is a missile": those in Cuba threatened U.S. security no more than the long-range nuclear weapons already deployed in the USSR. In any case, an air strike was impractical militarily and hence no action should be taken.[13] After an hour of patient listening and moustache-stroking, Acheson forcefully rebutted this line of thought. "Short-range missiles located 90 miles from our coast [are] a much surer bet than long-range ones located about 5,000 miles from our coast," was his reply.[14] Not only was the military impact of the missiles intolerable, but there was also a political cost to be reckoned. Toleration of offensive nuclear weapons so close to home would corrode relations with Latin America and other allies. The world would view the Monroe Doctrine as a farce. "Something should be done quickly," he said. He favored low-level conventional bombing, solely against the missile sites, to destroy the installations and the IL-28 bombers before the missiles became operational.

Although most historians and journalists have portrayed Acheson as the most articulate expositor of the hard line during the ExCom meetings, Acheson saw his own role in a different light. He considered his advocacy of a "surgical strike" on the remote bases, unpopulated except for Soviet technicians, to be the "middle ground solution" between the George Ball–Robert McNamara "doves" who saw no need for a martial response and the military establishment hardliners who wanted to use the missile crisis as a pretext for a full-scale invasion to overthrow Castro's government.[15] Acheson found the reasoning of both groups erroneous, emotional, and unsystematic, and was convinced that bombing the sites was the least dangerous tactic.

Acheson thought the Cuban events, like the Berlin crisis, a consequence of Soviet adventurism fueled by Kennedy's feeble leadership during the Vienna meeting and the failed Bay of Pigs invasion. The president had been passive again when the Berlin Wall was erected. Khrushchev could only conclude that the United States was too faint-hearted to fight. The fact that the Soviet leader had the temerity to put offensive missiles in Cuba in the first place was enough of a reason to demonstrate prompt, forceful American resolve to get them out.

Acheson told the group Khrushchev had three clear objectives: to increase Soviet nuclear first-strike capability by 50 percent; to debunk completely the notion of American hegemony in the Western hemisphere; and to exact from the United States such an exorbitant price for the removal of the missiles that JFK would be discredited both in Europe, where he had ambitions for his Grand Design, and in Asia, where the Russians hoped to promote communism. It would be treason, Acheson asserted, to permit the Soviets to obtain such a military and political stranglehold over the United States.[16]

Acheson regarded the joint chiefs' solution to the crisis as even less palatable. "For instance, it was pointed out that it would be a wise military step to take out the airfields in Cuba before mounting bombing expeditions. Surely, this is what any good planner would do, but it would be a stupid thing to do because the airfields were all right near Havana and other cities—you would have caused terrific casualties of Cubans which would be a very, very bad idea." Others from the military argued, "Well, if you're going to do all that, why don't we put six divisions in and take over the Island." Acheson thought that this was easier said than done, for once you invaded, it would be difficult to get out. "When you get soldiers talking about policy they want to go further and further in a military way so that all possibilities of doubt are removed, until their proposals are apt to be at least as dangerous as the original danger," an obvious allusion to General Douglas MacArthur's disregard for the principle of civilian control of the military during the Korean War.[17]

Issues of substance aside, Acheson was appalled by the formless, ad hoc nature of ExCom meetings—people coming and going; sandwiches and coffee delivered at the moment when the debate finally seemed to achieve coherence; irresponsible, sophomoric statements tossed into the discussion for no apparent reason. Acheson nervously wondered who was in charge of this "floating crap game for decisions." Why wasn't the president or the secretary of state in control?[18]

Robert Kennedy supplies a partial answer to this question in *Thirteen Days*: "During all these deliberations," RFK wrote, "we all spoke as equals. There was no rank, and in fact we did not even have a chairman. Dean Rusk, who as Secretary of State might have assumed that position, had other duties and responsibilities during this period of time and frequently could not attend our meetings."[19] RFK's portrait of ExCom as a nirvana of egalitarianism glosses over the fact that one of the problem-solvers was more equal: the president's brother.

Robert Kennedy, part of ExCom not by virtue of his official position as attorney general but by blood bond, eventually came to dominate the group. Acheson was accustomed to a formal, hierarchical approach to policy making, not an unwieldy, chaotic, pseudoegalitarian marketplace of ideas. Robert Kennedy's boast was Dean Acheson's grievance. The secretary of state should have been directing the ExCom sessions. What possible duties and responsibilities could have kept him from attending such critical meetings? "I can testify to the truth of the statement that members of the group did all speak as equals, were uninhibited, and that they had no chairman," Acheson commented in 1969. "But in any sense of constitutional and legal responsibility they were not equal and should have been under the direction of the head of government or his Chief Secretary of State for Foreign Affairs and his military advisors."[20]

Acheson acknowledged that Robert Kennedy assumed de facto control of ExCom, but he was not pleased with this state of affairs. Acheson's description of this "leaderless, uninhibited group, many of whom had little knowledge in either the military or diplomatic field" takes dead aim at RFK, for with the exception of Vice-President Johnson and Kenneth

O'Donnell, who attended only occasionally, ExCom was composed entirely of public servants seasoned in diplomacy and military matters.[21]

After witnessing a bravura performance by Acheson during the Berlin crisis, Robert Kennedy said he "would never wish to be on the other side of an argument with him."[22] But Dean Acheson was Robert Kennedy's most vocal challenger in the ExCom debates. The brash thirty-seven-year-old Kennedy was forced to take on the formidable elder statesman.

By the afternoon of October 17, Acheson's first full day of participation in the ExCom meetings, JFK had left the session to attend to other duties, leaving his brother in charge. When Acheson, Maxwell Taylor, and others began to push hard for destroying the missile sites, RFK countered that the president would never permit the sites to be bombed. The issue was moral: "My brother is not going to be the Tojo of the 1960's." Bombing the installations, he insisted, "would be a Pearl Harbor in reverse."[23]

Acheson attempted to demolish what he regarded as a "thoroughly false and pejorative analogy." The U.S. fleet at Pearl Harbor had been thousands of miles from Japanese shores, Acheson pointed out. In Cuba, by contrast, offensive nuclear weapons were only ninety miles from the U.S. coast.

Unlike the situation at Pearl Harbor, the Soviets had ample warning of how seriously the U.S. regarded the missiles. On October 3, Congress had authorized the president to prevent by whatever means necessary, including the use of arms, the creation in Cuba of a foreign military base that endangered security. The president himself recently had reiterated his warning against the placement of these offensive weapons in Cuba. Mocking the attorney general, Acheson asked whether it was "necessary to adopt the early nineteenth-century methods of having a man with a red flag walk before a steam engine to warn cattle and people to stay out of the way?" As if the political and military menace of the missile sites were not enough, Acheson continued, the Soviets had defied a historical principle that had stood since 1823: the Monroe Doctrine.[24]

The duel dragged on through the afternoon with no clear victor. As the discussion grew more acrimonious ExCom polarized into two camps: those who supported destroying the missile sites (the Acheson line) and those who supported applying pressure for their removal with a naval blockade of Cuba (the RFK line).[25] The next morning ExCom reconvened with the president in attendance. Following a brief discussion of ultimate U.S. policy objectives, President Kennedy asked Acheson and George Ball, both highly regarded international lawyers, to elucidate the legal difficulties that might arise were their respective courses of action followed.

Acheson led off by discounting "legal niceties" where the security of the United States was threatened. His philosophy was that "no law can destroy the state creating the law. The survival of states is not a matter of law."[26] Any talk of legality under these extreme circumstances was "pompous foolishness."[27] Summarizing his arguments at ExCom to a conference on international law some six months later, Acheson said, "The power, position and prestige of the United States had been challenged by another state. Law simply does not deal with such questions of ultimate power—power that comes close to the sources of sovereignty."[28] Acheson concluded his presentation by scrutinizing Cuba's treaty relationships. As Cuba was not a member of the Warsaw Pact, Acheson thought it unlikely the Soviets would risk nuclear war by coming to its aid. Cuba was in the American sphere delineated by the Monroe Doctrine. Khrushchev thus would be inclined to back off.

Ball tangled artfully with Acheson, charging that an air attack on Cuba would be an "unlawful blunder" that would damage America's standing in the international community. A naval blockade at least had the "color of legality."[29] Slowly, most ExCom members turned away from Acheson's aggressive stance to embrace the notion of a naval blockade of Cuba, which would avoid killing Soviet technicians and would provide Khrushchev with time to contemplate the gravity of the situation.

The assessment of Acheson's role in the Cuban crisis, including the sources of his obduracy and the degree of his bellicosity—a debate in which Acheson himself was a forceful participant—began almost immediately. In their accounts of the events, ExCom participants Robert Kennedy and Theodore Sorensen and the historian Arthur Schlesinger, Jr., paint a heedless and unrelenting Acheson, a man formed—and deformed—in the crucible of McCarthyism, so that having been accused of being soft on communism, he had become in response a right-wing reactionary. The United States and the Soviet Union were "eyeball to eyeball," in Dean Rusk's pungent phrase, waiting to see who would blink first,[30] and Theodore Sorensen relates the terrifying prospects raised by Acheson's "get tough" rhetoric:

> I remember Dean Acheson coming in our meeting and saying that he felt that we should knock out Soviet missiles in Cuba by air strike. Someone asked him, "If we do that, what do you think the Soviet

Union will do?" He said, "I think I know the Soviet Union well. I know what they are required to do in the light of their history and their posture around the world. I think they will knock out our missiles in Turkey." And then the question came again, "Well, then what do we do?" "Well," he said, "I believe under our NATO treaty with which I was associated, we would be required to respond by knocking out a missile base inside the Soviet Union." "Well, then what do they do?" "Well," he said, "then that's when we hope cooler heads will prevail, and, they'll stop and talk." Well, that was a rather chilling conversation for all of us.[31]

Acheson responded to his critics both during and after the crisis. Although he acknowledged that his proposal raised the possibility of a Soviet military response—a "spasmodic, reflex nuclear attack"—against the United States or an ally such as West Berlin, Greece, or Turkey, he dismissed this possibility as improbable. Acheson felt Khrushchev had wide latitude short of nuclear retaliation in which to maneuver. The Soviets, Acheson pointed out, had insisted they were not installing offensive nuclear weapons in Cuba. "So far, then, as the public record is concerned, a sudden air attack by us on a nonpopulated area of Cuba would have been an attack not on the Soviet Union but on something—not people—in Cuba," Acheson noted after the crisis. "This would hardly have called for a reflex attack on the United States at the expense of reciprocal destruction of the Soviet Union." Khrushchev would have had to charge that Washington "had nervously fired at shadows." "This would not have been easy to disprove," Acheson went on, pointing to the widely believed Soviet charge that America had used germ warfare during the Korean War. "Even the evidence of the photographs could be attacked as faked with dummies." If nuclear retaliation was deemed unlikely, the most pressing contingency was the Cuban missiles themselves. Only an air strike could immediately remove that threat.[32]

Acheson argued that a blockade actually posed "greater dangers without any assurance of compensating benefit." He believed there was a strong possibility that Soviet ships might try to run a blockade, leading to the very military confrontation the doves were trying to prevent. But even if the blockade were successful, the process would give Soviet technicians time to make some or all of the nuclear weapons operational. If they succeeded, "Cuba would become a combination porcupine and cobra," leaving America's survival in Khrushchev's hands.[33]

The decision to impose a blockade, Acheson thought, actually would leave the Soviet Union and Cuba in control of events. "I never quite believed that my younger colleagues really understood the nature of the decision," Acheson wrote his close friend Justice of the High Court Sir Patrick Devlin shortly after the crisis. "They thought that the choice was between beginning tough with some physical action, and risking its consequences, or beginning soft with the 'quarantine' and, if necessary, working up to tougher measures. They did not realize—though they were warned—that it is almost impossible today to work up."[34]

Following the afternoon ExCom meeting, the president invited Acheson to a private session at his White House office. There Kennedy listened closely to Acheson for nearly an hour.[35] Acheson reiterated his view that although an air strike involved grave risks, it was nevertheless a more effective course than a blockade, which, after all, was a means of keeping something from getting in, not of getting something out. When the president repeated his brother's Pearl Harbor comparison Acheson replied that the analogy was absurd, a position he maintained unapologetically to the last year of his life: "To talk about that [an air strike on the missile sites] as a Pearl Harbor in reverse seemed to me to be high school thought unworthy of people charged with the government of a great country."[36] Acheson acknowledged that Kennedy would have to bear the "terrible burden" of making the final decision. Kennedy responded that he was leaning toward a blockade. Their conversation finished, the president stood up from his rocking chair, walked to the French door looking out on the Rose Garden, and gazed out. "I guess I better earn my salary this week," he said. "I'm afraid you have to, I wish I could be more help," Acheson replied, and their meeting ended on that formal, somber note.[37]

On October 19, President Kennedy, in an effort to avoid raising public suspicions by altering his prearranged schedule, flew to scheduled pre-election appearances in Ohio and Illinois, leaving his brother in command of ExCom. Once more, Acheson engaged in a heated exchange with Robert Kennedy. But by this time the attorney general was making headway. He argued that his brother could not order an air strike, for the United States was "fighting for something more than just survival and ... our heritage and our ideals would be repugnant to such a sneak military attack."[38]

Many of the hawks, Maxwell Taylor and Douglas Dillon included, were swayed by the attorney general's moral arguments, and, as the clock ticked, frightened by the thought of actually bombing Cuba. After another long day of deliberation, it was clear that the air-strike advocates were losing. A consensus grew that a naval blockade represented the most sensible, least provocative measure available to the president. Acheson remained stubborn in his contrary convictions. The question then was how ExCom could get around the former secretary.[39] "During the course of ExCom . . . he [Acheson] just got fed up with all this brainstorming of things and everybody thinking out loud," recalled Deputy Secretary of Defense Roswell Gilpatric. "He liked to make a pronouncement and knock down any opposing ideas, which he did . . . very masterfully and then depart the scene. So he came and went . . . but if he was there in full force and wanted to make an issue of it, no frontal attack would overcome him."[40] Nearly a quarter of a century after the crisis, Acheson's long-time friend George Ball would say that "Dean's insistence on an immediate air attack was a real low point in an otherwise distinguished career."[41] And Douglas Dillon recalled that "none of us original bomb-first advocates matched Acheson in stridency of conviction."[42]

When Robert Kennedy suggested that ExCom split into two groups, each devising separate diplomatic and military position papers to submit to the president, Acheson, sensing the tide had turned against him, balked. After a brief discussion in an adjacent conference room with the other air-strike advocates, Acheson asked to be excused from further attendance, explaining that this was no place for a person not in government to be. "For an outsider to give advice and counsel when asked was one thing," Acheson told his colleagues. "It was quite another to participate in writing the most secret strategic and tactical plans of a vital military operation, which might soon be put into effect."[43] Content in knowing that he had tried his best to persuade the president to take firm, decisive action, Acheson left Washington and drove with his wife to his Maryland farm for the weekend.

Mission to Europe

On Saturday, October 20, as the Achesons were preparing to retire for the evening, Dean Rusk telephoned to say that the president had decided on an important matter and that it was contrary to Acheson's recommendation, a cryptic reference to the missile crisis. The president was anxious for Acheson to go to France to elucidate the circumstances and the decision for de Gaulle and the NATO Council.

In his private talk with the president on October 18, Acheson had stressed the importance of sending distinguished emissaries to inform the European and Latin American allies of the impending crisis and ask their support. He had suggested that Vice-President Johnson travel to Paris to meet de Gaulle, but now Rusk asked him to take on that task. Acheson, by way of reply, quoted an observation of Oliver Wendell Holmes, Jr.: "We all belong to the least exclusive and most expensive club in the world, the United States of America." He added, "I guess if I belong to that club, I better do what I'm asked to do." "You don't mind that your advice is not being followed?" asked Rusk. "Of course not," replied Acheson. "I'm not the President, and I'll do whatever I can do."[44] Rusk had no doubt that Acheson could present America's position to Europe with clarity and force and asked Acheson to come to the State Department the next morning for instructions before embarking for Europe as President Kennedy's ambassador plenipotentiary.[45]

Early the next morning Acheson discovered he had just seven dollars, no valid passport, and only country clothes to wear. His longtime personal secretary, Barbara Evans, was dispatched to the passport office at State, opened especially for her, to get his old passport validated. In an era before ubiquitous cash machines the banks were not so cooperative, and it being Sunday, various State Department officials were asked to chip in; they collected fifty dollars in cash for the special envoy. Acheson then hurried to his P Street house, packed a bag, met Barbara Evans with the passport, and was picked up by Bill Bundy, who rushed his father-in-law to a waiting Air Force 707 bound for Paris.[46]

On the flight was Walter "Red" Dowling, the U.S. ambassador to Germany, returning to Bonn from a leave; Sherman Kent of the CIA, who carried the aerial photographs of the missile sites; two other CIA men; and three armed bodyguards. Acheson and Kent reviewed the enlarged photographs while en route.

The plane refueled at Greenham Common Airfield, a SAC base north of London. There Acheson was met by his old patrician friend, David K. E. Bruce, the U.S. ambassador to Britain from 1961 to 1969. Together they went to a maximum security operations room at the base, where Bruce was left with a set of the photographs, one of the CIA men, and a guard and instructed to show Prime Minister Macmillan the pictures the following day.[47] After sharing some "nourishment" from a bottle of Scotch provided by Bruce, Acheson flew on to Evreux Air Force Base arriving at 1:30 A.M. local time. He was met by the U.S. chargé d'affaires, Cecil Lyon, and driven to Lyon's home. At 5:00 A.M. Acheson finally retired for a few restless hours. He had refused a soporific for fear of appearing groggy when he met de Gaulle.[48]

When Acheson awoke, he was confronted with the question of how to approach de Gaulle. He elected to tell the French president's chef de cabinet that he had come to Paris undetected in the middle of the night on a top-secret mission from President Kennedy and would like to see the general as soon as it was convenient. "I thought this was a matter of such complete secrecy that it would be wise for no one even to know that I was in town," Acheson later explained, "and, with that I was in his [de Gaulle's] hands."[49]

Arrangements were made for Acheson to meet Le Grand Charles at 5:00 P.M. De Gaulle would send a staff car so Acheson and company could arrive undetected. These arrangements settled, Acheson spent much of the afternoon briefing the American contingent of the Supreme Headquarters, Allied Powers, Europe (SHAPE) Command on the crisis. Although military personnel had previously checked the briefing room for listening devices, Acheson did not take any chances—he blasted the march from Verdi's *Aïda* on a large stereo phonograph as an extra precaution against Soviet bugs.[50]

Shortly before five, two small cars belonging to junior members of de Gaulle's staff picked up Acheson and the others. The police held up traffic around the Elysée Palace for several minutes while they were whisked in with nobody the wiser. Once on the grounds the cars drove through a tunnel and pulled up in front of a basement entrance. As Acheson, Sherman Kent, and Cecil Lyon climbed ancient stone steps, past musty wine closets, they passed through a series of steel doors with little peepholes through which security guards gazed and exchanged passwords. Acheson thought the scene straight out of *The Three Musketeers*. "Porthos, is your rapier loose in its scabbard?" Acheson stage-whispered to Kent. "I think some of the Cardinal's men may be lurking here." The CIA analyst, in no mood for jest, replied that he was ready.[51] They were led through a maze of passageways to a waiting room adjacent to de Gaulle's office. There they were greeted by an interpreter from the French embassy who said the president wished to see only Acheson and his interpreter, Lyon; Kent and the photographs were to wait outside.

"Your President has done me a great honor by sending so distinguished an emissary," de Gaulle said in greeting, as he entered his office. Acheson, at a rare loss for words, bowed politely. In an interview in the last year of his life, Acheson recalled that moment. De Gaulle was the epitome of dignity, but he had a bizarre appearance: "He struck me as looking like a pear on top of two toothpicks. He had narrow shoulders, a rather large nose, which was the stem of the pear. Then he went down to a rather round stomach and behind, and then two very long, very thin legs."[52] Acheson immediately handed de Gaulle a letter from President Kennedy outlining specific actions the United States would be taking regarding the Soviet missiles in Cuba. When de Gaulle finished reading, he asked whether he was being consulted or informed. "We must be very clear about this," Acheson responded, "I have come to inform you of a decision which has been taken—but I want to call to your attention that it is the kind of a decision which opens the way for a lot of advice from his allies, which he wishes to have."[53]

Acheson explained that rather than taking "sharp action" to begin with, President Kennedy had ordered a blockade of Cuba as a first step; only if Soviet ships attempted to run the blockade would further, more vigorous action be taken. De Gaulle thought the quarantine a "wise step."[54] Acheson then handed de Gaulle a copy of the speech Kennedy would be making on the missile threat in four hours to the American people. "I have outside the photographs of these missiles," Acheson continued. "They are extraordinary photographs and very impressive, and I think you might want to look at them." De Gaulle dismissed this suggestion. "Not now," he told Acheson. "These will only be evidence—a great nation like yours would not act if there were any doubt about the evidence. I accept what you tell me as fact, without any proof of any sort needed."[55]

De Gaulle asked what action the United States planned should the Soviets try to run the blockade. Acheson had not been briefed on this contingency but thought it best not to let on. "We will immediately tighten the blockade to include tankers," he ad-libbed. "This will bring Cuba to a standstill. If we have to go further, why of course we'll go further."[56] Acheson's impromptu reply apparently satisfied the French president, "though," Acheson maintained, "he would have approved something even more vigorous and incisive."[57] "If there is war, I will be with you. But there will be no war," de Gaulle told Acheson.[58]

De Gaulle ultimately agreed to look at the photographs. Kent was brought in. He handed the president a magnifying glass and explained the photographs in detail. De Gaulle was "delighted with them," Acheson recalled. "You could see the soldier really taking over at this point, as he studied every one of them. This really finished any doubt that he had about the seriousness of this matter." De Gaulle reiterated, "You may tell your President that France will support him in every way in this crisis." His mission completed, Acheson stood up to leave. "It would be a pleasure to me if these things [top-secret missions] were all done through you," de Gaulle said as Acheson left.[59] Henry Kissinger confirmed Acheson's impression in a letter to him that December. Kissinger wrote that he had spoken with a man who had an appointment with de Gaulle immediately following Acheson's. "He told me that de Gaulle said, 'Voilà un homme!' and that he went on at some length about how reassured he would be to have somebody he could send on missions like this."[60]

Acheson considered this a great compliment. "You know, this was Louis XIV saying a nice word to an ambassador from the Sultan of Turkey," he later commented.[61] "He [de Gaulle] is a man of great force and high intelligence," Acheson wrote a young friend later that October. "This does not prevent him from being a damned nuisance from time to time, but he has what has almost disappeared from the world, the dignity which comes from complete confidence in his values and the calm of unshakable convictions." Unlike Kennedy, de Gaulle possessed an inner voice and was not obsessed with opinion polls, media images, and second-guessing decisions already made. "He is the kind of 'hero as king' that Carlyle wrote about and everyone now, except me, makes fun of."[62]

In the evening following his meeting, Acheson addressed NATO's permanent council at an extraordinary session of the ambassadors from the fourteen other member states that lasted from 10:00 P.M. to midnight. Acheson briefed them on the measures ordered by President Kennedy to check the Soviet buildup of nuclear arms in Cuba, emphasizing the gravity of the situation. By the time the meeting ended, word of President Kennedy's seventeen-minute television speech announcing the blockade of Cuba had flashed across the international wires, beamed around the world in thirty-seven languages by the U.S. Information Agency.

Acheson retired for the evening, but his sleep was interrupted by an urgent telegram from President Kennedy instructing him to fly to Bonn at once for consultation with Chancellor Adenauer. Apparently, Walter Dowling had talked with Adenauer the night before and had found the chancellor "pretty excited" about the crisis over Cuba. The White House hoped Acheson could soothe Der Alte's nerves. "It turned out to be a good idea at that," Acheson later admitted.[63]

Acheson arrived in Bonn early the next morning. He immediately conferred at length with Defense Minister Strauss and other cabinet members. He spent the late afternoon with the chancellor and Strauss reviewing the aerial photographs of Cuba and the security precautions in West Berlin should Khrushchev respond to the blockade by disrupting access routes to that city.[64] Adenauer feared that Khrushchev had placed the missiles in Cuba as a bargaining chip to force the United States out of Berlin. "Der Alte wanted to talk and had to be confined, rather sternly, to talking sense," Acheson reported to Jean Monnet in November. "He wanted us to be more venturesome, without involving him."[65] Adenauer was puzzled, he said, by American policy: a blockade would not remove the missiles. What, he asked, was Kennedy's rationale. Acheson, who could not agree more with Adenauer's assessment, replied that he could only tell him one thing: "Faith moves mountains."[66] Unconvinced by such an anemic non-defense of U.S. policy, Adenauer replied that the United States should not have been so timid. Nevertheless, the chancellor gave Kennedy his full endorsement in a live nationwide television broadcast shortly after Acheson left Germany.

Pleased that he had once again succeeded in "lifting a stone" from the chancellor's heart, Acheson prepared to return home, his mission, he felt, accomplished with competence and style. To his dismay, however, he discovered himself marooned when his air force plane was ordered to Frankfurt to fly John J. McCloy to New York. McCloy was, Acheson noted, to "act as stiffening" in the UN for Adlai Stevenson, who had apparently been unnerved by the crisis and was, according to some in the administration, unable to fulfill his duties as ambassador. Acheson shared the president's concerns about whether Stevenson had the "judgment" or "stamina" necessary to handle the web of problems arising in the UN from the blockade, and so he naturally supported sending McCloy as reinforcement. But Acheson was piqued that it was "his" plane that was commandeered. Acheson was left to return in Ambassador Dowling's private train compartment from Bonn to Frankfurt, where he caught a Pan-Am commercial flight back to Washington.[67] "I was sent off to Europe as Paul Revere of the Cuban crisis, galloping through Paris and Bonn crying, 'The bombs are coming,'" Acheson reported to a friend once the crisis was over. "It was all very exciting and exhausting. Our European allies took it very calmly."[68]

Acheson arrived in tension-filled Washington on Wednesday afternoon; a showdown of some sort with the Soviets seemed imminent. Avoiding an ExCom meeting, Acheson reported on his mission directly to Dean Rusk and, the next day, to the president. He emphasized to both men that in the week that had passed new photographs clearly revealed "alarming progress" in mounting the missiles. "Time was running out," he recalled warning the president. "The air strike remained the only method of eliminating them and hourly was becoming more dangerous."[69] Other ExCom members also had begun leaning toward military action.

On Friday evening, Khrushchev sent a confused, rambling telegram to President Kennedy. Acheson, who had been asked by Rusk to stand watch with him at the State Department, sat in Rusk's seventh-floor office awaiting the translation. When it finally arrived, Acheson concluded that the Soviet premier was "either tight or scared."[70] The text was difficult to decipher, but it appeared Khrushchev was finally admitting the existence of offensive weapons in Cuba, while still emphatically denying their purpose was to attack the United States. The missiles were there to protect Cuba from another invasion like the Bay of Pigs, he claimed. If the United States would pledge never again to invade Cuba and call off the quarantine, the removal of the missile sites would be "an entirely different question."[71] This message was received with a sense of relief by the White House and the State Department—Khrushchev was looking for an escape hatch. Acheson, one of the few who remained skeptical, "felt we were too eager to liquidate this thing. So long as we had the thumbscrew on Khrushchev, we should have given it another turn every day."[72] Acheson's instincts proved correct, even if the "thumbscrew" image was another example of his harsh, irresponsible hyperbole.

At breakfast with Secretary McNamara on Saturday, October 27, Acheson learned that Moscow had followed up with a second, more formal telegram that ignored Khrushchev's prior rambling message. This time the condition for withdrawal of missiles in Cuba was withdrawal of American Jupiter missiles from Turkey. Months before, President Kennedy had considered dismantling the obsolete Jupiter missiles. Now the president felt he could not appear to capitulate under Soviet threat. ExCom quickly reconvened, Acheson again staying away. A majority agreed that the SAM sites in Cuba would have to be destroyed early the next morning in retaliation for the downing of an American U-2 plane by an operational SAM. The president, however, "quickly squelched the idea."[73]

At this juncture Robert Kennedy proposed that the president ignore Saturday's formal telegram and respond only to Khrushchev's Friday night ramblings. If the Kremlin councils were fractured like ExCom, the new American message should try to exploit this division. On Saturday night a response, drafted by Robert Kennedy and Ted Sorensen, accepted

Khrushchev's first proposal: the United States agreed not to invade Cuba, contingent on cessation of work on the missile sites and their supervised removal. And although the United States made no written pledge to withdraw the Turkish missiles, Robert Kennedy privately promised Soviet Ambassador Anatoly Dobrynin that the Jupiter missiles would be removed once the crisis had subsided, provided Moscow did not leak word of the deal. Robert Kennedy's ploy worked; on Sunday, October 28, 1962, the Soviet Union agreed and the missile crisis ended. "It was a gamble to the point of recklessness," Acheson later wrote of RFK's backroom maneuvers. "The amazing result was that this hundred-to-one shot certainly appeared to be paying off."[74] The only technicality that remained was an arrangement for verifying the dismantling of the missiles, which was to take place under UN supervision. "If the nuclear weapons and the IL-28s don't come out [of Cuba], we shall doubtless have to come in and get them out," a still-suspicious, saber-rattling Acheson wrote his friend the United States court of appeals circuit judge John C. Pickett on November 1. "Perhaps the Castro brothers may not survive this effort."[75]

But President Kennedy weathered the most serious test of his presidency and praise came pouring in from all corners, including Dean Acheson's. "With proper precautions for warding off the ill-luck which is said to attend upon and punish premature statements, may I congratulate you on your leadership, firmness and judgment over the past touchy week," he wrote the president of the denouement on October 29. "We have not had these qualities at the helm in this country at all times. It is good to have them again. Only a few people know better than I how hard these decisions are to make, and how broad the gap is between the advisors and the decider." Kennedy replied the following day that it was "a comforting feeling to have a distinguished captain of other battles in other years available for present duty." He later sent to all of the ExCom members a memento, a paperweight in the form of a calendar page for the month of October. Their initials were engraved on the page and the dates of October 16 through 28 were emboldened. Acheson thanked the president for the gift and "for the opportunity you opened to me to take part in the campaign so wisely conceived and vigorously executed. In its execution you confounded de Tocqueville's opinion that a democracy 'cannot combine its measures with secrecy or await their consequence with patience.'"[76]

Acheson's mission to the European allies served as reassurance that their concerns at this critical moment were not forgotten by the American president. Nevertheless, many Europeans resented the fact that Kennedy's envoy was sent merely to inform, not to consult. Only a few months later these resentments began to fester, leading many Europeans to perceive Kennedy's Grand Design—his call for an equal partnership between North America and Europe—as a rhetorical sham, a calculated charade designed to maintain U.S. power over the Continent. As the political commentator I. F. Stone noted in an article in 1966 that criticized the limited value of Acheson's journey to Europe: "Kennedy no more consulted NATO before deciding to risk World War over Cuba than Khrushchev consulted his Warsaw Pact satellites before taking the risky step of placing missiles on the island."[77]

Homage to Plain Dumb Luck

The ritual exchange of polite notes and compliments between Acheson and John F. Kennedy that followed the denouement of the missile crisis served to paper over, at least temporarily, the profound and heated policy disagreements between the elder statesman and the president—represented by his vicar, brother Bobby. But six years later, in 1968, Robert Kennedy himself actively was seeking the Democratic presidential nomination, a prospect that made Acheson uneasy. Due to "his money, his head start, and his irresponsible demagoguery," Acheson thought RFK might actually capture the nomination, he wrote to a friend in April 1968.[78] Two months later Robert Kennedy was assassinated in Los Angeles. When the Kennedy family posthumously published Robert Kennedy's self-serving memoir of the crisis, *Thirteen Days*, the fallout of the event and the book made permanent historical adversaries out of ExCom's two most forceful advocates.

Kennedy's revelation in his memoir that Acheson had been his primary antagonist in the ExCom debates led the elder statesman to respond with a scathing denunciation of the administration's handling of the entire crisis. In February 1969, less than a year after RFK's assassination, *Esquire* published an essay by Acheson, cast in the ill-fitting form of a book review of *Thirteen Days* and headlined "Dean Acheson's Version of Robert Kennedy's Version of the Cuban Missile Affair." There Acheson stripped the varnish off Robert Kennedy's account, exposing the hastily arranged ExCom meetings and describing what Acheson saw as the follies of JFK's circus approach to crisis management—minus the ringmaster.[79]

Acheson defended his call for an immediate air strike, chastised RFK for naiveté and ExCom for being a disorganized mess, and saluted the successful outcome by paying "homage to plain dumb luck." "It does not detract from President Kennedy's laurels in handling the Cuban crisis that he was helped by the luck of Khrushchev's befuddlement and loss of nerve," Acheson wrote. "The fact was that he succeeded. However, as the Duke of Wellington said of Waterloo, it was 'a damned near thing.' And one should not play one's luck so far too often."[80]

History, of course, has vindicated John F. Kennedy's judgment and strategy during those thirteen nerve-racking days as masterful. Most observers consider it the high point of his administration's foreign policy. The blockade was active, in that it flexed American military muscle, but also passive, in the sense of putting the next move in Khrushchev's hands—the major negative point, in Acheson's view. But labeling the blockade "passive" seems almost beside the point, for if any engagement of conventional forces were to take place, there could be no more advantageous circumstances for the United States than a naval engagement in the Caribbean. The blockade was a strong move but not an unnecessarily provocative one. It gave the Soviet Union time to realize the United States meant business but also allowed room to retreat without humiliation and with national pride intact.

For the Soviet Union, the long-term consequences of the Cuban showdown included Khrushchev's eventual purge from power and an acceleration of the Soviet nuclear effort. For the United States, an almost immediate consequence was the validation in the minds of many allies of de Gaulle's charge that when the chips were really down, the United States would always act unilaterally. To de Gaulle, as well as to many other European leaders, the crisis was proof positive that NATO was an organization designed to keep the United States strong and Europe impotent and dependent.[81]

How does one explain the gap between Acheson's letters of October 28 and November 30 to John F. Kennedy praising his leadership, firmness, and judgment and his later public dismissal of the successful Cuban outcome as primarily a consequence of plain dumb luck? One could interpret Acheson's letters as merely a display of diplomatic courtesy and good manners, an attempt to portray himself the good sport and remain a player in the White House. The dumb luck article can be read as arising from the sour grapes of an acerbic, rigid, aging cold warrior whose advice was disregarded. But this view ignores a profound difference in outlook between Kennedy and Acheson in how to conduct foreign relations in a nuclear world. Unlike Kennedy, Acheson failed to understand that in the nuclear age it is never wise to paint one's adversary into a corner. Beyond Acheson's gripes about style, misguided metaphors, circus atmosphere, ad hoc decision making, he was truly convinced that President Kennedy had missed an opportunity to damage the Soviet position in the world: Khrushchev should have been forced to pay dearly for his deceit, blunders, and hubris. Instead, Kennedy drifted into a successful outcome. "This is not really what I was looking for in the leadership of my country at this point," Acheson would comment nearly a decade after the Cuban missile crisis. "On other occasions, I'd had experience with him which led me to this conclusion; that he did not have incisiveness and he was really out of his depth where he was."[82]

On his part, President Kennedy came away from the crisis with even more respect for Dean Acheson the tireless public servant but less for the former secretary's foreign-policy judgment.[83]

Secretary of State Dean Acheson with his wife, Alice, waves goodbye to applauding State Department employees at an outdoor ceremony in Washington, D.C., on January 16, 1953. Courtesy of the Harry S Truman Library (HSTL).

Senator Joseph McCarthy and Secretary of State Dean Acheson share an elevator after leaving a closed-door hearing of the combined Armed Services and Foreign Relations committees.

Furniture making at Harewood Farm, a respite for Acheson while in and out of government.

General Dwight D. Eisenhower confers with Secretary of State Acheson at the State Department in 1951.

Longtime antagonists Dean Acheson, then secretary of state, and John Foster Dulles, then an ambassador-at-large, at the White House in 1951.

Former president Truman tries to negotiate a five-way conciliatory handshake between Democrats and Republicans at a conference on national security in early 1958. *Left to right*: Republican Senator Alexander Wiley, former secretary of state Dean Acheson, Truman, Senate Majority Leader Lyndon Johnson, and Minority Leader William Knowland.

Acheson, shown here with his wife, Alice, in Florence, traveled through Europe during September and October 1959, meeting dozens of statesmen and speaking out on behalf of a new Atlantic community.

UPI/Bettmann

President-elect John F. Kennedy and Acheson pose for photographers in the doorway of Acheson's home following a meeting on November 28, 1960. Kennedy referred more than once to Acheson's "intimidating seniority."

Courtesy LBJL

Secretary of Defense Robert McNamara and Acheson worked together throughout the Kennedy and Johnson years to develop the defense strategy known as flexible response.

Acheson arrives for the christening of the nuclear submarine the *George C. Marshall* in May 1965.

Courtesy of David C. Acheson

President Lyndon Johnson and Acheson at the White House in June 1965.

Courtesy LBJL

Courtesy LBJL

Acheson discusses the future of NATO at a White House meeting. Under Secretary of State George W. Ball, *left*, and Secretary of State Dean Rusk, *right*, were among those present. Acheson thought very highly of Ball but deemed Rusk "ineffective" at running the State Department.

Courtesy LBJL

When President Charles de Gaulle of France pulled out of NATO's integrated military command in March 1966, President Johnson put Acheson in charge of drafting appropriate American countermeasures. Here Acheson confers with members of his NATO crisis team. *Left to right*: Deputy Secretary of Defense Cyrus Vance, Under Secretary of State George W. Ball, and Ambassador to France Charles E. Bohlen.

President Johnson and Acheson stroll on March 14, 1968, only two days after LBJ had barely defeated the antiwar candidate Eugene McCarthy in the New Hampshire Democratic primary. A week later Acheson advised the president "to take steps to disengage" from Vietnam.

Courtesy LBJL

Former Truman administration official Clark Clifford, *right*, who became Johnson's secretary of defense in March 1968, joined forces with Acheson on a post-Tet reevaluation of Vietnam policy.

Acheson at a Washington address to the American Bar Association in 1968, where he charged that Britain and the U.S. were engaged in "bare-faced aggression" against Rhodesia. Acheson said the fact that Rhodesia did not wish to institute majority rule might not be "everyone's cup of tea," but "nor was it everyone's business."

Courtesy National Archives

Acheson liked the calm and intimacy of his meetings with Nixon, as opposed to the hurly-burly of Johnson's conferences. Pictured here, in April 1969, is the first of many White House sessions.

Courtesy of David C. Acheson

Truman administration cabinet members (*left to right*) John W. Snyder, Dean Acheson, and W. Averell Harriman visit their old "boss," former president Harry Truman, at his Independence, Missouri, home in 1970. This was the last time Truman and Acheson were together.

Dean Acheson at home.

Courtesy of David C. Acheson

CHAPTER SIX

Strains in the Atlantic Alliance, 1962–63

By early December 1962 JFK's handling of the Cuban missile crisis was regarded by most Americans as a diplomatic triumph. But this success in the realm of superpower relations had a deleterious impact on relations with the European allies. While Americans were transfixed by the attempted installation of offensive nuclear missiles a scant ninety miles from their shores, Charles de Gaulle was forcing Europeans to face critical issues in their relationship with each other and with the superpowers. Dean Acheson would play an important, if unintended, part in the fierce debates over the direction of European relations.

The elder statesman naturally was relieved to have the Cuban episode over and done with. He spent late November completing two articles and polishing an address to be delivered at West Point on December 5, a speech that would prove the most controversial of his postsecretarial years.

General William C. Westmoreland, the superintendent of the U.S. Military Academy at West Point, had invited Acheson to deliver the keynote address at a student conference on U.S. affairs. Acheson, who constantly received invitations to speak at colleges and universities, declined, he said, out of "sheer laziness." General Maxwell Taylor then intervened on Westmoreland's behalf. "Although I know you must receive many invitations of this kind, I hope that your busy schedule will permit you to accept this one," Taylor wrote Acheson. "I think it is fair to say that this annual event has attained a considerable reputation, and, with the theme of 'Atlantic Community,' it would be a forum particularly appropriate for an address from Dean Acheson."[1]

Acheson could not bear to say no to Taylor, who was one of the few men in Washington whom he unhesitatingly admired. He responded, "When you ask me to do it, that is something different."[2] So it was that Acheson found himself at West Point delivering a speech entitled "Our Atlantic Alliance: The Political and Economic Strands."

For the most part, the speech was vintage Acheson, a call for strengthening NATO and working toward a true Atlantic partnership. Midway through his address, however, Acheson pointed a finger at the country he saw as a spoiler:

> Great Britain has lost an empire and has not yet found a role. The attempt to play a separate power role—that is, a role apart from Europe, a role based on a "special relationship" with the United States, a role based on being the head of a "commonwealth" which has no political structure, or unity, or strength, and enjoys a fragile and precarious economic relationship by means of the Sterling area and preferences in the British market—this role is about played out. Great Britain, attempting to work alone and to be a broker between the United States and Russia, has seemed to conduct policy as weak as its military power.[3]

This excerpt, transmitted to England the following day, immediately was front-page news. The British were outraged, and the volcanic public outcry that ensued seemed out of proportion to the nature of the speech. "I wonder who the unsung reportorial genius was who read through the whole speech and found that paragraph to cable to London," an irritated Acheson wrote Arthur Schlesinger, Jr., in the midst of the controversy. "He ought to have a substantial raise."[4]

The notoriety of Acheson's speech in British newspapers and the "anguish," in diplomatic jargon, it caused at the Foreign Office and at Admiralty House (the temporary headquarters of Prime Minister Macmillan) forced the State Department on December 7 publicly to underscore two points. First, despite his sometime role as presidential adviser, Acheson on this occasion had spoken as a private citizen. Second, the general thrust of Acheson's discussion—support for British entry into the European Economic Community, increased economic cooperation by all Western nations, and a buildup of conventional military power in Europe—conformed to official State Department policy. Press Secretary Pierre Salinger added that President Kennedy had had no prior knowledge of the tenor of Acheson's speech.[5] Kennedy himself never publicly condemned the speech, but he approved a press release that said: "U.S.-U.K. relations are not based only on a power calculus, but also on [a] deep community of purpose and long practice of close cooperation. Examples are legion. . . . 'Special relationship' may not be a perfect phrase, but sneers at Anglo-American reality would be equally foolish."[6]

British pride had been too deeply wounded to be placated by State Department disclaimers. "He had stung us and we were temporarily numb," Acheson's close friend Sir Oliver Franks recalled.[7] Some British newspapers resorted to ad hominem attacks. The *Daily Express* denounced the American's "stab in the back." The *Sunday Times* hypothesized that Acheson's "tactless commentary" derived from America's success during the missile crisis, which must have "gone to his head." The *Daily Telegraph* noted that Acheson, who was always "more immaculate in dress than in judgment," was "extremely unlikely ever again" to hold high office.[8] The *Spectator* ruefully wrote: "In this transitional period . . . we have a right to ask that our friends should not make matters worse. It is the nature of nations diminished in power to feel humiliated when that fact is called to their attention."[9] The *Economist* alone refrained from blaming Acheson, saying his speech merely "sparked off what has always been the most disturbing feature of postwar Conservatism's inferiority complex; namely, the feeling that when in travail, it is an appropriate reflex to turn anti-American."[10]

Many of Acheson's British friends—for example, Sir Anthony Eden, Lord Patrick Devlin, Noel Annan, Desmond Donnelly, and Lord Frank Stowe-Hill—could not understand why Acheson had spoken so critically of their country and were concerned that his words would exacerbate anti-U.S. feeling throughout the United Kingdom. Acheson defended himself in a letter to Sir Frederick Leith-Ross: "Since both the *Times* and the *Telegraph* have printed my speech in full, you have seen that I did not deliberately start out to cause pain to my friends. In fact it was with great surprise that I found that a quite subsidiary sentence had been taken from a speech to a student conference, causing even the unflappable Mac [Harold Macmillan] to flap."[11]

The most galling phrase was "Great Britain has lost an empire and has not yet found a role." David Ormsby-Gore, the British ambassador to the United States at the time and an old friend of the president, was asked by the press what he thought of Acheson's remarks. The ambassador replied that many of its points were "much in line" with official British policy. Acheson, he pointed out, was pro-British; his record spoke for itself.[12]

David K. E. Bruce, the American ambassador in London, worked assiduously behind the scenes to calm Whitehall, emphasizing that except for the one unfortunate line, Acheson's speech was merely a reaffirmation of official Anglo-American foreign policy.[13]

Acheson had not foreseen the negative repercussions: "It had not occurred to me that a speech to a student conference would go ricochetting around the world in this way, nor furthermore, that the paragraph held the variety of meanings which seemed to be distilled from it," Acheson wrote Arthur Schlesinger, Jr. "Doubtless I should have known better." But Acheson meant what he said and never publicly apologized for his remarks.[14]

Unfortunately for Acheson, who was hoping the ruckus would subside quickly, Harold Macmillan had concluded that Acheson's comments had denigrated "the will and resolution of Britain and the British people" so thoroughly that they required an official response.[15] Although he understood that Acheson's remarks had placed Macmillan in an uncomfortable position, President Kennedy personally telephoned the prime minister to persuade him not to get drawn into a public debate that could only further damage Anglo-American relations.[16]

Macmillan decided he could not heed JFK's advice. He rebuked Acheson, in the form of a letter to the British public, printed in all the leading British newspapers, for committing "an error which [had] been made by quite a lot of people in the course of the last four hundred years, including Philip of Spain, Louis XIV, Napoleon, the Kaiser, and Hitler." He answered Acheson's assertion that Britain's "attempt to play a separate power role" was "about to be played out" by saying this applied to the United States and every other country in the West as well. "The doctrine of interdependence," the prime minister declared, "must be applied in the world today if peace and prosperity are to be assured."[17]

Macmillan also charged that Acheson had misdescribed the British Commonwealth as a sentimental organization without political structure, unity, or strength. "Mr. Acheson," the prime minister said, "seems wholly to misunderstand the role of the Commonwealth in world affairs." He feared that Acheson's denigration of Britain's world status would add to his government's difficulties in obtaining membership in the EEC.[18]

In retrospect, one can see that Acheson's speech received considerably more attention than it warranted because of the aspersion cast on the idea of the "special relationship" between the United States and Great Britain. "In his speech Acheson said quite rightly that Britain had lost her old role and was seeking a new one," recalled Sir Howard Beale, Acheson's friend and the Australian ambassador to the United States during the Kennedy years, "but in that inimitable way he sometimes uses in expressing words, he had given an impression quite unwittingly, which deeply hurt the feelings of the British people."[19]

To strike a blow at the special relationship was to attack the time-honored conventions of the Anglo-American relationship. Although many politically sophisticated Britons conceded that Acheson had said nothing that they themselves had not said privately, they were still angry that the former secretary of state made such remarks in a public address. Acheson accepted this criticism. "Macmillan came pretty close to saying the same thing when he said recently, as quoted by the *Washington Post*, that 'Britain could not expect to play a great power role in the new condition of the world,' " he wrote Francis Miller, special assistant to the Bureau of Educational and Cultural Affairs, Department of State. "But they are British and I, an alien. While they may justify my *Position*, I doubt, alas, if they justify my stating it."[20]

There was widespread speculation as to what motivated Acheson's remarks. Many attributed them to American cockiness in the aftermath of the missile crisis, although "cocky" is hardly the way Acheson felt. Others thought Acheson was a mouthpiece for President Kennedy, who was showing a typical Irish-American disrespect for Britain. The *Daily Mirror*, which had the largest newspaper circulation in Britain, emphasized that connection in an editorial in which it characterized Acheson as a key presidential adviser. The author noted that Britain had been "written off" by another American in 1940, "by a man who told Roosevelt we didn't have any hope in hell in Hitler's war." "That man," the editorial continued, "was President Kennedy's father—the rich, faint-hearted Mr. Joseph Kennedy, the American Ambassador to the Court of St. James in the days of Dunkirk."[21]

Not only had Acheson's ill-chosen words upset the British, who believed themselves consigned to a marginal role by Washington since the Suez war, but also they had raised questions about President Kennedy's political motivations. Some suspected that Kennedy had prodded Acheson into making the West Point speech as an attempt to damage Macmillan's government. These speculations were off the mark. Kennedy preferred the Conservative Macmillan, who favored—if somewhat reluctantly—British entry into the EEC, over the neutralist Labourites. He had no desire to hurt the Macmillan government. Asked years later by a graduate student whether he had been prodded by the Kennedy administration into making the speech, Acheson replied, "Nobody prods me, I prod myself."[22]

On both sides of the House of Commons, reaction to the speech was also strong. The Labour Party, led by Hugh Gaitskell, was slowly turning from the notion of joining the Common Market to pursuing a neutralist course. Labour interpreted pronouncements like Acheson's statement that Britain's future lay with Europe as interference in British domestic affairs. It was not Acheson's charge that Britain had not yet found a role in the post–1945 world order that irritated them. The source of their anger was Acheson's timing. His remarks—made just as Britain was experiencing a difficult transition period vis-à-vis Germany, France and other EEC members—weakened the country's bargaining position.[23]

There were exceptions to the prevailing critical view of Acheson's speech. "Your words of praise for the unfortunate West Point speech lost in the hurricane of British flap touched me and reassure me that, after all, it had a kernel of thought," a grateful Acheson wrote to Henry Kissinger, at that time a professor at Harvard.[24] Other friends offered their support. "Congratulations on your address at West Point and the worldwide attention which it aroused," wrote General Maxwell Taylor, the man who had recruited Acheson to deliver the speech. "You gave the cadets and their colleagues strong meat for their intellectual molars."[25] Felix Frankfurter wrote from the hospital, concerned about the clamor Acheson's speech had created. Acheson told Eugene V. Rostow, "[Frankfurter] has been very much exercised at the British press attacks on me, and worries a great deal about how to ensnare the Establishment so that we may subtly arrange for my reinstatement as a friend and not Public Enemy No. 1."[26]

Acheson's West Point speech is a useful occasion for reevaluating the common criticism of Acheson as too pro-British. In 1970 Chester Bowles tagged the former secretary of state as "one of the greatest Prime Ministers Britain ever had."[27] Many of Acheson's harshest critics, historians as well as his contemporaries, have given far too much weight to Acheson's Anglophilia; time and again Acheson has been seen, wrongly, as "more British than the British." This misperception stems from confusing appearance with substance. Acheson may have been brought up like an English gentleman, may have looked like an English gentleman, may have even talked like an English gentleman, but in reality he was a hard-nosed American pragmatist concerned primarily with enhancing his country's power and prestige abroad. There is no doubt that Acheson had a taste for British goods and style and an admiration for certain aspects of British political institutions, but there is no evidence that this admiration ever came at the expense of American interests.[28]

The historian Gaddis Smith has concluded that what Acheson admired most about Britain was its empire. In Smith's view Acheson wanted to create in the post–World War II period a loosely knit American empire that would replace Britain's declining construction. Acheson envisioned a global Monroe Doctrine—minus the Soviet sphere of influence—with the State Department emulating the role of the British Foreign Office as administrative overseer and protector.[29]

Acheson's debunking of the special relationship in his West Point speech was not an isolated, impulsive epigram. The statement is consonant with his longstanding views. From the time of the first postwar loans, Acheson always was among the first in Washington to counsel rebuffing British requests for special concessions. Acheson always felt Britain was a uniquely important partner of the United States, but this belief was accompanied by the recognition that it was an unequal partner and that "unique did not mean affectionate."[30]

Acheson's wariness was demonstrated in 1950, when he discovered that certain British Foreign Office and American State Department diplomats were drafting a paper defining the two countries' "special relationship." He immediately ordered all copies of the "wretched paper" destroyed. He thought that formalizing a privileged British position with the United States would perturb other allies, annoy the American public, and give "[Senator Joseph] McCarthy . . . proof that the State Department was a tool of a foreign power." No doubt constrained by his official position, Acheson did not call into question "the genuineness of the special relationship" but instead argued that "in the hands of troublemakers" the joint paper "could stir up no end of hullabaloo, both domestic and international."[31] In 1962 Acheson, no longer secretary of state, could take the gloves off and pummel the special relationship directly.

Near the end of his life Acheson got to the nub of his concern. "I've always thought that the special relationship was something which grew out of our past history and the fact that we spoke the same language, and that we had, to a very large extent, the same interests," he admitted. "That there was nothing basically political about it and that perhaps it was a mistake to talk about it at all."[32] Although one would be hard-pressed to explain why the grand Anglo-American collaboration of the Second World War was not "political," Acheson's criticism seems to be of sanctifying the special relationship.

A British friend once suggested to Acheson that if he favored a special relationship with another country it was West Germany, but Acheson emphatically denied this. "Please don't think I 'prefer' the Germans," Acheson protested. "No such suggestion can be found in the [West Point] speech; nor is it in my mind."[33]

A corollary of overweighting Acheson's Anglophilia is undervaluing his contributions to European integration. In fact, his eye was always on the larger picture—that is, Continental Europe—where a special relationship with Britain had no place and instead was perceived as an obstacle to the European Community movement. Acheson scoffed at the notion of a Pax Anglo-Americana in which Washington and London would run the world together.

One of the ironies about the West Point speech, however, was that Acheson had violated a cardinal principle of his own: Never criticize a NATO ally. John F. Kennedy, whom Acheson had chastised continuously for insensitivity to the problems of NATO members, did not turn the tables on Acheson; he refused to denounce him by name or to disassociate himself from the elder statesman.

The Skybolt Controversy and the Nassau Agreement

Late 1962 was littered with evidence of Britain's declining influence in America: lack of full consultation during the Cuban crisis and Acheson's West Point speech were prominent examples. London was also caught in a major defense crisis triggered by the Kennedy administration's abrupt cancellation of a promised air-to-surface missile called Skybolt, a weapon Britain regarded as essential for the Royal Air Force.[34] The British now perceived America as attempting to strip it of its recently acquired independent nuclear deterrent.

The Pentagon, led by Secretary of Defense Robert McNamara and armed with Acheson's NATO review of March 1961 and his cost-effectiveness analysis ($500 million had already been spent, and he projected that the weapon would cost an additional $2.8 billion), objected to independent nuclear capabilities for the European nations; they wanted the United States to maintain its nuclear monopoly. Ninety-seven percent of NATO's nuclear weapons were under U.S. control, for the United States had maintained that it was the only member with the technical know-how to manage them properly. The military was supported by President Kennedy and other civilian advisers like Acheson who also believed that a separate British nuclear force was superfluous, for it would duplicate what was already available for the defense of Europe and squander important resources. Therefore, shortly after the resolution of the Cuban missile crisis, McNamara, with the president's support, unilaterally cancelled the Skybolt program, which would have provided Britain with an independent intermediate-range missile. From the American point of view, the decision was logical and cost-effective, but it was another blow to British self-esteem. Britain had developed a hydrogen bomb and exploded it at Christmas Island in May 1958. The Royal Air Force, which could penetrate Soviet air space, thus had the capability to drop nuclear weapons. What Britain now needed was a long-range delivery system. The Skybolt missile would have allowed British bombers to attack from eight hundred miles off their target, well beyond the range of its opponents' air defenses.

Secretary of State Rusk had warned McNamara that the cancellation of Skybolt would cause the Macmillan government problems, but McNamara insisted that he would be able to iron them out with Britain's defense minister, Peter Thorneycroft. On December 7, in the midst of the furor over Acheson's West Point speech and before McNamara had had a chance to talk with Thorneycroft, the decision to cancel Skybolt was leaked to the press. When McNamara arrived in London to discuss alternative defense plans with Thorneycroft on December 11, he was met with an outraged British public, indignant over the dual affront from the United States. Thorneycroft maintained that Skybolt had been offered to Macmillan by Eisenhower in 1960 in exchange for the use of the Holy Loch Polaris base in Scotland. Now, after Britain had cancelled its own Blue Streak missile program on the strength of Eisenhower's promise, the United States was trying to renege. "This cancellation . . . went deeper than defense policy and went to the very root of any possibility of the British trusting America in defense dealings again," Thorneycroft reflected in 1966.[35] McNamara left Britain without reaching a new accord.

With this new strain in Anglo-American relations, Acheson's speech took on even more importance. "I suppose it was the coincidence of some reporter's coming across the sentence at just the time of the Skybolt incident that touched off the commotion," Acheson wrote in early 1963.[36] It would be up to Kennedy and Macmillan to try to revitalize British-American ties.

On December 19, 1962, Kennedy and Macmillan held a previously scheduled meeting at Nassau in the Bahamas to discuss both the status of negotiations for Britain's entrance into the EEC and the Skybolt issue.

Kennedy was met by a prime minister seething over American insolence toward his country. Macmillan, who wanted to reduce British defense expenditures without sacrificing his nation's pretensions to power, told Kennedy he could not accept Skybolt's cancellation, for this would surely dismantle his already wobbly parliamentary backing. Kennedy replied that the Skybolt program had been scrapped; the issue was not negotiable. To help the prime minister politically on the eve of British elections, Kennedy offered five Polaris missiles for British submarines on the condition that Whitehall pledge them to a NATO-wide nuclear force and not maintain an independent force of her own. Macmillan, though unhappy with the restrictions, realized that for political reasons he had to go along with them; he could not go home empty-handed. After negotiating an escape clause that permitted unilateral use of the weapons in case of a national emergency, Macmillan accepted Kennedy's watered-down offer, which became known as the Nassau Agreement, in order to save face and to camouflage yet another blow to British pride.

The Nassau Agreement was not a diplomatic success for Kennedy, however. The pact led to the abortion of his Grand Design for Europe before it had even begun to take shape. The replacement of Skybolt missiles with Polaris submarines provided de Gaulle with a pretext for vetoing British entry into the Common Market, which he did on January 29, 1963. The Nassau Agreement, de Gaulle declared, was clear evidence that Britain was more concerned with maintaining its incestuous ties with the United States, including the Anglo-American nuclear partnership, than with joining the European community. As an afterthought, Kennedy had offered de Gaulle Polaris submarines on the same terms as those accepted by Macmillan, but the general defiantly turned them down. He had not been consulted about the Nassau Agreement, so he would not accept any placating handouts from Kennedy and Macmillan.[37]

Four months after the West Point speech and the Skybolt controversy, Acheson was still embarrassed by the peculiar role he had played in the diplomatic drama. "As you have doubtless seen from the press, my purpose in life now is to make enemies," he wrote a young friend. "I shocked the British by accident, and really annoyed the allegedly phlegmatic people."[38] But the West Point speech was only one perturbation in a turbulent period of Anglo-American relations.

Britain had used the special relationship, coupled with plans for an independent nuclear deterrent, in order to maintain its image as a great power in a postwar order where the United States was dominant. The historian asks why Acheson's speech stirred such a commotion. It offered no novel insights; the decline of the British empire was obvious to everyone on both sides of the Atlantic. Nor was urging the British to reorient themselves away from the United States and toward closer integration with the European community a startling proposition; dozens of British statesmen had been saying the same thing for years. Acheson's speech had caused a stir in Britain simply because he had said aloud the unsayable: Britain's pretensions to imperial grandeur were illusions. And the United States was no longer willing to tolerate these illusions, which were sustained by Britain's bilateral orientation. London had to realize that, in American eyes, Britain was simply another European nation. Acheson's West Point speech, followed by Kennedy's cancellation of Skybolt, had shocked the British into realizing finally that their diplomatic self-image was unrealistic. Acheson erred not in saying what he did, but in saying it so bluntly.[39]

"Britain has lost an empire and not found a role" became a catchphrase used to describe nearly all of Britain's postwar woes. "One of the great troubles of the remark," Acheson told the journalist William Hardcastle in an interview for the *Listener* in 1970, "one which I struggled to overcome is that you must not be epigrammatic. The first requirement of a statesman is that he be dull. That is not always easy to achieve. And that statement suffered from being too epigrammatic and quotable. If I'd taken twice the number of words to express it, it would have been inoffensive and recognized as true at once. Since then it has been adopted by almost every British politician, though they have never given me credit for it at all."[40]

In his later years Acheson's dictum against criticizing NATO allies was honored often in the breach when it came to Britain. He openly scolded London for ordering economic sanctions against the white-minority government of Rhodesia. "Little England with a big mouth, and garnished with anti-Germanism," Acheson wrote Desmond Donnelly in 1966, "seems to describe a type which is a set-up for General de Gaulle."[41] Speaking before the American Bar Association in Washington in 1968, Acheson claimed Britain was involved in a conspiracy, "blessed by the United Nations," to overthrow Ian Smith's Rhodesian government.[42] In 1969 he charged that economic sanctions in southern Africa were a substitute for "the war Britain lacked heart and means to fight." The British by this time had developed some immunity to Acheson's goading barbs.

When asked in the House of Commons about these remarks, Prime Minister Harold Wilson responded that the charges were ludicrous. Wilson added, "Mr. Acheson is a distinguished figure who has lost a State Department and not yet found himself a role."[43]

French Nationalism versus the Atlantic Partnership

President Charles de Gaulle of France was not displeased about the Nassau Agreement, for it served to confirm his well-established doubts about allowing Britain entry into the Common Market. The agreement showed that the special relationship between the United States and Britain, the Anglo-Saxon conspiracy of which de Gaulle had complained since World War II, was alive and well. De Gaulle had begun to distance France from American hegemony in Western Europe as early as September of 1958, when his call for a NATO directorate in the form of a partnership among the United States, Great Britain, and France was squelched by Washington. By March 1959 he had withdrawn the French Mediterranean fleet from NATO's command and banned American nuclear weapons in France, while simultaneously initiating an independent nuclear force (*force de frappe*).

The Cuban missile crisis cemented de Gaulle's conviction that an independent nuclear force was the sine qua non of a great nation. France and, for that matter, all of Western Europe, could no longer rely solely on the American nuclear umbrella. Europe had to invent its own role vis-à-vis the two superpowers, and de Gaulle was determined that France lead the way with an independent foreign policy buttressed by an independent nuclear deterrent. De Gaulle also wanted to break out of the rigidities of the cold war game and reach détente with the Soviet Union.[44]

In the forefront of those working against the tide of archaic Gaullist nationalism was Dean Acheson. Acheson was viewed as the leading proponent of the new "Atlantic Partnership," the integrationist conception nourished by the persuasive power of Jean Monnet and his Action Committee for a United States of Europe (1955–75). Stimulated by Monnet's thinking and the committee's lobbying efforts, Acheson crusaded for the Partnership—greater European political unification within a larger trans-Atlantic framework that included British membership in the Common Market.[45] Acheson's advocacy took two forms. One depended on his direct access to the president. Whenever he had the opportunity, Acheson warned that the administration's frequent votes against European allies in the UN would weaken NATO and stall the European movement toward greater political unification. Acheson also used another avenue, his pipeline to the White House via like-minded thinkers such as George Ball. As under secretary of state, Ball, who had worked closely with Monnet on plans for the European Coal and Steel Community in the late 1940s and who later represented it and several other Common Market agencies in America, provided Acheson with a staunch integrationist ally in government. European friends—most notably Dirk Stikker and Jean Monnet—confirmed that Ball and his young deputy assistant secretary for European affairs, J. Robert Schaetzel, were respected throughout the Continent as experts on European trade policy and on the integration movement. So, throughout the Kennedy and Johnson years Acheson stayed in touch with both men in an attempt to influence policy and keep his thinking current. More than anything, though, it was the persuasive power of Monnet—who met with Acheson on March 3, 6, 13, and 18 of 1961 in Washington—that sparked Acheson's more visionary thinking on the future of U.S.–European relations.[46] Acheson and Monnet were working together again to launch a new institutional initiative: the Atlantic Partnership, which would unite the West by combining the two separate powers of the United States and a united Europe.[47] Acheson suggested to the president, through George Ball, that he invite Monnet to the White House to promote his Atlantic Partnership plan. This was a shrewd move; Acheson understood that such a meeting would remind Kennedy that de Gaulle spoke for only a fraction of Europeans and that the majority supported an economic and military partnership with the United States, Canada, and Great Britain. Kennedy was intrigued by the ideas of the Action Committee. In 1963 he would award the Freedom Medal to Monnet as the founder of the European Coal and Steel Community. Monnet was likewise impressed with Kennedy; his memoirs are filled with praise of the president's creative vision of the world and his strides toward achieving "an equal partnership between the United States and a united Europe."[48] Kennedy never shared Acheson and Monnet's extreme enthusiasm for an Atlantic partnership, however. He found it difficult to believe that transnational economic and military ties would in the long run prevail over narrow nationalism.

Monnet made another important three-week visit to Washington in April 1962 and began lining up appointments with highly placed friends in the Kennedy circle: Dean Rusk, Douglas Dillon, Walt Rostow, Henry Owen, McGeorge Bundy, J. Robert Schaetzel, and, of course, Dean Acheson and George Ball.[49] Monnet was on the circuit trying to sell his vision of partnership between the United States and a united Europe. James Reston of the *New York Times* wrote of Monnet on April 11: "He knows that there are immediate difficulties, but he assumes their solution and asks: What is the next step? And with the question he has at least started a quiet debate among some of the most powerful officials in Washington."[50] Working with Acheson at his P Street home in mid-June, Monnet put the finishing touches on a new Action Committee resolution which, given to Ball, Rostow, Owen, and Schaetzel, resurfaced in a slightly revised form in a major policy speech Kennedy delivered a week later.

In his famous Declaration of Interdependence speech at Independence Hall on July 4, 1962—to which at various draft stages Rostow, Acheson, Ball, Schaetzel, and Owen had contributed—Kennedy did promise that the United States would work with a united Europe to create "a concrete Atlantic partnership, a mutually beneficial partnership between the new union now emerging in Europe and the old American union founded here 173 years ago." The speech contained elements of the resolution issued during the previous week by the Action Committee. The resolution in many ways resembled the economic portion of Acheson's NATO policy review of 1961. The committee stated the following: "The economic political unity of Europe including Britain and the establishment of relations of equal partnership with the United States, alone will make it possible to consolidate the West and so create conditions for lasting peace between East and West."[51] Although Acheson liked both the resolution and Kennedy's speech, since he had a hand in writing both, he cringed at the phrase "equal partnership"; as a lawyer he had seen and been engaged in countless partnerships but never one that was equal, he declared.[52] Acheson had some private qualms about Kennedy's speech; it might be a sly attempt to obtain support for the Trade Expansion Act through New Frontier rhetoric. The act, which passed that August, gave the president authority to establish what amounted to a free trade zone embracing the United States and the Common Market.[53]

A month before the West Point speech in December 1962, Acheson wrote Monnet with a litany of complaints: weakness in the West, a U.S. dollar crisis, the hollowness of the Grand Design, de Gaulle's continuing anti-British bias, the mediocrity of world leadership, the slowness of the European integration process, and the endless crises in the Atlantic alliance that made the notion of a durable Atlantic Partnership appear unrealistic. Monnet disputed these bleak assessments.[54] But Acheson was growing pessimistic about the prospects for European integration. In a letter to J. Robert Schaetzel in April 1963, he noted that it was mandatory for Monnet to be optimistic. That was the purpose of the Action Committee: to promote all aspects of the European integration movement, to prod the Western leaders to think broadly and boldly. But although Acheson approved of its public relations activities, he thought Monnet's organization essentially weak, handcuffed by de Gaulle's obstructionism and by its own visionless bureaucratic members. De Gaulle had power; Monnet only had channels to like-minded people and could not counter the French president's continuing opposition to British entry into the Common Market. "Monnet and his people can help: they are good at organizing support for a new idea when the opponent is ignorance or inertia," Acheson wrote Schaetzel. "But they cannot lead against de Gaulle. They have no power base."[55] It had become clear to Acheson that Atlantic Partnership could not be fully developed until de Gaulle left the scene.

Acheson was writing out of bitter experience: on January 14, 1963, de Gaulle had stunned the Western world with the announcement that France would veto Britain's entry into the Common Market. De Gaulle gave three reasons for his decision: Britain's economic structure and monetary system differed from that of the six Common Market members, and it lacked the will to change it; the current member nations had more similarities with each other than differences, whereas with Britain they had more differences; Britain's admission to the EEC would be followed by applications from other nations, which if approved would lead to the formation of a "gigantic Atlantic Community that would be dependent on and be run by America."[56]

De Gaulle's position infuriated his Anglo-American allies, who thought him bent on undermining the Atlantic community and NATO. On January 29, six days after signing a bilateral treaty with Germany, France entered its official veto against British entry into the EEC, the only one of the six member nations to do so. These events brought to a climax a tumultuous period in postwar European history. In short order, de Gaulle had rejected JFK's Polaris submarine offer, turned his back on England, and embraced West Germany. His goal was to launch a new political alignment in Europe, based on the Paris-Bonn axis, that would counter U.S. hegemony while initiating an era of improved relations with the USSR.

Acheson believed that de Gaulle's actions had to be countered with a demonstration of unity within the Atlantic alliance. France must be reprimanded and persuaded to reconsider British entry into the EEC. "I have been hand-holding, encouraging, advising, and prodding on both sides of the Atlantic as General de Gaulle lowered the boom with such a resounding thud," Acheson wrote John Cowles. "Although the warning was ample and clear, no one thought the worst would really happen. . . . This threat is greater than that of last October [the missile crisis] and can't be handled with a blockade—or with bandaids. I have been sounding like a combination of Jeanne d'Arc and Henry V."[57] As Acheson saw it, the question was how to get de Gaulle to overcome his obsessive fear that the U.S. was trying to exercise control over NATO and had plans to absorb an expanded Common Market and turn France into an American satellite.

Some of Acheson's German friends asked the former secretary to contact Chancellor Adenauer personally to lobby against de Gaulle's announced veto, a tactic the State Department approved. "If anyone can affect General de Gaulle's decision you are surely that person," Acheson cabled Chancellor Adenauer on January 18. "I urge you to dissuade him from the disastrous course of breaking off negotiations with the British on their application to the Common Market. His indicated course will destroy the unity of Europe and of the West which you have so brilliantly and patiently worked to bring close to its pinnacle."[58]

Although Acheson could not dispel the chaos de Gaulle was wreaking on the alliance, he comforted himself with Jean Monnet's aphorism that the unification of Europe could only take a step forward in an atmosphere of crisis.[59] De Gaulle's vision of Europe, Acheson felt, held little appeal for other European nations, who would be less than enthusiastic about exchanging the French pipedream of renewed grandeur for American military and economic strength. De Gaulle's actions had done some damage, but Acheson did not believe they would change the course of Allied policy.[60] Acheson saw the Gaullist vision as resting on shaky grounds: one of de Gaulle's rationales for vetoing the British bid was that the six current Common Market members were not tied to an outside power by special political or military pacts. Acheson, on the contrary, "supposed that all six were tied to us or—at least equally important—that we were tied to them by the most special political and military pact in our history, one which reversed the whole course of our foreign relations since President Washington's Farewell Address—the North Atlantic Treaty."[61]

Undeterred by Acheson's efforts, de Gaulle turned his energies toward achieving Franco-German unity. On January 23, again to U.S. shock and dismay, he had signed a treaty with Chancellor Adenauer solidifying closer economic and military ties between their two nations.[62] Acheson had known that Adenauer was concerned about the Kennedy administration's commitment to Germany and that de Gaulle had been shrewdly cultivating his fellow conservative Catholic friend, but the treaty nevertheless came as a shock. "Chancellor Adenauer made a mistake—and I think a serious one—in signing the French treaty when he did," Acheson wrote to Dr. Kurt Birrenbach, an industrialist who was a CDU member of the Bundestag. "The Chancellor has never understood General de Gaulle's design [of French leadership in Europe] nor the undignified and demeaning role designed for him and for Germany. He has believed that his place in history would be that of the reconciler of France and Germany—a place long since occupied by Messieurs Schuman and Monnet. Neither nation has today the power, interest, or inclination to return to the futile hostilities of the past. His real role, if he but knew it, was to cement together Western Europe and North America."[63]

Since 1945, Acheson continued, the Western European countries had behaved toward Washington like "anemia patients with a blood bank.... We are happy that our friends are feeling so invigorated and confident that they class the United States with a host of other countries with which they do not wish to be involved. But we wonder whether General de Gaulle really expresses a view which Germans want the Chancellor to accept?"[64] American journalists as diverse in outlook as Walter Lippmann and James Reston joined Acheson in criticizing Adenauer's action.

Adenauer did not respond to Acheson's cable until after he had signed the Franco-German treaty. Then, in a detailed two-page confidential letter, he defended his action and maintained that he had previously procured the blessing of the Kennedy administration. "In some of the reports and articles [emanating from Washington], . . . the Federal Government and I, myself, have been criticized for having signed the German-French Treaty on January 22nd," Adenauer wrote Acheson. "Well, I had informed Secretary of State Rusk when he visited me last summer that we intended to establish closer ties with France; I asked him whether the United States had any reservations in this respect. Mr. Rusk answered at that time that the United States, of course, had no reservations, that, on the contrary, they would warmly welcome a close relationship between Germany and France and that they, themselves had special ties to Great Britain." Adenauer added that when he was informed in December that the treaty would be signed, the U.S. ambassador to Bonn, Walter Dowling, again conveyed American support of the Franco-German pact. "And now, everything is supposed to be interpreted in a different way because President de Gaulle, in his press conference on January 14, made his well known remarks on the entry of Great Britain into the EEC."[65]

Shortly after the treaty was signed, President Kennedy asked Acheson for a comprehensive analysis of why the Grand Design was coming unglued before it had even gotten started and what immediate steps the administration might take to counter de Gaulle's defiance and Adenauer's ambivalence. In "Reflections on the January Debacle," the sixteen-page memo he produced, Acheson called the chancellor's statements in his confidential letter preposterous. Did Adenauer really expect him to believe that the coincidence of the treaty signing with de Gaulle's remarks was merely fortuitous? Adenauer knew full well that de Gaulle was using Franco-German rapprochement as an instrument for reducing America's influence in Europe. Acheson wrote: "One cannot say that the West has not had ample warning [in Adenauer's summer meeting with Rusk] of the French and German action, yet it has been caught unprepared and been thrown into confusion. What was unexpected was not de Gaulle's wishes and desires; but that he acted, and acted so brazenly and revealingly. And what was surprising about Adenauer was that he acted so submissively in signing a treaty of Franco-German rapprochement and unity in effect as an acceptance of de Gaulle's anti-American, anti-Atlantic policy."[66]

Acheson urged the president to apply pressure on West Germany to make a choice between the United States and France, for the treaty was not immutable. To aid the Germans in understanding the long-term benefits of siding with the United States, Acheson recommended that they be provided with a written analysis of Gaullist policy and reasons why Bonn should reject it along with an in-depth prospectus of long-range political, economic, and military policies for European–North American collaboration. Acheson followed with his own detailed evaluation of the dangers posed by de Gaulle and a blueprint for strengthening the Atlantic alliance. The most important thing, Acheson told the president, was to reassure Bonn, in writing, that the United States stood firmly behind German reunification.[67]

Although Kennedy and Rusk concurred with Acheson's main objective—eliciting German disavowal of the recently signed treaty—they were not as enthusiastic as Acheson would have liked about the quid pro quo he was recommending. But given that de Gaulle was playing realpolitik poker and Germany was the stake, Kennedy decided it was advantageous to make use of Acheson. Who better to challenge the French leader than a distinguished American statesman known throughout Europe as a stalwart of NATO and a true believer in the Atlantic Partnership idea? "Any discussion we have on ... Germany," Kennedy instructed McGeorge Bundy in early February, "should include Dean Acheson."[68]

But as the months went by Acheson became more and more perturbed. Kennedy, he thought, was handling this crisis as he had Berlin and Cuba, by means of drift and indecision. "I have been carrying on a war on two fronts—one against the Chancellor in the Bundestag to minimize the damage caused by his stupidity in signing the French treaty when he did," Acheson wrote a friend in Düsseldorf, "the other, against my own government for its complete lack of perception of the intensity of German concentration on reunification and our silly dallying with Moscow over Berlin."[69]

There were also tensions over Adenauer's assertion in his letter to Acheson that Rusk had endorsed the idea of a Franco-German treaty and even had favorably compared it with America's intention to develop closer ties with Britain. Acheson thought Rusk was focused more on clearing himself of blame for the recent events than on meeting the crisis and altering its course. Instead of clearing his name, Rusk's lawyerly rebuttal of Adenauer's report of their conversation confirmed Acheson's suspicions that Rusk had made an inadvertent blunder.[70] "I did not refer in any way to any special relation with Britain in the context of the most general remarks about the importance of Franco-German reconciliation," Rusk wrote Acheson in an attempt to set the record straight with his former boss.[71]

Unconvinced that Kennedy and Rusk understood the urgency of getting Germany to reverse its course, Acheson, like a big-game hunter stalking his prey, pointed his pen and took aim at Charles de Gaulle, the true villain of the piece. In the January issue of *Foreign Affairs*, he published an article entitled "The Practice of Partnership," which examined the problems hindering better relations between NATO allies.[72] Acheson also supplied the White House with a detailed memorandum on how best to rattle de Gaulle's sublime self-confidence and to pressure him to terminate his plan to develop an independent French nuclear force.[73]

In early March Acheson set off for the university lecture circuit on the West Coast, this time with the specific aim of deflating de Gaulle and his anachronistic vision of a Europe united around one dominant nation-state. At his first stop, the California Institute of Technology, Acheson did not criticize de Gaulle by name.[74] But at a news conference following his lecture, Acheson explicitly stated that de Gaulle's vision of a Europe independent of the United States was "a mistaken policy." "We must press on with our policies," he continued. "I think he [de Gaulle] will slow things up . . . but it's no cause for despair." Sooner or later, Acheson said, Britain would become in effect, if not in name, a partner in the EEC.[75]

At his next stop, the University of California at Berkeley, Acheson lashed out at the French president in no uncertain terms. He warned de Gaulle he could not expect American military protection of a Europe that excluded American influence, although it was precisely this fantasy that undergirded the French president's notion of "a Europe from the Atlantic to the Urals" minus Great Britain. De Gaulle, buoyed by the first successful French atomic explosion in the Sahara in February 1960, envisioned a united Western Europe with conventional and nuclear power sufficient to balance the forces of Soviet-controlled Eastern Europe. But there was no possibility of actually attaining such a balance; a French nuclear force necessarily would be limited in both capacity for delivery and destructive power. In a crisis Europe ultimately would have to rely on American nuclear supremacy. De Gaulle's fatal error lay in believing that even after banishing the American presence from Europe, he could still, when push came to shove, rely on U.S. aid if he used his small nuclear force to start a war with the Soviets. Acheson characterized de Gaulle's policy as a "suicidal doctrine," for he sought the best of both worlds for his ideal Europe and assigned the worst part to America, and "it is difficult to conceive of any government in this country undertaking so unpromising a commitment."[76]

Acheson recited a list of optimal attitudes and actions for the United States: Remain confident that "the common allies" would not adopt de Gaulle's policy because it did not serve their common interest. (Europeans would realize that the United States was strong, while France was still "far from being a robust leader.") Base defense policy on an increase in conventional forces to deter Soviet expansionism into Western Europe; if the French delayed or frustrated NATO defense efforts, the United States would have to go forward "with nations able and willing to make progress." Maintain unequivocal support for German unification. Constant negotiations with the Soviets, he said, have "seemed to Germans to edge toward increasing recognition of the East German regime."[77]

The next day the Elysée publicly disputed Acheson's "attack," contending that a French nuclear force would be able to prevent Soviet invasion. The French, who viewed the tenacious Acheson as a stalking-horse for JFK, also claimed that Acheson had misinterpreted their attitude toward the alliance. De Gaulle, they insisted, believed in NATO but preferred national responsibility within the alliance to integration. Acheson's portrayal of the French position on the Common Market and on nuclear policy verged on caricature and was unworthy of serious response.[78]

France's leading newspapers had published the text of Acheson's Berkeley speech and debated the validity of its arguments. "I made the speech, in part, because of a curious modern phenomenon, the degree to which the French seem able to brainwash our correspondents in Paris," Acheson wrote Louis Halle. (He was referring to Cyrus L. ["Cy"] Sulzberger, Drew Middleton, and Crosby Noyes.) "The result is to give this country a mistaken sense of General de Gaulle's power. He has a considerable capability for doing harm or to block developments, due to the vital geographical position of France, as well as to the part which France has played in the history of Europe. But compared to the United States, France is feeble. It seemed important to put de Gaulle into proportion."[79]

In his "In the Nation" column Arthur Krock remarked that Acheson's warning to de Gaulle was "not likely to produce a fundamental change in French policy,"[80] but Krock was proved wrong, for by May the Gaullist vision no longer held sway in Europe. "I do not believe that the situation is as puzzling as the Administration appears to think," Acheson accurately noted to Truman early that May. "Germany is the present key to movement in Europe, and, I think, is ready to act with us."[81]

By the summer of 1963 it was clear that most in Bonn favored the Atlanticist vision over the Gaullist one and did not want to weaken Germany's ties with the United States: the Franco-German treaty had not been a commitment between two governments but rather the final act in the passionate fourteen-year political infatuation between de Gaulle and Adenauer. On June 26 President Kennedy made the historic speech in West Berlin in which he promised to defend free Berlin from Communist encroachment. His keynote phrase, "Ich bin ein Berliner," reverberated through the frenzied crowd. Shortly thereafter, the Bonn government added a preamble to the treaty with France that was widely interpreted as a reaffirmation of German ties to the United States and NATO. The Franco-German treaty slipped into oblivion, and the Kennedy administration gave a sigh of relief. At a dinner in July for French parliamentarians de Gaulle admitted he had been outflanked by the Americans. "You see, treaties are like young girls and roses; they do not last long," de Gaulle shrugged. "If the Franco-German Treaty is not to be implemented, it will not be the first time in history."[82] Although a rupture between Bonn and Washington had been averted, some commentators still believe that de Gaulle's announcement of January 14, 1963 marked the end of Kennedy's Grand Design.[83]

On September 18, 1963, Acheson spoke at The Hague before the European Movement, an organization formed in 1948 to promote European unity. Again he lashed out at de Gaulle's nationalist policies as a "lethal danger for both European and Atlantic unity" and characterized his views as "parochial nationalism."[84] Acheson's attacks on de Gaulle increased in frequency and sharpened in tone until the final crisis in 1966, when the general announced that France was pulling out of NATO's integrated military command. Acheson continued to describe Charles de Gaulle as "a great man" who "brought about a near miracle for France," but he deeply regretted and deplored "the havoc he wreaked on European unity."[85]

Disenchantment with Kennedy

By the time of the January debacle Acheson had lost all patience with the Kennedy administration's handling of both international and domestic affairs. The president continued to consult him on NATO-related matters and in February 1963 Acheson headed a special task force on the chronic payments imbalance and dangerous outflow of gold and dollars. But for his part Acheson was fed up with the "best and the brightest" crowd. "It seems to me interesting that a group of young men who regard themselves as intellectuals are capable of less coherent thought than we have had since Coolidge," Acheson complained to John Paton Davies. "They are pretty good at improvising; and, as Scotty Reston has observed, if we must get into trouble, it should be suddenly and unexpectedly, because they do best with this sort of a situation. But God help us, he says, if they are given any time to think!"[86] Acheson had lost faith in McGeorge Bundy, Robert McNamara, Walt Rostow, and Dean Rusk; in his eyes only George Ball and Paul Nitze, especially, had achieved the promise of their youth. "Paul Nitze's star is, I hope and believe, rising," Acheson wrote to Louis Halle. "It will be good for him, as he is now at the top of his capacity and needs to have all of it put to use. So does the country."[87]

Acheson adamantly was opposed to the administration's efforts to persuade Moscow to resume talks on a nuclear test ban, especially in the face of continuing crises in the Atlantic alliance. He doubted Moscow's bona fides. "Rusk spreads suspicion with his futile talks with the Russians," Acheson wrote Truman, "and, we continue to negotiate with ourselves in Geneva over a nuclear test ban which the Russians have no intention of accepting."[88] When the three-power talks (Britain, Soviet Union, United States) began in Moscow with Under Secretary of State for Political Affairs W. Averell Harriman representing the United States, Acheson shuddered. Didn't Kennedy realize that the more the United States negotiated with the Soviets, the more NATO was impaired, the more Bonn worried about a Moscow-Washington deal on Berlin, and the more determined de Gaulle would be to develop his own nuclear force? When the three powers signed the Limited Test Ban Treaty on August 5 prohibiting nuclear tests in space, the atmosphere, and underwater, Acheson wondered what possible gain Kennedy expected to achieve from the deal since de Gaulle had refused to sign the treaty. Kennedy had Acheson's promise not to lobby on the Hill against ratification of the treaty—which was regarded as the most important U.S.-Soviet agreement since the 1955 accord that ended the postwar occupation of Austria—but Acheson voiced his personal lack of enthusiasm for the test ban to John Cowles the day it was signed: "The way to win the Cold War may be difficult and unclear—though I am self-confident enough to believe that to plug away at the policies I have advocated since the end of the war will do it—but one thing seems to me as clear as day. That is that the one sure way to lose the Cold War is to lose Germany; and that the one sure way to lose Germany is to convince Germans that we are prepared to sacrifice German interests for an accord ... with Russia."[89]

In the fall, Dean and Alice Acheson traveled throughout Europe for five weeks. Acheson spoke at three large public occasions: a conference of the Dutch European Unity group at The Hague, a session of the Bundestag, and a meeting of the German American Club in Bonn. He also spoke at informal meetings, including a private session at the Institute of Strategic Studies in England attended by more than 150 defense experts from around the world, and had numerous private meetings with over a dozen high-ranking European government representatives.[90] While in Britain Acheson also tried to patch up old friendships derailed by his West Point speech. He told a friend that he found Britain in a ghastly state of decline, "moving swiftly to a Little England, almost Swedish position." France meanwhile, was in a "nationalist, anti-American—and if we act wisely—

isolated position," whereas Italy seemed wholly "self-concerned, prosperous and divided" but "hardly an international force"; only Germany, Acheson observed sadly, was subject to American influence.[91]

Before leaving for Europe, Dean Acheson had provided for Secretary of Defense McNamara a memorandum requested on the future of German-American relations. Acheson argued that America's policy of integrating and denationalizing Germany had achieved considerable success in the fifteen years since the creation of the FRG. At the present time the United States needed to be vigilant, for the good relations between the two nations brought about by the stability of the Adenauer era soon might be in jeopardy. Acheson pointed to "the emergence of a new German generation, untroubled by war guilt; increasing German preoccupation with the unity issue, and some doubts as to US intentions on this score; the retirement of the Chancellor and resulting vacuum in German politics; the heady example of de Gaulle's nationalism across the Rhine; and the slow down at Brussels—all contributed to make vocal those who are not in the way of grace and who believe that the Federal Republic now has a right and duty to look more to its own national interests." Acheson wrote that he did not fear "a revival of the Nazi movement, but rather the emergence of a Germany whose leaders are dedicated to national goals in the same sense that de Gaulle is."[92]

If a resurgence of German nationalism actually developed, Acheson believed, it would probably end the European unity movement. The British would view Germany with suspicion and hostility; the vitality and cohesion of the Atlantic alliance would be usurped, leaving German reunification to come about through a Soviet-German deal; and a new nationalist German government would seek independent negotiations with Moscow, as General Hans von Seeckt did after World War I. "You know my theme song only too well," Acheson wrote McNamara, "that Germany is the most important country in the world to us. It both holds, if not *the* key to Europe, at least a key, and is subject to be influenced by us in its use as the Soviet Union, France, and Britain are not."[93]

Although Acheson acknowledged that the FRG was still dependent on the United States for its security, he believed that this advantage would evaporate if the Christian Democratic party (CDU) was ousted from power by the pro-Gaullist Social Democrats (SPD). To keep the FRG moderate and compliant with American policies, the United States must decline to help France develop its own independent national nuclear capability and sell Germany on the MLF (multilateral force). This represented a reversal of Acheson's recommendation in his NATO review document of 1961. Acheson previously had been unenthusiastic about MLF, but given the French refusal to sign the test ban treaty, the NATO nuclear sharing proposal appeared the surest means of keeping Bonn from moving closer to de Gaulle's open arms and escaping the proliferation of national nuclear forces in Europe. Acheson was adamant about not helping France: should the United States opt to aid de Gaulle's nuclear endeavor, "it would set up an evident comparison between the independent nuclear forces which we would be helping France and Britain to achieve and the combined and *dependent* force which we would be asking Germany to join." Only by refusing to assist France—even if this meant yet another crack in the continuation of moderate, pro-American CDU leadership in the FRG under such leaders as Ludwig Erhard, Kai-Uwe von Hassel, and Gerhard Schroeder.[94]

Acheson went on to analyze internal German politics. Adenauer, recently forced to resign the chancellorship, due to an arrangement made in 1961 with his coalition partner, the Free Democrats, had refused to relinquish leadership of the CDU and was making life unbearable for the new chancellor, his fellow Christian Democrat Ludwig Erhard. Adenauer and Franz Josef Strauss openly were criticizing Erhard for his cold-shoulder attitude toward de Gaulle. If nothing was done to strengthen Erhard's hand, Acheson warned, the SPD easily would win election victory in 1965. The United States must "be prepared to suffer the slings and arrows of an outrageous General [de Gaulle] for sometime" in order to help CDU moderates maintain control of the Bonn government. Only if they were convinced that the United States was serious about developing a MLF in Europe would the West Germans chose Kennedy's Atlantic vision over de Gaulle's European one.[95]

Shortly after Acheson returned to Washington, President Kennedy asked for his views on the political climate in Europe with Adenauer and Macmillan newly out of office. Acheson related a story. The eighty-eight-year-old Adenauer, still steaming about being pushed aside, had scolded Erhard at the end of his two-hour inaugural address. "You're only going to be in office two years," he said, "and you took almost that long to say what you were going to do." Acheson told Kennedy, "The Germans are just different from everyone else. You have to treat them differently from everybody else." Adenauer died a few months later.[96]

Later that evening Kennedy repeated to Benjamin Bradlee, his close friend and *Newsweek*'s Washington bureau chief, his conversation with

Acheson. "I think Acheson . . . and Clark Clifford in a different way, are the two best advocates I have ever heard," the president said. "Acheson would have made a helluva Supreme Court justice, although he was sixty-seven or sixty-eight when I had my first vacancy."[97]

Although Acheson and Kennedy had policy differences, the two admired one another, Acheson somewhat begrudgingly. "Kennedy was very impressed with Acheson," recalls George Ball. "He retained that throughout, although they would occasionally get cross-wired. Jack was a little bit afraid of Dean. After all, Jack was a very young man and Acheson was a titan."[98] By spring of 1963 Kennedy had become somewhat more relaxed in his dealings with Acheson.

Acheson had been named by the Yale Club of Montclair, New Jersey, as the Outstanding Alumnus of Yale University, and a dinner was held in his honor in April 1963. Kennedy decided to have some fun with the occasion. He sent a telegram to Acheson at the dinner, praising the former secretary while at the same time getting in a few lighthearted jabs. He made reference to the honorary doctor of law degrees from Yale which had been awarded to each man in July 1962:

> As a member of the Yale Class of 1962, I am delighted to extend congratulations to Dean Acheson as he becomes the Outstanding Alumnus of Yale University. One of Mr. Acheson's own outstanding traits is his possession of an intimidating seniority, and it gives me some satisfaction that a year ago we were able to receive our advanced diplomas on the same platform. . . .
>
> As a Yale man I welcome this recognition, and as a Harvard man I want to assure Mr. Acheson of my reasonable confidence that in his new guise he will not be presiding over the decline of a first-rate power. It is fortunate for Yale that it has so long had so robust and experienced a leader as Mr. Acheson.[99]

The heavily Republican Montclair Yale Club roared with laughter at the president's telegram. "I particularly liked your attributing to me an 'intimidating seniority,'" Acheson wrote Kennedy in a handwritten thank-you note, "partly—I suppose—because innocuous characters like to imagine themselves impressively stern, but chiefly, I think, because of your own response to this alleged quality. Clearly no one is less intimidated by it than you are, and yet no one could have listened to the, perhaps, delusive certitude of my offerings over the past two years with more courtesy and close attention."[100]

When John F. Kennedy was assassinated on November 22, 1963, Acheson, along with the rest of the country, mourned. "No one knew what had happened," Acheson wrote a British friend. "We were like victims of an earthquake. Even the ground under our feet was shaking." But Acheson disputed the account of the emotional mood in America portrayed by the media. "Surely there was sorrow for the death of a brave young man and an inexpressibly gallant young widow and two utterly pathetic and heart-breaking children," Acheson wrote. But it was not the bewilderment attendant on losing a great leader, as it had been when FDR died, for Kennedy was not that. "It was fear from the utter collapse of all sense of security which lay at the bottom of the emotion."[101]

Acheson wrote to Jacqueline Kennedy, praising her for acting as "a symbol to us of what this sorrowing nation should be." Her stoicism brought to the country a much-needed "belief in the nobility of the human spirit."[102]

It was this quality of grace under pressure, the ability not to complain but to bear and endure life's hardships that Dean Acheson most admired in an individual; perhaps the same could be said of John F. Kennedy. Both also believed in courage—the courage to act boldly—but Acheson thought the debonair Kennedy only mimicked courage and was not inherently courageous, unlike Harry Truman, or himself. Acheson equally admired the ability to make firm decisions, a capacity General Marshall called "the rarest gift given to man." He thought that Truman had this gift.[103] Kennedy was too self-conscious, Acheson declared, too worried about what others thought of him. If action was over-deliberated, it was no longer decisive. This was Kennedy's fatal flaw, Acheson believed. From the Berlin crisis to the Cuban missile crisis to the collision with de Gaulle to the test ban treaty, Acheson found Kennedy's leadership wanting. Acheson acknowledged that Kennedy, like himself, wanted to beat back Soviet expansionist efforts and win the cold war. JFK, however, was not enough of a hawk; he often turned soft when the chips were down. On a personal level, Acheson had grown to like the young president and his ironic wit. He empathized with the president as he confronted difficult decisions, and he found Kennedy's foreign and defense policies light-years ahead of Eisenhower's. But Acheson still lamented what he saw as a continuing decline of presidential leadership since the Truman-Acheson team had left government.

Acheson believed Kennedy had drifted into what most considered foreign-policy successes. But at what cost? Kennedy seemed to equate averting confrontation with demonstrating strong leadership; to Acheson this represented timidity and mediocrity. The United States was the richest, most militarily powerful nation-state the world had ever seen. Its enemy, the Soviet Union, sought world domination. To Acheson's mind, there was no reason why the United States, with all its power and might, could not contain Soviet expansionism, develop an Atlantic Partnership, and win the cold war; all it would take would be single-minded resolve. But that resolve had to be undergirded by a strong, viable, and cohesive NATO and by American nuclear superiority. To Acheson, the Grand Design remained a direction rather than a policy, a prescription for the future rather than an honest-to-god program to be implemented. Kennedy, he claimed, was unable to commit himself to a real policy to unite the West beyond the veneer of exciting speeches about distant and vague goals.

In trying to please the entire world community, JFK had alienated several of America's European allies while reaping nothing but headaches from the developing nations. Kennedy was afraid to make enemies of the former colonial nations, and this showed lack of courage and of a sense of priorities. Great leadership, Acheson believed, rested on knowing who your friends were and who your enemies were, and then, with persistence and determination, working systematically to either co-opt or defeat your foes.[104]

An interview for the BBC in 1971 created yet another storm of controversy as Acheson gave a less-than-glowing assessment of John F. Kennedy. Although he was "attractive" and blessed "with real charm," Acheson declared, Kennedy was not "in any sense a great man." He explained, "I do not think he knew a great deal about any of the matters which it's desirable that a chief of state or a President of the United States should know about. He was not decisive."[105] Acheson, bound to the policies and attitudes of the bygone Truman era, was unable to appreciate that Kennedy had seized the mind and vision of a new generation and given it hope in America's future—even though the New Frontier rhetoric often outraced reality.

CHAPTER SEVEN

Repairing Cracks in NATO, 1964–67

The brief tenure of John F. Kennedy marked the starting point of a decade full of tumultous social change. His assassination on November 22, 1963, also brought an abrupt transition from East Coast elegance to the rough and tumble of politics writ Texas-style. If Acheson was unhappy with Kennedy's style of leadership, he found little solace in dealing with the often clumsy and heavy-handed LBJ.

At the same time, other large-scale forces were at work. The United States was faced with a serious dispute between two important NATO allies, Turkey and Greece, over the island of Cyprus. Dean Acheson would be called upon by the new president to preside over a futile attempt to solve the problem. Meanwhile, in the nearly two decades following the end of World War II there had been a robust economic recovery in Europe, and a new generation of leaders was arriving on the scene. Charles de Gaulle was forcing Europe to examine issues swept under the carpet during the convalescence from war: How could Europe shape its own destiny? What was the effect of American hegemony on the Continent? Was the superpower rivalry of the cold war necessary and did it have to be played out in Europe? Was America's commitment to European defense steadfast? De Gaulle's answers to some of these questions posed threats to the NATO Dean Acheson knew. And so, besides his proverbial prescription of American leadership to cure whatever ailed NATO, Acheson surprisingly began to favor MLF, as a means to help glue NATO back together. In another effort to regain the offensive from de Gaulle, Acheson proposed opening dialogue with the Warsaw Pact nations of

Eastern Europe. But this proposal went nowhere when President Johnson distanced himself from the suggestion.

A sea change in foreign policy bothered Dean Acheson and the other Europeanists. As a consequence of decolonization, more attention in the United States was focused on the emerging nations of Africa, and soon that focus would shift to the jungles of Vietnam. In the Achesonian worldview these areas were mere sideshows to where the real action lay—in Europe. Acheson's activities during the period from Kennedy's assassination through 1967, as the country became consumed by the issue of Vietnam, illuminate both his unwavering anticommunist convictions and his continued creative commitment to NATO.

Working for LBJ

Soon after Lyndon Johnson was sworn in as president on November 22, 1963, he turned to Dean Acheson for advice.[1] Johnson's immediate task was to reassure a nation stunned by Kennedy's slaying that government still worked and that he was in firm control of the country. Calling upon Acheson and other established statesmen for advice on foreign policy had symbolic as well as practical value, for it demonstrated continuity and stability in a time of turmoil and tragedy. For many, Dean Acheson embodied the Democratic legacy in U.S. foreign policy. He was viewed as a distinguished elder statesmen, along with such men as W. Averell Harriman, Robert Lovett, and John J. McCloy. Acheson brought not only unparalleled foreign-policy experience but also a sense of noblesse oblige to the task: he believed that it was his duty as a citizen to serve the president when asked.

Johnson had been profiting from Acheson's guidance since the late 1950s, when the former secretary's behind-the-scenes maneuvering had aided Johnson, then Senate majority leader, in the prodigious feat of steering through the Senate the most comprehensive civil rights bill since Reconstruction—the Civil Rights Act of 1957. Acheson had characterized the legislation as "among the greatest achievements since World War II and, in the field of civil rights, the greatest since the Thirteenth Amendment."[2] He helped Johnson to fend off liberal critics who predicted—accurately—that the act would not make it much easier for blacks to vote in the South. (Effective civil rights legislation would not be enacted until 1965, when LBJ was president.)

Acheson's imprint on the bill was considerable, from his legal advice on the bill's conception to his work for its passage, including his shrewd lobbying of the eighty-nine-year-old Democratic chairman of the Senate Foreign Relations Committee, Theodore Green of Rhode Island, and his advice on how to avoid a Dixie filibuster. The acceptance of his blunt recommendation to "dump part III" of the bill, which would have authorized the attorney general to institute civil actions for preventive relief in an array of civil rights cases, watered it down sufficiently to make the bill acceptable to Southern senators.[3] Together with Johnson's intimate friend Abe Fortas, Acheson crafted a realistic compromise bill that Congress passed, reshaping the perception of Johnson from that of a regional Southern politician to that of a Democrat of national stature. His civil rights credentials established with Eastern party leaders, LBJ began a drive for the Democratic presidential nomination in 1960. But if Johnson hoped to garner Acheson's support, he was in for a surprise.

Acheson continued to advise Johnson on an array of policy matters throughout the next several years, but eventually a rift of sorts developed. In early 1960 LBJ dispatched two envoys, former Kentucky senator Earle C. Clements and John Connally, soon to be governor of Texas, to Harewood to seek Acheson's backing for Johnson's bid for the presidential nomination. Although Acheson shared the Texas senator's staunch anticommunism, skepticism about the value of the UN, and advocacy of the flexible-response defense strategy, he told the emissaries that he had already committed himself to supporting Truman's personal choice for the presidency, Senator Stuart Symington.[4]

Johnson was hurt by Acheson's rebuff. He had assumed that Acheson naturally would gravitate to his corner. Johnson had courted the former secretary carefully since 1957, pouring on the flattery and supporting him on a number of Democratic Party and foreign-policy matters. Acheson, in turn, had provided the Texas senator with the legal, political, and foreign-affairs know-how of a seasoned member of the Eastern Establishment. Washington gossip had Acheson and LBJ forming a mutual admiration society with the ultimate purpose of transforming the party of Stevenson into the party of Johnson. This perception was fueled further by a series of statements by Johnson. For instance, asked in June 1959 what type of person he would appoint as secretary of state were he to become president, Johnson responded he "would like to see another Dean Acheson ... if he were first elected to Congress for two terms." "What I mean," Johnson elaborated, "is that you want a man who knows the world and who knows politics." Johnson often told Acheson—and the press—that the former secretary of state was "the most respected advisor I have."[5] Johnson regarded Symington as a mediocrity and concluded that Acheson was supporting him because of his unwavering devotion to Truman, at the expense of what was best for the party.[6]

Acheson and Johnson remained on outwardly cordial terms throughout the 1960 campaign, but the relationship was strained. During the Kennedy years Johnson occasionally called on Acheson to ask for advice or help with a speech, but Acheson usually begged off. In early 1961 LBJ asked him to write him a speech to deliver in Germany, but Acheson demurred, suggesting that instead he ask the able Europeanist Henry Owen.[7] "Their friendship rusted from 1960 right up until Kennedy's assassination," said the journalist Joseph Alsop in 1988. "Johnson felt that Acheson had snubbed him, while Acheson thought that Johnson was not so much an astute politician as a garrulous political operator."[8]

The exigencies of the assassination papered over their differences for the time being. A few days after assuming the presidency, Johnson phoned Acheson for advice on several pressing issues, including the formation of a commission to investigate the assassination. He dispatched Abe Fortas to confer with Acheson. Acheson believed neither Johnson's original plan to convene a state board of inquiry in Texas nor the star-studded federal commission advocated by others was the proper way to proceed. Instead, Acheson recommended that a group of senior state judges be named to a special investigatory commission, as they would have the time and concentration to get to the bottom of the assassination. The idea was quickly dismissed by Johnson. Outside pressure so favored what had come to be called the Warren Commission that LBJ was forced to capitulate.[9]

For Acheson, that final week of November, culminating in the media spectacle of Jack Ruby murdering Lee Harvey Oswald, JFK's accused assassin, was one of "horror and shame." "Tragedy was followed by the grossest ineptitude, incompetence, and sheer primitivism in Texas," Acheson wrote a friend. "To use a horrid word, the image of the United States as the world saw us was little, if any, better than that of the Congo [where revolutionary violence was running rampant]. The police and the bar of Texas have been a national disgrace."[10]

Although Acheson was relieved that Johnson had assumed control of the presidency in a smooth, confident, and professional manner, there was much that Acheson did not like about the new president—especially his foul mouth and constant double-dealings. Although he grudgingly admitted that Johnson was probably as well qualified as any person in America "to pick up the dead President's burden," his doubts were soon rekindled.[11]

On December 5, a day in advance of a scheduled meeting, Acheson had sent Johnson a seven-page memorandum outlining the essential do's and don't's of U.S. policy toward Germany. "Don't decrease our fighting strength in Europe; and don't talk about doing it," Acheson sternly warned. "Talk does only a little less harm than the actual withdrawal itself." Acheson also advised Johnson to discontinue the British-American-Soviet talks on Germany and not to help de Gaulle with his French nuclear program; pursuing either policy would only serve to alienate Germany. The Acheson "do's" boiled down to two overarching principles: continue working on the multilateral force (MLF) in Western Europe and do whatever is economically and politically necessary to help the Common Market prosper.[12]

Acheson had sent the memorandum to the president in advance so that Johnson would have time to prepare questions. McGeorge Bundy wrote a cover memo briefing the president on where the former secretary stood on foreign-policy issues:

> He is a determined believer in the "hard line." He sees Germany as the center of our policy and believes in paying no attention to General de Gaulle. . . . Acheson believed in action even during an election year (he remembers what Truman accomplished in [19]48) and he has little patience for less developed countries, the U.N., Adlai Stevenson, George Kennan, etc. He got along well with President Kennedy, although the President seldom took his advice but found him deeply stimulating. . . . After you see him you may want to see Averell Harriman who is at the opposite pole, if only to hold the liberal line.[13]

At the meeting Acheson, to his chagrin, found the president preoccupied with another matter. He entered the Oval Office to find Johnson pacing up and down, in a nearly uncontrollable rage because the Soviet Union had just denied permission for an American theatrical company to perform *Hello Dolly!* in Moscow. To make matters worse, the production's leading lady was a longtime friend of the president. The gall of those Reds, Johnson complained to Acheson in Texas barnyard language. No sooner had Johnson filled Acheson in on the details when an aide rushed into the office with a "crisis update." The "damn State Department," Johnson complained, had strongly advised against taking any action against the Kremlin. The president turned to Acheson: What should he do? Acheson replied that such a trivial issue was not worthy of the attention of the president of the United States. He had come there that afternoon to discuss Germany, the MLF, Gaullism, and other NATO-related issues. Expending executive time and energy over the cancellation of a play was absurd. "I don't care what the Russians think about *Hello Dolly!*," Acheson recalls saying. "And neither should you."[14]

The meeting turned briefly to American-European policy, but it was apparent to Acheson that the president still was preoccupied with *Hello Dolly!* Bewildered, Acheson left. (No sooner had he gone than Johnson ordered the stranded cast redirected to Saigon, to "show the Russians" by performing the musical for the American troops stationed there.) Johnson had behaved like the self-centered egotist Acheson always feared he was, unable to rise above the trivial. Even more worrisome was the aura of insecurity and amateurism emanating from the Oval Office. Acheson had learned years ago that with LBJ there was a direct correlation between bluster and self-doubt: the more bluster there was, the more doubt actually existed. Johnson, of course, also wounded Acheson's pride by his display of indifference to whatever the former secretary might have had to say about U.S. policy toward Europe.[15]

Johnson's attitude toward Dean Acheson was markedly ambivalent. Johnson respected the former secretary and agreed with him on most issues, but he refused to be awed by Acheson's formidable intellectual prowess. He made a conscious attempt to debunk what he saw as Acheson worship by the JFK entourage—McGeorge Bundy, Dean Rusk, Walt W. Rostow, George Ball, and other administration "elites." To demonstrate his immunity to Acheson's persuasive powers, Johnson often mocked the former secretary's aristocratic demeanor in front of journalists and cabinet members. "He used to raise his nose in the air in a haughty fashion and imitate Acheson's voice saying things like 'Mr. President, I will not succumb to your devilish ways,'" Joseph Alsop recalled.[16]

Part of Johnson's resistance to the Achesonian charm was his confidence that he understood what made the secretary tick. The secret was that Acheson was valuable because he was predictable. Press a button and out poured his vintage spiel: NATO was the pinnacle of postwar achievement, the backbone of the entire free world; its preservation and development must be the West's top foreign-policy priority if the cold war was to be won. Not that Johnson disagreed with any of this; for the most part he did not. But Acheson's invariableness, although useful to Johnson, diminished the president's respect for the former secretary.

Another source of Johnson's coolness was Acheson's membership in the East Coast Establishment, a derogatory term in the Texan's lexicon. The Easterners were a group he simultaneously venerated and loathed. The predictability of Acheson's strategic objectives, and thus his consistency as an adviser, made him one of LBJ's most useful unofficial foreign-policy spokesmen. If de Gaulle tried to cast aspersions on NATO, Johnson knew he could count on Acheson to counterattack. If the Soviets tried to stir up trouble in Berlin, Johnson knew Acheson would tell him to hold firm. Thus Johnson relied on Acheson not for innovative policy ideas and approaches but to reinforce his own cold war orthodoxy.[17]

Throughout his presidency, Johnson turned to Acheson as a foreign-policy sounding board, NATO watchdog, and special adviser and envoy. As he had in the 1950s, LBJ continued to pepper the former secretary with pictures of himself fulsomely inscribed, for example, "To Dean Acheson, a man of peace" or "To Dean Acheson, the American I admire most."[18] Following a lecture Acheson gave on American objectives in Western Europe at the National War College in January 1964, Johnson phoned to reiterate his support for the goals Acheson had enunciated. Acheson was unconvinced LBJ had read the speech and thought the president was trying to "butter him up" to make amends for their unpleasant *Hello, Dolly!* confrontation the month before.[19] The president flattered Acheson in public as well. At the conclusion of a White House affair celebrating NATO's fifteenth anniversary, Johnson introduced Acheson to the distinguished guests as "one of the great men of our time."[20] Acheson could not help but appreciate such gestures, although he recognized that flattery was part of Johnson's stock-in-trade, the gladhander's method of consolidating power.[21]

By spring, Acheson's initial disapproval of Johnson's presidential style had turned to grudging admiration for the remarkable job the accidental president had done in leading the country through the trauma of the Kennedy assassination. Acheson scouted the political landscape for a presidential candidate in 1964, only to decide that LBJ towered above all the rest. Acheson found the foreign-policy views of liberals like J. William Fulbright, Mike Mansfield, and Robert Kennedy intolerable. The Republican options were no better: Nelson Rockefeller ("a fatuous and rather cheap opportunist"), Richard Nixon ("cynical and bitter, . . . Everyman's enemy") and Barry Goldwater (who would "doubtless scare half the world . . . irreparably damaging . . . 'the American image' "). The candidates collectively appeared to Acheson "to have lost all semblance of

210 ▪ Cracks in NATO, 1964–67

intelligence."²² Johnson, despite glaring flaws, seemed the best equipped to be president. Acheson now saw himself as an important presidential adviser with a real stake involved in getting LBJ elected in November.²³ This allegiance was made apparent in July, when the State Department announced that Dean Acheson would go to Geneva as Special Representative of the President to "provide assistance that may be appropriate in helping to solve the Cyprus crisis."²⁴

The Cyprus Question

In February 1964, Under Secretary of State George Ball had asked Acheson to meet with him to discuss the far-reaching consequences of a dispute between two important NATO allies—Greece and Turkey. Although Acheson and Ball had had serious policy disagreements in the past (most notably during the Cuban missile crisis), they nevertheless maintained a deep mutual respect. Acheson's main political criticism of Ball was that he was too much the "soft," Stevensonian idealist, a peacemonger, as it were. But at the same time Acheson recognized that Ball was the most consistent and vigorous advocate in government of the EEC, NATO, the MLF, and the Atlantic Partnership idea. Acheson's respect was reinforced by the opinions of such leading European statesmen as Jean Monnet, Robert Marjolin, Dirk Stikker, Walter Hallstein, and Konrad Adenauer, all of whom viewed Ball as one of America's foremost experts on European trade policy.²⁵

At lunch the following day Ball asked Acheson if he would be available to "undertake quiet mediation," primarily with Athens and Ankara over the Cyprus conflict. Not only was Acheson a "brilliantly skillful negotiator," Ball thought, but he was also a legendary figure in Greece and Turkey, thanks to his key role in organizing and carrying out the 1947 Truman Doctrine (the $400 million aid program to the two nations that marked the transfer of Western leadership in the region from Britain to the United States).²⁶

More than most in Washington, Acheson knew that a Greco-Turkish war would not only create instability in the eastern Mediterranean but also shatter the cohesion of NATO and provide the Soviets with an ideal opportunity to undermine the organization's vulnerable southern flank. Acheson told Ball that he was at his disposal for this high-priority mission. He warned the under secretary that he should do whatever possible to keep the Cyprus mess out of the UN, a forum that would allow the

Soviets to nose into a NATO family feud. Ball said he did not have a specific assignment for Acheson yet, but he instructed State Department officials to begin briefing Acheson on the arcane complexities and nuances that made the Cyprus tangle a diplomat's nightmare.[27]

Following three centuries of Ottoman rule, in 1878 Cyprus became a British possession. Over decades Greek Cypriots persistently agitated for union with their mother country, and Turkish Cypriots reflexively demanded partition. In February 1959, following four years of intense struggle, the Republic of Cyprus was created. The governments of Britain, Greece, and Turkey signed the Zurich-London constitutional agreements, which provided for the independence, territorial integrity, and sovereignty of Cyprus and made Athens and Ankara co-guarantors of its stability. From its inception the new republic was plagued by the longstanding power struggle between the island's two main ethnic groups —Greek Cypriots (Greek-speaking Greek Orthodox Christians), who represented 80 percent of the population, and Turkish Cypriots (Turkish-speaking Sunni Muslims), who constituted 18 percent. Although the republic's new constitution provided for a pro-Western government, it did so by dividing the two communities educationally, culturally, and religiously. The constitution firmly rejected both the Greek Cypriots' demand for *enosis* (union) with Greece and the Turkish Cypriots' demand for *taksim*, that is, for creation of a relatively autonomous Turkish Cypriot territory within a loose federal framework.

Before the ink had dried on the Zurich-London agreements Greek Cypriots began complaining. The Greek Cypriot leader and first president of Cyprus Archbishop Makarios III took the lead in insisting that the new constitution was unfair to the majority. Makarios had been a reluctant signatory of the new arrangement, and his dissatisfaction was a forewarning of recurring instability to come.[28]

The new republic remained relatively calm for the next four years, until November 30, 1963, when President Makarios ignited a crisis by proposing thirteen new amendments to the constitution, all aimed at limiting Turkish Cypriot participation in government. The minority community, supported by the Turkish government, angrily denounced the proposals as an attempt to relegate those of Turkish descent to second-class citizenhood. When intercommunal violence erupted, the governments of Greece and Turkey entered the fray to protect their respective communities. Finally, on December 26, after nearly three hundred Cypriots, mostly Turkish, had died, the United States, Britain, Greece, and

Turkey achieved a negotiated truce. They created a British-patrolled neutral zone in the capital city of Nicosia. A British peace-keeping force was to patrol the island to prevent renewed violence. The cease-fire was short-lived. By the end of January 1964, despite LBJ's warnings to Makarios, local skirmishes mounted in intensity. Western leaders, at Britain's request, advanced a plan that would send a ten-thousand-man all-NATO force to the island for three months to oversee the observance of the cease-fire agreement. Since Cyprus was not a NATO member, this was seen by Makarios as a disingenuous plan to occupy his island nation with the aim of ending Cypriot sovereignty.[29]

To the Johnson administration's dismay, Makarios rejected the notion of a NATO peace-keeping force in favor of troops under UN supervision. He then turned to the Soviet Union to ask for support in case of a Turkish invasion. Many top State and Defense Department experts—including General Lyman Lemnitzer, the American commander of NATO, who had spoken recently to government officials in Ankara and Athens—predicted that if some sort of diplomatic initiative were not implemented at once, the United States would soon have a "Mediterranean Cuba" on its hands.[30] A crisis was at hand, and Britain had managed to hit the ball into Uncle Sam's court.

In early February President Johnson dispatched George Ball as his special representative to discuss the crisis with leading principals in Nicosia, Ankara, Athens, and London. After two weeks of shuttle diplomacy, a pessimistic Ball returned to Washington on February 16 to report to Johnson. "I believe the bomb has already gone off at Sarajevo and the archduke is dead," Ball wrote. "Both the governments and people of Turkey and Greece want peace, but they are like characters in a Greek tragedy. They cannot, by their own unaided efforts, avoid catastrophe. They can be pushed off a collision course only by some outside agency."[31] The president acknowledged the importance of restoring peace on the island in order to safeguard Western interests in the region. Washington found itself in the delicate position of trying to prevent war between two important NATO allies.

It was also vital, the State Department believed, to keep the Soviets out of what the West considered a fraternal conflict. Soviet interference in the Cypriot civil war—or even their continued support of Makarios—would serve only to undermine the peace process and turn Cyprus into an East-West battleground. Under UN Security Council Resolution 186, passed on March 5, a peace-keeping force was to be created and a mediator for the crisis was appointed. The resolution asked all states to refrain from interfering with Cypriot affairs. Makarios thought he had won a major contest against the United States in keeping his country from becoming a NATO protectorate. But Johnson ignored the UN resolution, as he had ignored the Cypriot president, opting instead to negotiate a Cyprus settlement directly with Greece and Turkey. Ball, frantically attempting to seek an alternative spokesperson to Makarios, found a candidate in an anticommunist hero of the Cypriot independence struggle, General George Grivas, who had recently reemerged from exile and apparently was willing to accept Washington's proposals in exchange for power. Ball also lobbied the Greek government to use its considerable influence over Makarios in order to stop his overtures to the Soviet Union.[32]

On June 22 and 24, the Turkish and Greek prime ministers, Ismet Inonu and George Papandreou, were invited to Washington to discuss Cyprus in separate meetings with the president. Johnson called Acheson in on both occasions to persuade the leaders to overcome their deep-rooted ethnic differences and consider the Cyprus situation as it related to NATO and the cold war. But, as George Ball notes in his memoirs, the two aging leaders "seemed incapable of comprehending the larger issues."[33] Inonu and Papandreou refused even to speak to one another, let alone to discuss a deescalation. Both men were dubious on their arrival about any U.S. role in the conflict. Inonu was shaken still by a harsh ultimatum sent by Johnson on June 5.[34] Papandreou had been suspicious about American intentions in Cyprus from the time he was elected prime minister in February 1964. Both left Washington even more doubtful that the United States could or should play a meaningful role in the ethnic conflict. The undaunted Ball pressed UN Secretary-General U Thant to endorse a new American mediation effort. The proposed meeting was to take place at Camp David, Maryland, between representatives of the Greek and Turkish governments. The Cypriots were not to be included, and the previously appointed UN mediator, Sakari Tuomioja of Finland, was to be replaced by Dean Acheson.

Although Acheson had been intimately involved in helping Ball review and evaluate possible settlement plans for Cyprus since February, U Thant balked at the idea of using Acheson as a mediator. The Burmese leader would not permit Washington to strip the United Nations of the diplomatic initiative. Moreover, Geneva, in neutral Switzerland, was clearly a more suitable site than the retreat of the United States president for delicate international negotiations. Ball reluctantly agreed to Geneva as the venue for the talks, but continued to assert that it was unrealistic to work for a settlement on Cyprus without an American mediator. U Thant made a partial concession. If Greece and Turkey did not object, Acheson would be allowed to "set up shop" near the site where the official UN negotiations were taking place; in this way participants could confer with Acheson as often as they saw fit. Ball grudgingly acquiesced to these informal arrangements, in the belief that "even in the wings, Acheson was such a strong personality that he could make his views felt."[35] Inonu readily agreed to have his delegates in Geneva consult with Acheson, and under considerable pressure from President Johnson, Papandreou reluctantly concurred. Johnson explicitly warned both prime ministers not to invade Cyprus while negotiations were proceeding.[36]

Acheson, accompanied by his wife and John D. Jernegan, the deputy assistant secretary of state for Near Eastern and South Asian affairs, left for Geneva on July 4. His attaché case bulged with briefing papers from George Ball, Phillips Talbot, and others at State on a number of possible solutions to the crisis. And thus, without formally supplanting the UN mediator and without recognition of the United States as the official diplomatic channel of negotiation, Acheson attempted to work out a settlement between two members of the NATO family.[37]

Thus, seventeen years after the proclamation of the Truman Doctrine, Acheson found himself in an unofficial role trying to save the nations the doctrine had originally helped—Greece and Turkey—from clashing over Cyprus. Archbishop Makarios, furious about the Geneva format, showed scant enthusiasm for Acheson's role. He correctly perceived that the ultimate goal of the United States was to dissolve the Republic of Cyprus. Makarios boycotted the conference, pointedly noting that although he respected Tuomioja, there were also in Geneva "certain self-invited mediators who have worked out unacceptable plans for solution of the Cyprus problem."[38]

On July 6 Acheson met with Tuomioja at the Palais des Nations to inform him that he was ready to assist in the negotiations. U Thant was under fire from both Makarios and Soviet Premier Khrushchev for allowing Acheson to participate. He issued a statement on July 9 stressing that it was up to Tuomioja to decide whether he needed "the assistance of anybody" and that the UN mediator was "free to seek the advice and cooperation of any member state."[39] Viscount Hood of the British Foreign Office also had arrived in Geneva to assist Tuomioja. Over the course of the next eight weeks Acheson and Hood often dined together, venting their frustration over Makarios's attempts at sabotage and the other obstacles they encountered in their difficult diplomatic assignments.[40]

Discussions began with Dr. Nihat Erim, an eminent professor of international law and chairman of the Committee on Foreign Relations of the Turkish Parliament, representing Turkey and Dimitrios Nicolareizis, a distinguished diplomat who at that time was his country's ambassador in London, representing Greece. However, it was the special presidential emissary from the United States, Dean Acheson, who was in command of the talks from the start.[41] By the end of July the so-called Acheson Plan had become the basis for all negotiations. His wide-ranging proposals fulfilled the wish list of all parties concerned, except one. The plan was ideal from the American point of view: it safeguarded U.S. interests in the region, provided Greece with its long-desired *enosis* with Cyprus, and created adequate guarantees for Turkish political rights and strategic concerns on the island as well. But to accomplish this feat the Acheson Plan had to ignore the Cypriots. The plan called for the demise of the independent Republic of Cyprus, and this provision Makarios, of course, could not embrace.[42]

Before negotiations began in Geneva, the State Department had concluded that the continuation of an independent state in Cyprus was a threat to American interests. Turkey was likely to invade the republic because of the treatment of ethnic Turks, and a Greco-Turkish war could follow, fracturing the previously good relations of both countries with the United States, strengthening the Soviet Union's position in Cyprus, placing a strain on the UN, and disrupting NATO harmony. For these reasons, and the more fundamental objective of wanting to bring Cyprus under direct NATO control, the U.S. government was convinced that the best solution to the Cyprus question was an end to Cypriot sovereignty.[43]

The Acheson Plan was also called "double *enosis*," a euphemism for the dissolving of the independent republic and carving up the island between Greece and Turkey. The plan contained the following general provisions:

1. The major part of Cyprus would be united with Greece.
2. Turkey would be granted a large military base on the island under a thirty-year lease, to serve as an important strategic outpost.
3. Cyprus would be divided into eight cantons, two of them to be established for the Turkish Cypriots, who would have full administrative control.

4. Greece would cede the small Dodecanese island of Kastellorizon (Meis) to Turkey. Turkish Cypriots wishing to emigrate would be resettled.
5. An international body would be formed with the responsibility of ensuring that human rights were not violated on Cyprus.[44]

The Turkish delegation accepted Acheson's proposals as the basis of discussion, but the Greeks were intimidated by Makarios's violent denunciation of the plan as a NATO trap. They publicly insisted on a settlement based only on the U.N. Charter that would guarantee "full and unrestricted independence that will afford the Cypriot people the right to decide freely on its future."[45] Acheson had offered the Greeks a way to finesse the issue of parliamentary approval of ceding a military base to Turkey via a secret NATO protocol providing for cession after *enosis* in the interest of allied unity and defense. Apparently neither Acheson nor the Johnson administration felt moral qualms about circumventing democratic rule in its very birthplace.

Acheson spent weeks trying to sell themes and variations of his basic proposals to Greece, but Papandreou ultimately rejected them all. Papandreou's intransigence incensed Acheson, for he had managed to convince the negotiators from both nations to accept most of his plan in principle. Convinced his measures satisfied the seemingly conflicting goals of *enosis* and *taksim,* thus eliminating the central source of interethnic tension, Acheson was angered by Makarios's undermining of his plan in Athens. Makarios was adamant about maintaining independence for Cyprus with no strings attached.[46]

Acheson regarded Makarios as a treacherous religious fanatic, "a political priest with considerable fits of demagogy and ruthlessness," and blamed Makarios for throwing "a monkey wrench into the machinery" of the negotiations.[47] "My Turkish and Greek colleagues became friends, if not of one another, at least of mine," Acheson wrote to Lucius Battle, then serving as U.S. ambassador to Egypt, "and we came close to an understanding which might have cropped the Archbishop's whiskers [Makarios had a long beard] and solved the idiotic problem of Cyprus."[48]

On August 7, Turkey sent a squadron of sixty-four planes to bomb Greek Cypriot forces that had besieged and threatened to overrun the town of Kokkina in northwest Cyprus. At least one hundred Greek Cypriots were killed and two hundred more wounded before the raids were halted by a UN Security Council cease-fire order a few days later. Although the Greek and Turkish representatives in Geneva returned to the negotiating table on August 14, the renewed violence on the island convinced Acheson his plan for Cyprus was dead. Two days later Tuomioja suffered a severe stroke, and a new UN mediator was called in to replace him; Acheson's instincts told him it was time to call it quits. On August 18 Acheson sent a telex to George Ball which noted that the odds of obtaining a settlement of the Cyprus question were "about the same as the odds on Goldwater [the Republican presidential nominee in the coming election]." It was time for him to return to Washington, where he would do whatever he could to prevent Cyprus from becoming "a Russian Mediterranean satellite."[49]

Ball was astonished: Was Dean Acheson really giving up? At 2:00 A.M. Washington time he was attempting to buck up Acheson's sagging spirits by teletype. Passing lightly over the Turkish bombardment of the prior week, Ball gave Acheson credit for successfully averting a Greco-Turkish war, persuading Papandreou to negotiate with Turkey, and toning down many of Turkey's earlier demands. "If the Geneva enterprise must die," Ball recalled telling Acheson, "its burial should be conducted not 'by an orthodox Archbishop but by the son of an Episcopal bishop,' which, of course, meant Acheson."[50] Ball had spent the early weeks of August trying to coax Makarios's archenemy, General Grivas, into accepting the terms of the Acheson Plan, and talk of a Grivas coup was in the air, so Ball was anxious to keep the talks alive.

Acheson agreed to stay on and try to find some magic solution to the conundrum. When Prime Minister Papandreou of Greece and President Makarios of Cyprus issued on August 25 a joint communiqué declaring that they wanted the Cyprus question handed over to the UN General Assembly in November, for all intents and purposes the Geneva negotiations finally had failed. Despite an encomium from Ball and Rusk saying Acheson had done a "superb job of establishing [the] confidence of both sides," the diplomatic deadlock in Geneva was a bitter pill for the former secretary to swallow.[51]

Acheson recognized that his proposals gave no voice to Makarios or the Cypriots as a group. He had gone out of his way, however, to woo Papandreou. Therefore, although it was understandable that the archbishop viewed Acheson's efforts with indignation, Papandreou, Acheson thought, behaved foolishly in rejecting the proposals on the pretext that the concession to Turkey was too high a price to pay. Acheson thought the prime minister seemed more responsive to the anti-American ravings of his irresponsible son Andreas and the whining of Makarios than to Lyndon Johnson's effort to avert war and contain Soviet expansionism in the region. "Our weakness was Papandreou's weakness, a garrulous, senile, windbag without power of decision or resolution," Acheson wrote Lucius Battle. "He gave away our plans at critical moments to Makarios, who undermined him with the Greek press and political left. A little money, which we had, the Greek 7th Division in Cyprus, which the Greeks had, and some sense of purpose in Athens, which did not exist, might have permitted a different result. The Turks could not have been more willing to cooperate."[52]

On August 31 the State Department announced that the Geneva negotiations had collapsed and Dean Acheson was coming home. Acheson stopped in London to discuss the Cyprus situation with R. A. Butler, the British foreign secretary, and Lord Louis Mountbatten, the chief of the defense staff. In a letter to a Turkish friend Acheson said that he had tried to reassure the British that at least the main points of his plan were still open and a settlement might still be possible. In reality he was deeply pessimistic; he expected a new explosion of violence on the island at any moment.[53]

Acheson was greeted by a swarm of journalists on his arrival at Dulles International Airport. He denied their assertion that the Geneva talks had broken down and instead called the dissolution a "recess." "We came a long way and covered a vast territory, and have greatly removed the differences between Greece and Turkey," he said. "Now we have come to a point where it is necessary to see where we are and where we are going from here." However, when asked what the future had in store for Cyprus, Acheson responded that the situation on the island was so grave that "war could break out in 25 minutes." Pushed to explain why the Acheson Plan had been rejected by Greece, Acheson put the brunt of the blame on Makarios, adding that the Cypriot president "has a rather intense dislike for me." The claim to Cypriot independence was reduced to a personality dispute.[54]

At a press conference the next day the president commended Acheson's efforts. "Although the situation in Cyprus . . . remains full of danger, all Americans can be very proud of Mr. Acheson's patient and skillful efforts to help find the honorable and peaceful solution. I believe when such a settlement is found, it will be clear that his work was a major constructive element in the process."[55]

Acheson was happy to be home. "Alice and I got back from Geneva where we spent two months in the worst rat race I have ever been in—trying to deny Greeks and Turks their historic recreation of killing one another," Acheson wrote an old Yale classmate. "When they really got going a month ago, they were unfortunately stopped before the Turks made a point which that bloody and bearded old reprobate Makarios badly needs to learn, that Turks are very dangerous people to fool with. It was an interesting experience from which I fear that I am not yet free."[56]

Acheson put together a report on his experiences in Geneva for the president, and on September 8 he met with Johnson, Rusk, McNamara, and Ball to discuss the impasse. Acheson told the group that "no negotiated solution was possible because of the weakness of Papandreou and the strength and intractability of Makarios." He believed a Turkish attack on Cyprus was imminent and argued that it was crucial for the United States to maintain the status quo, minimize the violence when it occurred, keep the Soviets out, and try to revive negotiations on the Acheson Plan, in its original form or with modifications.[57]

The Acheson Plan of 1964—a paradigm of great-power pressure in the arena of small-power diplomacy—would remain the basis for all negotiations over Cyprus for the next ten years. Acheson's proposals, disregarding as they did a small, troublesome but deeply divided state and its leaders, were a classic example of *realpolitik,* which has no place for the hopes and aspirations of a powerless and divided people.

For nearly a decade, a UN peacekeeping force was able to prevent full-blown war, until a Greek military junta overthrew Makarios in July 1974. The Turkish army responded by invading, and occupying northern Cyprus. The United States objected vociferously to Turkey's actions, and Congress, under pressure from the Greek-American lobby, imposed an arms embargo on Turkey, exacerbating tensions in U.S. relations with Ankara.[58] Partition of Cyprus was brought about by force. Into the 1990s the Acheson Plan remained the working model for U.S. negotiations over Cyprus, but no agreements were forthcoming and the Turkish army remained on the island.

Campaign Victory

On September 9, President Johnson announced that he was forming a permanent panel of sixteen senior foreign-policy advisers, including Acheson. Critics charged that Johnson had created the bipartisan panel to project an image of unity in foreign affairs for the upcoming presidential election. Acheson, not surprisingly, saw the panel as a sensible, innovative mechanism for approaching international problem solving.[59] From that time through March 1968, when the war shattered any semblance of order in the administration's foreign-policy hierarchy, Acheson was regarded as LBJ's unofficial NATO troubleshooter.

Some days later Johnson made another pointedly friendly overture to Acheson by conferring upon the seventy-one-year-old statesman the highest civilian honor, the Presidential Medal of Freedom. In the East Room of the White House, Acheson and twenty-nine other prominent Americans (including Aaron Copland, Willem de Kooning, Walt Disney, T. S. Eliot, John L. Lewis, Reinhold Niebuhr, Carl Sandburg, and John Steinbeck) received a gold medal and a presidential handshake while high-ranking government officials looked on. Acheson, who was asked to respond for the group of honorees, was impressed by the good company he was in that afternoon and grateful that the president had thought to honor him in this way. He continued to support the president, and he put himself at Johnson's disposal for the homestretch of the presidential campaign.

While Acheson was in Geneva, Barry Goldwater, the right-wing Republican presidential nominee, had attacked the cold war policy of containment first implemented under President Truman and had called instead for "total victory" over communism. Once freed from the obligations of mediation Acheson hastened to defend LBJ's foreign policy. In an op-ed piece in the *Washington Post* he attributed the Arizona senator's hyperbole to "the naiveté of inexperience."[60]

In short order Acheson praised the Tonkin Gulf Resolution for enhancing executive authority in foreign affairs, lent his name to the bipartisan National Lawyers Committee for Johnson-Humphrey, and joined another special bipartisan presidential panel, this one chaired by former under secretary of defense Roswell Gilpatric and charged with devising new policies to help prevent nuclear proliferation.[61]

Acheson also advised the president on a variety of foreign-policy issues during the course of the campaign. In a detailed memorandum he urged LBJ to support the Kennedy Round, a series of talks begun in 1963 and aimed at a mutual reduction of tariffs between the United States and the Common Market nations. He warned LBJ of potential political threats to NATO, first in Britain, where the electorate had turned out the Conservatives for the first time in thirteen years and installed Labourite Harold Wilson as prime minister, and second in France, from the ever-disruptive Charles de Gaulle.[62] Acheson also played morale booster for

LBJ. When the president gave a stirring speech in New Orleans, Acheson poured on the flattery: "It was a fine, brave speech, simple, clear and forthright, in the best American political tradition and temper."[63]

Johnson won in a landslide victory on November 3, securing the largest popular majority in history and 486 electoral votes to Goldwater's 52. "I wrote [LBJ] after the election to congratulate him, as I said, not primarily upon his majority, to which his opponent made a substantial contribution, but upon the achievement which was his alone of pulling together a shattered country and bringing us through grave troubles to a new unity," Acheson wrote to his friend Lady Pamela Berry. "Like all powerful men, he has his faults; and some are not small, including his vanity. But I believe the election will do him far more good than harm. It will not, I think, feed his vanity, but will give him assurance, which he sometimes lacks, and bring home to him the vast responsibility which has been placed upon him."[64] Acheson's hopes were shortlived.

Johnson—with Acheson's blessing—set about cleaning house throughout the executive departments and White House staff, weeding out many New Frontier appointees and replacing them with his own men.[65] Acheson had lost confidence in Kennedy administration holdovers Dean Rusk and McGeorge Bundy and was starting to sour on Robert McNamara. Nevertheless, he was dismayed by LBJ's abusive treatment of his most important foreign-policy subordinates. Sometimes, for instance, the president insisted they take dictation while he sat on the toilet.[66]

At one White House session Acheson bore witness to Johnson's boorishness, disrespect for others, and unconcern for protocol. The president ridiculed his top foreign-policy advisors. He chided George Ball for compiling a "disgraceful" list of ambassadorial candidates, he lambasted Robert McNamara for his ignorance of congressional affairs, he mocked Dean Rusk, and he insulted Dean Acheson by calling him "the man who got us into war in Korea," adding, "[we had to] get Eisenhower to get us out of it." As the badgering continued, Acheson's indignation grew. "Mr. President," Acheson finally interrupted, "you don't pay these men enough to talk to them that way—even with the federal pay raise." His comment caused a burst of laughter from all present, breaking the tension in the room. When discussion resumed, Johnson's voice had taken on a more respectful, congenial tone.[67] Acheson remained annoyed at Johnson's arrogance. "A gentleman whom we used to call 'Old Stone Face' is trying to look down his nose and elevate it at the same time," Acheson wrote Sir Patrick Devlin that December, referring to LBJ.[68]

Acheson thought that Johnson was so intimidated by Eastern Establishment intellectuals, Acheson himself included, that he had to resort to humiliating his own in an attempt to overcome his inferiority complex. He hoped to impress them and frighten them with his abrasive disregard of social niceties.[69] Acheson also became concerned that Johnson was obsessively preoccupied with public opinion, congressional support, and consolidation of domestic power and that he was neglecting Europe and failing to provide impassioned leadership for the free world.[70]

Acheson urged the president to take advantage of changes occurring in the Soviet power structure. In October 1964 an intraparty struggle had led to the overthrow of Premier Khrushchev by Aleksei Kosygin and Leonid Brezhnev. Acheson argued to the president that the power scramble in Moscow could be turned into a Western advantage, if only Johnson would "give direction to a Europe marked by economic affluence but having little sense of responsibility for world affairs." Khrushchev had "lost his job," Acheson wrote in another memorandum, because the United States had held firm in Berlin and forced the Soviet Union to back down during the Cuban missile crisis. It was now up to Johnson to press his advantage in a vigorous new campaign designed to showcase the American economic and military miracle throughout the globe, most particularly to the developing nations. The United States had the carrot and the stick and should not be afraid to use either on any underdeveloped nation toying with the idea of establishing a communist system of government.[71]

Despite Acheson's advice, over the next four years LBJ pursued a more conciliatory approach to Moscow—initiating credit-based grain sales; promoting cultural exchanges; holding meetings with Chairman Kosygin for two days in Glassboro, New Jersey; and, in 1968, signing a nuclear nonproliferation treaty with the Soviets. All of these experiments in détente occurred while the United States was enmeshed in the Vietnam War. Johnson's overtures to Moscow seemed ludicrous and hypocritical to Acheson at a time when American lives were being lost in a war aimed at containing communist expansion in Southeast Asia. But of more concern to Acheson was that LBJ's efforts toward a cold war thaw were sending confusing and contradictory signals to Western Europe, which already was losing faith in Washington's commitment to NATO and confidence in its ability to win the Vietnam War.[72]

Soon after the 1964 election, pundits as different in their thinking as Arthur Krock and Walter Lippmann began predicting an imminent "European crisis."[73] Acheson began showering Johnson with long, detailed memorandums on policy initiatives designed to enhance Atlantic solidarity. Acheson ticked off the problems: de Gaulle daily further distanced his nation from NATO; Britain's Labour government was more concerned with their balance-of-payments deficit than with bolstering NATO militarily; an important election was set for 1965 in West Germany, and Adenauer and Franz Josef Strauss were pressuring Chancellor Ludwig Erhard to adopt a Gaullist line; the dispute between Greece and Turkey over Cyprus was still unresolved; the Kennedy Round tariff talks were stalled; and there was a heated debate within the administration on the MLF. All of Acheson's memorandums of November and December urged Johnson to affirm publicly America's dedication to the Atlantic Partnership idea, the Common Market, and NATO.

One of Acheson's suggestions is surprising: he argued that allowing the Europeans to have a say in their own nuclear defense via the MLF would be the first step in knitting the allies back together. Acheson thought that certain Western European nations were approaching political disarray, but he predicted optimistically that fresh U.S. initiatives could easily reverse the deterioration. "The United States is the most powerful nation in the world, the most concerned with the broad international public interest," Acheson wrote to Johnson, who had publicly supported the MLF program in April 1964. "Our President has had the greatest endorsement of any leader in decades. And yet our press is calling for the reconsideration of policies which we have been following for years, because Harold Wilson and General de Gaulle, the first of whom has no influence outside of his own country and the second of whom has been trying futilely to block our policies, do not like them. All that is needed is a clear lead from you to set things straight and get us started forward."[74]

Five memorandums from this period reiterated three programs of action Acheson endorsed to keep the Atlantic alliance cohesive: developing a joint Atlantic nuclear force (some variation of MLF), while simultaneously working to control the spread of nuclear weapons; holding more frequent meetings between NATO ministers and even creating a new Atlantic Assembly or "directorate," as McNamara soon would call it; and moving toward more effective trade policies by pressing ahead with the Kennedy Round.[75] All of these steps, Acheson wrote Johnson, were "solidly based on the principle that collective, not national, action is the key to progress."[76]

LBJ paid serious attention to the MLF enthusiasts in the administration (including Acheson, Ball, Bruce, McNamara, Henry Owen, J. Robert Schaetzel, and Gerard C. Smith) but ultimately decided against going ahead with the NATO nuclear force, deeming it unrealistic for several reasons for an American president to push for a strategic program of this sort. By and large, the allies seemed lukewarm about it, partly for reasons of cost. Johnson also had concluded, after consulting with senators Henry Jackson, Clinton Anderson, Mike Mansfield, and J. William Fulbright, among others, that the Congress would overwhelmingly reject MLF. Liberals opposed giving Germany even a semblance of control of nuclear weaponry, for that would hinder disarmament proposals; conservatives wanted America to maintain its nuclear monopoly. Johnson was also influenced by McGeorge Bundy, who thought MLF was unrealistic and unnecessary. Bundy at first viewed the Atlanticists in the administration with mild derision, but as the MLF debate grew, he pejoratively dubbed these Eurocentric statesmen "theologians" for constantly preaching the Jean Monnet gospel of Atlantic Partnership. Bundy unearthed a memorandum he had written for JFK in 1963, remarking to Johnson that Kennedy's reaction to it was, "If the Europeans don't want it, then the hell with it." Johnson decided that would be his attitude, too.[77]

At Dean Rusk's suggestion the president placed the burden of MLF's future on the Europeans; he asked London and Bonn to hammer out an agreement between themselves. If they could come up with a new mutual defense program—something along the lines of Harold Wilson's Atlantic Nuclear Force (ANF), which included a vast array of weapons sharing, from British V bombers to U.S. Polaris submarines—the United States would be glad to consider it. But until such a time Washington would remain noncommittal. Thus, for all practical purposes MLF was stillborn; the United States continued to maintain unilateral control of all nuclear capabilities in NATO. Contrary to Acheson's recommendation, Johnson had made clear that MLF would not be the focal point of U.S. nuclear policy toward Europe. Chancellor Erhard continued to push hard for MLF, but within nine months even he had given up.[78]

Acheson and the other so-called MLF theologians had lost an important battle. They decried LBJ's refusal to lead the Atlantic alliance. Johnson "told Wilson and Erhard to go off and work out their differences together, which of course they were unable to do," Acheson complained to Sir Anthony Eden. Acheson saw Johnson as too stubborn and narrowminded, too much the parochial politician to be educated in European affairs. By July 1965 the president had become engulfed by the Vietnam

War and by his civil rights and Great Society social programs. European affairs were relegated to the back burner, and there they would stay, to Acheson's dismay, for the remainder of the Johnson presidency. "LBJ tends to concentrate where the most noise is coming from," Acheson told Eden. "The way our system works, instruction in foreign affairs does not play much of a part in the education of prospective presidents."[79] The consummate Europeanist had lost an important policy struggle, but he did not give up trying to persuade the president that European integration and Atlantic cooperation, not victory in Vietnam, should be America's foreign-policy priority.

Morning and Noon

In early 1965 Acheson was pessimistic about the world situation. "We have troubles at home and abroad and handle most of them like clumsy plumbers," he wrote Noel Annan, the provost of King's College, Cambridge. "Our neighbors, the Canadians, seem to be held together with string and safety pins and a flag to end all flags. Germany is in really bad shape. A good many of the cracks in Weimar are appearing in Bonn. My office has become a wailing wall for visiting German friends. Mon General [de Gaulle] alone seems happy over the approaching troubles which will engulf him, too. Italy, Turkey, Greece, Britain—all are in the grip of painful circumstances. But I shall not become a one man wailing wall myself."[80]

Although Acheson stayed in touch with Ball, Bundy, and Rusk and was on the record books as a presidential foreign-policy adviser, he had not conferred with the president once between December 1964 and March 1965. Acheson dropped a not-so-subtle hint to Johnson that the time was ripe for the president to seek his counsel on European affairs. "The strategy of the Great Society—the most dynamic idea in the world today—is inseparable from foreign policy, and especially from the world's second greatest producing area, Europe," Acheson wrote LBJ on March 15. "Europe can make the Great Society, here and elsewhere, possible, or by narrow policies, slow it or prevent it. Trade, agriculture, finance, politics—all come back to European cooperation."[81] Apparently buoyed by his memo to the president, Acheson wrote Noel Annan on the same day: "Already some of us are at work to get LBJ out of his fixation on Alabama and Vietnam and back on to the even more—or, at least, equally important problem of leadership in Europe."[82]

On March 31 Acheson fired off another memo to LBJ urging him to commission a new NATO review—modeled after the study Acheson had undertaken for JFK in 1961—to "get the facts straight about Europe as a whole" before disaster struck the alliance and America was caught unprepared. Johnson's noncommittal reply promised to discuss the memorandum with Rusk, McNamara, and Bundy but hinted that Acheson's proposal would be superfluous, as Ball already was overseeing an interdepartmental study along similar lines.[83]

And so the seventy-two-year-old Acheson, already depressed by the death of his dearest friend, Felix Frankfurter, on February 22,[84] found himself snubbed by the president. The fiftieth reunion of his class at Yale, a visit to Missouri to see Truman, and the honor of christening the nuclear submarine the *George C. Marshall* were tonics to a year that had begun dismally, but chronic stomach ailments and a worsening thyroid condition that affected his eyes contributed to spring doldrums.[85] Acheson dealt with his melancholia by lending his literary talents and legal expertise to George Ball, who was working on peace plans for Vietnam,[86] and completing a memoir of his Connecticut childhood and the early years in Washington when he had worked for Brandeis and FDR. The memoir, *Morning and Noon*, dedicated to the memory of Felix Frankfurter, was published that October.[87]

Although somewhat buoyed by the success of *Morning and Noon*, Acheson remained deeply troubled by LBJ's obsession with Vietnam and hesitancy toward action in Europe. The president, Acheson believed, was unable to understand that the United States was capable of undertaking many commitments at once. He related an anecdote to an interviewer in 1969 to underscore his view. "I remember my father had a mythical Mississippi steamboat that he always used as an illustration," Acheson said. "This steamboat could not go upstream and blow the whistle at the same time. It didn't have enough steam. Now, the United States has got enough steam, we can have a European policy, we can have a Vietnam policy, we can have a domestic policy."[88] Acheson did not believe that the United States needed a larger federal budget to assert itself globally; it merely needed more vigorous executive leadership. His experiences at various White House meetings throughout the summer of 1965 left Acheson exasperated at the lack of a can-do approach to foreign policy and at Johnson's penchant for "endlessly reconsidering decisions" while simultaneously feeling victimized by the press and the liberal wing of his own party.[89]

In April 1965 in violation of the Organization of American States charter, President Johnson dispatched five hundred U.S. marines followed by more than 22,000 combat-ready soldiers to the Dominican Republic in an effort to protect American and other non-Dominican citizens and to prevent the island nation from turning communist.[90] Many Americans were aghast at Johnson's unwarranted intervention and charged that the president's fear of another Cuban-style revolution had led him to overreact. Acheson, however, was impressed by LBJ's decisive action to thwart what he thought was an attempt by Castro and his Dominican puppet Juan Bosch to make the country a Cuban satellite. He wrote Erik Boheman, the former Swedish ambassador to the United States, that LBJ had given the "Lilliputians a healthy reminder that the threads with which they have been trying to bind Gulliver for twenty years don't even bother him when aroused. This realization upsets the liberals and intellectuals; but has brought considerable relief in Latin America."[91]

Acheson thought LBJ ought now to tackle other international dilemmas with equal energy and decisiveness. The Dominican success, to Acheson's disappointment, did not inoculate the president against self-doubt, and a scant two months later LBJ, under criticism from the press, was second-guessing his decision. He called his advisory panel together for a three-hour session on Europe, Latin America, and Vietnam. "Finally I blew my top," Acheson wrote to Truman, "and told him that he was wholly right in the Dominican Republic and Vietnam, that he had no choice except to press on, that explanations were not as important as successful action; and that the trouble in Europe (which was more important than either of the other spots) came about because under him and Kennedy there had been no American leadership at all."[92]

Acheson, likely smarting from LBJ's decision to sideline MLF, pulled no punches at this White House meeting. To allow the Europeans to formulate their own nuclear policy was foolish and served only to strengthen de Gaulle's freewheeling, independent foreign-policy and defense postures. Acheson had grown hoarse warning LBJ of the French president's corrosive effect on NATO. "Time—and the General—will not stand still while we wonder whether this is the moment to save the Alliance," Acheson wrote in a letter to the *Atlantic Community Quarterly* in November. "We probably have only until early in 1966 either to assert the strong leadership required or else face difficulties greater than any yet experienced in the Atlantic Alliance."[93] In a talk delivered the following week Acheson predicted that de Gaulle soon would insist that all NATO forces on French soil come under French direction; as it turned out, he underestimated de Gaulle's boldness.[94] Through his friend Chip Bohlen, Acheson knew that studies were underway at the Quai d'Orsay on modifications in the various Franco-American bilateral agreements on U.S. bases in France. Nonetheless he was totally unprepared when the general brazenly announced that all French forces were being withdrawn from NATO's two integrated military commands—Allied Command Europe (ACE) and Allied Forces Central Europe (AFCENT)—and that NATO headquarters would have to be moved from Paris. An unprecedented crisis was at hand and at stake was the very survival of NATO. De Gaulle's tactics once again catapulted Dean Acheson into action.[95]

The France-NATO Crisis of 1966

On March 7, 1966, Charles de Gaulle sent President Johnson a handwritten letter outlining his reasons for removing French forces from the integrated NATO military system and for ousting all foreign troops and most NATO installations and bases from French soil. De Gaulle had been telegraphing for years his belief that NATO had outlived its usefulness. As opposed to the situation in 1949, when the North Atlantic Treaty was ratified, Western Europe was now economically sound; the Soviet Union appeared to be less of a military threat; France had nuclear capabilities of her own; and a nuclear balance of terror between the Soviet Union and the United States had replaced the American nuclear monopoly. France had extended diplomatic recognition to Communist China in January 1964. De Gaulle was adamantly opposed to America's involvement in Vietnam and feared that Washington would try to draw NATO into the conflict. Nevertheless, he stated unambiguously that, although he was pulling his country out of the NATO organization, France would not leave the Atlantic alliance proper "unless events in the years to come were to bring about a radical change in East-West relations."[96]

President Johnson immediately designated Dean Acheson as senior consultant for a study of the long-term implications of the French withdrawal. Acheson was assigned a private office in the State Department, complete with staff, and was asked to begin drafting, in consultation with the other thirteen NATO allies, a joint reply to France, reaffirming the allegiance of the remaining members to NATO and to the principle of Western military integration and collective defense.[97]

On March 16 and 17, LBJ summoned Acheson to the White House, along with Rusk, Ball, Deputy Secretary of Defense Cyrus R. Vance, Ambassador to France Charles E. Bohlen, and Assistant Secretary of State for European Affairs John M. Leddy to discuss the crisis. Bohlen, whose antipathy to the general's policies matched Acheson's, led off the first day's discussion by explicating the French motivation for the withdrawal. He advised the president to comply with de Gaulle's "tall order" that all NATO forces in France be removed and bases closed by April 1, 1967.[98] Johnson agreed with Bohlen that Washington should respond to de Gaulle's "fervent nationalism" with "restraint and patience" and not, as the Pentagon was recommending, with a direct challenge to the request on technical and legal grounds. "When a man asks you to leave his house," Johnson told McNamara, "you don't argue; you get your hat and go." LBJ was against letting himself or his advisers be drawn into a direct confrontation with de Gaulle, preferring to let the French president bear total responsibility for the crisis.[99]

Acheson agreed with Bohlen, but to the surprise of many at the meeting, he minimized the military damage the French withdrawal would cost NATO. His major worry was that the virus of independence could spread to West Germany and other NATO nations. It would be impossible, Acheson believed, "to persuade, bribe, or coerce" the French president; therefore, the allies should use the crisis to bolster and perfect the NATO system.[100] He told the group what he would tell Congress that April: only by maintaining military integration could the NATO nations both withstand a major Soviet attack with conventional weapons and guarantee that there would not be a revival of West German militarism.[101]

Throughout the end of March and early April, Acheson and the other top foreign-policy advisers tried to find symbolic ways to "contain" the damage caused by de Gaulle. This was done through upbeat press briefings and by sending a constant stream of reassuring State Department telegrams to European leaders. On March 22 Johnson sent the maverick general a wistful letter in which he expressed the hope that de Gaulle would reconsider his expulsion order.[102] At a ceremony on April 4 celebrating the seventeenth anniversary of the signing of the North Atlantic Treaty, he refrained from criticizing de Gaulle or even mentioning the French withdrawal; instead he extolled "the years of peace" that the integrated-command system had brought to the alliance.[103]

If the president was reluctant to attack de Gaulle personally, Dean Acheson was not. In a television interview with Marvin Kalb later that same afternoon, Acheson called de Gaulle's criticisms of the alliance system "utter nonsense." "Once you take away the very protection that has made Europe grow and prosper and be wealthy and happy," Acheson argued, "all the dangers come back again." Both de Gaulle and Adenauer had been behaving irresponsibly in saying of the Red Army, "Ah, you see the tiger is just lying there perfectly quiet and purring, it isn't doing anything." Naturally the tiger appeared docile, for he was caged, "but if you took the bars away, I wouldn't want to be out in front. The bars are NATO." Asked about de Gaulle's contention that the integrated NATO command only served to enhance America's hegemony over Europe, Acheson scoffed: "It's a curious situation of a recovered patient, a convalescent who has been weak, who has been ill and has finally been built up and had good food and good care, been in a warm house and warm bed and suddenly he says: 'I'm a big man, I don't need anymore food, no more doctors, no more house, I want to get out in the wind and the rain, the ice and the snow. I don't need any of this protection.'"[104]

Acheson contended that de Gaulle had decided to make his "atavistic" demands in March because he planned a state visit to the Kremlin in June and did not want the other Western nations to view his actions as a quid pro quo offered in exchange for Soviet support of his political visions. De Gaulle, Acheson asserted, clearly was not going to Moscow "to have a pleasant glass of vodka with some of the Russian leaders" but to establish closer political and economic ties with the USSR.[105]

Whether Johnson had given Acheson the green light to criticize de Gaulle is unclear, but the president apparently did not discourage him, for throughout the spring Acheson continued to speak out against the French withdrawal. In private, he attacked the Gaullist worldview as an anachronism. "De Gaulle seems bent on undoing the past twenty years," Acheson wrote Desmond Donnelly. "It is not merely an argument about the organization of NATO. He wants the Americans out of Europe—bag, baggage, and troops—and the Entente Cordiale revived. To him the enemy is Germany (and perhaps the U.S.) and must be put and held in place by the Triple Entente. He is not aware of the European Revolution or that the British, French, and German empires of his youth are gone. Nor does he seem to understand that the USSR has power and ambitions unknown to Imperial Russia."[106]

By the end of April Acheson's public condemnation of de Gaulle was being echoed by George Ball, Dean Rusk, John J. McCloy, J. Robert Schaetzel, and U.S. Ambassador to NATO Harlan Cleveland. An all-out anti–de Gaulle offensive was under way. Using diplomatic channels, congressional hearings, and the news media to get their point across, this formidable team of Atlanticists began a public relations offensive in hopes of convincing French voters to reject de Gaulle's stance in the 1967 French parliamentary elections. In the process they hoped to cement cohesion among the fourteen other NATO allies, particularly among the United States, Britain, and West Germany.[107] Acheson wrote most of the anti-French speeches and notes that poured from the State Department that spring.

Assault on de Gaulle

Acheson took his campaign to save NATO to Congress on April 27. He testified as the lead witness in hearings on the Atlantic alliance before a Senate subcommittee on national security chaired by Senator Henry M. Jackson of Washington. Acheson testified that de Gaulle's France was not now "a dependable or an effective ally," and he recommended the United States follow an "empty chair" policy in response. "We should keep her place ready and work for her return." He added that there was a strong uneasiness in France over de Gaulle's radical policy of "isolation," which aimed at eliminating the American presence in Europe by undermining NATO's military arrangements.[108]

Senator Milward L. Simpson asked about the durability of the French decision. Acheson replied that he did not think the French policy would survive without de Gaulle. Senator Edmund Muskie asked Acheson why he thought de Gaulle had not removed France from the North Atlantic Council proper. Acheson stepped into de Gaulle's shoes to speculate: "If I were to go to Moscow [in June] to try an independent policy, it would seem to me there would be advantages in shaking myself loose from any possible connection with the effective part of NATO, but still retaining church membership in it. This has advantages both ways. It recommends one to a new ally or new friendship. You are both in and out. This is not a bad position diplomatically to be in."[109]

Acheson went on to cite what he termed errors in an article by Max Frankel that had appeared in the *New York Times* that morning. Frankel declared that Dean Acheson had persuaded George Ball and Dean Rusk to shelve indefinitely the idea of joint sharing in NATO's nuclear defense.[110] "The attitude attributed to me is fantastically wrong," Acheson testified. Responding to Senator Robert F. Kennedy's probes regarding the future of MLF, Acheson said that what was under current consideration was not

MLF but Britain's Atlantic Nuclear Force (ANF), adding that in recent months London had started backing away from her own proposal, while Bonn was moving toward it. There is a "minuet going on here," Acheson noted, and the Johnson administration was looking to West Germany and Britain to agree first. Acheson noted that he personally believed that joint management and ownership of some type of allied nuclear weapons system under NATO was desirable, but he demurred when asked to comment on the official position on nuclear sharing.[111]

Senator Jacob Javits raised a different subject: Why were purportedly loyal NATO allies like Great Britain and West Germany not supporting the Johnson administration's Vietnam efforts? Acheson said it was a mistake to "crybaby" about being alone in Vietnam and to "nag" the allies for more help: "I think the fact has to be faced that the European nations are not interested in Vietnam. They don't understand it. It is a long way off. France had its try and it missed, and is now opposed to the part we are playing, and the others just don't want to be bothered. We wish it were otherwise, but it is not. I think if we try to mix too much up in NATO we will weaken and not strengthen the arrangement. It would be fine to have help but they are not disposed to it. . . . We are the only power that has a sense of world responsibility. This is too bad but it is a fact. The fact of the matter is that these other powers, which were great, are no longer great powers."[112]

Acheson characterized as inexcusable the Johnson administration's failure to consult Bonn about the temporary transfer of fifteen thousand U.S. troops from West Germany to Vietnam. Such protocol failures only gave credence to recurring European fears, fed by de Gaulle, that the United States would never risk a major war on the allies' behalf and that Washington was using NATO for her own hegemonic purposes.

Later that day Acheson also testified before a House subcommittee on foreign affairs. Following White House directions, Acheson stressed in his opening statement that NATO was more than a static anti-Soviet defensive alliance; it was also an innovative political organization prepared even to engage in an "imaginative and conciliatory" series of discussions with Eastern Europe. What NATO had in mind in this regard, Acheson told the committee in a bid to outflank de Gaulle by publicly hinting at the possibility of establishing better relations with the Warsaw Pact nations, was eventually to develop a "good neighbor policy" in Central Europe. "The time has arrived to enter a new era for NATO, an era of vigorous creative actions," he declared.[113]

The congressmen questioned Acheson as if he were the Oracle of Delphi; if Dean Acheson did not know what the future had in store for the NATO alliance, who did? The *New York Times* chose to interpret Acheson's remarks on Eastern Europe as indication of a major policy shift by the Johnson administration—turning from a defensive posture to an attempt to present NATO as a potent, forward-looking organization.[114] Acheson cautiously shared the interpretation of the *Times*: "We are presently engaged in a series of studies aimed at strengthening the Alliance through improved consultation, a reorganization of the Organization and an agreed strategy in Europe," he wrote Kurt Birrenbach on May 26. "How successful we will be remains to be seen, but I am optimistic—particularly since de Gaulle's recent moves, hopefully, have reduced France's ability to prevent change."[115]

Acheson's lucid and optimistic testimony helped to reassure Europe of the American commitment to NATO and helped mold domestic opinion against France. It received widespread media attention. The American press lauded Acheson's commanding performance as a refreshing reminder of the durability of NATO itself.[116] For a few days NATO received far more media attention than the killings in the far-away hamlets and garrisons of Vietnam. The Acheson-led Europe-firsters had taken the offensive and gotten their point across: de Gaulle was a temporary nuisance whose grandstanding was inconsequential.

Some senators and journalists disagreed with Acheson's assessment of de Gaulle's motivations. Senators Mike Mansfield, Frank Church, and J. William Fulbright, and columnist Walter Lippmann, for example, praised de Gaulle for, in Lippmann's phrase, "opening the valve" to long-needed changes in NATO.[117] Acheson tried to persuade LBJ not to pay any attention to that "silly ass" Fulbright and the other de Gaulle devotees.[118] "For more than two months now I have been working full time for Dean Rusk, trying to take off his shoulders the problems created for NATO by General de Gaulle," Acheson wrote Anthony Eden in May. "What a tiresome creature that man [de Gaulle] is. Just as we had gotten to the point where NATO might have turned some of its attention to devising a sensible political policy for Central Europe, we are thrust back into military improvisation. If this weren't trouble enough, all the so-called liberals in this capital city, led by Walter Lippmann, castigate everyone who does not give three cheers for de Gaulle every morning at breakfast. I can also remember times when the Government of the United States was what we horsemen call 'more collected' than it is today."[119]

Acheson was running himself ragged as quarterback of the NATO public relations campaign. "I am too old to work as hard as I have been doing," Acheson wrote his friend Sir William Elliot.[120] He was rankled that Rusk seemed so unconcerned about what Acheson called the "Battle of the NATO Bulge."[121] "I recommended Rusk to Kennedy when he wanted to appoint, of all people, Fulbright, and had high hopes of him," Acheson wrote Truman in October, after he had stepped down as senior NATO consultant at State. "He had been a good assistant to me, loyal and capable. But as number one he has been no good at all. For some reason, unknown to me, he will not disclose his mind to anyone. The Department is totally at a loss to know what he wants done or what he thinks."[122] Acheson had tried to compensate for Rusk's apparent indifference by assuming control of the crisis response within the State Department, but he found he was spinning his wheels to some degree: "I have also learned that in order to run things it is a help to have the power as well as the thoughts."[123]

Acheson spent the remainder of May and June heading an interagency crisis management group, for which he wrote various top-secret position papers, memos, and speeches on U.S.-NATO policy for the president, only to have LBJ distance himself from Acheson's positions.[124] "While I was doing my best to advise him [LBJ] on NATO, and while he was writing messages and making speeches I wrote for him, he was circulating rumors in the press that my views were not his," Acheson wrote Truman. "If they were not, a half hour's talk could have gotten us together. . . . I never did find out what he wanted done differently."[125] At Senator Jackson's suggestion, Acheson also ghost wrote a "forward-looking letter," which Harry Truman agreed to sign, underscoring the former president's staunch advocacy of NATO.[126] The NATO loyalists and State Department Atlanticists were taking advantage of every opportunity they could to bring their message of continued commitment to Europe home to the American people.

After nearly four months of "unrequited toil" without pay as a State Department "volunteer," Acheson submitted his resignation to Dean Rusk on July 15.[127] He had done all he could to avert a Gaullist chain reaction, and on the whole, the transition to a NATO military command without France was accomplished smoothly, facilitated by the fact that no other member challenged the premise that Atlantic solidarity remained the essential element to the national security of each. "My chief duty since the NATO crisis began—besides helping Rusk on that dreary and discouraging job of moving [transferring headquarters from Rocquencourt,

France, to a complex near Brussels], etc.—has been to get prepared, cleared, presented to and decided by the President a series of policy questions regarding Europe, our relations with our allies there, and what we hope NATO might be inspired to be and do," Acheson wrote Dirk Stikker. "This has been pretty well accomplished."[128]

If Acheson left his temporary assignment buoyed by the other NATO members' disregard of de Gaulle, he still was "frustrated," unconvinced that Rusk had a firm grip on the situation. "There must be an easier way of doing things than those presently in vogue," Acheson wrote Lord Richard Casey.[129] With George Ball preparing to leave the State Department soon, Acheson was concerned that European policy would become even less of an administration priority and that his action-oriented long-range NATO position papers would end up gathering dust in some file cabinet in Rusk's office.[130]

Rusk wrote Acheson in response to his resignation: "I have received your letter of July 15 with mixed feelings—deep gratitude for all you have done, regret that we may not be seeing so much of you for a while. Your wisdom and counsel during this sticky period for the Western Alliance has been tonic for all of us. You have tied all the loose strands together into a coherent pattern when it would have been easy for us to have diffused our energies."[131] In a letter to Anthony Eden Acheson angrily commented on Rusk's commendation: Rusk had been secretary of state for over five years, Acheson asserted. *He* should have been the one tying all the loose strands together. "I have not seen the [State] Department so disorganized since the end of the [Cordell] Hull regime."[132]

Johnson also wrote Acheson to thank him for his service and perfunctorily to reassure him that his administration's Atlantic policy "will reflect your papers."[133] Over the next two years Acheson would get an occasional word in about NATO to LBJ at White House meetings, but the president ignored the point of Acheson's message; Vietnam was his obsession. Acheson continued to crusade for NATO and the Atlantic Partnership idea, but after the spring of 1966, no one seemed to care. Asked by a student in October 1967 what he thought about the French, Acheson responded with characteristic candor: "We [Americans] have inbred a sort of Methodist dogoodism. That isn't shared by France, who are the most . . . selfish people in the . . . world, which doesn't mean they aren't the most civilized. They are. But they won't part with a franc for anything. The French are both the greatest creative force in Europe and the greatest nuisance."[134] An interviewer inquired in December 1967 what would happen to the Atlantic alliance if de Gaulle renounced the NATO treaty. Acheson snapped, "France is worth nothing to NATO—absolutely nothing whatever—and NATO will be improved by the absence of this France rather than helped by it."[135] Harsh words from a former secretary of state who always promoted Atlantic harmony, but an America absorbed in Vietnam paid scant attention.

CHAPTER EIGHT

The Vietnam War, 1961–68

In dealing with Asian policy Dean Acheson was never as ideological or dogmatic as John Foster Dulles. Indeed, most of the Asian hardliners in the 1950s—for instance, Henry and Clare Boothe Luce, William Knowland, and Walter Judd—were the very "primitives" he had beaten back, in the MacArthur hearings and elsewhere, at great personal and political cost. Acheson made his decisions case by case: no to intervention in China's civil war, yes to countering the invasion of South Korea, no to attempting through the war to unify Korea and no to threatening China, yes to aiding the French at Dienbienphu, no to the creation of SEATO (the Southeast Asian Treaty Organization), and no to possible war over what he deemed the meaningless islands of Quemoy and Matsu.[1]

Acheson's positions on Asian issues were shaped by two axioms: First, the United States should not get mired in areas of the world that were of considerably less strategic importance than Europe. Second, the Soviet Union, not China, was Washington's chief adversary. Acheson, unlike many on the Republican right, even as he grew more conservative was too knowledgeable to regard the Soviet Union and China as one communist monolith. As the text of his well-known Press Club speech of January 12, 1950, makes abundantly clear, Acheson was aware of the historical antagonism between the two countries and worked to exploit this friction. (Likewise, he encouraged support of Marshal Tito of Yugoslavia, who had broken away from the Soviet bloc.) He nevertheless believed failing to stand up to communist pressure on developing nations would erode confidence in the United States throughout the world. Thus, when North Korea invaded the South in 1950, he argued that the United States had to act firmly and decisively. Although he regarded Ho Chi Minh and the Viet Cong as more under Chinese than Soviet influence, Acheson also thought that Premier Khrushchev had targeted Vietnam as a testground for his "wars of national liberation" policy. Acheson subscribed to the domino theory in Asia and so pushed the necessity to contain Mao Tse-tung's expansionism or Khrushchev's adventurism wherever they arose.[2]

Throughout the Kennedy presidency Acheson paid scant heed to the growing U.S. presence in Southeast Asia. He was well aware of the seriousness of the internal strife in Vietnam and of the possibility that Kennedy might have to dispatch combat troops to fight communism in the region, but his focus was on strengthening the Atlantic community.[3]

With the assassinations in November 1963 of John F. Kennedy and Ngo Dinh Diem, the fiercely anticommunist Catholic president of the Republic of Vietnam since 1955, two new leaders, Lyndon Johnson and General Duong Van Minh (Big Minh), assumed power.[4] Johnson was able to effect a smooth transition by following his predecessor's already well established domestic and foreign agenda, including the supplying of advisers and military aid to Vietnam. In late 1961 Kennedy had initiated the Strategic Hamlet counterinsurgency program, under which by late 1963, sixteen thousand "combat support" troops had been dispatched to Vietnam. Big Minh, an inept pro-American figurehead, could not consolidate support for his regime and came under daily attack from opposition military groups. Secretary of Defense McNamara flew to Saigon at Johnson's behest in late December 1963. He found Minh's government disastrously weak. The Viet Cong had made considerable inroads in the South. McNamara concluded that the United States might well have to increase its military presence should the situation continue to deteriorate. Instability and deeply rooted pessimism prevailed in Saigon as 1963 ended. A coup in January 1964 toppled Minh's wobbly government, a scenario reenacted seven times during the next year.

Prologue to Escalation

As Lyndon Johnson assumed the presidency, inheriting the Vietnam quagmire, Acheson offered no novel advice on how to deal with Ho Chi Minh. He believed that no matter how difficult the situation might appear, the United States had the resources and power to save South Vietnam from falling into Hanoi's hands—just as American power had succeeded in the "almost exactly analogous" situation in Korea when Acheson was secretary of state—so long as U.S. resolve and determination remained firm.[5] Tugging in the opposite direction was anxiety at the prospect that the Administration would be trapped into spending much of its time on Vietnam, at the expense of European affairs and domestic problems.

In early February 1964 LBJ authorized a covert operation known as OPLAN 34A, which was designed to force North Vietnam to withdraw from South Vietnamese territory. The tactics, for the most part unsuccessful, were continued throughout the spring. During this time Acheson was one of the first private citizens to urge the president to pay closer attention to Vietnam, primarily, however, for its potential ramifications on the upcoming presidential election.

In early May Johnson had appointed Douglass Cater, the national affairs editor of the *Reporter*, as a special White House assistant. Cater's precise duties were unclear; LBJ only told him to be "his reporter" and "to think ahead." Cater, who knew from long press experience that proximity to the Oval Office correlated directly with access to the president, insisted that his desk be situated in the West Wing. Walter Jenkins, a senior White House special assistant, put Cater in the strategically located situation room of the National Security Council. On his first day on the job Cater found himself ensconced in a huge room full of electronic maps and phones of every hue—without a secretary, without a concrete assignment, and with no clue as to what he was supposed to do. Suddenly, a staff secretary announced a call from Mr. Acheson, inviting him to his house that night for drinks. Cater, who knew Acheson only slightly, recalled that he thought to himself, "Perhaps [this] is the way it works." He accepted the invitation.[6]

That evening, at a small gathering in Acheson's Georgetown home, Acheson pulled Cater aside and said, "Doug, somebody needs to tell Johnson that things are going to hell faster than he knows in Vietnam. The Pentagon is not keeping him adequately informed. . . . What is likely to happen is that it will move dramatically bad sometime during the Democratic convention or fall campaign. He needs to worry about this because we all know that is a vulnerable period in American politics." Impressed by Acheson's tone of urgency, Cater scurried back to the White House and typed his first memo to the president. He relayed Acheson's concern that "the situation in Vietnam will soon enter [a] phase when new initiatives become impossible because of [the] convention and campaign period here at home. He [Acheson] urged that any assessment of stepping up involvement in Indo-China take into account that we must act quickly or be prepared to stall for a while."[7]

To Cater's astonishment, the next morning he was moved out of the

NSC situation room, which, for the next four days, became the round-the-clock gathering spot for "all of the chieftains in government." Johnson had sent word down that he wanted to know "what the hell the true story in Vietnam is." A full-fledged review of U.S. policy in Southeast Asia was under way and Cater believed that his memo may have been the catalyst. William Bundy pointed out that this was a strong, and ultimately unprovable, claim, but Bundy acknowledged that the memo may have been a cause of the frenzy of activity that followed.[8]

On May 20, the day Cater's memo arrived on LBJ's desk, the president ordered his advisers to formulate separate military and political plans of action in Vietnam for his immediate consideration. On May 21 Secretary of State Rusk sent Henry Cabot Lodge, Jr., the ambassador to South Vietnam, an "eyes-only" cable relaying alarm at South Vietnam's failure to organize effectively against the Communists and soliciting advice on how the American people should be made aware that their government soon might have to send substantial military and economic aid to Saigon.

McGeorge Bundy reported to LBJ on the Vietnam action plans of the four working groups. John T. McNaughton at Defense recommended that the United States "strike to hurt but not to destroy, and strike for the purpose of changing the North Vietnamese decision on intervention in the south." William Sullivan, special assistant to the under secretary of state for political affairs, was devising a plan to integrate Americans and Vietnamese "at every level, both civilian and military." Chester Cooper of the NSC staff was evaluating possible North Vietnamese reactions to various U.S. offensive moves, such as strategic bombing and blockades. Under Secretary of State George Ball was drafting a variety of congressional resolutions, so that the president could consider different means of acquiring concurrence to wider U.S. involvement in Vietnam. Ball advised the president that "such a resolution is essential before we act against North Vietnam, but . . . it should be sufficiently general in form not to commit you to any particular action ahead of time."[9]

Top-secret reports, memos, contingency plans, and schemes for covert operations proliferated throughout the rest of May and early June. U.S. officials from Washington and Saigon were ordered to attend the Honolulu Conference from June 1 to 3. The agenda: developing plans to reverse North Vietnamese military and political gains in the South, strengthen the crumbling South Vietnamese government, stop communist encroachment in Vietnam, and sell increased U.S. involvement in Vietnam to the American people. Ultimately little came of the spring review in terms of concrete decisions, but it did make clear that Vietnam was the administration's most pressing foreign-policy dilemma. It could not be tucked away and forgotten until the election was over.[10]

Johnson took seriously Acheson's warnings that Vietnam could become the president's Achilles' heel. Always suspicious of the so-called Eastern Establishment cabal, Johnson may have given credence to Acheson's views in the belief that Acheson had obtained a detailed assessment of events in Vietnam from his son-in-law, Assistant Secretary of State for Far Eastern Affairs William Bundy. Johnson asked his advisers to sketch a congressional resolution that would shelter him from Republican critics and, in particular, that would force Goldwater to support his Vietnam program or risk being more isolated than he already was. William Bundy drafted an intentionally vague war-powers resolution, but Johnson thought it too ambiguous. He concluded that such an open-ended resolution—in the tradition of the Formosa Resolution of 1955, which authorized President Eisenhower to defend Formosa in the event of armed attack—would get hung up in Congress. Several senators, Wayne Morse of Oregon in particular, would find reasons to filibuster it to death. The National Security Council advised waiting for a more opportune moment to present a resolution on Southeast Asia.[11]

LBJ's opportunity to rally Congress and the public to support increased involvement in Vietnam came in early August. North Vietnamese torpedo boats were alleged to have fired twice on U.S. naval vessels in the international waters of the Gulf of Tonkin, off the shores of North Vietnam. Johnson immediately ordered air strikes on North Vietnam as reprisal and asked Congress to empower him to repel any future attacks. By an overwhelming vote of 416 to 0 in the House and 88 to 2 in the Senate, Congress passed the Tonkin Gulf Resolution, giving Johnson a virtual blank check to prosecute the war in Southeast Asia. Concern over the election prevented any further escalation of the war for the time being.[12]

From Geneva, where he was mediating the dispute between Greece and Turkey over Cyprus, Acheson applauded Johnson's firm action and congratulated him on the Tonkin resolution, which he considered a political masterstroke. In his speeches in support of Johnson's election, Acheson did not refer to Vietnam. On December 9, however, barely a month after LBJ's landslide victory over Senator Barry Goldwater, Acheson alluded to critics of the administration's "policy in Southeast Asia" in an address at Amherst College entitled "Ethics in International Relations Today." In the previous month the Viet Cong had conducted a mortar attack at an air base in Bien Hoa in which six B-57 fighter planes were destroyed and five Americans killed. Acheson, moved by that incident, said that for the United States to deny to itself the option of military force "seems to me not only a bad bargain but a stupid one. . . . I would almost say an immoral one."[13]

Liberals in the Democratic Party charged that once again Dean Acheson seemed incapable of comprehending that restraint was not always a sign of weakness but constituted a realistic posture in a nuclear world where miscalculation could be catastrophic. They also maintained that Acheson's willingness to resort to force rather than use moral suasion tarnished the image of America that JFK had worked so diligently to project. Under his guidance the United States would be transformed from citadel of democracy to international bully.[14] Acheson responded in the pages of the *New York Times Magazine*. "A country half slave—or all slave—to foreign criticism cannot stand, except as a mental institution," Acheson wrote. "Our 'image' will take care of itself, if we get on with what we have to do."[15]

The Escalation of 1965

By January 1965 coup-ridden South Vietnam and its institutions—military, religious, political, and social—were in disarray. Many administration officials predicted imminent anarchy if the United States did not increase its military commitment. Acheson's friend General Maxwell Taylor had become U.S. ambassador to Saigon in June 1964; by January 1965 Taylor was telling Washington that because of the intense internal political conflicts plaguing the South Vietnamese government (GVN) and army (ARVN), it was imperative for Washington to take control of the war to prevent a communist takeover. Taylor agreed with Robert McNamara: Saigon needed massive American economic and military assistance.[16] Against a backdrop of Viet Cong attacks against U.S. facilities at Pleiku on February 6 and 7 that killed nine American soldiers and wounded seventy-six, their recommendations led President Johnson to order retaliatory air strikes (called Operation Flaming Dart) on North Vietnam, further escalating U.S. involvement. Following these strikes, Johnson ordered a more sustained bombing campaign on restricted targets, which was named Operation Rolling Thunder. The campaign, which began on March 19, 1965, continued uninterrupted until March 31, 1968, except for occasional pauses to explore cease-fire agreements. During this three-year period Rolling Thunder dropped over 400,000 tons of bombs on North Vietnam, killing hundreds of thousands of Vietnamese peasants and destroying the American image that Acheson had said would take care of itself.[17]

The Johnson administration was hopeful that systematic bombing of the North soon would force Hanoi to surrender and that a stable, pro-American regime could then be installed in South Vietnam. Further, Washington would have demonstrated to the world that it had the will and might to contain the spread of communism in Asia and that it would make good on its SEATO obligations.

Johnson also had committed two marine battalions of 3,500 men to South Vietnam that March to protect American installations. By May 1965 there were 35,000 U.S. troops in Vietnam; by September 130,000; by December over 180,000; by June 1966, 270,000; by December of that year, 380,000. This massive U.S. military build-up continued—in 1967 it increased by another 100,000—until the Tet offensive in early 1968, which finally convinced Johnson that Americanizing the war had failed to bring the North Vietnamese to their knees. Johnson had plunged the United States into the midst of a Vietnamese civil war, and one consequence was division in the United States. Dissenting college students and other outraged citizens around the country were calling peace rallies and protest marches to voice their opposition to the war. Johnson began to recognize that the Vietnam engagement was having an unhealthy effect upon America.[18]

Acheson initially favored the military build-up, although he believed that the Rolling Thunder bombardment was a retaliatory move to punish North Vietnam for Bien Hoa and Pleiku. When the bombing persisted into March and early April, Acheson assumed this was a get-tough tactic designed to intimidate Hanoi and to bolster morale in Saigon, but he was skeptical that it would be effective. His approval of Rolling Thunder was contingent on its success in getting Hanoi speedily to come to terms with the United States, thereby freeing the president to turn his energies to more significant problems. By mid-April Acheson had grown frustrated by the lack of progress.[19]

The Acheson-Ball Peace Plan

Under Secretary of State George Ball knew that his friend Dean Acheson was concerned by LBJ's disregard of European affairs as the war intensified. Ball, who strongly opposed both the bombings and increased American military intervention in Vietnam, began a desperate bid to persuade the president to replace military escalation with a more sensible, efficient, and economical political compromise. Ball was convinced that Johnson, Rusk, McNamara, and McGeorge Bundy were all misjudging the political and military consequences of Operation Rolling Thunder and of the ground-force deployments. In late April Ball made "an emotional plea that the President not take such a hazardous leap without further exploring the possibilities of a settlement." Johnson replied, "All right, George, I'll give you until tomorrow morning to get me a settlement plan. If you can pull a rabbit out of the hat, I'm all for that."[20]

Ball had a memorandum on the president's desk by nightfall. Calling Operation Rolling Thunder a failure, Ball proposed that the United States should undertake the following actions: call a bombing halt; announce a general amnesty, allowing all Viet Cong to move to the North if they so desired; ask an international control commission to oversee a cease-fire; and promise a complete U.S. withdrawal from Vietnam once a new government in Saigon was established. Johnson read the memo that evening and called Ball into his office the next morning. He was sufficiently impressed to convene a number of his top foreign-policy advisers to explore alternatives to the bombing campaign and troop increases.[21]

Ball, sensing this might well be his only opportunity to sway LBJ from a continuing military escalation, knew that he did not have an influential ally within the administration's inner circle. "I desperately needed at least one high-level confrere on my side," he wrote in his memoirs, *The Past Has Another Pattern*. "How could the President be expected to adopt the heresies of an Under Secretary against the contrary views of his whole top command."[22] Ball decided to try to enlist the support of Dean Acheson in finding a political solution in Vietnam. "Dean, I want to put you to work," he recalled telling Acheson over the telephone.[23]

On May 7 Acheson, Ball, and Lloyd Cutler, a powerful and astute Washington attorney, submitted to the president a thirty-five-page document entitled "A Plan for a Political Resolution in South Viet-Nam."[24] It was soon to be known as the Acheson-Ball Peace Plan. Acheson used Ball's original memo as a starting point, but wrote nearly the entire document himself. He set aside his concern over how America would be perceived by other nations should it pull out of Vietnam and instead kept in mind Ball's premise that the war was unwinnable. "Acheson was convinced that the war in Vietnam was going nowhere and we had to have a settlement," Lloyd Cutler recalled.[25]

On the assumption that the Rolling Thunder bombardment would prove ineffective and that the North Vietnamese soon would defeat the South, the plan called for an immediate bombing pause while proposals were presented; phased withdrawal of all American, North Vietnamese, and Viet Cong troops; general amnesty for "all Viet Cong adherents who cease fighting;" the establishment of a government in South Vietnam by local elections, including Viet Cong participation; the economic rebuilding of South Vietnam; and the eventual withdrawal of all foreign troops.[26]

Lamenting that the United States government had become a "puppet of the puppet," Acheson and Ball argued that it was imperative to turn the conflict "from the military to the political arena." Acheson, who viewed official negotiations with communists as undesirable, tried to semantically finesse the issue by "*not* requir[ing] South Vietnam to enter into negotiations." He offered instead a vague formulation: the United States should adopt a "posture of willingness to hold discussions with any government concerned."[27] As late as December 1967, Acheson ruled out any "possibility of negotiating our way out of Vietnam . . . anybody who states that bombing will increase the possibility of negotiating just doesn't understand the Communist point of view at all."[28]

Acheson's willingness to help Ball reflected his skepticism about the effectiveness of the bombing campaign, his concern over LBJ's neglect of European affairs, his irritation with Dean Rusk's lackluster performance, his personal liking for George Ball and his respect for Ball's intellectual acumen, and his dismissal of Southeast Asia as a secondary concern in the larger scheme of things.

On May 16 Acheson and Ball presented their plan to Johnson, Rusk, and McNamara. Discussion at the meeting centered primarily on criticism from the *New York Times* and Congress for the administration's recent ending of a week-long bombing pause, but the president also expressed willingness to give the new plan a try, so long as the South Vietnamese government could be persuaded to go along with its terms.[29]

Encouraged by LBJ's green light, Acheson immediately set to work writing three top-secret memorandums to George Ball focusing on how to sell the plan first to Ambassador Taylor and then to the South Vietnamese government.[30] "This Plan will touch hypersensitive Vietnamese nerves, and enlisting the kind of Vietnamese cooperation necessary for its successful execution will not be easy," Acheson wrote. "Because of Vietnamese feelings and concerns . . . particularly their continuing fear of a United States disengagement which would leave them isolated, and their resultant suspicion of any United States actions which could conceivably be construed as preparations for such a disengagement—our approach to the Vietnamese will have to be a trifle disingenuous if it is to have any chance of succeeding." Acheson suggested Washington package the plan for South Vietnamese consumption by initially emphasizing those aspects that would strengthen the position, image, and efforts of the South Vietnamese government. "Once Vietnamese interest and, with luck, enthusiasm has been aroused over these points," Acheson continued, "we can then proceed to point out the Plan's broader (and, in our eyes, principal) features, though . . . we should initially soft-pedal our desire to curtail military involvement and actions *per se*."[31]

Acheson also recommended that the administration "avoid giving the appearance of leading from weakness," saying it would be inadvisable to "announce or attempt to initiate execution of the Plan during a period of intensive military activity, particularly a period in which United States and GVN forces are suffering tactical reverses."[32] Another of Acheson's memos was written in question-and-answer form, and the third summarized the fundamentals of a political settlement in South Vietnam. Both of these documents were designed to provide Ball with ammunition to meet whatever reservations Taylor and his senior staff might have.[33]

In late May Ball dispatched his personal assistant, Thomas Ehrlich, to Saigon to present the peace plan to Ambassador Taylor and Deputy Ambassador U. Alexis Johnson and to sound them out on possible revisions before the plan was taken to the South Vietnamese government. Taylor flatly rejected the plan as "a giveaway program of the worst sort," although he did extend Ball the courtesy of sending him a detailed list of objections.[34] Ball replied with a long telegram addressing most of Taylor's points but glossing over his primary concern: the Acheson-Ball plan called for total disengagement from Vietnam, which for Taylor was tantamount to a U.S. stamp of approval for Hanoi's takeover of South Vietnam.[35] Such an outcome he found unacceptable. Incensed that the plan had gone as far as it had, Taylor made his objections known to Acheson and Ball in person during a visit to Washington in June. Despite its pragmatic ingenuity, the Acheson-Ball plan was stillborn. "The episode confirmed an opinion I had not wanted to accept," Ball wrote in his memoirs. "America had become a prisoner of whatever Saigon military clique was momentarily in power."³⁶ The plan was also dismissed by the more vehement anticommunists in the administration because it provided for "the peaceful participation of Viet Cong adherents in the national life of South Vietnam."³⁷

Acheson apparently had little emotional commitment to the plan, for he took its rejection in stride. If Johnson and Taylor wanted to play hardball in Southeast Asia, that was fine by him, as long as they realized that the more committed the U.S. became militarily, the harder it would become to disengage should the situation deteriorate. "The State Department has drawn me—flatteringly but a little too persistently—into trying to penetrate the mists of the unfolding future and devise measures to help it unfold more advantageously than it otherwise might," Acheson wrote a friend shortly after the plan was defeated.³⁸ He still hoped for a political solution but noted, "Hanoi does not want a settlement and won't have one until they're convinced that they cannot win the war and will suffer from continuing it." He added, "We are not looking for a face-saving surrender."³⁹ To Acheson, the problems in South Vietnam were "less difficult and baffling" than the administration made out.⁴⁰ And on July 8, at the first of what came to be known as the meetings of the Wise Men on Vietnam, if Acheson harbored any doubts about South Vietnam's ability to persevere in its fight against the North, he kept them to himself. Rather, he took the familiar role of bucking up LBJ, saying that like Truman in Korea, Johnson had no choice but to provide Saigon with men, money, and matériel for an all-out pursuit of military victory in Vietnam.⁴¹

At that meeting, in addition to the administration's foreign-policy team, were Robert Lovett, John J. McCloy, General Omar Bradley, John Cowles, former under secretary of state Robert Murphy, and David K. E. Bruce. They were asked by Rusk and McNamara to meet individually with various administration officials for an assessment of the rapidly deteriorating situation in South Vietnam and then reconvene to consider General Westmoreland's month-old request for 44 battalions—nearly 200,000 men—from the United States and its allies. William Bundy, who attended the joint session, reported to LBJ that most of the participants "felt that there should be no question of making whatever combat force increases were required. Several . . . thought that our actions had been perhaps too restrained, and had been misconstrued by Hanoi that we were less than wholly determined." Withdrawal, Bundy told the president, was an unacceptable option to the Wise Men.⁴²

At day's end LBJ invited the group to the White House for drinks.

The president's greeting was immediately followed by a litany of his Vietnam woes, which left Acheson longing for bygone days: "I got to thinking about you and General Marshall and how we never wasted time 'fighting the problem,' or endlessly reconsidering decisions, or feeling sorry for ourselves," Acheson wrote Truman. Acheson, finally unable to tolerate Johnson's whining any longer, assailed the president's peevish self-doubt, telling LBJ that he had no choice but to increase the American military presence in Vietnam. "With this lead my colleagues came thundering in like the charge of the Scots Greys at Waterloo," Acheson told Truman, with evident glee. "They were fine; old Bob Lovett, usually cautious, was all out, and, of course, Brad [Omar Bradley] left no doubt that he was with me all the way.... I think ... we scored."[43]

Two days after the meeting Johnson wrote to Acheson that he was "strengthened by [Acheson's] support of our work in Vietnam, and I continue to feel that anything men of your standing can say to the country will be of great help."[44] McGeorge Bundy is not alone in contending that this meeting, in which Acheson's "mustache was voluble," was a highly significant episode in the saga of the Vietnam War.[45] For on July 28, fortified by the prowar consensus of the elder statesmen, LBJ announced his fateful decision to commit American combat troops to fight in an open-ended ground war in South Vietnam. Intentionally misleading reporters, he stated only that U.S. forces would be increased from 75,000 to approximately 125,000. Now that the war in Vietnam had been Americanized, Acheson hopped firmly on the bandwagon. "Acheson was an all-or-nothing type of man," George Ball noted later. "[After Korea] he was uncomfortable with the notion of limited war."[46]

The Pro-War Committees

Acheson's support of LBJ's Vietnam policy and his concomitant contempt for the antiwar protesters were manifested publicly in early September when he joined the Committee for an Effective and Durable Peace in Asia, a prowar organization established by Arthur H. Dean, the chief U.S. Korean War negotiator, to provide "the American people [with] a better understanding of Vietnam." The group, composed of former high-ranking government officials and of financiers, college presidents, business executives, and university professors, ran full-page advertisements in the *New York Times* and other newspapers endorsing the president's measures "to meet the increased aggression against South Vietnam."[47]

In November Acheson joined more than one hundred other American luminaries, including Richard Nixon, Lucius D. Clay, James B. Conant, Douglas Dillon, Sidney Hook, Max Lerner, John Dos Passos, and Rex Stout, in denouncing, by way of a signed manifesto, the antiwar movement. They urged Americans who supported U.S. policy in Vietnam to "shout" their approval so that it "will ring as loudly in Peking as in Peoria, that it will be understood in Hanoi as in Houston." Acheson also signed a statement—distributed by Freedom House, a nonpartisan, self-described centrist, educational center based in New York City that had been circulating statements on public issues since 1941—urging patriotic prowar Americans to speak up in their hometowns on Vietnam; to make their views known to their congressmen; to draft and circulate locally resolutions expressing support for using "whatever national resources are required" to win the war; and to contribute time and money to voluntary humanitarian agencies serving the poor and injured in South Vietnam.[48]

Over the next two years Freedom House issued and Acheson signed numerous prowar statements. As antiwar protests grew more vehement, Freedom House statements grew more jingoistic. A press release in November 1966 endorsed by more than one hundred prominent Americans, including Acheson and former president Eisenhower, charged that protesters were failing to distinguish between "responsible" and "irresponsible" criticism. The statement accused the antiwar "extremists" of propounding "fantasies," as for example: "That this is Lyndon Johnson's war or McNamara's war or any other individual's war . . . That the American leaders are committing 'war crimes' or indulging in 'genocide' . . . That this is a 'race' war of white versus colored people . . . That this nation's leaders are obsessed with some compulsion to play 'world policeman' or to conduct some 'holy war' against the legitimate aspirations of underdeveloped people." Acheson and the other signatories further argued that these public charges encouraged Hanoi to continue the war and avoid negotiations, because communists tended to misread the significance of dissent in free societies.[49]

From the perspective of the White House the only problems with the Freedom House campaign were that its statements were issued irregularly and that the organization lacked the resources for the media blitz necessary to counter the well-publicized antiwar demonstrations. Popular sentiment in America strongly supported the war in Vietnam, the prowar contingent in the administration believed; the question was how to rally the country around the flag and drown out the antiwar minority.

One response was to create two new organizations meant to consolidate support for Johnson's war policies: the White House Information Group, responsible for cultivating favorable news coverage, and the Citizens Committee for Peace and Freedom in Vietnam, a public-relations organization claiming to speak for the "silent center" of prowar opinion.[50]

The idea of creating the committee came from Secretary of Health, Education, and Welfare John Gardner and one of his business friends. At a meeting in early 1967 they convinced White House staffers John P. Roche and Harry McPherson of its value. Roche drew together a group of private citizens to form the organization in an effort to deflect accusations that they were creating a propaganda arm of the government.[51] He corralled seventy-five-year-old Senator Paul Douglas as chairman and Charles Tyroler II as director of the committee.

Roche quickly exited the stage, leaving Douglas and Tyroler to enlist members and raise funds. Their initial targets were former presidents Eisenhower and Truman. They added, among others, Dean Acheson, James Byrnes, Lucius Clay, Omar Bradley, Lewis Strauss, and Douglas Dillon from government; labor leaders George Meany and Joe Beirne; academics Paul Seabury, Louis Hacker, James MacGregor Burns, Allan Nevins, Oscar Handlin, and T. Harry Williams; writers Eric Hoffer, Ralph Ellison, James T. Farrell, Howard Lindsay, and Ralph E. McGill, and several Nobel laureates in science and medicine. The committee's purpose, Senator Douglas wrote Acheson, was to "mobilize the 'silent center' opposed to capitulation and general war in Asia." Of the committee's roughly 130 members, more than two-thirds were over sixty years of age; nearly a third were past seventy. Although the objective of garnering distinguished names clearly tilted the averages, it was becoming obvious that the Vietnam War was dividing America along generational lines.[52]

In October 1967 Senator Douglas, flanked by General Bradley, held a press conference in Washington to announce the official formation of the Citizens Committee for Peace and Freedom in Vietnam. The committee declared in a statement of purpose that the American objective in Vietnam was "to make the price too high and the risk too great" for Hanoi to continue trying to "impose a government and political system upon their neighbors by internal subversion, insurrection, infiltration and invasion." It continued, "Our objective as a committee is not to suppress the voice of opposition—[but] to make sure that the majority voice of America is heard—loud and clear—so that Peking and Hanoi will not mistake the strident voices of some dissenters for American discouragement and a weakening of will."[53]

Acheson believed that from July 1965 onward the liberals in the media had attempted to turn popular opinion against LBJ's policies by portraying protesters as heroes and G.I.'s as bloodthirsty murderers of peasants. "If not a word were printed or spoken in the press, radio, or television for six months about Vietnam the situation would be immeasurably improved," Acheson wrote the newspaper publisher John Cowles, his close friend, in October 1965. "What is being done [by LBJ] is in my judgment right except for the pressure which comes from the public controversy to confine the bombing in the North . . . but this blabbermouth society of ours makes any sensible procedure impossible."[54] In a television interview in December 1967, Acheson expressed his hope that Douglas's committee would send prowar pamphlets to Chambers of Commerce and Kiwanis Clubs in towns and cities across America, so that the hardworking, tax-paying American citizenry would be informed properly about Vietnam and public discussion would be broadened.[55]

The Vietnam Buildup

While Acheson was exhorting others to speak out, he himself maintained a certain distance from the discussion of Vietnam between July 1965, when he met with the Wise Men, and October 1967, when he joined Douglas's committee. Acheson signed prowar petitions and occasionally consulted with the president, but by and large he stayed aloof from the day-to-day vicissitudes of the war strategy. During this two-year period of escalating U.S. air and ground action, of bombing pauses and resumptions, of peace initiatives and failures, Acheson played no real role in decision making. On the few occasions when he publicly weighed in for the debate—most notably by joining the prowar organizations such as Freedom House and the Citizens Committee for Peace and Freedom—it was always as promoter, trying to lend credence to LBJ's efforts to achieve an American victory.

Acheson's analysis of risks during this period reflects a certain ambivalence. He saw parallels between the Vietnamese situation and Korea, and he feared antagonizing the Chinese Communists should LBJ expand aerial assaults north of Hanoi as some Republicans and Pentagon officials were urging.[56] But when a student pressed him to speculate whether Peking would enter the war, Acheson answered, "The Chinese don't want to get into the Vietnam situation and they won't."[57] Only if LBJ initiated a massive bombing campaign in the North would Peking contemplate getting directly involved.

Acheson favored intervention in Vietnam not because of SEATO commitments but to demonstrate that communist expansionism of any kind was doomed when met head-on by American military might. Thus once troops were committed, the only option was to see the conflict through to a victorious conclusion. Acheson asserted in dozens of letters to friends that the loss of Vietnam would mean a dramatic loss of confidence in America's ability to lead the free world. "There can be no question that the crowning disaster for the western position would be an American withdrawal without any defensible arrangement," he wrote Anthony Eden in October 1967.[58] Acheson's concern about loss of national prestige in the event of a withdrawal mounted, particularly after the de Gaulle-NATO crisis of spring 1966. He refused to believe that the overextension of American power in Asia could cause as much, if not more, national humiliation as a straightforward admission that U.S. intervention had been a gross miscalculation. Throughout the war, Acheson sounded one theme. Vietnam was like Korea, with only one glaring difference: unlike Johnson, Harry Truman had had the self-confidence and stamina to see his commitment through. As William Bundy later said of Acheson, "Vietnam really rang his Korea bell."[59]

In letters to friends Acheson vacillated about the value of bombing pauses, as well as about LBJ's overall policy of massive strategic bombing. He wrote Anthony Eden that, as he did not possess current military information, he "must leave it to those who do to decide whether any relaxation of air bombing is possible if the military position is to be held as it must be for ultimate negotiations."[60] Yet he suspected that LBJ was afraid to bring the bombing to a halt lest it appear, in an election year, that America was losing the war. "The fact is that the bombing of the North started as a morale builder for the South when things were very bad there," he wrote John Cowles in August 1967. "We have now run out of targets but the Republican hawks keep calling for more which produces useless casualties and encourages some air force fire eaters to urge population bombing. LBJ has not HST's courage to say no to political pressures. Our damned election is too far off . . . bombing like this for fifteen months looks impossible."[61]

In attempting to understand Acheson's stance, one must also bear in mind that unlike the case with the European crises of these years—where Acheson was called in by the State Department, thoroughly briefed, and accorded access to top-secret government documents—with respect to Vietnam Acheson's information came from secondhand sources. Newspapers, occasional consultations with White House staffers, the Pentagon rumor mill (often by way of Paul Nitze), and the Washington cocktail circuit (which he generally tried to avoid) all led Acheson to believe that the United States would ultimately prevail in Vietnam.

Denied insider knowledge of the day-to-day conduct of the war, Acheson took the hard line partially out of reflex. Furthermore, he apparently buried any doubts he might have had about the reliability of the Pentagon's assurances that the war was winnable, although he had himself warned in 1964 that the president was not getting all the facts, and his difficulty in dealing with General MacArthur during the Korean War might have led him to be suspicious of the military's gung-ho rhetoric. Acheson was preoccupied with practicing law and writing *Present at the Creation*, although he must have been thinking about Asian foreign policy as he wrote the chapters on the Korean War and the French war in Indochina. But isolated at Harewood in the summer, Acheson found Vietnam peripheral to his primary concern: Europe. And so, on Vietnam Acheson dutifully played the role of reassuring elder statesman backing the administration's policies, not foreign-policy conceptualizer.

Acheson's Eurocentrism and his ambivalent feelings toward LBJ prevented him from ever seeking out in the Vietnam arena anything more than a secondary role as morale booster.[62] Acheson felt that the best he could provide the president was a course in character-building. Asking him a question about the soundness of LBJ's stand at any time during this period always would elicit essentially the same response: "We might have gotten out ten years ago, but we didn't. It's a hard job and a tough job, and it's got to be done."[63]

He was a role model for the president. "You do not know how heartening the example of Dean Acheson as Secretary of State has been even in the past few years both to me and my own Secretary of State," LBJ wrote Acheson in April 1968. "Your conduct in the Truman years taught us both how to endure and to accept the calumnies, the outrages, and yes, the viciousness which too often is loosed upon American Presidents and Secretaries of State in times of international strain."[64]

On November 1 and 2, 1967, President Johnson invited members of his senior foreign-policy advisory group to the White House for a dose of reassurance and enlightenment. Acheson had refrained from discussing Vietnam with LBJ since the summer of 1966, when his experiences during the NATO crisis had left him disappointed with the president.[65] "[LBJ] is a strange man, by no means a hero of mine," Acheson wrote the historian Barbara Tuchman in June of 1967. "I am one of the few people who have told him to his face what I think of some of his performances, rather than the world at large."[66] But, at the urging of Tuchman and other friends, Acheson put aside his distaste and accepted the invitation.

Acheson and the other advisers (George Ball, Omar Bradley, McGeorge Bundy, General Lucius Clay, Clark Clifford, Arthur Dean, Douglas Dillon, Abe Fortas, W. Averell Harriman, Henry Cabot Lodge, John J. McCloy, Robert Murphy, General Matthew Ridgway, Maxwell Taylor, and Cyrus Vance) met for cocktails on the evening of November 1. The chairman of the Joint Chiefs of Staff, General Earle Wheeler, and George Carver of the CIA briefed them on the war. Both were upbeat, saying victory in Vietnam appeared within reach. The group also spoke of the antiwar movement, Korea, and the Wise Men meeting of July 1965 before adjourning. In a memo to Johnson, Walt W. Rostow confidently wrote: "I detect in this group no sentiment for pulling out of Vietnam."[67]

The next morning Johnson greeted his guests cheerfully as they entered the Cabinet Room. Turning to Acheson first, LBJ asked for his thinking on Vietnam. Acheson responded first with an ad hominem and apparently gratuitous attack, sympathizing with the president for having to deal with "a dilettante fool" like J. William Fulbright, chairman of the Senate Foreign Relations Committee. Acheson went on to recite, chapter and verse, how the Truman team had persevered in Korea. He said he had been reassured that "this was a matter we can and will win" by Wheeler's presentation the previous evening. Acheson reiterated his belief that no matter how many bombs were dropped on the North Vietnamese, Hanoi would not be moved to negotiate. "We must understand that we are not going to have negotiations," he told Johnson. "When these fellows decide they can't defeat the South, then they will give up. This is the way it was in Korea, this is the way the Communists operate." On this day the advice of all the Wise Men—with the notable exception of George Ball—was fundamentally the same: ignore the critics and press on to a military victory in Vietnam. Johnson, understandably elated by the nearly unanimous support of this group, was, for the moment, more convinced than ever that his policies were correct.[68]

A month later Acheson defended the president's Vietnam policy in a two-hour debate with four college students televised on the Public Broadcasting System in New York. His only criticism of LBJ was for devoting too much time to trying to placate "peacenik" senators like Fulbright and Morse. "There seems to have been a great worry grown up about getting along with Congress," Acheson said, disposing of the legislative branch of government as an annoying inconvenience when it came to making a sensible foreign policy. "This I always considered to be a waste of time." Asked how President Johnson could possibly ignore the fierce antiwar opposition, Acheson acknowledged that it was a formidable force. "This is why I'd like to see the President get out on his high horse and go ride around the country and beat the drum," he added. "Let's get this thing going." Acheson also reasserted his belief that there was no possibility of negotiating a way out of Vietnam.[69]

W. Averell Harriman expressed his dismay with his friend's TV appearance in a visit to Acheson's home a week later. Harriman attempted to convince Acheson that Vietnam was not Korea and that it would be impossible for the United States to score a military victory without draining its resources and rending the fabric of its society. To his pleasant surprise, Harriman found Acheson much less rigid than he had supposed.[70]

Indeed, by late December Acheson was beginning to sour on Vietnam. A crisis in Europe was at hand, thanks to another veto by de Gaulle of British entry into the EEC, and there were riots in the ghettos of many U.S. cities. Acheson's mood was dark as he contemplated the limits of American power. "Vietnam plus the riots is very bad," he wrote Anthony Eden on December 31. "It spells frustration and a sense of feebleness at home and abroad. Everyone pushes the USA around. Yellow men in Asia, black men at home, de Gaulle a ridiculous type in Europe, and Nasser threatens to have the Arab states seize what is regarded as 'our' oil properties. Americans aren't used to this, and LBJ is not a loveable type. He is the one to blame."[71]

The Tet Offensive

By January 1968 many observers felt that both President Johnson's domestic economic policies and his conduct of the war in Asia were unraveling. America's international balance of trade, which had been declining since the early 1960s, nosedived dramatically during the first ten weeks of 1968, and the value of the dollar on the exchange market was dropping daily. LBJ was also faced with an unanticipated crisis in the Sea of Japan. On January 23 North Korean patrol boats seized the USS *Pueblo*, an unarmed surveillance ship in international waters, and imprisoned the crew and officers. The *Pueblo* incident frustrated LBJ; he was unable sufficiently to retaliate for the killing of an American sailor in the seizure for fear of getting more Americans killed and other complications. Johnson sent 370 formerly inactive airplanes to U.S. bases in South Korea and mobilized 15,000 reservists against further aggression, but he was forced to work through diplomatic channels to obtain the captives' release, a process that took eleven months and sapped much of his energy.[72]

In late January 1968—as the new year, or Tet, brought in the Year of the Monkey—Hanoi caught Washington off guard. In a surprise attack the Viet Cong hit the American stronghold of Saigon and other South Vietnamese cities. The offensive was aimed at targets freighted with symbolism: the U.S. Embassy, the Presidential Palace, the South Vietnamese military headquarters, Tan Son Nhut Airport, as well as other airbases in the South. U.S. retaliatory ground and air strikes saw to it that the Viet Cong paid a heavy price in casualties for the Tet offensive. From a purely military standpoint it was a Communist failure, but from the American perspective it was a public relations disaster. Belying the optimistic reports that Ambassador Ellsworth Bunker and General Westmoreland had given the American public in late 1967, Tet exposed the weakness of the Saigon regime and demonstrated that the North Vietnamese were still enormously powerful and imbued with a fighting spirit. Newspaper columnists, middle-of-the-road politicians, and college students all over America turned up the volume of their outrage against what they saw as the indiscriminate and immoral mass destruction LBJ was overseeing in Vietnam.

Shaken by the Tet offensive and by the ongoing siege of marines at Khe Sanh, LBJ called Acheson to the White House in late February for consultation. Johnson was in desperate need of allies. He asked Acheson what he thought of General Westmoreland's "search and destroy" missions, which were designed to wear the Communists down through attrition, and of the bombing of Hanoi's supply routes and war industries in an attempt to cripple the Communists' warmaking capabilities. Acheson responded that his opinion would be of little value, as it was based on the misinformation that he had been handed before Tet. He told Johnson that he was tired of getting erroneous canned briefs from the Pentagon: "With all due respect, Mr. President, the Joint Chiefs of Staff [JCS] don't know what they're talking about." Johnson said that this statement was quite shocking. Acheson curtly rejoined, "Then maybe you should be shocked." Pressed repeatedly to give his candid assessment of post-Tet policy, Acheson stood firm: it would be impossible to do so unless Acheson conducted his own inquiry and was given access to all the data on Vietnam, not just the drivel the joint chiefs and Rostow had been feeding him. Hearing the determination in Acheson's voice, Johnson agreed to the condition. He granted him complete access to all top-secret intelligence information and promised the full cooperation of State and Defense, the CIA, and the JCS so he could conduct a special Vietnam investigation of his own.[73]

Acheson went to work immediately, conferring privately with Rusk; McNamara (who had announced in November his resignation as secretary of defense effective March 1, and his new position as head of the World Bank); Clark Clifford, the incoming secretary of defense; and the CIA director, Richard Helms. His most illuminating briefings, however, were with second-level officials recommended by William Bundy, particularly with Philip Habib at the State Department, George Carver at the CIA, and Major General William De Puy of the JCS. Acheson interrogated these officials at his Georgetown home, seeking the raw data their respective agencies ostensibly had used in making their most recent reports. He was dismayed by his findings. "The situation in VN is very bad," he wrote Cowles on February 27, 1968.[74] The more raw data Acheson uncovered, the more closely he examined documents and cable traffic between Washington and Saigon, the more persuaded he grew that the United States had to narrow its military and political responsibilities in Vietnam.

Acheson also concluded that it was time for Washington to get tough with the South Vietnamese government (GVN), as the Truman administration had done with Seoul during the Korean War. Saigon must be pressed to work harder in implementing area pacification programs and to quash guerrilla belligerency in areas under the control of the South Vietnamese army (ARVN). But even more important, Acheson wrote Cowles, the United States had to make sure that the Saigon government did not collapse, for "if that collapses, we have no future there and must be able to extricate ourselves."[75]

His Vietnam study complete, Acheson met with Johnson on March 14 to discuss his findings. LBJ led off by telling Acheson that although morale in South Vietnam following Tet was at an all-time low, U.S. and ARVN military losses were not great. Hanoi had miscalculated in thinking that the South Vietnamese people would rally against their government in popular support of the Viet Cong. In that sense the GVN had suffered no significant loss, Johnson optimistically noted. Westmoreland had informed him that the ARVN was preparing a major offensive and that additional American troops were required. Although the army wanted 200,000 reserves, Westmoreland claimed he could get the job done with

80,000 to 90,000 fresh troops. Johnson told Acheson that he would not mobilize the reserves, although he might make piecemeal additions of between 25,000 and 50,000 men and women within the next four months, primarily in the persons of nurses and doctors, supply troops, and air reserves to send to Korea. His recital finished, LBJ asked Acheson for his opinion based on his own assessment of the data.[76]

Acheson said that, based on the information he had garnered, the JCS was leading the administration "down the garden path." What Westmoreland was attempting in Vietnam would take unlimited resources and at least five long years. The American public was not prepared to bear such a burden for Vietnam, Acheson believed, due in part to the ongoing gold crisis and concern over the stability of the dollar.[77] A force of half a million Americans had been insufficient to prevent the Viet Cong from creating havoc in Saigon and other cities and hamlets throughout the region.

America's objective in Vietnam after Tet, Acheson concluded, should be to enable the GVN to survive long enough "to acquire public support [and] to stand alone for a period of time at least with only a fraction of the foreign military support it has now."[78] If the GVN could not meet these conditions, the United States should disengage. Should Washington detect some measurable success in these areas, it should reorient its strategic policy to keeping a limited military presence in the South until the ARVN proved self-sufficient.

Impressed with the competent men who had briefed him, Acheson urged LBJ to have their counterparts in other departments prepare similarly accurate and unvarnished reports on Vietnam to be relayed directly to the president. Acheson said it was imperative to freeze policy until the president had received the same unadulterated information from Rusk and Clifford that Acheson had received from Habib, Carver, and De Puy; then the president would understand what had gone wrong in South Vietnam. Acheson added that he was convinced that Hanoi now had absolutely no interest in negotiations, nor would they buy any solution that left a government in the South that they could not control. "Therefore, while negotiations at some point might be the only choice, at the present time to engage in them could only do great harm to the standing of the GVN."[79]

Acheson said the time had come for the United States to devise a new, long-range strategy in Vietnam, conditioned on the GVN demonstrating a modicum of competence in fulfilling assigned tasks, with U.S. ground troops in Vietnam stabilized at their post-Tet strength. Thenceforward, strategy must be based on accurate data in order to "appraise the ultimate as well as immediate possibilities and objectives." America's two-pronged mission should be to strengthen and aid the GVN in establishing a system of government with popular support while simultaneously U.S. forces were engaging Viet Cong forces in combat as far from population centers as possible. Acheson did not think it was necessary for the United States to call it quits in Southeast Asia, but if the GVN could not maintain stability in the South, disengagement had to be an option.[80]

Johnson was shaken by Acheson's report. On the same day as their meeting, LBJ received the discouraging news that the United States had taken a shellacking in gold trading and that because of pressure from Washington the London gold market was shut down. Acheson had noted that Westmoreland's mobilization request would result in a financial drain. Worse yet, he thought, it was a strategic mistake and bad politics. Others in the administration, most notably Clark Clifford, recently had voiced similar sentiments, adding to the president's alarm. LBJ could have concluded, but did not, that there was a conspiracy of the old Truman war horses—Acheson, Clifford, Harriman, and Nitze—to undermine him and save the containment policy by liquidating the war. The fact was that pressure to curtail U.S. involvement in Vietnam was coming from all corners, and these former Trumanites were only the parade leaders of other Establishment critics. Acheson even went so far as to have disseminated throughout the State and Defense departments an editorial entitled "Vietnam Quo Vadis," written by Wallace Carroll, his longtime friend and editor and publisher of the *Winston-Salem Journal*. Carroll called the Vietnam War a folly and urged the White House to get its global priorities straight.[81] To make matters worse for LBJ, he had won the New Hampshire Democratic primary on March 12 by a mere 5 percent margin over the antiwar candidate, Senator Eugene McCarthy. When Senator Robert Kennedy announced his candidacy for president on March 16, LBJ faced a dilemma. Not only had hawks like Acheson soured on his Vietnam policies, but he rapidly was losing the rank and file of his party.[82]

On March 20 LBJ summoned his UN ambassador, Arthur Goldberg, to the White House to discuss a bombing halt memo Goldberg had recently sent the president. Two days later Johnson announced that General Westmoreland would be stepping down from his command to represent the Army on the Joint Chiefs board. All of Washington sensed that a dramatic shift in Vietnam policy was in the air. Shortly thereafter, Johnson, urged on by Dean Acheson, Clark Clifford, and others, reconvened the senior foreign-policy advisory group (mainly the same individuals who had met in November), to attend briefings at the State Department and the White House.[83]

The fourteen senior advisers assembled at the State Department on March 25 for a working dinner. After scanning detailed data and reports prepared by Paul Nitze, Paul Warnke, and Alain Enthoven at the Pentagon, they heard a pessimistic briefing from Clark Clifford on just how badly things were going in Vietnam. More focused briefings followed: Philip Habib on the political situation, General De Puy on the post-Tet military outlook, and George Carver on pacification and the fighting strength of the Viet Cong. By evening's end November's near unanimity of prowar sentiment had been shattered. Acheson's change of heart had had an especially profound impact on the other advisers.[84]

The next morning the Wise Men met for a breakfast session at the White House. General Wheeler, just returned from Saigon, gave an upbeat report: Tet had severely damaged the Communist forces; the South Vietnamese had fought with commendable valor; things finally were looking up for the administration. General Maxwell Taylor vigorously endorsed escalating the bombing and dispatching more combat troops. This time, however, most of the audience was unmoved by Wheeler's optimism and Taylor's call to fight on to victory. Later that afternoon, General Creighton Abrams, Westmoreland's replacement, told the advisers and other high-level officials how the United States was transforming Vietnamese peasants into a formidable fighting force. Afterwards, LBJ politely dismissed Rusk and other administration officials directly involved in policy so that the advisers might feel free to express their views candidly. (Only Vice-President Humphrey and General Wheeler stayed on.)[85]

McGeorge Bundy, who had left government in early 1966 to become president of the Ford Foundation, was asked by the group to summarize. He led off by telling Johnson that there had been a dramatic shift in attitude since November. Most of the group present now were disenchanted with the situation in Vietnam and believed that a new counterinsurgency strategy was necessary. With public support for the war waning, Vietnam policy had reached an impasse; administration objectives were unattainable without the expenditure of unlimited resources. Bundy repeated the statement Acheson had made at the morning session: "We can no longer do the job we set out to do in the time we have left and we must take steps to disengage."[86]

Acheson, who was seated next to the president, told LBJ that he thoroughly concurred with Bundy's assessment: military victory in Vietnam was not possible unless the administration dramatically expanded the scope of the war. Only a change of goals and strategy could free America from the crisis at hand. Acheson urged the president to begin disengaging no later than midsummer. "One thing seems sure," he said. "The old slogan that success is just around the corner won't work."[87] Europe and the gold crisis were at the forefront of Acheson's agenda. He stressed that Vietnam was tarnishing the prestige of the American military and limiting the nation's economic might abroad. Disengagement from Vietnam was a prerequisite to grappling with more pressing foreign-policy concerns. "Our broader interests in Southeast Asia, Europe and in connection with the dollar crisis require a decision now to disengage within a limited time," Acheson told LBJ.[88]

Many of the others supported Acheson's views. McGeorge Bundy, Douglas Dillon, Cyrus Vance, Arthur Goldberg, George Ball, and Matthew Ridgway believed that Tet was the final blow, and disengagement the only rational option. But not all present agreed. General Maxwell Taylor, Abe Fortas, and Robert Murphy defended LBJ's policy of attrition. They proposed a bombing escalation and insisted that the war still was winnable. John McCloy, Henry Cabot Lodge, Arthur Dean, and Omar Bradley thought that the war had taken a turn for the worse but were unwilling to conclude that disengagement was the best solution. Johnson had invited the JCS chairman, Earle Wheeler, a diehard supporter of the war, to answer questions. Wheeler took exception to Acheson's call for disengagement and his assertion that the Pentagon was "bent on victory." Westmoreland and the joint chiefs realized that a "classic military victory" in Vietnam was impossible, he told the group. "Then what in the name of God are five hundred thousand men doing out there?" Acheson asked bluntly. "Chasing girls?" Wheeler, Acheson insisted, was playing semantic games. If the United States did not seek a military solution with that many troops engaged in combat, then words were meaningless.[89]

LBJ was deeply troubled by Acheson's about-face and the concurrence of so many other advisers. Someone "had poisoned the well," he said later.[90] "I think our general recommendation [to LBJ on March 25] was that we were trying to perform the wrong role . . . that it was basically a South Vietnamese enterprise in which we were auxiliaries and not principals," Acheson commented in an interview in 1969.[91]

The next day Acheson recorded in a memo for his personal files (with copies sent to the publishers J. H. P. Gould and John Cowles) why he had reversed his attitude on Vietnam. Tet had demonstrated that the North Vietnamese and Viet Cong could move freely about South Vietnam, able to attack and withdraw at will. It was only a matter of time before the GVN would lose what little credibility it still had. Furthermore, the South Vietnamese people themselves were apathetic toward the GVN. The United States could provide Saigon with supplies and firepower, but it could not give them what they needed most—popular support. The United States had to disengage and see if the GVN could stand on its own.[92] "Any satisfactory solution of the Vietnam effort is impossible.... I believe we must opt for an unsatisfactory one," Acheson wrote Cowles on March 29.[93]

On March 31 Lyndon Johnson gave a televised speech in which he announced a new plan for peace in Vietnam. He called for a bombing halt above the 20th parallel and an opportunity for Hanoi to agree to negotiations. He then stunned the nationwide audience by announcing his withdrawal from the presidential election campaign.[94] The Johnson administration's policy of escalation in Vietnam, begun in 1965, had ended. "We had been wrong," Acheson wrote, "in believing that we could establish an independent, non-communist state in South Vietnam"; the U.S. military could not "keep the North Vietnamese off the backs of the South Vietnamese while they [dealt] with the Viet Cong and [built] a state."[95]

The harsh medicine Acheson had prescribed for LBJ must have been equally unpalatable for the physician. Acheson had been forced to confront his own misperception that the United States had unlimited resources and could undertake correspondingly wide commitments abroad. Acheson also demonstrated once more his flexibility conceiving of U.S.-Asian issues. Johnson was not unaware of the difficulty Acheson had faced in reaching his conclusion to recommend withdrawal.[96]

Shortly after announcing that he would not seek reelection, LBJ wrote to Acheson: "You and I both know there have been a number of times when I did not like the advice you gave me. I am aware that you were aware that I would not like it when you gave it to me—and I am also aware that as you define your duty, my dislike was, and had to be, an irrelevancy."[97] Acheson's growing sense of the limits of U.S. power would become evident in his criticism of the Nixon administration for its actions in Laos and Cambodia, which Acheson saw as only prolonging the agony of the inevitable.

CHAPTER NINE

Reconciled with Nixon

For nearly two decades Dean Acheson and Richard Nixon had been bitter enemies. With the possible exceptions of Joseph McCarthy, John Foster Dulles, and Nelson Rockefeller, there was no man Acheson loathed more than Nixon.[1] In the McCarthy period Nixon had gained national notoriety as an adept practitioner of the political smear. It was he who successfully tarred the fiercely anticommunist Acheson with the epithet "Red Dean" in the early 1950s. Running on the Eisenhower ticket in 1952 against the Democratic team of Adlai Stevenson and John Sparkman, Nixon charged that Acheson, then secretary of state, had "a form of color blindness—a form of pink eye—toward the Communist threat in the United States." He attacked Stevenson by linking him to Acheson: "Mr. Stevenson has a degree alright—a Ph.D. from the Acheson College of Cowardly Communist Containment." Nixon also derogated Acheson for his role in the firing of General Douglas MacArthur, for neglecting to mention Korea in his defense perimeter speech, for losing Eastern Europe and China to communism, and for "bare-faced appeasement" in his attempts to end the Korean War. In a typical example of his campaign rhetoric, he attacked Acheson's Chinese policy as the "spineless school of diplomacy which cost the free world 600 million former allies in the past seven years of Trumanism."[2] Nixon also was an ardent enthusiastist of McCarthy's attempts to purge the State Department of the so-called American communist fifth column. Taking advantage of Acheson's well-publicized refusal to "turn his back" on his former colleague Alger Hiss, Nixon hammered the Democrats on this issue.[3]

In his memoirs, published long after Acheson's death, Nixon recalls with a degree of remorse that in the 1952 campaign, Acheson's "clipped moustache, his British tweeds, and his haughty manner made him the perfect foil for my attacks on the snobbish kind of foreign service personality and mentality that had been taken in hook, line, and sinker by the Communists." Nixon confessed that, while he still believed Acheson was "wrong about Asia," he was "right about Europe, where he helped make NATO a strong, durable bastion against communist aggression."[4] But after nearly two decades of animosity between the two men, it is not surprising that in 1968 Acheson thought the country would be "going to hell in a hack with Mr. Nixon as our inspiring leader."[5]

Acheson's concerns about Nixon did not signal happiness with his own party. When Hubert Humphrey won the Democratic Party's nomination for the presidency at the chaotic 1968 convention in Chicago, the elder statesman breathed a sigh of relief. Outside the convention hall antiwar demonstrators and civil rights activists, joined by hippies and yippies, clashed with Mayor Richard Daley's Chicago police force; inside, a deeply divided party chose President Johnson's vice-president as their candidate. To Acheson, a man who had devoted his career to creating and restoring order, the street violence in Chicago and the assassinations of Martin Luther King, Jr., and Robert F. Kennedy were deeply disturbing.[6]

Acheson put part of the blame for the unrest of the 1960s on sensationalized, irresponsible television news coverage. Shortly after Robert F. Kennedy was murdered Acheson wrote to a friend that "the television from gangster movies for the teenager to battlefront murder in Vietnam to the political and sentimental frenzy of the Kennedy funeral keeps this country in an emotional frenzy."[7] Acheson did not own a television and only would watch "the boob-tube" at a friend's on special occasions.[8]

Acheson was depressed by the worldwide "mediocrity of leadership," especially in the United States, where, he commented, "No one rises above the level of what we used to expect of respectable mayors." Still, as a loyal Democrat, he had little choice but to go all out for Hubert Humphrey.[9] He personally liked and respected Humphrey and thought it unfair that so many branded him with responsibility for the war by virtue of his unenviable (and powerless) position as Johnson's vice-president. In September, with Humphrey trailing Nixon by a large margin in the polls, Acheson tried to counter his party's ideological divisions and defeatist mood in an article for the *Washington Post* entitled "HHH Is in Truman's Shoes." Harking back to Truman's upset of Dewey in 1948, Acheson dismissed public opinion polls as fraudulent. He scoffed at those who tried to equate Nixon with John F. Kennedy: "To begin with, it takes too much 'beautification' to transform Nixon into the fresh young challenger of 1960, to say nothing of the difficulty of maintaining the role."[10]

Acheson refrained from publicly attacking Nixon as he had during the 1960 election campaign. In the intervening years he had come to regard Nixon with grudging approval. "Painful experience," he explained, "has improved and sophisticated Nixon's political technique." He characterized Nixon as clearly an "authentic conservative" who had the backing of big business interests. Humphrey, he argued, represented the liberal progressive tradition, the predominant current of American political thought since the days of FDR. But Acheson realized that the campaign would turn on the Vietnam War, not on political ideology. Cognizant that Humphrey would necessarily lose some votes from association with LBJ's Vietnam policy, Acheson nevertheless did not want Humphrey in consequence to become too vocal an advocate of military withdrawal from the region. In Acheson's view the importance of the election lay in relieving Hanoi "of any expectation that a peacenik administration, a peace at any price group, might come to power in Washington."[11]

When Nixon won, then, Acheson took his victory in stride, although he expressed a few doubts about the notorious president-elect. In a letter to former British prime minister Anthony Eden shortly after the election, Acheson reflected, "It may not hurt the Democratic Party to let their opponents chew for a while on the problems we have not been able to solve. At best, the next four years are likely to be boring here in Washington. And next to worse, we may be scared to death."[12]

Henry Kissinger Plays Matchmaker

Acheson thought Nixon got off to an uninspired start by appointing William P. Rogers as secretary of state. Rogers, a successful New York Republican lawyer, had been counsel to several postwar investigating committees, including the McCarran Committee, whose members were convinced that the State Department under Acheson was riddled with subversives. Rogers focused on developing comprehensive antisubversion legislation. His performance on the committee eventually led to his appointment in 1957 as attorney general in the Eisenhower administration. His association with Nixon and the unsavory side of the Republican Party compromised him in Acheson's eyes.[13]

Acheson remained critical of Rogers to the end of his life. He thought him vacuous, narrow-minded, and inept as secretary of state. "Bill Rogers' difficulties, including his inability to speak effectively to representatives of foreign governments which you mention, spring from his own inadequacies and not from Henry Kissinger or anyone else," Acheson wrote Dean Rusk in 1971. "One conclusion I hold after some experience is that a quiet word with Bill Rogers is not only a waste of time, but it's far better left unspoken."[14]

But if Acheson disapproved Nixon's choice for secretary of state, he was delighted at the appointment of his friend Henry Kissinger as national security adviser. The German-born Kissinger—a Rockefeller protégé, Council on Foreign Relations rapporteur, and Harvard professor—had, interestingly enough, first attracted Acheson's attention in 1957 when Acheson served as the chairman of the foreign-policy committee of the Democratic Advisory Council. Kissinger's book *Nuclear Weapons and Foreign Policy* impressed Acheson with its unrelenting assault on the massive retaliation doctrine and its bold claim that a limited nuclear war could be won. "It is a hard book to read because of its repetitive Germanic style and the first section is infuriating because of its academic superiority," Acheson wrote a friend. "But the damned cuss has brains and has thought a lot."[15] An intellectual bond quickly developed between the two, with Acheson as mentor. Kissinger, in his turn, energetically endorsed Acheson's *Power and Diplomacy*, in a review entitled "Acheson's Wise, Lucid Analysis of Our Foreign Policy Problems."[16]

So impressed was Acheson by Kissinger's intellectual prowess that in February 1960 he actually tried to recruit him for the DAC.[17] Kissinger, who was then working on Nelson Rockefeller's presidential campaign, politely declined. But the two corresponded frequently during the 1960s. Kissinger occasionally breakfasted with Acheson at his Georgetown home, and they discussed military policy and strategy.[18] During the Berlin crisis of 1961 Kissinger wrote to tell Acheson that "only your presence" at a White House meeting in July "prevented a real disaster."[19] In 1964 Kissinger suggested that Acheson use the services of his research assistant, Marina Finkelstein, to help him prepare his second volume of memoirs, *Present at the Creation*; Acheson did and was forever grateful for the referral, further solidifying their relationship.[20] "One sees no Dean Achesons anywhere and I wonder whether we are still capable of producing them," Kissinger said to Acheson in 1966. "What will happen to our clever young men when they are still clever young men at the age of 70."[21]

Acheson and Kissinger shared the same conception of the proper role for the United States in world affairs. Both adhered to the realist school of thought, which asserts the primacy of pragmatic organization and balance of power over legal and moral principles in the making of foreign policy. They held strikingly similar views on the need to downplay the role of Congress when it came to foreign-policy decisions. Both also had a deep distrust of the emerging third world and the United Nations. They stressed the importance to the United States of remaining the supreme military power in the world.[22]

Kissinger's Harvard doctoral dissertation (later published as *A World Restored: Metternich, Castlereagh, and the Restoration of Europe, 1812–1822*) assessed European diplomacy during the post-Napoleonic period.[23] Kissinger maintained that Metternich, Austria's foreign minister, brought order, stability, and a "hundred years of peace" to Europe by creating a balance of power in which all countries involved had a vested interest. Acheson likewise admired the conservative Austrian statesman and was not unhappy at being called by his critics "a Metternich born out of time."[24] The alliance-building approach of the Congress of Vienna was the paradigm for Acheson and Kissinger of successful diplomatic method.

The general tone of the Acheson-Kissinger correspondence from the sixties is illustrated in a letter Acheson wrote Kissinger in 1964: "I have been reading your book—*A World Restored*—with great enthusiasm and giving it to others. I do it slowly as I like to taste it and think about it as I go along. It also refreshes me from the too arid discussions of the present."[25] Acheson's personal library contained many volumes inherited from his father on nineteenth-century British statesmen.[26] Acheson especially admired the way England had used its navy in the conduct of imperial foreign policy, and he urged the study of nineteenth-century Britain upon Kissinger. He also prodded Kissinger to continue writing "more history from the point of view of political theory. No one is doing it. We need to understand our past."[27]

The diplomatic historian Walter LaFeber has commented of Kissinger and Acheson: "The Jewish emigre and the son of an Episcopalian minister from Connecticut came to see the globe in much the same way." LaFeber goes on to connect their vision to the American tradition of pragmatism: "The two statesmen differed from the rest of their countrymen only in being able to make that view more coherent, historically rooted, and politically effective."[28] An abhorrence of instability and an intolerance for moralism in the conduct of foreign policy were key features of each man's approach to international power politics.

When Kissinger became national security adviser, he immediately turned to Dean Acheson for guidance. Kissinger felt history had awarded Acheson "its highest accolade—it proved him right."[29] It is not surprising, therefore, that he would make use of Acheson's experience, prestige, and political acumen to ease his move from studying balance-of-power issues in Harvard Yard to acting on the world stage in the ultimate seat of power—the White House. When Kissinger wrote his memoirs, *The White House Years*, in 1979, he praised Acheson as he never had any other public official.[30]

The First Meeting

Shortly after Nixon's inauguration, Kissinger told the president that he ought to consider employing Dean Acheson as an unofficial adviser. Acheson's attitude of near-reverence toward the institution of the presidency would outweigh his previous acrimony toward Nixon. In the beginning Acheson apparently found it difficult to live up to this high-minded principle: he said of the inaugural weekend that it was like "finding oneself pregnant and trying to fall in love as quickly as possible."[31]

Despite their long careers in government, Acheson and Nixon had never met, and while Nixon took the first step agreeing to consult with Acheson from time to time, it was Acheson who brought about their first face-to-face meeting—"the first overture to de-escalate our ancient feud" in the elder statesman's words—by introducing himself to the president at a Gridiron Club dinner in March 1969. Acheson congratulated the president on his recent announcement of the Safeguard antiballistic missile program. Nixon responded by saying he would like to talk with Acheson privately sometime soon. The elder statesman accepted the invitation with assurances to the president that he "would always be at his service."[32] Kissinger wrote in *The White House Years*, "Nixon's shabby treatment of him in the 1952 campaign did not keep Acheson from assisting the President when he was needed almost two decades later. His loyalty ran to the office, not the man."[33] Asked in late 1969 about his reconciliation with Nixon, Acheson himself explained, "I feel about political battles the way Mr. Truman did, that 'If you can't stand the heat you better stay out of the kitchen.' I said pretty harsh things about Mr. Nixon. I think it's a mistake to allow that to interfere with relations. I don't think either one of us now are affected by what happened 20 years ago."[34]

Three days later Kissinger called Acheson to relay two messages from his boss. The president wanted to see Acheson the next day, and he was also extending an invitation to attend a White House dinner for the NATO foreign ministers.

The first official Acheson-Nixon meeting took place on March 19, 1969, in the Oval Office with Henry Kissinger present. Nixon's opening gambit in dealing with the man he had called the Red Dean was to commend Acheson's long experience in government, particularly his role in the Marshall Plan, which Nixon called one of the great acts of statesmanship in American history. The discussion turned to Lyndon Johnson, whom Nixon felt would be treated more kindly by historians than he had been by contemporary commentators. Nixon thought LBJ was a stronger man than he was given credit for being, although he was perplexed by Johnson's inability to establish good relations with certain Democratic members of Congress, for instance, J. William Fulbright. Nixon asked Acheson why he thought this was so. The elder statesman replied, "No President could maintain any relationship with Fulbright, who [is] a dilettante, an egoist, and a prima donna." Acheson's candor on this point was, he felt, the "curtain raiser" to the new rapprochement, for Nixon heartily agreed with this description of Fulbright. To their mutual surprise the former adversaries had found a common ground.[35]

Talk turned to the serious business of extracting the United States from Vietnam. Exasperated by President Johnson's piecemeal efforts to end the war, Acheson urged Nixon to find a reasonable solution to the stalemate as soon as possible. Nixon said he opposed the overwhelming opinion of the business, financial, and legal world in New York, which favored "scuttling Vietnam at any price." The whole situation was "frustrating and puzzling." Nixon then asked Acheson for his view of the current Paris peace talks on Vietnam.

Acheson replied that the discussions in Paris were irrelevant to U.S. objectives and advocated "so reduc[ing] the belligerency in Vietnam that with minimum, competent help from us the South Vietnamese could survive in an attempt to reach a political modus vivendi with the Vietcong." To support his recommendation, Acheson pointed out that "the years of discussion at Panmunjom in Korea had not brought about an armistice and the beginning of an American withdrawal until the Chinese discovered that they could not defeat Ridgway on the Kansas line and simply stopped fighting." But, Acheson also noted, the United States still had no political settlement in Korea, and he doubted whether a political settlement was possible in Vietnam. Thus the sound strategy was to reduce the fighting in Vietnam to "tolerable proportions." Acheson added that the new administration should follow the course decided upon "relentlessly, regardless of criticism." Johnson's trouble, Acheson told the president, was that he "flinch[ed] in a pinch."

Acheson cautioned that Johnson had suffered through blindly relying on information received from the Pentagon. He suggested adhering to General Abrams's policy of strengthening the South Vietnamese military so that eventually it would take over the offensive. Acheson stressed that under no circumstances should the United States resume bombing North Vietnam. If bombing seemed militarily desirable, the South Vietnamese should be the ones to do it. The withdrawal of American troops should begin as soon as possible to signal to the Soviets and the North Vietnamese that Washington was indeed beginning to deescalate. To Acheson's surprise, Nixon agreed completely with his analysis.

Nixon thought there should soon be a U.S.-Soviet summit. Acheson, as usual, was adamantly opposed. He remarked that he had learned as Truman's secretary of state that "the Russians don't negotiate under pressure—only when the correlation of forces makes it seem to their advantage." Nixon brought up the Glassboro meetings between Kosygin and Johnson in June 1967, at which time he thought the Soviets were yearning for a new era of détente. Acheson snapped that so "did the yearning for a heaven, but it proved nothing." The president reserved judgment. He said he "wished to think it [the summit issue] over very carefully" and pursue the subject with Acheson again.

The first meeting ended with Acheson criticizing U.S. policy toward South-West Africa [now Namibia]. The president cut off that discussion for lack of time but asked to see the former secretary again soon.

Acheson left the meeting impressed with the president. He wrote his close friend J. H. P. Gould that he "got a feeling of orderliness and concentration rather than of Napoleonic drive and scattered attention," as in the Johnson White House. Acheson admired Nixon's grasp of world affairs and, Acheson joked, his wisdom, which he had demonstrated by listening to Acheson's advice. He had told his wife his opinion of Nixon had "been moved toward a more favorable one and in this process I am quite conscious that a change in his attitude from abusive hostility to respect with a dash of flattery has played a part." To William Tyler Acheson gave a more qualified portrait; Nixon was a "definite relief from L.B.J., not from definable positive virtues, but from the absence of a swinish bullying boorishness which made his last three years unbearable."[36]

In a talk before the American Society of Newspaper Editors, Acheson assessed the first hundred days of the Nixon administration. Nixon, he said, had scored "a hit at both times at bat." The two "hits" were the president's whirlwind trip abroad and his decision to go forward with the antiballistic missile program (ABM). Nixon's European visit had been a surprising success, and Acheson, in a rare demonstration of public humility, admitted it: "A good many of us are in the position of having to concede that, in deciding to go to Europe, President Nixon's judgment was better than ours."[37]

The Fight for the ABM

Acheson supported Nixon's decision to push forward with development of the ABM and to proceed with a limited program to protect Minuteman silos. To do away with an ABM system, Acheson had commented in his Newspaper Editors talk, "would have been foolish and dangerous ... [for] a going program could always be intensified if necessary, but it might well be impossible, starting from scratch, to catch up [with the Soviets]."[38] If the United States wished to convince Moscow to limit its ICBMs, the ABM system would be a useful bargaining chip.

There had been a mood swing on Capitol Hill from 1967, when Congress essentially forced ABM appropriations on the reluctant McNamara. By 1969 opposition to the ABM was growing rapidly in Congress, as well as in the academic and scientific communities.[39] One concern was the increase in defense spending triggered by the unpopular and costly Vietnam War. Nixon needed allies in his campaign to convince Congress to approve ABM funding. His program called for twelve separate sites for area defense, four of which would also protect Minuteman missiles; nineteen radar installations; and several hundred interceptor missiles, slated for completion by 1973. President Nixon named his system "Safeguard," a revision of Johnson's "Sentinel." The two systems differed mainly in that Safeguard ostensibly would cover the United States with radar installations and would concentrate more on defending ICBM silos.

Nixon's announcement of Safeguard provoked a fierce debate lasting from March to August 1969. Acheson and Paul Nitze lobbied on behalf of the program. They viewed ABM development as crucial to maintaining military superiority of the United States over the Soviet Union. Liberal Democrats countered that the ABM program would accelerate the nuclear arms race and hinder the prospect of arms control agreements. Acheson, who long ago had broken with the liberals, now was publicly aligned with Nixon in attacking them. "The whole [ABM] issue is a phony and a cover for a general attack on the whole U.S. policy toward the U.S.S.R. over the past twenty years," Acheson wrote his friend Lady Pamela Berry. "The protagonists are a group of wooly-headed Democrats—Fulbright-Mansfield-Proxmire-McCarthy and so on. The swing to the right may replace some of them next year but I shall save my tears for worthier weeping."[40]

Acheson, Nitze, and Albert Wohlstetter, a leading nuclear strategist from the University of Chicago, founded the Committee to Maintain a Prudent Defense Policy as a lobbying organ, although its self-proclaimed purpose was to contribute to a more thoughtful and public national security debate. On May 26 they sent a letter to members of Congress that declared, "On an issue of this kind, connected as it is with avoiding nuclear war and nuclear coercion, it is all too easy to stimulate an emotional rather than a reasoned public response."[41]

The main objective of this letter was to reveal the flawed reasoning of the ABM opponents, especially of those members of Congress who wanted to suspend the ABM but proceed with Strategic Arms Limitation talks (SALT) with the Soviets. The chief purpose of Safeguard, as the committee saw it, was to defend U.S. war-making capability by protecting Minuteman silos, manned bombers, and the facilities necessary in an emergency to coordinate strategic forces. The existence of these structures gave the United States a better position in the SALT talks. Secondarily, the program would provide some protection to the civilian population against "accidental, irrational or desperate small attack" by taking out an incoming weapon. The committee characterized the projected program as modest in cost. It was clear, they charged, that the "anti-ABM campaign ha[d] capitalized on the disenchantment with the Vietnamese war, on a general feeling of alienation from government, and on the desire to wish away problems of national defense."[42]

Acheson looked back to the bipartisan policy of the Truman-Acheson-Vandenberg period as having been very beneficial for world policy, as it had led to the formation of NATO and to years of peace in Western Europe. Acheson sought a new bipartisan defense consensus around the ABM. "I have finally agreed to go before Senator William Proxmire's Joint Committee [Economic]," Acheson wrote J. H. P. Gould, "to add to the large doses of visible gas which it is discharging on the country."[43] In June he testified before the committee.

Acheson began his testimony with a broad statement: "In the more than 20 years during which I have been dimly conscious of the world around me, I have been strongly impressed that the Congress . . . has underspent rather than overspent on the defense of the United States." During this period, he continued, Congress and the American people "have been greatly distracted from considering the real problems they have to face by witch hunts and clichés, all of which have taken their minds off the point," namely, that the United States could no longer count on its distance from Europe and Asia to provide adequate national security. America needed a defensive system to protect against Soviet or possibly even Chinese nuclear attack.[44]

Acheson testified that Safeguard was the "best that present technology can provide for the active defense of the land-based retaliatory forces." Voting for ABM would not diminish the possibility of an arms control agreement with the Soviet Union but actually would strengthen it by bringing about "that calculation of forces by the Russians which induces them to make a deal." Acheson viewed the ABM as a defensive program and was confident that the Soviets would perceive it as such. The Soviets were developing an ABM system of their own and would recognize that the sole purpose of Safeguard was to destroy incoming weapons. Rejecting Safeguard could mean real trouble for the United States in the future, Acheson warned, whereas proceeding with its development "cannot mean terrible trouble. It may indeed bring great assurance. If you lose the whole investment, it is not a very serious [financial] loss."

Senator Proxmire commented on recent testimony by John Kenneth Galbraith and others that the U.S. government had unrealistic expectations for its military systems. Expenditures for major weapons systems exceeded cost estimates by two to three times; the systems were delivered years after they were promised; and more often than not they failed to come close to meeting the technical capabilities specified. Proxmire said the ABM could cause citizens to lose faith in the country's basic defense. Acheson's only response was an ad hominem remark: "So far as Ken Galbraith is concerned, he is the greatest humorist in the world."

The committee appearance aroused Acheson's appetite for a battle on Capitol Hill that summer. America had just demonstrated technological prowess by landing the *Apollo 11* astronauts in the lunar module *Eagle* on the moon. The achievement aided Acheson's cause; if the United States could send a man to the moon, surely it could develop an effective ABM system. Acheson began lobbying full time for the Safeguard program.

To do what Nitze called "the necessary nitty-gritty of drafting papers to combat the arrant nonsense, the inaccuracies and logical tripe being perpetrated by the other side," the committee enlisted "four worker bees": Peter Wilson and Paul Wolfowitz (students of Wohlstetter), Richard Perle (who had studied at UCLA and Princeton), and Edward Luttwak (a strategic analyst and military historian).[45] The four produced analyses on which the committee could base its lobbying efforts.

Acheson insisted on registering the committee as an official lobbying organization, since its purpose was to affect legislation; this meant that contributions to its support were not tax-deductible. Nitze recalls that he insisted the committee not "accept any money from any organizations having any interests in defense industry, and that cut off all kinds of other sources of possible contributions. The upshot was that we raised a total of $15,000, of which I put up 50 percent, so that we had the smallest budget of any lobbying group you ever heard of."[46]

Senator Charles Percy of Illinois, a Republican and an opponent of Safeguard, debated Acheson on the nationally televised David Frost Show in mid-July. Frost asked Acheson to respond to Percy's speculation that ABM quickly might become technically obsolete. Acheson said, "I think everything is open to that danger, everything. Science is moving very fast. But you cannot turn over one whole field of development to the opponent with any degree of safety. One must stay with it, Mr. Frost, one has got to stay all the time with it. If you delay and delay, and delay, and the other person experiments and develops and develops, you are losing ground." The televised debate helped focus the attention of the American people on the issues, and Acheson's performance elicited dozens of laudatory letters. Having a distinguished American statesman speaking out so forcefully on television was a public relations coup for Safeguard.[47]

Acheson continued his lobbying efforts throughout the summer, most notably in an article entitled "A Citizen Takes a Hard Look at the ABM Debate," in the *Washington Sunday Star*.[48] In a letter to a friend, Acheson wrote that the ABM vote was "still close but moving toward our side, first by firming up our own votes as our committee boys have gotten the real arguments to our senators, and second by picking up a few votes."[49]

Three amendments, each of which would have halted ABM construction, were introduced in Congress on August 6. All were defeated. On the first and most important amendment, prohibiting Safeguard deployment, the Senate vote was tied 50-50. Vice-President Spiro Agnew cast the tie-breaking vote, defeating the bill and giving President Nixon his first major legislative victory—congressional authorization for Safeguard. Paul Nitze believes that "without the work of Dean Acheson, and the Committee to Maintain a Prudent Defense Policy, the ABM never would have passed."[50] Richard Nixon went further. He wrote in 1978 that he was "absolutely convinced that had we lost the ABM battle in the Senate, we would not have been able to negotiate the first nuclear arms control agreement in Moscow in 1972."[51] In other words, no ABM, no SALT I. Acheson himself, however, would have been none too thrilled by the connection of his efforts to SALT. By 1970 he was cynical about SALT, believing that the Kremlin could not be trusted and that there were insurmountable difficulties preventing the verification of Soviet nuclear stockpiles. "The whole subject is so complex and in many respects so unknowable at present that to plan a chess game on the theory that either or both sides may cheat is too complicated to me," Acheson wrote the former prime minister of Rhodesia Sir Roy Welensky. "Man has educated himself above his intelligence."[52]

A year after the ABM victory, Acheson and Henry Cabot Lodge, Jr., founded the Citizens' Committee to Safeguard America in support of Nixon's proposal to expand ABM. With Foy Kohler, formerly ambassador to Moscow, as their spokesman, the committee argued that bolstering the Safeguard system would enhance, not hinder, the SALT talks.[53]

Present at the Creation

No single project occupied more of Acheson's time and energy during his postsecretarial years than the writing of his 350,000-word memoir, *Present at the Creation: My Years in the State Department*. The book is perhaps the most historically significant American political autobiography of the twentieth century. Acheson's reminiscences of his early life, published under the title *Morning and Noon*, had been, to his surprise, a popular and critical success. Nevertheless, for a long time he forswore any intention of writing about his State Department career. He feared, he said, that his "detachment and objectivity would become suspect," and the "element of self-justification could not be excluded."[54]

His son, David, as well as others, pointed out that if he did not get his own story down for the record, revisionist historians would do it for him after his death, and this warning finally led Acheson to write about his State Department years.[55] The epigraph attributes the book's title to Alphonso X (called Alphonso the Learned), King of Spain from 1252 to

1284: "Had I been present at the creation I would have given some useful hints for the better ordering of the universe." Some critics thought the title revealed Acheson's hubris in the implied equivalence between the creation of the postwar order and the creation of the universe, as described in Genesis. Others thought the title self-effacing, for Acheson was not merely "present," he was a master architect of the new Europe and a dynamic strategist of foreign policy who brought the United States from prewar isolationism to postwar internationalism.

With the help of several research assistants, Acheson pored over hundreds of documents in his private papers and in the State Department archives. Acheson was determined to avoid, insofar as it was within his power, having his memoirs seen as self-serving. His objective was a thoroughly documented, historically accurate account of his years in the State Department. He also wanted to introduce a new generation to the heroic figures of Harry S Truman, George C. Marshall, and other, less well known, public servants of that era. He ultimately dedicated the book to Truman, "the captain with the mighty heart." After a year of researching and taking notes, Acheson began to write, mostly in longhand on yellow legal pads.[56]

Acheson worked on the memoirs from August 1966 until early 1969. During this period his letter writing dramatically increased, as he solicited information, opinions, and suggestions from old associates and friends. Outside, the Vietnam War raged and the NATO allies skirmished, but at his writing desk Acheson was reliving through letters "the splendid years" of Korea and the triumphant early years of Atlantic unity. The process energized Acheson, as he felt connected again to the time when he was secretary of state and America seemed more noble, a time when American men did not burn their draft cards and American women did not burn their bras. "In writing about those years," Acheson told Truman shortly before the book's publication, "I came close to reliving them again with you and hope I have captured some of your spirit and purpose that made them such a wonderfully satisfying adventure."[57]

Present at the Creation, published in September 1969, was an immediate success. Dozens of newspapers and journals reviewed the book admiringly, and Acheson received hundreds of letters from around the globe praising his lucid and literate account of his State Department years.[58] The book, brimming with admiration for Truman, Marshall, and Churchill, also contained scathing portraits of Douglas MacArthur, Joseph McCarthy, and Walter Lippmann, which raised eyebrows and caused a swirl of press attention. But perhaps most impressive is Acheson's thoughtful and respectful description of the less well known diplomats and bureaucrats who worked with him. Lucius Battle, William L. Clayton, Joseph C. Grew, Ernest Gross, Loy Henderson, John D. Hickerson, Robert Lovett, Edward G. Miller, Jr., and Dean Rusk, among other government officials, emerge from Acheson's pages as patriots of the first order, tireless public servants who helped America awake from its isolationist slumber to assume leadership of the free world. "Even George Kennan writes praising my treatment of him," an astonished Acheson wrote J. H. P. Gould.[59] Such longtime Acheson detractors as John Kenneth Galbraith and Chester Bowles grudgingly admired *Present at the Creation*. "The reception the book has had has given me great pleasure," Acheson wrote to Lewis Douglas, formerly the U.S. ambassador to Great Britain. "As Macaulay put it—'Even the ranks of Tuscany could scarse forbear to cheer'—in the person of Ken Galbraith."[60]

Acheson appeared on three television news shows and at countless book-signing parties and speaking engagements. By November *Present at the Creation* was on most of the nonfiction bestseller lists, and it remained there well into the spring of 1970. The book was translated into German and Japanese. Other foreign editions followed, as did anthologies of excerpts for college use.[61]

The capstone for Acheson was the Pulitzer Prize for history awarded the book in May 1970. Acheson had suffered a stroke earlier in the month. "The Pulitzer Prize," he wrote to Lawrence S. Eagleburger, a State Department official, "was a great boon to my rather sagging spirits, and they have been further lifted by notes from my friends telling me of their approval of the book and the prize."[62] With Nixon and Kissinger seeking his advice and a new celebrity status, as a consequence of his television appearances (including a thirty-minute, prime-time *CBS News Special* interview with Eric Sevareid), Acheson, not surprisingly, felt rejuvenated. "I was delighted to hear the news of your Pulitzer Award but I must confess I was not surprised," Robert Lovett wrote Acheson. "If you keep on at that rate you will probably collect an Oscar, an Emmy—and anything else that is not nailed down."[63]

Only New Left historians and the columnists who wrote for the *Nation* criticized Acheson's book, saying that underneath the eloquence and urbanity lay the philosophy of a conservative cold warrior who had led America into the global overcommitment from which it was still struggling to disengage, especially in Vietnam.

278 ▪ *Reconciled with Nixon*

The "Silent Majority" Speech

Following the ABM victory and the publication of *Present at the Creation*, Acheson returned to reminding President Nixon that the Vietnam clock was ticking; he must pull out as soon as possible—without losing South Vietnamese and American honor—or else face political disaster at home. Domestic unrest was continuing, and Acheson saw danger in these efforts to discredit Nixon. In early summer Acheson's concern for Nixon's position was evident. "Poor Nixon is beginning to need an 'act of God' like the Antigua rain to silence his opposition," he wrote. "I never thought that I would sympathize with him. Senility, I guess."[64]

Acheson began to see in the Nixon White House the kind of indecisiveness that had characterized the Johnson administration. "The [Nixon] administration is made up on the whole of pretty good men, intelligent, high-minded, conservative, but wholly inexperienced in government and—so it seems to me—naive beyond words," Acheson wrote Sir Roy Welensky. "If the Administration would focus its mind on three principal issues—Vietnam, internal order, and inflation—it could, I believe, easily expand its present minority position in the center by accretions from right and left into a majority position. What is required are quite simple actions aimed at fairly short-range objectives. The great trouble seems to be the absence of any objectives."[65]

Millions of other Americans were likewise deeply troubled over Nixon's inability to end the Vietnam War. By autumn 1969 violent antiwar demonstrations had erupted at colleges and universities throughout the nation. Nixon dug in, determined not to let the demonstrators disrupt his peace-with-honor disengagement strategy. He later wrote that his "real concern was that these highly publicized efforts aimed at forcing me to end the war were seriously undermining my behind-the-scenes attempts to do just that."[66] In a *New York Times* interview in October 1969 Acheson spoke of the rough waters into which President Nixon was sailing and warned Americans, "We're going to have a major constitutional crisis if we make a habit of destroying Presidents. We'll have the situation we had after the Civil War, when the Presidency practically disappeared from Andrew Johnson to McKinley."[67]

Acheson repeated his warnings to a group of members of his own party. "The important thing for the United States is that the next three years should not be spent in tearing down the present President," he told the Women's National Democratic Club. "When we come to 1972, that is another matter. We will have our internal battle, and we will fight it lustily and strong. But we cannot have a period of three years before the next election in which the entire energies of the whole, perhaps dominant, party in the United States spends time in destroying the credibility of the government."[68]

On October 20 in a letter to Henry Kissinger, Acheson commented on the president's scheduled television response on November 3 to the critics of his phased withdrawal program. Following his explanation of the administration's goals, Acheson suggested, Nixon should make a special plea to the American people for their support. If he could rally the nation emotionally around the flag, his supporters would drown out the unpatriotic demonstrators whom Acheson believed represented only a small fraction of the population.[69]

Speaking on the television program *Issues and Answers* Acheson noted: "I can't do any more than say that I think the President would greatly strengthen his position if he could carry to the people a conviction that he is trying to do what everybody wants to do, which is to reduce the thing [Vietnam] in a sensible and wise way."[70]

On October 27 Acheson met with the president. Kissinger, briefing him beforehand, said that a paragraph from Acheson's letter of the previous week had been incorporated into the speech. The president also was considering speaking about the rate of troop withdrawal or on time limits for withdrawal. Acheson said he would "most emphatically advise against it." Kissinger concurred with Acheson on this point.[71]

Nixon opened the meeting by thanking Acheson for his support expressed on *Issues and Answers*. He next asked the question Kissinger had warned was coming, whether to include a schedule of troop withdrawals and a deadline for completion. Acheson advised against doing so. Disclosure of these details, Acheson felt, would be a sign of "weakness and yielding to pressure" and would be "wholly the wrong way . . . to use the withdrawal to have the maximum effect on the South Vietnamese, the North Vietnamese, the Russians, and the Chinese." As for the American people, no statement would "appease those who criticized him or reassure the great mass of people that he was in command of the situation and was operating under a definitive plan." What the public needed was a president resolute in purpose and in clear control of the international political trading over Vietnam. Once again Acheson cautioned the president not to raise public expectations by suggesting that a total armistice with the North Vietnamese was being discussed in Paris.

Early on November 3 Henry Kissinger phoned Acheson to say that the president had requested him to convey his gratitude for Acheson's help on the tone and substance of the speech. The last two paragraphs of the speech had been taken from Acheson's letter of October 20 to Kissinger. Nixon had also heeded Acheson's advice not to state numbers and dates for troop withdrawals.[72]

In what came to be known as the "silent majority" speech, the president described in general terms his plan for ending the war by "Vietnamization": gradual withdrawal of American troops while military responsibility was transferred to the South Vietnamese until such time as a "fair and honorable peace" could be arranged. As Acheson had advised, Nixon offered no timetable for withdrawal; his goal, he stated, was to convince the "great silent majority" of Americans that he was doing everything humanly possible to end the war without losing American honor and prestige abroad. Nixon closed by pledging to carry out his presidential responsibilities in Vietnam with "all of the strength and wisdom I can command, in accordance with your hopes, mindful of your concerns, sustained by your prayers."[73]

Acheson's letter to Kissinger had advised that the president adopt precisely this tone. An excerpt from that letter reveals its profound influence on the tonality of the "silent majority" speech:

> We would respond to a Lincolnian touch of patience and sadness, of understanding beneath determination; and above all an indication that the goal is a common one, though the heavy responsibility for picking the path to it, for better or for worse, has been laid on him. He cannot abdicate it, cannot escape it. He hopes for strength and wisdom to achieve this common goal in accordance with the hopes, mindful of the interests, and aided by the prayers of all.[74]

Nixon called Acheson after delivering the speech and "most touchingly expressed his gratitude," Acheson noted.[75]

The response to the speech was overwhelmingly favorable; the president had struck the responsive chord Acheson had hoped he would. Acheson applauded both content and delivery. "It was a courageous speech and I think will reassure the silent majority of the country that he is acting forcefully and temperately to bring an end to the fighting in Vietnam," he wrote to Sir Roy Welensky. "He will not dissuade the extremists or the violent young people who do not understand the intractability of humanity. If the President is successful in quieting down the belligerency, I think the extremist youth movement will begin to run out of steam."[76]

Nixon himself later came to regard the silent majority speech as "both a milestone and turning point" for his administration. Not so much what the president said as the way he said it favorably impressed the war-weary nation. Acheson, who helped guide him, deserves some of the credit.[77]

In the months that followed, Acheson continued to support the president's Vietnam policy, although he was concerned by the overuse of the term *Vietnamization*. He had warned in October that it would be a mistake to "guarantee" the success of the policy, citing Korea as an example of how difficult military extrication could be.[78]

Acheson's relationship with the president continued to solidify. "To my vast surprise and due to a series of accidents, Mr. Nixon and I have become very friendly, an almost unbelievable possibility, and I have been drawn into the White House more as a comforter than an advisor," Acheson wrote Lincoln MacVeagh in December. "I have, I believe, propelled the President in the right direction in his Vietnam policy . . . I find that I like him better than I thought it would be possible to do."[79] Acheson was impressed by Nixon's calm dignity and by the courtesy he extended to a senior statesman, as opposed to Lyndon Johnson's vulgarity and Eisenhower's snub of most Truman administration officials.[80] Nixon, who always addressed Acheson as Mr. Secretary, in turn, developed special regard for his former political dartboard. He wrote in his memoirs, "Acheson and I became friends, and he was one of my most valued and trusted unofficial advisers."[81]

Acheson lent his name to a statement that appeared in the *New York Times* on November 17, supporting President Nixon's Vietnam policy.[82] Other backers included Charles Bohlen, Lucius Clay, Arthur Dean, Alfred Gruenther, George Humphrey, and Lewis Strauss. A week later in a letter to the *Times* Acheson wrote: "The most responsible course for 'war foes,'—and surely that term means all of us—is to focus on finding out what the issue is. No one has yet proposed a quicker and more practicable manner of ending the war."[83] Acheson wanted the carping to stop in order to give the president's plan a chance. What he failed to comprehend was that Nixon's "plan" was not a plan at all, but rather a vague series of ad lib moves and cosmetic countermoves that would prolong American participation for three more years.

In December Nixon invited Acheson to the White House along with former governor of New York Thomas E. Dewey and retired general

Lucius D. Clay to seek their counsel on Vietnam, Latin American policy, the SALT talks, and tensions in the Middle East. Nixon said that he would like to consult with them monthly on pressing international matters, a shrewd political move by a president anxious to broaden support for his foreign and domestic policies.[84] By now Nixon had turned Acheson, a lifelong Democrat, into a lobbyist on behalf of his policies. How far Acheson had changed is indicated by his comment to Charles Burton Marshall during this time that, of all the presidents he had known, only Harry Truman had had a firmer grip on foreign policy than Nixon.[85] Nearly twenty years later Alice Acheson still viewed her husband's transformation into a "Nixon man" with incredulity. She thought that "Nixon was wooing Dean for his own political purposes" and regretted that her husband had fallen prey to a campaign of flattery waged by Nixon and Kissinger.[86] Acheson succumbed because of his devotion to the institution of the presidency coupled with the need to be connected to the most powerful individual in the world—the occupant of the Oval Office—even though that individual was his erstwhile tormentor. Commenting to Anthony Eden on his relationship with Nixon, Acheson admitted as much: "We get along well, and I find the pleasure of being listened to seductive."[87]

The Nixon White House now regarded Acheson as a stalwart ally, one to whom they could turn for favors. J. Edgar Hoover, the director of the FBI, had conducted domestic political surveillance at the behest of many presidents. In December 1969 he informed the White House that wiretaps had revealed that Clark Clifford, the former secretary of defense, would soon be "sharpening up his attack on Nixon" in an article on Vietnam for *Life* magazine. An aide to H. R. Haldeman, one of the presidential assistants, sent Hoover's letter to Special Assistant to the President Jeb Magruder, urging that the staff "get ourselves springloaded to a position from which we can effectively counter whatever tack Clifford takes." Magruder learned that Clifford would attack Nixon's policies "utilizing quotes and information he has regarding the President, and probably suggesting complete troop withdrawal by the end of 1970." He thought Dean Acheson could be asked to counterattack by writing a defense of the policies for *Look* magazine, but he dropped the idea when Kissinger told him that Acheson would never publicly attack his old Truman administration pal, even though he disagreed with Clifford's criticisms of Nixon.[88]

An illustration of just how determined the White House was to keep Acheson on board was the special communication link the president, on

Kissinger's suggestion, had set up through the U.S. Marine station on Antigua. The arrangement allowed the White House to confer with Acheson by cable on national security affairs while he vacationed on the island. One night as the elder statesman was preparing for bed, two men drove over from the Marine station with a long message from Kissinger. The president wanted Acheson's opinion on sending relief help to the starving Biafran natives who had become refugees during the Nigerian civil war. Various groups in the United States were, in Acheson's words, "hot for large scale relief" in "amounts and methods" that the Nigerian federal leader General Yakubu Gowon did not approve. Acheson recommended acting slowly and offering only moderate assistance, as General Gowon opposed organized relief efforts. It was absurd, he maintained, to antagonize the general with an overwhelming amount of unwanted American aid. Acheson was surprised that the president had gone to such lengths to seek his counsel on a question the answer to which appeared obvious, but he admitted that "one appreciates such gestures." Nixon did heed Acheson's advice. He did not provide any immediate direct aid to the Biafrans but did name on February 22 a special coordinator of U.S. relief to civilian victims of the Nigerian civil war. Acheson clearly had become politically important to Nixon, but when it came to a change of policy in Indochina, Acheson was not even consulted. Nixon's incursion into Cambodia would in some ways rupture their improbable relationship.[89]

Cambodian Incursion

In January 1970 U.S. intelligence reported rapidly increasing Communist infiltration from North Vietnam into the South. The Viet Cong had also begun moving troops and equipment into "sanctuaries" along the Cambodian–South Vietnamese border. On March 18 Washington was further shaken by an unexpected event: while visiting Moscow, Prince Norodom Sihanouk, Cambodia's crafty neutralist head of state, was overthrown in a bloodless military coup d'état staged by the fiercely anticommunist general Lon Nol. Kissinger was reporting little progress at secret peace talks in Paris, and the Communists now controlled a quarter of Cambodia, while intelligence reports indicated that they were gaining ground on the capital, Phnom Penh. Nixon concluded that Lon Nol's new pro-U.S. regime needed help to survive; a Communist victory in Cambodia, he thought, would pose a threat to South Vietnam from the west as well as the north. It would jeopardize "our troop withdrawal program" and would also "virtually assure a Communist invasion of South Vietnam as soon as the last American had left."[90]

Dean Acheson believed that Prince Sihanouk had blundered when he left Cambodia to visit Moscow, opening the door to Lon Nol. Despite his friendship with the prince, he did not believe events in Cambodia should alter the objective of disengaging American troops from the region. In a letter to Sir Robert Menzies of Australia on April 6, Acheson wrote, "My foolish friend Sihanouk has pretty well loused things up, but even that may cool off. As I see it, the essential policy is to move without hesitation or wavering toward withdrawal to token strength, or if necessary altogether."[91]

The Acheson-Sihanouk relationship dated from 1961, when the prince had hired Acheson to represent Cambodia in a sovereignty dispute with Thailand over a ninth-century Buddhist temple. To avoid war, the two nations brought the dispute to the International Court of Justice at The Hague. After a year of deliberations the court ruled in Cambodia's favor. The Thai government was forced to withdraw its troops from the temple. Acheson became a national hero in Cambodia and was awarded the Grand Cross of the Royal Cambodian Order.[92] Dean and Alice Acheson themselves visited the temple and had been entertained by Sihanouk. "The Prince has, indeed, charm, verve, and a gay and dynamic nature," Acheson wrote to Philip Sprouse, who had recently become U.S. ambassador to Cambodia. "He has done a superb job with his little country, in holding it together and guiding it steadily along, not only through the difficult relations with its stronger and more turbulent neighbors, but in adjusting itself to modernity."[93]

The day after the coup Acheson shared his misgivings with Lord Stowe-Hill. The candidness in this letter is surprising because Acheson typically avoided expressing negative thoughts about any of the presidents to his foreign correspondents. After questioning whether Vietnamization was a real policy or merely a clever but dangerous political ploy to placate antiwar activists, the elder statesman criticized Nixon's rhetoric. His own years in government, he commented, had taught him never to "talk as though something was succeeding that in the nature of things cannot succeed in the popular sense of that word." South Vietnam, Acheson thought, would never become the democracy portrayed in Nixon's speeches. Thus he regarded it as "a mistake to talk as though we hoped to build a brilliant and stable democracy in South Vietnam, which would last until Judgment Day."[94]

By the end of March, however, with Communist assaults on Cambodian towns mounting daily, the White House debated the need for a "bold move" in Asia. The president suggested sending Dean Acheson to Cambodia to consult with General Lon Nol. Kissinger disagreed; he felt "it would just trigger an enormous debate and would probably be overtaken by decisions of the NSC." Kissinger said what was needed was presidential action, not consultation. Nixon dropped the notion of using Acheson as a diplomatic troubleshooter.[95]

In early April Acheson became concerned that the military was making use of the media to promote a policy different from the president's. A series of newspaper articles in both Saigon and Washington reported that General Creighton Abrams in Vietnam and General William Westmoreland, the army chief of staff in Washington, were urging Nixon to postpone further troop withdrawals for up to six months. Acheson thought the president should continue his withdrawal policy and disregard his generals. "What puzzles me is that two officers on opposite sides of the world should be talking to the press in a manner inconsistent with what appears to be the President's policy," Acheson wrote his friend Sir William Elliot. "This, of course, happened to us from Tokyo when General MacArthur was there, but it never happened from the Pentagon also."[96]

On April 26, 1970, President Nixon ordered U.S. forces to cross the border in order to attack North Vietnamese sanctuaries and destroy arms depots in neutral Cambodia. Many of his top foreign-policy advisers, including Secretary of State William Rogers and Secretary of Defense Melvin Laird, vigorously opposed widening the war. But the president bought the Pentagon's line: the invasion was necessary to buy a year's grace from enemy attacks against South Vietnam, allowing time for Vietnamization to progress while simultaneously fortifying Lon Nol's government.[97]

Acheson thought Nixon's decision most unwise. "This new version of search and destroy strategy is bound to lead us a chase around Cambodia," he told a friend. "The chances of cornering any substantial number of enemy forces seems small." He added that the president had underestimated the negative domestic consequences of the incursion: "The university population is getting more and more upset, the market is declining, and the Nixon Administration is getting into trouble."[98] After six students were killed by national guardsmen in demonstrations at Kent State University in Ohio and Jackson State College in Mississippi, a protest march in Washington drew more than a hundred thousand participants. Acheson longed, he told another friend, for "what the Constitution defines as one of our primary domestic needs—domestic tranquility." He wanted Nixon to accelerate the troop withdrawal.[99]

Acheson feared that Senator Mike Mansfield, the Democratic majority leader, might use the Cambodian incursions as grounds for cutting NATO and scrapping the ABM. He also was irritated that the GVN was still influencing American policy. Had he been consulted, he would have warned Nixon of the impossibility of scoring a military victory in Cambodia. "The country is very large and is a very difficult area in which to operate," he noted. Further, Nixon's statement that the United States would keep no troops in Cambodia made no sense; the enemy would simply come back after the troops left.[100]

Although Acheson had little regard for William Rogers, he was dismayed to learn that the secretary of state had been left out of the discussions on the Cambodian incursion until it was a fait accompli. Rogers told him that he agreed with Acheson that the Cambodian escapade was a mistake and that the time had come to get out of the Southeast Asian morass. Nonetheless, Rogers refused to convey his anger at being excluded from the decision-making process to the president. Acheson, who hated seeing the office of secretary of state derogated in any way, was more furious with Rogers for not presenting his views forcefully to Nixon than he was with Kissinger for allowing the president to steer the country down such a manifestly wrong course.[101]

"Mr. Nixon put me off by his incursion into Cambodia and his handling of it," Acheson wrote some months later; and to some degree he would remain put off. The Acheson-Nixon honeymoon was over. He refused to see the president for months after the bombing raid and declined numerous requests for consultation on Cambodia in late May, "making it clear that since I disagree strongly with the policy, I could not be of any help."[102] The elder statesman now saw Nixon as "unlikely material out of which a first-class president, equal to the challenge of our times, will emerge." He added, "Unfortunately he does not seem to be a very coolheaded or wise man. . . . However, I am not in favor of scoring points on him and wish him the best of luck."[103]

In early June Acheson collapsed with what doctors called a ministroke, "although it didn't seem so very mini at the time," he wrote Desmond Donnelly. "I am using the excuse of my illness—no mere excuse at that—not to be drawn into the White House for so-called consultation in any way."[104] After a two-week hospitalization he was released under doctor's orders not to exert himself. Acheson spent the remainder of the summer at Harewood, relaxing, swimming, gardening, and seeing a few close friends.

By early August Acheson was drawn back into the Washington fray, meeting with Kissinger for the first time since the Cambodian incursion. Kissinger scolded Acheson for staying away from the White House when summoned. The elder statesman "pleaded illness as well as dislike of flogging a dead horse." Acheson got Kissinger off the subject of Southeast Asia—"which is an obsession with him"—and turned the conversation to what Acheson considered the more pressing problems of Germany and the Middle East. Kissinger told Acheson that when the president returned from California he urgently wanted to discuss these matters with him. Acheson agreed to meet Nixon in a few weeks, although he privately complained that the "visits across Lafayette Square are very depressing experiences."[105]

Although Acheson had strongly objected in private to the Cambodian venture, he never rebuked Nixon publicly for the decision. He had lost faith in the president's judgment but saw nothing to be harvested by making Nixon's life more difficult. "Somehow or other we will get out of Southeast Asia without leaving too many of our tail feathers in the door jamb," Acheson wrote his Australian friend Sir Howard Beale in late August. "My real worries center about Willy Brandt's foolish flirtations with the Russians and Rogers' even more foolish ones with them in regard to the Middle East. These two escapades will, I fear, cost us dearly."[106]

Intelligent Neglect of the Middle East

Acheson strongly opposed the so-called Rogers Plan for the Middle East, which linked proposals for Israeli-Egyptian peace and Israeli-Jordanian peace. Presented first to the Soviet Union in October 1969, the plan was announced publicly by Rogers to the belligerent Middle East nations in December. Rogers asserted that the U.S. proposal was balanced: both Israel and the Arab states would have to make concessions. His plan called on Israel to pull out of Arab territory they had occupied since the Six-Day War in 1967 in return for a "binding commitment to peace" on the part of the Arab nations. This was to include the obligation to prevent terrorist attacks originating from their territories. The Rogers Plan alarmed Israel on two counts: it reopened the Palestinian refugee question and advocated that both Israel and Jordan participate "in the civic, economic, and religious life" of Jerusalem. Although the belligerents rejected the initial proposal, by 1970 Rogers had succeeded in securing Egyptian, Jordanian, and Israeli agreement to a cease-fire and a resumption of negotiations, with UN ambassador Gunnar Jarring mediating.[107]

Acheson had long viewed the disharmony in the Middle East as insoluble. He had objected to the creation of Israel in 1948, but, unlike many commentators on the Middle East, Acheson did not believe Truman's strong pro-Israeli stance was motivated primarily by internal American politics. "The President had his mind concentrated on the hundred thousand Jewish refugees that we had in our refugee camps in Europe," Acheson told Edward P. Morgan of ABC in October 1969. "He was being pressed very strongly by the soldiers to do something about this. He tried to have our immigration laws broadened here so they could come in and was unsuccessful. Then there was this tremendous pressure from the Jewish organizations, the Zionist organizations and from the refugees themselves to go to Palestine. He put pressure on the British; this mounted and mounted until it finally came nearly to a breach between us and the British, and ultimately the refugees went there, not only 100,000 but over a million."[108]

Acheson believed that Truman should have followed his advice and "kept them in the camps and brought them ultimately to the United States rather than to put a million Jews in the center of this lot of dynamite over there."[109] Felix Frankfurter was an avid supporter of Israel. For years the two were a familiar sight walking from their Georgetown homes to Foggy Bottom. To prevent a rupture in their friendship, they agreed at some point never again to mention Israel in any conversation; they both felt too strongly—in opposite directions—to engage in dialogue on the subject.[110]

Disturbed that Israel refused to concede the need for a Palestinian homeland, Acheson told Morgan that the Israelis not only had "refugees outside of the area for which they now have responsibility, but they have a large Arab population which is sure to become larger within that area. Inevitably they can not go forward with the idea of a purely Jewish state."[111] Nonetheless, Acheson thought threatening Israel—our only responsible ally in the region—was a waste of time. He could not envision any plan favored by the British, French, Soviets, and Americans that would have a chance of being adopted by the Arabs and Jews.

Kissinger and Rogers, neither of whom had any expertise in Middle

Eastern affairs when they joined the administration, were at odds over the region. Acheson sided with Kissinger, for both viewed foreign affairs in global terms and through the prism of the cold war. One of Rogers's innumerable deficiencies, Acheson believed, was that he, like John Foster Dulles, could only concentrate on a single issue at a time; he did not conceptualize, he plodded. In public Acheson toned down these criticisms. "[Rogers] has a great deal of ability in many fields," he told a reporter in December 1970. "But he puzzles me as Secretary of State. I've been puzzled about our intentions in the Middle East . . . our moralistic approach. I don't understand what Rogers wants to do."[112]

A division of labor had been established by the president. Kissinger was to formulate global foreign policy; Rogers was assigned to specific projects, including the current Middle East situation. The arrangement was motivated in part by Nixon's desire to distance the White House from Middle East policy, where he perceived the chances of success as slim and the risk of tangling with the pro-Israeli lobby in the United States great. Nixon also thought that the fact Kissinger was Jewish would in some people's minds be seen as an obstruction to any attempts to establish better relations with the Arab nations.[113]

Despite Nixon's strategy, Kissinger conceived a Middle East peace plan of his own and forced deliberations into the NSC framework. In a campaign to sway Nixon to his views, he asked Dean Acheson to appraise the Rogers Plan. To no one's surprise, Acheson's "Memorandum to Mr. Kissinger" hammered Rogers for inviting the Soviets to participate in the peace process and said nothing had been achieved: "Secretary Rogers' effort was, I think, so far as producing any movement toward peace or any effect in enhancing the prestige of the United States, a complete failure. Further efforts can only result in continued failure." Acheson recommended the administration say it had no further suggestions to make and saw no utility in continued talks between outside powers that aimed either at encouraging the parties involved to agree on a plan or at imposing one upon them.[114]

He advised that Washington not set an embargo on arms to Israel so long as the Soviet bloc was supplying arms to some of the Arab states. Instead, it should permit arms sales, not gifts, as a balance to military imports from the Communist bloc. The United States would look foolish if it took a moral position against any country's supplying arms to the Middle East; such high-mindedness would have no effect on the Soviets, and eventually the U.S. would be forced to recant and again supply arms to Israel. He urged that the United States not try to assert leadership in the UN on this issue, nor should it be "put into a position of being Israel's lawyer."[115]

The Soviet's had their own objectives in the region. "Long before Israel was established the Russians were interested in Middle Eastern oil and a route through the Persian Gulf," Acheson noted. Referring to reports that the Russian oil industry was outmoded and that it "may be both easier financially and more productive politically for them to gain control over some or all Middle Eastern oil than to invest in new facilities to exploit their own," he suggested that the great oil reserves of the Middle East would "beckon alluringly to the Soviet Union. It is almost certain to heed that invitation."[116] Acheson told friends he was convinced that the Soviets had a further goal; they were "hell-bent" on supplanting the British and Americans in the Middle East in order to control the economic lifeblood of Europe—Arabian oil. A battle between the superpowers for control of oil was at hand. Thus, involving the Soviets in Middle East negotiations was a dreadful mistake.[117]

Kissinger passed the memorandum on to President Nixon. Early in January of 1970 Acheson sent a letter to the president urging that he adopt an attitude of "intelligent neglect" toward the Middle East. Initially Nixon agreed, but he changed his mind in February when it appeared the Soviets might send arms to Egypt. The president wrote to Kissinger, "I think it is time to talk directly with the Soviets on this. Acheson's idea—'let the dust settle'—won't work." Kissinger continued to endorse Acheson's approach, but he lost out to the State Department, for, as he later commented, "On the Middle East I was not in the dominant position."[118]

By fall 1970 the peace talks still had failed to produce a settlement. "Rogers or rather [Joseph] Sisco's Middle East initiative really never got off the ground and never deserved to," Acheson wrote Anthony Eden. "A good measure of RMN's character is that he never believed in it and never dared to stop it. The idea that it is good policy to try to keep the peace when it is impossible or—better—where no one is prepared to do what is necessary to do in order to keep peace, is not a sound or sensible policy."[119] Already disenchanted with Nixon's extension of the Vietnam War into Cambodia, Acheson added Middle East policy to his list of grievances. He told J. Robert Schaetzel, former U.S. ambassador to the European Economic Community, that in the upcoming congressional elections he would be voting a straight Democratic ticket, as "a small defiance of all this nonsense."[120]

In the summer of 1971, with no progress in the Middle East peace efforts, Nixon came under increasing pressure from Jewish Americans and a host of others to sell aircraft to Israel as a counter to reported increases in Soviet aid to Egypt. Acheson had maintained public silence on Middle Eastern affairs during the Rogers initiative, but in an op-ed piece for the *New York Times* written just a few days before his death in the autumn of 1971, he reiterated the warnings against Soviet adventurism in the region he had made in private to the administration:

> The first aim of American policy should be to convince the Soviet leaders that direct involvement of their own forces in the Middle East involves unacceptable risks. They are already substantially present in Egypt. Secretary Rogers proposes to compound the evil by having combined Russian-American forces there (to keep the peace). The true American interest is to keep both out. It is also the true interest of both Israelis and Arabs.[121]

Acheson probably also would have been critical of Kissinger's widely acclaimed Jerusalem to Cairo to Damascus "shuttle diplomacy" of the mid-1970s, for Kissinger did not give advance information to the Western European nations of U.S. intentions. Intelligent neglect of the Middle East was not meant to lead to unintelligent neglect of Western Europe.

Confronting Ostpolitik

A nightmare came true for Acheson when a coalition between the Social Democratic Party (SPD) and the smaller Free Democratic Party (FDP) ousted Kurt Kiesinger and the Christian Democrats from power in the West German general election of September 1969. The Social Democratic leader Willy Brandt was elected chancellor. Although the coalition held only a two-member majority in the Bundestag and Acheson sneered that "a bad cold on somebody's part may produce a different result,"[122] he was afraid of Brandt's announced policy of *Ostpolitik*. This plan to pursue normal relations with the Soviet Union and Warsaw Pact countries would irreparably damage the Atlantic alliance, Acheson believed, and would simultaneously enhance the Kremlin's power and prestige. Acheson went on the offensive. He attacked *Ostpolitik* as a threat to the very existence of NATO and perhaps to the integrity of Germany itself. *Ostpolitik*, he thought, was simply a new name for traditional German nationalism. "Fear I am not sufficiently au courant to see anything new in Ostpolitik or

Brandt's Rapallo mentality," Acheson wrote J. Robert Schaetzel. "It seems recrudescence of German illusions in moments of frustration as evidenced by Rathnenau, Schumacher, Adenauer in de Gaulle period and so on. The opposite end of the pendulum's swing we know well enough."[123]

Acheson's primary concern was not that West Germany would become more dependent on the Soviets but rather that under Brandt it would become less dependent on the United States. Following World War II, the main American objective concerning West Germany was to cement the republic firmly within the Western bloc, NATO, and, later, the European Economic Community. Brandt's diplomacy—centered on reducing East-West tensions in Central Europe by establishing friendly relations with East Germany, Poland, and the Soviet Union—might produce a détente, led by Bonn, that would undermine U.S. leadership in Europe. "Our common interest is in the development of a united Europe with the strength that comes from common interests, carried out by common means and common policies, including common political purposes vis-à-vis the Soviet Union," Acheson wrote to Countess Marion Donhoff, the editor-in-chief of *Die Zeit*, West Germany's leading daily newspaper.[124]

Acheson thought Nixon and Kissinger too sanguine about the new German chancellor. He remarked to Schaetzel, "One cannot make a silk purse out of Brandt or any other German politician I know."[125] As always, Acheson believed that any bilateral discussions with the Soviet Union had to be undergirded by a solid base of European-American unity lest they divide the countries of Europe, and Europe from America. He wanted Washington to confront Brandt. "I am sick of being told that he [Brandt] is 'sincere,'" Acheson wrote Sir Roy Welensky. "All fools and rascals are sincere. Hitler was, Chamberlain was, Khrushchev was."[126]

George Ball recalls that the period of Brandt's tenure heightened Acheson's ever-present worry that NATO was not receiving enough attention. He thought that Nixon and Kissinger, like LBJ and Rusk before them, were ignoring Europe because of their preoccupation with Southeast Asia and the Middle East. Other factors strained the alliance: Britain weak, France independent, and now West Germany dabbling with the communists. Meanwhile, the Soviets were gaining strategically over the West through dogged persistence and the exertion of brute force, as the invasion of Czechoslovakia in 1968 had demonstrated. Acheson wanted Nixon to review all U.S.-European policies (military, political, and economic), with a view toward future joint action, such as nuclear sharing and the lifting of certain trade barriers.[127]

"I am being drawn back in without enthusiasm into Presidential consultations," Acheson told a friend in December 1970. In recent weeks he had discussed European affairs with a committee chaired by John McCloy, advised the president on disarmament issues, and, at the president's request, written a position paper for a White House meeting on U.S.-Soviet relations.[128]

Present at this meeting, on December 7, 1970, were Nixon, Kissinger, Acheson, McCloy, Thomas Dewey, and General Lucius Clay.[129] McCloy, the former U.S. high commissioner in Germany, and Clay, the American representative on the Allied Control Council during the 1948–49 Berlin blockade, proclaimed their distrust of Chancellor Brandt and the rest of the current leadership in Germany. Then Acheson took the floor to denounce *Ostpolitik* and to offer several recommendations to strengthen NATO. Acheson wanted the president to deliver a series of forceful speeches reaffirming some long-neglected principles of U.S. foreign policy: the necessity for a united Europe, the importance of maintaining close European-American relations, and commitment to mutual defense.

A few days after his meeting with the president, Acheson told a group of reporters that Chancellor Brandt "should be cooled off" as part of an effort to slow down "the mad race to Moscow." Assuming that pursuit of *Ostpolitik* depended on a Berlin settlement, Acheson vehemently asserted that the status of Berlin must never be compromised. During Brandt's recent visit to Warsaw he had pledged to regard the Oder-Neisse line, established in 1945, as the boundary between Poland and East Germany. Acheson hyperbolically suggested that Brandt's next move would be the wholesale giveaway of Berlin.

Acheson was incensed about two treaties Brandt had signed in the previous months. The Treaty of Moscow (August 1970) was a nonaggression pact in which both the USSR and West Germany renounced the use of force and eschewed claims on the territory of each other or on that of any other state. Under the Treaty of Warsaw (December 1970) "full normalization" of relations with Poland was established. Brandt was not coordinating his actions with the Big Four talks on Berlin, and Acheson lamented that "West Germany rather than the U.S., Britain, and France [is] in a position 'to call the tune' on Berlin."[130]

Acheson told newsmen that the U.S. government should make it clear it favored Western European unity and British entry into the Common Market. Such a step would hinder Brandt's attempts to seek accommodation with the Soviets and discourage other European nations from following the separatist policies of France. Although he noted that he was a friend and admirer of Henry Kissinger's, Acheson commented that Kissinger "does not believe as strongly as I do in supranational organizations in Europe to balance Soviet power. They can do it only by organizing."[131]

Brandt was infuriated by Acheson's remarks, especially because they came only a day after the ex-secretary had attended a White House meeting; the timing would lead to speculation that Acheson was representing President Nixon's views. The West German Embassy filed an official complaint with the State Department over Acheson's comments. They asked the State Department to disavow Acheson's statements publicly. Martin Hillenbrand, the U.S. ambassador to West Germany, assured the FRG that the request would be taken under advisement, but there was no further action.[132] It appeared to many observers that Acheson had been encouraged by the White House to speak his mind, and the White House made no attempt to dispel the notion.

Rolf Pauls, the West German ambassador to the United States, personally telephoned Acheson on December 11 in an effort to correct what he saw as a misperception of the Bonn-Moscow pact. Although his tone was civil, Pauls made it clear he was upset by the severity of Acheson's criticism and, in particular, by his irresponsible phrase "the mad race to Moscow." After politely listening awhile as Pauls defended FRG policy— Bonn's priority was the unity of Western Europe and NATO; Brandt did not have two foreign policies, an Eastern policy and a Western policy, but only a pro-Western one—Acheson broke in. He reiterated his opposition to Brandt's efforts at rapprochement with Moscow. *Ostpolitik*, he told Pauls, was a hazardous policy and the Treaty of Warsaw a dangerous precedent. Acheson said he would not retract his earlier statement. "The individual attempt of Germany to attempt separately to negotiate with the Soviet Union a recognition of the *status quo*," he argued, "not only [is] an exercise in futility but [is] divisive with regard to united policies both within Europe and between Europe and North America." Finding Acheson unwavering, Pauls coolly but politely terminated the conversation.[133]

West German officials soon let it be known that Brandt and the Nixon administration were close to a crisis of confidence over *Ostpolitik*. Asked what role Acheson's criticisms had played in the deteriorating relations between Bonn and Washington, a German official responded, "We feel this is only the tip of the iceberg. Our concern is that when we ask the Americans what we should think of such criticism we always get positive and approving declarations. Nevertheless these criticisms keep emerging, from Acheson and from many others. We can localize the sources of the criticism but we are unable to get precise definitions of them. It is never in the open. It has become an unknown factor for us and that is what oppresses us."[134]

On December 19, journalists asked Acheson if he wished to clarify his recent remarks. Instead of using the opportunity to ease the tensions between Bonn and Washington, Acheson chose to pour gasoline on the fire. He said he could only reiterate his belief—which was shared by John McCloy, General Lucius Clay, Thomas Dewey, and George Ball—that *Ostpolitik* was a domestic political maneuver Brandt was using to hold together his wobbly coalition. He and his colleagues, all with long experience in U.S.-Soviet relations, viewed Brandt's policy "with great alarm." Acheson also charged that Brandt's courting of the USSR and Eastern Europe was undermining the West's bargaining position on Berlin, as well as other negotiating issues.[135]

This time the State Department immediately disputed Acheson's contentions. Brandt was not using *Ostpolitik* as a domestic political ploy, they maintained; Brandt's coalition partner, the Free Democrats, had themselves occasionally criticized his policy as moving too close to the Soviet Union too quickly. John McCloy also was disturbed by Acheson's remarks. "I was very much taken aback by Dean Acheson's statement after our meeting," he wrote Kissinger. "I was out of town when he made it but he didn't consult me about it before or since. I had been disturbed by what appeared to me to be the pressures on the Chancellor to reach an agreement with the Soviets and the GDR without definite and significant concessions on the part of the Soviet Union, but the last thing in the world I would have thought of doing would have been to 'sound off' after our visit to the White House."[136]

In his memoir *People and Politics* Brandt wrote that he never encountered opposition to *Ostpolitik* policy in conversation with Nixon and Kissinger but was well aware that Acheson and other leading statesmen had "transmitted their objections to the President." Brandt thought Acheson an antediluvian incapable of understanding the need for policy renovation and change.[137]

Acheson continued to worry that *Ostpolitik* played right into the Kremlin's hands. Independent West German policy, furthermore, would cripple NATO and the Common Market. "The Russians win by everyone else losing," Acheson observed to C. L. Sulzberger. "The worse things get, the better off they themselves are."[138]

The Mansfield Amendment and the Pentagon Papers

Acheson's opinion of President Nixon and his administration continued to seesaw. The positive impression Nixon had given at the December 7 meeting had dissipated by the start of the new year.[139] Acheson avidly supported Nixon's policy of "positive communication" with the white-ruled governments of southern Africa and endorsed his expansion of the ABM program, but he had nagging doubts about his abilities to deal with West Germany and the Middle East, or with domestic strife.

Frustrated with the snail's pace of troop withdrawal in Vietnam, Acheson believed that the president was misleading the American people about Indochina. "In person, in a small company, I don't mind Nixon and sometimes like him," Acheson wrote a friend. "But on T.V. the phoney in him is overpowering. The fact of the matter is that the credibility gap, both ways—that is my disbelief in the government and my disbelief in the media—is complete."[140] Acheson contended that the public indignation over Nixon's intentions in Vietnam stemmed from what the president had said, not from what he had done.

When Nixon announced the start of troop withdrawals in 1969, the United States had some 550,000 soldiers in Vietnam. Acheson noted, in an article published in the *New York Times*, that by December 31, 1971, 365,000 troops would have been withdrawn, leaving roughly 185,000 men in Vietnam.[141] The average pull-out rate over the thirty months of the operation had been 12,000 per month. Acheson pointed out that that rate of withdrawal would leave only 40,000 men in Vietnam by the end of 1972, fewer than remained in Korea. If Vietnamization was successful, Acheson argued, those troops would not be needed to prevent a sudden takeover of South Vietnam by the North. If it was not successful, they would be too few to do the job. America, in any case, had done all that any country could do for another by giving it the opportunity to free itself from a communistic, totalitarian way of life. Acheson added that if Vietnamization was to be successful, Nixon would have to avoid mindless sorties such as those into Cambodia in 1970 and Laos in 1971. As he wrote some months earlier, he wanted the administration to "stop talking, testifying, denouncing, and invading—and move steadily out."[142]

In early May, Acheson lunched with Henry Kissinger. Kissinger asked his opinion about why Nixon was so widely mistrusted. Acheson acknowledged that he shared the public's perception of the president and repeated Justice Louis Brandeis's dictum "To give the whole variety of reasons for what one [is] about to do or not do always [leads] to doubts as to the firmness of one's decision." This, according to Acheson, was Nixon's chronic problem; "every time he makes an unalterable decision he gives different reasons."[143]

The Nixon-Kissinger team was occupied in the early part of 1971 with working to cut North Vietnamese communications with neighboring Laos, reestablishing relations with China, and breaking the logjam in the SALT talks with the Soviet Union on linking defensive and offensive weapons. In May 200,000 antiwar protestors marched on Washington in an unsuccessful attempt to shut down the federal government for a day. Given this flurry of activity, Europe was not in the forefront of the president's mind—not, that is, until Senator Mike Mansfield began stirring up the pot.

Mansfield was planning to resurrect his "perennial proposal," as Kissinger called it, to cut U.S. NATO forces in half, a reduction of 150,000 men.[144] America's failure in Vietnam had led to a wave of isolationist sentiment in Congress, and Republican congressional leaders informed the White House that the persistent Mansfield had enough votes to get his proposal passed as an amendment to the Draft Extension Act.

Nixon, Kissinger, and Acheson all had been arguing for years that U.S. forces in Europe needed to be increased, not decreased. The passage of the Mansfield amendment would, for all practical purposes, destroy NATO, but the Nixon administration was cornered by a Senate controlled by the Democrats. Kissinger recalled:

> It was symptomatic of the bitter and destructive mood of the period and of the substantial breakdown of national consensus that a bill of such magnitude could reach the floor of the Senate without committee hearing and that it stood a serious chance of passage. Our massive balance-of-payments deficit lent weight to any call to cut overseas expenditures; respect for Mansfield made his colleagues reluctant to vote against him.... [A] national malaise ... made the United States Senate willing to hazard institutions built up on a bipartisan basis over more than twenty years and five administrations.[145]

For Kissinger and other policy makers the Mansfield amendment was a threat to the entire thrust of America's foreign policy.

Kissinger asked Acheson to join the battle to defeat the amendment.

Acheson replied that he would "call any Senators where he could help, or any newspaper—though he might have outworn his welcome with the *New York Times* and the *Washington Post.*" He gave Kissinger a list of other "worthies"—including John McCloy, George Ball, McGeorge Bundy, Cyrus Vance, and Robert Lovett—to enlist.

Kissinger reported back to Acheson that his luck had been mixed: Lovett and McCloy had signed on; Ball advised seeking a compromise; and Vance, Bundy, and others had offered only lukewarm support. Acheson girded for battle: "It seems to me what we want is a little volley firing and not just a splattering of musketry." He began lining up former secretaries of defense, high commissioners for Germany, NATO commanders, and chairmen of the Joint Chiefs of Staff. He even convinced McCloy to fly to Germany to elicit Chancellor Willy Brandt's support. Nixon and Kissinger were both overjoyed with Acheson's vigorous campaign. Kissinger observed that Nixon "reveled in the prospect that for the first time, and in the event the only, time in his public life he would have the Establishment on his side—the men he revered and despised, whose approbation he both cherished and scorned."[146]

The "Old Guard," as Kissinger called them, met on May 13 in the Cabinet Room at the White House. Among the grey eminences in attendance were Acheson, Ball, Vance, Clay, Henry Cabot Lodge, Jr., Alfred Gruenther, Lauris Norstad, and Lyman Lemnitzer. Nixon opened the meeting by saying that he, like Acheson, had been "present at the creation" and understood that NATO was the backbone of America's defense posture. He urged the gathering to help him preserve the alliance that they had developed and nurtured.

The senior statesmen all agreed the amendment had to be derailed, but some felt a compromise was possible. Acheson pounced on the word *compromise* as treasonous and, Kissinger recalls, "effectively squelched" the notion. Acheson, whom Kissinger describes as having "none of Nixon's reluctance to engage in face-to-face confrontations," took charge of the discussion. At a key moment he introduced a statement supporting Nixon's position for the others to sign. Kissinger recorded that "Rogers—unaware that Nixon himself had originated the notion of an Acheson draft, perhaps put off by the elegant self-assurance of his predecessor, perhaps worried about Mansfield, with whom he would have to continue to work—urged that it be kept in abeyance." Acheson, fearing that delay might cause the consensus he had just fashioned to dissipate, argued for a press release within the next two days. Nixon pressured Rogers to go along, and Acheson was chosen to report the outcome of the meeting to the press.[147]

Acheson and Ball immediately went to the White House briefing room to speak to the media about the Mansfield amendment. Acheson told the reporters that "the President was absolutely adamant against it" and "was prepared for no compromise at all." Asked if he foresaw a time when the NATO troop commitment could be cut, Acheson replied that it would be "absolutely asinine" and "sheer nonsense" to cut NATO forces without a corresponding cut in Soviet forces. He described how the president had called upon the men responsible for the creation of NATO and for its development over the past twenty years to come to his aid. And they did, Acheson concluded, with "fighting gloves on." Asked why the meeting had lasted for over ninety minutes, Acheson dismissed the debate with a joke: "Did you ever see twenty men get together without everybody wanting to outtalk the others? We are all old and we are all eloquent." George Ball added that a compromise was no longer a possibility.[148]

As agreed at the meeting, a presidential statement opposing the Mansfield amendment was released on May 15 and immediately endorsed by those who had been present, as well as by former president Lyndon Johnson; former secretary of state Dean Rusk; former secretaries of defense Robert Lovett, Neil McElroy, and Thomas Gates; senior Defense Department officials such as Roswell Gilpatric; diplomats such as C. Douglas Dillon, Livingston Merchant, and Robert Murphy; NATO commander General Matthew Ridgway; and former high commissioners for Germany John McCloy and Lucius Clay.

The *New York Times* applauded the efforts of "the Establishment" and published an editorial captioned "Senator Mansfield's Folly" that criticized the proposal as damaging to national security interests. Acheson cheered the paper on, for he, too, was outraged that Congress was interfering with the president's foreign-policy prerogatives. "You are the President," the seventy-eight-year-old Acheson had barked at Nixon. "You tell them to go to hell."[149]

The press had predicted a close vote on the amendment, but on May 19 the administration achieved an astounding 61-36 victory. Acheson was jubilant. "We have had a fine old ding-dong fight down here in which those of us who rallied to the President's side have been subjected to a degree of vilification unequaled since the McCarthy days," he wrote John Cowles (with no apparent recognition that the last time he had been so vilified Richard Nixon was among his tormentors). "It has been great fun and resulted in a most satisfying victory."[150] Kissinger wrote Acheson that it had been "a great privilege and pleasure" to work with him in the battle against the Mansfield amendment: "You were magnificent, as usual, and you deserve a substantial part of the credit for the successful outcome."[151]

The day after the Senate vote, Nixon also sent Acheson a letter of appreciation:

> Yesterday's votes in the Senate on the Mansfield Amendment have been interpreted in the morning newspapers as an Administration victory. This, of course, is technically true. But in a deeper sense the votes yesterday represented a victory for five Administrations which since World War II have on a bipartisan basis been committed to support for the NATO Alliance.
>
> You were among the few present at our meeting in the Cabinet Room Thursday afternoon who could truly claim to have been Present at the Creation. All, however, can now proudly look back to the events of the past few days and with some degree of truth say that they were "Present at the Resurrection."[152]

Acheson responded, "It was an honor to have had a part in the second battle of NATO." He was pleased to have been part of the Resurrection, although, he added, "the way some of my fellow Democrats and the so-called liberal press have categorized us, they seem to have cast me for both the thieves at the Crucifixion for whom no such outcome is recorded."[153]

Walter Isaacson and Evan Thomas, in their book *The Wise Men*, depict Acheson's role in defeating the Mansfield amendment as "the dedicated warrior's last hurrah, his final defense of duty and honor in an age that seemed increasingly dominated by expediency."[154] Acheson would have agreed with this assessment. He was proud of his activities in the days leading up to the amendment's defeat and wrote friends glowing reviews of his own performance. "The White House was ambushed and panicked," Acheson told Sir Roy Welensky. "Talk of compromise flew about; I was called on for suggestions and urged a battle royal with no quarter asked or given."[155]

Shortly after the defeat of the amendment, the *Washington Post* called on Nixon to reduce U.S. troops elsewhere than Europe as a gesture of presidential goodwill. Acheson was furious. He wrote a vehement letter to the *Post* attacking the newspaper for asking the president "not to fight, and even if you lick 'em, join 'em." The liberals were engaging in unwarranted interference with the chief executive's handling of foreign affairs.

"The President had every right, indeed, the duty to face up to a constitutional confrontation and return the Senate to its proper interest in foreign policy and not accept your mistaken notion of it," Acheson scolded.[156]

In July 1971 the *Washington Post* and the *New York Times* published what came to be known as the Pentagon Papers, documents about the Vietnam War illegally taken from government custody. Acheson again exploded at the press in a piece for the July 7, 1971, *New York Times* editorial section entitled "The Purloined Papers." He was not shocked at what the papers revealed—that Vietnam had been an "American war" in which official Washington was guilty of duplicity—but at the actions of the press in publishing excerpts from a top-secret Pentagon study. "The Pentagon Papers," he charged, "belong to the United States of America as clearly as does the battleship Missouri or the White House silver. To jump from the assertion that the papers do not belong to any public figure to the conclusion that they do belong to all the two hundred million inhabitants of the United States violates Mr. Johnson's advice to Boswell not 'to think foolishly.'"[157]

Acheson scorned Neil Sheehan, the *Times* reporter who had accepted the documents obtained by Daniel Ellsberg. Reporters like Sheehan were on a "crusade . . . to protect suffering humanity from all governments everywhere, even if in so doing they usher all of us into a well-intentioned state of anarchy."[158] Acheson argued for the principle of executive secrecy. The British Official Secrets Act had always appealed to him, and he began promoting the adoption of similar legislation in the United States. "We need a severe Official Secrets Act," Acheson wrote to the *New York Times* on July 7, "to prevent irresponsible or corrupt transfer of secret papers from the government to publishers."[159] According to Acheson, the lesson to be drawn by the U.S. government from the Pentagon Papers incident was never to trust the press, a sentiment shared by Kissinger and Nixon.

By summer 1971 Acheson once again was back in the White House fold. He began seeing Kissinger and other administration members more frequently. "The liberals will excommunicate me for good when they learn that I have lunched with Mr. Agnew," Acheson joked to John Cowles. The prospect of Nixon's reelection in 1972 did not appear to bother Acheson, and he noted "that minimum good sense and luck on the President's part would bring him in going away almost by default."[160] David Acheson believes that, had he lived until 1972, his father for the first time would have broken with his party and voted for the Republican candidate in the Nixon-McGovern election.[161] Writing to the powerful

Washington attorney Edward Bennett Williams in 1970, Acheson went so far as to claim that "if the President would fire that old fart [John] Mitchell and make you Attorney General I would become a Republican."[162] In some ways, Acheson had come to see himself as part of the administration. He was much closer ideologically to conservatives like Nixon than to Democrats like Fulbright, McGovern, and Mansfield, whom he had long regarded with contempt.[163] Although their characters and operational codes could not have been more different, the two old warhorses had come to share a political worldview. Nowhere did their viewpoints coincide with greater alacrity than in their support for the white minority governments in southern Africa.

CHAPTER TEN

Southern Africa Policy, 1961–71

Following the Second World War Dean Acheson was antipathetic and condescending to the European colonies struggling to become independent states. A passage he wrote in 1964 fairly captures his views on the subject:

> Whatever may be said about colonialism, one thing must be said about our attitude toward it, an attitude which we have had for nearly a hundred and fifty years, and that is that anti-colonialism is not a policy. It is merely an attitude of mind and not a very sensible one at that.[1]

Insensitive to the cries for freedom and liberation by the black majorities in Africa, Acheson was downright belligerent to Americans who supported these aspirations. His antagonism was fed by many sources. The traditional values of Western civilization—individualism, capitalism, scientific thinking, and the rule of law—informed his every thought and action. Europe, the progenitor of these values, was central to his worldview. A colonialist view toward the peoples of the region, an attitude of white and Western superiority, became more pronounced in his postsecretarial years. According to Acheson, colonialism, far from being responsible for Africa's poverty, provided skills and infrastructure; the region had become worse off economically the further from colonialism it moved.

Acheson was unable to accept the notion that African blacks had their own nationalist agendas for decolonization and were not bound to accept a future designed by other architects. He could not conceive that the colonies were capable of organizing to gain their freedom or that they could establish efficient, economically solvent democratic governments once independence was achieved. Thus, behind African struggles for freedom he looked for—and found—Soviet or communist influence. He scoffed at neutralism, nonalignment, and racial equality and therefore ignored the growing strength of the forces outside the U.S. or Soviet axes.[2] As the historian Gaddis Smith has pointed out, Acheson "gave only glancing attention to the mass of the world's population who did not have white skins, advanced industrial economies, and homes in Western Europe or the United States."[3]

Acheson was vocal in his contempt for the emerging nonwhite states of Africa, beginning in 1957 with Ghana's independence. During his last years he crusaded for the idea that the United Nations had no right to interfere in the "domestic jurisdiction" of the white-ruled African states—Angola, Mozambique, Rhodesia, and South Africa—even if their racial policies posed a threat not only to their indigenous populations but to neighboring states.[4]

Given Acheson's paternalistic stance toward nonwhites and his constant fear of Soviet subversion, he was increasingly critical of the United Nations. If few of the new nonwhite, nonindustrialized governments could influence international politics, the United States nevertheless had a stake in their votes at the United Nations, as well as in their resources, their cold war posture, and their attitudes toward American traders and investors, Acheson recognized.[5]

In 1945 only four UN countries (counting Egypt) were African. By 1965, 36 of the 115 member-states were African, 15 Asian, and 11 Middle Eastern. In 1959, Acheson had asserted that the United Nations had no real power and would never acquire any. Conceding only that the UN could be a useful meeting place at which diplomats could hobnob and exchange frivolous niceties, Acheson dismissed the debates and votes as a waste of time.[6] He reiterated this position in a televised interview in 1965. Asked to assess the importance of UN resolutions, Acheson replied that they "really amount to very little. . . . The votes in the United Nations mean less than nothing . . . [they] have departed far from any conception of diplomacy."[7]

Acheson spoke derisively of "the international orphan asylum, the United Nations," refusing to accept the legitimacy of what he usually called the Afro-Asian bloc.[8] The major states, he believed, should dominate in international affairs. He also was wary of peoples and leaders of the emerging third world. As he himself confessed, he had no tolerance for so-called neutralist leaders, such as the prime minister of India, Jawaharlal Nehru. His feelings extended to the people of Nehru's country. "One of my other prejudices is Indians," Acheson wrote to Lord Patrick Devlin in 1959. "I know I ought to like them, and, indeed, have liked some. But by and large they and their country gives me the creeps."[9] Undergirding all of these sentiments was Acheson's belief in the obvious superiority of white Western culture and institutions.

The Portuguese Colonies

In the 1960 presidential election John Kennedy had campaigned against Eisenhower's African policy, and he took office convinced his administration should adopt an agenda more favorable to the emerging nations. "Africa is for the Africans," Assistant Secretary of State for African Affairs G. Mennen Williams declared in a stunning speech in Nairobi which met with sharp criticism from Acheson, Congress, and Europe. Williams's words became a catchphrase for JFK's approach as eleven African leaders entered the White House portals in 1961 alone to discuss international affairs with the sympathetic new president.[10]

Acheson was unhappy with the team Kennedy assembled to deal with African issues; key figures such as Chester Bowles, Adlai Stevenson, G. Mennen Williams, and his deputy head of the African bureau, Wayne Fredricks, were all relatively pro-African. It was this "Africanist" liberal wing of the Democratic Party that Acheson had tried to muscle out of the decision-making apparatus of the foreign-policy committee of the DAC while he was chairman from 1957 to 1960. Acheson considered none of them intellectually suited to international affairs; they were altruistic "woolyheaded liberals" whose only asset was their political clout.[11]

Acheson also feared that unrealistic expectations were being generated by these vocal pro-African policies. For instance, with only a trickling of financial aid forthcoming, the gap between word and deed would become glaring. Kennedy's pro-African public pronouncements were also at odds with U.S. relations with the NATO allies, who were still caught up, for the most part, in the work of disengaging from colonial rule.[12] Acheson argued that, with a crisis in Berlin looming and with de Gaulle attempting to undermine NATO, it made no sense to place Africa high on a list of economic or political priorities. He pointed out that in 1960 Africa accounted for less than 4 percent of America's imports and only 3.5 percent of its exports.

On the other hand, of course, Acheson was not about to ignore the new African nations, for the United States had to ensure that they not fall under the influence of the Soviet Union or the People's Republic of China.[13] His African policy was articulated with missionary zeal and an explicit judgment of inferiority on the recipient of the proffered good. "We are, and should be, deeply concerned with social, political, and economic development in Latin America, Asia, and Africa," Acheson wrote in an article for the *Yale Review* in 1961. "In all of these areas revolutionary movements are pressing hard for change and improvement. In many of them independence has been wrested from weakened colonial powers by people wholly incompetent to manage their own affairs and, therefore in desperate need of disinterested help and instruction."[14]

Whenever U.S. policy toward southern Africa was discussed—whether casually with friends or officially at White House conferences or NSC meetings—Acheson's belief in the overarching importance of NATO, his antenna tuned to the concerns of fading colonial powers, his fear of Khrushchev's socialist revolution via third-world "wars of national liberation," and his insensitivity to the aspirations of black Africans made him impervious to all but the most conservative options.[15] Time and again he referred to the bloody tribal and provincial uprisings in the Congo (soon to be Zaire) as proof that black Africans were unable to handle the responsibility inherent in being a sovereign state. In this case, Belgium left in 1959 and then "all hell broke out."[16]

Acheson consistently backed Portugal's struggle to maintain its unique brand of racial and political domination over the black majorities of Angola and Mozambique. For the elder statesman, Portugal was more than a NATO member; his "emotionalism" on the subject of the colonies, as Lucius Battle put it, stemmed in part from his affection for Portugal itself and for its dictator, Antonio de Oliveira Salazar.[17] "A convinced libertarian . . . could understandably disapprove of Salazar," Acheson rationalized in *Present at the Creation*, "but I doubt whether Plato would have done so."[18]

During the Second World War, Washington had extensive dealings with Salazar—who simultaneously acted as prime minister, foreign minister, and minister of war—in an effort to obtain for the Allies as much as possible of Portugal's resources, particularly tungsten. Following the war Acheson played a pivotal role in obtaining from Salazar free rights to a U.S. base on the strategically located Azores Islands. This fine bargain, and his dealings with the Portuguese leader at the historic NATO Conference in Lisbon in 1952, produced in Acheson a "deep respect for Salazar's competence," even though his regime was propped up by the military, a ubiquitous secret police, corrupt judges, and draconian laws.[19] Acheson's brief stay in Portugal in 1952 developed into a lifelong attachment. He wrote:

> Lisbon was no longer just a name; the Portuguese, no longer merely the subjects of a king to whom the Pope had apportioned half the world; Salazar, no longer solely a ruler about whom authoritarians and liberals disputed. "I am a part of all that I have met," said Ulysses. From then on some of my fleece was left behind, and some of Portugal came with me."[20]

If, as some said, John J. McCloy was the "godfather of Germany," McGeorge Bundy has remarked, then Dean Acheson was surely the "godfather of Portugal."[21] Acheson, who generally had no kind words to spare for the Eisenhower administration, heaped kudos on it throughout 1960 for agreeing to provide Portugal with two warships; concluding an accord for U.S. arms production in Portugal; and abstaining from UN Resolution 1514, which demanded self-determination in dependent territories. Acheson worried that Kennedy would turn on this trusted Atlantic ally, displaying the same insensitivity to Portugal that he had to France when as a senator in 1957 he supported Algerian nationalism. Acheson expressed his concern to Truman. "We are about to alienate a most essential ally by our silly attitude in the U.N.," he wrote in August 1961. "And our ally [Portugal] is about to go bankrupt trying to suppress an uprising which it probably can't suppress. I think that we could help by trying to quiet things down on the basis of more participation in government by blacks and economic development in both Portugal and Angola. This means some give by Salazar and a silencer on Soapy [Williams] and Adlai [Stevenson]."[22]

At the time Kennedy took office, in January 1961, Portugal was the only European nation that had not been shaken by anticolonial rebellion in its African territories. The Portuguese had claimed that the climate of "racial equality" in Angola and Mozambique made political independence for its native inhabitants unnecessary. Nationalist violence did erupt in Angola in February 1961, and Portugal refused to recognize the revolutionary movement. Salazar announced his intention to fight to retain control of the colonies. "Nationalism does not exist in either Angola or Mozambique," Salazar proclaimed. "You Americans have invented it. Portugal will continue its 400 year old effort to build a multi-racial society."[23]

The staunch anticommunist dictator had hoped for U.S. support or, at the very least, that the United States would abstain from voting on UN resolutions condemning Portugal. Salazar argued that the United States, as a NATO ally, had a contractual obligation to back Portugal in its struggle to hold onto its "overseas provinces." In his view, Angola was, as much as Lisbon, a part of Portugal.

But on March 15, 1961, the United States voted in favor of a Liberian-sponsored Security Council resolution calling for a UN investigation into the recent violence in Angola and an end to Portuguese colonialism. The motion failed, and on April 20 the United States again voted in favor of an unsuccessful resolution demanding that Portugal immediately move toward granting Angola independence.[24] Salazar claimed that American support for these resolutions was encouraging a "communist revolution" in Angola and prompted anti-American demonstrators to storm the U.S. embassy in Lisbon. Acheson was furious about the votes on two additional counts: "I think what this [U.N.] agitation does is to push them [Angola] forward toward an independence for which they are not ready, for which they do not have the cultural attainments or economic or military or governmental experience," he later reflected. "It is solely to make an agitation against Portugal. The Portuguese are allies and friends. They have made available to us and NATO important military advantages. It is important that we play fair with them."[25]

Acheson had become an adviser to President Kennedy on the Portugal-Angola crisis by chance. On March 15 Acheson, Dean Rusk, and Deputy Assistant Secretary Woodruff Wallner were on their way to the White House to attend an NSC meeting on NATO. Wallner, unaware of Acheson's special attachment to Portugal, showed him a draft of a telegram instructing U.S. Ambassador to the U.N. Adlai Stevenson to vote for the resolution calling for an investigation into the violence in Angola. Acheson argued against sending the telegram, on the grounds that it would alienate Portugal.[26] At the White House, however, the president held a whispered conference with Rusk, Wallner, and G. Mennen Williams, and a few minutes later Kennedy signed the cable, which was sent to Stevenson at the UN.

While presenting his recommendations on NATO, Acheson, riled by the proceedings over the telegram, and the news that military aid to Portugal for 1961 had been reduced from a promised $25 million to only $3 million, asserted that the Atlantic alliance was in a state of dreadful decline because "some people" in the administration were "much too lighthearted about kicking our friends around." Kennedy heard the obvious irritation in Acheson's voice and urged him to talk about his concerns. "It's silly to talk about it," Acheson replied. "You already sent the telegram and we're going to take this step. . . . What we are doing is . . . acting for the purpose of appeasing the Afro-Asian group. This is all we will accomplish. We will accomplish nothing in Angola. . . . We will alienate the Portuguese. Now this is not the way to run an alliance." Acheson's remarks triggered a heated discussion. He told the group that the administration could "write all the papers on NATO in the world," but if the president continued to support UN resolutions denouncing an important ally, NATO soon would dissolve into thin air.[27]

For the balance of 1961, Kennedy continued to instruct Stevenson to support all UN resolutions denouncing Portugal's colonial policy and instructed the U.S. ambassador in Lisbon, C. Burke Elbrick, to tell Salazar that America could not tolerate Portugal's African policies. Kennedy also sent arms and money through the CIA to Holden Roberto's Movimento Popular de Libertação (UPA), the most powerful Angolan nationalist group, thus involving the United States in covert action against Salazar.[28] Before long Roberto was placed on the CIA payroll, where he remained until 1969. Although the Stevenson-Bowles-Williams group was still carrying the day, Acheson thought he had "made some headway" in awakening the president to the folly of their disastrous advice. "One of the greatest traps in the UN is to allow small countries to maneuver responsible powers into voting on every conceivable issue," he wrote Kennedy on March 19. "We can refuse to vote on alleged issues which do not advance solutions and our very greatness and responsibility requires us to look at every situation in light of the whole."[29] While he remained tormented by Stevenson's continued UN pontificating he was much relieved when his Europeanist friend George Ball replaced the Africanist Chester Bowles as under secretary of state in November 1961.

Bowles blamed his ouster on a conspiracy lead by "the Achesons" in the State Department and White House who opposed his call for self-determination in Africa and wrote Stevenson that he and Williams would soon meet a similar fate. "When I bumped into Acheson at the State Department shortly after Kennedy canned Bowles, he pointed at his waist and said, 'Soapy, yours will be the next scalp on my belt,'" Williams recalled.[30]

Preoccupied with the Berlin crisis throughout the summer of 1961, Acheson put his African lobbying efforts on hold. By autumn he had returned to his defense of Portugal and NATO solidarity against Kennedy's "misguided idealism." In an article in the *Yale Review*, Acheson claimed that the air and sea bases in the Azores were "perhaps the single most important [set of bases] we have anywhere."[31] In fiscal 1961 alone the air bases on Teheira and Santa Maria islands in the Azores had handled over fourteen thousand takeoffs, amounting to the departures of more than forty long-range planes each day. The lease from Portugal was due to expire on December 31, 1962. Acheson argued that America could not risk the loss of these important refueling, communications, and antisubmarine bases because of an ill-conceived African policy.

The Kennedy administration was split on policy toward Portugal. General Maxwell Taylor, CIA director John McCone, Dean Rusk, and the entire Defense Department supported assistance for Portugal in its war with the Angolan nationalists. Salazar had the Azores; if he wanted, he could blackmail the United States into halting its support of UPA. To prevent this outcome, Acheson argued, all the United States had to do was to stop supporting the UPA and other nationalist groups, abstain from voting against Portugal in the UN, and embrace Salazar as a sensible ally whose admirable leadership had prevented revolution in the Iberian peninsula.[32]

The Angola-Azores Debate

By early 1962 word had spread that Dean Acheson was the most powerful backer of Salazar's Portugal in Washington. The Portuguese hired the New York public relations firm Selvage & Lee, publicized Acheson's views on the Angola crisis as identical to Salazar's, and offered to sponsor Acheson on a fact-finding mission to Angola. Prominent Portuguese officials and lobbyists wrote him impassioned letters of thanks for aiding their cause.[33] Because of Acheson's clout with high Portuguese officials, JFK invited him to the White House in April to recruit him for a diplomatic mission to Lisbon. He and McGeorge Bundy got right down to business: Would Acheson go to Lisbon to negotiate for the extension of the Azores lease? Acheson hesitated; he would go, he said, provided the United States adopt a "sensible" policy. Acheson gave the president a dose of I-told-you-so's: had the president followed his sound advice at the March 15 NSC meeting, negotiations now would be unnecessary; Salazar would have granted an extension, no questions asked. "Portugal is a devoted and loyal ally," Acheson went on. "She would like nothing better than to extend the lease. On the other hand, if you're going [to go] ahead and fight what they're doing in Angola, you won't get the extension anyway. Nobody can get it. I can't—nobody can."³⁴

The problem lay not so much in the immediate negotiations with the Portuguese, but in determining the future direction of U.S. policy. The battle would take place not in Lisbon but in Washington. The administration's pro-Afro-Asian group (Harlan Cleveland, G. Mennen Williams, Adlai Stevenson, John Kenneth Galbraith) believed that relations with Portugal should be sacrificed to maintain the favor of the new black African states. Such thinking was unacceptable to Acheson. "We voted in the United Nations for resolutions 'condemning' Portugal for maintaining order in territory unquestionably under Portuguese sovereignty," he pointed out to Kennedy. "The Portuguese [are] proud people especially sensitive because they [have] declined to such an impotent position after such a glorious history. They would rather proceed to the ruin of their empire in a dignified way . . . than be bought or wheedled into cooperating in their own destruction."

Acheson proposed that the United States should refrain during the upcoming UN General Assembly session from joining in any debates or votes critical of Portugal. The White House stance should be that such resolutions are futile; the interests of all concerned are better served by quiet, friendly discussions. Second, he should try to mount a plan for economic development in both Portugal and Angola with Brazilian and West German participation.

This course of action, Kennedy responded, would represent a very considerable change in U.S.-African policy, and he would be accused of revising direction solely to keep the Azores. Kennedy was trapped by the conflict between his commitment to the principle of self-determination and his obligation to and dependence on a NATO ally. Acheson counseled the president that, if he now recognized the folly of adhering to the policies of the pro-African group, "the best thing was to change it as soon as possible and accept the embarrassment of doing so." But Kennedy raised another point: the existing relationship between Portugal and its colonies could not continue indefinitely; independence for Angola and Mozambique was inevitable. Acheson responded that an enlightened American policy could facilitate the transition "with the greatest advantage to all concerned and the least possible disruption." The relationship of France with its African colonies (except, of course, Algeria) should be the model.

Kennedy acknowledged during the meeting that the United States was aiding Holden Roberto's UPA, but the purpose, he said, was "to keep the Angolan nationalist movement out of the hands of the communist

Ghanians . . . and keep it in the most moderate hands possible." Acheson remarked that this motivation did not make American support of the rebels "any more palatable" to the Portuguese. He went on to charge, correctly as it happens, that the United States was "smuggling Angolese out of Angola and educating them in Lincoln College outside of Philadelphia [a predominantly black school] in the most extreme nationalist views." Furthermore, the president of that college had "secretly and illegally entered Angola and on his return had engaged in violent anti-Portuguese propaganda."[35]

Acheson mentioned rumors emanating from the State Department that the United States was contemplating the overthrow of the Salazar regime. Whoever might be advocating such action, Acheson asserted, clearly lacked knowledge of what Portugal was like from 1910 to 1928, when "with a revolution every six months . . . , it had been reduced to abject poverty, anarchy, and despair." Acheson added, "It was Salazar, whom everybody criticize[s] now, who . . . produced almost a miraculous change in the country."[36]

By meeting's end, it was clear to Kennedy that Acheson was not the man for the negotiating job. However, Acheson was lunching the next day with Portugal's ambassador to the United States, Pedro Pereira, and Kennedy asked whether Acheson would be willing to broach the possibility of a more cooperative attitude on the part of the Portuguese with the ambassador. Acheson said he would.[37]

Acheson's arguments had influenced Kennedy's thinking about the Angola-Azores issue. The president began looking for ways to "balance" support for the Angolan nationalists and Portugal. The pro-African group protested. From his desk in New Delhi, Ambassador John Kenneth Galbraith wrote: "I have difficulty in appreciating your use of Dean Acheson. He is able. He has established himself with the political right. But I cannot think he is capable of loyalty. He will be a source of trouble, for he wants the policy that serves his ego, not your needs."

Adlai Stevenson urged that Kennedy "firmly resist Portuguese efforts to link the Azores to U.S. policy in Angola. Rather, we should insist that the Azores base is vital not only to the defense of the United States but to all NATO, including Portugal. We should, therefore, treat it as a NATO matter."[38]

Acheson targeted G. Mennen Williams, then assistant secretary of state for African affairs, as the main source of "confusion regarding our interests in Africa."[39] In June 1961 Williams had organized a task force on the Portuguese territories that recommended increasing pressure on

Salazar to endorse a "timetable" for Angolan freedom. He later recalled Acheson's response to these efforts: he "wouldn't have a thing to do with me once he heard that I did not feel that maintaining U.S. bases on the Azores was worth undermining our whole new African policy. To Acheson, black Africans just did not exist."[40]

In late April 1962 Senator Henry M. Jackson came to Acheson's aid. He publicly blamed Stevenson and Williams for "the disproportionate amount of energy" the administration had been expending on UN issues such as Angola at the expense of NATO. When Jackson charged that Stevenson was not "a second Secretary of State" and that it was "unfortunate" that he had been given cabinet rank, Stevenson suspected Dean Acheson of maliciously pulling strings behind his back. Stevenson wrote his sister that the attack was a "plot," part of "a well coordinated movement going back to Dean Acheson a dozen years ago and deriving its momentum today from the Pentagon, the European division at State, and the Dulles-line diplomats who favor Europe over the new states." He assailed Acheson's "everlasting backbiting and negativism."[41] Beyond this complaint, Stevenson and the other Africanist members of the administration feared that Kennedy was abandoning them in favor of the Europeanists; in essence, he was.[42]

The Acheson-Stevenson feud, which dated from their policy disputes in the Democratic Advisory Council in the late fifties, had mushroomed into a bitter personal and political rivalry; by 1962 they were no longer on speaking terms. When Stevenson died suddenly of a heart attack in London in 1965, Acheson wrote a letter to Lord Patrick Devlin that reveals the depths of his rancor:

> We have been busy eulogizing Adlai for virtues he never had. He was not eloquent. He was not a great elevator of American politics, nor a potent factor for peace. Adlai was glib, a quipster, and often a wit. He did not have a glimmer about politics but started a new interest in politics among the educated young which opened the way for Kennedy. He had no judgment and his ideas on foreign policy were disastrous—or would have been if followed. A man of great personal charm, he could have played a useful part if fate had not carried him beyond his capabilities.[43]

By summer 1962 Stevenson's influence with the president had vastly diminished. Kennedy had come under the sway of Acheson and the Joint Chiefs, who argued for the strategic indispensability of the Azores. He had begun implementing a two-track approach that he hoped would appeal to both Salazar and the Angolan nationalists. "We are trading our African policy for a few acres of asphalt in the Atlantic," Galbraith reproved.[44] In a reversal of policy, secret arms shipments first intended for the Angolan nationalists were rerouted to Salazar to use against the nationalists.[45]

While Kennedy continued his anticolonialist rhetoric in public, he ceased pressuring Portugal to relinquish its African territories. He feared not only the loss of the Azores military bases but the election-year attacks from Republicans that surely would have followed. The State Department ordered all aid and contact with Roberto's UPA severed, with only a fraction of the original CIA money still to be funneled into clandestine efforts in Angola. Kennedy did try to induce Salazar to relinquish control of Angola by offering a half billion dollars in aid in return for a promise to pull out of Africa within five years. But Salazar would not be bought. Kennedy threw his support behind an abortive coup in Portugal staged by Botelho Moniz, the minister of defense, but Salazar artfully managed to maintain firm control of the country. By his iron resolve and his skillful play of his role as landlord of the Azores, Richard Mahoney points out, Salazar forced Kennedy to abandon support of the Angolan nationalists.[46] In December 1962 the U.S. voted for the first time against two UN Security Council resolutions denouncing continued Portuguese colonialism. This abrupt and dramatic reversal of policy united the previously disparate Angolan black nationalist groups with a bond of anti-Americanism.[47]

When the Azores lease officially expired on December 31, 1962, no new agreement was drawn up between Portugal and the United States. Instead, Salazar permitted his American tenants to remain on a day-to-day basis. As Arthur Schlesinger, Jr., starkly stated in a July 1, 1963, memorandum to Attorney General Robert F. Kennedy, the president continued to face a dilemma: "the military risk of losing the Azores and the (NASA) Southern African tracking station [versus] the political risk of losing Africa."[48] But by this time it was clear that Kennedy had sided with Acheson and the other pro-NATO members of the administration; the "two-track" policy in fact headed squarely toward Lisbon.[49] It would take a decade of guerrilla war before Angola finally gained independence in 1975, as Kennedy had known it eventually would. And, as many in the Kennedy administration had predicted, the protracted struggle ended with establishment of a Marxist regime, unrecognized by Washington.

Acheson naturally was pleased that Kennedy had adopted the Europeanist position, but he wanted more: he thought the president should renounce support for African nationalism, which the liberal Democrats compared to the American civil rights movement.⁵⁰ For Acheson, black rule in Africa translated to chaos across the "dark continent," the perfect soil for communism to flourish in.

When Lyndon Johnson took the oath of office in the wake of JFK's assassination, Acheson was hopeful that in African affairs the Texas politician would be guided by pragmatism, not by the idealism of his predecessor. Acheson's hopes were short-lived. To his dismay Johnson also supported the principle of democratic rule in Africa, to the extent of following the UN call to impose economic sanctions on Rhodesia. Acheson expended much energy trying to convince LBJ to lift the sanctions and formally recognize Ian Smith's white minority government.

Rhodesian Independence

On November 11, 1965, Rhodesia, formerly a self-governing colony of Great Britain, declared independence. The unilateral declaration of independence (UDI), the government claimed, was modeled on the American declaration of 1776. For the next four years, Rhodesia's white-ruled regime under Prime Minister Ian D. Smith withstood—in addition to guerrilla warfare, terrorist attacks, strikes, and urban riots—escalating economic sanctions imposed by Britain and the United Nations to pressure the white regime to revoke its declaration of independence and eventually to permit black majority rule.⁵¹

Even though whites accounted for less than 5 percent of Rhodesia's population, they completely dominated the country's social, economic, and political structure. Since World War II Britain had been dismantling its empire by granting independence to its colonies with the stipulation that the new governments follow the principle of majority rule. In the case of Rhodesia, Britain did not require immediate transition to majority rule, but in 1965 did insist that a timetable for eventual majority rule be drawn up.

The UDI brought protests throughout the world. Nationalist parties in Rhodesia, which were banned, demanded immediate independence with one person–one vote democracy. Prime Minister Harold Wilson of Britain called the declaration "treasonable"; his government "condemn[ed] the purported declaration of independence by the former government of Rhodesia as an illegal act." Nearly all of the UN member-states adamantly opposed Smith's government as an outlaw regime based on white exploitation and urged Britain to do whatever was necessary to reverse Rhodesia's action. The United States supported the British position in the UN. Further, it withdrew its consular officials, terminated the diplomatic status of the minister for Rhodesian affairs in the British embassy in Washington, established an arms embargo on Rhodesia, refused Rhodesian applications for loans, and discouraged American investment in and private travel to Rhodesia.

On November 12, the day after Rhodesian independence was proclaimed, the UN Security Council unanimously "condemn[ed] the unilateral declaration of independence made by a racist minority in Southern Rhodesia" and called on "all states not to recognize this illegal racist minority regime in Southern Rhodesia and to refrain from rendering any assistance to that illegal regime."[52] Arthur Goldberg, then ambassador to the United Nations, and the African bureau of the State Department wanted to move Britain toward even stronger action against the Smith regime.

Acheson was infuriated at the outside interference with Smith's white, Christian, stable, anticommunist government. His first public statement on the Rhodesian imbroglio came in a speech at the University of Virginia in May 1966. What went on within Rhodesia's borders, he contended in this talk, should not concern other nations: "Rhodesia follows policies toward the black people within her territory, regarding qualifications for voting and apportionment of parliamentary representatives, which if attempted in the United States, would be held to violate the fourteenth and fifteenth amendments to our Constitution," he acknowledged, but he quickly added that "this would not always have been the case."[53] To Acheson, Smith's government was a beacon of European light in a dark continent being overrun by anarchy, Marxism, and demonic black-power propaganda.

In reiterating the position he had taken during the Cuban missile crisis that international law should not serve as the basis of U.S. national security policy, Acheson observed that in the post–World War II era the world was going through "a withdrawal of the legal order" in which might made right, or, perhaps more accurately, might was the source of right. The pursuit of peace through law was "illusory." "The conclusion seems plain," Acheson went on, "that in the search for ways to maintain our values and pursue them in an orderly way, we must look beyond the resources of law."[54]

In the first of a series of lectures at Columbia University in memory of his predecessor at the UN, Adlai Stevenson, Arthur Goldberg disputed Acheson's views. Against Acheson's characterization of the UN as incapable of developing an alternative to national power, Goldberg quoted

Stevenson: "Let none of us mock its weakness, for when we do, we are mocking ourselves." In a direct rebuttal to Acheson's assertion that the idea of peace through law was "illusory," Goldberg claimed that in international disputes, as in other legal matters, it was wrong to separate issues of law and power because "in real life, law and power operate together." "Power not ruled by law is a menace," Goldberg declared, "but law not served by power is a delusion."[55]

No other Johnson administration official irritated Acheson more than the man he called "that ass Goldberg."[56] As head of the U.S. delegation to the UN, Goldberg had been doing an effective job of advancing the rights of black Africans, but from the early days of the Kennedy administration, Acheson had harangued both the State Department and White House to revise the Stevenson-Goldberg policies toward Portuguese Africa, Rhodesia, and South Africa because they were "not calculated to help in any way the black people about whom we profess to be disturbed." On the contrary, Acheson asserted, these policies were making life harder for African blacks while creating chaos throughout the region. "We are concerned with postures and not with realities," Acheson wrote Sir Frederick Leith-Ross in May. "Unfortunately, I seem to have made no headway at all."[57]

In October 1966, with the blessings of LBJ and Dean Rusk, Goldberg introduced a resolution in the UN General Assembly declaring that South Africa had forfeited its right to administer the area called South-West Africa and that a commission should be formed to start the process of self-determination. To Acheson it seemed that the United States now was not merely supporting measures aimed at crippling the governments of faithful allies like Rhodesia and South Africa, it was initiating them.

In December the British submitted a resolution calling for sanctions against Rhodesia. In an interview for the *Washington Evening Star* Acheson objected that the UN would be "completely out of hand" if it imposed sanctions on Rhodesia. The political system of Rhodesia was "totally an internal matter," of no concern to the UN or to the United States. The United States should veto the British resolution on the grounds that it violated the UN charter.[58] The following day, in a letter to the *Washington Post*, Acheson repeated his case that the Smith regime was a de facto state. Thus the UN had no right to interfere in what was clearly an "internal matter" of a sovereign nation. The black African states that called for UN sanctions were the real "threat to peace." The thinking of the UN, Acheson mocked, was "worthy of the Red Queen in *Through The Looking Glass*." Harold Wilson, who had initiated the resolution, Acheson dismissed as a "loony."[59]

Goldberg responded on January 8, 1967, in a letter to the *Post*, that Rhodesia had not been recognized as a state by any "responsible" nation in the world. The UN had acted "at the request of and with the concurrence of the legitimate sovereign, the United Kingdom," and the situation was not a "domestic" one; it involved the international responsibilities of the United Kingdom. Goldberg termed the Smith regime's claim to the right of self-determination ludicrous, in view of the fact that Rhodesian whites represented a tiny fraction of the population.[60]

Spurred on, and widely hailed, by many of the new African and Asian states for his bold initiative on the South-West African issue, Goldberg sided with Britain and the majority of the UN Security Council (the resolution passed by a vote of 11-0 with four abstentions) to impose mandatory sanctions on Rhodesia. By this vote, the Johnson administration made it clear that it considered the Rhodesian situation a "threat to the peace" within the meaning of the UN charter.[61]

A host of conservative and right-wing politicians criticized the UN sanctions, including senators Barry Goldwater and Paul Fannin of Arizona, James Eastland of Mississippi, and Strom Thurmond of South Carolina, and Governor George Wallace of Alabama. Acheson began a singularly strident crusade to gain popular support for his pro–Ian Smith views. He also worked frenetically behind the scenes trying to undo the administration's UN policy, which he claimed pandered to "the international juvenile delinquents" of the third world.[62]

He wrote to a British conservative, "In my view if Britain cannot—and she cannot—coerce a colony, it isn't one, and she had better not call the Black Mafia [the African nationalists in the UN] in. Why we blunder along behind Harold Wilson, God only knows."[63] And, to the historian Barbara Tuchman, Acheson said, "The U.N. is useless, and U-Thank[sic] a contemptible little rat who provides cover for Nasser, Makarios and that whole tribe when they want protection and who scuffles when they say, 'seat!'"[64]

Acheson's lobbying efforts received a boost when his friend Charles Burton Marshall, a Johns Hopkins University professor and former State Department colleague, published *Crisis over Rhodesia: A Skeptical View*. Marshall sided with Acheson's contentions that white rule in Rhodesia was a domestic matter and that UN interference in the form of sanctions set a dangerous precedent.[65] Acheson favorably reviewed Marshall's book for the *Washington Post*, and used the opportunity to ridicule Goldberg's logic by comparing it to the reasoning the Soviet spokesman Andrei Vyshinsky had used during the Korean War. Vyshinsky contended that

South Korea was not a state, but rather was part of a state that had been divided. Therefore North Korea's invasion of South Korea did not constitute an act of international aggression but should be seen instead as civil war.[66]

In private discussion with Johnson, Acheson called the United States a patsy of the UN and of Harold Wilson. Goldberg was creating instability and providing Moscow with an opportunity to encroach on the region. The only accomplishment of sanctions, Acheson told the president, was to cut off American access to strategic mineral resources in Rhodesia. The president paid little attention to these arguments. "[The administration's] reply has been to go ahead in their own happy way and just ignore me," Acheson complained.[67] Acheson later privately asserted that LBJ had struck a deal with Wilson in November 1965 by which the United States would support Britain's economic warfare against Rhodesia in return for Wilson's promise not to criticize U.S. policy in Vietnam.[68]

Frustrated that his arguments had fallen on deaf ears, Acheson turned up the heat in public. In an address to the International and Comparative Law Section of the American Bar Association in May 1968, he charged that the United States was "engaged in an international conspiracy, instigated by Britain and blessed by the United Nations, to overthrow the government of a country [Rhodesia] that has done us no harm and threatens no one." He claimed that Rhodesia's UDI had the moral status of the American Declaration of Independence. Acheson also asserted that the Rhodesian government planned to give blacks an increasing voice, but would stop short of majority rule. "This was not everyone's cup of tea," Acheson declared, managing to denigrate the aspiration for political liberty to a choice of Lipton's over Earl Grey. "Neither was it everyone's business; nor was it apartheid." He closed with a poke at the Arthur Goldbergs of the world: "One of the troubles of the troubled age in which we live is that too many people are trying to achieve harmony of interest by forcing everyone to harmonize with them."[69] Asked by the press for a comment on Acheson's talk, Goldberg replied, "The Secretary of State is a very distinguished man, but what he has said is sheer nonsense."[70]

The differences between the theoretical views Acheson and Goldberg held on the role of international law were unbridgeable. Acheson's position was grounded on the right of sovereign states to manage their own domestic affairs; Goldberg's position was grounded on the obligation to defend individual human rights, even as against the abuses of a nation's own leaders. Acheson also insisted that a sensible U.S. foreign policy required avoiding excess in moralizing and emotion, at least in regard to those issues he deemed trivial or those people he found unworthy to make serious moral claims. His posture short-circuited any examination of the question of whose standards of morality should prevail, and his legalistic invocation of the status quo gave no consideration to the wellsprings of "political" emotions—anger and frustration over powerlessness and injustice. Of course, Acheson himself was not above pleading a higher morality to buttress his case when it suited him or playing upon the emotions in furtherance of his own views. His double standard when it came to the underdeveloped world infuriated his critics.

The strength of Acheson's feelings is revealed in a startling letter to Philip Jessup in August 1968: "It is barefaced aggression. That the UN attempts to do this to Rhodesia does not make it any more palatable to me than the Soviet Union's attempt to do it to Czechoslovakia."[71] Acheson's comparison conveniently overlooks the fact that the Soviets had brutally intervened to end Alexander Dubcek's domestic experiment with "socialism with a human face" in August 1968. They had used military force to maintain their dictatorial rule over Eastern Europe, whereas the UN intervened with economic force for the purpose of ensuring democratic and human rights for all Rhodesians. "I cannot understand why we follow the stupid policy of a bewildered country [Great Britain] under a third-rate Prime Minister, thereby heading for problems with much-needed friends," Acheson said to the Rhodesian minister of external affairs, Lord Angus Graham. "If the Afro-Asian group in the United Nations continues to manipulate Harold Wilson along his present path, I see possibilities for greater trouble."[72]

Following Hubert Humphrey's loss to Richard Nixon in the 1968 presidential election, Acheson wrote a newspaper article urging Lyndon Johnson to launch a house-cleaning of the State Department by purging the liberal Africanists. He should drop Rhodesian sanctions, disregarding UN whining, and recognize Ian Smith's government before the Nixon administration took over:

> The Johnson Administration, like a tidy and conscientious housewife, will want to clean out rubbish, failures, and broken-down contraptions rather than leave them to embarrass the new tenant. There is no better place to start than with Rhodesian policy, bought by the present occupant in an absentminded moment from a smart salesman [Arthur Goldberg]. It never did work. The salesman is trying

desperately to escape from all connection with it; and to leave the old non-starter to clutter up the garage would be a scurvy trick.[73]

LBJ did not "clean house." Although many regarded enforcement of sanctions against Rhodesia as a failed policy because it did not end the rebellion, others praised Johnson for maintaining solidarity with Great Britain, for showing respect for the United Nations, for displaying moral courage, and for winning the devoirs and confidence of black African nations.[74]

To Acheson's pleasant surprise, his long years of frustration over African policies during the Kennedy-Johnson era would largely evaporate with the installation of the Nixon-Kissinger team.

Positive Communication

During his first White House meeting with President Nixon, in March 1969, Acheson brought up U.S. policy toward southern Africa and found the president in accord with his views. Both thought the two previous presidents had been misguided in opposing anticommunist allies such as Portugal, South Africa, and Rhodesia because of their conduct of internal affairs. With the Suez Canal shut, the United States needed to use South Africa's ports. The African continent was in disarray, and both men saw the white-ruled governments as the only centers of stability and order. Seizing upon this opening Acheson urged upon Nixon the advice he had offered Kennedy and Johnson: clean out the remaining Africanists in the State Department. Nixon soon followed Acheson's advice.[75]

Throughout 1969 and 1970, while Acheson continued his public attacks on the UN trade embargo against Rhodesia, Nixon and Kissinger were developing a new policy toward the white-ruled nations of southern Africa. Their strategy was described in National Security Study Memorandum 39 (NSSM 39) of April 10, 1969, a top-secret policy review undertaken without Acheson's direct participation. In effect, NSSM 39 called for a compromise between the Acheson–Defense Department line of noninterference in the domestic affairs of the white regimes in southern Africa (referred to as Option 1 or the "Acheson Approach") and the Johnson-Kennedy policy advanced by the African Bureau, which aimed at enhancing American political influence in Africa (referred to as Option 3). The study declared that "force [applied by nationalist groups] is not an appropriate means to bring about constructive change in southern Africa," and it wrongly predicted that there was "no likelihood in the foreseeable future that liberation movements could overthrow or seriously threaten" either white-ruled Rhodesia or Portuguese-ruled Angola and Mozambique.[76] Acheson's impassioned memorandum supporting the white regimes was used to give a veneer of intellectual legitimacy and bipartisanship to the new Option 2—"positive communication." Roger Morris, who served on Nixon's NSC staff on southern African matters, characterized Acheson's influence as "atmospheric" rather than "political." Acheson's rationale provided "the icing on the cake" for Nixon's conciliatory approach to, and defense ties with, the white rulers of southern Africa.[77]

Encouraged by his first White House meeting, Acheson submitted a lengthy memorandum entitled "U.S. Policies toward Southern Africa Require Change" in April 1969.[78] He warned that continued pressure against the white-led regimes of southern Africa would lead to the independence of Angola and Mozambique, to the "subjugation of Rhodesia to majority rule," and to Soviet gains in Africa—all contrary to U.S. national interests. "The Portuguese," he explained, "discovered Angola a decade before Columbus discovered the Western Hemisphere. Portuguese rule has been undisputed since the sixteenth century." While praising Salazar's strong-armed rule, he blamed the Soviet Union and the People's Republic of China for infecting Angolans with revolutionary fever. He warned that the end of Portuguese rule in Angola would result in not "one-man-one-vote but a bloody Nigerian type shambles."[79]

As for economic sanctions, Acheson said, in a letter to the editor of the *Washington Post*: "Two and a half years of sanctions have served only to encourage the British Government to frustrate a settlement by insisting on untenable conditions, to push the isolated Rhodesian electorate sharply rightward, to retard the Blacks' economic progress and to make the United States improvidently dependent on the Soviet Union for chrome."[80]

In July 1969 Acheson submitted another memorandum to the White House. The British were about to expel the Rhodesian consul general from London. Acheson argued that maintaining a U.S. consulate in Rhodesia did not constitute recognition of the regime. He concluded, "The real purpose of sanctions is to foment race war in Rhodesia. American liberals might be too fuzzy-headed to see it. But both British right and left see it; and the left cheers it on. This is no policy for the United

States government to accept in an alleged search for peace."[81] Kissinger began requesting from Acheson a series of memorandums on all facets of Washington's relationship with Africa. In a position paper written in October Acheson once again stressed the need to preserve U.S. independence in the conduct of foreign relations and protect access to essential strategic minerals. And again disagreed with economic sanctions:

> It is now almost four years since the Rhodesian assertion of independence. The government of Rhodesia is in full control of the country. It is ready to fulfill its international obligations. A new Constitution has been submitted and adopted by the electorate. The last connection with the British Crown has been severed. No threat to international peace and security has materialized. Rhodesian forces readily cope with sporadic terrorist infiltrations attempted from Zambia in an earlier phase. More than a year has passed since the last such attempt. The countryside is secure. Police in the cities go unarmed. Rhodesia is quiet and peaceful.[82]

Given Acheson's belief in the inherent superiority of the white Western rulers and limitations of the native populations, he viewed the attempt to inflict enough hardship on the white governments to force them to pursue a more democratic and egalitarian policy as unwise and dangerous. Nor, he argued, did the sanctions achieve that end. Larded with pages of statistics obtained from conservative friends in Britain, Acheson's memorandum meant to demonstrate that sanctions had inconvenienced but not economically injured Rhodesia. Their main effect had been to reduce employment among blacks, he claimed. On the other hand, sanctions could damage the American economy. Acheson predicted a shortage of chrome and petalite, a lithium ore used by U.S. glass manufacturers. He closed with a familiar legal argument for lifting the sanctions.

In November 1969 Acheson and Charles Burton Marshall appeared before the House subcommittee on Africa, chaired by Charles Diggs, a black congressman from Michigan. Acheson testified that diplomatic recognition of a foreign state did not imply approval of its ideology or policies. He based his argument on the principle of noninterference in the internal affairs of other countries—a principle, he noted, that would have prevented the devastation caused in Europe by the religious wars of the Middle Ages. Africa's best hope for stability and development, he continued, lay with the competent, highly cultured white people "who [rule] southern Africa." He contrasted their orderly regimes with the "return to primitive tribalism" which, he said, had occurred in Nigeria and the Congo and which would ensue should the white governments of southern Africa fall. The entire "dark continent" would become "black[,] and hostile" to Western economic interests and Western democratic principles. Prime Minister of South Africa John Vorster and Foreign Minister Dr. Hilgard Muller, he averred, sincerely believed that apartheid served the best interests of all their countrymen, regardless of their color.[83]

A letter Acheson wrote General Johannes Steinhoff of West Germany captures the tone of his many messages to European friends urging activity in support of lifting the UN sanctions on Rhodesia:

> It seems to me that the policy of the Western nations toward Africa is most ill-advised. Instigated by Great Britain and supported with fanatical zeal by the Third World through the United Nations, we are all helping the Soviet Union cause as much trouble as it can to our interests in the Middle East. I believe a great deal could be done to strengthen our position in the Indian Ocean and to bring about a more stable situation in Southern Africa, both in the white areas and in the black areas, by a more sensible policy toward the white governments.[84]

Acheson expanded on the more general point of the importance of conducting American foreign policy in terms of American interests in a meeting with the president in December 1969. He cautioned Nixon against "differentiating in our policy . . . against those countries that [have] dictatorships." At a luncheon with Acheson a few days later, Secretary of State Rogers said, "It would be easier to make overtures to South Africa if that country would do something such as letting in the well-known black tennis player, Arthur Ashe." Acheson responded that the South African ambassador was "a sensible man" and might accept some such suggestion from Rogers.[85]

By the late 1960s Acheson, the lawyer who had helped to draft LBJ's 1957 Civil Rights Bill, greatly feared pressure by blacks—whether in Africa or in America—for political rights. He most often expressed this anxiety to Sir Roy Welensky, the former prime minister of Rhodesia. Acheson never met Welensky; their common friendship with Anthony Eden led to a satisfying relationship through letters. Welensky had initiated the correspondence by writing Acheson in 1968 to ask that he use his influence to alter American policies toward Rhodesia. Within a year the two had exchanged letters on race relations, British policy toward

Rhodesia, and the Rhodesian and American constitutions. In the hour before he died of a stroke on October 12, 1971, Acheson wrote an enthusiastic letter to Anthony Eden in anticipation of their planned joint trip to Africa in January 1972. It would have been Acheson's first trip to southern Africa, and he was looking forward to meeting Welensky and Smith in Rhodesia, as well as to visiting other white leaders in Angola, South-West Africa, South Africa, and Mozambique.[86]

In Acheson's eyes men like Ian Smith and Roy Welensky were idealistic white knights in rebellion against an unjust sovereign, not racists whose primary objective was the preservation of privilege. Acheson dismissed black African leaders as powerless, politically unreliable, and unable "to create a modern territorial state" because of their adherence to "tribalism." Ghana's leader Kwame Nkrumah, for instance, suffered from "vanity, corruption, absolutism and inability to manage," while the Belgian Congo, Acheson maintained, had been destroyed by Patrice Lumumba's "schizophrenic leadership." Acheson wrote in 1971: "Among emerging African leaders the perverse stimulation of personal ambition operating in areas of almost total ignorance [contributes] to a full measure of confusion. A bright child at the controls of a car on a major thruway could produce comparable disaster."[87]

Acheson, normally reticent about criticizing American leaders and policies to foreigners, was almost immediately outspoken with Welensky in denouncing U.S. policy in Africa: "Our attitude toward Rhodesia is unnecessary to appease our blacks and liberals who have very little choice beyond the Democratic party." Convinced that Soviet activity in the eastern Mediterranean had made the Cape of Good Hope route even more important for trade and defense purposes, Acheson lamented, "We go blithely on antagonizing all three Cape governments. Talleyrand, Metternich, and Castlereagh, as well as our own Ben Franklin, would not regard this as wise."[88] U.S. policy toward southern Africa was "as mistaken as that toward Israel in the other direction." He admonished, "Foreign Policy should not be regarded as a popularity contest."[89]

In early August 1971 Welensky made a speech in Bulawayo, Rhodesia, that appeared to Acheson to advocate considerable political advancement for blacks. He grew alarmed that Welensky's proposal would sound the death knell for continued white control and warned him against using the United States as his model for Rhodesia's future:

> I do not decry the energy and daring with which FDR attacked the problems of a society and economy, disintegrating almost as fast as

were those of Europe in 1946–47. A little more thought by him of the dim and distant future twenty years away would have been appreciated by those of us who lived to see it as he did not. Some of it—such as the movement of southern blacks to northern cities and high relief payments could have been foreseen if anyone had looked. We now face black urban government in many northern cities accompanied by white exodus. We furnish a good forecasting model for Rhodesia, including the make-up and control of armed forces and police. . . . As the two wars brought about the black movement from rural agriculture to urban industry and relief in this country, does it furnish you with guides to policies of free movement and the effect of certain policies on population drift?[90]

Acheson's question is rhetorical. The letter reflects his longing to return to an arcadian past when black Americans could be manipulated, exploited, and discouraged from making political and moral claims based on democratic and egalitarian principles. By no means a visceral racist, Acheson held an attitude toward the plight of black America that perhaps can be best described as old-fashioned paternalism.

Backing the white regimes of southern Africa gained Acheson a new coterie of followers made up of Americans on the far right and British conservatives. Such individuals and organizations as Patrick Buchanan, the speechwriter for Nixon; William Loeb, the publisher of the *Manchester Union Leader* (New Hampshire); Young Americans for Freedom; the Liberty Lobby; the John Birch Society; the American group Friends of Rhodesia; and the Rhodesian Information Bureau quoted him often. The Friends of Rhodesia, a white supremacist organization, used the line "Former Secretary of State Dean Acheson stated that our Government's position on Rhodesia is both immoral and illegal. What do you think?"[91] The Rhodesian Information Bureau issued a special bulletin entitled "Dean Acheson on the Rhodesian Question." William F. Buckley praised the "new Acheson" in editorials in the *National Review* and in books. He earned persona non grata status from Kenneth Kaunda, the president of Zambia, for republishing Acheson's denunciation of U.S. sanctions against Rhodesia. The right-wing columnist James J. Kilpatrick joyously proclaimed, "Would you believe: 'Acheson is the greatest!'"[92]

During this period, Acheson often found himself in heated arguments with family and friends. They did not want to see him end his distinguished public career as a spokesman for the crumbling and anachronistic Rhodesian government and a supporter of apartheid in South Africa.[93]

"I find [Acheson's] views unrealistic and quite unfortunate," W. Averell Harriman told an interviewer in 1970. "His policies on South Africa and Rhodesia—that they are our best friends—I find atrocious. He [is] entirely a European man. A great statesman for a certain period in history, [Acheson] has long since been of another era. He is not what you call a universal statesman, he is not one of those men who has transcended time."[94] Even Acheson's immediate family viewed his thinking as outdated. "My daughters—natural and by marriage—think I am an old reactionary," Acheson lamented in May 1971. He had no reply to the rebellion stirring in his own back yard but a firmly stated denial: "They are wrong about that."[95]

Acheson's final effort on behalf of what he called "the white states of southern Africa"—a term instructive in itself for obliterating, by sheer obstinacy, the black majority—was to join the lobbying effort on behalf of an amendment by Sen. Harry F. Byrd of Virginia. The amendment would reverse United States policy against buying chrome and seventy-two other "strategic and critical materials" from Rhodesia despite the continuing UN-imposed sanctions. Acheson's final appearance on the public stage was before the Senate Subcommittee on African Affairs on July 7 and 8, 1971, to argue the merits of the amendment.[96]

Assistant Secretary of State for African Affairs David Newsom and Congressman Charles Diggs of Michigan fought the bill, as did the Congressional Black Caucus, the United Steelworkers of America, and the American Committee on Africa. Their opposition centered on issues of international law and human rights. Their major claims—that the legislation would undermine the positive image of the United States in Africa and in the UN, give financial support to the illegal Ian Smith Rhodesian regime, and place the United States in clear violation of an international treaty obligation—were borne out. At the time their arguments did not prevail. While Nixon did not publicly support the amendment, he refused to embrace the State Department's efforts to defeat the bill. The amendment's well-organized supporters concentrated on two issues: the American domestic economy and national security interests. Acheson's lobbying was part of a team effort that included industrial giants such as Union Carbide. They were able to tip the scales in favor of the amendment on November 17, 1971; Acheson, however, did not live to see its final passage.[97] The United States thus joined South Africa and Portugal as the only nations to defy the UN sanctions.

To his last breath Dean Acheson was an unrepentant, unreconstructed colonialist where black Africa was concerned. As early as 1952 he had opposed pressuring South Africa on the South-West Africa question. The collapse of the Portuguese African empire in 1973–74 and the subsequent demise of Rhodesia and birth of Zimbabwe a scant decade after his death revealed the wrongheadedness of his apocalyptic vision of the future should African blacks achieve freedom and independence.

Once, in an appearance before the House Committee on Foreign Affairs, Acheson closed his testimony by quoting Lord Salisbury: "The commonest error in politics is sticking to the carcasses of dead policies. When a mast falls overboard, you do not try to save a rope here and a spar there, in memory of their former utility; you cut away the hamper altogether."[98] It is a sad irony that after a lifetime devoted to his country, he was unable to cut away the hampers from his own boat. His support for the white regimes in southern Africa was rooted in a cluster of prejudices and attitudes that were beyond the reach of rational opposition. He would never try to appreciate the aspirations for political freedom of the peoples of the third world.

Epilogue: Death at Harewood

With the successful denouement to the "battle of Mansfield" and his well-publicized support of the Byrd amendment behind him, and a beautiful Maryland autumn ahead, Acheson decided to remain at Harewood to write and relax. September was blocked off for writing articles and letters on Rhodesia, Berlin, the Middle East, and China. His health seemed to be improving, and he was planning a six-week tour of southern Africa with Anthony Eden in January. His letters to W. Averell Harriman, John Cowles, and Archibald MacLeish that September were filled with reminiscences of his Connecticut childhood. Buoyed by the service he had rendered the nation during the past year, he was looking forward to helping Nixon and Kissinger develop constructive policies toward China and Rhodesia.

On October 12, 1971, Acheson spent the day preparing his garden for winter. Late in the afternoon he went to his study and wrote Anthony Eden a lengthy letter filled with enthusiasm at the prospect of their upcoming journey to Africa.[1] At six o'clock the seventy-eight-year-old statesman was found by his groundskeeper slumped over his desk, dead of a stroke.

When news of Acheson's death reached President Nixon, he immediately issued a statement: "The nation, the Western alliance and the world all share in the loss of one of their staunchest champions." He noted that it was "a measure of Dean Acheson's stature as a man and statesman that almost 20 years after his service as Secretary of State he continued to be recognized as one of the towering figures of his time. He was a man not only of great achievement but also of rare intellect, of rigorous conscience and of profound devotion to his country." He added a personal note: "I shall greatly miss both his wise counsel and his penetrating wit."[2]

Given the erratic course of politics in America, it is perhaps unsurprising that a man who once was vilified for being soft on communism should later be condemned for being too hard an anticommunist. In fact, Acheson's position did not change much over the years. He viewed the cold war as the central foreign-policy reality and wanted the United States to remain economically, militarily, and politically superior to the Soviet Union. "Negotiation from strength" became synonymous with Achesonian diplomatic method during the cold war. There was no room for morality as such in diplomacy; it spoiled the game and led to fanaticism. All his career he scorned the liberal habit of trying to "exorcise evil spirits by moral incantation."[3]

Twenty years after Dean Acheson's death, his son David recalled that a hallmark of his father's style was his refusal "to dabble around the edges of foreign affairs." Instead he preferred to "immerse himself in an issue, direct upon it all of his formidable powers of concentration and persuasion, and become a dedicated, even ruthless, advocate of the proposal he thought needed." In the years from 1953 to 1971, David Acheson admitted, his father occasionally "allowed himself too much fun and brushed the edges of the outrageous, savoring the freedom from official constraints that went with his private status."[4]

Hundreds gathered at the public funeral at the National Cathedral in Washington to pay their last respects to Dean Acheson. While distinguished diplomats and world leaders reminisced about Acheson's great foreign-policy achievements during the Truman years, those in Washington who knew him best grieved the loss of a man who, as James Reston wrote in tribute, "told Presidents what he truly believed about the realities of power in the world and not what they wanted to hear."[5] Arthur Schlesinger, Jr., in a *New York Times* essay titled "The Style Was Always Bravura," noted that "in a city of gray and anonymous men, Dean Acheson stood out like a noble monument from another and more vivid era."[6] The loss of Dean Acheson's candor, clarity, intelligence, and devotion to public service would be mourned by those who had had the benefit of his counsel. For those who value an American foreign policy grounded in global realpolitik and clad in eloquence, urbanity, and wit, the death of Dean Acheson left an unfillable void.

NOTES

Abbreviations

AF	*Among Friends: Personal Letters of Dean Acheson*, ed. McLellan and Acheson
CT Papers	Charles Tyroler II Papers
DGA	Dean G. Acheson
DGA-Yale	Dean Acheson Papers, Manuscripts and Archives, Yale University Library, New Haven, Connecticut
HST	Harry S Truman
HSTL	Harry S Truman Library, Independence, Missouri
LBJ	Lyndon Baines Johnson
LBJL	Lyndon Baines Johnson Library, Austin, Texas
JFK	John Fitzgerald Kennedy
JFKL	John Fitzgerald Kennedy Library, Boston, Massachusetts
NYT	*New York Times*
RMN	Richard Milhous Nixon
S, B, F	Series, Box, Folder
TVER	*This Vast External Realm* by Dean Acheson

Introduction: Intimidating Seniority

1. Dean Acheson, "Idle Thoughts of an Idle Fellow," notes for speech at the Century Club, Washington, D.C., March 19, 1968, S 3, B 54, F 75, DGA-Yale.
2. DGA to Hans J. Morgenthau, March 23, 1963, S 1, B 23, F 284, DGA-Yale.
3. DGA to Anthony Eden, July 7, 1969, S 1, B 9, F 119, DGA-Yale.
4. JFK to DGA, April 19, 1963 (telegram), S 1, B 18, F 223, DGA-Yale.
5. Ferrell and McLellan, "Dean Acheson: Architect of a Manageable World Order," in Merli and Wilson, eds., *Makers of American Diplomacy*, pp. 219–20.
6. The Reminiscences of Chester Bowles, Oral History Research Office, Columbia University, 1963, Vol. 5, p. 785.

7. David K. E. Bruce Diaries, November 27, 1957, Virginia Historical Society, Richmond, Va.

8. Paul H. Nitze, Introduction, *Dean Acheson and the Making of U.S. Foreign Policy*, ed. Brinkley, xxii.

9. W. Averell Harriman Memoirs, Miscellany Interview, June 28, 1970, Harriman Papers, Box 874, Library of Congress, MSS.

10. Robert Bowie, interview, January 1991, Washington, D.C.

11. Clifford, *Counsel to the President*, 142.

Chapter 1. Into the Fray against John Foster Dulles

1. Acheson, *Present at the Creation*, 632–33. For documents dealing with the administrative aspects of the transition, see U.S. Department of State, *Foreign Relations of the United States* (hereafter, *FRUS*), 1952–1954, vol. 1, pt. 1, pp. 1–44. Also see DGA to Frank M. Shea, Feb. 4, 1958, S 1, B 28, F 362, DGA-Yale.

2. Anthony Leviero, "Truman, Too, Gets His Blaze of Glory," *NYT*, Jan. 21, 1953, p. 1. For Acheson's recounting of inauguration day, see Acheson, *Present at the Creation*, 721.

3. HST to DGA, Feb. 7, 1953, Acheson-Truman Correspondence (hereafter, A-T Corres.), 1953, Box 166, HSTL.

4. Leviero, "Truman, Too . . . ," p. 1.

5. Much has been made of the cordial working relationship between Acheson and Truman. For their praiseful assessments of each other, see Acheson, *Present at the Creation*, and Truman, *Memoirs: Years of Trial and Hope*. For useful explanations of why the two men remained friends for life, see David C. Acheson, "Truman-Acheson Friendship"; and Gaddis Smith, "The Improbable Partnership: Truman and Acheson," (Paper delivered at the Dean Acheson Conference, Yale University, April 24, 1982).

6. Leviero, "Truman, Too . . . ," p. 1.

7. Acheson's *Present at the Creation* offers a detailed account of his years in the State Department. His devotion and admiration for Marshall is best revealed in chapter 7 of *Sketches from Life of Men I Have Known*, by Dean Acheson. For further discussion of the Acheson-Marshall working relationship, see Pogue, *George C. Marshall*.

8. For important studies concentrating on Acheson's tenure as secretary of state, see Acheson, *Present at the Creation*; Smith, *Dean Acheson*; McLellan, *Dean Acheson*; Stupak, *Shaping of Foreign Policy*; Perlmutter, "Acheson and American Foreign Policy" (Ph.D. diss.); Rosenau, "Senate and Dean Acheson" (Ph.D. diss.); and Salmon, "Statesmanship of Dean Acheson" (Ph.D. diss.).

9. McCarthy is quoted in Brandon, *Special Relationships*, 96. For Eisenhower's victory in the 1952 presidential election, see Parmet, *Eisenhower and the American Crusades*, 118–49; Ambrose, *Eisenhower: Soldier, General . . .*, 550–71; and Bernstein, "Election of 1952," 215–66.

10. Quoted in Ambrose, *Eisenhower: The President and Elder Statesman*, 14.

11. Brendon, *Ike*, 237. A fascinating portrayal of the Truman-Eisenhower feud can be found in Brauer, *Presidential Transitions*, 1–32. For their own conflicting views on the deterioration of their relationship, see Truman, *Memoirs* 2:501–05; and Eisen-

hower, *Mandate for Change*, 84–85. Truman's disdain for Eisenhower is captured best in *Where the Buck Stops*, ed. Margaret Truman, chap. 8, "Why I Don't Like Ike."

12. Acheson, *Present at the Creation*, 686–714. A harsher, less statesmanlike critique of Eisenhower's campaign tactics can be found in [Dean Acheson], Advisory Council of the Democratic National Committee [hereafter, DAC], "How to Lose Friends and Influence: The Decline of American Diplomacy 1953–1959," Democratic Programs for Action, no. 3, June 1959, CT Papers, Washington, D.C. Tyroler was executive director of the Democratic Advisory Council from 1957 to 1960. This pamphlet was written by Acheson, with the assistance of Sidney Hyman, as a politically useful summary of the Eisenhower administration's foreign-policy record.

13. Acheson, *Present at the Creation*, 693–95. Also Lucius Battle, interview, March 1988, Washington, D.C.

14. Acheson, *Present at the Creation*, 690–93. Acheson was infuriated when, at a speech in Cincinnati during the 1952 presidential campaign, Eisenhower revived Robert Taft's criticisms of him and "grossly distorted" his Press Club speech. Throughout his later years Acheson continued to defend that speech by insisting he had not excluded Korea from America's "defense perimeter" in the Pacific area: "On the contrary, I referred specifically to these 'other areas in the Pacific.'" Arthur Schlesinger, Jr., in an interview in March 1988, was helpful on the Acheson-Stevenson relationship in 1952.

15. Acheson, *Present at the Creation*, 651–721. See also Mosher, Clinton, and Lang, *Presidential Transitions*, 135–54.

16. DGA to Dulles, Nov. 25, 1952, S 1, B 9, F 111, DGA-Yale. See also Memorandum of conversation with John Foster Dulles, Dec. 24, 1952, Acheson Papers, Box 67, HSTL. Dulles determined early on to run the State Department differently than Acheson had; he wanted to spend more time on policy and less on personnel and administrative concerns. See interviews with Roderic L. O'Conner (pp. 28, 58); John W. Haines, Jr. (pp. 124–26); and Herbert Brownell (p. 27); John Foster Dulles Oral History Collection.

17. Isaacson and Thomas, *Wise Men*, 563. For an overview of the topics Acheson and Dulles discussed during the interregnum, see Acheson, *Present at the Creation*, 710–13; and Acheson, "Thoughts about Thought in High Places," *NYT Magazine*, Oct. 11, 1959 (reprinted in Acheson, *Grapes from Thorns*, 106–22).

18. DGA to Robert Spivak, July 1961, S 1, B 27, F 352, DGA-Yale.

19. For Dulles's role in negotiating the peace treaty, see Pruessen, *John Foster Dulles*, 432–98; and Hoopes, *Devil and John Foster Dulles*, 89–113. For how Acheson and Dulles worked together on the treaty, see Takeshi Igarashi, "Dean G. Acheson and the Japanese Peace Treaty" in Brinkley, *Dean Acheson and the Making of U.S. Foreign Policy*.

20. It was Louis J. Halle who first dubbed Dulles a "single-minded concentrator"; Acheson readily concurred (Halle to DGA, Nov. 16, 1962, S 1, B 15, F 189, DGA-Yale). Halle had been a member of the Policy Planning Staff under Acheson. Nitze became a Democrat as a result of his abhorrence of Republican acquiescence to Joe McCarthy.

21. Interviews with Paul H. Nitze (Sept. 1987, Washington, D.C.); Charles Burton Marshall (March 1987, Washington, D.C.); and Dorothy Fosdick (Dec. 1987, Washington, D.C.). All three were members of the State Department Policy Planning Staff during the Truman years.

22. Quoted in Pruessen, *John Foster Dulles*, 454.
23. Quoted in Sidney Hyman, "Mr. Dulles in a China Shop" (Unpublished paper sent to Acheson to use as ammunition against the Eisenhower administration when Acheson was serving as chairman of the foreign-policy committee of the Democratic Advisory Council) Acheson Papers, DAC-Foreign Policy, Box 92, HSTL.
24. Ibid.
25. Quoted in Hoopes, *Devil and John Foster Dulles*, 176.
26. DGA to HST, July 21, 1953, A-T Corres., 1953, Box 166, HSTL. (Included in *AF*.) Also interviews with Nitze, Sept. 1987; and Lucius Battle, March 1987, Washington, D.C.
27. Alice Acheson, interview, Dec. 1987, Washington, D.C.
28. DGA to HST, Feb. 10, 1953, A-T Corres., 1953, Box 166, HSTL.
29. DGA to David Acheson, Feb. 19, 1953, *AF*, p. 80.
30. Barbara Evans, interview, Oct. 1987, Washington, D.C.
31. DGA, interview by Margaret Ingram, Oct. 1958, Cambridge, England (transcript in author's possession).
32. DGA to HST, April 14, 1953, A-T Corres., 1953, Box 166, HSTL. (Also in *AF*.)
33. DGA to HST, April 6, 1953, A-T Corres. 1953, Box 166, HSTL.
34. DGA to Adlai Stevenson, Dec. 5, 1955, S 1, B 29, F 373; DGA to Arthur Schlesinger, Jr., Sept. 27, 1954, S 1, B 28, F 359; DGA-Yale.
35. DGA to Stevenson, Dec. 20, 1955, Stevenson Papers, Box 408.
36. "Acheson in Farewell to Department Aides," *NYT*, Jan. 17, 1953, p. 7. Also Acheson, *Present at the Creation*, 718–20.
37. DGA to HST, April 14, 1953, A-T Corres., 1953, Box 166, HSTL. (Also in *AF*.)
38. Rearden, *Evolution of American Strategic Doctrine*, offers a comprehensive analysis of Nitze's influence on the making of U.S. national security policy. Also see Wells, "Sounding the Tocsin," 116–58. For a discussion of the Acheson-Nitze relationship, see Callahan, *Dangerous Capabilities*, 60–61, 95–96, 141, 154–55; and Talbott, *Master of the Game*, 46, 50–51.
39. Acheson, *Present at the Creation*, 373.
40. Ibid., 375.
41. DGA to HST, April 14, 1953, A-T Corres. 1953, Box 166, HSTL.
42. DGA to Lucius Battle, Aug. 6, 1953, S 1, B 2, F 26, DGA-Yale.
43. For Nitze's account of his mistreatment, see Nitze, *From Hiroshima to Glasnost*, 146–48.
44. Paul H. Nitze, interview, Sept. 1987.
45. Quoted in Cabell Philips, "Dean Acheson Ten Years Later," *NYT Magazine*, Jan. 18, 1959, p. 56. For Acheson's own account of his early career as a lawyer, including his relationships with Brandeis and Frankfurter, see Acheson, *Morning and Noon*.
46. Interviews with Nitze, Sept. 1987; and Battle, March 1988. Acheson's most important legal cases from 1953 to 1971 are discussed in Westwood, *Covington & Burling*. The firm was named Covington, Burling, Rublee, Acheson & Shorb in 1934; Acheson's name was dropped from the shingle when he became assistant secretary of state in 1941.
47. DGA to George Perkins, Sept. 16, 1953, Acheson Papers, Princeton Seminars, microfilm reel 1, Correspondence, HSTL. The transcript of the proceedings exceeds 2,000 pages in length. The extent of Acheson's poor health during this period was

emphasized by William P. Bundy in an interview in June 1988 in Princeton, New Jersey.

48. Acheson's dinner speech when the FDR Four Freedoms Award was given to Truman on September 28, 1953, and his remarks at a dinner given in honor of the former president and Mrs. Truman at the Mayflower Hotel in Washington, D.C., on June 23, 1953, are both stirring tributes to his old boss (S 3, B 47, F 17, DGA-Yale).

49. Acheson, "Post-War Foreign Policy" (Speech delivered at Woodrow Wilson Foundation Dinner, Oct. 1, 1953), S 3, B 47, F 18, DGA-Yale. A slightly changed version of the speech can be found in *TVER*. For Acheson's assessment of his reentry into national politics, see DGA to HST, Oct. 8, 1953, Post Pres-Sec Off. File, Box 1, HSTL.

50. For various Democratic leaders' responses to the address, see Russell Porter, "Acheson Attacks Arms Budget Cuts," *NYT*, Oct. 2, 1953, p. 1.

51. Published as John Foster Dulles, "The Evolution of Foreign Policy," 108. For a scholarly evaluation of the New Look, see Gaddis, *Strategies of Containment*, 147. Chapter 5, "Eisenhower, Dulles and the New Look," offers the best overview of the Eisenhower administration's defense policies. Also see Snyder, "The 'New Look' of 1954"; Kinnard, *President Eisenhower and Strategy Management*; Rosenberg, "A Smoking Radiating Ruin"; and Wells, "Origins of Massive Retaliation." For unfavorable historical assessments of the New Look, see Brands, "Age of Vulnerability"; and Schlesinger, *Cycles of American History*, 387–405.

52. Hoopes, *Devil and John Foster Dulles*, 200. For an early elucidation of Dulles's thinking on massive retaliation, see Dulles, "Policy of Boldness."

53. [Dean Acheson] DAC, "How to Lose Friends and Influence."

54. Dulles, "Policy for Security and Peace."

55. Aliano, *American Defense Policy*, 33. Also see Morgenthau, *Restoration of American Policies* 3: 129, for the discussion of "the maximum deterrence at bearable cost." For a well-documented account of Eisenhower's nuclear policy, see Rosenberg, "Origins of Overkill," 3–71.

56. Gaddis, *Strategies of Containment*, 147–63; and Hoopes, *Devil and John Foster Dulles*, 191–201.

57. Bowles, "Plea for Another Great Debate." Reichard, in "Domestic Politics of National Security," p. 25, argues that though Bowles and Acheson nominally were criticizing Dulles's massive retaliation policy, their articles also revealed a fundamental division in the Democratic Party. Bowles's "moralist" approach and Acheson's "realist" argument were representative of what would by 1959 be seen as a split between the Stevenson–Eleanor Roosevelt liberals and the Truman-Acheson cold warriors. In 1963 Bowles noted, "I think Dulles and Acheson are very hard to distinguish between, although Acheson thinks of Dulles as his arch enemy, antagonist" (Reminiscences of Chester Bowles, 1963, Oral History Research Office, Columbia University, p. 593).

58. Acheson, "'Instant Retaliation'. . . ," March 28, 1954. (Reprinted in *TVER*. David C. Acheson, the only son of Dean Acheson, selected for publication in this volume articles he felt best expressed the principles his father thought crucial to the successful conduct of foreign affairs.)

59. DGA to HST, March 1954, S 1, B 30, F 392, DGA-Yale. Acheson and Bowles were not the only ones to pen negative critiques of massive retaliation during the Eisenhower years. For other important critical assessments see Brodie, "Unlimited

Weapons and Limited War"; Kaufmann, "Requirements of Deterrence"; Liddell Hart, *Deterrent or Defense*; Ridgway, *Soldier*; Kissinger, *Nuclear Weapons and Foreign Policy*; Taylor, *Uncertain Trumpet*; and Wohlstetter, "Delicate Balance of Terror."

60. Eleanor Lansing Dulles, interview, May 1987, Washington, D.C.

61. DGA, interview by Gaddis Smith, Oct. 12, 1969, S 3, B 54, F 81, DGA-Yale (published in *NYT* Oct. 12, 1969).

62. Acheson, *TVER*, 29–41.

63. DGA to Stevenson, Nov. 14, 1955, S 1, B 29, F 273, DGA-Yale.

64. For a discussion of the policy's shortcomings, see Peeters, *Massive Retaliation*.

65. Acheson, "NATO and Nuclear Weapons," *New Republic*, Dec. 30, 1957, p. 16.

66. Acheson, *TVER*, 35–39. Also see, for instance, Acheson, *Power and Diplomacy*, 87.

67. [Acheson], DAC, "How to Lose Friends and Influence." Also Gaddis, *Strategies of Containment*, 165. Morgan's *Eisenhower versus the Spenders* offers a detailed critique of Democratic attacks on the New Look.

68. Dulles, "Challenge and Response in United States Policy," 31. For an analysis of the two statesmen's differing approaches to deterrence policy, see George and Smoke, *Deterrence in American Foreign Policy*, 245–47. Eleanor Lansing Dulles, in her unpublished comparative biography of Acheson and Dulles, argues that the Truman and Eisenhower deterrence policies were not as far apart as many commentators have claimed (Eleanor Lansing Dulles Papers). Acheson's views of the inherent problems of the massive retaliation approach are nearly identical to those outlined by Henry Kissinger in Kissinger, *Necessity for Choice*.

69. DGA, interview by Gaddis Smith.

70. For example, see letters to Lucius Battle, John Cowles, Patrick Devlin, Wilmarth Lewis, Robert Lovett, Ranald MacDonald, Sir Robert Menzies, Edward G. Miller, Jr., and Harry S Truman (DGA-Yale).

71. Acheson, "Foreign Policies toward Asia," Sept. 18, 1950, p. 460.

72. Acheson, "Strategy of Freedom," Dec. 18, 1950, p. 962.

73. Acheson, "Plowing a Straight Furrow," Nov. 27, 1950, p. 840.

74. Acheson, "Freedom—The Key to Hemisphere Solidarity and World Peace," April 9, 1951, p. 573.

75. Acheson, "'Instant Retaliation'. . . ," 77. Also see "Acheson: 'I Don't Share the Sense of Panic,'" *U.S. News & World Report*, Jan. 18, 1957, pp. 126–31.

76. Acheson, *Power and Diplomacy*, 137.

77. Arthur Schlesinger, Jr., "The Great Debate: Kennan vs. Acheson," *New York Post*, March 2, 1958. Also Arthur Schlesinger, Jr., interview, March 1988, New York.

78. Acheson, "Morality, Moralism and Diplomacy," June 1958.

79. This point is argued in Vaughn, "Comparison of Foreign Policy Viewpoints . . . ," (Master's thesis), p. 55.

80. DGA, interview by Gaddis Smith.

81. Quoted in Herring, *America's Longest War*, 18–19.

82. Quoted in Gibbons, *U.S. Government and Vietnam War, Part 1*, p. 120. For a useful discussion of Secretary of State Acheson's attitude toward Indochina, see Smith, *Dean Acheson*, 305–29.

83. Eisenhower, Annual Message to the Congress on the State of the Union, Feb. 2, 1953, *Public Papers of the Presidents . . . Eisenhower, 1953*, 16. For a good

account of the press conference at which Eisenhower developed his "domino thesis," see Gardner, *Approaching Vietnam*, 196–97.

84. Summary of Dean Acheson's remarks to Ranald MacDonald (telephone conversation; hereafter, Telcon), April 28, 1954, S 4, B 68, F 172, DGA-Yale.

85. Memorandum of conversation [hereafter, Memcon] between James Reston and Dean Acheson, March 30, 1954, S 4, B 68, F 172, DGA-Yale.

86. Summary of Acheson's remarks to MacDonald (telcon), April 28, 1954.

87. Memcon Reston and Acheson, March 30, 1954.

88. DGA to HST, June 16, 1954, A-T Corres., 1954, Box 166, HSTL. United Action was a coalition of the U.S., Great Britain, France, Australia, New Zealand, Thailand, and the Philippines, and the Associated States of Indochina. It was committed to the defense of Indochina and the rest of Southeast Asia.

89. Summary of Acheson's remarks to MacDonald (telcon), April 28, 1954. While the Republican Party had slim majorities in Congress (48-47-1 in the Senate and 221-212-1 in the House), Eisenhower had used cooperative Democrats to push his proposals through Congress. However, bipartisanship could not be counted on in an election year and the Democrats had already challenged the administration's material support to French Indochina even before the Dienbienphu crisis.

90. Memcon Reston and Acheson, March 30, 1954.

91. For a detailed account of the conference, see Randle, *Geneva, 1954*. For an interpretive historical overview of this important conference, see Immerman, "United States and Geneva Conference."

92. Notes on telephone conversation between Dean Acheson and James Reston, Dec. 23, 1954, S 4, B 68, F 172, DGA-Yale.

93. Quoted in "Indo-China Crisis Linked to Acheson," *NYT*, May 16, 1954, p. 2.

94. "Asia Split in Senate Widens as Two Parties Sharpen Attack," *NYT*, July 10, 1954, pp. 1, 6.

95. William S. White, "Dulles Is Assured 2-Party Support on Geneva Parley," *NYT*, April 21, 1954, pp. 1, 44.

96. [Acheson], DAC, "How to Lose Friends and Influence." For a recent study which, as Acheson did, finds much to be desired in the Republicans' handling of Indochina in 1954, see Anderson, "J. Lawton Collins, John Foster Dulles, . . . ," 127–47.

97. See, e.g. DGA to David K. E. Bruce, Sept. 14, 1953, S 1, B 4, F 50; and DGA to Frank M. Shea, Feb. 4, 1958, S 1, B 28, F 364; DGA-Yale. Also George Ball, interview, Sept. 12, 1990, Hyde Park, N.Y.

98. McLellan, *Acheson*, 347–81, traces the origins of the EDC and Acheson's early advocacy of it. Also see Gillingham, *Coal, Steel and . . . Europe*, 348–53; and Fursdon, *European Defense Community*; and Brinkley, "Dean Acheson and European Unity."

99. Acheson, *Sketches from Life*, 107–21. See also Acheson, "U.S. Encouraged by European Unity," Sept. 29, 1952, p. 447.

100. Telegram, Secretary of State to the Embassy in France, Sept. 6, 1952, U.S. Department of State, *FRUS*, 1952–54, vol. 5, Western European Security, pt. 1, p. 692.

101. Acheson, State Department farewell address, Jan. 14, 1953, Accession 89-M-44, B 1, F 6, DGA-Yale.

102. [Acheson], DAC, "How to Lose Friends and Influence." Throughout 1953 Acheson remained confident about the chances of a Euroarmy due to Bruce's optimistic reports. See DGA to Harold Linder, Oct. 5, 1953, S 2, B 38, F 8, DGA-Yale.

103. Acheson, *Sketches from Life*, 55.

104. [Acheson], DAC, "How to Lose Friends and Influence." For Monnet's reasons why the EDC failed, see Monnet, *Memoirs*, 393–404.

105. Hoopes, *Devil and John Foster Dulles*, 293–94. For an evaluation of Dulles's negotiation of the Austrian State Treaty, see Larson, "Crisis Prevention and the Austrian State Treaty."

106. Dulles to DGA, May 15, 1955, S 1, B 9, F 111, DGA-Yale. Also see "Dulles Sends Thanks to His Predecessors," *NYT*, May 16, 1955, p. 6; and Dulles to Konrad Adenauer, Dec. 27, 1955, General Correspondence and Memorandum Series, Box 2, Dulles Papers.

107. DGA to Dulles, May 16, 1955, S 1, B 9, F 111, DGA-Yale. Acheson also supported the Trieste agreement (1954) providing for partition of the free territory between Italy and Yugoslavia.

108. Memorandum of conversation [hereafter, Memcon] between James Reston and Dean Acheson, July 1, 1955, S 4, B 68, F 172, DGA-Yale.

109. Quoted in Sulzberger, *Seven Continents*, 185.

110. Memcon between Reston and Acheson, July 1, 1955.

111. For Acheson's early postsecretarial views of Eastern Europe, see Acheson, *Power and Diplomacy*.

112. Quoted in Sulzberger, *Seven Continents*, 185–86.

113. The best source on the development of the Open Skies proposal is Rostow, *Open Skies*. Also see Strong, "Eisenhower and Arms Control." For a useful, brief narrative of the Geneva Conference, see Eubank, *Summit Conferences*, 144–59.

114. Paul H. Nitze, interview, Sept. 1987.

115. Memorandum of discussion at the 231st meeting of the National Security Council, Jan. 13, 1955 (Drafted by S. Everett Gleason, deputy executive secretary of the NSC), *FRUS*, 1955–57, vol. 2, China. A copy of the memo was provided to the author by Ronald W. Pruessen.

116. Arthur Krock, Memorandum, April 6, 1960, Correspondence-Felix Frankfurter File, Box 26, Arthur Krock Papers.

117. Transcript of "A Conversation with Dean Acheson" (*CBS News Special*, television interview by Eric Sevareid, Nov. 4, 1969), pp. 4–5.

Chapter 2. A Democrat Looks at His Party and at Eisenhower's Foreign Policy

1. Acheson, "Responsibility for Decision," Sept. 1954, pp. 1–12. The Eisenhower administration was also opposed to the Bricker Amendment, which was finally defeated after heated debate throughout February 1954. For a judicious and readable account of the crusade for the legislation, see Tananbaum, *Bricker Amendment Controversy*.

2. "Achesons to Visit Trumans," *NYT*, Feb. 13, 1955, p. 42. Also see "Truman and Acheson Both For Stevenson in 1956," *NYT*, Feb. 17, 1955, p. 10. Acheson and Harriman's friendship dated back to 1905, when they met as schoolboys at Groton. During the Truman years the two worked closely together in government. Acheson also represented Harriman in 1959, arguing that his client be given permission to visit Communist China as a newspaper correspondent. In endorsing Stevenson over

Governor Harriman in 1956, Acheson trod carefully lest he rupture his longstanding friendship with Harriman. For a discussion of their relationship, see Isaacson and Thomas, *Wise Men*.

3. Paul H. Nitze, interview, Sept. 1987, Washington, D.C.

4. Acheson served as a member of the Yale University Corporation, the school's governing body, for more than twenty years. His friend Eugene V. Rostow recalled that shortly after stepping down as secretary of state, Acheson had doubts about returning to his law firm. Friends began exploring the possibility of a career for him in academia. Archibald MacLeish was dispatched by Harvard to offer Acheson a university professorship there. "It's perfect, Dean," the poet-laureate enthused. "There are no fixed rules about residence or teaching. We could go to Antigua in the winter just as we do now. The pay is good and the company is wonderful." "But there is an obstacle, Archie. I just can't do it," Acheson responded. "What is the obstacle?" MacLeish asked. Acheson replied, "The train to Boston goes through New Haven." See Eugene V. Rostow, "In Commemoration of Dean Acheson" (Luncheon speech at Dean Acheson Conference, Yale University, April 24, 1982; unpublished transcript).

For Acheson's correspondence concerning Yale University matters see S 1, B 34–37, F 446–78, DGA-Yale. Of particular interest are Acheson's letters to James R. Angell, Kingman Brewster, Henry Sloane Coffin, A. Whitney Griswold, Wilmarth S. Lewis, and Charles Seymour. The Yale Law School was of singular concern to Acheson and he often wrote Eugene V. Rostow and Harry Shulman to discuss ways of improving the curriculum. See S 1, B 36, F 461–62, DGA-Yale.

5. Acheson, *A Democrat Looks at His Party*, 11–12. Correspondence concerning publication and reviews of the book can be found in S 3, B 57, F 90–93, DGA-Yale.

6. For details of Acheson's trip to Great Britain see "Achesons Visit Eden," *NYT*, Sept. 23, 1955, p. 3; and "Acheson Guest of Macmillan," *NYT*, Sept. 24, 1955, p. 20.

7. Acheson, "The Parties and Foreign Policy," Nov. 1955. See also James Reston, "Acheson Criticizes Dulles and G.O.P. Foreign Policy," *NYT*, Oct. 27, 1955, p. 1.

8. "Acheson Is Denounced," *NYT*, Oct. 28, 1955, p. 16. Similarly, Senator John W. Bricker of Ohio, in an address before the Chicago Executives' Club on December 2, 1955, called Acheson's book a "distorted vision" riddled with "foolish statements" (S 3, B 57, F 93, DGA-Yale).

9. Joseph R. McCarthy, "Acheson Looks at Acheson," *National Review*, Dec. 28, 1955.

10. Quoted in Nash, *Conservative Intellectual Movement*, 151. Shortly after the McCarthy article appeared Kirk asked, for other reasons, that his name be removed from the masthead of the *National Review*.

11. "Hiss-Acheson Link Charged by G.O.P.," *NYT*, Nov. 12, 1955, p. 12.

12. William S. White, "Acheson's Uncomplaining Testament," *NYT, Book Review*, Nov. 20, 1955, p. 1.

13. Larson, *A Republican Looks at His Party*. For analysis of Larson's book, see Reichard, *Reaffirmation of Republicanism*, 228–29; and Hamby, *Liberalism and Its Challengers*, 121.

14. Kennedy, "A Democrat Looks at Foreign Policy."

15. Acheson, Speech before the Women's National Democratic Club, Washington, D.C., Jan. 12, 1956, S 3, B 48, F 24, DGA-Yale. For coverage of the speech, see "Acheson Charges U.S. Policy Fails," *NYT*, Jan. 13, 1956, p. 2.

16. Acheson, "To Meet the Shifting Soviet Offensive," NYT Magazine, April 15, 1956, pp. 11, 69, 70, 76.
17. Acheson, Speech before Women's National Democratic Club, Jan. 12, 1956.
18. Ibid.
19. [Acheson], Advisory Council of the Democratic National Committee [hereafter, DAC], "How to Lose Friends and Influence: The Decline of American Diplomacy 1953–1959," Democratic Programs for Action, no. 3, June 1959, CT Papers.
20. Churchill's mistrust of Eisenhower is discussed in Schlesinger, *Cycles of American History*, 393–94, 401.
21. Acheson, *Power and Diplomacy*, 105–35.
22. Information about Acheson's health was supplied by William P. Bundy and Mary Acheson Bundy in an interview in June 1988 in Princeton, New Jersey.
23. Acheson, "A Critique of Current Foreign Policy" (Address at the Colgate Foreign Policy Conference, Hamilton, N.Y., June 30, 1959), p. 1, S 3, B 50, F 44, DGA-Yale.
24. Acheson, "The Middle East" (Unpublished essay written in September 1956), S 3, B 48, F 26, DGA-Yale. The essay may have been written for Stevenson to use during the 1956 presidential campaign.
25. DGA to Henry Byroade, Aug. 21, 1956, S 1, B 4, F 55, DGA-Yale.
26. Ibid.
27. Acheson was pleased when Sir Anthony Eden wrote in his memoirs that Dulles's handling of Suez was horrendous. See Acheson's comments on Anthony Eden's memoirs, Jan. 20, 1960, Speeches and Articles, 1936–1971, Box 140, HSTL. Eden also described Dulles's behavior during the Suez crisis as "dishonest." See Louis, "Dulles, Suez, and the British," 134. For an evaluation of Eden's role during Suez, see James, *Anthony Eden*, 441–598.
28. DGA to Frank Altschul (a New York financier) Oct. 4, 1956, S 1, B 1, F 9, DGA-Yale.
29. "As ruthless . . ." remark in Acheson, Commencement Address at Brandeis University, June 11, 1956, S 3, B 48, F 25, DGA-Yale.
30. See, e.g., DGA to David C. Acheson, Aug. 3, 1956, S 1, B 1, F 4, DGA-Yale. Also see Isaacson and Thomas, *Wise Men*, 581.
31. Dulles quoted in Foot and Jones, *Guilty Men*, 125. Britain and France tried to gain American support by comparing their relationship to the Suez Canal with that of the United States vis-à-vis the Panama Canal.
32. DGA to Henry Byroade, Aug. 21, 1956.
33. Ibid.
34. Acheson, "Foreign Policy and Presidential Moralism," May 2, 1957, p. 11.
35. Dean Acheson, interview by Gaddis Smith, Oct. 12, 1969, S 3, B 54, F 81, DGA-Yale.
36. John F. Fenton, "Acheson Critical of Both Parties," NYT, Oct. 26, 1957, p. 3. See also [Acheson], DAC, "How to Lose Friends and Influence."
37. Acheson, *Power and Diplomacy*, 109–16.
38. Acheson, Comments, Princeton Seminar transcript, March 14, 1954, Acheson Papers, HSTL.
39. For Acheson's views on U.S.–Middle East relations and the UN, see Acheson, "Foreign Policy and Presidential Moralism," May 2, 1957, p. 11.

40. For revisionist interpretations of the Eisenhower-Dulles Suez diplomacy, see Bowie, "Eisenhower, Dulles, and the Suez Crisis," in Louis and Owen, *Suez 1956*; and Louis, "Dulles, Suez, and the British," in Immerman, *John Foster Dulles*.

41. See chap. 4, "Political Precepts for Coalitions of Free States," in Acheson, *Power and Diplomacy*, 105–35. For critical studies of Dulles's Suez diplomacy, see Hoopes, *Devil and John Foster Dulles*; and Finer, *Dulles over Suez*.

42. "Truman Accuses President in Crisis," *NYT*, Nov. 4, 1956, p. 68. Truman was speaking of Suez.

43. Robert Bowie, interview, January 1991, Washington D.C.

44. Quotes from DGA to Lord Frank Stowe-Hill, April 21, 1971, S 1, B 29, F 377, DGA-Yale.

45. Paul H. Nitze, interview, Sept. 1987. Also C. L. Sulzberger, "Making an Omelet out of Eggheads," *NYT*, Aug. 15, 1956, p. 28. Other members of the Acheson platform committee included Chester Bowles; Ben Cohen, a former State Department counselor; Clayton Fritchey, deputy chairman of the Democratic National Committee; and several congressmen.

46. Quoted in Russell Baker, "Acheson Advises Restudy of China," *NYT*, Sept. 29, 1959, p. 18.

47. C. L. Sulzberger, "Local Politics and Foreign Policy," *NYT*, Aug. 18, 1956, p. 16. See also Robert H. Estabrook, "Acheson Plan Overruled on Foreign Policy Plank," *Washington Post*, Aug. 16, 1956. For Dulles's Goa remarks, see Bender, "American Policy toward Angola," 111.

48. G. Mennen Williams, interview, Nov. 1987, Detroit, Michigan.

49. Sulzberger, "Local Politics and Foreign Policy," p. 16.

50. Sulzberger, "Making an Omelet out of Eggheads."

51. For how Stevenson ran the 1956 presidential campaign, see Martin, *Adlai Stevenson and the World*, 232–398. Also see Thomson and Shattuck, *The 1956 Presidential Campaign*. Acheson and Nitze wrote several speeches for Stevenson, but he never delivered them. See DGA to Stevenson, Aug. 23, 1956, Box 425, Stevenson Papers.

52. Acheson, "The Shape of Foreign Policy Issues in 1956" (Address before the Western Suburban Democratic Club of Maryland, Sept. 26, 1956), S 3, B 48, F 26, DGA-Yale. "Acheson Sees Ike's Foreign Policy as 'Bluster and Bluff,'" *U.S. News & World Report*, Oct. 5, 1956, gives the entire text of Acheson's speech. The *New York Times* printed the text on Sept. 27, 1956, p. 24.

53. "The Transcript of Eisenhower's News Conference on Foreign and Domestic Affairs," *NYT*, Sept. 28, 1956, p. 14.

54. Martin, *Adlai Stevenson and the World*, 365–79.

55. DGA to Stevenson, Oct. 9, 1956, Acheson File, Box 425, Stevenson Papers.

56. DGA to Mrs. Jack Chadderdon, Nov. 4, 1957, S 1, B 5, F 57, DGA-Yale.

57. Pruessen, "Predicaments of Power," 30–31.

58. Quoted in Eisenhower, *Waging Peace*, 177–78. Also Notes on meeting with Congressional leaders, Jan. 1, 1957, Whitman File, Legislative Meeting Series, B 2, Dwight D. Eisenhower Library, Abilene, Kansas.

59. U.S. Congress, Senate, Committee on Foreign Relations, *A Select Chronology and Background Documents Relating to the Middle East*, p. 144.

60. Divine, *Eisenhower and the Cold War*, p. 91.

61. House Committee on Foreign Affairs. *Economic and Military Cooperation with Nations in the General Area of the Middle East: Hearings on the Middle East Resolution*, H.J. Res. 117, 85th Cong., 1st sess., Jan. 7–10, 15–17, 22, 1957. (Hereafter, *House Hearings*.)

62. "Mideast Windmill Tilt Seen," *NYT*, Jan. 7, 1957, p. 16.

63. Acheson, "The Administration's Proposed Joint Resolution Relating to the Middle East," Jan. 10, 1957, *House Hearings*.

For the best explanation of Acheson's attitude toward the Eisenhower Doctrine, see McLellan, *Dean Acheson*, 414–15. Shortly after the doctrine was announced, Truman, to Acheson's dismay, offered Eisenhower his support. Acheson responded by writing Truman a rare angry letter accusing him of hindering Democratic efforts to "put some sense into the Administration's foreign policy" (DGA to HST, Jan. 15, 1957, A-T Corres., 1957, Box 166, HSTL).

64. Acheson, "The Administration's Proposed Joint Resolution Relating to the Middle East," Jan. 10, 1957, *House Hearings*. Acheson was not alone in his criticism of the Eisenhower Doctrine. Senator Humphrey called it "essentially . . . a psychological and public relations matter." And, not without some bitterness, Britain's Prime Minister Harold Macmillan would characterize Eisenhower's Middle East policy as "a recantation—an act of penitence unparalleled in history." See Senate Committee on Foreign Relations, "The President's Proposal on the Middle East," Hearings, Jan.–Feb. 1957, 85th Cong., 1st sess., 1957; Stebbins, *United States in World Affairs, 1957*, 177; Macmillan, *Riding the Storm*, 511. For Democratic criticisms of the Eisenhower Doctrine, see Schulzinger, "Impact of Suez on United States Middle East Policy," 254.

65. DGA to Eugene Milligan, Feb. 19, 1957, S 1, B 20, F 255, DGA-Yale. In a letter to Philip Jessup, Acheson explained his ideas about policing the Israeli-Arab area with a United Nations force that would be "maintained and used on all borders of Israel, with an underwriting from us that, if it were attacked in force, the United States would come to its assistance" (DGA to Philip Jessup, Jan. 16, 1957, S 1, B 16, F 205, DGA-Yale).

66. Acheson, "Foreign Policy and Presidential Moralism," 14.

67. "Acheson Talks about Middle East Conflict to Laurel Rotarians" (Unidentified clipping, probably from a Laurel, Maryland, newspaper), S 2, B 39, F 19, DGA-Yale.

68. Wilson, *Congressional Government*. Acheson's Stettinius Lectures were published in book form as *A Citizen Looks at Congress*. One chapter of Acheson's book was excerpted before publication in the Summer 1956 issue of the *Yale Review*. Acheson noted that although President Wilson achieved brilliant diplomatic successes, he suffered disastrous defeats in dealing with Congress.

69. Correspondence concerning publication and reviews of *A Citizen Looks at Congress* can be found in S 3, B 57, F 87–89, DGA-Yale. The book was well received. E. W. Kenworthy, in a review for the *New York Times*, wrote: "If Citizen Acheson still bears the scars of Secretary Acheson's battles on Capitol Hill, he does not show them in this urbane political essay, where personal experience is called upon not for vindication but for illustration" (*NYT*, April 21, 1957).

70. DGA to Katherine Taylor, Dec. 15, 1959. S 1, B 29, F 380. DGA-Yale.

71. Parmet, *Democrats*, 151.

72. CT Papers, DAC, Index. For papers pertaining to the creation of the DAC, also see Acheson Papers, Post-Administration Files, Democratic Advisory Council—

Meetings, 1957–1960, Box 94, Folders 1–3, HSTL; and Democratic National Committee Executive, Committee Resolution Authorizing Advisory Council, Box 58, Butler Papers.

73. Cotter and Hennessy. *Politics without Power*, 213.

74. Parmet, *Democrats*, 124–29. Also Charles Tyroler II, interview, Oct. 10, 1987, Washington, D.C. Butler's role in the creation of the DAC can be found in Roberts, *Paul M. Butler*, 103–05.

75. For an explanation of why leading Senate Democrats refused to join the DAC, see Lazarowitz, "Years in Exile" (Ph.D. diss.).

76. Tyroler, interview. Oct. 1987.

77. Tyroler, interview, Feb. 1988, Washington, D.C.

78. Butler quote in Cotter and Hennessy, *Politics without Power*, 222. The additional DAC committees focused on labor policy, science and technology; and urban and suburban problems. In early 1960 five more committees were created: Civil Rights, chaired by Eleanor Roosevelt; Farm Policy, chaired by Gov. Herschel Loveless of Iowa; Health Policy, under Dr. Michael DeBakey; Natural Resources, led by Oregon national committeeman C. Girard Davidson; and Social Security, with Arthur J. Altmeyer as chairman.

79. DAC, Statement on Foreign Policy, May 5, 1957, CT Papers. Also Tyroler, interview, Oct. 1987.

80. Tyroler, interview, Oct. 1987.

81. Truman and Acheson always tried to avoid contradicting each other in public. For an example of this "united front" strategy, see DGA to HST, June 5, 1957, S 1, B 31, F 395, DGA-Yale.

82. Tyroler, interview, Oct. 1987.

83. Ibid.

84. DGA to Katherine Taylor, Dec. 14, 1969, S 1, B 29, F 380, DGA-Yale.

85. DGA to Chester Bowles, Aug. 22, 1957. Acheson Correspondence File, Bowles Papers. Acheson wrote a practically identical letter to William Benton on August 22, 1957 (Charles Murphy Papers, HSTL).

86. Tyroler, interview, Oct. 1987. Acheson himself later complained: "It is a difficult job which I have mapped out for myself in getting these pamphlets written and published. People have a lot of enthusiasm about them until it comes to writing them. I remember years ago Mr. Dwight Morrow saying that broadly speaking there were two classes of people—those who did things and those who didn't, and the first class was fairly small" (DGA to Paul Ziffren, Dec. 30, 1958, DAC, Box 92, HSTL).

87. DGA to LBJ, Dec. 18, 1958, S 1, B 18, F 215, DGA-Yale.

88. LBJ to DGA, LBJA, Famous Names, Box 1, LBJL. Acheson, of course, was not a unique recipient of his flattery; Johnson sent admiring notes and autographed photos to many.

89. [Acheson and Nitze], DAC, "The Democratic Approach to Foreign Policy and United States Defense," DAC File, Box 61, Butler Papers.

90. Donovan, *Cold Warriors*, 134. Chap. 6 examines the process by which the Gaither Report was prepared.

91. Quoted in Herken, *Counsels of War*, 113. This book offers the best evaluation of the Gaither Report.

92. Donovan, *Cold Warriors*, 131. See also Talbott, *Master of the Game*, 67–70.

93. Nitze's contributions to the report are examined best in Callahan, *Dangerous Capabilities*, 166–75.

94. [Acheson], DAC, "America's Present Danger and What We Must Do About It," Jan. 13, 1958, CT Papers.

95. Ibid. See also John D. Morris, "Democrats Declare U.S. Is Unprepared," *NYT*, Feb. 2, 1958, p. 1; and Reichard, "Domestic Politics and National Security," 225.

96. Parmet, *Democrats*, 158–59. Also Tyroler, interview, May 1987.

97. DGA to John Cowles, Oct. 8, 1957, S 1, B 6, F 83, DGA-Yale. Acheson told Cowles that Niels Bohr had told him more than twelve years before that he knew "the Russian and German scientists who were working on these matters [Sputnik]" and that "they were quite as good as we." Bohr also told Acheson at that time that he doubted whether the U.S. had more than a two-to-five-year lead in satellite technology.

98. While Acheson was one of the leading perpetrators of the missile gap myth, it is clear that even as late as November 1959 he was unsure whether or not the Soviets actually did have a missile edge. "You believe that I believe that at the present time Russian nuclear capacity exceeds ours," Acheson responded to a letter from a citizen in Boston, Bronson W. Chanler. "Whether it does or does not at the present time, I do not know. But even the Secretary of Defense agrees that Russian intercontinental missile capacity will exceed ours in a few years. At this point Russian nuclear capacity *will* exceed ours" (DGA to Bronson Chanler, Nov. 20, 1959, S 1, B 5, F 57, DGA-Yale). See also [Acheson], DAC, Statement on the Satellite, Oct. 11, 1957, CT Papers.

99. The Democratic National Committee issued a press release explaining to the public how this pamphlet had met DAC approval. Acheson's pamphlets all were endorsed in this way: "The original draft was written by Mr. Acheson. He submitted it to the members of the Advisory Committee on Foreign Policy, first by mail and then during an all-day meeting of the Committee on January 20. A revised version was then submitted to the Advisory Council, first by mail, then during a two-day session of the Council in Washington on February 1 and 2. The final version was then prepared by Mr. Acheson, reflecting the discussion and suggestions" (quoted in Cotter and Hennessy, *Politics without Power*, 220). The Democratic National Committee Files at JFKL contain more than fifty articles pertaining to the DAC in the period 1957–60.

100. Earl Mazo, "Democratic Advisers: 'Shadow Government,'" *New York Herald Tribune*, May 22, 1960. Mazo was the first to call the DAC the Democratic shadow cabinet. By 1960 it was commonly referred to by this name.

101. Tyroler, interview, Oct. 1987. All of the pamphlets written by Acheson can be found in the Acheson Papers, Post-Administration Files, Democratic Advisory Council—Meetings 1957–1960, Box 94, Folders 1–3, HSTL.

102. DGA to Bowles, March 5, 1958, S 1, B 3, F 42, DGA-Yale.

103. [Acheson], DAC, "Where We Are: The World Today and How It Got That Way," May 1958, CT Papers.

104. Harriman is quoted in Isaacson and Thomas, *Wise Men*, 584.

105. [Acheson], DAC, "Where We Are," 16, CT Papers. Acheson worked the contents of this pamphlet into a speech delivered at a Jefferson-Jackson Day dinner in Detroit, Michigan. For excerpts, see *NYT*, May 4, 1958, p. 42.

106. For discussions of the Formosa Straits Crises of 1954–55 and 1958, see

Brands, "Testing Massive Retaliation," 124–51; Chang, "To the Nuclear Brink," 96–123; and George and Smoke, *Deterrence in American Foreign Policy*, 361–89. Acheson's views regarding the 1954–55 crisis can be found in [Acheson], DAC, "How to Lose Friends and Influence," CT Papers.

107. Acheson, "Statement on Quemoy Crisis," Press release, Acheson Papers, Speeches and Articles 1936–1971, Box 139, HSTL. See also E. W. Kenworthy, "Acheson Sees Risk of War; Nixon Defends," *NYT*, Sept. 7, 1958, p. 1.

108. DGA to Beverly Admomaitis, Nov. 20, 1958, S 1, B 1, F 1, DGA-Yale.

109. DGA to HST, Sept. 15, 1958, S 1, B 31, F 395, DGA-Yale. See also DGA to HST, Sept. 17, 1958, S 1, B 31, F 395, DGA-Yale.

110. For Acheson's early prediction that the 1958 elections would return both houses of Congress to the Democrats, see Acheson, Jefferson-Jackson Day dinner address in Detroit, Michigan, May 3, 1958, Acheson Papers, Speeches and Articles, 1936–1971, Box 139, HSTL.

111. DGA to Sir Patrick Devlin, Nov. 7, 1958, S 1, B 7, F 96, DGA-Yale. Acheson comments on how the Democratic victories of 1958 would benefit the DAC in DGA to John Grange (Review and Development Department, Asian Foundation), Dec. 4, 1958, S 1, B 12, F 160, DGA-Yale.

112. Galbraith, *A Life in Our Times*, 359. For another recounting of the Galbraith-Acheson feud in the DAC, see Galbraith, "Dean Acheson Recalls His Life and Good Brawling Times." This review of *Present at the Creation* can be found in the Vertical File, HSTL. Chester Bowles recalled, "It was really very vigorous, rough talk that went on. Very strong disagreements. Acheson, of course, likes not only to disagree with people but to destroy them if he can" (Reminiscences of Chester Bowles, Oral History Research Office, Columbia University, vol. 5, 1963, p. 785).

113. Charles Burton Marshall, interview, March 1987, Washington, D.C. Also, DGA to Charles Tyroler II, Oct. 17, 1969, S 1, B 32, F 406, DGA-Yale.

114. John Kenneth Galbraith, interview, Aug. 1991, St. John's, Canada.

115. Quoted in Martin, *Adlai Stevenson and the World*, 402.

116. Tyroler, interview, Oct. 1987; and Paul H. Nitze, interview, Sept. 1987, Washington, D.C.

117. DGA to Lord Frank Stowe-Hill, April 21, 1971, S 1, B 29, F 377; DGA-Yale.

118. Quoted in Isaacson and Thomas, *Wise Men*, 583.

119. DGA to HST, Jan. 27, 1959, S 1, B 31, F 396, DGA-Yale. Also G. Mennen Williams, telephone interview, Nov. 1987, Detroit, Mich.; and Porter McKeever, interview, Oct. 12, 1990, Hyde Park, N.Y.

120. DGA to Eugene V. Rostow, Aug. 14, 1958, *AF*, 143.

121. "Mrs. FDR Says Acheson Is behind Times," *Washington News*, Oct. 22, 1959.

122. DGA to Eric Swenson, Aug. 25, 1971, *AF*, 332. Swenson was Acheson's editor at W. W. Norton, the publisher of *Present at the Creation*. He had sent Acheson a copy of Joseph Lash's *Eleanor and Franklin*. Acheson's letter in response expressed his mixed feelings toward Mrs. Roosevelt.

123. DGA to HST, Aug. 14, 1958, S 1, B 31, F 396, DGA-Yale.

124. [Acheson] DAC, "Where We Are," CT Papers; and [Acheson], DAC, "Why We Need Allies and They Need Us to Preserve the Free World," Feb. 1959, CT Papers.

125. [Acheson], DAC, "Why We Need Allies," 22.

126. DGA to HST, Jan. 27, 1959, S 1, B 31, F 396, DGA-Yale.
127. Quoted in Sulzberger, *Seven Continents and Forty Years*, 285.
128. Tyroler, interview, Oct. 1987.
129. DGA to Louis Halle, Nov. 21, 1962, S 1, B 15, F 190, DGA-Yale.
130. [Acheson], DAC, "How to Lose Friends and Influence." Fellow DAC member Sidney Hyman helped Acheson write the first draft of this pamphlet.
131. *NYT*, Jan. 26, 1958, p. 61.
132. [Acheson], DAC, "How to Lose Friends and Influence."
133. [Paul Nitze], DAC, "The Military Forces We Need and How to Get Them," June 1959, CT Papers.
134. Sam Pope Brewer, "Acheson Assails G.O.P. on Defense," *NYT*, July 1, 1959, p. 2. In a nine-page Senate rebuttal to Acheson's speech, Senator Leverett Saltonstall asked the former secretary to explain how he planned to finance the $7.5 billion increase in annual military spending proposed by the DAC. "Do they contend," the Republican leader asked, "that we should raise taxes or do they argue that we should go further into debt and in effect simply support these expenditures by more inflation?" Neither Acheson nor anyone else from the DAC responded to Saltonstall's questions. (See "Democrats Chided on Arms Spending," *NYT*, July 3, 1959, p. 7).
135. Cotter and Hennessy, *Politics without Power*, 217. Kennedy and Symington joined the DAC and its foreign-policy committee in late 1959. The group had been headed by Dean Acheson in the previous two years, with Paul Nitze as vice-chairman and Eugenie Anderson, William Benton, Barry Bingham, Chester Bowles, James B. Carey, Ben Cohen, Silliman Evans, Jr., Abraham Feinberg, Dorothy Fosdick, Philip Jessup, Estes Kefauver, Herbert Lehman, David J. McDonald, Edward G. Miller, Jr., Hans J. Morgenthau, J. G. Patton, Edith Sampson, and G. Mennen Williams as members.
136. Berman, "Democratic Advisory Council," Unpublished paper.
137. JFK to Paul Butler, Feb. 7, 1957, Box 9, Sorensen Papers, JFKL.
138. Parmet, *Struggles of John F. Kennedy*, 477.
139. Nitze, interview, Sept. 1987.
140. Marshall, interview, March 1987.
141. Schlesinger, *A Thousand Days*, 552–53. For examples of JFK's criticism of France's Algerian policy, see Kennedy, *Strategy of Peace*, 66–81, 99–102, 212–15.
142. Acheson, *Power and Diplomacy*, 122.
143. Acheson, interview by Lucius Battle, April 27, 1964, JFKL.
144. Quoted in Schoenbaum, *Political Profiles*, 593.
145. Stuart Symington, interview, Nov. 1987, New Canaan, Conn. Acheson and Truman corresponded throughout 1959 and 1960 about ways to help Symington's presidential ambitions, even though they realized he had little chance of being elected.

Acheson supported Symington in strong terms: "What amazes me is that all which was accomplished from 1950 through 1952 to restore our defenses has been willfully thrown away by a President who has been bemused by the ideas of [Secretary of the Treasury] George Humphrey that we cannot afford to survive," he wrote to Symington on one occasion. "Apparently the Nixon-dominated Republican National

Committee, like the Bourbons, never learns anything, but, unlike the Bourbons, forgets everything. It chooses to forget that you, as the first Secretary of the Air Force, established it, and, in a matter of months, put its administration and its strategic role on a par with services which had existed since the founding of the Republic" (DGA to Symington, Jan. 21, 1959, S 1, B 29, F 379, DGA-Yale).

146. DGA to HST, Aug. 31, 1959, *AF*, 170–71. This is one of a number of letters to Truman appraising the possible contenders for the Democratic nomination.

147. [Acheson and Nitze], "The Decision in 1960: The Need to Elect a Democratic President," Dec. 1959, CT Papers.

148. Quoted in W. H. Lawrence, "Stevenson Makes a Flat Rejection of '60 Candidacy," *NYT*, June 14, 1959, p. 1.

149. DGA to Lord Patrick Devlin, Nov. 7, 1958, S 1, B 7, F 96, DGA-Yale. For similar complaints, see DGA to Dirk Stikker, Dec. 2, 1959, S 1, B 29, F 375; and DGA to W. W. Rostow, Jan. 21, 1959, S 1, B 26, F 338; both in DGA-Yale.

150. DGA to Chester Bowles, Dec. 30, 1959, S 1, B 3, F 42, DGA-Yale.

151. DGA to Halle, March 12, 1959, S 1, B 15, F 189, DGA-Yale.

152. Quoted in *U.S. Daily News*, Nov. 18, 1959.

153. "Democrats Praise Report on Policy," *NYT*, Dec. 8, 1959, p. 25.

154. Copies of these statements can be found in Acheson Papers, Post-Administration Files, Democratic Advisory Council—Press Releases, 1957–1960, Box 94, HSTL.

155. DGA to Linda Walsh, May 12, 1960, S 1, B 32, F 415, DGA-Yale. Walsh had written to ask Acheson how the DAC functioned.

156. Krock and Mazo articles quoted in Cotter and Hennessy, *Politics without Power*, 223.

157. John D. Morris, "Democrats End Advisory Council," *NYT*, March 12, 1961.

158. Parmet, *Democrats*, 161.

Chapter 3. The Changing Political Climate in Europe, 1957–60

1. For an elucidation of Acheson's adherence to the principles and institutions of European integration, see Brinkley, "Dean Acheson and European Unity," in Heller and Gillingham, *NATO*. Also see Acheson, "The American Interest in European Unity" (Speech delivered at The Hague, Netherlands, Sept. 19, 1963), Acheson Papers, Speeches and Articles 1936–1971, Box 140, HSTL. Although the Common Market and Euratom Treaties were signed in March 1957, they were not ratified until December 1957. An excellent monograph on the Treaties of Rome is von der Groeben, *The European Community*.

2. Quote from DGA to Robert Menzies, Nov. 13, 1958, S 1, B 22, F 282, DGA-Yale; Jean Monnet influence from George Ball, interview, Feb. 1988, Princeton, N.J.; Brinkley and Hackett, *Jean Monnet*; and Brinkley, "Dean Acheson and Jean Monnet" (unpublished paper).

3. Acheson, "Illusion of Disengagement," 379.

4. Kennan, *Memoirs, 1950–1963*, 229–30.

5. For the texts of the Reith Lectures, see Kennan, *Russia, the Atom and the West.*

6. *NYT*, June 21, 1956. Also see Christopher Emmet, Memorandum (n.d.), S 1, B 9, F 123, DGA-Yale; and Green, "Political Thought of George F. Kennan" (Ph.D. diss.). For an overview of the difficulties in the Kennan-Stevenson relationship, see Mayers, *George Kennan and the Dilemmas of U.S. Foreign Policy,* 226–30.

7. Christopher Emmet, Memorandum, Dec. 19, 1957, S 1, B 9, F 123, DGA-Yale.

8. David Klein (former Director of American Council on Germany, Inc.), interview, Sept. 1987, Princeton, N.J.

9. Emmet to DGA, Dec. 24, 1957, S 1, B 9, F 123, DGA-Yale.

10. Acheson, "A Vital Necessity," *Western World,* Aug. 1957, 40.

11. Ollenhauer, "An Outdated Policy," 33–39. The Ollenhauer and Acheson articles were part of the magazine's Debate of the Month series.

12. DGA to Harriman, Aug. 8, 1957, S 1, B 15, F 193, DGA-Yale. General Lauris Norstad, the supreme commander of the Allied Powers in Europe, wrote Acheson that his *Western World* article "would do a great deal of good" in combating the disengagement advocates in Europe (Norstad to DGA, [n.d.], S 1, B 23, F 297, DGA-Yale).

13. DGA to Emmet, Dec. 30, 1957, S 1, B 9, F 123, DGA-Yale. The Kennan-Acheson disagreement is discussed in Brinkley, "Kennan-Acheson Disengagement Debate."

14. Emmet, Memorandum, Jan. 2, 1958, S 1, B 9, F 123, DGA-Yale.

15. Emmet to DGA, Jan. 4, 1958, S 1, B 9, F 123, DGA-Yale.

16. Acheson, "Reply to Kennan," Press release, Jan. 11, 1958, S 1, B 9, F 123, DGA-Yale.

17. Ibid.

18. Ibid.

19. Christopher Emmet, Memorandum, April 21, 1958, S 1, B 9, F 123, DGA-Yale. Emmet kept track of all press commentary coming out of West Germany, Britain, and the United States.

20. Quoted in Merli and Wilson, *Makers of American Diplomacy,* 277–78.

21. Kennan, *Memoirs, 1950–1963,* 251.

22. King, "Kennanism and Disengagement."

23. Denis Healey (British Labour Party leader), interview, April 1988, Princeton, N.J.

24. Ninkovich, *Germany and the United States,* 119–20.

25. Kissinger to DGA, Jan. 24, 1958, S 1, B 18, F 226, DGA-Yale.

26. Quoted in "Refusal of Missile Bases Seen as Danger to Europe's Future," *NYT,* March 19, 1958, p. 5.

27. Douglas to DGA, Jan. 17, 1958, S 1, B 9, F 111, DGA-Yale.

28. Adenauer to DGA, Feb. 20, 1958, S 1, B 1, F 6, DGA-Yale.

29. Harry Gilroy, "Brentano Chided on Kennan Issue," *NYT,* Jan. 21, 1958, p. 3.

30. Dulles to DGA, Jan. 13, 1958, S 1, B 9, F 11, DGA-Yale. Dulles also wished Acheson a speedy recovery from a "thoroughly annoying accident," a double fracture of his arm. Throughout the period of the Kennan-Acheson debate Acheson was in extreme pain. He wrote of the accident: "Last week I carelessly stepped on a bit of very slippery ice, took one of the world's most spectacular falls, and broke my left arm in two places. I am now encased in a plaster cast, have to sleep sitting up, and have no

clothes which will go over the whole troublesome new contour of my body. However, this can be worked out and will be" (DGA to Thomas Stone [Canadian ambassador to The Hague], S 1, B 29, F 376, DGA-Yale).

31. DGA to Dulles, Jan. 17, 1958, S 1, B 9, F 111, DGA-Yale.
32. RMN to Emmet, Jan. 17, 1958, Nixon Pre-Presidential Papers.
33. DGA to Canfield, Feb. 1958, S 1, B 5, F 64, DGA-Yale.
34. William Shannon, "Washington Column," NYT, Jan. 23, 1958.
35. Edith Evans Asbury, "Truman Proffers Ties to President," NYT, Jan. 13, 1958, p. 20.
36. Leith-Ross to DGA, S 1, B 19, F 238, DGA-Yale.
37. DGA to Leith-Ross, S 1, B 19, F 238, DGA-Yale.
38. "Acheson Blames G.O.P. for 'Crisis,'" NYT, Jan. 21, 1958, p. 1.
39. Kennan, *Memoirs 1950–1963*, p. 241. Also see Mayers, *George Kennan and the Dilemmas of U.S. Foreign Policy*, 236–237; Hixson, *George F. Kennan: Cold War Iconoclast*, 180; and Hoopes, *Devil and John Foster Dulles*, 461.
40. Acheson, *Power and Diplomacy*. The five chapters in this book had been delivered as the William L. Clayton Lectures on International Economic Affairs and Foreign Policy at the Fletcher School of Law and Diplomacy in October 1957. For correspondence concerning publication and reviews of *Power and Diplomacy*, see S 3, B 57–58, F 94–96, DGA-Yale.
41. Quincy Howe, "Opportunity and Danger," NYT, Jan. 12, 1958, p. 7. This is the most penetrating review of *Power and Diplomacy*. Henry Kissinger reviewed the book favorably in "Acheson's Wise, Lucid Analysis of Our Foreign Policy," *New York Herald Tribune*, Jan. 12, 1958.
42. See also Acheson, Remarks at the New York Herald-Tribune book and author luncheon, February 17, 1958, Acheson Papers, Speeches and Articles, 1936–71, Box 139, HSTL.
43. Acheson, *Power and Diplomacy*. According to William L. Ryan, an Associated Press foreign-news analyst, Soviet radio denounced *Power and Diplomacy* as a continuation of Acheson's "bankrupt position-of-strength policy" (William L. Ryan, "Acheson's New Book Draws Red Fire before Publication Date," *Charleston Gazette* (W.Va.), Jan. 13, 1958).
44. Joint statement released by American Council on Germany, Inc, "Experts Oppose German Neutralization," Press release, S 2, B 9, F 123, DGA-Yale. The release was written by James B. Conant and Christopher Emmet. The other signatories were Professor Carl J. Friedrich, Eaton Professor of the Science of Government, Harvard University; H. V. Kaltenborn, commentator on foreign affairs for the National Broadcasting Company; Hans Kohn of City College, New York, an authority on current affairs; Rev. John LaFarge, S.J., former editor-in-chief of *America* and a commentator on German affairs; Louis Lochner, former head of the Associated Press bureau in Berlin and author of *The Goebbels Diaries* and other books on Germany; Norbert Muhlen, a foreign correspondent; George Nebolsine, an attorney in international law; Fritz Oppenheimer, former legal staff officer to SHAEF, former special assistant to General Lucius D. Clay, and former special assistant to the U.S. Department of State on Germany; Lithgow Osborne, former United States ambassador to Denmark and counsellor at the U.S. Embassy in Berlin; Samuel Reber, former U.S. deputy high com-

missioner in Germany and executive secretary for Goethe House; Gerhart Seger, the New York correspondent for the *Berlin Telegraf* and former Reichstag member from the Social Democratic Party; Dr. George N. Shuster, the president of Hunter College and former U.S. land commissioner of Bavaria; Professor Robert Strauss-Hupe, the director of the Foreign Policy Research Institute at the University of Pennsylvania and chairman of the International Relations Group Committee; Hans Wallenberg, former editor of the *Neue Zeitung*, an American-owned daily with one of the largest newspaper circulations in Germany; and Professor Arnold Wolfers, the director of the Washington Center of Foreign Policy Research, former director of the Berlin School of Politics, and former consultant on Germany for the State Department.

45. DGA to Emmet, Jan. 27, 1958, S 1, B 9, F 123, DGA-Yale.
46. Armstrong to DGA, Jan. 17, 1958, S 1, B 49, F 35, DGA-Yale.
47. DGA to Armstrong, Jan. 23, 1958, S 1, B 49, F 35, DGA-Yale.
48. Kennan to Bonn, Feb. 10, 1958, Kennan Papers.
49. DGA to Kennan, March 13, 1958, S 1, B 17, F 222, DGA-Yale.
50. Kennan to DGA, March 20, 1958, S 1, B 17, F 222, DGA-Yale.
51. DGA to Jessup, March 25, 1958, S 1, B 17, F 213, DGA-Yale.
52. Acheson, "Illusion of Disengagement," 371. One of Acheson's most widely acclaimed articles, this essay was later reprinted in the posthumously published collection of Acheson's articles, letters, and speeches, *Grapes from Thorns*.
53. Ibid., pp. 374–75.
54. DGA to Sir Alexander Spearman, June 26, 1958, S 1, B 29, F 370, DGA-Yale.
55. Acheson, "Illusion of Disengagement," 375–76.
56. Ibid., 378.
57. Dana Adams Schmidt, "Acheson vs. Kennan on a German Policy," *NYT*, Jan. 19, 1958, p. 5.
58. Kennan, "Disengagement Revisited," 207–08.
59. JFK letter is quoted in Derman, "Riddle of Containment," (Ph.D. diss.), p. 199. Chapter 2 is an excellent evaluation of the Kennan vs. Acheson debate. The JFK letter is also found in the George F. Kennan oral history interview (transcript), March 23, 1965, JFKL.
60. Arthur Schlesinger, Jr., "The Great Debate: Kennan vs. Acheson," *New York Post*, March 2, 1958.
61. DGA to Bonbright, June 23, 1958, S 1, B 3, F 40, DGA-Yale.
62. Kennan to Acheson, Oct. 28, 1958, S 1, B 17, F 222, DGA-Yale. The speech was published as "Meetings at the Summit: A Study in Diplomatic Method," in *TVER*. This was a lecture given by Acheson on May 8, 1958, as part of the Distinguished Lecture Series of the University of New Hampshire.
63. DGA to Kennan, Nov. 4, 1958, S 1, B 17, F 222, DGA-Yale. Acheson wrote a speech during August 1959 that he was planning to deliver at the War College. He sent an advance copy to Walter Hahn, the executive editor at the Foreign Policy Research Institute in Philadelphia, to be published in the institute's journal. "The only [change] not in the interest of clarity is to delete George Kennan's name," Acheson wrote Hahn. "He feels that I have been brutal to him. While that can be debated so far as the past is concerned, I have no desire to develop the argument into a feud" (DGA to Walter F. Hahn, Aug. 24, 1959, S 1, B 16, F 206, DGA-Yale).

64. Charles Burton Marshall, interview, March 1987. Also see DGA to Leo Cherne, Oct. 28, 1959, S 1, B 5, F 57, DGA-Yale.

65. Joseph Alsop, interview, March 1988, Washington, D.C. For other examples of Acheson's denigration of Kennan, see DGA to Bessie Randolph, April 25, 1958, S 1, B 25, F 320; and DGA to Perry Laukhugf, Oct. 23, 1959, S 1, B 19, F 234; both in DGA-Yale.

66. George F. Kennan, Oral history interview, March 23, 1965, JFKL.

67. Stuart Symington, interview, Nov. 1987, New Canaan, Conn.

68. DGA to John P. Frank, [n.d.; responding to Frank's letter of Nov. 29, 1967]; S 1, B 11, F 137; DGA-Yale. Frank, a young lawyer from Phoenix, Arizona, occasionally wrote to Acheson for advice.

69. For a discussion of the importance of the Kennan-Acheson debate to the military situation in Europe, see Joynt, "Disengagement and Beyond," 161–68.

70. For a discussion of Acheson's belief in the strategic importance of Berlin, see Acheson, *Present at the Creation*, 262–63. Acheson's involvement in the Berlin blockade is evaluated in Shlaim. *United States and the Berlin Blockade*.

71. See Schick, *Berlin Crisis*, 5–27. Also Hoopes, *Devil and John Foster Dulles*, 460–79. It should be noted that the Soviets controlled the rail and highway traffic of the Western Allies; other access into Berlin was controlled by the East Germans. Khrushchev was threatening to turn over *all* access to the East Germans once the peace treaty was signed.

72. Quotes are from Acheson, "Berlin" (Notes for a lecture at the School of Advanced International Studies, Johns Hopkins University, Washington, D.C., Dec. 11, 1958), S 4, B 68, F 172, p. 3. DGA-Yale, pp. 3–9.

73. Ibid., pp. 3–6.

74. Emmet to DGA, Feb. 16, 1959, S 1, B 9, F 123, DGA-Yale.

75. Ibid.

76. Acheson, "Berlin," 4–6.

77. Kissinger, *Nuclear Weapons and Foreign Policy*; and Paul Nitze, interview, Sept. 1987, Washington, D.C.

78. Acheson, "Berlin," 4–6.

79. DGA to HST, Jan. 27, 1959, S 1, B 31, F 395, DGA-Yale.

80. Acheson, "Wishing Won't Hold Berlin," *Saturday Evening Post*, March 7, 1959, pp. 32–36. For a summary of this article, see "Acheson Gives View," *NYT*, March 3, 1959, p. 27.

81. Ibid.

82. Ibid.

83. DGA to W. W. Rostow, March 17, 1959, S 1, B 26, F 338, DGA-Yale.

84. General Lauris Norstad, telephone interview, Aug. 1988, Tucson, Ariz.

85. DGA to General Maxwell D. Taylor, July 27, 1959, S 1, B 30, F 385, DGA-Yale.

86. Taylor, *Uncertain Trumpet*, 6, 8. Taylor believed his deterrent strategy of "flexible response," unlike "massive retaliation," would enable the United States to defend itself against anything from general war to infiltration, aggression, or subversion.

87. Norstad, telephone interview, Aug. 1988.

88. Schlesinger, *A Thousand Days*, 310. Schlesinger points out that, in addition to Taylor and Norstad, former army chief of staff Matthew B. Ridgway and the army

deputy chief of staff for plans and research, James M. Gavin, also tried to rehabilitate the notion that limited wars still were possible in a nuclear world.

89. Quoted in Schick, *Berlin Crisis*, 51–52.
90. DGA to William Tyler, March 18, 1959, S 1, B 31, F 404, DGA-Yale.
91. DGA to LBJ, March 17, 1959, S 1, B 17, F 215, DGA-Yale.
92. Ibid.
93. LBJ to DGA, March 23, 1959, S 1, B 17, F 215, DGA-Yale.
94. For a discussion of Herter and Berlin, see Noble, *Christian A. Herter*.
95. DGA to Harold Stein, June 5, 1959, S 1, B 29, F 371, DGA-Yale. For a more detailed analysis of why he thought negotiating with Khrushchev was dangerous and futile, see Acheson, "On Dealing with Russia: An Inside View," *NYT Magazine*, April 12, 1959. The article was later reprinted in *TVER*, 75–87.
96. DGA to HST, Aug. 31, 1959, S 1, B 31, F 395, DGA-Yale.
97. Clipping (no newspaper identification), July 21, 1959, S 2, B 40, F 27, DGA-Yale.
98. For a lively review of the Camp David meeting, see Beschloss, *Mayday*, 187–215.
99. Sergio Frosali, "Dean Acheson in Florence Speaks on the World Situation," *La Nazione* (Florence daily), Sept. 19, 1959, S 3, B 50, F 40, DGA-Yale. See also "Acheson Is Skeptical," *NYT*, Sept. 19, 1959, p. 12.
100. Acheson, "On Dealing with Russia: An Inside View," *NYT Magazine*, April 12, 1959, p. 27.
101. Acheson, "Meetings at the Summit," *TVER*, 45–48.
102. Frosali, "Dean Acheson in Florence." See also "Acheson Ties Soviet Jabs to Balanced-Power Test," *Christian Science Monitor*, Sept. 19, 1959. Acheson loved Italian and in 1959 began teaching himself the language via records. He would write letters in Italian to Manlio Brosio, the Italian Ambassador to the United States. (See DGA letters to Manlio Brosio, S 1, B 4, F 48, DGA-Yale.)
103. Russ Braley, "Acheson Has New NATO Plan," *Washington Post*, Oct. 5, 1959. On October 3, Acheson had made an important speech in Bonn articulating his vision for a new Atlantic community. See also Arthur J. Olsen, "Acheson Favors a Broader NATO," *NYT*, Oct. 4, 1959, p. 1; and Olsen, "Acheson Details Wider NATO Plan," *NYT*, Oct. 5, 1959, p. 6. Among the American delegates were John J. McCloy, the former U.S. high commissioner; and his successor, former ambassador James B. Conant; retired general James Gavin; and three senators.
104. Braley, "Acheson Has New NATO Plan." Also see DGA to Mrs. W. A. Camps, Dec. 18, 1959, S 1, B 5, F 63, DGA-Yale. In actuality Acheson's plan was similar to a report developed in June 1959 by a special Atlantic congress of leaders from the NATO countries. See Report of the Atlantic Economic Committee, reproduced in the *Atlantic Congress Report* (London: International Secretariat of the NATO Parliamentarians' Conference, 1959). The Acheson Plan received some press support. For example, see "Atlantic Community" (Editorial), *Washington Post*, Oct. 9, 1959; Olsen, "Acheson Favors a Broader NATO"; and Olsen "Acheson Details Wider NATO Plan."
105. DGA to Mrs. W. A. Camps, Dec. 18, 1959.
106. Olsen, "Acheson Details Wider NATO Plan," *NYT*.
107. Editorial, "Atlantic Community," *Washington Post*, Oct. 9, 1959.
108. Olsen, "Acheson Details Wider NATO Plan," *NYT*.

109. Kissinger to DGA, Oct. 23, 1959, S 1, B 18, F 226, DGA-Yale.
110. DGA to Frankfurter, Oct. 15, 1959, S 1, B 11, F 147, DGA-Yale.
111. See DGA to Wilmarth S. Lewis [undated], *AF*, 143–44.
112. "Acheson Is Scornful of President's Trips," *NYT*, Nov. 17, 1959, p. 18.
113. Acheson, Speech before the parliamentarians of the North Atlantic Treaty Organization, Washington, D.C., Nov. 21, 1959, S 3, B 50, F 40, DGA-Yale.
114. Ibid. Also Robert E. Baker, "Acheson Warns Berlin Negotiations Will Mean Only Retreat by West," *Washington Post*, Nov. 19, 1959, A25. When asked by the French delegation precisely what he meant by arms reduction talks, Acheson replied: "It is perfectly true that if one attempts to abolish all atomic weapons it is impossible. That is why total disarmament is dangerous. We should shorten our reach, the objective being to prevent the possibility of a saturation attack. Conventional forces would be permitted for defense."
115. William J. Jorden, "Herter Defends Parleys with Russians on Berlin," *NYT*, Nov. 25, 1959, p. 1. For a transcript of Herter's news conference, see *NYT*, Nov. 25, p. 6.
116. DGA to Bernadotte Schmidt, Nov. 25, 1959, S 1, B 28, F 359, DGA-Yale.
117. Baker, "Acheson Warns Berlin Negotiations Will Mean Only Retreat by West," *Washington Post*.
118. "Pravda Prints Acheson Speech," *NYT*, Nov. 23, p. 4.
119. "Pravda Chides Acheson," *NYT*, Nov. 28, 1959, p. 3.
120. Hans J. Morgenthau, "Berlin Negotiations," *NYT*, Dec. 2, 1959, p. 42. Other journalists also came to Acheson's defense. For example, see Melvin K. Whiteleather, "Acheson's Sage Counsel," *Philadelphia Evening Bulletin*, Nov. 25, 1959.
121. For a discussion of the U-2 affair, see Beschloss, *Mayday*.
122. DGA to HST, May 23, 1960, *AF*, 181–82. For other instances of Acheson's rage with Eisenhower's behavior during the U-2 affair, see DGA to John Dickey, March 18, 1959, S 1, B 8, F 102, DGA-Yale; and Acheson, "Ethics in International Relations Today," in *TVER*, 127–28.

Chapter 4. JFK, NATO Review, and the Berlin Crisis of 1961

1. Dean Acheson, Oral history interview, April 27, 1964, JFKL. Lucius D. Battle, assistant to Acheson when he was secretary of state, conducted the interview.
2. Jacqueline Kennedy to DGA, March 1958; and DGA to Mrs. Kennedy, March 1958, S 1, B 18, F 223, DGA-Yale. For his criticism of JFK, see Acheson, *Power and Diplomacy*, 122.
3. Acheson, Oral history interview, April 27, 1964, p. 2. Also interviews with Paul Nitze, Sept. 1987, Washington, D.C.; and David Acheson, Dec. 1987, Washington, D.C.
4. Acheson, Oral history interview, April 27, 1964, p. 2. Also see Clifford, *Counsel to the President*, 321.
5. Reminiscences of Chester Bowles, Oral History Research Office, Columbia University, vol. 5, 1963, p. 785; and Bowles, Oral history interview, Feb. 2, 1965, JFKL, p. 6.
6. DGA to JFK, July 17, 1960, S 1, B 18, F 223, DGA-Yale.

7. DGA to Dirk Stikker, Sept. 1960, S 1, B 29, F 375, DGA-Yale.
8. DGA to HST, Aug. 12, 1960. S 1, B 31, F 396, DGA-Yale. (Also in *AF*.)
9. Quoted in Schlesinger, *A Thousand Days*, 68.
10. From a speech in Houston, Texas. Quoted in Parmet, *JFK*, 43.
11. DGA to HST, Sept. 14, 1960, S 1, B 31, F 396, DGA-Yale.
12. DGA to HST, Nov. 22, 1960, *AF*, 199.
13. Isaacson and Thomas, *Wise Men*, 591.
14. Democratic National Committee, News release, Oct. 21, 1960, Box 789, Stevenson Papers. Also see Paterson, "Fixation with Cuba," 126.
15. Acheson, Oral history interview, April 27, 1964, p. 5. Also see Acheson, Memorandum, "Points for Senator Kennedy on Cuba," Oct. 1960, Acheson Papers, Democratic Party Files, 1957–68, Democratic Party—1960 Campaign, Box 96, Folder 2, HSTL.
16. DGA to MacLeish, Sept. 14, 1960, *AF*, 196–97.
17. DGA to Stikker, Nov. 1, 1960, S 1, B 29, F 375, DGA-Yale.
18. DGA to Count Alvise Gustiniani (Venezia, Italy), Nov. 21, 1960, S 1, B 13, F 166, DGA-Yale.
19. Acheson, Oral history interview, April 27, 1964, p. 6.
20. Charles Burton Marshall, interview, March 1987, Washington, D.C.
21. Acheson, Oral history interview, April 27, 1964, p. 6.
22. Ibid.
23. Quoted in Halberstam, *Best and the Brightest*, 324.
24. For Rusk's governmental career before he became secretary of state, see Cohen, *Dean Rusk*; and Schoenbaum, *Waging Peace and War*.
25. Acheson, *Present at the Creation*, 432.
26. Acheson, Oral history interview, April 27, 1964, pp. 7–8.
27. Ibid., p. 8. Also see Mosher, Clinton, and Lang, *Presidential Transitions and Foreign Affairs*, 159–76, for a discussion of the gold outflow problem that faced Kennedy in December 1960.
28. Acheson, Oral history interview, April 27, 1964, p. 9.
29. Ibid.
30. DGA to Stikker, Dec. 27, 1960, S 1, B 29, F 375, DGA-Yale. Also see Beschloss, *Crisis Years*, 242.
31. Ibid.
32. Isaacson and Thomas, *Wise Men*, 594–95.
33. Dean Rusk, telephone interview, March 1988, Athens, Ga.
34. Quoted in Paterson, "Bearing the Burden," 198.
35. Theodore Sorensen, interview, Feb. 1988, New York, N.Y.
36. Schlesinger, *A Thousand Days*, 380.
37. Arthur M. Schlesinger, Jr., interview, March 1988, New York, N.Y.
38. McGeorge Bundy, letter to author, May 10, 1988.
39. DGA to John Cowles, June 8, 1961, S 1, B 6, F 830, DGA-Yale.
40. *Public Papers of the Presidents of the United States: John F. Kennedy, 1961*, p. 229. Also Acheson, Oral history interview, April 27, 1964, p. 11.
41. Kaufmann, *McNamara Strategy*, 106.
42. DGA to Edward B. Burling, Sept. 20, 1961, S 1, B 4, F 53, DGA-Yale.

43. Dean Acheson, "A Review of North Atlantic Problems for the Future" (hereafter, Acheson Report on NATO), March 1961, National Security File, Box 220, JFKL. See also Acheson Papers, Post-Administration Files, State Department and White House Advisor (hereafter, Post-Admin. Files, State and WH), Box 85, April–June 1961, HSTL.

44. DGA to Raymond L. Thurston, SHAPE Liaison Office, April 3, 1961, Acheson Papers, Post-Admin. Files, State and WH, Box 85, April–June 1961, HSTL.

45. For Acheson's views on the Grand Design, see Acheson, "Practice of Partnership." Also see Kraft, *Grand Design*, and Costigliola, "Pursuit of the Atlantic Community," 24–56.

46. Robert Bowie, "The North Atlantic Nations: Tasks for the 1960's" (Report to Secretary of State Herter, Aug. 1960, Bowie Report 1), Norstad Files, Box 28, Dwight D. Eisenhower Library, Abilene, Kansas. Also see Winand, "Presidents, Advisers and the Uniting of Europe" (Ph. D. diss.).

47. Acheson Report on NATO.

48. See Schwartz, *NATO's Nuclear Dilemmas*, 150.

49. Acheson Report on NATO.

50. Rusk to DGA, April 5, 1961, Acheson Papers, Post-Admin. Files, State and WH, Box 85, April–June 1961, HSTL.

51. JFK to DGA, April 24, 1961, S 1, B 18, F 223, DGA-Yale.

52. Kennedy, "Address before the Canadian Parliament in Ottawa, May 17, 1961," *Public Papers of the Presidents of the United States: John F. Kennedy, 1961*, 385.

53. Schwartz, *NATO's Nuclear Dilemmas*, 152.

54. Acheson, Oral history interview, April 27, 1964, pp. 12–13. For a statistical overview of American military commitments in Europe see Senate Committee on Foreign Relations, *United States Policy toward Europe (and Related Matters)*, 89th Cong., 2d sess. (Washington, D.C.: GPO, 1986).

55. DGA to Stikker, Dec. 27, 1960, *AF* 200–202.

56. Acheson, Oral history interview, April 27, 1964, p. 13.

57. McGeorge Bundy, interview, April 1988, New York, N.Y.

58. DGA to Cowles, Feb. 6, 1961, S 1, B 6, F 83, DGA-Yale.

59. Quoted in Catudal, *Kennedy and the Berlin Wall Crisis*, 52.

60. Schlesinger, *A Thousand Days*, 375.

61. McGeorge Bundy, Memorandum for the President, April 4, 1961, NSF-84, JFKL.

62. Acheson, Memorandum for the President, April 3, 1961, Declassified Documents Collection, 1985/2547, Center for Research Libraries, Chicago, Illinois.

63. Schlesinger, *A Thousand Days*, 380–81. The account that follows depends on this work.

64. Ibid. For Prime Minister Macmillan's recollections of his 1961 trip to Washington see Macmillan, *Pointing the Way, 1959–1961*, chap. 11.

65. Quoted in Schlesinger, *A Thousand Days*, 381.

66. Schlesinger to JFK, April 6, 1961, Box 5, Schlesinger Papers, JFKL.

67. Acheson, Oral history interview, April 27, 1964, pp. 13–14.

68. Ibid.

69. Acheson, Remarks at Foreign Service lunch, Washington, D.C. (transcribed

June 29, 1961), S 3, B 51, F 52, DGA-Yale. The speech was delivered sometime between June 13 and 25.

70. DGA to HST, May 3, 1961, S 1, B 31, F 396, DGA-Yale.

71. Acheson, *Sketches from Life of Men I Have Known*. Chapter 8, "Konrad Adenauer," offers colorful vignettes of the chancellor. For correspondence and reviews of *Sketches from Life*, see S 3, B 58, F 101–103, DGA-Yale. The final draft and earlier versions are located in S 3, B 58, F 97–100, DGA-Yale.

72. Acheson, Oral history interview, April 27, 1964, pp. 16–17.

73. Beschloss, *Crisis Years*, 240–41. The JFK article Adenauer objected to was "A Democrat Looks at Foreign Policy."

74. Acheson, Oral history interview, April 27, 1964, pp. 16–17.

75. Ibid. Also Gruson, "Adenauer Tells Acheson of Fear for NATO Power," *NYT*, April 10, 1961.

76. Adenauer to DGA, April 28, 1961, Acheson Papers, Post-Admin. Files, State and WH, Box 85, HSTL. For Adenauer's impressions of JFK, see Adenauer, *Erinnerungen, 1959–1963*, 90–99; and Prittie, *Konrad Adenauer*, 283–84.

77. Quoted in Beschloss, *Crisis Years*, 241.

78. Catudal, *Kennedy and the Berlin Wall Crisis*, 59–62. Also see Memorandum of conversation between Kennedy, Rusk and Adenauer re: Berlin Contingency Planning, April 13, 1961, JFKL; and Adenauer to DGA, April 28, 1961. For a detailed evaluation of German views on defense strategy in the 1960s, see Kelleher, *Germany and the Politics of Nuclear Weapons*; and Richardson, *Germany and the Atlantic Alliance*.

79. Acheson, "An Unofficial Ambassador," in *Grapes from Thorns*. For de Gaulle's attitude toward NATO in this period, see de Gaulle, *Memoirs of Hope: Renewal and Endeavor, 1958–1962*, 256–57.

80. Acheson, Oral history interview, April 27, 1964, p. 16.

81. Robert C. Doty, "Acheson Confers with de Gaulle," *NYT*, April 21, 1961.

82. Quoted in ibid.

83. Acheson, Remarks at Foreign Service Lunch, June 29, 1961, S 3, B 51, F 52, DGA-Yale.

84. Ibid.
85. Ibid.
86. Ibid.
87. Ibid.

88. Quoted in Ambrose, *Rise to Globalism*, 201.

89. Acheson, Remarks at Foreign Service Lunch.

90. "The Two-Hatted Dean," *Battle Line*, Republican National Committee 1961, no. 20, April 14, 1961. Also, "Acheson Attacked by G.O.P. on Trip," *NYT*, April 15, 1961. David Brinkley read the Republican National Committee press release on his nightly news telecast and erroneously added that Acheson was traveling in Europe as a "representative of the United States Government." Acheson's law firm asked for and received a public retraction. See Extract from script used by Mr. David Brinkley on NBC-TV, Acheson Papers, Post-Admin. Files, Box 85, April–June 1961, HSTL.

91. DGA to HST, May 3, 1961, S 1, B 31, F 396, DGA-Yale.

92. Quoted in Catudal, *Kennedy and the Berlin Wall Crisis*, 118. For detailed accounts of the Vienna summit, see Gelb, *Berlin Wall*, 73–96; and Sorensen, *Kennedy*, 658–60. Also Khrushchev, *Khrushchev Remembers*, 566–69.

93. Quoted in Marguerite Higgins, "Acheson Heads Task Force to Watch Berlin," *New York Herald Tribune*, June 17, 1961.
94. Mike Mansfield, Oral history interview, June 23, 1964, JFKL. Also *NYT*, June 15, 1961, p. 1.
95. Quoted in Isaacson and Thomas, *Wise Men*, 603–04.
96. DGA to HST, June 24, 1961, S 1, B 31, F 396, DGA-Yale.
97. Acheson, Remarks at Foreign Service Lunch.
98. Ibid.
99. Lucius Battle, interview, Oct. 1987, Washington, D.C.
100. John Ausland to Honoré Catudal, Aug. 15, 1978, quoted in Catudal, *Kennedy and the Berlin Wall Crisis*, 297.
101. DGA to JFK, Aug. 18, 1961, S 1, B 18, F 223, DGA-Yale.
102. Transcript of "A Conversation with Dean Acheson," pt. 2 (*CBS News Special*, television interview by Eric Sevareid, Nov. 4, 1969), p. 3, DGA-Yale.
103. See Bundy, *Pattern of Responsibility*.
104. McGeorge Bundy, interview, April 1988, New York, N.Y.
105. Quoted in Isaacson and Thomas, *Wise Men*, 611.
106. McGeorge Bundy, interview, April 1988.
107. McGeorge Bundy, letter to author, May 10, 1988.
108. Although Acheson's paper is still classified, in the interview of April 1964 he quotes directly from it. Also see Memorandum for record discussion at NSC meeting, June 29, 1961, drafted by McGeorge Bundy (hereafter, Memorandum, NSC meeting, June 29, 1961), NSC meeting 486, Box 313, JFKL; Bundy, *Danger and Survival*, 372; and Marquis Childs, "The Acheson View on Holding Berlin," *The Washington Post*, July 28, 1961. Childs stresses the similarities between the purported recommendations of Acheson's Berlin plan (which had not been made public) and his March 7, 1959, *Saturday Evening Post* article, "Wishing Won't Hold Berlin."
109. DGA to Adenauer, June 28, 1961, Acheson Papers, Post-Admin. Files, State and WH, Box 85, HSTL.
110. Quoted in Schoenbaum, *Waging Peace and War*, 338. For Rusk's recollection of the Berlin Crisis, see Rusk, *As I Saw It*, 218–28.
111. Catudal, *Kennedy and the Berlin Wall Crisis*, 143.
112. Acheson, Oral history interview, April 27, 1964, pp. 19–20. Also Memorandum, NSC meeting, June 29, 1961.
113. Acheson, Oral history interview, April 27, 1964, pp. 19–20.
114. Ibid. Also Catudal, *Kennedy and the Berlin Wall Crisis*, 144–45.
115. Schlesinger, *A Thousand Days*, 382.
116. Memorandum, NSC meeting, June 29, 1961.
117. Schlesinger, *A Thousand Days*, 356–57.
118. DGA to William S. Stone, July 10, 1961, Acheson Papers, Post-Admin. Files, State and WH, Box 85, July 1961, HSTL.
119. U. Alexis Johnson, interview, Feb. 1988, Princeton, N.J.
120. Foy Kohler, telephone interview, Feb. 1988. See also Kohler, *Understanding the Russians*, 329.
121. Adenauer to DGA, July 21, 1961, Acheson Papers, Post-Admin. Files, State and WH, Box 85, July 1961, HSTL.
122. Abram Chayes, Oral history interview, JFKL, p. 17.

123. Quoted in Isaacson and Thomas, *Wise Men*, 610–11.
124. Catudal, *Kennedy and the Berlin Wall Crisis*, 150.
125. See DGA to Wilmarth Lewis, June 30, 1961, *AF*, 207–08.
126. Memorandum of discussion in the National Security Council on July 13, 1961, drafted by McGeorge Bundy (hereafter, Memorandum, NSC meeting, July 13, 1961), NSC meeting 487, Box 313, JFKL.
127. Catudal, *Kennedy and the Berlin Wall Crisis*, 173.
128. Paul H. Nitze, interview, Sept. 1987, Washington, D.C.
129. Catudal, *Kennedy and the Berlin Wall Crisis*, 174–75.
130. Ibid.
131. Memorandum, NSC meeting, July 13, 1961.
132. Quoted in Catudal, *Kennedy and the Berlin Wall Crisis*, 175.
133. DGA to HST, July 14, 1961, *AF*, 208. For similar criticism by Acheson of the administration's handling of the Berlin crisis, see DGA to David K. E. Bruce (U.S. ambassador to the U.K.), July 5, 1961, Acheson Papers, Post-Admin. Files, State and WH, Box 85, HSTL.
134. Memorandum of Minutes of the National Security Council, July 20, 1961, drafted by McGeorge Bundy, NSC meeting 488, Box 313, JFKL.
135. Sidey, *John F. Kennedy*, 230–31.
136. *Public Papers of the Presidents of the United States: John F. Kennedy, 1961*, p. 534.
137. Ibid., 533–39. Also Miroff, *Pragmatic Illusions*, 76–77.
138. McGeorge Bundy, letter to author, May 10, 1988.
139. Senate Committee on Foreign Relations, *Documents on Germany, 1944–1961*, 718–20.
140. Acheson's notes of the July 29 and 30 meetings with Strauss and Nitze are in the Acheson Papers, Post-Admin. Files, State and WH, Box 85, August 1961, HSTL. For Strauss's critique of flexible response, see Stromseth, *Origins of Flexible Response*.
141. Acheson Report, "Berlin: A Political Program," Aug. 1, 1961, NSF, Box 82, JFKL. For JFK's response to the paper, see JFK to DGA, Aug. 14, 1961, S 1, B 18, F 223, DGA-Yale.
142. DGA to HST, Aug. 4, 1961, S 1, B 31, F 396, DGA-Yale.
143. Ibid.
144. Ibid.
145. DGA to Eden, Aug. 4, 1961, S 1, B 9, F 117, DGA-Yale.
146. Quotes from McGeorge Bundy, *Danger and Survival*, 375–76. Acheson's article "Wishing Won't Hold Berlin" was discussed in chapter 3. Also see McGeorge Bundy, interview, April 1988, New York, N.Y.
147. DGA to Lady Pamela Berry [undated], S 1, B 3, F 32, DGA-Yale.
148. Eliot Janeway, interview, May 1990, New York, N.Y.
149. JFK to DGA, Aug. 14, 1961, S 1, B 18, F 223, DGA-Yale.
150. Dean Acheson, Oral history interview, May 27, 1964, JFKL, p. 21.
151. Ibid.
152. McGeorge Bundy, interview, April 1988.
153. DGA to HST, Sept. 21, 1961, S 1, B 31, F 396, DGA-Yale. Truman replied that he was not at all pessimistic about the future of Berlin. Acheson's pessimism lifted slightly by November. "I wish, too, that I were making a useful contribution to the

handling of the Berlin problem," he wrote to John H. Ferguson, a lawyer in the firm of Cleary, Gottlieb, Steen, and Hamilton. "As you say, I am regarded as a very hard boiled egg. Not many people within the government will argue with me. On the other hand, my ideas have a curious way of turning up in government action with their clothes on backward" (DGA to John H. Ferguson, Nov. 3, 1961, Acheson Papers, Post-Admin. Files, State and WH, Box 85, Oct.–Dec. 1961, HSTL).

154. DGA to Joseph Johnson, Nov. 21, 1961, S 1, B 4, F 54, DGA-Yale.

155. See DGA to General Lucius Clay, Jan. 4, 1962, Acheson Papers, Post-Admin. Files, State and WH, Box 85, HSTL.

156. Ibid. For a further discussion of Acheson's desire for a united Germany, see DGA to Eelco van Kleffens, Sept. 6, 1961, Acheson Papers, Post-Admin. Files, State and WH, Box 85, HSTL. Van Kleffens was the Netherlands Ambassador to the United States from 1947 to 1950 and Chief Representative in the United Kingdom of the European Coal and Steel Community during the Kennedy years.

157. DGA to Marshall Shulman, Nov. 23, 1961, S 1, B 29, F 367, DGA-Yale.

158. Acheson, Memorandum on meeting with Chancellor Adenauer, Nov. 21, 1961, Acheson Papers, Post-Admin. Files, State and WH, Box 85, HSTL.

159. Ibid.

160. Acheson, Statement before the Subcommittee on Foreign Economic Policy of the Joint Economic Committee, Dec. 5, 1961, S 3, B 51, F 53, DGA-Yale.

Chapter 5. The Cuban Missile Crisis

1. "Acheson Sees Gain in Vietnam," *NYT*, Jan. 26, 1962, p. 2; "Acheson in Australia," *NYT*, Jan. 28, 1962, p. 79; "Acheson Gives Case on Cambodia Temple," *NYT*, March 2, 1962, p. 24.

2. Charles Burton Marshall, interview, March 1987, Washington, D.C. Also Marshall, letter to author, Oct. 1988.

3. Marshall, letter to author, Oct. 1988.

4. Acheson, "Revising Forward Political Strategies and Improving the Organization of the Free World" (Text of remarks at National Strategy Seminar, National War College, Washington D.C., July 21, 1959), Acheson Papers, Speeches and Articles, 1936–1971, Box 139, HSTL. For the Eisenhower administration's view of Castro, see Rabe, *Eisenhower and Latin America*.

5. DGA to HST, Oct. 8, 1962, S 1, B 31, F 396, DGA-Yale.

6. Allison, *Essence of Decision*, 185. The members of ExCom are also listed in Brugioni, *Eyeball to Eyeball*, 239–40. They included Secretary of State Dean Rusk, Secretary of Defense Robert McNamara, Director of the CIA John McCone, Special Assistant for National Security Affairs McGeorge Bundy, Secretary of the Treasury Douglas Dillon, Special Counsel Theodore Sorensen, Chairman of the Joint Chiefs of Staff Maxwell Taylor, Under Secretary of State George Ball, Deputy Under Secretary of State U. Alexis Johnson, Assistant Secretary of State for Latin American Affairs Edwin Martin, State Department Soviet expert Llewellyn Thompson, Deputy Director of the CIA General Marshall Carter, Deputy Secretary of Defense Roswell Gilpatric, Assistant Secretary of Defense for International Security Affairs Paul Nitze, and Attorney General Robert F. Kennedy. Vice President Lyndon B. Johnson, Appointments Secre-

tary Kenneth O'Donnell, U.S. Information Agency Deputy Director Donald Wilson, Ambassador to the United Nations Adlai Stevenson, and former Secretary of Defense Robert Lovett were also present at some or all of the meetings.

7. Thaddeus Holt, Memorandum 9 November 1962, S 1, B 16, F 199, DGA-Yale. In early November of 1962, after a U.S.-Soviet hot war over the missiles had been avoided, Acheson gave a talk to his colleagues at Covington & Burling on his part in the Cuban affair. Holt, a member of the firm, took detailed, handwritten notes that he later incorporated into a memorandum. On March 3, 1967, Holt, then Deputy Under Secretary of the Army in the Johnson administration, sent Acheson a copy (Holt to DGA, March 3, 1967, S 1, B 16, F 199, DGA-Yale). See also Acheson, Memorandum on the Cuban Missile Crisis, Acheson Papers, Post-Administration Files, (hereafter, Post-Admin. Files), Box 86, January–December 1963, HSTL.

8. Holt, Memorandum 9 November 1962. Also Abel, *Missile Crisis*, 11–54.

9. Isaacson and Thomas, *Wise Men*, 620. Also Acheson, "Dean Acheson's Version . . . of the Cuban Missile Affair." The article, a review of Robert Kennedy's book *Thirteen Days*, was later reprinted as Acheson, "Homage to Plain Dumb Luck."

10. Acheson, Oral history interview, April 27, 1964, JFKL, p. 22.

11. Acheson, "Homage to Plain Dumb Luck," 197–98.

12. Steel, "Endgame." This review of Robert Kennedy's *Thirteen Days* is an extended essay on the missile crisis. It was reprinted in Divine, *Cuban Missile Crisis*, as "Lessons of the Missile Crisis."

13. Isaacson and Thomas, *Wise Men*, 620. Also Abel, *Missile Crisis*, 60.

14. Acheson, Oral history interview, April 27, 1964, p. 23.

15. Ibid.

16. DGA to Michael Janeway, Oct. 31, 1962, S 1, B 16, F 209, DGA-Yale. See also Acheson, "Homage to Plain Dumb Luck," 206. "The Cuban exercise was a most reckless act on the part of the Russians and I think it probably grew out of an appraisal that Khrushchev made of President Kennedy when they met in Vienna," Acheson asserted in 1966. "I think he thought, 'I can outbluff this fellow' and proceeded to attempt it" (Testimony of Dean Acheson before U.S. Joint Committee on Foreign Affairs, Subcommittee on Europe, "The Crisis in NATO", May 17, 1966, S 3, B 53, F 71, DGA-Yale).

17. Acheson, Oral history interview, April 27, 1964, p. 23.

18. Brugioni, *Eyeball to Eyeball*, 244; and Acheson, "Homage to Plain Dumb Luck," 206. For formlessness of ExCom meetings, see Medland, "American-Soviet Nuclear Confrontation of 1962" (Ph.D. diss).

19. Kennedy, *Thirteen Days*, 46.

20. Acheson, "Homage to Plain Dumb Luck," 206.

21. Ibid., 207.

22. Kennedy, *Thirteen Days*, 16. For a more thorough discussion of Robert Kennedy's difficult relationship with Dean Acheson, see Schlesinger, *Robert Kennedy and His Times*, 507–30.

23. Quoted in Acheson, "Homage to Plain Dumb Luck," 198. Also quoted in Abel, *Missile Crisis*, 64; and Isaacson and Thomas, *Wise Men*, 621. Allison, *Essence of Decision*, discusses the relevancy of the Pearl Harbor analogy (pp. 60, 124, 132, 203, 296–97).

24. Acheson, "Homage to Plain Dumb Luck," 198–99. A year after the missile crisis Acheson wrote an essay redolent with the phraseology of the Monroe Doctrine. He concluded: "The Monroe Doctrine should be kept alive—and, one has no doubt, will be kept alive—to suggest to our Soviet friends that the people and government of the United States still 'considered any attempt on their part to extend their system to any portions of this Hemisphere as dangerous to our peace and safety,' and, furthermore, that we would view an interposition to control the destiny of any part of the hemisphere 'as the manifestation of an unfriendly disposition toward the United States.' If they should be in doubt as to the meaning of this stilted and old-fashioned phrase, there would be a way, though a dangerous way, to find out" (Acheson, "The Monroe Doctrine: Dead or Alive?" *Think*, Oct. 1963, Acheson Papers, Speeches and Articles 1936–1971, Box 140, HSTL).

25. The account in this paragraph depends upon Abel, *Missile Crisis*, 65–73.

26. See Acheson, Remarks at the American Institute of International Law panel on Cuban Quarantine (hereafter, Remarks on Cuban Quarantine), April 25, 1963, S 1, B 51, F 57, DGA-Yale, p. 3. Dean Rusk was often criticized by Acheson for giving too much weight to law in the making of foreign policy. After Rusk retired from government, he taught at the University of Georgia Law School. His first exam consisted of two quotations, he writes: "One was from Dean Acheson: 'The survival of nations is not a matter of law' and one from myself: 'In a nuclear world, the survival of nations may depend on law.' I let my students sweat those two statements out" (Dean Rusk, "Reflections on Foreign Policy," 196).

27. Abel, *Missile Crisis*, 72.

28. Acheson, Remarks on Cuban Quarantine. Also quoted in Chayes, *Cuban Missile Crisis*, 1. Chayes notes that in addition to Acheson, six other lawyers participated in ExCom: George Ball, Roswell Gilpatric, Robert Kennedy, Dean Rusk, Theodore Sorensen, and Adlai Stevenson. Although he profoundly disagreed with much of Acheson's thinking, George Kennan shared Acheson's conviction that American foreign-policy makers often overvalue legal considerations. See Kennan, *American Diplomacy*, 95–103.

29. See Ball, *Past Has Another Pattern*, 291.

30. Dean Rusk, telephone interview, March 1988, Athens, Ga.

31. Theodore Sorensen, Oral history interview, March 24, 1964, JFKL. Acheson's tit-for-tat approach is discussed in Blight and Welch, *On the Brink*, 47; and Sagan, "Nuclear Alerts and Crisis Management," 106–22.

32. Acheson, "Homage to Plain Dumb Luck," 199–201.

33. Ibid., 200.

34. DGA to Devlin [undated; probably January 1963], S 1, B 8, F 97, DGA-Yale.

35. Meeting described in Acheson, Oral history interview, April 27, 1964, JFKL, p. 24.

36. Kenneth Harris, "Pungent Memories from Mr. Acheson," *Life*, July 23, 1971, p. 53. Harris was a British journalist who also had interviewed Acheson for BBC television.

37. Acheson, Oral history interview, April 27, 1964, p. 24.

38. RFK is quoted in Schlesinger, *Robert Kennedy and His Times*, p. 509.

39. Abel, *Missile Crisis*, 88–89.

40. Roswell Gilpatric, Oral history interview, May 5, 1970, JFKL.
41. George W. Ball, interview, Feb. 1988, Princeton, N.J.
42. C. Douglas Dillon, interview, June 1989, New York, N.Y.
43. Acheson, "Homage to Plain Dumb Luck," 203. Also Acheson, Oral history interview, April 27, 1964, p. 24.
44. Acheson, Oral history interview, April 27, 1964, pp. 24–25. CIA Director John McCone convinced President Kennedy to dispatch a special envoy to seek European support. Kennedy sent Livingston T. Merchant to brief Prime Minister Diefenbaker of Canada.
45. Dean Rusk, telephone interview, March 1988, Athens, Ga.
46. Thaddeus Holt, Memorandum 9 November 1962, S 1, B 16, F 199, DGA-Yale.
47. Acheson, Oral history interview, April 27, 1964, pp. 25–26. Also Beschloss, *Crisis Years*, 477.
48. Holt, Memorandum 9 November 1962.
49. Acheson, Oral history interview, April 27, 1964, p. 26.
50. Holt, Memorandum 9 November 1962.
51. Acheson, Oral history interview, April 27, 1964, p. 26. Acheson retailed this story often, changing details as needed.
52. Harris, "Pungent Memories from Mr. Acheson," 52.
53. Acheson, Oral history interview, April 27, 1964, p. 26.
54. Harris, "Pungent Memories from Mr. Acheson," 52.
55. Acheson, Oral history interview, April 27, 1964, p. 26.
56. Ibid.
57. DGA to Jean Monnet, Nov. 1962, S 1, B 23, F 288, DGA-Yale.
58. Quoted in Schlesinger, *A Thousand Days*, 815.
59. Acheson, Oral history interview, April 27, 1964, p. 29.
60. Henry Kissinger to DGA, S 1, B 18, F 226, DGA-Yale.
61. Acheson, Oral history interview, April 27, 1964, p. 29.
62. DGA to Michael Janeway, Oct. 31, 1962, S 1, B 16, F 209, DGA-Yale.
63. Acheson, Oral history interview, April 27, 1964, p. 29.
64. Sydney Gruson, "Germans Bracing for Soviet Move," *NYT*, Oct. 24, 1962, p. 20. West Berlin's mayor, Willy Brandt, praised America's toughness and described JFK's blockade decision as "earnest, courageous, determined, and reasonable."
65. DGA to Monnet, Nov. 1962, S 1, B 23, F 288, DGA-Yale.
66. Acheson is quoted in Sulzberger, *Seven Continents and Forty Years*, 530.
67. Quotes from DGA to Michael Janeway, Oct. 31, 1962, S 1, B 16, F 209, DGA-Yale. For a discussion of Stevenson's assertion that Acheson and McGeorge Bundy were trying to "smear" his reputation and stifle his voice within the Kennedy administration, see Robert S. Allen and Paul Scott, "Deep-Laid Political Power Play Lies behind Charges against Stevenson," *Camden Courier Press* (N.J.), Jan. 12, 1963, Newspaper clipping in Acheson Papers, Post-Admin. Files, State and WH, Box 85, HSTL.
68. DGA to Blair Butterworth, Nov. 21, 1962, S 1, B 4, F 54, DGA-Yale. For McCloy's being dispatched to "stiffen" Stevenson at the UN, see Brugioni, *Eyeball to Eyeball*, 318–19.
69. Acheson, "Homage to Plain Dumb Luck," 204.
70. Quoted in Isaacson and Thomas, *Wise Men*, 629.

71. Acheson, "Homage to Plain Dumb Luck," 204. Also see Bromley Smith, Summary meeting of NSC Executive Committee meeting no. 7, October 27, 1962, 10:00 A.M., Box 316, Meetings and Memorandum, National Security Files, JFKL.
72. Quoted in Abel, *Missile Crisis*, 182.
73. Acheson, "Homage to Plain Dumb Luck," 204–05; Abel, *Missile Crisis*, 185–200; and Bromley Smith, Summary meeting of NSC Executive Committee meeting No. 8, October 27, 1962, 4:00, Box 316, Meetings and Memorandum, National Security Files, JFKL.
74. Ibid., 205.
75. DGA to Pickett, Nov. 1, 1962, Acheson Papers, Post-Admin. Files, State and WH, Box 85, HSTL.
76. DGA to JFK, Oct. 28, 1962; JFK to DGA, Oct. 29, 1962; and DGA to JFK, Nov. 30, 1962; S 1, B 18, F 223, DGA-Yale.
77. I. F. Stone, "The Brink," *New York Review of Books*, April 14, 1966, pp. 12–16. Reprinted in Divine, *Cuban Missile Crisis*, 155–65.
78. DGA to Desmond Donnelly, April 24, 1968, S 1, B 8, F 108, DGA-Yale.
79. McGeorge Bundy has noted that "Acheson's review of Kennedy's book is one of the important documents in the missile crisis and it appeared in that unlikely journal [Esquire]" (Bundy, "Kennedy and the Nuclear Question," 217).
80. Acheson, "Homage to Plain Dumb Luck," 205–06. Also see Lazo, *Dagger in the Heart*. Lazo implies that Acheson's belated criticism of the handling of the Cuban missile crisis stemmed from the desire of Acheson and his law firm to establish a cordial relationship with the new Nixon administration.
81. Three years after the missile crisis, de Gaulle made his decision to pull France out of NATO's integrated military command. At a news conference on February 21, 1966, he noted that "while the prospects of a World War breaking out on account of Europe are dissipating, conflicts in which America engages in other parts of the world—as the day before yesterday in Korea, yesterday in Cuba, today in Vietnam—risk by virtue of that famous escalation, being extended so that the result would be a general conflagration. In that case Europe—whose strategy is, within NATO, that of America—would be automatically involved in the struggle, even when it would not have so desired" (Quoted in Stone, "The Brink," 167).
82. Harris, "Pungent Memories from Mr. Acheson," *Life*, July 23, 1971, p. 53. Acheson believed that Kennedy's reputation for crisis management was overinflated because of the martyrdom surrounding his assassination. For a line of arguments similar to Acheson's, see Cohen, "Why We Should Stop Studying the Cuban Missile Crisis."
83. Arthur Schlesinger, Jr., interview, March, 1988, New York, N.Y.

Chapter 6. Strains in the Atlantic Alliance, 1962–63

1. Taylor to DGA, July 27, 1962, S 1, B 30, F 385, DGA-Yale.
2. DGA to Taylor, July 30, 1962, S 1, B 30, F 385, DGA-Yale. Because Acheson was not acquainted with Westmoreland, his invitation did not carry the same weight as the request from Taylor, whom Acheson knew and respected. For the Acheson-Taylor alliance during ExCom, see Brugioni, *Eyeball to Eyeball*, 240–44.

3. Acheson, "Our Atlantic Alliance: The Political and Economic Strands" (Speech delivered at the United States Military Academy, West Point, New York, Dec. 5, 1962). Reprinted in *Vital Speeches of the Day* 29, no. 6, Jan. 1, 1963, pp. 162–66.

4. DGA to Schlesinger, Jan. 31, 1963, S 1, B 28, F 359, DGA-Yale. Schlesinger, who was in England, had sent Acheson a clipping of Selwyn Lloyd's commentary from the Sunday *Telegraph*.

5. State Department telegram, Dec. 7, 1962, NSF Countries, Box 170A, "UK 12/6/62," JFKL. Also Max Frankel, "Acheson Speech Irks British; U.S. Terms Criticism Minor," *NYT*, Dec. 7, 1962, p. 1.

6. See McGeorge Bundy to Robert J. Manning, Dec. 7, 1962, National Security Files 170A/34, JFKL. The statement is also quoted in Dimbleby and Reynolds, *An Ocean Apart*, 255.

7. Lord Oliver Franks, interview, Washington, D.C., April 1989.

8. Quoted in Nunnerley, *President Kennedy and Britain*, 1. The author provides a fascinating account of the collapse of Anglo-American relations during the Kennedy years. Also see Pierre, *Nuclear Politics*, 225.

9. "New Power Arising," *Spectator*, Dec. 14, 1962, p. 920.

10. Quoted in Pierre, *Nuclear Politics*, 225.

11. DGA to Leith-Ross, Jan. 16, 1963, S 1, B 19, F 238, DGA-Yale.

12. Quoted in Max Frankel, "Acheson Speech . . . ," *NYT*.

13. See, e.g., Hathaway, *Great Britain and the United States*, 75.

14. DGA to Arthur Schlesinger, Jr., Jan. 14, 1963, S 1, B 28, F 259, DGA-Yale.

15. Drew Middleton, "Macmillan Rebukes Acheson on Speech," *NYT*, Dec. 8, 1962, pp. 1, 8.

16. Nunnerley, *President Kennedy and Britain*, 1–2.

17. Published letter to Lord Chandos, Dec. 7, 1962, reprinted in Macmillan, *At the End of the Day, 1961–1963*, 339. Macmillan's statement was a reply to a letter he had received from Lord Chandos, president of the Institute of Directors and former Conservative cabinet member; Sir Louis Spears; and Sir Robert Renwick, requesting that the prime minister seek a disavowal from Acheson before he met with Kennedy in the Bahamas on December 19.

18. Ibid. The British Foreign office also wired Macmillan's statement to Dean Rusk as an official government telegram (Dec. 8, 1962, NSF Countries, Box 170A, "UK 12/6/62," JFKL).

19. Sir Howard Beale, Oral history interview, April 16, 1964, JFKL. Beale recalls that he was in England when the furor over Acheson's remarks hit the London papers: "I spent the next few days in England defending him and when I came back, I took him to task and asked him why I should have to defend him! He told me it was one of those inadvertent things; he had thought the words he used were all right, some of his people had read the speech and saw nothing wrong—it occurred to nobody that it could be interpreted in any way wrong."

20. DGA to Miller, Jan. 24, 1963, S 1, B 20, F 255, DGA-Yale.

21. Quoted in Middleton, "Macmillan Rebukes Acheson."

22. Quoted in Vaughn, "a Comparison of . . . Acheson as Secretary of State and as Elder Statesman" (Master's thesis), 88–89.

23. Frankel, "Acheson Speech Irks British; U.S. Terms Criticism Minor," *NYT*,

Dec. 7, 1962, pp. 1, 19. Also Nunnerley, *President Kennedy and Britain*, 1–13; and Camps, *Britain and the European Community*, 463–65.

24. DGA to Kissinger, Jan. 7, 1963, S 1, B 18, F 236, DGA-Yale.
25. Taylor to DGA, Dec. 7, 1962, S 1, B 30, F 385, DGA-Yale.
26. DGA to Eugene V. Rostow, Dec. 13, 1962, *AF*, 240–41. Acheson began to refer to himself in letters as "Public Enemy No. 1 in England." See, for example, DGA to McGeorge Bundy, Dec. 13, 1962, S 1, B 4, F 51, DGA-Yale.
27. Chester Bowles, Second oral history interview, July 1, 1970, JFKL.
28. For discussions of Acheson's supposed Anglophilia, see Brinkley, "Dean Acheson and European Unity," in Heller and Gillingham, *NATO and the Founding of the Atlantic Alliance* ; Kaplan, "Dean Acheson and the Atlantic Community," in Brinkley, *Dean Acheson and the Making of U.S. Foreign Policy*; and "The Diplomat Who Did Not Want to Be Liked," *Time*, Oct. 26, 1971, pp. 19–20. For a superb evaluation of Anglo-American ties, see Hitchens, *Blood, Class and Nostalgia*.
29. Smith, *Dean Acheson*, 416.
30. Acheson, *Present at the Creation*, 387–88.
31. Ibid.
32. "Hard Words from the Veteran American Statesman Dean Acheson, in Conversation with William Hardcastle," *Listener*, June 19, 1970.
33. DGA to Leith-Ross, Jan. 16, 1963, S 1, B 19, F 238, DGA-Yale.
34. Schwartz, *NATO's Nuclear Dilemmas*, 96–103, offers excellent evaluations of the decision to cancel Skybolt, the McNamara-Thorneycroft meeting, and Kennedy and Macmillan at Nassau. Also see Pierre, *Nuclear Politics*, 224–43; Freedman, *Britain and Nuclear Weapons*, 10–18; and Hathaway, *Great Britain and the United States*, 61–67.
35. Lord Thorneycroft, Oral history interview by David Nunnerley, June 18, 1969, JFKL, p. 16.
36. DGA to Leith-Ross, Jan. 16, 1963.
37. Barnet, *Alliance*, 212–13. Chapter 5 offers a fascinating profile of the personal relationship of Kennedy and de Gaulle.
38. DGA to Michael Janeway, March 5, 1963, S 1, B 16, F 209, DGA-Yale.
39. Nunnerley, *President Kennedy and Britain*, 3–13. For an overview of Acheson's attitude toward Anglo-American relations, see Acheson, Address at the 1963 conference on Anglo-American relations sponsored by the English-Speaking Unions of the United States and the Commonwealth, New York, New York, May 1, 1963, S 3, B 51, F 57, DGA-Yale.
40. "Hard Words," *Listener*, June 19, 1970.
41. DGA to Donnelly, April 11, 1966, Acheson Papers, Post-Administration Files, State Department and White House Advisor (hereafter, Post-Admin. Files, State and WH), 1965–1968, Foreign Aid and NATO, Folder 4, Box 88, HSTL.
42. Quoted in Peterson, *Rhodesian Independence*, 122–23.
43. Quoted in "Acheson's Gibe Returns with Some English on It," *NYT*, Nov. 23, 1969, p. 17.
44. Cook, *Charles de Gaulle*, 355–72. Chapter 18 explains the Gaullist vision of Europe in detail. Also see Barnet, *Alliance*, 212–16; Stebbins, *United States in World Affairs*, 94–139; and Camps, *European Unification in the Sixties*, 1–28.
45. Interviews with George Ball, Feb. 1988, Princeton, N.J.; J. Robert Schaetzel,

May 1989, Bethesda, Md.; and Pierre Uri, Oct. 1990, Hempstead, N.Y. Monnet created the Action Committee in 1955 to promote European integration measures and began promoting his Atlantic Partnership concept in 1959. See also Acheson-Monnet correspondence, S 1, B 23, F 288, DGA-Yale.

46. Jean Monnet, travel diary, "Voyages de Jean Monnet, 1955–1975," Monnet Papers, Fondation Jean Monnet, Ferme Dorigny, Lausanne, Switzerland.

47. Memorandum for the President, Subject: Luncheon meeting with Jean Monnet, March 6, 1961, National Security Files, Box 321, JFKL.

48. Monnet, *Memoirs*, 472. For the Ball-Monnet relationship, see Ball, "Introduction," in Brinkley and Hackett, *Jean Monnet*; and Ball, *Past Has Another Pattern*, 69–99.

49. Monnet travel diary.

50. James Reston, *NYT*, April 11, 1961.

51. For a discussion of JFK's Independence Day speech and Monnet's Action Committee resolution, see Duchene, "Jean Monnet's Methods," in Brinkley and Hackett, *Jean Monnet*, 184–209. For the text of JFK's speech, see *Public Papers of the Presidents of the United States: John F. Kennedy, 1962*, 538. For Monnet's proposal, see "Joint Declaration, June 26, 1962," in *Action Committee for the United States of Europe: Statements and Declarations, 1955–1967*, 62–65. My understanding of the JFK-Monnet relationship comes from my interviews with J. Robert Schaetzel, May 1989; and François Duchene, October 1990, Hyde Park, N.Y.

52. Quoted in Schaetzel, *Unhinged Alliance*, 41.

53. DGA to Hans J. Morgenthau, March 25, 1963, S 1, B 23, F 289, DGA-Yale. Also DGA to William L. Clayton, April 12, 1963, S 1, B 6, F 77, DGA-Yale. For a good brief discussion of the Trade Expansion Act, see Castigliola, "The Pursuit of Atlantic Community," 30–31.

54. DGA to Jean Monnet, Nov. 1962; Monnet to DGA, Nov. 23, 1962, S 1, B 23, F 288, DGA-Yale.

55. DGA to J. Robert Schaetzel, April 1, 1963, S 1, B 28, F 356, DGA-Yale.

56. De Gaulle is quoted in Grosser, *Western Alliance*, 206–08.

57. DGA to Cowles, Jan. 31, 1961, S 1, B 6, F 83, DGA-Yale.

58. Telegram, DGA to Adenauer, Jan. 18, 1963, Acheson Papers, Post Admin. Files, State and WH, Box 86, HSTL. The following day Acheson wrote Truman that he had urged Adenauer by cable "to move General de Gaulle from the disastrous course he has chartered, which, if followed, will go far to destroy the Chancellor's life work" (DGA to HST, Jan. 19, 1961, S 1, B 31, F 396, DGA-Yale).

59. Acheson, "De Gaulle and the West," *New Leader*, April 1, 1963, pp. 17–22.

60. Acheson, "The Obstacles to Partnership" (Speech delivered at California Institute of Technology, Pasadena, Cal., March 7, 1963), S 3, B 51, F 56, DGA-Yale.

61. DGA to Birrenbach, Feb. 19, 1963, S 1, B 3, F 36, DGA-Yale. Also in *AF*, 242–44.

62. Acheson wrote Michael Janeway that he had given his German friends "hell for the Chancellor's stupidity in signing the treaty with France on his visit to Paris" (DGA to Janeway, March 5, 1963, S 1, B 16, F 209, DGA-Yale).

63. DGA to Birrenbach, Feb. 19, 1963.

64. Ibid.

65. Adenauer to DGA [no date], Acheson Papers, Post-Admin. Files, State and WH, January–December 1963, Box 86, HSTL.
66. Acheson, Memorandum, "Reflections on the January Debacle," Jan. 31, 1963, Acheson Papers, Post-Admin. Files, State and WH, Box 86, HSTL.
67. Ibid.
68. Quoted in Castigliola, "Pursuit of Atlantic Community," 50.
69. DGA to Roger Warren Evans, May 20, 1963, S 1, B 9, F 115, DGA-Yale.
70. Acheson, Memorandum, Feb. 20, 1963, Acheson Papers, Post-Admin. Files, State and WH, Box 86, HSTL.
71. Rusk to DGA, Feb. 3, 1963 [Private and Confidential], Acheson Papers, Post-Admin. Files, State and WH, Box 86, HSTL.
72. Acheson, "Practice of Partnership," Jan. 1963.
73. Acheson, Memorandum, Feb. 20, 1963.
74. Acheson, "The Obstacles to Partnership" (Speech delivered at California Institute of Technology, Pasadena, California, March 7, 1963), S 1, B 51, F 56, DGA-Yale.
75. "Acheson Says U.S. Must Help NATO," *NYT*, March 8, 1963, p. 3. After ten bitter years of fratricidal European infighting, Britain was admitted to the Community in 1973.
76. Acheson, "Europe: Kaleidoscope or Clouded Crystal" (Speech delivered at the University of California, Berkeley, March 13, 1963), S 3, B 51, F 56, DGA-Yale. Also excerpted in *NYT*, March 14, 1963, p. 2.
77. Ibid.
78. Drew Middleton, "French Contest Acheson Attack," *NYT*, March 15, 1963, p. 3.
79. DGA to Louis Halle, March 19, 1963, S 1, B 15, F 190, DGA-Yale. Acheson went on to say that this brainwashing phenomenon did not happen in Bonn, London, or Rome, but that in Paris, "Cy Sulzberger, Drew Middleton, Crosby Noyes—all seemed to be putty in the hands of M. Maurois' Minion."
80. Arthur Krock, "Improbable Hypothesis for De Gaulle," *NYT*, March 15, 1963, p. 6.
81. DGA to HST, May 6, 1963, S 1, B 31, F 396, DGA-Yale.
82. Quoted in Ball, *Past Has Another Pattern*, 273.
83. See, e.g., Grosser, *Western Alliance*, 208; and Kleiman, *Atlantic Crisis*, 21–46.
84. See Edward T. O'Toole, "Acheson Calls Nationalism of de Gaulle Peril to Unity," *NYT*, Sept. 19, 1963, pp. 1, 2.
85. DGA to T. C. Bryant, Dec. 1, 1970, S 1, B 2, F 20, DGA-Yale. Also *AF*, 319. For Acheson's most candid complaints about de Gaulle, see Acheson, Interview with Public Broadcasting Corporation, Dec. 3, 1967 (reels 1–3), S 3, B 53, F 74, DGA-Yale.
86. DGA to Davies, April 18, 1963, S 1, B 7, F 93, DGA-Yale. Davies, a senior Foreign Service officer, was one of the so-called old China hands in the State Department when Acheson was secretary. See also Acheson, Oral history interview, April 27, 1964, JFKL, 31–34.
87. DGA to Halle, March 19, 1963, S 1, B 15, F 190, DGA-Yale.
88. DGA to HST, May 6, 1963, S 1, B 31, F 396, DGA-Yale.
89. DGA to Cowles, Aug. 5, 1963, S 1, B 6, F 83, DGA-Yale. Also *AF*, 250–51.
90. Alice Acheson, interview, Dec. 1986, Washington, D.C. See also Acheson,

Statement at the Institute of Strategic Studies, Cambridge, England, Sept. 20–23, 1963, S 3, B 52, F 59; Acheson, "The American Interest in European Unity" (Speech delivered at The Hague, Sept. 1963), S 3, B 52, F 58; and Acheson, "Germany in the New Europe" (Address to the German American Club, Bonn, West Germany, Oct. 18, 1963), S 3, B 52, F 59, DGA-Yale.

91. DGA to Mrs. Mortimer Seabury, Oct. 29, 1963, S 1, B 28, F 360, DGA-Yale. Mortimer and Frida Seabury were friends of the Achesons in Antigua. Also *AF*, 254–55.

92. DGA to Robert S. McNamara, Memorandum, Sept. 16, 1963, Acheson Papers, Post-Admin. Files, Box 86, HSTL.

93. Ibid.

94. Ibid.

95. Ibid. For a good short discussion of U.S.-German relations during the Adenauer to Erhard transition, see Gatzke, *Germany and the United States*, chap. 8.

96. The Erhard inaugural story is told in Bradlee, *Conversations with Kennedy*, 224–25.

97. Ibid.

98. George Ball, interview, Feb. 1988, Princeton, N.J.

99. Telegram, JFK to DGA, April 19, 1963, S 1, B 18, F 223, DGA-Yale.

100. DGA to JFK, May 6, 1963, S 1, B 18, F 223, DGA-Yale.

101. Acheson, "Thoughts Written to a British Friend on the Assassination of President Kennedy," in Acheson, *Grapes from Thorns*, 81–82.

102. DGA to Jacqueline Kennedy, Nov. 28, 1963, S 1, B 18, F 223, DGA-Yale.

103. Acheson, Remarks on the Occasion of the Diamond Jubilee Celebration for the Honorable Harry S Truman, May 8, 1959, Acheson Papers, Post-Admin. Files, Speeches and Articles, 1936–1971, Box 139, HSTL.

104. DGA to John Paton Davies, April 18, 1963, S 1, B 7, F 93, DGA-Yale.

105. Kenneth Harris, "Pungent Memories from Mr. Acheson," *Life*, July 23, 1971, p. 53. Of his controversial comments on Kennedy, Acheson wrote: "Only two other speeches since I returned to private practice have, I think, stirred up so much interest. My secretary tells me that two-thirds of the letters are violently hostile and some downright scurrilous" (DGA to William B. Loeb, July 29, 1971, S 1, B 20, F 246, DGA-Yale).

Chapter 7. Repairing Cracks in NATO, 1964–67

1. Ben A. Franklin, "20 Johnson Aides Form Cadre for an Enlarged Personal Staff," *NYT*, Nov. 24, 1963. See also Ben Bagdikian, "The 'Inner Inner Circle' around Johnson," *NYT Magazine*, Feb. 25, 1965, p. 82.

2. DGA to LBJ, Aug. 13, 1957, S 1, B 17, F 215, DGA-Yale. Also *AF*, 127–29.

3. For an overview of Acheson's role in drafting and lobbying for the Civil Rights Act of 1957, see Evans and Novak, *Lyndon B. Johnson*, 147–53; Shogan, *Question of Judgment*, 88; and Acheson, Memorandum of conversation with Lyndon Johnson, July 22, 1957, S 5, B 73, F 1, DGA-Yale. After the bill was passed, LBJ wrote Acheson: "A breath of fresh air has finally been brought into the civil rights issue and minds

once closed are now receptive to logic. The result is due in no small measure to your wise counsel and to your selfless willingness to help in a difficult situation" (LBJ to DGA, Aug. 8, 1957, S 5, B 73, F 1, DGA-Yale).

4. Evans and Novak, *Lyndon B. Johnson*, 262.

5. Johnson is quoted in C. L. Sulzberger, "A Confident Man at the Helm," *NYT*, Nov. 27, 1963.

6. Stuart Symington, interview, Nov. 1987, New Canaan, Conn.

7. Henry Owen, interview, Sept. 1990, Washington, D.C.

8. Joseph Alsop, interview, March 1988, Washington, D.C.

9. Murphy, *Fortas*, 117. Also William P. Bundy, interview, Aug. 1988, Princeton, N.J.

10. DGA to Arthur J. Freund, December 3, 1963, S 1, B 12, F 152, DGA-Yale. Also in *AF*, 257.

11. DGA to Sir William Haley, Dec. 2, 1963, S 1, B 15, F 187, DGA-Yale. Also in *AF*, 256.

12. Acheson, Memorandum on United States policy toward Germany, Dec. 5, 1963, Acheson Papers, Post-Administration Files, State Department and White House Advisor (hereafter, Post-Admin. Files, State and WH), January–December 1963, Box 86, HSTL. These ideas also appear in Acheson, "Withdrawal From Europe? 'An Illusion,'" *NYT Magazine*, Dec. 15, 1963, p. 7.

13. McGeorge Bundy to LBJ, Dec. 6, 1963, LBJL. Quoted in Isaacson and Thomas, *Wise Men*, 645.

14. See account in Campbell, *Foreign Affairs Fudge Factory*, 70–74. Acheson gave Campbell permission to publish the *Hello, Dolly!* cancellation story, but he later asked him to tone down the language. See John Franklin Campbell to Barbara Evans (Draft of chap. 4), Oct. 6, 1970, Brookings Institution File, S 1, B 4, F 47, DGA-Yale.

15. Ibid.

16. Joseph Alsop, interview, March 1988, Washington, D.C.

17. For examples of LBJ's need to surround himself with yes-men, see Geyelin, *Lyndon B. Johnson and the World*, 133–34; Conklin, *Big Daddy from the Pedernales*, 173–207; and Barnet, *Alliance*, 234–80.

18. Isaacson and Thomas, *Wise Men*, 647. For other examples of his flattery of Acheson, see Photocopies of correspondence from LBJL, B 73, F 2, DGA-Yale.

19. Alsop, interview, March 1988. The speech was Acheson, "U.S. Interests and Objectives in Free Europe" (Speech delivered at the National War College, Washington, D.C., Jan. 20, 1964), S 3, B 51, F 62, DGA-Yale.

20. Quoted in Tom Wicker, "President Urges NATO Head Trend in Eastern Bloc," *NYT*, April 4, 1964, p. 1.

21. Mary Acheson Bundy, interview, Aug. 1988, Princeton, N.J.

22. DGA to Anthony Eden, June 18, 1964, S 1, B 9, F 118, DGA-Yale.

23. See, e.g., DGA to Patrick Devlin, April 2, 1964, S 1, B 8, F 97, DGA-Yale. Acheson wrote Devlin that "Lyndon Johnson has been doing so well that one looks for a return to more normal governmental confusion. A section of the press complains that he is not Kennedy—but little can be done about that; another, that he cannot by a 'bold new policy' (Fulbright) cause de Gaulle, Castro and Ho Chi Minh

to disappear—but, again, this is normal American adolescent annoyance with that intractible external realm."

24. Quoted in Kosut, *Cyprus*, 131. Much of this section on Acheson and Cyprus appeared in Brinkley, "The Cyprus Question: Dean Acheson as Mediator," 5–19.

25. Ball, interview, Feb. 1988. Acheson and Ball became friends in 1933 when Acheson was serving as under secretary of the treasury and Ball, fresh out of Northwestern University Law School, worked for the Farm Credit Administration and the Treasury Department. Over the next thirty-eight years they grew increasingly close. In fact, by 1964 Acheson had more respect for Ball's abilities than for those of any other Johnson administration figure. This is ironic when one considers that Ball was known throughout Washington as a "Stevenson man." Acheson was willing to overlook this normally fatal flaw because Ball was an outspoken "Europe-firster." Ball, in his turn, considered Acheson "a courageous giant." Ball's memoirs note that one of his most cherished possessions was a handwritten note Acheson sent him just two weeks before his death: "Keep on making sense; you have the field to yourself" (Ball, *Past Has Another Pattern*, 358).

26. See Ball, *Past Has Another Pattern*, chap. 23, for Ball's analysis of the mediation efforts in Cyprus.

27. Ball, interview, Feb. 1988.

28. There are a number of valuable monographs that detail the creation and the collapse of the first Cypriot republic. For example, see Ehrlich, *Cyprus, 1958–1967*; Crawshaw, *Cyprus Revolt*; Markides, *Rise and Fall of the Cyprus Republic*; Foley and Scobie, *Struggle of Cyprus*; and Couloumbis, *United States, Greece and Turkey*, chap. 2. On the possibilities of the survival of the London-Zurich constitutional arrangements, see Intelligence Report 8047/U.S. Department of State/INR, "Analysis of the Cyprus Agreements," July 14, 1959, published in *Journal of the Hellenic Diaspora* 11, no. 4 (Winter 1984), pp. 9–31. It is interesting to see how well this document anticipated the troubles of 1963–64.

29. For details of the NATO plan of 1964, which would have virtually eliminated the Cyprus government, see Coufoudakis, "U.S. Foreign Policy and the Cyprus Question: An Interpretation"; and Windsor, "NATO and the Cyprus Crisis," *Adelphi Papers*, no. 14, 11/1964.

30. See Coufoudakis, "United States Foreign Policy and the Cyprus Question: A Case Study in Cold War Diplomacy"; and Hitchens, *Hostage to History*.

31. Quoted in Brands, "America Enters the Cyprus Tangle," 360.

32. Joseph, *Cyprus*, 130–31.

33. See Ball, *Past Has Another Pattern*, 355–57, for the events described in this section.

34. The text of the famous Johnson letter to Inonu can be found in Cyprus, Public Information Office, *Cyprus: The Problem in Perspective*.

35. Ball, *Past Has Another Pattern*, 355–56.

36. Ibid.

37. "Acheson Assumes Cypriot Mission," *NYT*, July 4, 1964, p. 1; and Max Frankel, "Johnson Renews Plea to Premiers for Cyprus Talks," *NYT*, July 5, 1964, p. 1.

Acheson was impressed with the "first class competence" Jernegan displayed during their eight-week Geneva ordeal (DGA to George W. Ball, Oct. 12, 1964, Acheson Papers, Post-Admin. Files, State and WH, 1964, Box 87, HSTL.

38. Quoted in Joseph, *Cyprus*, 132.

39. See Thomas J. Hamilton, "Thant Proposes Vietnam Parley to End Fighting," *NYT*, July 9, 1964, p. 2.

40. "Acheson and Briton Confer," *NYT*, July 10, 1964, p. 3.

41. For Acheson's own account of the Geneva talks, in an address to the Chicago Bar Association, see Acheson, "Cyprus: The Anatomy of the Problem," May 1965. Acheson concluded that his experience in Geneva "was not the brightest chapter in the diplomacy of the west." A transcript of the address can be found in Acheson Papers, Post-Admin. Files, Speeches and Articles, 1936–1971, Box 141, HSTL.

42. The most comprehensive evaluation of the Acheson Plan can be found in Coufoudakis, "United States Foreign Policy and the Cyprus Question: A Case Study," 114–17.

43. Ibid., 116–17. For Acheson's pre-Geneva views on how to mediate the Cyprus dispute, see Acheson, Memorandum, July 1, 1964, Acheson Papers, State and WH, 1964, July–October, Box 86, HSTL. Also Ball, interview, Feb. 1988.

44. Coufoudakis, "United States Foreign Policy and the Cyprus Question: A Case Study," 115.

45. Quoted in Joseph, *Cyprus*, 132.

46. See, e.g., "Makarios Scores Acheson's Views," *NYT*, July 31, 1964, p. 1.

47. Quoted in Acheson, "Cyprus: The Anatomy of the Problem," May 1965.

48. DGA to Luke Battle, Dec. 7, 1964, Acheson Papers, Post-Admin. Files, State and WH, 1964, Nov.–Dec., Box 87, HSTL.

49. Ball, *Past Has Another Pattern*, 358. Also Ball, interview, Feb. 1988.

50. Ball, *Past Has Another Pattern*.

51. Memorandum for the Record, Background briefing to press by Dean Rusk and George Ball, Sept. 4, 1964, Acheson Papers, Post-Admin. Files, State and WH, 1964, Sept.–Oct., Box 87, HSTL.

52. DGA to Luke Battle, Dec. 7, 1964. For Acheson's belief that "the Greeks with all their gifts have no sense," see DGA to Harlan Cleveland, Feb. 23, 1966, S 1, B 6, F 77, DGA-Yale. For an excellent journalistic evaluation of why the Acheson Plan failed, see Crosby Noyes, "Acheson Had Wide-Ranging Plan," *Washington Star*, Sept. 2, 1964.

53. DGA to Dr. Nihat Erim, Dec. 21, 1964, Acheson Papers, State and WH, 1964, Nov.–Dec., Box 87, HSTL. Acheson's meetings with Butler and Mountbatten are discussed in McGeorge Bundy, Memorandum for the record, Sept. 8, 1964, National Security Council Files of McGeorge Bundy, Boxes 18–19, LBJL.

54. Tad Szulc, "Acheson Warns of Peril in Cyprus," *NYT*, Sept. 5, 1964, p. 1.

55. Lyndon B. Johnson, News conference, Sept. 5, 1964, in George W. Johnson, *Johnson Presidential Press Conferences* 1:207.

56. DGA to Ranald MacDonald, Sept. 6, 1964. S 1, B 21, F 264, DGA-Yale.

57. McGeorge Bundy, Memorandum for the record, Sept. 8, 1964.

58. For a discussion of the role the Greek American lobby played in U.S. foreign-policy decision making, see Hackett, "Role of Congress and Greek-American Relations."

The 1974 Cyprus crisis is discussed in Coufoudakis, "American Foreign Policy and the Cyprus Problem." For an informative analysis of the role the Acheson Plan played in Henry Kissinger's handling of Cyprus in 1974, see Coufoudakis, "Cyprus—July 1974"; and Bell, *Diplomacy of Detente*, 138–55.

59. McGeorge Bundy to DGA, Sept. 15, 1964, Photocopies of correspondence from LBJL, B 73, F 2, DGA-Yale; Semple, "Johnson Selects Foreign Advisors," NYT, Sept. 10, 1964, p. 1; and DGA to LBJ, March 16, 1965, Acheson Papers, Post-Admin. Files, State and WH, 1965–68, NATO Folder 2, Box 87, HSTL.

60. Acheson, "Trust and Confidence," *Washington Post*, Oct. 7, 1964. See also Statement by Dean Acheson (Press release), Oct. 4, 1964, S 3, B 51, F 63, DGA-Yale.

61. See Dean Acheson interview with Public Broadcasting Corporation, December 3, 1967 (reel 2), S 3, B 53, F 74, DGA-Yale; "Johnson Supported by Lawyers' Group," NYT, Oct. 3, 1964, p. 16; and "President Appoints Panel to Seek Halt in Nuclear Spread," NYT, Nov. 2, 1964, p. 1.

62. Acheson, Memorandum to McGeorge Bundy, Oct. 26, 1964, Acheson Papers, Post-Admin. Files, State and WH, Sept.–Oct. 1964, Box 86, HSTL.

63. DGA to LBJ, Oct. 11, 1964, Photocopies of correspondence from LBJL, B 73, F 2, DGA-Yale.

64. DGA to Berry, Nov. 20, 1964, S 1, B 3, F 33, DGA-Yale. Also in AF, 262–63.

65. Acheson, Memorandum to LBJ, Dec. 21, 1964, Acheson Papers, Post-Admin. Files, State and WH, Nov.–Dec. 1964, Box 87, HSTL. Acheson provided LBJ with a list of "good men" who deserved an ambassadorial appointment, or a promotion within the State Department.

66. Isaacson and Thomas, *Wise Men*, 644.

67. See account in Geyelin, *Lyndon B. Johnson and the World*, 162.

68. DGA to Devlin, Dec. 6, 1964, S 1, B 8, F 97, DGA-Yale.

69. David Acheson, interview, Dec. 1987, Washington, D.C.

70. Acheson, "U.S. Policy toward Europe," Memorandum to LBJ, Nov. 19, 1964, Acheson Papers, Post-Admin. Files, State and WH, Nov.–Dec. 1964, Box 87, HSTL.

71. Ibid.; and Acheson, Memorandum to LBJ, Dec. 14, 1964; Acheson Papers, Post-Admin. Files, State and WH, Nov.–Dec. 1964, Box 87, HSTL.

72. For examples of Acheson's disapproval of LBJ's efforts at détente with the Soviet Union, see DGA to General Earle G. Wheeler, Nov. 1, 1965, S 1, B 34, F 433, DGA-Yale; Dean Acheson interview with Public Broadcasting Corporation, Dec. 7, 1967 (Transcript of reels 1–3), S 3, B 53, F 74, DGA-Yale; and Testimony of Dean Acheson, House Committee on Foreign Affairs, Subcommittee on Europe, Hearings on the Crisis in NATO, May 17, 1966, pp. 182–84. Also interviews with George Ball, Feb. 1988, Princeton, N.J.; and Paul Nitze, Sept. 1987, Washington, D.C.

73. See Ronald Steel, *Walter Lippmann and the American Century*, 538. Also see Joseph Alsop, interview, March 1988, Washington, D.C.

74. DGA to LBJ, Nov. 25, 1964, Acheson Papers, Post-Admin. Files, State and WH, Nov.–Dec. 1964, Box 87, HSTL.

75. See DGA memorandums to LBJ, Nov. 19, Nov. 30, Dec. 3, Dec. 14, and

Dec. 21, 1964; Acheson Papers, Post-Admin. Files, State and WH, Nov.–Dec. 1964, Box 87, HSTL.

76. DGA, "Forward March for the Alliance," Memorandum for LBJ, Nov. 30, 1964.

77. For Bundy story, see Geyelin, *Lyndon B. Johnson and the World*, 171. The MLF debate within the Johnson Administration is discussed on pages 159–80 of that work, and in Stromseth, *Origins of Flexible Response*, 75–85.

78. For an evaluation of the obstacles which advancing MLF would have created, see McGeorge Bundy, Memorandum to Rusk, McNamara, Ball, Nov. 25, 1964; Subject: The Future of MLF, National Security File, Aides File, Box 2, McGeorge Bundy—Memos to the President, vol. 7, LBJL.

79. DGA to the Earl of Avon [Anthony Eden] [undated, 1965], S 1, B 9, F 118, DGA-Yale.

80. DGA to Annan, March 15, 1965, S 1, B 1, F 12, DGA-Yale. Also in *AF*, 265–66.

81. DGA to LBJ, March 15, 1965, Acheson Papers, Post-Admin. Files, State and WH, 1965–68, NATO (Folder 2), Box 87, HSTL.

82. DGA to Annan, March 15, 1965. Also in *AF*, 265–66. For an overview of Acheson's concerns for Europe in spring 1965, see Acheson, "Ambivalences of American Foreign Policy," in *TVER*, 138–56. The article is a transcript of a speech Acheson delivered at Indiana University on March 5, 1965.

83. Acheson, "Study Needed of U.S. Policy towards Europe," Memorandum for the President, March 31, 1965, Acheson Papers, Post-Admin. Files, State and WH, 1965–68, NATO (Folder 2), Box 87, HSTL; and LBJ to DGA, April 1, 1965, Photocopies of Correspondence from LBJL, B 74, F 2, DGA-Yale.

84. For Acheson's tribute to Frankfurter, see Acheson, "Felix Frankfurter, 1882–1965," in *Fragments of My Fleece*, 219–22.

85. See DGA to Erik Boheman, July 7, 1965, S 1, B 3, F 40, DGA-Yale. Also in *AF*, 270–72. For an explanation of Acheson's various ailments, see DGA to Ada and Archibald MacLeish, June 24, 1965, *AF*, 269.

86. Ball, interview, Feb. 1988.

87. Correspondence concerning publication and reviews of *Morning and Noon* can be found in S 3, B 59–60, F 105–15, DGA-Yale.

88. Dean Acheson interview with PBC, Dec. 3, 1967, reel 1 transcript, pp. 16–17.

89. DGA to HST, July 10, 1965, S 1, B 31, F 397, DGA-Yale. Also in *AF*, 272–73. For Acheson's most comprehensive assessment of the Great Society, which he called "the greatest idea President Johnson ever had," see Acheson interview with PBC, Dec. 3, 1967 (reel 3 transcript), S 3, B 53, F 74, DGA-Yale.

90. For the most authoritative account of the Dominican crisis, see Lowenthal, *Dominican Intervention*. A brief overview of the Johnson administration's Latin American policy can be found in LaFeber, "Latin American Policy." The complicated negotiations which Ambassador Ellsworth Bunker undertook to settle the Dominican crisis are evaluated in Bracey, *Resolution of the Dominican Crisis*.

91. DGA to Boheman, July 7, 1965, S 1, B 3, F 40, DGA-Yale. Also in *AF*, 270–71.

92. DGA to HST, July 10, 1965, S 1, B 31, F 397, DGA-Yale. Also in *AF*, 272–73.

93. DGA to the Editor, *Atlantic Community Quarterly*, Nov. 4, 1965, S 3, B 53, F 68, DGA-Yale.

94. Acheson, Speech to Brooks School, *Fence View*, November 11, 1965 (unidentifiable newspaper clipping), S 3, B 60, F 115, DGA-Yale.

95. See de Gaulle, Memoranda to the NATO nations, March 11, and 29, 1966, reprinted as Appendixes A and C in Hunt, "NATO without France," 22–25. For brief overviews of the 1966 NATO crisis, see Stebbins, *United States and World Affairs, 1966*, 154–66; Kaplan, *NATO and the United States*, 115–22; and Stromseth, *Origins of Flexible Response*, 108–20.

96. Quoted in Stromseth, *Origins of Flexible Response*, 109. For a detailed overview of why de Gaulle decided to withdraw from NATO, see Harrison, *Reluctant Ally*, 134–63.

97. Benjamin Welles, "14 in NATO Draft Reply to France," *NYT*, March 12, 1966, p. 1; "NATO: A Question of Survival," *Newsweek*, March 28, 1966; DGA to Sir William Elliot, May 17, 1966, S 1, B 9, F 122, DGA-Yale; and J. Robert Schaetzel, interview, June 1990, Bethesda, Md.

98. Bohlen, *Witness to History*, 507.

99. Johnson, *Vantage Point*, 305.

100. Quoted in Barnet, *Alliance*, 238.

101. Testimony of Dean Acheson, Senate Subcommittee on National Security and International Operations, *Hearings on the Atlantic Alliance*, 89th Cong., 2d sess. (Hereafter, *Alliance Hearings*.) April 27, 1966 (Washington, D.C.: G.P.O., 1966), S 3, B 53, F 70, DGA-Yale.

102. LBJ's letter to de Gaulle is part of the State Department Administrative History, Section 5, French withdrawal and NATO counter-measures, LBJL.

103. Quoted in Benjamin Welles, "Johnson Pledges U.S. Won't Abandon NATO," *NYT*, April 5, 1966, p. 13.

104. Transcript of television interview of Dean Acheson by Marvin Kalb, *CBS News*, April 4, 1966, S 3, B 53, F 70, DGA-Yale.

105. Ibid.

106. DGA to Donnelly, April 11, 1966, Acheson Papers, Post-Admin. Files, State and WH, 1965–68, Foreign Aid and NATO, Folder 4, Box 88, HSTL.

107. "The Undiplomatic Diplomats," *Newsweek*, April 25, 1966, p. 39; J. Robert Schaetzel, interview, Dec. 1987, Bethesda, Md.

108. Testimony of Dean Acheson, *Alliance Hearings*, April 27, 1966.

109. Ibid.

110. Max Frankel, "U.S. to Ask Bonn to Forgo Share in Nuclear Arms," *NYT*, April 27, 1966, p. 1. Acheson remained furious with Frankel for distorting his views on nuclear sharing. "I consider the April 27 article in the *New York Times* to be one of the most irresponsible and misleading pieces I have seen in some time," Acheson wrote his German friend Kurt Birrenbach. "I can well appreciate the problems that reports like this cause our German friends. I hope my statement [before the Jackson subcommittee] did something to repair the damage" (DGA to Birrenbach, May 25, 1966, Acheson Papers, Post-Admin. Files, State and WH, 1965–68, Foreign Aid and NATO, Folder 4, Box 88, HSTL). Rusk, also perturbed by Frankel's "misstatement of facts," issued a disclaimer on April 27, saying that the United States had "made no decision to foreclose a possible Atlantic nuclear force or any other collective approach" that would allow Bonn to participate in "the management of nuclear power." See Max Frankel, "Bar to Atom Role for Bonn Denied," *NYT*, April 28, 1966, p. 1.

111. Testimony of Dean Acheson, *Alliance Hearings*, April 27, 1966.
112. Ibid.
113. Testimony of Dean Acheson, House Committee on Foreign Affairs, Subcommittee on Europe, Hearings on the crisis in NATO, May 17, 1966, pp. 171–95, S 3, B 53, F 71, DGA-Yale. For a brief discussion of the shift in administration policy, see Rostow, *Diffusion of Power*, 400.
114. Benjamin Welles, "U.S. Wants NATO to Develop Policy to Reduce Tension," *NYT*, May 18, 1966, p. 1.
115. DGA to Birrenbach, May 25, 1966, Acheson Papers, Post-Admin. Files, State and WH, 1965–68, Foreign Aid and NATO, Folder 4, Box 88, HSTL.
116. For example, see Max Frankel, "NATO as Acheson Conceived It," *NYT*, May 1, 1966, IV, p. 3.
117. See Richard L. Strout, "Acheson Stiffens NATO Line on France," *Christian Science Monitor*; and Steel, *Walter Lippmann and the American Century*.
118. PBC interview, Dec. 3, 1967, reel 2 transcript, p. 21. For an unambiguous statement of Acheson's contempt for Fulbright, see DGA to the Editor, *Washington Post*, Dec. 29, 1967, "Acheson on Fulbright," S 3, B 53, F 74, DGA-Yale.
119. 9, F 118, DGA to Eden, May 17, 1966, S 1, B 9, F 118, DGA-Yale.
120. DGA to Elliot, May 17, 1966, S 1, B 9, F 122, DGA-Yale.
121. DGA to W. Averell Harriman, April 18, 1966, JFK-LBJ Administrations, Special Files, Public Service, Acheson File, Box 429, MSS, Harriman Papers.
122. DGA to HST, Oct. 3, 1966, S 1, B 31, F 398, DGA-Yale.
123. DGA to Elliot, May 17, 1966.
124. DGA memorandums to LBJ: "Broad Lines of Approach toward the France-NATO Crisis," March 26, 1966; "Broad Lines of Approach toward Negotiations with France in NATO Crisis," May 13, 1966; "The Nuclear Problem in NATO," May 24, 1966; "Measures to Increase Cohesion of NATO, Final Response to NSAM 345," June 3, 1966; and "Bilateral Negotiations with France on Re-entry Rights and Facilities," June 27, 1966; State Department Administrative History, French withdrawal and NATO counter-measures, LBJL.
125. DGA to HST, Oct. 3, 1966, S 1, B 31, F 398, DGA-Yale. Also in *AF*, 281–82.
126. DGA to HST, June 28, 1966, Acheson Papers, Post-Admin. Files, State and WH, 1965–68, Europe-Foreign Aid-NATO, Folder 5, Box 88, HSTL. (Acheson draft for Truman letter attached.)
127. DGA to HST, Oct. 3, 1966. See also DGA to Lord Richard Casey, Aug. 15, 1966, Photocopies of correspondence from LBJL, B 73, F 2, DGA-Yale.
128. DGA to Stikker, July 11, 1966, Acheson Papers, Post-Admin. Files, State and WH, 1965–68, Europe-Foreign Aid-NATO, Folder 5, Box 88, HSTL. On June 21 the Belgian Chamber of Representatives approved the transfer of SHAPE to Belgium. Later, on October 26, the North Atlantic Council decided to move NATO headquarters to Brussels.
129. DGA to Casey, Aug. 15, 1966, Photocopies of correspondence from LBJL, B 73, F 2, DGA-Yale. For further evidence of Acheson's unhappiness with the way the State Department was being run, see DGA to Edward E. Wright, May 19, 1966, S 1, B 33, F 422, DGA-Yale.
130. DGA to Casey, Aug. 15, 1966. Also see DGA to the Earl of Avon (Anthony Eden), June 29, 1966, S 1, B 31, F 398, DGA-Yale (also in *AF*, 278–79).

131. Rusk to DGA, July 18, 1966, Acheson Papers, Post-Admin. Files, State and WH, 1965–68, Europe-Foreign Aid-NATO, Folder 5, Box 88, HSTL.

132. DGA to the Earl of Avon, June 29, 1966.

133. LBJ to DGA, July 15, 1966, Acheson Papers, Post-Admin. Files, State and WH, 1965–68, Europe-Foreign Aid-NATO, Folder 5, Box 88, HSTL.

134. Quoted in William Pannill, "Former Secretary of State Speaks His Mind at U-M Seminar," *Detroit Free Press*, Oct. 8, 1967, p. 14C.

135. PBC interview, Dec. 3, 1967, reel 2 transcript. For Acheson's continued disillusion with LBJ's Atlantic policy, see DGA to J. Robert Schaetzel, March 31, 1967, S 1, B 28, F 357, DGA-Yale.

Chapter 8. The Vietnam War, 1961–68

1. For Acheson's China policy while he was secretary of state, see Cohen, "Acheson, His Advisors, and China"; and Tucker, *Patterns in the Dust*. Asian policy also is discussed in Smith, *Dean Acheson*, chaps. 5, 7, 8, 10, 11, and 12. The point about Acheson's flexibility in Asian affairs was made by William P. Bundy in a letter to the author (May 16, 1990).

2. Salmon, "Statesmanship of Dean Acheson" (Ph.D. diss.). Also interview with George Ball, Feb. 1988, Princeton, N.J.

3. Dean Acheson, interview with Public Broadcasting Corporation, Dec. 3, 1967 (hereafter, PBC interview), (reel 1 transcript), S 3, B 53, F 74, DGA-Yale. For an evaluation of the Kennedy administration's policies toward Vietnam, see Gibbons, *U.S. Government and the Vietnam War*, vol. 2: *1963–1964*; Pelz, "John F. Kennedy's 1961 Vietnam War Decisions"; and Rust, *Kennedy in Vietnam*.

4. For the transition in Vietnam policy from JFK to LBJ, see Herring, *America's Longest War*, 108–14. The decision to support the overthrow of Diem is best recounted in Berman, *Planning a Tragedy*, 23–30.

5. Acheson, PBC interview, reel 1 transcript, S 3, B 53, F 74, DGA-Yale.

6. Douglass Cater, interview, Dec. 1988, Baltimore, Md.

7. Ibid.; and Cater, Memorandum to LBJ, May 19, 1964, Cater Memos, National Security Name File, LBJL.

8. Cater, interview, Dec. 1988; and Bundy, letter to author, May 16, 1990.

9. All quotes are from Gibbons, *U.S. Government and the Vietnam War*, Vol. 2: *1963–1964*, pp. 252–60.

10. See William P. Bundy, unpublished manuscript on the Vietnam War, chap. 13: "To the Brink and Back: May and June of 1964." A copy was provided to the author by Mr. Bundy. The manuscript is available to scholars at the Lyndon B. Johnson Library.

11. Halberstam, *Best and the Brightest*, 403–04.

12. For detailed narratives of the Gulf of Tonkin episode, see Goulden, *Truth Is the First Casualty*; and Galloway, *Gulf of Tonkin Resolution*.

13. Acheson, "Ethics in International Relations Today" (Address delivered at Amherst College, Dec. 9, 1964), Acheson Papers, Post-Admin. File, Speeches and Articles 1936–71, Box 140, HSTL. Also in *TVER*, 127–37. For why Acheson approved of the Tonkin resolution, see Acheson, PBC interview, reel 2 transcript.

Acheson's Amherst address left an indelible and unfavorable impression on Democratic Party liberals, who had respected Acheson as secretary of state but now thought him an atavistic cold warrior. "We will pay a growing price in blood, money and futility if we allow Mr. Acheson's theories to dominate current policy," wrote Wayne Morse, one of the two senators to vote against the Tonkin resolution, in direct reference to Acheson's Amherst address (Morse, "Morse on Acheson," *Washington Post*, Dec. 24, 1967). For Acheson's response, see "Acheson on Morse," *Washington Post*, Dec. 30, 1967. Both letters to the *Post* can be found in Acheson Papers, Post-Admin. File, Speeches and Articles 1936–71, Box 141, HSTL.

14. "Acheson Speech Assailed," *NYT*, Dec. 18, 1964, p. 32.

15. Acheson, "The American Image Will Take Care of Itself," *NYT Magazine*, Feb. 28, 1965, p. 24. Reprinted in Acheson, *Grapes from Thorns*, 160–68.

16. Taylor, *Swords and Plowshares*, 323–47.

17. Military details are from Herring, *America's Longest War*, 127–34.

18. Ibid. See also Schandler, *Lyndon Johnson and Vietnam*, chap. 1.

19. Television interview of Dean Acheson by Eric Sevareid, *CBS News—Who, What, When, Where, Why*, Sept. 28, 1969 (transcript), S 3, B 54, F 80; and Acheson, "Vietnam: An Asian Greece," *Detroit News*, Jan. 14, 1966, S 3, B 53, F 69, DGA-Yale. Also George Ball, interview, Feb. 1988, Princeton, N.J.; and Dean Rusk telephone interview, April 1989, Athens, Ga.

20. Quoted in Ball, *Past Has Another Pattern*, 392–93.

21. Ibid., 393–94.

22. Ibid., 394.

23. Ball, interview, Feb. 1988.

24. Dean Acheson and George Ball, Memorandum for the President: A Plan for a Political Resolution in South Viet-Nam (hereafter, "Plan for Resolution"), May 1965, Ball Papers. For a valuable overview of the Acheson-Ball peace plan, see DiLeo, *George Ball, Vietnam and the Rethinking of Containment*, 89–90.

25. Lloyd Cutler, telephone interview, Dec. 1988, Washington, D.C.

26. Acheson and Ball, "Plan for Resolution."

27. Ibid.

28. Acheson, PBC interview, reel 3 transcript, S 3, B 53, F 74, DGA-Yale.

29. Isaacson and Thomas, *Wise Men*, 649.

30. Acheson memorandums to George Ball (all marked *top secret*): "Questions and Comments relating to 'A Plan for a Political Resolution in South Viet-Nam,'" "Fundamental Factors in a Political Settlement in South Vietnam," and "The Mechanics of Executing the Proposed 'Plan for a Political Resolution in South Viet-Nam,'" May 20, 1965, Ball Papers.

31. Acheson, Memorandum to Ball: "Mechanics of Executing the Proposed 'Plan for a Political Resolution in South Viet-Nam.'"

32. Ibid.

33. Acheson, Memorandums to Ball: "Questions and Comments Relating to 'A Plan for a Political Resolution in South Viet-Nam'" and "Fundamental Factors in a Political Settlement in South Vietnam."

34. Ball, interview, Feb. 1988.

35. Telegram, Under Secretary of State George Ball to Ambassadors Taylor and Johnson (9 pages), May 25, 1965, Ball Papers. For Taylor's meetings with Acheson, see Maxwell Taylor Diary notes, June 7–12, Maxwell Taylor Papers, U.S. National Defense University, Washington, D.C.

36. Ball, *Past Has Another Pattern*, 395.

37. Acheson and Ball, "Plan for Resolution," Ball Papers.

38. DGA to Erik Boheman, July 7, 1965, S 1, B 3, F 40, DGA-Yale. Also in *AF*, 270–72.

39. DGA to Donnelly, July 6, 1965, S 1, B 8, F 106, DGA-Yale.

40. DGA to Boheman, July 7, 1965.

41. Isaacson and Thomas, *Wise Men*, 646. Throughout the remainder of LBJ's presidency, these elder statesmen were called by administration officials the Wise Men. Acheson despised the term; he told Dean Rusk that they were all "just a bunch of S.O.B.'s from out of town."

42. Ibid., 650. Bundy is quoted in ibid., 651. For a detailed evaluation of the advisory debate and the monumental decisions Johnson made in July 1965, see Berman, *Planning a Tragedy*, 94–129; and Gibbons, *U.S. Government and Vietnam War*, 3:349–65.

43. DGA to HST, July 10, 1965, S 1, B 31, F 397, DGA-Yale. Also in *AF*, 272–73.

44. LBJ to DGA, July 10, 1965, Photocopies of correspondence from LBJL, B 73, F 2, DGA-Yale.

45. McGeorge Bundy, interview, April 1988, New York, N.Y. "Mustache" quote in Isaacson and Thomas, *Wise Men*, 652.

46. Ball, interview, Feb. 1988.

47. See "U.S. Leaders Back Johnson in Vietnam," *NYT*, Sept. 9, 1965, p. 2.

48. Ralph Blumenthal, "Vietnam Backers Urged to 'Shout'," *NYT*, Nov. 29, 1965, p. 1. For Acheson's advice to LBJ on Vietnam in fall 1965, see DGA to Joseph A. Califano, Jr., Dec. 3, 1965, S 1, B 5, F 62, DGA-Yale.

49. Maurice Carroll, "138 U.S. Leaders Chide War Foes," *NYT*, Nov. 14, 1966, p. 11.

50. See DeBenedetti, "Lyndon Johnson and the Antiwar Opposition." For Johnson's endorsement of the warning from Freedom House that "extremist" attacks on U.S. Vietnam policy could delay negotiation of a peaceful settlement, see Robert E. Kintner, Memorandum for Walt Rostow, Nov. 21, 1966, S 5, B 73, F 2, DGA-Yale.

51. McPherson, *Political Education*, 402–03.

52. Charles Tyroler II, interview, March 1988, Washington, D.C.; Membership Roster of the Committee for Peace with Freedom in Vietnam, S 4, B 67, F 167, DGA-Yale; and Douglas to DGA, Oct. 11, 1967, S 1, B 9, F 111, DGA-Yale.

53. Paul Douglas, Press release memo, Oct. 23, 1967, S 1, B 9, F 111, DGA-Yale. See also McPherson, *Political Education*, 403.

54. DGA to Cowles, Oct. 27, 1965, S 1, B 7, F 84, DGA-Yale.

55. Acheson, PBC interview, reel 3 transcript.

56. DGA to John Cowles, Aug. 27, 1967, S 1, B 7, F 84, DGA-Yale.

57. William Pannill, "Former Secretary of State Speaks His Mind at U-M Seminar," *Detroit Free Press*, Oct. 8, 1967, p. 14C.

58. DGA to Eden, Oct. 14, 1967, S 1, B 9, F 119, DGA-Yale.
59. Quoted in Isaacson and Thomas, *Wise Men*, 654.
60. DGA to Eden, Oct. 14, 1967.
61. DGA to Cowles, Aug. 27, 1967.
62. Walt W. Rostow, telephone interview, March 1988, Austin, Tex.; McGeorge Bundy, interview, April 1988, New York, N.Y.
63. Newspaper clipping (n.p., n.d.) describing Acheson's speech entitled "Fence View," delivered to Brooks School, Nov. 11, 1965, S 3, B 60, F 115, DGA-Yale.
64. LBJ to DGA, April 11, 1968, S 1, B 17, F 215, DGA-Yale.
65. DGA to HST [n.d.; probably April 1967], S 1, B 31, F 398, DGA-Yale. The November 1967 advisory group was different from the group chosen in July 1965; LBJ had dropped some names and added others.
66. DGA to Tuchman, June 1, 1967, S 1, B 31, F 401, DGA-Yale. Tuchman had written Acheson to urge him to talk to LBJ about the folly of America's policies in Vietnam.
67. Isaacson and Thomas, *Wise Men*, 677–79.
68. Quotes in ibid., 679. For a more detailed account of Acheson's role in the November 1967 meetings, see Berman, *Lyndon Johnson's War*, 96–113.
69. Acheson, PBC interview, reels 1–3, transcripts, S 3, B 53, F 74, DGA-Yale. Also see John Sibley, "Acheson Dubious of Talks on War," *NYT*, Dec. 4, 1967, p. 3.
70. Isaacson and Thomas, *Wise Men*, 681–82. Former senator Eugene McCarthy remembered Acheson from 1965 to 1967 as hostile to even the mention of withdrawal, while Harriman had embarked on a crusade to alter administration policies on Vietnam. McCarthy recalls Harriman saying, "Remember folks, I was the one who first warned Truman of the Russian threat, and I'm now going to tell Johnson to get out of Vietnam" (Eugene McCarthy, interview, March 1990, Toronto, Canada).
71. DGA to Eden, Dec. 31, 1967, S 1, B 9, F 118, DGA-Yale. Also quoted in Isaacson and Thomas, *Wise Men*, 683–84.
72. For a brief discussion of why the *Pueblo* incident failed to affect Vietnam policy, see Berman, *Lyndon Johnson's War*, 144–45.
73. Hoopes, *Limits of Intervention*, 204. Also see Schandler, *Lyndon Johnson and Vietnam*, 257–58.
74. DGA to Cowles, Feb. 27, 1968, S 1, B 7, F 85, DGA-Yale. Also in *AF*, 288–91.
75. Ibid.
76. Acheson, Confidential memorandum, Meeting with the President Re: Vietnam and the Gold Crisis, March 14, 1968 (hereafter, Vietnam and Gold Crisis), S 4, B 68, F 173, DGA-Yale. Also in *AF*, 292–94. See Lorry, "Hawks' Shift Precipitated Bombing Halt," *Washington Post*, May 31, 1968, p. A2.
77. Hoopes, *Limits of Intervention*, 205. Also Townsend Hoopes, interview, Jan. 1991, Bethesda, Md.
78. Acheson, Confidential memorandum, Vietnam and Gold Crisis.
79. Ibid.
80. Ibid. Also see Schandler, *Lyndon Johnson and Vietnam*, 258; and Oberdorfer, *Tet*, 294–95.
81. Carroll's editorial can be found in DGA to Wallace Carroll file, S 1, B 5, F 65,

DGA-Yale. Also see George C. Herring, "Vietnam and American National Security" (Paper presented at the U.S. Military Academy 1988 History Symposium, April 13–15, 1988, pp. 29–30).

82. For Johnson's interpretation of the March 1968 events, see Johnson, *Vantage Point*, 401–24.

83. Ibid. Also see Isaacson and Thomas, *Wise Men*, p. 698.

84. Interviews with McGeorge Bundy, April 1988, New York, N.Y.; and William Bundy, Feb. 1988, Princeton, N.J.

85. For accounts of the March 25 and 26 Wise Men meetings, see Berman, *Lyndon Johnson's War*, 194–203; Isaacson and Thomas, *Wise Men*, 698–706; Schandler, *Lyndon Johnson and Vietnam*, 259–65; Taylor, *Swords and Plowshares*, 390–92; Johnson, *The Vantage Point*, 416–18; Halberstam, *Best and the Brightest*, 635–40; and Hoopes, *Limits of Intervention*, 201–13. For Acheson's recounting of the Wise Men meeting, see DGA to Cowles, March 29, 1968, S 1, B 7, F 85, DGA-Yale; and Acheson, Confidential memorandum, "DA's Views Regarding Vietnam" (hereafter, "DA's Views"), March 26, 1968, S 4, B 68, F 173, DGA-Yale.

86. Isaacson and Thomas, *Wise Men*, 702. At the morning breakfast session, LBJ had taken down Acheson's very words in a bold hand. See Lyndon Johnson, Meeting Notes Files, March 26, 1968, Box 2, LBJL.

87. Acheson, Confidential memorandum, "DA's Views."

88. Quoted in Oberdorfer, *Tet*, 312.

89. Ibid., 312–14. Also see Isaacson and Thomas, *Wise Men*, 702; Karnow, *Vietnam: A History*, 562; and Clifford, *Counsel to the President*, 517.

90. Johnson, *Vantage Point*, 414–24.

91. Television interview of Dean Acheson by Eric Sevareid, *CBS News*. Sept. 28, 1969.

92. Dean Acheson, Confidential memorandum, "DA's Views."

93. DGA to Cowles, March 29, 1968, S 1, B 7, F 85, DGA-Yale.

94. For text of President Johnson's televised speech of March 31, 1968, see *Public Papers of the Presidents of the United States: Lyndon B. Johnson, 1968*, 469–76.

95. DGA to Jane Acheson Brown, April 13, 1968, S 1, B 5, F 69, DGA-Yale.

96. For a good brief discussion of how Acheson was able to rethink his cold war attitudes, see Chace and Carr, *America Invulnerable*, 258–64.

97. LBJ to DGA, April 11, 1968, S 1, B 17, F 215, DGA-Yale.

Chapter 9. Reconciled with Nixon

1. For Acheson's dislike of Dulles, see chap. 1. On the basis of his official dealings with Rockefeller, he believed the wealthy Republican to be a dishonest, disloyal, incompetent opportunist who was incapable of thinking, let alone administering. In 1945, when Secretary of State James Byrnes asked Acheson to be his under secretary, Acheson agreed, on one condition: Rockefeller must not hold a position in the State Department. Byrnes accepted Acheson's precondition and fired Rockefeller. For the Acheson-Rockefeller relationship, see DGA to Desmond Donnelly, April 24, 1968, S 1, B 8, F 107, DGA-Yale; and Alsop, *Nixon and Rockefeller*, 89.

2. Voorhis, *Strange Case of Richard Milhous Nixon*, 15. Also see Ambrose, *Nixon*:

The Education of a Politician, 1913–1960, 214–16, 296–97, 336, 349, 357, 499–501, 582, 613. Ambrose discusses Nixon's continuing attacks on Acheson until the 1960 election.

3. McLellan, *Dean Acheson*, 220.
4. Nixon, *Memoirs of Richard Nixon*, 110–11.
5. DGA to Jane Acheson Brown, April 13, 1968, *AF*, 297.
6. DGA to J. H. P. Gould, June 11, 1968, *AF*, 299. Also see DGA to Donnelly, April 24, 1968.
7. DGA to J. H. P. Gould, June 11, 1968.
8. Alice Acheson, interview, Dec. 1986, Washington, D.C.
9. DGA to Lincoln MacVeagh, Aug. 19, 1968, *AF*, 300. For his views on why there was such a paucity of leadership, see Acheson, Speech to the Women's National Democratic Club, Washington, D.C., Sept. 29, 1969, S 3, B 54, F 80. DGA-Yale.
10. Acheson, "HHH Is in Truman's Shoes," *Washington Post*, Outlook sec., Sept. 22, 1968.
11. Ibid.
12. DGA to Eden, Dec. 11, 1968, *AF*, 301.
13. Morris, *Uncertain Greatness*, 85–86. Also Roger Morris, telephone interview, Aug. 1987, Santa Fe, N.M. Morris served on the National Security Council staff under Kissinger from February 1969 to May 1970. Also see DGA to HST, Feb. 28, 1969, Post-Presidential Name File, Box 1, HSTL.
14. DGA to Rusk, March 10, 1971, S 1, B 27, F 341, DGA-Yale.
15. DGA to Charles B. Gray, June 20, 1957, S 1, B 13, F 162, DGA-Yale.
16. Kissinger, "Acheson's Wise, Lucid Analysis of Our Foreign Policy Problems," *New York Herald Tribune*, Jan. 12, 1958.
17. Acheson to Kissinger, Feb. 16, 1960, S 1, B 18, F 226, DGA-Yale.
18. Alice Acheson, interview, Dec. 1986.
19. Kissinger to DGA, July 18, 1961, S 1, B 18, F 226, DGA-Yale.
20. See "Acknowledgments," in Acheson, *Present at the Creation*.
21. Kissinger to DGA, Dec. 14, 1966, S 1, B 18, F 226, DGA-Yale.
22. D'Auria, "Present at the Rejuvenation," 404.
23. Kissinger, *World Restored*.
24. DGA to Sir Roy Welensky, Aug. 28, 1970, *AF*, 309.
25. DGA to Kissinger, Dec. 15, 1964, S 1, B 18, F 226, DGA-Yale.
26. Mrs. Alice Acheson was kind enough to let me look at the books in Dean Acheson's private library.
27. DGA to Kissinger [n.d., 1966], S 1, B 18, F 226, DGA-Yale.
28. LaFeber, "Kissinger and Acheson."
29. Kissinger, *White House Years*, 943.
30. See ibid., 942–43.
31. DGA to J. Robert Schaetzel, Jan. 31, 1969, Schaetzel Papers, Bethesda, Md.
32. DGA to J. H. P. Gould, March 21, 1969, *AF*, 302. See "Ballistic Missile Defense System: Statement by the President Announcing His Decision on Deployment of the System," March 14, *Presidential Documents*, Vol. 5, 406.
33. Kissinger, *White House Years*, 943.
34. Eric Sevareid interview of Dean Acheson, *CBS News Special* (transcript), Nov. 4, 1969, p. 6, S 3, B 54, F 82, DGA-Yale.

35. Dean Acheson, Memorandum of meeting at the White House, March 19, 1969, S 4, B 68, F 173, DGA-Yale. This is a detailed, five-page account of the meeting. See also, D'Auria, "Present at the Rejuvenation," 394–95; and Ambrose, *Nixon: The Triumph of a Politician, 1962–1972*, 259–60.

36. DGA to J. H. P. Gould, March 21, 1969, *AF*, 303; and DGA to William Tyler, March 21, 1969, S 1, B 32, F 405, DGA-Yale.

37. Acheson, "The First Hundred Days," Remarks to the American Society of Newspaper Editors, Washington, D.C. April 16, 1969, S 3, B 54, F 78, DGA-Yale. His remarks included a brief history of how previous presidents had fared in their first hundred days in the White House.

38. Ibid.

39. Kissinger, *White House Years*, 204–15. Kissinger offers a brief account of the ABM debate. The best historical assessment of the ABM controversy is Talbott, *Master of the Game*.

40. DGA to Lady Pamela Berry, June 24, 1969, S 1, B 3, F 33, DGA-Yale.

41. Letter of May 26, 1969, from Dean Acheson, Paul H. Nitze, and Albert Wohlstetter for the Committee to Maintain a Prudent Defense Policy. The letter was sent to all members of Congress to ask them to join the committee and to support President Nixon's ABM proposal. For a discussion of the committee, see Talbott, *Master of the Game*, 111–14.

42. Ibid. See also William Beecher, "Acheson Group Seeks 'Balanced' Defense Budget," *NYT*, May 27, 1969, p. 14.

43. DGA to Gould, June 7, 1969, S 1, B 13, F 169, DGA-Yale.

44. Joint Economic Committee, Subcommittee on Economy in Government, *Security and Foreign Policy in the 1970's*, June 11, 1969, Dean Acheson Statement and Testimony. Acheson's testimony was published in pamphlet form by the Committee to Maintain a Prudent Defense Policy as Report No. 1, June 26, 1969. Citations are to this pamphlet.

45. Nitze quote from Talbott, *Master of the Game*, 112.

46. Paul H. Nitze, interview, Sept. 1987, Washington, D.C.

47. *David Frost Show*, Discussion of the ABM program with former secretary of state Dean Acheson and Senator Charles Percy of Illinois (Telecast July 15, 1969). The transcript of the *David Frost Show* debate was made part of the *Congressional Record* by Senator William Saxbe (*Cong. Rec.*, July 23, 1969). See also DGA to Charles H. Percy, July 17, 1969, S 1, B 24, F 311, DGA-Yale.

48. Acheson, "A Citizen Takes a Hard Look at the ABM," *Sunday Star*, July 27, 1969. Also see *Cong. Rec.*, July 28, 1969. This article was introduced into the *Record* by Senator John Stennis, who thought that it "should be read by everyone who is interested in the ABM issue. It is a forthright exposition by a distinguished American."

49. DGA to J. H. P. Gould, July 24, 1969, S 1, B 13, F 169, DGA-Yale.

50. Nitze, interview, Sept. 1987.

51. Nixon, *Memoirs of Richard Nixon*, 417–18.

52. DGA to Welensky, Jan. 11, 1970, S 1, B 33, F 431, DGA-Yale.

53. See "Prominent Citizens Back Nixon on ABM Expansion," *NYT*, June 25, 1970, p. 91.

54. Acheson, "Apologia Pro Libre Hoc," in Acheson, *Present at the Creation*.

55. David Acheson, interview, April 1988, Washington, D.C.

56. The working papers for *Present at the Creation* are at Yale University (S 3, B 60–65, F 115–150, DGA-Yale). Acheson's extensive correspondence with his research assistants at the Historical Office of the State Department, Marina Finkelstein, Corinne Lyman, and William Franklin, can be found in boxes 63–64.

57. DGA to HST, Aug. 12, 1969, Acheson-Truman Correspondence, 1965–1971, Box 166, HSTL.

58. Reviews of *Present at the Creation* can be found in S 3, B 64–65, F 144–47, DGA-Yale.

59. DGA to Gould, Oct. 28, 1969, S 1, B 13, F 169, DGA-Yale.

60. DGA to Douglas, Oct. 26, 1969, S 1, B 9, F 110, DGA-Yale. Also see DGA to Galbraith, Oct. 21, 1969, S 1, B 12, F 160, DGA-Yale.

61. Two such anthologies were entitled *The Korean War* (New York: W. W. Norton, 1971) and *The Struggle for a Free Europe*. (New York: W. W. Norton, 1971).

62. DGA to Eagleburger, June 25, 1970, S 1, B 9, F 116, DGA-Yale. Also see "Dean Acheson Wins Pulitzer for History," *NYT*, May 5, 1970, p. 48.

63. Lovett to DGA, May 5, 1970, S 1, B 20, F 248, DGA-Yale.

64. DGA to J. H. P. Gould, June 7, 1969, S 1, B 13, F 169, DGA-Yale.

65. DGA to Welensky, Aug. 28, 1969, S 1, B 33, F 431, DGA-Yale.

66. Nixon, *Memoirs of Richard Nixon*, 401.

67. Israel Shenker, "Acheson Sees Danger in Attempts to 'Destroy' Nixon," *NYT*, Oct. 10, 1969, p. 17.

68. Acheson, Address to the Women's National Democratic Club, Sept. 29, 1969, S 3, B 54, F 80, DGA-Yale.

69. DGA to Kissinger, Oct. 20, 1969, S 1, B 13, F 226, DGA-Yale.

70. Interview of Dean Acheson by Edward P. Morgan, *Issues and Answers* (ABC television program), Oct. 26, 1969, S 3, B 54, F 81, DGA-Yale.

71. Acheson, Memorandum of conversation with the President, Oct. 27, 1969, S 4, B 68, F 173, DGA-Yale. The text below relies on this detailed account of the meeting.

72. Acheson, Notes of telephone call from Henry Kissinger, Nov. 3, 1969, S 4, B 68, F 173, DGA-Yale.

73. "Text of President Nixon's Address to Nation on U.S. Policy in the War in Vietnam," *NYT*, Nov. 4, 1969, p. 1. The speech can also be found in S 4, B 67, F 167, DGA-Yale.

74. DGA to Kissinger, Oct. 20, 1969.

75. DGA to Welensky, Nov. 5, 1969, S 1, B 33, F 430, DGA-Yale.

76. Ibid.

77. Nixon, *Memoirs of Richard Nixon*, 410–11. Also see Safire, *Before the Fall*, 171–80. Safire has a chapter on the making of the silent majority speech.

78. DGA to Kissinger, Oct. 20, 1969.

79. DGA to MacVeagh, Dec. 2, 1969, S 1, B 22, F 276, DGA-Yale.

80. DGA to Anthony Eden, Jan. 19, 1970, S 1, B 9, F 118, DGA-Yale.

81. Nixon, *Memoirs of Richard Nixon*, 110.

82. "Statement in Support of President Nixon's Policy in Vietnam," *NYT*, Nov. 17, 1969, p. 54.

83. Acheson, "Nixon Policy Backed," *NYT*, Nov. 24, 1969.

84. Acheson, Memorandum of meeting with the President, Dec. 11, 1969, S 4, B 68, F 173, DGA-Yale. The memo is a ten-page narrative of his afternoon with Nixon.
85. Charles Burton Marshall, interview, March 1987, Washington, D.C.
86. Alice Acheson, interview, Dec. 1987, Washington, D.C.
87. DGA to Eden, Nov. 3, 1969, S 1, B 9, F 117, DGA-Yale.
88. Lukas, *Nightmare*, 59–60.
89. Acheson, Memorandum of conversation with Henry Kissinger, Dec. 29, 1969, and Acheson, Memo, Jan. 17, 1970, S 4, B 68, F 173, DGA-Yale.
90. Nixon, *Memoirs*, 445.
91. DGA to Menzies, April 6, 1970, S 1, B 22, F 282, DGA-Yale.
92. Westwood, *Covington & Burling*, 142–43. For the legal case, see "Case Concerning the Temple of Preah Vihear (Cambodia vs. Thailand)," Preliminary Objections, 1962 International Court of Justice 17.
93. DGA to Sprouse (American Embassy, Phnom Penh, Cambodia), Jan. 21, 1963, S 1, B 29, F 370, DGA-Yale. Also see DGA to Barbara Evans, Jan. 18, 1962, S 1, B 10, F 126, DGA-Yale; and Barbara Evans, interview, Oct. 1987, Washington, D.C. Acheson wrote his long-time secretary glowing accounts of his trip to Cambodia.
94. DGA to Lord Stowe-Hill, March 19, 1970, S 1, B 29, F 377, DGA-Yale.
95. Kissinger, *White House Years*, 490.
96. DGA to Elliot, April 3, 1970, S 1, B 9, F 122, DGA-Yale.
97. Nixon, *Memoirs*, 449–50. The Cambodian episode is one of the most emotionally charged in recent times. For differing evaluations of U.S. Cambodian policy, see Shawcross, *Sideshow*, especially 112–27; and Kissinger, *White House Years*, 457–521. An excellent brief summary of the Cambodian incursion can be found in Herring, *America's Longest War*, 233–40.
98. DGA to John Cowles, May 5, 1970, S 1, B 7, F 86, DGA-Yale.
99. DGA to Sir Roy Welensky, June 30, 1970, *AF*, 315–16.
100. DGA to Cowles, May 5, 1970.
101. See DGA to Anthony Eden, June 30, 1970, S 1, B 9, F 119, DGA-Yale. In July 1971 Acheson published an article in *Foreign Affairs* entitled "The Eclipse of the State Department," which lamented the decline of leadership in Foggy Bottom. It was later reprinted in *TVER*, 276–97.
102. Both quotes from DGA to Ranald MacDonald, Dec. 10, 1970, S 1, B 21, F 264, DGA-Yale.
103. DGA to Lord and Lady Stowe-Hill, May 21, 1970, S 1, B 29, F 377, DGA-Yale.
104. DGA to Desmond Donnelly, June 22, 1970, S 1, B 8, F 108, DGA-Yale.
105. DGA to J. Robert Schaetzel, Aug. 9, 1970, Schaetzel Papers, Bethesda, Md.
106. DGA to Beale (Australia), Aug. 17, 1970, S 1, B 3, F 28, DGA-Yale.
107. See Spiegel, *Other Arab-Israeli Conflict*, 181–88.
108. Dean Acheson, interview by Edward P. Morgan, *Issues and Answers*.
109. Ibid.
110. William P. Bundy, interview, Feb. 1988, Princeton, N.J.
111. Dean Acheson, interview by Edward P. Morgan, *Issues and Answers*.
112. Quoted in Chalmers M. Roberts, "Acheson Urges Brandt's 'Race to Moscow' Be 'Cooled Off,'" *Washington Post*, Dec. 11, 1970.
113. See Kissinger, *White House Years*, 558–60.

114. Acheson, Memorandum to Mr. Kissinger, Dec. 29, 1969, S 4, B 68, F 173, DGA-Yale.
115. Ibid.
116. Ibid.
117. DGA to J. H. P. Gould, Aug. 18, 1970, S 1, B 13, F 169, DGA-Yale. Acheson sent a nearly identical letter to Sir Howard Beale (Aug. 17, 1970; in *AF*, 317–18).
118. Kissinger, *White House Years*, 562.
119. DGA to Eden, Sept. 8, 1970, S 1, B 9, F 119, DGA-Yale. Joseph Sisco, assistant secretary of state for Near Eastern and South Asian affairs, conducted most of the day-to-day negotiations with Soviet Ambassador Anatoly Dobrynin during the spring and summer of 1969.
120. DGA to Schaetzel, Nov. 2, 1970. Schaetzel Papers.
121. Acheson, "Russia's Goals in the Mideast," *NYT*, Oct. 14, 1971.
122. Dean Acheson, interview by Edward P. Morgan, *Issues and Answers*. Acheson nonetheless wrote Brandt a warm congratulatory courtesy note. See DGA to Willy Brandt, Oct. 23, 1969, S 1, B 4, F 43, DGA-Yale.
123. DGA to Schaetzel, July 31, 1970, Schaetzel Papers. Acheson wrote dozens of letters to Schaetzel about U.S.–West German relations.
124. DGA to Donhoff, Dec. 16, 1970, *AF*, 320–21.
125. DGA to Schaetzel, July 31, 1970, Schaetzel Papers.
126. DGA to Welensky, July 18, 1970, S 1, B 33, F 431, DGA-Yale.
127. George Ball, interview, Feb. 1988, Princeton, N.J.
128. DGA to J. H. P. Gould, Dec. 3, 1970, *AF*, 320.
129. Throughout his first administration, Nixon called on these four statesmen for consultation on European affairs. The account that follows is taken from Acheson, Memorandum, Meeting at the White House, Dec. 7, 1970, S 4, B 68, F 173, DGA-Yale.
130. Quoted in Roberts, "Acheson Urges Brandt's 'Race to Moscow' Be 'Cooled Off,'" *Washington Post*.
131. Ibid.
132. Confidential Telegram 201525, Department of State, Dec. 11, 1970, Subject: FRG Complaint about Alleged Remarks of Dean Acheson. Schaetzel Papers. A copy of this telegram was given to the author by J. Robert Schaetzel, former U.S. Representative to the European Communities. See also J. Robert Schaetzel, interview, Dec. 1987.
133. Acheson, Memorandum of conversation with West German Ambassador Rolf Pauls, Dec. 11, 1970, S 4, B 68, F 173, DGA-Yale.
134. Quoted in David Binder, "Strain in U.S.-Bonn Relations Reported," *NYT*, Dec. 20, 1970, p. 1.
135. Ibid. For further discussion of what Acheson called "Brandt's stupidities," see DGA to Anthony Eden, Dec. 15, 1970, S 1, B 9, F 119, DGA-Yale.
136. McCloy to Kissinger, Dec. 30, 1970, Nixon Presidential Project Papers, White House Special File: White House Central Files: Confidential Files [CF] CO 1–5, Europe. I would like to thank John Robert Greene for alerting me to the existence of this letter.
137. Brandt, *People and Politics*, 288. For an American critique of Acheson's treatment of Brandt, see Arthur J. Goldberg, "The Cold Warriors vs. Willy Brandt," *NYT*,

Jan. 5, 1971, p. 35. The Nixon-Brandt relationship is best captured in Barnet, *Alliance*, 283–321.

138. C. L. Sulzberger, "Foreign Affairs: The Sage of Sandy Spring," *NYT*, Sept. 20, 1970, sec. 4, p. 16.

139. See DGA to John Cowles, Jan. 12, 1971, S 1, B 7, F 86, DGA-Yale.

140. DGA to John Cowles, March 27, 1971, S 1, B 7, F 86, DGA-Yale.

141. Acheson, "Dean Acheson: On Winding Down," *NYT*, May 25, 1971.

142. DGA to Cowles, March 27, 1971, S 1, B 7, F 86, DGA-Yale.

143. DGA to Desmond Donnelly, May 4, 1971, S 1, B 8, F 108, DGA-Yale.

144. Kissinger, *White House Years*, 938–49. Kissinger's retelling of these events is subtitled "The Mansfield Amendment: The Old Guard Steps into the Breach."

145. Ibid.

146. Ibid., 944–45.

147. Ibid.

148. White House Press Conference of Dean Acheson, former secretary of state, and George Ball, former under secretary of state, May 13, 1971 (Press release of the Office of the White House), S 3, B 55, F 85, DGA-Yale. Also George Ball interview, Feb. 1988, Princeton, N.J.

149. Quoted in Isaacson and Thomas, *Wise Men*, 718.

150. DGA to John Cowles, May 21, 1971, S 1, B 7, F 86, DGA-Yale.

151. Kissinger to DGA, May 21, 1971, S 1, B 18, F 226, DGA-Yale.

152. RMN to DGA, May 23, 1971, S 1, B 23, F 296, DGA-Yale.

153. DGA to RMN, May 24, 1971, S 1, B 23, F 296, DGA-Yale.

154. Isaacson and Thomas, *Wise Men*, p. 718.

155. DGA to Welensky, June 2, 1971, *AF*, 326–27.

156. Acheson, "Dean Acheson on 'The Right Way to Defeat Mike Mansfield'," *Washington Post*, May 25, 1971, p. A19.

157. Acheson, "The Purloined Papers," *NYT*, July 7, 1971, p. 37.

158. DGA to Matthew H. Fox, Research Associate, Twentieth Century Fund, Sept. 1, 1971, *AF*, 332–34.

159. Quoted in Wise, *Politics of Lying*, 228. The British Official Secrets Act is actually a series of acts. The first was passed in 1889, the basic law was enacted in 1911 and then amended in 1920 and 1939.

160. DGA to Cowles, May 21, 1971, S 1, B 7, F 86, DGA-Yale.

161. David Acheson, interview, Dec. 1987, Washington, D.C.

162. Quoted in Thomas, *The Man To See*, 253.

163. See DGA to Allen Early, July 16, 1971, S 1, B 9, F 114, DGA-Yale. This letter, filled with vituperation toward the liberal wing of the Democratic Party, is one among many.

Chapter 10. Southern Africa Policy, 1961–71

1. Acheson, "Foreign Policy of the United States," *Arkansas Law Review and Bar Association*, June 4, 1964, p. 232, Acheson Papers, Speeches and Articles, 1936–1971, Box 140, HSTL.

2. Acheson, *Grapes from Thorns* 171–93. The chapter "Southern Africa" is a reprint of Acheson's statement before the Subcommittee on Africa of the House

Committee on Foreign Affairs of November 19, 1969. It is his most comprehensive statement on U.S. policy toward southern Africa. Much of the sections on the third world and on Portugal in this chapter first appeared in Douglas Brinkley and G. E. Thomas, "Dean Acheson's Opposition to Liberation in Africa." Thomas was formerly U.S. ambassador to Guyana and to Kenya.

3. Smith, *Dean Acheson*, 16.

4. Acheson, "Address to International and Comparative Law Section of the American Bar Association," Washington, D.C., May 24, 1968, S 3, B 54, F 76, DGA-Yale.

5. See Lake, *Tar Baby Option*, 61.

6. Acheson, "Revising Forward Political Strategies and Improving the Organization of the Free World" (Speech delivered at the National Strategy Seminar, National War College, Washington, D.C., July 21, 1959), p. 26. Acheson Papers, Speeches and Articles, 1936–1971, Box 139, HSTL.

7. Dean Acheson, interview by Edward P. Morgan, *Issues and Answers* (ABC television program), Oct. 24, 1965, S 3, B 53, F 67, DGA-Yale.

8. Acheson, "Ambivalences of American Foreign Policy" (Speech delivered at Indiana University, March 5, 1965), Acheson Papers, Speeches and Articles, 1936–1971, Box 141, HSTL.

9. DGA to Devlin, March 18, 1959, S 1, B 7, F 96, DGA-Yale. Acheson went on in this letter to criticize Nehru: "I remember when Owen Dixon went out as the United Nations Commissioner to try to do something about the Kashmir crisis, he came to see me after his struggles with Nehru, and said, Dean, if you ever allow that man to influence any action of yours in any respect whatsoever, you ought to go to an institution where they can examine your head. I have felt that way about him and about Menon."

In his foreword to *The Third World*, by former Portuguese foreign minister Alberto Franco Nogueira, Acheson attacked Western nations as being "overimpressed by the elegance, not to say saintliness, with which Mr. Nehru could cut a purse or slit a throat and cover the operation with the new legitimacy of the Third World."

10. Williams was the Kennedy administration's staunchest advocate of African self-determination. See G. Mennen Williams, *Africa for Africans*. See also Noer, *Cold War and Black Liberation*, 61–95.

11. DGA to John Cowles, Feb. 6, 1961, S 1, B 6, F 85, DGA-Yale.

12. Lake, *Tar Baby Option*, 74. For Acheson's criticism of JFK's early pro-African approach, see Acheson, "Foreword" in Nogueira, *Third World*, 13–16.

13. Noer, "New Frontiers and Old Priorities in Africa," 258.

14. Acheson. "Fifty Years After," *Yale Review* 61, no. 1 (Oct. 1961), p. 7.

15. For examples, see Acheson, *Grapes from Thorns*, pp. 171–93; Acheson, *TVER*; and Acheson, *Dean Acheson on the Rhodesian Question*.

16. On the Congo crisis of the early 1960s, see Acheson, "Foreign Policy of the United States," Acheson Papers, Speeches and Articles, 1936–1971, Box 140, HSTL, 232.

17. Lucius Battle, interview, March 1988, Washington, D.C.

18. Acheson, *Present at the Creation*, 628.

19. Quote from Acheson, *Sketches from Life of Men I Have Known*, 97.

20. Ibid., 103.

21. McGeorge Bundy, interview, March 1988, New York, N.Y. Acheson wrote to the former Rhodesian prime minister Sir Roy Welensky: "I have tried to befriend Portugal against silly policies of the Kennedy and Johnson administrations and have been adopted as a godfather whose neglect would cause pain" (DGA to Welensky, Aug. 5, 1969, S 1, B 33, F 430, DGA-Yale).

22. DGA to HST, Aug. 4, 1961, S 1, B 31, F 396, DGA-Yale.

23. Salazar is quoted in Mahoney, *JFK: Ordeal in Africa*, 187.

24. Marcam, *Angolan Revolution*, Vol. 1: *Anatomy of an Explosion*, 181. Chapter 6 offers a first-rate interpretation of U.S.-Portuguese relations in 1961. Also see UN General Assembly Resolution 1603(xv), April 20, 1961; and UN doc. 5/4768 in *State Department Bulletin*, April 3, 1961, pp. 498–99. The resolution of March 15, 1961, failed by a vote of 5 (Ceylon, Liberia, the USSR, the United Arab Republic, and the United States) to 0, with 6 abstentions (Chile, China, Ecuador, France, Turkey, and the United Kingdom).

25. Acheson, "Foreign Policy of the United States," 234.

26. Acheson, Oral history interview, April 27, 1964, JFKL, pp. 14–15.

27. Ibid. Also see Acheson, "Foreword" in Nogueira, *Third World*, 14–15.

28. See Mahoney, *JFK: Ordeal in Africa*, 191–202. Also see Bender, "American Policy toward Angola," 111; and Noer, *Cold War and Black Liberation*, 72. Roberto's group was called the UPA at the time of the revolt in 1961. In early 1962 it changed its name to the more radical Movimento Popular de Libertação de Angola (MPLA). It became the predominant black nationalist group.

29. DGA to Eelco van Kleffens, Aug. 7, 1961, Acheson Papers, Post-Admin. Files, State Department and White House Advisor, Box 85, HSTL; and DGA to JFK, March 19, 1961, S 1, B 18, F 223, DGA-Yale.

30. Bowles to Stevenson, July 23, 1961, Box 301, Bowles Papers; and G. Mennen Williams, telephone interview, Nov. 1987, Detroit, Mich.

31. Acheson, "Fifty Years After," 9.

32. Acheson, Oral history interview, 14–17.

33. See, e.g., DGA's correspondence with Pedro Pereira, S 1, B 24, F 311, and Nogueira, S 1, B 23, F 293, DGA-Yale; and U.S. Congress, Senate, Committee on Foreign Relations, *Activities of Foreign Powers in the U.S.* For a summary of Selvage & Lee's propaganda campaign, see Wayne Fredricks, Memorandum to Chester Bowles, July 14, 1962, Box 299, Bowles Papers.

34. Acheson, Memorandum of conversation with the President, April 2, 1962, S 1, B 68, F 172, DGA-Yale, pp. 1–4. The account that follows depends on this document.

35. Ibid. See Mahoney, *JFK: Ordeal in Africa*, 206, for an explanation of the State Department's educational program at Lincoln College, which infuriated the Portuguese foreign minister, Franco Nogueira.

36. Acheson, Memorandum, April 2, 1962. In June 1961 de Gaulle similarly had cautioned Kennedy that deposing Salazar might lead to violent revolution in Portugal and in Spain. Although Acheson admired Salazar, he had nothing but contempt for Francisco Franco, the dictator of Spain.

37. Ibid. When Ambassador Pereira was interviewed in 1966 he commented that he considered "the brilliant former Secretary of State Dean Acheson" to be "one of my most distinguished and most constant friends" (Pereira, Oral history interview, Dec. 18, 1966, JFKL).

38. Galbraith and Stevenson are quoted in Mahoney, *JFK: Ordeal in Africa*, 211.

39. Acheson, "Foreword" in Nogueira, *Third World*, 14. Nogueira was foreign minister in the Portuguese government. He corresponded regularly with Acheson in the late 1960s.

40. G. Mennen Williams, telephone interview, Nov. 1987, Detroit, Mich. See G. Mennen Williams, "Report to the Task Force on the Portuguese Territories in Africa" (n.d.), NSF: Angola, Box 5, JFKL.

41. Adlai Stevenson to Elizabeth Stevenson Ives, Oct. 19, 1961, Stevenson Papers.

42. Martin, *Adlai Stevenson and the World*, 702–04. Chester Bowles saw the "real problem" of Kennedy's presidential foreign policy as his shift in 1962 to the "European-oriented view" of Acheson, Rusk, and McGeorge Bundy (Bowles, Oral history interview, July 1, 1970, JFKL).

43. DGA to Lord Patrick Devlin, July 19, 1965, S 1, B 8, F 97, DGA-Yale.

44. Quoted in Mahoney, *JFK: Ordeal in Africa*, 214.

45. Ibid., 220–22. Also Marcum, *Angolan Revolution* 1:275–77. By September 1962 Dean Rusk had instructed the African bureau of the State Department and the U.S. mission to the UN to halt all contact with the UPA/MPLA and all other African nationalists.

46. Mahoney, *JFK: Ordeal in Africa*, 222; and Noer, *Cold War and Black Liberation*, 93–94.

47. Marcum, *Angolan Revolution* 1:277. Marcum points out that "one of the consequences of the American decision to choose NATO over Africa, or the Azores over Angola, was to drag the cold war deeper into Angolan nationalist politics."

48. Schlesinger, Memorandum for the Honorable Robert Kennedy, Subject: Our Policy in Africa, July 1, 1963, Declassified Documents Reference System (Carrollton, Tex.: Carrollton Press, 1979), 327A.

49. Mahoney, *JFK: Ordeal in Africa*, 222.

50. G. Mennen Williams recalled Acheson saying to him that just because Williams was from "the dark city of Detroit" he should not think that America had "to pander to the dark and delirious continent of Africa" (G. Mennen Williams, telephone interview, Nov. 1987.)

51. For valuable studies of Rhodesian independence in 1965, see Good, *UDI*; Loney, *Rhodesia*; Vulindela, *Rhodesia*; Windrich, *Britain and the Politics of Rhodesian Independence*. British policy toward Rhodesia is detailed in Young, *Rhodesia and Independence*. For Acheson's views on Rhodesia in the 1960s, see Brinkley and Thomas, "Dean Acheson's Opposition to African Liberation," 70–72.

52. See Peterson, *Rhodesian Independence*, 30–73.

53. The speech was published as Acheson, "Lawyer's Path to Peace." Excerpts from this speech were reprinted in Acheson, *Dean Acheson on the Rhodesian Question*, 3–4.

54. Ibid.

55. Quoted in Sam Pope Brewer, "Goldberg Rebuts Acheson View That Peace by Law Is 'Illusory,'" *NYT*, May 19, 1966, p. 6.

56. DGA to Ranald McDonald, Nov. 20, 1969, S 1, B 34, F 264, DGA-Yale.

57. DGA to Leith-Ross, May 27, 1966, S 1, B 19, F 238, DGA-Yale.

58. Quoted in Crosby S. Noyes, "Veto Sanctions on Rhodesia, Acheson Urges,"

Washington Evening Star, Dec. 10, 1966. Clipping found in Acheson Papers, Speeches and Articles, 1936–1971, Box 141, HSTL.

59. "Acheson on Rhodesia," *Washington Post*, Dec. 11, 1966. Reprinted in Acheson, *Dean Acheson on the Rhodesian Question*, 7–11.

60. "Goldberg Responds to Acheson on Rhodesia," *Washington Post*, Jan. 8, 1967, p. 6. The Acheson vs. Goldberg debate on Rhodesia is discussed in Lake, *Tar Baby Option*, 112–16; and Noer, *Cold War and Black Liberation*, 230.

61. See Nielsen, *Great Powers and Africa*, 316–17.

62. Acheson, "Ambivalences of American Foreign Policy." For the responses of Acheson and other critics to Rhodesian sanctions, see Lake, *Tar Baby Option*, 116–22; and Noer, *Cold War and Black Liberation*, 230–37. Noer's chapter 8, "The U.S.A. and UDI," is the best scholarly analysis of U.S. policy toward Rhodesia under the Johnson administration.

63. DGA to Sir William Elliot, Jan. 2, 1967, S 1, B 9, F 122, DGA-Yale.

64. DGA to Tuchman, June 1, 1967, S 1, B 31, F 401, DGA-Yale.

65. Marshall, *Crisis over Rhodesia*. Also Charles Burton Marshall, interview, March 1987, Washington, D.C.

66. Acheson, "Legality and Loyalty in Rhodesia," *Washington Post*, June 4, 1967. See also Lake, *Tar Baby Option*, 115–16.

67. Dean Acheson, interview with Public Broadcasting Company, Dec. 3, 1967, Reel 3, transcript, S 3, B 53, F 74, pp. 8–9, DGA-Yale. Also Marshall, interview, March 1987.

68. Roger P. Morris (NSC staff member responsible for African affairs), telephone interview, Aug. 1987, Santa Fe, N.M.

69. Acheson, "Arrogance of International Lawyers," July 1968. The article can be found in Acheson Papers, Speeches and Articles, 1936–1971, Box 141, HSTL. It was later reprinted in Acheson, *Fragments of My Fleece*, 155–67.

70. Goldberg is quoted in "Rhodesia Sanctions Scored by Acheson," *NYT*, May 25, 1968, p. 5.

71. DGA to Philip Jessup, Aug. 25, 1968, S 1, B 17, F 213, DGA-Yale. The reference is to the Russian invasion of Czechoslovakia, which had just occurred.

72. DGA to Graham, July 23, 1968, S 1, B 13, F 170, DGA-Yale.

73. Acheson, "Drop 'Reformist Intervention' in Rhodesia," *Sunday Star* (Washington, D.C.), Dec. 22, 1968.

74. For a summation of LBJ's Rhodesian policy, see Noer, *Cold War and Black Liberation*, 237.

75. Acheson, "Meeting at the White House," Memorandum, March 19, 1969, S 4, B 68, F 172, DGA-Yale.

76. See El-Khawas and Barry Cohen, *Kissinger Study of Southern Africa*. The book contains the text of National Security Study Memorandum 39 and of the study prepared by the U.S. National Security Council Interdepartmental Group for Africa in response to NSSM 39.

77. Roger Morris, interview, Aug. 1987.

78. Acheson, "U.S. Policies toward Southern Africa Require Change," Memorandum, April 30, 1969, S 4, B 68, F 173, DGA-Yale.

79. Acheson, "U.S. Policies toward Southern Africa." Acheson used the same

argument in his statement before the Subcommittee on Africa of the House Committee on Foreign Affairs, Washington, D.C., November 19, 1969.

80. DGA to the Editor, *Washington Post*, June 20, 1969.

81. Acheson, "The U.S. Consul General in Salisbury Should Not Be Withdrawn," Memorandum, July 7, 1969, S 4, Box 68, Folder 173, DGA-Yale.

82. Acheson, Memorandum to Mr. Kissinger, Oct. 1, 1969, S 4, B 68, F 173, DGA-Yale. This memorandum offers Acheson's most comprehensive review of U.S.-Rhodesian relations.

83. Acheson, Statement made before the Subcommittee on Africa of the House Committee on Foreign Affairs, Washington, D.C., Nov. 19, 1969. An altered version of this statement appears as "Southern Africa" in Acheson, *Grapes from Thorns*, 171–93.

84. DGA to Steinhoff, July 1, 1970, S 1, B 29, F 371, DGA-Yale.

85. Acheson, Memorandum for the record, Luncheon meeting with Secretary of State Rogers, Dec. 12, 1969, Accession 89-M-44, B 1, DGA-Yale.

86. Acheson had also been impressed by the "intelligence" of Welensky's autobiography. See Welensky, *Welensky's 4,000 Days*. For other correspondence on southern African matters see the files at Yale for Lord Graham, H. L. T. Tasswell, Kenneth Tousey, Ted Xanathu, Denis Black, and Ernest Lefever.

87. Quotes taken from his interpretation of African history in Acheson, "Statecraft in Black Africa," *Sunday Star*, Feb. 21, 1971, p. C-2. This article is a review of Lefever, *Army, Police and Politics in Tropical Africa*.

88. DGA to Welensky, July 11, 1968, S 1, B 33, F 430, DGA-Yale.

89. DGA to James Conant, Oct. 17, 1969, S 1, B 6, F 80, DGA-Yale.

90. DGA to Welensky, Aug. 3, 1971, S 1, B 34, F 432, DGA-Yale.

91. Acheson had become friendly with James R. Smeed, the national chairman of the Los Angeles-based Friends of Rhodesia lobbying group. They corresponded with each other in the late 1960s and Smeed would send Acheson copies of his speeches. Because of his criticisms of Great Britain, Smeed was denied entry to the U.K. See DGA-James Smeed Correspondence, S 1, B 29, F 347, DGA-Yale.

92. Acheson, *Dean Acheson on the Rhodesian Question*; Buckley, *Inveighing We Will Go*, 206; and quote in James J. Kilpatrick, "Would you believe: 'Acheson is the greatest!'" (Dec. 1967, Newspaper clipping), Accession 89-M-44, B 2, F 8, DGA-Yale.

93. Lucius Battle, interview, Oct. 1987, Washington, D.C.

94. W. Averell Harriman miscellany interview, June 28, 1970, Box 874, MSS, Harriman Papers.

95. DGA to John Cowles, May 29, 1971, S 1, B 7, F 86, DGA-Yale.

96. Statement of Dean Acheson to the Byrd Subcommittee [Senate Subcommittee on African Affairs], July 7, 1971, S 3, B 55, F 85, DGA-Yale.

97. Lake, *Tar Baby Option*. Also David Newsom, interview, March 1988, Washington, D.C.

98. Acheson, *Grapes from Thorns*, 192–93.

Epilogue: Death at Harewood

1. DGA to Lord Avon (Anthony Eden), Oct. 12, 1971, S 1, B 9, F 119, DGA-Yale.

2. Quoted in "Dean Acheson Dies on His Farm at 78," *NYT*, Oct. 13, 1971, p. 1. The *New York Times* published a full-page obituary.

3. "The Diplomat Who Did Not Want to Be Liked," *Time*, Oct. 25, 1971, pp. 19–20.

4. David Acheson, letter to author, Feb. 7, 1991.

5. James Reston, "The Dean," *NYT*, Oct. 17, 1971, p. 11. Reston recalled that after suffering several strokes and developing other physical handicaps resulting from old age, Acheson became fearful that "he might loiter down like his old friend Felix Frankfurter and dwindle slowly and unconsciously into the grave, a burden to his loved ones." His nightmare did not materialize. Acheson died quickly in the midst of life's fullness and was buried on a beautiful Indian summer day in Rock Creek Park Cemetery in Georgetown, only a few blocks from his P Street home.

6. Arthur Schlesinger, Jr., "The Style Was Always Bravura," *NYT*, Oct. 17, 1971, sec. 3, p. 4.

BIBLIOGRAPHY

This bibliography is divided into the following sections: Manuscript Collections, Works by Dean Acheson, Books, Articles, Unpublished Material, Public Documents, Newspapers, and Personal Interviews.

Manuscript Collections

Acheson, Dean. Papers. Manuscripts and Archives, Yale University Library, New Haven, Connecticut.
Acheson, Dean G. Papers. Harry S Truman Library, Independence, Missouri.
Ball, George W. Papers. Princeton, New Jersey. (Private.)
Bowles, Chester. Papers. Sterling Memorial Library, Yale University, New Haven, Connecticut.
Bruce, David K. E. Papers and Diaries. Virginia Historical Society, Richmond, Virginia.
Butler, Paul. Papers. Notre Dame University, South Bend, Indiana.
Dulles, Eleanor Lansing. Papers. Washington, D.C. (Private.)
Dulles, John Foster. Oral History Collection. Seeley Mudd Library, Princeton University, Princeton, New Jersey.
Dulles, John Foster. Papers. Seeley Mudd Library, Princeton University, Princeton, New Jersey.
Eisenhower, Dwight D. Presidential Papers. Dwight D. Eisenhower Library, Abilene, Kansas.
Harriman, W. Averell. Papers. Library of Congress, Washington, D.C.
Johnson, Lyndon B. Presidential Papers. Lyndon B. Johnson Library, Austin, Texas.
Kennan, George F. Papers. Seeley Mudd Library, Princeton University, Princeton, New Jersey.

Kennedy, John F. Oral History Collection. John F. Kennedy Library, Boston, Massachusetts.
Kennedy, John F. Presidential Papers. John F. Kennedy Library, Boston, Massachusetts.
Kennedy, Robert. Oral History Collection. John F. Kennedy Library, Boston, Massachusetts.
Krock, Arthur. Papers. Seeley Mudd Library, Princeton University, Princeton, New Jersey.
Monnet, Jean. Papers and Travel Diary. Fondation Jean Monnet, Ferme Dorigny, Lausanne, Switzerland.
Nixon, Richard M. Papers. Presidential Materials Project. National Archives, Alexandria, Virginia.
Nixon, Richard M. Vice-Presidential Papers. Federal Archives, Laguna Niguel, California.
Norstad, Lauris. Papers. Dwight D. Eisenhower Library, Abilene, Kansas.
Schaetzel, J. Robert. Papers. Bethesda, Maryland. (Private.)
Schlesinger, Arthur M., Jr. Papers. John F. Kennedy Library, Boston, Massachusetts.
Sorensen, Theodore. Papers. John F. Kennedy Library, Boston, Massachusetts.
Stevenson, Adlai E. Papers. Seeley Mudd Library, Princeton University, Princeton, New Jersey.
Taylor, Maxwell. Papers and Diary. National Defense University, Washington, D.C.
Truman, Harry S. Papers. Harry S Truman Library, Independence, Missouri.
Tyroler, Charles II. Papers. Washington, D.C. (Private.)

Works by Dean Acheson

BOOKS

A Democrat Looks at His Party. New York: Harper & Brothers, 1955.
A Citizen Looks at Congress. New York: Harper & Brothers, 1957.
Power and Diplomacy. Cambridge, Mass.: Harvard University Press, 1958.
Sketches from Life of Men I Have Known. New York: Harper & Brothers, 1961.
Morning and Noon. Boston: Houghton Mifflin, 1965.
Dean Acheson on the Rhodesian Question. Washington, D.C.: Rhodesian Information Office, 1969.
Present at the Creation: My Years in the State Department. New York: W. W. Norton, 1969.
Fragments of My Fleece. New York: W. W. Norton, 1971.
Grapes from Thorns. New York: W. W. Norton, 1972.
This Vast External Realm. New York: W. W. Norton, 1973.

ARTICLES

Note: Over the course of his postsecretarial years, Dean Acheson wrote numerous articles. Listed here are only those cited in this study.

"Foreign Policies toward Asia," *Department of State Bulletin* 23, no. 585 (September 18, 1950): 460–64.

"Plowing a Straight Furrow," *Department of State Bulletin* 23, no. 595 (November 27, 1950): 839–41.

"Strategy of Freedom," *Department of State Bulletin* 23, no. 598 (December 18, 1950): 962–67.

"Freedom—The Key to Hemisphere Solidarity and World Peace," *Department of State Bulletin* 24, no. 614 (April 9, 1951): 569–73.

"Defenses Against Menace of External and Internal Attack," *Department of State Bulletin* 25, no. 628 (July 9, 1951): 46–52.

"What Is Point Four?" *Department of State Bulletin*, 26, no. 658 (February 4, 1952): 155–59.

"'Instant Retaliation': The Debate Continued," *New York Times Magazine*, March 28, 1954.

"The Responsibility for Decision in Foreign Policy," *Yale Review* 44, no. 1 (September 1954): 1–12.

Introduction to *Civilization and Foreign Policy: An Inquiry for Americans* by Louis J. Halle. New York: Harper, 1955.

"The Parties and Foreign Policy," *Harpers Magazine*, November 1955.

"To Meet the Shifting Soviet Offensive," *New York Times Magazine*, April 15, 1956.

"I Don't Share the Sense of Panic," *U.S. News & World Report*, January 18, 1957.

"Foreign Policy and Presidential Moralism," *Reporter*, May 2, 1957.

"A Vital Necessity for America and Europe," *Western World*, August 1957.

"NATO and Nuclear Weapons," *New Republic*, December 30, 1957.

"The Illusion of Disengagement," *Foreign Affairs*, 36, no. 3 (April 1958): 371–82.

"Morality, Moralism and Diplomacy," *Yale Review* 47, no. 4 (June 1958): 481–93.

"Wishing Won't Hold Berlin," *Saturday Evening Post*, March 7, 1959.

"On Dealing with Russia: An Inside View," *New York Times Magazine*, April 12, 1959.

"Fifty Years Later," *Yale Review* 51, no. 1 (October 1961): 1–10.

"Our Atlantic Alliance: The Political and Economic Strands." In *Vital Speeches of the Day* 29, no. 6 (January 1, 1963): 162–66.

"The Practice of Partnership," *Foreign Affairs* 41 (January 1963): 247–60.

"The Monroe Doctrine: Dead or Alive?" *Think*, October 1963.

"Withdrawal from Europe? 'An Illusion,' " *New York Times Magazine*, December 15, 1963.
"Foreign Policy of the United States," *Arkansas Law Review and Bar Association*, June 4, 1964.
"Goldwater and NATO," *Washington Post*, October 7, 1964.
"The American Image Will Take Care of Itself," *New York Times Magazine*, February 28, 1965.
"Cyprus: The Anatomy of the Problem," *Chicago Bar Record* 46, no. 8 (May 1965).
"The Lawyer's Path to Peace," *Virginia Quarterly Review* 42, no. 3 (Summer 1966).
"Legality and Loyalty in Rhodesia," *Washington Post*, June 4, 1967.
"Acheson on Morse," *Washington Post*, December 30, 1967.
Foreword to *The Third World* by Alberto Franco Nogueira. London: Johnson Publications, 1968.
"The Arrogance of International Lawyers," *International Lawyer*, July 1968.
"Dean Acheson's Version of Robert Kennedy's Version of the Cuban Missile Affair," *Esquire*, February 1969.
"Homage to Plain Dumb Luck." In *The Cuban Missile Crisis*, ed. Robert A. Divine. Chicago: Quadrangle Books, 1971.
"The Purloined Papers," *New York Times*, July 7, 1971.

Books

Abel, Elie. *The Missile Crisis*. Philadelphia: J. B. Lippincott, 1966.
Adenauer, Konrad. *Erinnervungen, 1959–1963*. Stuttgart: Deutsche Verlags-Anstalt, 1968.
Adomeit, Hannes. *Soviet Risk Taking and Crisis Behavior: A Theoretical and Empirical Analysis*. London: George Allen & Unwin, 1982.
Aliano, Richard A. *American Defense Policy from Eisenhower to Kennedy*. Athens: Ohio University Press, 1975.
Allison, Graham T. *Essence of Decision: Explaining the Cuban Missile Crisis*. Boston: Little, Brown, 1971.
Alsop, Stuart. *Nixon and Rockefeller: A Double Portrait*. Garden City, N.Y.: Doubleday, 1960.
Ambrose, Stephen E. *Eisenhower: Soldier, General of the Army, President-Elect, 1890–1952*. New York: Simon & Schuster, 1983.
———. *Eisenhower: The President and Elder Statesman, 1952–69*. New York: Simon & Schuster, 1984.
———. *Nixon: The Education of a Politician, 1913–1960*. New York: Simon & Schuster, 1987.

———. *Nixon: The Triumph of a Politician, 1962–1972*. New York: Simon & Schuster, 1989.

———. *Rise to Globalism*, 4th rev. ed. New York: Penguin, 1985.

Ball, George W. *The Past Has Another Pattern*. New York: W. W. Norton, 1982.

Barnet, Richard. *The Alliance*. New York: Simon & Schuster, 1983.

Bell, Coral. *The Diplomacy of Detente: The Kissinger Era*. New York: St. Martin's Press, 1977.

Berman, Larry. *Lyndon Johnson's War*. New York: W. W. Norton, 1989.

———. *Planning a Tragedy: The Americanization of the War in Vietnam*. New York: W. W. Norton, 1982.

Beschloss, Michael R. *Mayday: Eisenhower, Khrushchev, and the U-2 Affair*. New York: Harper & Row, 1986.

———. *The Crisis Years: Kennedy and Khrushchev, 1960–1963*. New York: HarperCollins, 1991.

Blight, James G., and David A. Welch. *On the Brink: Americans and Soviets Reexamine the Cuban Missile Crisis*. New York: Hill & Wang, 1989.

Bohlen, Charles. *Witness to History, 1929–1969*. New York: W. W. Norton, 1973.

Borg, Dorothy, and Waldo Heinrichs. *Uncertain Years: Chinese–American Relations, 1947–1950*. New York: Columbia University Press, 1980.

Bracey, Audrey. *Resolution of the Dominican Crisis, 1965*. Washington, D.C.: Institute for the Study of Diplomacy, 1980.

Bradlee, Benjamin C. *Conversations with Kennedy*. New York: W. W. Norton, 1975.

Brandon, Harry. *Special Relationships: A Foreign Correspondent's Memoirs from Roosevelt to Reagan*. New York: Atheneum, 1988.

Brandt, Willy. *People and Politics: The Years 1960–1975*. Boston: Little, Brown, 1978.

Brauer, Carl M. *Presidential Transitions: Eisenhower through Reagan*. New York: Oxford University Press, 1986.

Brendon, Piers. *Ike: His Life and Times*. New York: Harper & Row, 1986.

Brinkley, Douglas, ed. *Dean Acheson and the Making of U.S. Foreign Policy*. New York: St. Martin's Press, 1992.

Brinkley, Douglas, and Clifford Hackett, eds. *Jean Monnet: The Path to European Unity*. New York: St. Martin's Press, 1991.

Brown, Seyom. *The Faces of Power: Constancy and Change in United States Foreign Policy from Truman to Reagan*. New York: Columbia University Press, 1983.

Brugioni, Dino A. *Eyeball to Eyeball: The Inside Story of the Cuban Missile Crisis*. New York: Random House, 1991.

Buckley, William F., Jr. *Inveighing We Will Go*. New York: G. P. Putnam's Sons, 1972.

Bundy, McGeorge. *Danger and Survival: Choices about the Bomb in the First Fifty Years*. New York: Random House, 1988.
———, ed. *The Pattern of Responsibility: Speeches and Statements of Dean Acheson*. Cambridge, Mass.: Riverside Press, 1951.
Callahan, David. *Dangerous Capabilities: Paul Nitze and the Cold War*. New York: HarperCollins, 1990.
Campbell, John Franklin. *The Foreign Affairs Fudge Factory*. New York: Basic Books, 1971.
Camps, Miriam. *Britain and the European Community, 1955–1963*. Princeton: Princeton University Press, 1964.
———. *European Unification in the Sixties: From the Veto to the Crisis*. New York: McGraw-Hill, 1966.
Catudal, Honoré M., Jr. *The Diplomacy of the Quadripartite Agreement*. Berlin: Berlin Verlag, 1978.
———. *Kennedy and the Berlin Wall Crisis*. Berlin: Berlin Verlag, 1980.
Chace, James, and Caleb Carr. *America Invulnerable: The Quest for Absolute Security from 1812 to Star Wars*. New York: Summit Books, 1988.
Chayes, Abram. *The Cuban Missile Crisis: International Crises and the Role of the Law*. New York: Oxford University Press, 1974.
Cleveland, Harlan. *NATO: The Transatlantic Bargain*. New York: Harper & Row, 1970.
Clifford, Clark, with Richard Holbrooke. *Counsel to the President: A Memoir*. New York: Random House, 1991.
Cohen, Warren I. *Dean Rusk*. The American Secretaries of State and Their Diplomacy, edited by Robert H. Ferrell. New York: Cooper Square Publishers, 1980.
Conklin, Paul K. *Big Daddy from the Pedernales: Lyndon Baines Johnson*. Boston: Twayne Publishing, 1986.
Cook, Don. *Charles deGaulle: A Biography*. New York: G. P. Putnam's Sons, 1983.
Cotter, Cornelius P., and Bernard C. Hennessy. *Politics without Power*. New York: Atherton Press, 1964.
Couloumbis, Theodore A. *The United States, Greece and Turkey: The Troubled Triangle*. New York: Praeger, 1983.
Couloumbis, Theodore A., and John O. Iatrides, eds. *Greek-American Relations: A Critical Review*. New York: Pella, 1980.
Crawshaw, Nancy. *The Cyprus Revolt: An Account of the Struggle for Union with Greece*. London: George Allen & Unwin, 1978.
Cyprus, Public Information Office, *Cyprus: The Problem in Perspective*. Nicosia: Public Information Office, 1969.
de Gaulle, Charles. *Memoirs of Hope: Renewal and Endeavor, 1958–1962*. New York: Simon & Schuster, 1971.

Detzer, David. *The Brink: Cuban Missile Crisis, 1962*. New York: Thomas Crowell, 1979.
DiLeo, David Lewis: *George Ball, Vietnam and the Rethinking of Containment*. Chapel Hill: University of North Carolina Press, 1991.
Dimbleby, David, and David Reynolds. *An Ocean Apart: The Relationship between Britain and America in the Twentieth Century*. New York: Random House, 1988.
Divine, Robert. *Eisenhower and the Cold War*. New York: Oxford University Press, 1981.
———, ed. *Exploring the Johnson Years*. Austin: University of Texas Press, 1981.
———, ed. *The Johnson Years*. Volume 2, *Vietnam, the Environment, and Science*. Lawrence: University Press of Kansas, 1987.
———, ed. *The Cuban Missile Crisis*. Princeton, N.J.: Wiener, 1988.
Donovan, John C. *The Cold Warriors: A Policy-Making Elite*. Lexington, Mass.: D. C. Heath, 1974.
Ehrlich, Thomas. *Cyprus, 1958–1967: International Crises and the Role of Law*. New York: Oxford University Press, 1974.
Eisenhower, Dwight D. *Mandate for Change: 1953–1956*. Garden City, N.Y.: Doubleday, 1963.
———. *Waging Peace: 1956–1961*. Garden City, N.Y.: Doubleday, 1965.
El-Khawas, Mohamed, and Barry Cohen, eds. *The Kissinger Study of Southern Africa: National Security Study Memorandum 39*. Westport, Conn.: Lawrence Hill, 1976.
Evans, Rowland, and Robert Novak. *Lyndon B. Johnson: The Exercise of Power*. New York: New American Library, 1966.
———. *Nixon in the White House: The Frustration of Power*. New York: Random House, 1971.
Finer, Herman. *Dulles over Suez: The Theory and Practice of His Diplomacy*. New York: Quadrangle Books, 1984.
Finletter, Thomas K. *Power and Policy*. New York: Harcourt, Brace & Co., 1954.
Foley, Charles, and W. I. Scobie. *The Struggle of Cyprus*. Stanford, Cal.: Hoover Institution Press, 1975.
Foot, Michael, and Mervun Jones. *Guilty Men, 1957: Suez and Cyprus*. New York: Rinehart and Co., 1957.
Freedman, Lawrence. *Britain and Nuclear Weapons*. London: Macmillan, 1980.
Fursdon, Edward. *The European Defence Community: A History*. London: Macmillan, 1980.
Gaddis, John Lewis. *Strategies of Containment: A Critical Appraisal of Postwar American National Security Policy*. New York: Oxford University Press, 1982.

Galbraith, John Kenneth. *A Life in Our Times: Memoirs.* Boston: Houghton Mifflin, 1981.

Galloway, John. *The Gulf of Tonkin Resolution.* Rutherford, N.J.: Farleigh Dickinson University Press, 1970.

Gardner, Lloyd C. *Approaching Vietnam: From World War II through Dienbienphu.* New York: W. W. Norton, 1988.

Gatzke, Hans W. *Germany and the United States.* Cambridge: Harvard University Press, 1980.

Gelb, Norman. *The Berlin Wall: Kennedy, Khrushchev, and a Showdown in the Heart of Europe.* New York: Times Books, 1986.

George, Alexander L., and Richard Smoke. *Deterrence in American Foreign Policy: Theory and Practice.* New York: Columbia University Press, 1974.

Geyelin, Philip. *Lyndon B. Johnson and the World.* New York: Praeger, 1966.

Gibbons, William Conrad. *The U.S. Government and the Vietnam War: Executive and Legislative Roles and Relationships, Vol. 1: 1945–1960.* Princeton: Princeton University Press, 1986.

——— . *The U.S. Government and the Vietnam War: Executive and Legislative Roles and Relationships, Vol. 2: 1961–1964.* Princeton: Princeton University Press, 1986.

——— . *The U.S. Government and the Vietnam War: Executive and Legislative Roles and Relationships, Vol. 3: January–July 1965.* Princeton: Princeton University Press, 1989.

Gillingham, John. *Coal, Steel and the Rebirth of Europe, 1945–1955.* Cambridge: Cambridge University Press, 1991.

Goldman, Eric F. *The Tragedy of Lyndon Johnson.* New York: Alfred A. Knopf, 1969.

Good, Robert. *UDI: The International Politics of the Rhodesian Rebellion.* London: Faber & Faber, 1973.

Goulden, Joseph C. *Truth Is the First Casualty: The Gulf of Tonkin Affair.* Chicago: Rand McNally, 1969.

Graebner, Norman A., ed. *The National Security: Its Theory and Practice, 1945–1960.* New York: Oxford University Press, 1986.

Graff, Henry. *The Tuesday Cabinet: Deliberation on Peace and War under Lyndon Johnson.* Englewood Cliffs, N.J.: Prentice Hall, 1970.

Grosser, Alfred. *The Western Alliance: European American Relations since 1945.* New York: Vintage Books, 1982.

Gurtov, Melvin. *The First Indochina Crisis.* New York: Columbia University Press, 1967.

Halberstam, David. *The Best and the Brightest.* New York: Random House, 1972.

Halperin, Morton H. *Contemporary Military Strategy.* Boston: Little, Brown, 1967.

Hamby, Alonzo L. *Liberalism and Its Challengers: FDR to Reagan.* New York: Oxford University Press, 1985.
Hammer, Ellen. *The Struggle for Indochina: 1950–1955.* Stanford, Cal. Stanford University Press, 1955.
Harrison, Michael. *The Reluctant Ally: France and Atlantic Security.* Baltimore: Johns Hopkins University Press, 1981.
Hathaway, Robert M. *Great Britain and the United States: Special Relations since World War II.* Boston: Twayne Publishing, 1990.
Heller, Francis H. and Gillingham, John R., eds. *NATO: The Founding of the Atlantic Alliance and the Integration of Europe.* New York: St. Martin's, 1992.
Herken, Gregg. *Counsels of War.* New York: Oxford University Press, 1987.
Herring, George C. *America's Longest War: The United States and Vietnam, 1950–1975.* 2d ed. Philadelphia: Temple University Press, 1986.
Higgins, Trumbull. *The Perfect Failure: Kennedy, Eisenhower, and the CIA at the Bay of Pigs.* New York: W. W. Norton, 1987.
Hitchens, Christopher. *Blood, Class and Nostalgia: Anglo-American Ironies.* New York: Farrar, Straus & Giroux, 1990.
———. *Hostage to History: Cyprus from the Ottomans to Kissinger.* New York: Farrar, Straus & Giroux, 1989.
Hixson, Walter L. *George F. Kennan: Cold War Iconoclast.* New York: Columbia University Press, 1989.
Hoopes, Townsend. *The Devil and John Foster Dulles.* Boston: Atlantic–Little, Brown, 1973.
———. *The Limits of Intervention.* New York: David McKay, 1969.
Hunt, Michael H. *Ideology and U.S. Foreign Policy.* New Haven, Conn.: Yale University Press, 1987.
Immerman, Richard H., ed. *John Foster Dulles and the Diplomacy of the Cold War.* Princeton: Princeton University Press, 1990.
Irving, Ronald. *The First Indochina War: French and American Policy, 1945–1954.* London: Croom Helm, 1975.
Isaacson, Walter, and Evan Thomas. *The Wise Men: Six Friends and the World They Made.* New York: Simon & Schuster, 1986.
James, Robert Rhodes. *Anthony Eden: A Biography.* New York: McGraw-Hill, 1987.
Johnson, Lyndon Baines. *The Vantage Point: Perspectives of the Presidency, 1963–1969.* New York: Holt, Rinehart & Winston, 1971.
Joseph, Joseph S. *Cyprus: Ethnic Conflict and International Concern.* New York: Peter Lang, 1987.
Kaplan, Lawrence S. *NATO and the United States.* Boston: Twayne Publishing, 1989.
Kaufmann, William W. *The McNamara Strategy.* New York: Harper & Row, 1964.

Kay, Hugh. *Salazar and Modern Portugal*. New York: Hawthorn, 1970.
Kelleher, Catherine M. *Germany and the Politics of Nuclear Weapons*. New York: Columbia University Press, 1975.
Kennan, George F. *American Diplomacy: 1900–1950*. New York: New American Library, 1951.
———. *Russia, the Atom and the West*. New York: Harper & Brothers, 1958.
———. *Memoirs, 1950–1963*. Boston: Little, Brown, 1972.
Kennedy, John F. *The Strategy of Peace*. Edited by Allan Nevins. New York: Harper & Brothers, 1960.
Kennedy, Robert F. *Thirteen Days*. New York: W. W. Norton, 1969.
Khrushchev, Nikita S. *Khrushchev Remembers*. Boston: Little, Brown, 1970.
———. *Khrushchev Remembers: The Last Testament*. Translated and edited by Strobe Talbott. Boston: Little, Brown, 1974.
Kinnard, Douglas. *President Eisenhower and Strategy Management: A Study in Defense Politics*. Lexington: University Press of Kentucky, 1977.
Kissinger, Henry. *Nuclear Weapons and Foreign Policy*. New York: Harper & Row, 1957.
———. *The Necessity for Choice*. New York: Harper & Brothers, 1960.
———. *A World Restored: The Politics of Conservatism in a Revolutionary Era*. Boston: Houghton Mifflin, 1957.
———. *The White House Years*. Boston: Little, Brown, 1979.
Kleiman, Robert. *Atlantic Crisis: American Diplomacy Confronts a Resurgent Europe*. New York: W.W. Norton, 1964.
Kohler, Foy D. *Understanding the Russians: A Citizen's Primer*. New York: Harper & Row, 1971.
Kosut, Hal, ed. *Cyprus: 1964–68*. New York: Facts on File, 1970.
Kraft, Joseph. *The Grand Design: From Common Market to Atlantic Partnership*. New York: Harper & Row, 1962.
Lake, Anthony. *The Tar Baby Option: American Policy toward Southern Rhodesia*. New York: Columbia University Press, 1973.
Larson, Arthur. *A Republican Looks at His Party*. New York: Harper & Brothers, 1956.
Lazo, Mario. *Dagger in the Heart: American Policy Failures in Cuba*. New York: Twin Circle, 1970.
Ledwidge, Bernard. *DeGaulle*. New York: St. Martin's Press, 1982.
Lefever, Ernest W. *Army, Police and Politics in Tropical Africa*. Washington: Brookings Institution Press, 1971.
Liddell Hart, B.H. *Deterrent or Defense: A Fresh Look at the West's Military Position*. New York: Praeger, 1960.
Lineberry, William P. *The United States in World Affairs, 1970*. New York: Simon & Schuster, 1972.
Loney, Martin. *Rhodesia: White Racism and Imperial Response*. London: Penguin Books, 1975.

Louis, William Roger, and Hedley Bull, eds. *The Special Relationship: Anglo-American Relations since 1945*. New York: Oxford University Press, 1986.
Louis, William Roger, and Roger Owen, eds. *Suez 1956: The Crisis and Its Consequences*. New York: Oxford University Press, 1989.
Lowenthal, Abraham F. *The Dominican Intervention*. Cambridge: Harvard University Press, 1972.
Lukas, Anthony J. *Nightmare: The Underside of the Nixon Years*. New York: Viking, 1976.
Macmillan, Harold R. *Riding the Storm: 1956–1959*. New York: Harper & Row, 1971.
———. *Pointing the Way: 1959–1961*. London: Macmillan, 1972.
———. *At the End of the Day: 1961–1963*. London: Macmillan, 1973.
Mahoney, Richard P. *JFK: Ordeal in Africa*. New York: Oxford University Press, 1983.
Marcam, John. *The Angolan Revolution*. Vol. 1, *The Anatomy of an Explosion*. Cambridge: MIT Press, 1969.
Markides, Kyriacos. *The Rise and Fall of the Cyprus Republic*. New Haven, Conn.: Yale University Press, 1977.
Marshall, Charles Burton. *Crisis over Rhodesia: A Skeptical View*. Baltimore: Johns Hopkins University Press, 1967.
Martin, John Bartlow. *Adlai Stevenson and the World*. Garden City, N.Y.: Doubleday, 1977.
Mayers, David. *George Kennan and the Dilemmas of U.S. Foreign Policy*. New York: Oxford University Press, 1988.
McKeever, Porter. *Adlai Stevenson: His Life and Legend*. New York: William Morrow, 1989.
McLellan, David S. *Dean Acheson: The State Department Years*. New York: Dodd, Mead, 1976.
McLellan, David S., and David C. Acheson, eds. *Among Friends: Personal Letters of Dean Acheson*. New York: Dodd, Mead, 1980.
McPherson, Harry. *A Political Education*. Boston: Little, Brown, 1972.
Melanson, Richard A., and David Mayers, eds. *Reevaluating Eisenhower: American Foreign Policy in the 1950's*. Urbana: University of Illinois Press, 1987.
Merli, Frank J., and Theodore A. Wilson, eds. *Makers of American Diplomacy: From Theodore Roosevelt to Henry Kissinger*. New York: Charles Scribner's Sons, 1974.
Miroff, Bruce. *Pragmatic Illusions: The Presidential Politics of John F. Kennedy*. New York: Longman, 1976.
Monnet, Jean. *Memoirs*. Translated by Richard Mayne. Garden City, N.Y.: Doubleday, 1978.
Morgan, Iwan W. *Eisenhower versus the Spenders*. New York: St. Martin's Press, 1990.

Morgenthau, Hans. *The Restoration of American Policies in Politics of the 20th Century*, vol. 3. Chicago: University of Chicago Press, 1958.

Morris, Roger. *Uncertain Greatness: Henry Kissinger and American Foreign Policy*. New York: Harper & Row, 1977.

Mosely, Philip. *The Kremlin and World Politics*. New York: Viking, 1960.

Mosher, Fredrick C., W. David Clinton, and Daniel G. Lang. *Presidential Transitions and Foreign Affairs*. Baton Rouge: Louisiana State University Press, 1987.

Murphy, Bruce Allen. *Fortas: The Rise and Ruin of a Supreme Court Justice*. New York: William Morrow, 1988.

Nash, George H. *The Conservative Intellectual Movement since 1945*. New York: Basic Books, 1976.

Neff, Donald. *Warriors at Suez: Eisenhower Takes America into the Middle East*. New York: Simon & Schuster, 1981.

Nielsen, Waldemar. *The Great Powers and Africa*. New York: Praeger, 1969.

Ninkovich, Frank. *Germany and the United States*. Boston: G.K. Hall, 1983.

Nitze, Paul H. *From Hiroshima to Glasnost: At the Center of Decision—A Memoir*. New York: Grove Weidenfeld, 1989.

Nixon, Richard M. *The Memoirs of Richard Nixon*. New York: Grosset & Dunlap, 1978.

Noble, George Bernard. *Christian A. Herter*. The American Secretaries of State and Their Diplomacy, edited by Robert H. Ferrell and Samuel Flagg Bemis. New York: Cooper Square Publishers, 1972.

Noer, Thomas J. *Cold War and Black Liberation: The United States and White Rule in Africa, 1948–1968*. Columbia: University of Missouri Press, 1985.

Nunnerley, David. *President Kennedy and Britain*. London: Bodley Head, 1972.

Oberdorfer, Don. *Tet!* Garden City, N.Y.: Doubleday, 1971.

Osgood, Robert Endicott. *NATO: The Entangling Alliance*. Chicago: University of Chicago Press, 1962.

Parmet, Herbert S. *Eisenhower and the American Crusades*. New York: Macmillan, 1972.

———. *The Democrats: The Years After FDR*. New York: Macmillan, 1976.

———. *The Struggles of John F. Kennedy*. New York: Dial, 1980.

———. *JFK: The Presidency of John F. Kennedy*. New York: Dial, 1983.

Paterson, Thomas G., ed. *Kennedy's Quest for Victory: American Foreign Policy, 1961–1963*. New York: Oxford University Press, 1989.

Peeters, Paul. *Massive Retaliation*. Chicago: Henry Regnery Company in cooperation with the Foundation for Foreign Affairs, 1959.

Peterson, Robert W., ed. *Rhodesian Independence*. New York: Facts on File, 1971.

Pierre, Andrew J. *Nuclear Politics: The British Experience with an Independent Strategic Force, 1939–1970*. New York: Oxford University Press, 1972.

Pogue, Forrest C. *George C. Marshall, Statesman, 1945–1959*. New York: Viking, 1987.
Prados, John. *The Sky Would Fall: Operation Vulture*. New York: Dial, 1983.
Prittie, Terence. *Konrad Adenauer*. London: Tom Stacey, 1971.
Pruessen, Ronald W. *John Foster Dulles: The Road to Power*. New York: Free Press, 1982.
Rabe, Stephen G. *Eisenhower and Latin America: The Foreign Policy of Anticommunism*. Chapel Hill, N.C.: University of North Carolina Press, 1988.
Randle, Robert. *Geneva, 1954*. Princeton: Princeton University Press, 1969.
Rearden, Stephen L. *The Evolution of American Strategic Doctrine: Paul H. Nitze and the Soviet Challenge*. Boulder, Col.: Westview Press, 1984.
Reichard, Gary W. *The Reaffirmation of Republicanism: Eisenhower and the Eighty-third Congress*. Knoxville: University of Tennessee Press, 1975.
Reynolds, David. *An Ocean Apart: The Relationship between Britain and America in the Twentieth Century*. New York: Random House, 1988.
Richardson, James. *Germany and the Atlantic Alliance*. Cambridge, Mass.: Harvard University Press, 1966.
Ridgway, Matthew B. *Soldier: The Memoirs of Matthew B. Ridgway*. New York: Harper, 1956.
Roberts, George C. *Paul M. Butler: Hoosier Politician and National Political Leader*. Lanham, Md.: University Press of America, 1987.
Rostow, W. W. *The Diffusion of Power: An Essay in Recent History*. New York: Macmillan, 1972.
———. *Open Skies: Eisenhower's Proposal of July 21, 1955*. Austin: University of Texas Press, 1982.
Rusk, Dean. As told to Richard Rusk. *As I Saw It*. New York: W. W. Norton, 1990.
Rust, William J. *Kennedy in Vietnam*. New York: Scribner's, 1985.
Safire, William. *Before the Fall: An Inside View of the Pre-Watergate White House*. New York: Belmont Tower, 1975.
Schaetzel, J. Robert. *Unhinged Alliance*. New York: Harper & Row, 1975.
Schandler, Herbert Y. *Lyndon Johnson and Vietnam: The Unmaking of a President*. Princeton: Princeton University Press, 1977.
Schick, Jack M. *The Berlin Crisis, 1958–1962*. Philadelphia: University of Pennsylvania Press, 1971.
Schlesinger, Arthur M., Jr. *Robert Kennedy and His Times*. Boston: Houghton Mifflin, 1978.
———. *A Thousand Days: John F. Kennedy in the White House*. Boston: Houghton Mifflin, 1965.
———. *The Cycles of American History*. Boston: Houghton Mifflin, 1986.
Schoenbaum, Eleanora W., ed. *Political Profiles: The Eisenhower Years*. New York: Facts on File, 1977.

Schoenbaum, Thomas J. *Waging Peace and War: Dean Rusk in the Truman, Kennedy and Johnson Years.* New York: Simon & Schuster, 1988.

Schwartz, David N. *NATO's Nuclear Dilemmas.* Washington, D.C.: Brookings Institution Press, 1983.

Seaborg, Glenn T., and Benjamin S. Loeb. *Kennedy, Khrushchev, and the Test Ban.* Berkeley: University of California Press, 1981.

Shawcross, William. *Sideshow: Kissinger, Nixon and the Destruction of Cambodia.* New York: Simon & Schuster, 1979.

Shlaim, Avi. *The United States and the Berlin Blockade, 1948–1949: A Study in Crisis Decision-Making.* Berkeley: University of California Press, 1983.

Shogan, Robert. *A Question of Judgment: The Fortas Case and the Struggle for the Supreme Court.* Indianapolis, Ind.: Bobbs-Merrill Co., 1972.

Sidey, Hugh. *John F. Kennedy, President.* New York: Atheneum, 1964.

Slusser, Robert. *The Berlin Crisis of 1961: Soviet-American Relations and the Struggle for Power in the Kremlin.* Baltimore: Johns Hopkins University Press, 1973.

Smith, Gaddis. *Dean Acheson.* The American Secretaries of State and their Diplomacy, edited by Robert H. Ferrell and Samuel Flagg Bemis. New York: Cooper Square, 1972.

Sorensen, Theodore C. *Kennedy.* New York: Bantam, 1966.

Spiegel, Stephen L. *The Other Arab-Israeli Conflict: Making America's Middle East Policy from Truman to Reagan.* Chicago: University of Chicago Press, 1985.

Stebbins, Richard P. *The United States in World Affairs, 1957.* New York: Harper & Brothers for the Council on Foreign Relations, 1958.

———. *The United States in World Affairs, 1963.* New York: Harper & Row, 1964.

———. *The United States in World Affairs, 1966.* New York: Harper & Row, 1967.

Steel, Ronald. *Walter Lippmann and the American Century.* Boston: Little, Brown, 1980.

Stikker, Dirk U. *Men of Responsibility: A Memoir.* New York: Harper & Row, 1960.

Stoessinger, John G. *Henry Kissinger: The Anguish of Power.* New York: W. W. Norton, 1976.

Stromseth, Jane E. *The Origins of Flexible Response: NATO's Debate over Strategy in the 1960's.* New York: St. Martin's Press, 1988.

Stupak, Ronald. *The Shaping of Foreign Policy: The Role of the Secretary of State as Seen by Dean Acheson.* Cleveland: Odyssey, 1969.

Sulzberger, C. L. *Last of the Giants.* New York: Macmillan, 1970.

———. *Seven Continents and Forty Years: A Concentration of Memoirs.* New York: Quadrangle, 1977.

Talbott, Strobe. *The Master of the Game: Paul Nitze and the Nuclear Peace.* New York: Alfred A. Knopf, 1988.

Tananbaum, Duane. *The Bricker Amendment: A Test of Eisenhower's Political Leadership.* Ithaca, N.Y.: Cornell University Press, 1988.

Taylor, Maxwell D. *Swords and Plowshares.* New York: W. W. Norton, 1972.

———. *The Uncertain Trumpet.* New York: Harper & Brothers, 1960.

Theoharis, Athan G. *The Yalta Myths: An Issue in U.S. Politics, 1945–1955.* Columbia: University of Missouri Press, 1970.

Thomas, Evan. *The Man to See: Edward Bennett Williams: Ultimate Insider, Legendary Trial Lawyer.* New York: Simon & Schuster, 1991.

Thompson, Kenneth W., ed. *The Kennedy Presidency.* Lanham, Md.: University Press of America, 1985.

Thomson, Charles A. H., and Frances M. Shattuck. *The Presidential Campaign.* Washington, D.C.: Brookings Institution Press, 1960.

Treadgold, Donald. *Twentieth Century Russia.* Chicago: Rand McNally, 1972.

Troen, S. I., and M. Shemesh, eds. *The Suez-Sinai Crisis, 1956: Retrospective and Reappraisal.* New York: Oxford University Press, 1990.

Truman, Harry S. *Memoirs: 1945, Year of Decisions.* Garden City, N.Y.: Doubleday, 1955.

———. *Memoirs: Years of Trial and Hope, 1946–1952.* Garden City, N.Y.: Doubleday, 1956.

Truman, Margaret, ed. *Where the Buck Stops: The Personal and Private Writings of Harry S Truman.* New York: Warner Books, 1989.

Tucker, Nancy Bernkopf. *Patterns in the Dust.* New York: Columbia University Press, 1983.

Ulam, Adam. *Expansion and Coexistence: A History of Soviet Foreign Policy, 1917–1967.* New York: Praeger, 1968.

Von der Groeben, Hans. *The European Community: The Formative Years.* Luxembourg: Office for Official Publications of the European Communities, 1987.

Voorhis, Jerry. *The Strange Case of Richard Milhous Nixon.* New York: Paul S. Eriksson, 1972.

Vulindela, Mtshali B. *Rhodesia: Background to Conflict.* New York: Hawthorn, 1967.

Weintal, Edward, and Charles Bartlett. *Facing the Brink: An Intimate Study of Crisis Diplomacy.* New York: Charles Scribner's Sons, 1967.

Welensky, Sir Roy. *Welensky's 4,000 Days: The Life and Death of the Federation of Rhodesia and Nyasaland.* London: Collins, 1964.

Westwood, Howard C. *Covington & Burling, 1919–1984.* Washington, D.C.: Covington & Burling, 1986.

Williams, G. Mennen. *Africa for Africans.* Grand Rapids, Mich.: William B. Eerdmans, 1969.

Wilson, Woodrow. *Congressional Government.* Cambridge, Mass.: Houghton Mifflin, Riverside Press, 1885.
Windrich, Elaine. *Britain and the Politics of Rhodesian Independence.* New York: Africana, 1978.
Wise, David. *The Politics of Lying: Government Deception, Secrecy, and Power.* New York: Random House, 1973.
Young, Kenneth. *Rhodesia and Independence: A Study of British Colonial Policy.* London: Eyre & Spottiswoode, 1967.
———. *Negotiating with the Chinese Communists: The United States Experience, 1953–1967.* New York: McGraw-Hill, 1968.

Articles

Accinelli, Robert. "Eisenhower, Congress and the 1954–55 Offshore Island Crisis," *Presidential Studies Quarterly* 20, no. 2 (Spring 1990): 329–48.
Acheson, David C. "The Truman-Acheson Friendship," *Whistlestop Newsletter*, 1984. (Vertical Files, HSTL).
"Acheson Sees Ike's Foreign Policy as 'Bluster and Bluff,'" *U.S. News & World Report*, October 5, 1956.
Anderson, David C. "J. Lawton Collins, John Foster Dulles, and the Eisenhower Administration's 'Point of No Return' in Vietnam," *Diplomatic History* 12, no. 2 (Spring 1988): 127–47.
Bagdikian, Ben. "The 'Inner Inner Circle' around Johnson," *New York Times Magazine*, February 25, 1965.
Bender, Gerard J. "American Policy toward Angola: A History of Linkage." In *African Crisis Areas and U.S. Foreign Policy*, ed. Gerald J. Bender, James S. Coleman, and Richard L. Sklar. Berkeley: University of California Press, 1985.
Bernstein, Barton J. "Election of 1952." In *History of American Presidential Elections, 1789–1968*, ed. Arthur M. Schlesinger, Jr. New York: Chelsea House, 1971.
Bowie, Robert R. "Eisenhower, Dulles, and the Suez Crisis." In *Suez 1956*, ed. Louis and Owen.
Bowles, Chester. "A Plea for Another Great Debate," *New York Times Magazine*, February 28, 1954.
———. "America Enters the Cyprus Tangle," *Middle Eastern Studies* 23:3 (July 1987).
Brands, H. W., Jr. "Testing Massive Retaliation: Credibility and Crisis Management in the Taiwan Strait," *International Security* 12 (September 1988): 124–51.
———. "The Age of Vulnerability: Eisenhower and the National Security State," *American Historical Review* 94, no. 4 (October 1989): 963–89.

Brinkley, Douglas. "The Kennan-Acheson Disengagement Debate," *Atlantic Community Quarterly* 25, no. 4 (Winter 1987–88): 413–25.

―――. "The Cyprus Question: Dean Acheson as Mediator," *Journal of the Hellenic Diaspora* 15, nos. 3 and 4 (1988):, pp. 5–18.

―――. "Dean Acheson and the 'Special Relationship': The West Point Speech of December 1962," *Historical Journal* 33, 3 (1990).

―――. "Dean Acheson and European Unity." In *NATO*, ed. Heller and Gillingham.

Brinkley, Douglas, and G. E. Thomas. "Dean Acheson's Opposition to Liberation in Africa," *TransAfrica Forum* 5, no. 4 (Summer 1988): 62–81.

Brodie, Bernard. "Unlimited Weapons and Limited War," *Reporter*, November 18, 1954.

Bundy, McGeorge. "Kennedy and the Nuclear Question." In *The Kennedy Presidency*, ed. Thompson.

Chang, Gordon H. "To the Nuclear Brink: Eisenhower, Dulles, and the Quemoy-Matsu Crisis," *International Security* 12 (Spring 1988): 96–123.

Childs, Marquis. "The Acheson View on Holding Berlin," *Washington Post*, July 28, 1961.

Clubb, Edmund O. "Formosa and the Offshore Islands in American Foreign Policy, 1950–1955," *Political Science Quarterly* 74, no. 4 (December 1959): 518–31.

Cohen, Eliot A. "Why We Should Stop Studying the Cuban Missile Crisis," *National Interest* (Winter 1985/86): 3–13.

Cohen, Warren I. "Acheson, His Advisors, and China." In *Uncertain Years*, ed. Borg and Heinrichs.

Costigliola, Frank. "The Pursuit of Atlantic Community: Nuclear Arms, Dollars, and Berlin." In *Kennedy's Quest for Victory*, ed. Paterson.

Coufoudakis, Van. "Cyprus—July 1974, or, Acheson's Failure, Kissinger's Success," *Journal of the Hellenic Diaspora* 1(4), 1974: 35–42.

―――. "United States Foreign Policy and the Cyprus Question: A Case Study in Cold War Diplomacy." In *U.S. Foreign Policy toward Greece and Cyprus: The Clash of Principle and Pragmatism*, ed. Theodore A. Couloumbis and Sallie M. Hicks. Washington, D.C.: Center for Mediterranean Studies, 1975.

―――. "U.S. Foreign Policy and the Cyprus Question: An Interpretation," *Millennium Journal of International Studies* (London School of Economics), vol. 5, no. 3 (Winter 1976–77): 245–68.

―――. "American Foreign Policy and the Cyprus Problem, 1974–1978: The 'Theory of Continuity' Revisited." In *Greek-American Relations*, ed. Couloumbis and Iatrides.

D'Auria, Gregory T. "Present at the Rejuvenation: The Association of Dean Acheson and Richard Nixon," *Presidential Studies Quarterly* 28, no. 2, (Spring 1988): 393–412.

DeBenedetti, Charles. "Lyndon Johnson and the Antiwar Opposition." In *The Johnson Years*. Vol. 2, ed. Divine.

Dulles, John Foster. "A Policy of Boldness," *Life*, May 19, 1952.

———. "The Evolution of Foreign Policy," *Department of State Bulletin*, January 25, 1954.

———. "Policy for Security and Peace," *Foreign Affairs* 32 (April 1954): 353–64.

———. "Challenge and Response in United States Policy," *Foreign Affairs* 36 (October 1957).

Ferrell, Robert H., and David S. McLellan. "Dean Acheson: Architect of a Manageable World Order." In *Makers of American Diplomacy*, ed. Merli and Wilson.

Galbraith, John Kenneth. "Dean Acheson Recalls His Life and Good Brawling Times," *Book World*, October 12, 1969.

Gelfand, Mark I. "The War on Poverty." In *Exploring the Johnson Years*, ed. Divine.

Gordon, Leonard H. D. "United States Opposition to Use of Force in the Taiwan Strait, 1954–1962," *Journal of American History* 72 (December 1985): 637–60.

Graebner, Norman A. "Eisenhower and Communism: The Public Record of the 1950's." In *Reevaluating Eisenhower*, ed. Melanson and Mayers.

Hackett, Clifford P. "The Role of Congress and Greek-American Relations." In *Greek American Relations*, ed. Couloumbis and Iatrides.

Hunt, Brigadier Kenneth. "NATO without France: The Military Implications," *Adelphi Papers*, no. 32. London: Institute for Strategic Studies, 1966.

Immerman, Richard H. "Between the Unattainable and the Unacceptable: Eisenhower in Dienbienphu." In *Reevaluating Eisenhower*, ed. Melanson and Mayers.

———. "The United States and the Geneva Conference," *Diplomatic History* 14, no. 1 (Winter 1990): 43–66.

Joynt, Carey B. "Disengagement and Beyond," *Queen's Quarterly* 65, no. 2 (Summer 1958): 161–68.

Kaplan, Lawrence S. "Dean Acheson and the Atlantic Community." In *Dean Acheson and the Making of U.S. Foreign Policy*, ed. Brinkley.

Kaufmann, Walter. "The Requirements of Deterrence." In *Military Policy and National Security*, ed. Walter Kaufmann. Princeton: Princeton University Press, 1956.

Kennan, George. "Disengagement Revisited," *Foreign Affairs* 37 (January 1959): 187–210.

Kennedy, John F. "A Democrat Looks at Foreign Policy," *Foreign Affairs* 36 (October 1957): 44–49.

King, James E., Jr. "Kennanism and Disengagement," *New Republic*, April 7, 1958.
LaFeber, Walter. "Kissinger and Acheson: The Secretary of State and the Cold War," *Political Science Quarterly* 92, no. 2 (Summer 1977).
———. "Latin American Policy." In *Exploring the Johnson Years*, ed. Divine.
Larson, Deborah Welch. "Crisis Prevention and the Austrian State Treaty, " International Organization 41 (Winter 1987): 27–60.
Lerner, Max. "Memoirs of a Statesman with Style," *Life*, October 29, 1965.
Louis, William Roger. "Dulles, Suez and the British." In *John Foster Dulles and the Diplomacy of the Cold War*, ed. Immerman.
Lyndon B. Johnson News Conference, September 5, 1964. In *The Johnson Presidential Press Conferences*, vol. 1, ed. George W. Johnson. New York: Earl M. Coleman, 1978.
McCarthy, Joseph R. "Acheson Looks at Acheson," *National Review*, December 28, 1955.
"New Power Arising," *Spectator*, December 14, 1962.
Noer, Thomas J. "New Frontiers and Old Priorities in Africa." In *Kennedy's Quest For Victory*, ed. Paterson.
Ollenhauer, Erich. "An Outdated Policy," *Western World*, August 1957.
Paterson, Thomas G. "Bearing the Burden: A Critical Look at JFK's Foreign Policy," *Virginia Quarterly Review* 54, no. 1 (Spring 1978): 193–212.
———. "Fixation with Cuba: The Bay of Pigs, Missile Crisis, and Covert War against Fidel Castro." In *Kennedy's Quest For Victory*, ed. Paterson.
Pelz, Stephen. "John F. Kennedy's 1961 Vietnam War Decisions," *Journal of Strategic Studies* 4 (December 1981): 356–85.
Perkins, Bradford. "Unequal Partners: The Truman Administration and Great Britain." In *The Special Relationship*, ed. Louis and Bull.
Philips, Cabell. "Dean Acheson Ten Years Later," *New York Times Magazine*, January 18, 1959.
Pruessen, Ronald W. "Predicaments of Power." In *John Foster Dulles*, ed. Immerman.
Reichard, Gary W. "The Domestic Politics of National Security." In *The National Security*, ed. Graebner.
Reston, James. "Acheson Criticizes Dulles and G.O.P. Foreign Policy," *New York Times*, October 27, 1955, p. 1.
Rosenberg, David Alan. "A Smoking Radiation Ruin at the End of Two Hours: Documents of American Plans for Nuclear War with the Soviet Union, 1954–55," *International Security* 6 (Winter 1981–82): 3–38.
Rusk, Dean. "The President," *Foreign Affairs* (April 1960): 353–69.
———. "Reflections on Foreign Policy." In *The Kennedy Presidency*, ed. Thompson.

Sagan, Scott D. "Nuclear Alerts and Crisis Management," *International Security* 9 (Spring 1985): 106–22.
Schulzinger, Robert D. "The Impact of Suez on United States Middle East Policy, 1957–1958." In *The Suez-Sinai Crisis*, ed. Troen and Shemesh.
Snyder, Glen H. "The 'New Look' of 1954." In *Strategy, Policies, and Defense Budgets*, ed. Warner H. Schilling, Paul Y. Hammond, and Glen H. Snyder, pp. 383–524. New York: Columbia University Press, 1962.
Steel, Ronald. "Endgame," *New York Review of Books*, March 13, 1969.
Stone, I. F. "The Brink," *New York Review of Books*, April 14, 1966.
Strong, Robert A. "Eisenhower and Arms Control." In *Reevaluating Eisenhower*, ed. Melanson and Mayers.
Thompson, Kenneth W. "The Kennan-Acheson Debate," *Commonweal*, April 4, 1958.
"The Two-Hatted Dean," *Battle Line*, April 14, 1961.
Welles, Benjamin. "NATO: A Question of Survival," *Newsweek*, March 28, 1966.
Wells, Samuel F., Jr. "Sounding the Tocsin: NSC-68 and the Soviet Threat," *International Security* 4 (Fall 1979): 116–58.
―――. "The Origins of Massive Retaliation," *Political Science Quarterly* 96 (Spring 1981): 31–52.
White, William S. "Acheson's Uncomplaining Testament," *New York Times Book Review*, November 20, 1955, p. 1.
Windsor, Philip. "NATO and Cyprus Crisis," *Adelphi Papers* no. 14, London: Institute for Strategic Studies, 1964.
Wohlstetter, Albert. "The Delicate Balance of Terror," *Foreign Affairs* 37 (January 1959): 211–34.

Unpublished Material

Berman, W. G. "The Democratic Advisory Council: A Foreign Policy for Democrats, 1957–1960." Unpublished paper.
Brinkley, Douglas. "Dean Acheson and Jean Monnet: The Pioneers on the Path to Atlantic Partnership." Paper delivered at conference on Jean Monnet and the Americans, Franklin D. Roosevelt Library, Hyde Park, N.Y., October 11, 1990.
Bundy, William P. Vietnam War Manuscript, Lyndon B. Johnson Library, Austin, Texas.
Derman, Dorothy I. "The Riddle of Containment: As Rejected in the Advice and Dissent of George F. Kennan." Ph.D. diss., University of Miami, 1975.
Green, James F. "The Political Thought of George F. Kennan." Ph.D. diss., American University, 1972.
Herring, George C. "Vietnam and American National Security." Paper pre-

sented at the U.S. Military Academy history symposium, April 13–15, 1988.

Kaplan, Larry. "Dean Acheson and the Atlantic Community." Paper delivered at conference on Dean Acheson, Johns Hopkins School of Advanced International Studies, Washington, D.C., April 6, 1989.

Lazarowitz, Arlene. "Years of Exile: The Liberal Democrats, 1950–1959." Ph.D. diss., vol. 2, University of Southern California, 1987.

Medland, William James. "The American-Soviet Nuclear Confrontation of 1962: An Historiographical Account of the Cuban Missile Crisis." Ph.D. diss., Ball State University, 1980.

Perlmutter, Oscar. "Acheson and American Foreign Policy: A Case in the Conduct of Foreign Affairs in a Mass Democracy." Ph.D. diss., University of Chicago, 1959.

Rosenau, James. "The Senate and Dean Acheson: A Case Study in Legislative Attitudes." Ph.D. diss., Princeton University, 1957.

Rostow, Eugene V. "In Commemoration of Dean Acheson." Luncheon speech at conference on Dean Acheson, Yale University, April 24, 1982.

Salmon, Jeffrey. "The Statesmanship of Dean Acheson." Ph.D. diss., Catholic University, 1985.

Smith, Gaddis. "The Improbable Partnership: Truman and Acheson." Paper presented at conference on Dean Acheson, Yale University, April 24, 1982.

Vaughn, Cecil Ellis. "A Comparison of the Foreign Policy Viewpoints of Dean Acheson as Secretary of State and as Elder Statesman." Master's thesis, University of Miami, 1967.

Winand, Pascaline. "Presidents, Advisers and the Uniting of Europe." Ph.D. diss., University of Brussels, Belgium, 1990.

Public Documents

Acheson, Dean. Memorandum for the President, April 3, 1961. Declassified Documents Collection, Center for Research Libraries, Chicago, Illinois.

Action Committee for the United States of Europe: Statements and Declarations 1955–1967. European Series No. 9. London: Chatham House, 1969.

Congressional Record. Washington, D.C., July 23, 1969.

Congressional Record. Washington, D.C., July 28, 1969.

International Secretariat of the NATO Parliamentarians Conference. Atlantic Congress Report. London, 1959.

Public Papers of the Presidents of the United States: Dwight D. Eisenhower, 1953. Washington, D.C.: Government Printing Office, 1964.

Public Papers of the Presidents of the United States: John F. Kennedy, 1961–1963. Washington, D.C.: United States Government Printing Office, 1964.

Schlesinger, Arthur, Jr. "Memorandum for the Honorable Robert Kennedy.

Subject: Our Policy in Africa." Declassified Documents System, Carrollton, Texas: Carrollton Press, 1979.

U.S. Congress. Joint Committee on Foreign Affairs. Subcommittee on Europe. *The Crisis in NATO.* May 17, 1966.

———. Joint Economic Committee. Subcommittee on Economy in Government. *Security and Foreign Policy in the 1970's.* June 11, 1969.

U.S. Congress. House. Committee on Foreign Affairs. *Dean Acheson Statement.* November 19, 1969.

———. *Hearings on the Atlantic Alliance.* 89th Cong., 2d sess., 1966.

———. *Economic and Military Cooperation with Nations in the General Area of the Middle East.* 85th Cong., 1st sess., 1957.

U.S. Congress. Senate. Committee on Foreign Relations. *A Select Chronology and Background Documents Relating to the Middle East,* rev. ed. 91st Cong., 1st sess., 1969.

U.S. Congress. Senate. Committee on Foreign Relations. *Activities of Non-Diplomatic Representatives of Foreign Powers in the U.S.* 88th Cong., 1st sess., 1963.

———. *Documents on Germany 1944–1961.* New York: Greenwood Press, 1968.

———. *The President's Proposal on the Middle East.* 85th Cong., 1st sess., 1957.

———. Subcommittee on Foreign Economic Policy of the Joint Economic Committee. *Dean Acheson Statement.* December 5, 1961.

———. Subcommittee on National Security and International Operations. Dean Acheson testimony, *Hearings on the Atlantic Alliance.* 89th Cong., 2d sess., 1966.

U.S. Department of State. *Foreign Relations of the United States [FRUS], 1952–1954.* Vol. 1, pt. 1, and vol. 5, pt. 1. Washington, D.C.: Council on Foreign Relations, 1983.

———. *Intelligence Report 8047, Analysis of the Cyprus Agreements,* July 14, 1959. (Published in *Journal of the Hellenic Diaspora* 11, no. 4 (Winter 1984):9–31.

Newspapers, 1952–71

Charleston (West Virginia) Gazette
Christian Science Monitor
Detroit Free Press
Detroit News
National Observer
New York Herald Tribune
New York Post
New York Times

Philadelphia Evening Bulletin
Sunday Star
U.S. Daily News
Washington Post
Washington Star

Personal Interviews
INTERVIEWS BY AUTHOR

Acheson, Alice. December 1986 and December 1987, Washington, D.C.
Acheson, David. February 1987, December 1987, and April 1988, Washington, D.C.
Alsop, Joseph. March 1988, Washington, D.C.
Ball, George W. February 1988, Princeton, N.J.; and September 1990, Hyde Park, N.Y.
Battle, Lucius. March 1987, October 1987, and March 1988, Washington, D.C.
Bowie, Robert. January 1991, Washington, D.C.
Bundy, Mary Acheson. June 1988 and August 1988, Princeton, N.J.
Bundy, McGeorge. April 1988, New York, N.Y. Also letter to author, May 1988.
Bundy, William P. February 1988, June 1988, and August 1988, Princeton, N.J.
Carver, George. August 1990, Canton, N.Y.
Cater, Douglass. December 1988, Baltimore, Md.
Cutler, Lloyd. December 1988 (telephone), Washington, D.C.
Dillon, C. Douglas. June 1989, New York, N.Y.
Duchene, François. October 1990, Hyde Park, N.Y.
Dulles, Eleanor Lansing. May 1987, Washington, D.C.
Evans, Barbara. October 1987, Washington, D.C.
Fosdick, Dorothy. December 1987, Washington, D.C.
Franks, Sir Oliver. April 1989, Washington, D.C.
Galbraith, John Kenneth. August 1991, St. John's, Newfoundland, Canada.
Healey, Denis. April 1988, Princeton, N.J.
Janeway, Eliot. May 1990, New York, N.Y.
Johnson, U. Alexis. February 1988, Princeton, N.J.
Kleiman, Robert. January 1992, Washington, D.C.
Klein, David. September 1987, Princeton, N.J.
Kohler, Foy. March 1988 (telephone), West Palm Beach, Fla.
Marshall, Charles Burton. March 1987, Washington, D.C. Also letter to author, October 1988.
McCarthy, Eugene. March 1990, Toronto, Canada.
McKeever, Porter. October 1990, Hyde Park, N.Y.

Morris, Roger. August 1987 (telephone), Santa Fe, N.M.
Newsom, David. March 1988, Washington, D.C.
Nitze, Paul H., September 1987, Washington, D.C.
Norstad, Lauris. June 1988 (telephone), Tucson, Ariz.
Owen, Henry. March 1988, and September 1990 (telephone), Washington, D.C.
Reston, James. August 1991, St. John's, Newfoundland, Canada.
Rostow, Walt W. March 1988 (telephone), Austin, Tex.
Rusk, Dean. March 1988 (telephone), and April 1989, Athens, Ga.
Schaetzel, J. Robert. December 1987, Bethesda, Md.
Schlesinger, Arthur M., Jr. March 1988, New York, N.Y.
Sorensen, Theodore. February 1988, New York, N.Y.
Swenson, Eric. March 1990, New York, N.Y.
Symington, Stuart. November 1987, New Canaan, Conn.
Tyroler, Charles II. October 1987, February 1988, and May 1988, Washington, D.C.
Uri, Pierre. October 1990, Hempstead, N.Y.
Westwood, Howard C. October 1987 (telephone), Washington, D.C.
Williams, G. Mennen. November 1987 (telephone), Detroit, Mich.

INTERVIEWS OF DEAN ACHESON

By Margaret Ingram. Cambridge, England, October 1958.
By Kenneth Harris. "Pungent Memories from Mr. Acheson," *Life*, July 23, 195
By Lucius D. Battle. April 27, 1964. John F. Kennedy Library, Boston, Massachusetts.
By Edward P. Morgan. American Broadcasting Corporation, ABC "Issues and Answers," October 24, 1965.
By Marvin Kalb. "CBS News" (transcript), April 4, 1966.
Public Broadcasting Corporation. Reels 1–3 (transcript), December 3, 1967.
By David Frost. "ABM Discussion with Former Secretary of State Dean Acheson and Senator Charles Percy of Illinois," "The David Frost Show," July 15, 1969.
By Gaddis Smith. September 24, 1969. Published in the *New York Times Book Review*, October 12, 1969.
By Eric Sevareid. "A Conversation with Dean Acheson," "CBS News Special," November 4, 1969.
By William Hardcastle. "Hard Words from the Veteran American Statesman: Dean Acheson in Conversation with William Hardcastle," *Listener*, June 19, 1970.

INDEX

ABM. *See* Antiballistic missile system
Abrams, Creighton, 260, 270, 285
Acheson, Alice, 6, 13–14, 15, 47, 83–84, 197, 214, 218, 282, 284
Acheson, David, 3, 14, 275, 301, 330
Acheson, Dean Gooderham
—as advocate of ABM system, 271–75
—Africa: attitude toward colonies in, 303–10, 321–28, 386n2, 389n50; as adviser to Nixon on, 321–23
—Asian policies of, 237–38
—as proponent of Atlantic solidarity, 186–96, 202, 223–25, 234–35
—Austrian State Treaty, view of, 32–33
—Berlin: as adviser to Kennedy on, 124–26, 135–39, 144–46, 147–48; report of on crisis in, 139–44; role of in deadline crisis of *1958–59*, 93–100
—books by, 3–4, 39–41, 53–54, 226, 275–77
—Willy Brandt: concerns regarding, 291–96
—Fidel Castro, encounter with, 154–55
—Cuban missile crisis: as adviser to Kennedy during, 156–64; as emissary to Europe during, 164–69, 171–72; retrospective view of, 172–74
—Cyprus conflict: role of in, 210–19
—death of, 329–30, 391–92n5
—Democratic Advisory Council: as member of, 55–63, 65–67, 71–72, 305
—and John Foster Dulles, 10–12, 11–13, 15–16, 17, 19, 23–26, 48, 83; and nuclear policy of, 20–23, 39, 335n57, 336n68
—early career of, 1–2
—as elder statesman, 2–5, 204, 253
—as critic of Dwight D. Eisenhower, 23–26, 35–37, 38, 41–49, 50–53, 59–60, 63–64, 67–69, 71–73, 333n12, 342n63
—Europe: as advocate for, 75–76, 79–85, 101–7, 119–24, 197–99, 223–26, 227–28, 231–36, 291–96, 347n1; diplomatic missions to, 126–34; 164–69, 171–72
—and European Defense Community, 29–32
—foreign-policy pamphlets by, 58–62, 66–67, 68–69, 343n86, 344n99
—Great Britain: criticism of in West Point speech, 176–82, 185
—and Indochina controversy, 27–29
—Lyndon B. Johnson: as adviser to, 58, 99, 203–10, 219–25
—George F. Kennan: debate with, 80–92, 348–49n30, 350n63
—John F. Kennedy: as adviser to, 113–16, 117, 118, 139–46, 156–64, 199–200; as critic of, 201–2, 368n105; relationship with, 108–12, 200
—Henry Kissinger: as admirer of, 266–68; relationship with, 279–80, 287, 294, 296–98, 300
—Mansfield amendment: as opponent of, 297–300
—memoirs of, 275–77
—on Middle East policy, 51–53, 287–91
—and morality as yardstick in foreign policy, 24–26

418 ■ Index

Acheson, Dean Gooderham (continued)
—NATO: as chairman of Advisory Committee on, 117–24; commitment of to, 203, 204, 228–36, 292, 309–10
—and Paul H. Nitze, 16–18, 35–36, 43, 48, 56, 57, 68–69, 74, 119, 144
—Richard M. Nixon: Acheson's view of, 263–64; as admirer of, 270–71; as adviser to, 268–70, 283
—Pentagon Papers: reaction to, 299
—Portugal: as supporter of, 305–14
—and presidential election of 1952, 8–10
—and presidential election of 1956, 47–50
—and presidential election of 1960, 109–12
—as private citizen, 13–19
—Pulitzer Prize awarded to, 277
—as target of Republicans, 39–41
—Rhodesia: differences with Arthur Goldberg over, 316–20
—as critic of William P. Rogers, 265–66, 286, 289
—as secretary of state, 1, 6–8
—Sihanouk: relationship with, 284
—Adlai Stevenson: rift with, 65–67, 362n67; as supporter of, 38–39, 47–49
—and Suez crisis, 42–47
—Stuart Symington: as supporter of, 71
—Harry S Truman: as admirer of, 19, 332n5, 335n48; correspondence of with, 14–15, 16, 17, 21, 66, 127–28, 136–37, 145, 148, 151, 197, 227, 234, 248, 276, 346–47n145, 366n58
—on U.S.-Soviet disengagement, 79–93
—Vietnam: as adviser to Eisenhower on, 27–29; as adviser to Johnson on, 238–42, 256–62; as supporter of Johnson's policy, 248–55; as adviser to Nixon on, 278–82
—as supporter of Yale University, 39, 339n4
Acheson, Jane, 14
Acheson, Mary, 14
Acheson-Ball Peace Plan: for Vietnam, 243–48
Acheson Plan: to resolve Cyprus conflict, 215–16, 217, 218, 219
Achilles, Theodore, 102
Action Committee for a United States of Europe, 186, 187, 188
ADA. *See* Americans for Democratic Action
Adams, John, 14
Adenauer, Konrad, 33, 79, 82, 101, 127, 223, 230; Acheson's meetings with, 128–29, 152; and Berlin crisis, 136, 140, 152; and Cuban missile crisis, 168–69; as ally of de Gaulle, 190–93, 366n58; Kennedy's first meeting with, 130; resignation of, 199
Africa, southern: Acheson's view of colonies in, 303–5, 311, 321–28; Nixon's policy toward, 321–22; Portuguese colonies of, 305–10. *See also* Rhodesia
Agnew, Spiro, 274, 301
Algeria, 70
Allemann, Fritz René, 78
Allied Command Europe (ACE), 228
Allied Forces Central Europe (AFCENT), 228
Alphonso X, 275–76
Alsop, Joseph, 84, 91, 206, 208
Altmeyer, Arthur J., 343n78
American Council on Germany, Inc., 349–50n44
Americans for Democratic Action (ADA), 94
Amory, Robert, 143
Anderson, Clinton, 224
Angola, 306, 307–9, 310, 311
Annan, Noel, 177, 225
Antiballistic missile (ABM) system: Acheson as advocate of, 271–75
ANZUS Treaty, 42
Armstrong, Hamilton Fish, 87
ARVN. *See* Vietnam
Asian-African Conference, 33
Aswan Dam: Dulles's policy on, 43
Atlantic Nuclear Force (ANF), 224, 232
Atlantic Partnership: Acheson as advocate of, 223–25, 234–35; versus French nationalism, 186–96
Atomic policy. *See* Nuclear weapons policy, U.S.
Ausland, John, 138
Austrian State Treaty, 32–33
Azores Islands: debate over U.S. presence in, 310–14; U.S. bases on, 306, 310

Baghdad Pact, 41–42
Ball, George, 158, 160, 161, 164, 187, 188, 196, 200, 208, 221, 224, 226, 229, 230, 231, 235, 292, 298, 309, 370n25; and Cyprus conflict, 210–11, 212, 213–14, 217; and U.S. involvement in Vietnam, 240, 243–46, 248, 254, 261
Bandung, Indonesia, 33
Bao Dai, 28
Barkley, Alben, 6

Batista, Fulgencio, 154
Battle, Lucius, 17, 138, 216, 218, 277, 306
Bay of Pigs: invasion of, 127–28
Beale, Sir Howard, 179, 287, 364n19
Beirne, Joe, 250
Belgian Congo, 132, 306, 325
Belgium: Acheson's meeting with prime minister of, 132
Bennett, Wallace F., 39
Benson, Ezra Taft, 65
Benton, William, 57, 66
Berlin: Acheson as adviser on, 134–39; Acheson's report on, 139–44; control of access to, 351n71; deadline crisis of *1958–59*, 93–101; Kennedy's policy toward, 124–26, 135–36, 146–48; NSC deliberations on, 144–46; wall built by Soviets, 148–53
Berlin Wall, 108, 148–53
Berry, Lady Pamela, 221, 272
Bevan, Aneurin, 82
Bingham, Barry, 57
Birrenbach, Kurt, 191, 233, 374n110
Black, Eugene, 115
Boheman, Erik, 227
Bohlen, Charles E. ("Chip"), 228, 229, 281
Bohr, Niels, 344n97
Bonbright, James C., 90–91
Bonn, N. J., 87
Bosch, Juan, 227
Boure, Robert, 47
Bowie, Robert, 5, 47, 119, 120
Bowie Report, 120
Bowles, Chester, 4, 21, 49, 55, 57, 61, 66, 109, 112, 137, 142, 180, 277, 305, 309, 335n57, 345n112
Bradlee, Benjamin, 199
Bradley, Omar, 247, 248, 250, 254, 261
Brandeis, Louis, 1, 18, 297
Brandt, Willy, 287, 298; Acheson's concerns regarding, 291–96
Brentano, Heinrich von, 83, 103
Bretton Woods agreement, 7
Brezhnev, Leonid, 222
Bricker Amendment, 38, 338n1
Bridges, Styles, 16
Brinkley, David, 356n90
Brown, George, 105
Bruce, David K. E., 4, 31, 114, 165, 178, 224, 247
Buchanan, Patrick, 326
Buckley, William F., 40, 326

Bulganin, Nikolai, 33, 34, 35, 84–85
Bundy, McGeorge, 47, 118, 124, 125, 138, 139, 144, 148–49, 150, 151, 187, 196, 207, 208, 221, 224, 298, 307, 310, 359n6; and Vietnam War, 244, 248, 254, 260–61
Bundy, William P., 118, 165, 240, 241, 247, 252, 257
Bunker, Ellsworth, 256, 373n90
Burling, Edward, 119
Burns, James MacGregor, 250
Butler, Paul, 54, 55, 66, 69, 70
Butler, R. A., 218
Byrd, Harry F.: amendment proposed by, 327
Byrnes, James F., 7, 250, 380n1
Byroade, Henry, 43, 45

Cambodia: as threat to South Vietnam, 283–86
Canfield, Cass, 83
Carroll, Wallace, 259
Carter, Marshall, 359n6
Carver, George, 254, 257, 258, 260
Casey, Lord Richard, 235
Castro, Fidel, 227; Acheson's encounter with, 154–55. *See also* Cuban missile crisis
Cater, Douglass, 239–40
CDU. *See* Christian Democratic Party
CENTO. *See* Central Treaty Organization
Central Treaty Organization (CENTO), 41
Chamberlain, Neville, 88, 109
Chamoun, Camille, 53
Chayes, Abram, 139, 142
Chiang Kai-shek, 8, 63
China, People's Republic of (PRC): and Indochina, 27–28; and Korean armistice, 15–16; and Quemoy and Matsu, 62–64; and Soviet Union, 33; U.S. policy toward, 48
Christian Democratic Party (CDU), 79, 198–99, 291
Church, Frank, 233
Churchill, Winston, 32, 42
A Citizen Looks at Congress (Acheson), 3, 53–54, 342nn68,69
Citizens Committee for Peace and Freedom in Vietnam, 250
Citizens' Committee to Safeguard America, 275
Civil Rights Act of *1957,* 204–5, 368–69n3
Clausewitz, Carl von, 130
Clay, Lucius, 150, 151, 249, 250, 254, 281, 282, 293, 295, 298, 299

Clayton, William L., 153, 277
Clements, Earle C., 205
Cleveland, Harlan, 230, 311
Clifford, Clark, 5, 115, 138, 200, 254, 257, 259, 260, 282
Cohen, Ben, 57
Common Market. *See* European Economic Community
Communism: as issue under Acheson, 2, 8; in Indochina, 27–29. *See also* China, People's Republic of; Soviet Union
Conant, James B., 79, 86, 249, 349n44
Congo. *See* Belgian Congo
Congressional Government (Wilson), 53
Connally, John, 205
Cooper, Chester, 240
Copland, Aaron, 220
Covington, Burling & Rublee, 1, 334n46; Acheson's return to, 18
Cowles, John, 14, 60, 124, 197, 247, 251, 252, 257, 262, 299, 301, 329, 344n97
Crisis over Rhodesia: A Skeptical View (Marshall), 318
Cuba: Bay of Pigs invasion, 127–28; Kennedy's position on, 111–12; U.S. relations with, 154–55. *See also* Cuban missile crisis
Cuban missile crisis: Acheson's role in, 156–64, 169–71; Acheson's retrospective view of, 172–74; advisers during, 359–60n6; European reaction to, 164–68, 171–72; Khrushchev's response to naval blockade during, 170–71
Cunningham, Joe, 133
Cutler, Lloyd, 244–45
Cyprus conflict: Acheson's role in, 210–19

DAC. *See* Democratic Advisory Council
Daley, Richard, 264
Davies, John Paton, 196
Davidson, C. Girard, 343n78
Dean, Arthur H., 248, 254, 261, 281
DeBakey, Michael, 343n78
Defense policy, U.S.: under Eisenhower, 19–23; under Kennedy, 118–19. *See also* Nuclear weapons policy, U.S.
de Gaulle, Charles, 76, 127, 130–31, 175, 223; as opponent to British entry into Common Market, 186, 189–90; and Cuban missile crisis, 166–68; seeks treaty with Germany, 189–96, 366n58; response of to Nassau Agreement, 184, 186; as threat to NATO, 203, 227–28, 231–36; threatens to withdraw from NATO, 228–31, 363n81; refusal of to sign test ban treaty, 197, 199
de Kooning, Willem, 220
Democratic Advisory Council (DAC), 54–63, 305, 343n78, 346n135; foreign-policy positions of, 56–63, 65–67, 68–69, 71–72, 73–74
Democratic National Committee (DNC), 54
Democratic Party: Acheson as foreign-policy spokesman for, 54–58
A Democrat Looks at His Party (Acheson), 3, 39–41
De Puy, William, 257, 258, 260
Devlin, Sir Patrick, 64, 163, 221, 313
Dewey, Thomas E., 281–82, 293, 295
Diefenbaker, John, 362n44
Dienbienphu. *See* Indochina
Diggs, Charles, 323, 327
Dillon, C. Douglas, 115, 157, 163, 164, 187, 249, 250, 254, 261, 299, 359n6
Dillon, Read & Co., 115
Disney, Walt, 220
Dixon, Owen, 387n9
DNC. *See* Democratic National Committee
Dobrynin, Anatoly, 171, 385n119
Dominican Republic, 227, 373n90
Donhoff, Countess Marion, 292
Donnelly, Desmond, 177, 185, 247, 286
Dos Passos, John, 249
Douglas, Lewis, 277
Douglas, Paul H., 83, 250
Douglas-Home, Sir Alec. *See* Home, Sir Alec Douglas-
Dowling, Walter ("Red"), 165, 168, 169, 191–92
Draft Extension Act: Mansfield amendment to, 297–300
Dubcek, Alexander, 320
Dulles, Allen, 142
Dulles, Eleanor Lansing, 336n68
Dulles, John Foster: Acheson's view of, 11–13, 15–16, 17, 19, 23–26, 36–37, 39, 41, 42, 48, 50, 65; as supporter of Acheson, 83–84; appointment of as secretary of state, 10–11, 333n16; negotiations with China, 63, 64; death of, 67; as supporter of Eisenhower Doctrine, 51; and European Defense Community, 31; Indochina policy of, 28–29;

nuclear defense policy of, 19–22, 23, 39, 335n57; as secretary of state, 32–36; and Suez crisis, 43–47, 340n27
Duong Van Minh ("Big Minh"), 238

Eagleburger, Lawrence S., 277
Eastern Europe. *See* Europe (Eastern)
East Germany: Eisenhower administration policy toward, 15; Khrushchev's relationship with, 135. *See also* Berlin; Berlin Wall
Eastland, James, 318
Eaton, Cyrus, 82
ECSC. *See* European Coal and Steel Community
EDC. *See* European Defense Community
Eden, Anthony, 2, 35, 39, 44, 82, 148, 177, 224, 233, 235, 252, 255, 265, 282, 290, 329, 340n27
EEC. *See* European Economic Community
Egypt: Soviet aid to, 291; role of in Suez crisis, 43–46
Ehrlich, Thomas, 246
Eisenhower, Dwight D., 3, 6, 249; Acheson's criticism of, 19, 23–26, 35–37, 38, 41–49, 50–53, 59–60, 63–64, 68–69, 71–73, 102, 333n12; and Berlin deadline crisis of *1958–59, 93*–101; defense policy under, 19–23, 69; and *1952* presidential election, 8–10; European policy of, 31; foreign policy under, 15–16, 32–37, 41–42, 68–69; Indochina policy of, 26–29, 68, 337n89; Latin American policy of, 67–68; Middle East policy of, 68, 342n64; and Quemoy and Matsu crisis, 63–64; and Rapacki Plan, 85; and Suez crisis, 42–47; and Truman, 8–9, 36–37, 332–33n11, 342n63
Eisenhower Doctrine, 50–53, 342n63
Elbrick, C. Burke, 309
Eliot, T. S., 40, 220
Elliot, Sir William, 234, 285
Ellison, Ralph, 250
Ellsberg, Daniel, 301
Emmet, Christopher, 79, 80, 83, 86, 95, 349n44
England. *See* Great Britain
Enthoven, Alain, 118, 260
Erhard, Ludwig, 199, 223, 224
Erim, Nihat, 215

Euratom. *See* European Atomic Energy Commission
Europe (Eastern): Dulles's policy toward, 13, 46; NATO's role in, 232–33; Soviet domination of, 35, 81, 96, 320
Europe (Western): Acheson's diplomatic missions to, 126–34, 164–69, 171–72; Acheson's view of, 75–76, 101–7; reaction of to Cuban missile crisis, 164–69, 171–72; Kennan's view of, 77–78; Kennedy's approach to, 119–24; multilateral force (MLF) in, 198–99, 203, 207, 223–24; Nixon's visit to, 271; U.S. military presence in, 79–85; reaction of to U.S. nuclear policy, 23; U.S.-Soviet disengagement from, 77–93; concerns of regarding Vietnam, 232. *See also* Berlin; Berlin Wall; European Economic Community; North Atlantic Treaty Organization
European Atomic Energy Commission (Euratom), 75–76
European Coal and Steel Community (ECSC), 8, 30, 187
European Defense Community (EDC), 10, 79; France's rejection of, 29–32
European Economic Community (EEC; Common Market), 75, 102–3, 122; controversy over British entry into, 186, 188–89
European Movement, 196
Evans, Barbara, 3, 14, 165
ExCom, members of, 359–60n6. *See also* Cuban missile crisis

Fanfani, Amintore, 132
Fannin, Paul, 318
Farrell, James T., 250
Faure, Edgar, 35
Ferrell, Robert H., 3
Finkelstein, Marina, 266
Finletter, Thomas K., 19, 55–56, 66
Finletter Group, 54–55
Fontaine, André, 131–32
Foreign Affairs, 41, 76, 87, 90
Foreign policy, U.S.: Acheson as influence on, 1–5; Acheson-Kennan debate over, 80–92; as campaign issue in *1954,* 21–22; as campaign issue in *1956,* 47–50; as campaign issue in *1960,* 110–12; as advocated by the Democratic Advisory Council, 54–63, 65–67, 68–69, 71–72, 73–74; Democratic

Foreign policy, U.S. (continued)
position papers on, 48; under Eisenhower and Dulles, 10–13, 15–37, 41–42; toward Europe, 76–93; and Great Britain, 182–86; in Latin America, 67–68; in Middle East, 50–53, 68, 287–91; as advocated by NATO advisory committee, 117–24; in Suez Canal zone, 44–46; and U.S.-Soviet disengagement from Europe, 77–93; after World War II, 1, 6–8. *See also* Africa, southern; Berlin; Cuban missile crisis; Europe (Western); European Defense Community; Indochina; Korean War; Nuclear weapons policy, U.S.; Soviet Union; Vietnam
Formosa Resolution, 36, 63
Fortas, Abe, 205, 206, 254, 261
Fosdick, Dorothy, 57
Fragments of My Fleece (Acheson), 3
France: and Algeria, 70; and Euratom, 76; and European Defense Community, 29–32; and Indochina, 26–29; nationalist policies of, 186–96; and Suez crisis, 44–46; as ally of West Germany, 189–96. *See also* de Gaulle, Charles
Franco, Francisco, 388n36
Frank, John P., 92
Frankel, Max, 231, 374n110
Frankfurter, Felix, 18, 103, 154, 180, 226, 288, 392n5
Franks, Sir Oliver, 177
Fredricks, Wayne, 305
Free Democratic Party (FDP), 291
Freedom House, 249, 378n50
Friedrich, Carl J., 349n44
Frost, David, 274
Fulbright, J. William, 57, 94, 112, 113, 136, 143, 209, 224, 233, 234, 254, 269

Gaither, H. Rowan, 59
Gaither Committee, 59–60
Gaitskell, Hugh, 82, 180
Galbraith, John Kenneth, 55, 62, 65, 137, 273, 277, 311, 312, 314, 344n112
Gardner, John, 250
Gates, Thomas, 299
Gaulle, Charles de. *See* de Gaulle, Charles
Gavin, James M., 352n88
Geneva Conference of 1955, 33–35
German Democratic Republic. *See* East Germany

German Federal Republic. *See* West Germany
Germany. *See* East Germany; West Germany
Ghana, 304
Gilpatric, Roswell, 123, 164, 220, 299, 359n6
Glassboro, N.J.: Johnson-Kosygin meeting in, 222
Goldberg, Arthur, 259, 261; debate with Acheson over Rhodesia, 316–20
Goldwater, Barry, 209, 220, 241, 318
Gould, J. H. P., 262, 270, 272, 277
Gowon, Yakubu, 283
Graham, Lord Angus, 320
Grapes from Thorns (Acheson), 3
Great Britain: and controversy over Acheson's West Point speech, 176–82, 185; entry of into Common Market, 186, 189–90; and Skybolt controversy, 182–84, 185; and Suez crisis, 44–46; relations with U.S., 182–86
Greece: assistance program to, 7. *See also* Cyprus conflict
Green, Theodore, 205
Grew, Joseph C., 277
Grivas, George, 213, 217
Gross, Ernest, 277
Gruenther, Alfred, 281, 298
Gustiniani, Count Alvise, 112
GVN. *See* Vietnam

Habib, Philip, 257, 258, 260
Hacker, Louis, 250
Hahn, Walter, 350n63
Haldeman, H. R., 282
Halle, Louis, 67, 72, 196, 333n20
Hammarskjöld, Dag, 132
Handlin, Oscar, 250
Hardcastle, William, 185
Harper's Magazine, 38
Harriman, W. Averell, 4, 38, 49, 55, 62, 65, 66, 80, 136, 197, 254, 320, 327, 338–39n2; views of on Berlin, 126, 142, 143; views of on Vietnam, 255, 259
Hay, John, 4
Healey, Denis W., 82
Helms, Richard, 257
Henderson, Loy, 277
Herter, Christian, 100, 102, 104–5, 120
Heuss, Theodor, 78
Hickerson, John D., 277
Hillenbrand, Martin, 294
Hiss, Alger, 40, 263

Hitch, Charles, 118
Ho Chi Minh, 26, 28, 29, 238. *See also* Vietnam
Hoffer, Eric, 250
Holland. *See* Netherlands
Holmes, Oliver Wendell, Jr., 14, 165
Home, Sir Alec Douglas-, 125–26, 143
Hood, Viscount Samuel, 214–15
Hook, Sidney, 249
Hoover, J. Edgar, 282
Howe, Quincy, 85
Humphrey, George, 72, 281, 347n145
Humphrey, Hubert H., 55, 57, 66, 67, 73, 260, 320, 342n64; as Democratic nominee, 264–65
Hungary: U.S. policy toward, 46
Hyman, Sidney, 333n12

Indochina: U.S. policy toward, 26–29
Inonu, Ismet, 213, 214
Isaacson, Walter, 300
Israel: Acheson's view of, 52; reaction of to Rogers Plan, 287–88; and Suez crisis, 45; U.S. policy toward, 289–91
Ives, Buffy, 47

Jackson, Henry ("Scoop"), 112, 224, 231, 234, 313
Janeway, Eliot, 149
Janeway, Michael, 149
Japan: treaty with, 11–12, 42
Jarring, Gunnar, 288
Javits, Jacob, 232
Jefferson, Thomas, 4, 14
Jenkins, Walter, 239
Jenner, William E., 9, 16, 29
Jernegan, John D., 214, 371n37
Jessup, Philip, 57, 88, 320, 342n65
John Birch Society, 326
Johnson, Joseph, 151
Johnson, Lyndon B., 26, 64, 71, 159, 165, 359n6, 369–70n23; Acheson as adviser to, 58, 99, 203–10, 219–25, 228–31, 235; African policy of, 315, 317, 319, 320–21; and Berlin crisis, 145; and Cyprus conflict, 212–14, 218–19; and Democratic Advisory Council, 54, 55, 58; foreign-policy priorities of, 223–25, 226–28; and threatened French withdrawal from NATO, 228–31; Nixon's view of, 269; as advocate of U.S. involvement in Vietnam, 239–43, 251–55; Vietnam as priority for, 226, 235, 238; reaction of to Vietnam peace plan, 244–48; reevaluation of U.S. involvement in Vietnam, 255–62
Johnson, U. Alexis, 142–43, 246, 359n6
Judd, Walter, 237

Kalb, Marvin, 229
Kaltenborn, H. V., 349n44
Kaufmann, William, 118
Kaunda, Kenneth, 326
Kefauver, Estes, 55, 57, 69
Kennan, George F., 76–78, 94, 277, 350n63; Acheson's debate with, 80–92, 348–49n30
Kennedy, Jacqueline, 108, 201
Kennedy, John F., 2, 41, 67, 90; Acheson as adviser to, 113–16, 117, 118, 139–46, 199–200; Acheson's relationship with, 108–9; Acheson's view of, 173–74, 193, 196, 201–2, 368n105; response of to Acheson's West Point speech, 176–77, 182; African policy of, 305, 308–9; assassination of, 201; and negotiations over Azores, 310–14; Berlin policy of, 124–26, 134–39, 143–45, 146–48; response of to Berlin Wall, 148–53; cabinet appointments of, 113–16; and Cuban missile crisis, 156–64, 169–72, 363n80; as member of Democratic Advisory Council, 70, 71; and Nassau Agreement, 184; NATO policy of, 117–24; debates with Nixon, 111; as presidential hopeful, 69–70, 73–74, 107, 109–12; and Skybolt controversy, 182–84; Vietnam policy of, 238
Kennedy, Joseph, 109, 179
Kennedy, Robert F., 115–16, 209, 231, 264, 314, 359n6; and Cuban missile crisis, 159–60, 161, 163, 164, 170–71, 172–73, 259
Kennedy Round, 220, 223
Kent, Sherman, 165, 166, 167
Kenworthy, E. W., 342n69
Keyserling, Leon, 60
Khrushchev, Nikita, 33, 34, 108, 214, 306; declares ultimatum over Berlin, 134–35, 140–43, 144–45; role of in Berlin crisis of 1958–59, 93–101, 351n71; and Berlin Wall, 150–53; overthrow of, 222; and Vietnam, 238. *See also* Cuban missile crisis; Soviet Union

Kiesinger, Kurt, 103, 291
Kilpatrick, James J., 326
King, Martin Luther, Jr., 264
Kirk, Russell, 40
Kissinger, Henry, 73, 82–83, 96, 103, 168, 180, 336n68; Acheson as admirer of, 266–68; Acheson's relationship with, 279–80, 287, 294, 296–98, 300, 323; and reconciliation of Acheson and Nixon, 268–69; African policies of, 321; as opponent of Mansfield amendment, 297–300; as adviser to Nixon, 266, 283, 285, 288–289, 290, 293
Knowland, William, 16, 237
Kohler, Foy, 119, 136, 142, 143, 275
Kohn, Hans, 349n44
Komer, Robert, 119
Korean War, 22; Acheson's role in, 8–9, 10; Dulles's role in, 12–13; end of, 15–16; moral issues relating to, 25, 26
Kornilov, V., 105
Kosygin, Aleksei, 222
Krock, Arthur, 36, 73, 105, 195, 222

LaFarge, John, 349n44
LaFeber, Walter, 267
Laird, Melvin, 285
Laniel, Joseph, 28
Larson, Arthur, 41
Laski, Harold, 14
Latin America: Eisenhower's policy toward, 67–68
Lawrence, D. H., 132
Lebanon: U.S. policy toward, 53
Leddy, John M., 229
Lehman, Herbert, 55, 57, 65
Leith-Ross, Sir Frederick, 84, 177, 317
Lemnitzer, Lyman, 212, 298
Lerner, Max, 249
Lewis, John L., 220
Liberty Lobby, 326
Lindsay, Howard, 250
Lippman, Walter, 61, 94, 117, 222, 233, 276
Lochner, Louis, 349n44
Lodge, Henry Cabot, Jr., 240, 254, 261, 275, 298
Loeb, William, 326
London Conference, 44
Lon Nol, 283, 284, 285
Loveless, Herschel, 343n78

Lovett, Robert, 114, 115, 116, 247, 248, 277, 298, 299, 360n6
Luce, Clare Boothe, 237
Luce, Henry, 237
Lumumba, Patrice, 325
Luttwak, Edward, 274
Lyon, Cecil, 165, 166

MacArthur, Douglas, 276
McCarran, Patrick, 16
McCarthy, Eugene, 259
McCarthy, Joseph, 8, 9, 16, 19, 35, 40, 181, 263, 276
McCloy, John J., 114, 169, 230, 247, 254, 261, 293, 295, 298, 307, 362n68
McCone, John, 157, 310, 359n6, 362n44
McCormack, John, 48
MacDonald, Ranald, 27
McElroy, Neil, 299
McGill, Ralph E., 250
MacLeish, Archibald, 14, 112, 329, 339n4
McLellan, David S., 3–4
Macmillan, Harold, 39, 47, 82, 97, 124–25, 126, 143, 165, 177, 342n64; reaction of to Acheson's West Point speech, 178, 179; and Skybolt controversy, 183–84
McNamara, Robert, 118, 119, 144–46, 157, 158, 170, 182–83, 196, 198, 219, 221, 223, 224, 229, 359n6; and U.S. involvement in Vietnam, 238, 242, 244, 245, 257
McNaughton, John T., 240
McPherson, Harry, 250
MacVeagh, Lincoln, 281
Magruder, Jeb, 282
Mahoney, Richard, 314
Makarios III, 211–219
Malenkov, Georgi, 33
Mansfield, Mike, 48, 94, 95, 135–36, 143, 209, 224, 233, 286, 297–300
Mansfield amendment, 297–300
Marshall, Charles Burton, 155, 282, 318, 323
Marshall, George C., 7, 9, 32, 35, 76, 276, 332n7
Marshall Plan, 7, 17
Martin, Edwin, 359n6
Matsu. *See* Quemoy and Matsu crisis
Mazo, Earl, 73
Meany, George, 250
Memoirs, 1925–50 (Kennan), 92
Mendès-France, Pierre, 31

Menzies, Sir Robert, 284
Merchant, Livingston, 299, 362n44
Middle East: Eisenhower's policy toward, 50–53, 68; Rogers Plan for, 287–91; Soviet influence in, 41, 44, 46. *See also* Suez Canal crisis
Middleton, Drew, 195
Miller, Edward G., Jr., 277
Miller, Francis, 179
Milligan, Eugene, 52
Mitchell, John, 302
Molotov, V. M., 98
Moniz, Botelho, 314
Monnet, Jean, 30, 76, 131, 169, 186, 187–89, 190
Monroe Doctrine, 361n24
Morgan, Edward P., 288
Morgenthau, Hans J., 2, 57, 105
Morning and Noon (Acheson), 3, 226, 275
Morris, Roger, 322
Morrow, Dwight, 343n86
Morse, Wayne, 241, 377n13
Moscow Conference, 11
Mountbatten, Lord Louis, 218
Movimento Popular de Libertação (UPA), 309, 310, 311, 388n28
Mozambique, 306, 307, 311
Muhlen, Norbert, 349n44
Muller, Hilgard, 324
Murphy, Charles, 55–56, 66
Murphy, Robert, 247, 254, 261, 299
Muskie, Edmund, 231

Nassau Agreement, 184, 186
Nasser, Gamal Abdel, 42, 68; and Suez crisis, 43–45
National Lawyers Committee for Johnson-Humphrey, 220
National Review, 39–40
National Security Council (NSC): deliberations over Berlin, 144–46
NATO. *See* North Atlantic Treaty Organization
Nebolsine, George, 349n44
Nehru, Jawaharlal, 304–5, 387n9
Netherlands: Acheson's meeting with prime minister of, 132
Nevins, Allan, 250
Newsom, David, 327
Ngo Dinh Diem, 28, 238

Niebuhr, Reinhold, 220
Nigerian civil war, 283
Nitze, Paul H., 12, 16–18, 39, 43, 48, 56, 57, 65, 68–69, 74, 112, 114, 119, 123, 142, 144, 157, 196, 259, 260, 271, 272, 274, 275, 333n20, 359n6
Nixon, Richard M., 3, 29, 44, 67, 209, 249, 293, 320; as advocate of ABM system, 271–75; Acheson as adviser to, 268–70, 278–82, 321–23; Acheson's first meeting with, 268–70; Acheson's view of, 263–65, 270–71, 296; as supporter of Acheson, 83; African policies of, 321–23; response of to Cambodian threat, 283–86; debates with Kennedy, 111; as opponent of Mansfield amendment, 297–300; reaction of to Pentagon Papers, 301; as presidential nominee, 110; "silent majority" speech of, 280–81; Vietnam policies of, 269–70, 278–81, 296, 297
Nkrumah, Kwame, 325
Norodom Sihanouk. *See* Sihanouk, Norodom
Norstad, Lauris, 98, 119, 122, 151, 298
North Atlantic Treaty Organization (NATO), 8, 23, 30, 79, 89–90, 93, 97, 102–4; Acheson as chairman of Advisory Committe on, 117–24; de Gaulle's threat to withdraw from, 228–31, 363n81; nuclear strategy for, 120–21; as deterrent to Soviet aggression, 130–31; threats to, 220, 223, 227–28. *See also* Europe
North Vietnam. *See* Vietnam
Noyes, Crosby, 195
NSC-68, 17, 22, 59–60, 114
Nuclear Weapons and Foreign Policy (Kissinger), 266
Nuclear weapons policy, U.S., 7, 19–23, 60–61, 122, 196–97, 222, 353n114; as debated by Acheson and Dulles, 23–24, 39; as issue in Indochina policy, 29; as issue in Quemoy and Matsu crisis, 63–64; and Skybolt controversy, 182–84. *See also* Cuban missile crisis

O'Donnell, Kenneth, 159–60, 360n6
Ollenhauer, Erich, 79
Operation Rolling Thunder, 242–43, 244, 245. *See also* Vietnam
Oppenheimer, Fritz, 349n44
Oppenheimer, J. Robert, 19

Organization of American States (OAS), 227–28
Ormsby-Gore, David, 177
Osborne, Lithgow, 349n44
Ostpolitik: Acheson's opposition to, 291–96
Oswald, Lee Harvey, 206
Owen, Henry, 187, 188, 206, 224

Panmunjom, South Korea, 15
Papandreou, Andreas, 218
Papandreou, George, 213, 214, 216, 217–18
The Past Has Another Pattern (Ball), 244
Pauls, Rolf, 294
Pentagon Papers, 301
People and Politics (Brandt), 295
Percy, Charles, 274
Pereira, Pedro, 312, 388n37
Perle, Richard, 274
Perlman, Phillip, 55, 66
Philippine security treaty, 42
Pickett, John C., 171
Pleven, René, 30
Portugal: Acheson as supporter of, 387–88n21; African colonies of, 305–10; negotiations with over Azores, 310–14
Potsdam Accords of 1945, 100
Power and Diplomacy (Acheson), 3, 25, 46, 85, 86, 108, 266
Present at the Creation: My Years in the State Department (Acheson), 3, 114, 253, 266, 332n7; critical success of, 275–77
Proxmire, William, 272, 273
Pueblo incident, 255–56

Quemoy and Matsu crisis, 62–64, 68

Radford, Arthur, 27–28
Rapacki, Adam, 84
Rapacki Plan, 84–85
Rayburn, Sam, 54, 58, 99
Reber, Samuel, 349–50n44
Reedy, George, 99
A Republican Looks at His Party (Larson), 41
Reston, James ("Scotty"), 28, 29, 34, 43, 82, 188, 196, 330, 391–92n5
Rhodesia: Acheson-Goldberg debate over, 316–20; declaration of independence of, 315–21; UN trade embargo against, 321, 323; U.S. policies toward, 321–28
Ridgway, Matthew B., 254, 260, 261, 299, 351–52n88
Rio Treaty, 42
Roberto, Holden, 309, 311, 314
Roche, John P., 250
Rockefeller, Nelson, 209, 380n1
Rogers, William P., 285; Acheson's view of, 265–66, 286, 289; Middle East plan of, 287–91
Rogers Plan: for Middle East, 287–91
Roosevelt, Eleanor, 49, 55, 57, 66, 343n78, 345n122
Roosevelt, Franklin: and Acheson, 1–2
Rostow, Eugene V., 66, 180, 339n4
Rostow, Walt W., 97, 119, 136, 142, 145, 187, 188, 196, 208, 254
Rowen, Henry S., 118, 119
Ruby, Jack, 206
Rusk, Dean, 114–15, 187, 208, 224, 266, 277, 374n110, 359n6; Acheson as adviser to, 117, 123, 157, 219; Acheson's view of, 134, 137, 145, 148, 196, 221, 234, 235, 245, 361n26; and Cuban missile crisis, 157, 161, 165, 169–70; as secretary of state, 140, 183, 191, 193, 217, 229, 230, 231, 244, 257, 310, 317
Russia. *See* Soviet Union
Russia, the Atom, and the West (Kennan), 90

Safeguard. *See* Antiballistic missile system
Salazar, Antonio de Oliveira, 306, 307, 308, 309, 310, 322, 388n36; and negotiations over Azores, 310, 313, 314
Salinger, Pierre, 176
SALT talks. *See* Strategic Arms Limitation Treaty (SALT) talks
Sampson, Edith, 57
Sandburg, Carl, 220
San Francisco Conference, 11
Schaetzel, J. Robert, 187, 188, 189, 224, 230, 290, 292
Schlesinger, Arthur, Jr., 25, 55, 70, 90, 118, 124–25, 126, 142, 143, 161, 176, 178, 314, 330
Schmid, Carlo, 103
Schmidt, Bernadotte, 105
Schroeder, Gerhard, 199
Schuman, Robert, 30, 31, 191
Seabury, Paul, 250
SEATO. *See* Southeast Asian Treaty Organization

Index ■ 427

Seger, Gerhart, 350n44
Selvage & Lee, 310
Sethe, Paul, 78
Sevareid, Eric, 36, 277
Shannon, William, 61, 84
SHAPE. *See* Supreme Headquarters, Allied Powers, Europe
Sheehan, Neil, 301
Shulman, Marshall, 152
Shuster, George N., 350n44
Sidey, Hugh, 146
Sihanouk, Norodom, 283, 284
Simpson, Milward L., 231
Sisco, Joseph, 290, 385n119
Sketches from Life of Men I Have Known (Acheson), 2, 128, 332n7
Skybolt controversy, 182–84
Smeed, James R., 391n91
Smith, Gaddis, 181, 304
Smith, Gerard, 120, 224
Smith, Ian, 185, 315, 316, 318, 320, 325. *See also* Rhodesia
Smith, Walter Bedell, 29
Social Democratic Party (SPD), 78, 198, 291
Sorensen, Theodore, 118, 143, 161, 170, 359n6
South Africa, 324, 326–28
Southeast Asia: U.S. policy in, 26–29, 68
Southeast Asian Treaty Organization (SEATO), 41
South Vietnam. *See* Vietnam
Soviet-American Relations, 1917–1920: The Decision to Intervene (Kennan), 87
Soviet Union: as signers of Austrian State Treaty, 32; Berlin as source of conflict with U.S., 125–26, 134–44, 146–48; role of in Berlin deadline crisis of 1958–59, 93–101; and Berlin Wall, 149–53; and Cuban missile crisis, 156–64, 169–71; Democratic stance toward, 57–58, 59–61; and disengagement debate, 84–93; as dominant force in Eastern Europe, 35, 46, 81; foreign policy of, 33–35; at Geneva Conference of 1955, 33–35; Kennan's view of, 76–78; as influence in Middle East, 41, 44, 46, 51–52, 53; nuclear capability of, 22, 24, 33, 60–61; satellites launched by, 59, 60–61; as threat to U.S. and Europe, 118–19, 121–24; and U-2 incident, 106
SPD. *See* Social Democratic Party
Sprouse, Philip, 284

Stalin, Joseph, 33
Steel, Ronald, 157
Steinbeck, John, 220
Steinhoff, Johannes, 324
Stevenson, Adlai E., 8–10, 16, 19, 22, 26, 69, 112, 137, 360n6; Acheson as supporter of, 38–39, 43, 47–49; rift with Acheson, 65–67, 313, 362n67; views of on Berlin, 126; and Cuban missile crisis, 169; as member of Democratic Advisory Council, 55; Nixon's attack on, 263; position of on Portugal, 309, 311, 312; as UN ambassador, 306, 308, 309
Stikker, Dirk, 110, 112, 116, 124, 187, 235
Stokes, Thomas, 61
Stone, I. F., 172
Stout, Rex, 249
Stowe-Hill, Lord Frank, 177, 284
Strait, Clarence, 102
Strategic Arms Limitation Treaty (SALT) talks, 275
Strategic Hamlet counterinsurgency program, 238
Strauss, Franz Josef, 147, 168–69, 199, 223
Strauss, Lewis, 250, 281
Strauss-Hupe, Robert, 350n44
Suez Canal crisis, 42–47, 340n27
Sullivan, William, 240
Sulzberger, C. L., 34, 195, 296
Summerfield, Arthur E., 29
Supreme Headquarters, Allied Powers, Europe (SHAPE), 166
Swenson, Eric, 345n122
Symington, Stuart, 67, 69, 70–71, 73, 205, 206, 346–47n145

Taft, Robert, 333n14
Taiwan: Eisenhower's agreement with, 36
Talbot, Phillips, 214
Taylor, Maxwell, 98, 157, 163, 175–76, 180, 254, 310, 351n86, 359n6; and U.S. involvement in Vietnam, 242, 245, 246, 247, 260, 261
Tet offensive: effect of on Johnson's Vietnam policy, 256–62
Thant, U, 213, 214
Thirteen Days (Kennedy), 159; Acheson's reaction to, 172–73
This Vast External Realm (Acheson), 3
Thomas, Evan, 300

Thompson, Llewellyn, 359n6
Thorneycroft, Peter, 183
Thurmond, Strom, 318
Tito, Josip Broz, 33, 237
Tonkin Gulf Resolution, 241, 377n13
Treaties of Rome, 75, 102
Treaty of Moscow, 293
Treaty of Warsaw, 293, 294
Truman, Harry S: as Acheson's advocate, 48, 56, 84, 332n5; Acheson's correspondence with, 14–15, 16, 17, 21, 66, 127–28, 136–37, 145, 148, 151, 197, 227, 234, 248, 276, 346–47n145, 366n58; Acheson as secretary of state under, 1, 6–8, 47; Acheson's view of, 19, 41, 276, 332n5; defense policy under, 20, 21; as member of Democratic Advisory Council, 55; and Dulles, 11, 12–13, 26; and Eisenhower, 8–9, 36–37, 332–33n11; foreign alliances formed under, 42; concerns of regarding Kennedy, 111; and 1956 presidential campaign, 47, 49
Truman Doctrine, 7, 51, 210
Tuchman, Barbara, 254, 318
Tuomioja, Sakari, 213, 214, 217
Turkey: assistance program to, 7. *See also* Cyprus conflict
Twilight in Italy (Lawrence), 132
Tyler, William, 98, 270
Tyroler, Charles, II, 55–56, 57, 65, 66, 250

U-2 incident, 106
UDI (unilateral declaration of independence). *See* Rhodesia
Ulbricht, Walter, 151
The Uncertain Trumpet (Taylor), 98
Union of Soviet Socialist Republics. *See* Soviet Union
United Action, 337n88
United Arab Republic, 53
United Kingdom. *See* Great Britain
United Nations (UN): Acheson's view of, 304; African countries as members of, 304; and Korean War, 8
UPA. *See* Movimento Popular de Libertação

Vance, Cyrus R., 229, 254, 260, 261, 298
Viet Cong. *See* Vietnam
Viet Minh, 26, 28
Vietnam: Cambodian involvement in, 283–87; Eisenhower's policy toward, 27–29; lack of European support for, 232; Johnson's policies toward, 238–42; as concern for Johnson, 226, 238; Nixon's policies on, 269–70, 278–81, 296, 297; peace plan proposed for, 243–48; Pentagon Papers on, 301; protests against, 248–51, 285–86, 297; and prowar movement, 248–51; impact of Tet offensive on, 256–62; increasing U.S. involvement in, 242–43
von Hassel, Kai-Uwe, 199
von Seeckt, Hans, 198
Vorster, John, 324
Vyshinsky, Andrei, 318–19

Wallace, George, 318
Wallenberg, Hans, 350n44
Wallner, Woodruff, 308
Warburg, James, 55
Warnke, Paul, 260
Warsaw Pact, 34, 35. *See also* Europe (Eastern)
Welensky, Sir Roy, 275, 278, 280, 292, 300, 324–25, 387–88n21
West Berlin, Germany. *See* Berlin
Western Europe. *See* Europe (Western); European Defense Community
West Germany: France's relationship with, 189–96; *Ostpolitik* in, 291–96; rearmament of, 29–31, 78, 93; rebuilding of, 8; U.S. presence in, 77–78, 79; U.S. relations with, 198–99. *See also* Adenauer, Konrad; Berlin; Berlin Wall
Westmoreland, William C., 175, 256, 259, 260, 285
West New Guinea, 132
West Point speech, Acheson's: controversy generated by, 176–82
Wheeler, Earle, 254, 260, 261
White, William S., 40
White House Information Group, 250
The White House Years (Kissinger), 268
Williams, Edward Bennett, 302
Williams, G. Mennen, 55, 57, 137, 305, 311, 312, 389n50
Williams, T. Harry, 250
Wilson, Charles E., 17–18
Wilson, Donald, 360n6
Wilson, Harold, 186, 220, 223, 224, 317, 318, 320

Wilson, Peter, 274
Wilson, Woodrow, 53
Wilstach, Paul, 14
The Wise Men (Isaacson and Thomas), 300
Wohlstetter, Albert, 119, 272
Wolfers, Arnold, 350n44
Wolfowitz, Paul, 274
World Bank, 7
A World Restored: Metternich, Castlereagh, and the Restoration of Europe, 1812–1822 (Kissinger), 267

Yale University: Acheson as supporter of, 39, 339n4
Yale University Corporation, 39, 339n4
Yalta Conference, 13
Young Americans for Freedom, 326
Yugoslavia, 33

Zaire. *See* Belgian Congo
Zimbabwe. *See* Rhodesia
Zurich-London constitutional agreements, 211